POSTCARDS FROM

Frommer

W9-ANY-640

Alaska 2005

Glaciers flow down from Mount McKinley, the tallest peak in North America. The dark
streaks in the glacial ice are called moraine and are accumulations of rock pushed to
the side as the glacier flows slowly downhill. Those in the center of the flow are called
median moraine and are produced when two glaciers flow together. See chapter 8.
© Ken Graham/Accent Alaska.

A kayaker explores the iceberg-filled waters in Tracy Arm. The South Sawyer Glacier, located at the end of the Arm, calves off many tons of ice daily, giving the channel an otherworldly look. See chapter 5. © Jeff Foott/Alaska Stock Images.

A sled dog race in Fairbanks. The city and the surrounding area host the Yukon Quest International Sled Dog Race in February and the North American Sled Dog Championships in March. See chapter 9. © Gary Schultz/Alaska Stock Images.

One of the most distinctive representations of Native culture in Southeast Alaska, totem poles, like this one in Juneau, are carved to depict the genealogy and history of their people. You'll see them throughout the region, particularly at Ketchikan's several totem parks and heritage centers and at the Sitka National Historic Park, which has a totem trail and a workshop where Native artists craft new poles. See chapter 5. © Randy Brandon/Alaska Stock Images.

Denali State Park borders the southeast corner of Denali National Park, and provides wonderful views of the south side of Mt. McKinley. See chapter 8. © Mike Jones/Accent Alaska.

An angler displays his trophy, a king, or chinook, salmon, considered the best-fighting salmon species in Alaska. Kings commonly grow to over 30 pounds in 5 to 7 years; the largest ever, taken by a commercial fisherman near Petersburg, weighed a whopping 126 pounds. For more on fishing, see chapter 2. © Chip Porter/Getty Images.

Visitors to Denali National Park encounter one of the locals. The park's buses are the only way to traverse the park in a vehicle. It's a system that keeps visitors from overwhelming the ecosystem, so the animals are still there to watch, and their behavior remains essentially normal. It may be the only $20 safari in the world. See chapter 8. © Kim Heacox/Accent Alaska.

The Yorktown Clipper cruises among the towering cliffs of Punchbowl Cove in Rudyerd Bay in the Misty Fjords National Monument. This is extreme topography: Cliffs rise vertically more than 3,000 feet from the surface of water that is 900 feet deep. For more on cruising Alaska, see chapter 4; for more on Misty Fjords, see chapter 5. © Wolfgang Kaehler Photography.

A humpback whale breaching in Frederick Sound. No one knows for sure why they leap from the water like this—it may just be because they enjoy it. Humpbacks are easy to recognize by their huge, mottled tails, by the hump on their backs, and by their arm-like flippers, which can grow to be 14 feet long. See chapter 5. © David Hoffmann/Accent Alaska.

A cow moose with calf in tow crosses the rolling Glenn Highway, with the Chugach Mountains rising majestically beyond. See chapter 6. © Ken Graham/Accent Alaska.

Boat tours on Prince William Sound let travelers get up close and personal with mammoth glaciers. See chapter 7. © Hugh Rose/Accent Alaska.

Frommer's

Alaska

2005

by Charles Wohlforth

Here's what the critics say about Frommer's:

"Amazingly easy to use. Very portable, very complete."

—*Booklist*

"Detailed, accurate, and easy-to-read information for all price ranges."
—*Glamour Magazine*

"Hotel information is close to encyclopedic."

—*Des Moines Sunday Register*

"Frommer's Guides have a way of giving you a real feel for a place."
—*Knight Ridder Newspapers*

WILEY
Wiley Publishing, Inc.

About the Author

Charles Wohlforth is a lifelong Alaskan who has been a writer and journalist since 1986. His *Frommer's Family Vacations in the National Parks* covers parks all over the United States based on insights from the Wohlforth family's own camping experiences. Wohlforth lives in Anchorage with his wife, Barbara, sons Robin and Joseph, and daughters Julia and Rebecca. Last year, Farrar, Straus and Giroux published his new book about Eskimos experiencing warming in the Arctic, titled *The Whale and the Supercomputer: On the Northern Front of Climate Change.* Wohlforth welcomes reader questions and comments through his website, www.wohlforth.net.

Published by:

Wiley Publishing, Inc.

111 River St.
Hoboken, NJ 07030-5774

ISBN 0-7645-7146-X

Editor: William C. Fox
Production Editor: Blair J. Pottenger
Cartographer: Tim Lohnes
Photo Editor: Richard Fox
Production by Wiley Indianapolis Composition Services

Front cover photo: Matanuska Glacier, SC: Woman in raft in glacial pool
Back cover photo: Denali National Park: Wonder Lake, moose pair kiss in greeting

For information on our other products and services or to obtain technical support, please contact our Customer Care Department within the U.S. at 800/762-2974, outside the U.S. at 317/572-3993 or fax 317/572-4002.

Wiley also publishes its books in a variety of electronic formats. Some content that appears in print may not be available in electronic formats.

Manufactured in the United States of America

5 4 3 2 1

Contents

8   The Denali National Park Region   317

9   The Alaskan Interior   355

10   The Bush   406

Appendix: Alaska in Depth   440

List of Maps

Acknowledgments

I couldn't put together a book such as this without a lot of help in covering Alaska's great distances and tracking its fast-changing visitor businesses. This is my eighth edition, and over the years so many friends have contributed their knowledge and support that the book seems to belong to a great community. A few had a special part this year, the reliable core team of researchers whom I would trust with any assignment: Karen Datko (the real reason the book got finished), Kris Capps (a wolf can't stretch at Denali without her knowing it), and Kathleen Tessaro (always cheerful, accurate, and on time). Many other friends and family members helped with this and previous editions, and I'm grateful to all of them.

—Charles Wohlforth

An Invitation to the Reader

In researching this book, we discovered many wonderful places—hotels, restaurants, shops, and more. We're sure you'll find others. Please tell us about them, so we can share the information with your fellow travelers in upcoming editions. If you were disappointed with a recommendation, we'd love to know that, too. Please write to:

Frommer's Alaska 2005
Wiley Publishing, Inc. • 111 River St. • Hoboken, NJ 07030-5774

An Additional Note

Please be advised that travel information is subject to change at any time—and this is especially true of prices. We therefore suggest that you write or call ahead for confirmation when making your travel plans. The authors, editors, and publisher cannot be held responsible for the experiences of readers while traveling. Your safety is important to us, however, so we encourage you to stay alert and be aware of your surroundings. Keep a close eye on cameras, purses, and wallets, all favorite targets of thieves and pickpockets.

Other Great Guides for Your Trip:

Frommer's Alaska Cruises & Ports of Call
Alaska For Dummies

Frommer's Star Ratings, Icons & Abbreviations

Every hotel, restaurant, and attraction listing in this guide has been ranked for quality, value, service, amenities, and special features using a **star-rating system.** In country, state, and regional guides, we also rate towns and regions to help you narrow down your choices and budget your time accordingly. Hotels and restaurants are rated on a scale of zero (recommended) to three stars (exceptional). Attractions, shopping, nightlife, towns, and regions are rated according to the following scale: zero stars (recommended), one star (highly recommended), two stars (very highly recommended), and three stars (must-see).

In addition to the star-rating system, we also use **seven feature icons** that point you to the great deals, in-the-know advice, and unique experiences that separate travelers from tourists. Throughout the book, look for:

Finds	Special finds—those places only insiders know about
Fun Fact	Fun facts—details that make travelers more informed and their trips more fun
Kids	Best bets for kids and advice for the whole family
Moments	Special moments—those experiences that memories are made of
Overrated	Places or experiences not worth your time or money
Tips	Insider tips—great ways to save time and money
Value	Great values—where to get the best deals

The following **abbreviations** are used for credit cards:

| AE | American Express | DISC | Discover | V | Visa |
| DC | Diners Club | MC | MasterCard | | |

Frommers.com

Now that you have the guidebook to a great trip, visit our website at **www.frommers.com** for travel information on more than 3,000 destinations. With features updated regularly, we give you instant access to the most current trip-planning information available. At Frommers.com, you'll also find the best prices on airfares, accommodations, and car rentals—and you can even book travel online through our travel booking partners. At Frommers.com, you'll also find the following:

- Online updates to our most popular guidebooks
- Vacation sweepstakes and contest giveaways
- Newsletter highlighting the hottest travel trends
- Online travel message boards with featured travel discussions

What's New in Alaska

Here are some changes in Alaska travel since the last edition of *Frommer's Alaska*.

PLANNING YOUR TRIP For more planning information, see chapters 2 and 3.

Visitation to Alaska was way up in 2004. Business owners said they were busier than they had been since before Sept. 11, 2001. Good for them, but not so good for you. Bargains became scarce and base prices rose. The idea of showing up without reservations was riskier than ever in the high season. Whether this continues in 2005 probably depends on the economy and the world political situation.

A change that's spread all over Alaska in a year has been the availability of wireless Internet. If you want to bring your laptop, it's not hard to find a hotel where you can log onto a high-speed connection through a wireless networking card (these cost about $60 at any computer or office supply store).

On the other end of the technology spectrum, driving Alaska's gravel highways is easier for visitors now thanks to more companies that will allow their rental vehicles to be used off pavement. These are listed under "Equipped for the Backroads," in chapter 9, and in "Getting Around" in chapter 6.

Outdoor adventuring has changed forever: No longer is it necessary to be out of touch in the backcountry. I tried renting an Iridium satellite phone for the first time on a 3-week wilderness trip. It was easy to use and cheap for the security provided—that of knowing help was easy to summon if someone got sick or was injured. On the other hand, the world seems to have shrunk alarmingly. Details on renting these phones are on p. 31.

Alaskan Bicycle Adventures stopped operating in 2004.

THE SOUTHEAST For more, see chapter 5.

The state's catamaran-hull fast ferry *Fairweather* went into service in 2004. The governor changed its homeport from Sitka to Juneau amid great controversy. That means its primary run is from Juneau up Lynn Canal to Haines and Skagway. Only 2 days a week does it runs from Juneau to Sitka. Whatever the route, the boat's speed cuts the running time in half. Fares are 10% higher than the conventional ferries.

In **Ketchikan** there's a new, relatively inexpensive option for bear viewing. Instead of flying out on a floatplane, take a bus or your rental car to **Alaska Rainforest Sanctuary** (© 907/225-5503), on a creek south of town where black bears congregate in pursuit of salmon returning to a hatchery. They've built a beautiful trail and boardwalk; guides lead all guests in groups to see the bears and other wildlife.

Wrangell's long-awaited new museum, the **Nolan Center Museum** (© 907/874-3770), is a big, impressive building that holds the town's substantial collections of historic and Native artifacts and contains a new visitor center staffed by both town guides and rangers from the Tongass National Forest.

There's a cool place to stay in town, a small houseboat that's either tied up in the harbor or anchored in a picturesque remote spot. It is offered for a bargain price by **Rainwalker Expeditions** (© **907/874-2549;** www.rainwalkerexpeditions.com).

In **Sitka** a terrific little restaurant has opened, offering the town's most sophisticated food: **Ludwig's Bistro** (© **907/966-3663**).

Juneau's historic **Wickersham House** will probably be closed throughout 2005 for much-needed restoration and repair. The restaurant **DiSopra** (© **907/586-3150**) has hit its stride and now is one of Alaska's best. Sadly, another of Alaska's best, the **Summit Restaurant,** sold out to yet another cruise-ship-oriented jewelry store. That establishment also took over the pension-style hotel upstairs from the restaurant to house its imported summer workers.

At **Glacier Bay National Park** a new concessionaire, ARAMARK, took over the services offered to visitors and immediately set about updating the drab rooms at the lodge.

ANCHORAGE & ENVIRONS
For more, see chapter 6.

The **Alaska Native Heritage Center** is making things easier for visitors by offering shuttles from downtown. Call for current arrangements (© **800/315-6608** or 907/330-8000; www.alaskanative.net).

Downtown, two superb new galleries are showing the best contemporary art in museumlike rooms. Both are entirely artistic rather than commercial in approach—so you better look fast while they're still in business. They are **The Center for Contemporary Visual Art of Alaska,** at 621 W. 6th Ave., and **International Gallery of Contemporary Art,** at 427 D Street.

One of the hardest parts of assembling the book each year is finding decent budget lodgings in Anchorage. I'm happy to say the **Caribou Inn** (© **800/272-5878** or 907/272-0444; www.cariboubnb.com) has made major improvements and now is an amazing bargain. For families, the **Parkwood Inn** (© **800/478-3590** or 907/563-3590; www.parkwoodinn.net) is the best bet, with big, clean apartments that rent for reasonable rates by the night (a similar place downtown, **Duke's 8th Avenue Hotel,** is no longer available).

Birch Trails, my favorite dog mushing tour, stopped operating, and I was unable to find another that I wanted to recommend. Ask at the visitor center or Alyeska Resort, as I am sure someone will fill the void.

KENAI PENINSULA & PRINCE WILLIAM SOUND For more, see chapter 7.

Prince William Sound is due to get a new fast ferry like the one in Southeast Alaska. (They sold the old one on Ebay. Everyone said the guy was getting an incredible bargain when he paid $389,500 for a 193-foot ship capable of carrying 29 cars and 236 passengers. Like many a last-minute Ebay purchase, however, the ship may have looked better before it was delivered, as I saw it 8 months later tied up at a dock in Seattle with a for sale sign on it. Meanwhile, a fill-in ferry ran the route while waiting for the new fast ferry.) The new catamaran, should it start service on time, will be cutting travel times in half between Prince William Sound ports during the 2005 season.

Mitch Seavey, owner of the **Seward** dog mushing tour company **Idida-Ride** (© **800/478-3139** or 907/224-8607; www.ididaride.com) won the Iditarod himself in 2004. His son had previously won the Junior Iditarod.

Homer seems to deserve its own book—so much is happening there and there are so many great places to stay and eat. I have added several lodgings in town and more across Kachemack Bay. Instead of limiting myself to wilderness lodges, I've expanded that across-the-bay section to interesting B&Bs and a "Center For Creative Renewal." There's also a cool new restaurant with a brick oven in Homer called **Fat Olives** (© 907/235-8488).

Cordova has a new museum focused on the local Eyak culture called the **Ilanka Cultural Center,** 110 Nicholoff Way (near the Fishermen's Memorial at the small boat harbor; © 907/424-7903). I've included a full description of the **Orca Adventure Lodge** (© 866/424-ORCA or 907/424-7249; www.orcaadventure lodge.com), which is the first lodging to really take advantage of Cordova's wonderful outdoors.

DENALI NATIONAL PARK For more, see chapter 8.

Most of the work in the frontcountry area finally will be complete in 2005, adding a new educational component to a visit and a more pleasant environment. Improvements along the highway's built-up area were completed in 2004 and make that area much more attractive and easier for pedestrians to navigate. The major hotels have also gone through expensive upgrades.

The next project for the Park Service is to replace the Eielson Visitor Center, closing that traditional destination of shuttle bus rides 66 miles along the Park Road at least through 2006. I have adjusted my shuttle bus advice accordingly, but remember I had to write that advice a year in advance—you should ask plenty of questions when you make your reservations.

The park has finally instituted online booking for the all-important advance reservations for shuttle buses and campsites at www.reservedenali. com.

The new **Skyline Lodge** (© 907/683-1223; www.katair.com), in the Kantishna backcountry, offers a great bargain on rooms near Mount McKinley deep within the park.

THE INTERIOR For more, see chapter 9.

The spectacular expansion project at the **University of Alaska Museum of the North** should be completed during the 2005 season. I toured the construction site: this may be Alaska's most beautiful building, and certainly should not be missed. I am sorry to say the tours at the **Fort Knox Gold Mine** are no longer being offered.

Construction at the **Westmark Fairbanks Hotel & Conference Center** © 800/544-0970 reservations, or 907/456-7722; www.westmarkhotels. com) was completed in 2004, creating the best hotel in town and one of the best in the state. For once, they've done something fashionable rather than something "Alaskan."

Strange doings out at **Chena Hot Springs Resort** (© 800/478-4681 or 907/451-8104; www.chenahotsprings. com): construction of a hotel made entirely of ice. It lasted through the winter but melted in the spring, despite the owner's best efforts to insulate it from the sun. He promises to build it again next winter.

On the **Dalton Highway,** the Bureau of Land Management has completed a large new **Arctic Interagency Visitor Center,** at mile 175 on the west side of the highway in Coldfoot (© 907/678-5209).

1

The Best of Alaska

As a child, when my family traveled outside Alaska for vacations, I often met other children who asked, "Wow, you live in Alaska? What's it like?" I never did well with that question. To me, the place I was visiting was far simpler and easier to describe than the one I was from. The Lower 48 seemed a fairly homogeneous land of freeways and fast food, a well-mapped network of established places. Alaska, on the other hand, wasn't even completely explored. Natural forces of vast scale and subtlety were still shaping the land in their own way, inscribing a different story on each of an infinite number of unexpected places. Each region, whether populated or not, was unique far beyond my ability to explain. Alaska was so large and new, so unconquered and exquisitely real, as to defy summation.

In contrast to many places you might choose to visit, it's Alaska's unformed newness that makes it so interesting and fun. Despite the best efforts of tour planners, the most memorable parts of a visit are unpredictable and often unexpected: a humpback whale leaping clear of the water, the face of a glacier releasing huge ice chunks, a bear feasting on salmon in a river, a huge salmon chomping onto your line. You can look at totem poles and see Alaska Native cultural demonstrations, and you can also get to know indigenous people who still live by traditional ways. And sometimes grand, quiet moments come, and those are the ones that endure most deeply.

As the writer of this guidebook, I aim to help you get to places where you may encounter what's new, real, and unexpected. Opening yourself to those experiences is your job, but it's an effort that's likely to pay off. Although I have lived here all my life, I often envy the stories visitors tell me about the Alaskan places they have gone to and what happened there. No one owns Alaska, and most of us are newcomers here. In all this immensity, a visitor fresh off the boat is just as likely as a lifelong resident to see or do something amazing.

1 The Best Views

- **A First Sight of Alaska:** Flying north from Seattle, you're in clouds, so you concentrate on a book. When you look up, the light from the window has changed. Down below, the clouds are gone, and under the wing, where you're used to seeing roads, cities, and farms on most flights, you see instead only high, snowy mountain peaks, without the slightest mark of human presence, stretching as far as the horizon. Welcome to Alaska.

- **Punchbowl Cove** (Misty Fjords National Monument): A sheer granite cliff rises smooth and implacable 3,150 feet straight up from the water. A pair of bald eagles wheels and soars across its face, providing the only sense of scale. They look the size of gnats. See p. 104.

- **From the Chugach Mountains Over Anchorage, at Sunset:** The city sparkles below, on the edge of an orange-reflecting Cook Inlet, far below the mountainside where you stand. Beyond the pink and purple silhouettes of mountains on the other side of the inlet, the sun is spraying warm, dying light into puffs of clouds. And yet it's midnight. See "Getting Outside" in chapter 6.
- **Mount McKinley from the Air** (Denali National Park): Your bush pilot guides his plane up from the flatlands of Talkeetna into a realm of eternal white, where a profusion of insanely rugged peaks rises in higher relief than any other spot on earth. After circling a 3-mile-high wall and slipping through a mile-deep canyon, you land on a glacier, get out of the plane, and for the first time realize the overwhelming scale of it all. See "Attractions & Activities Outside the Park" and "Talkeetna: Back Door to Denali" in chapter 8.
- **The Northern Lights** (Alaska's Interior): Blue, purple, green, and red lines spin from the center of the sky, draping long tendrils of slow-moving light. Bright, flashing, sky-covering waves wash across the dome of stars like ripples driven by a gust of wind on a pond. Looking around, you see that your companions' faces are rosy in a silver, snowy night, all gazing straight up with their mouths open. See p. 364.

2 The Best Alaska Cruises

Cruises provide comfortable, leisurely access to the Inside Passage and the Gulf of Alaska. Here are some of the best bets. See chapter 4 for details.

- **Best Up-Close Alaska Experience:** Glacier Bay Cruiseline's *Wilderness Adventurer* and *Wilderness Explorer* sail itineraries that shun overcrowded port towns in favor of wilderness areas and small fishing villages. Both carry sea kayaks for off-ship exploration, and both feature naturalist-led hikes as central features of the experience. The line is owned by an Alaska Native corporation and the ships are small (carrying 74 and 36 passengers, respectively) and very casual. They're not fancy, but that's the point—it's where they take you that counts.
- **Most Comfortable Small Ships:** Cruise West's *Spirit of Endeavor* and *Spirit of '98* (a 19th-c. coastal steamer re-creation) and Clipper's *Yorktown Clipper* offer a higher level of comfort than the other small ships in Alaska while still giving you an intimate, casual, up-close small-ship experience.
- **Most Luxurious Big Ships:** *Crystal Harmony* is the top-of-the-line ship in the Alaska market, with superb cuisine, elegant service, lovely surroundings, great cabins, and sparkling entertainment. If you want a more casual kind of luxury, Radisson Seven Seas' *Seven Seas Mariner* (which is slightly smaller than the *Harmony*) offers just that. Among the mainstream cruise ships, Celebrity's *Mercury, Infinity,* and *Summit* are the big winners, offering cutting-edge modern ships with great service, dining, and design.
- **Best Cruisetours:** Holland America Line and Princess are the leaders in linking cruises with land tours into the Interior, either before or after your cruise. They own their own hotels, deluxe motor coaches, and railcars, and after many years in the business,

Alaska

MILEAGE CHART
Approximate driving distances in miles between cities.

	Anchorage	Circle	Dawson City	Eagle	Fairbanks	Haines	Homer	Prudhoe Bay	Seattle	Seward	Skagway	Tok	Valdez
Anchorage		520	494	501	358	775	226	847	2234	126	832	328	304
Circle	520		530	541	162	815	746	1972	2271	646	872	368	526
Dawson City	494	530		131	379	548	713	868	1843	619	430	189	428
Eagle	501	541	131		379	620	727	868	1974	627	579	173	427
Fairbanks	358	162	379	379		653	584	489	2121	484	710	206	364
Haines	775	815	548	620	653		1001	1142	1774	901	359	447	701
Homer	226	746	713	727	584	1001		1073	2455	173	1058	554	530
Prudhoe Bay	847	1972	868	868	489	1142	1073		2610	973	1199	695	853
Seattle	2243	2271	1843	1974	2121	1774	2455	2610		2493	1577	1931	2169
Seward	126	646	619	627	484	901	173	973	2493		958	454	430
Skagway	832	872	430	579	710	359	1058	1199	1577	958		504	758
Tok	328	368	189	173	206	447	554	695	1931	454	504		254
Valdez	304	526	428	427	364	701	530	853	2169	430	758	254	

Chukchi Sea

Little Diòmede Island

Nome

Norton Sound

Yukon Delta National Wildlife Refuge

Bethel

Yukon Delta National Wildlife Refuge

Bering Sea

Nunivak Island

Bristol Bay

Attu Island

Pribilof Islands

Cape St. Stephen

Rat Islands

Alaska Peninsula

Unimak Island

Cold Bay

Dutch Harbor

Adak

Atka Island

Adak Island

Atka

Unalaska

Aleutian Islands

PACIFIC

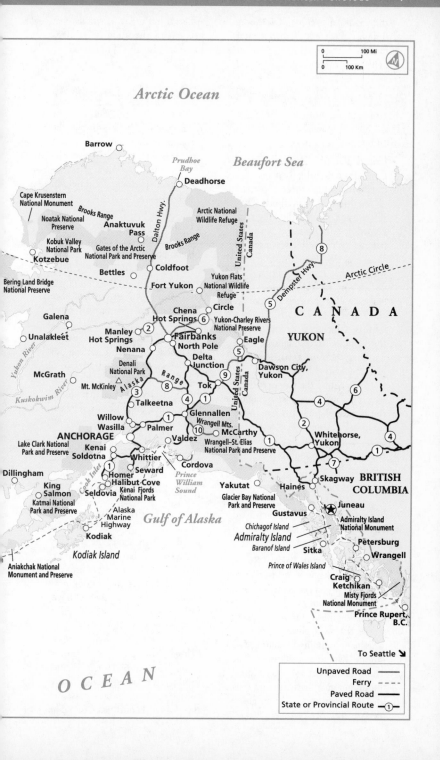

Arctic Ocean

Prudhoe Bay

Barrow

Deadhorse

Beaufort Sea

Cape Krusenstern
National Monument

Noatak National
Preserve

Brooks Range

Anaktuvuk
Pass

Arctic National
Wildlife Refuge

Kobuk Valley
National Park

Gates of the Arctic
National Park and Preserve

Dalton Hwy.

Brooks Range

United States
Canada

(8)

Kotzebue

Bettles

Coldfoot

Dempster Hwy.

Arctic Circle

Bering Land Bridge
National Preserve

Fort Yukon

Yukon Flats
National Wildlife
Refuge

(5)

Galena

Chena
Hot Springs

(6)

Circle

Yukon-Charley Rivers
National Preserve

Eagle

C A N A D A

YUKON

Unalakleet

Manley
Hot Springs

(2)

Fairbanks
North Pole

Yukon River

Nenana

Denali
National Park

Delta
Junction

(9)

(5)

Dawson City,
Yukon

McGrath

Mt. McKinley △

Alaska

Range

(3)

(8)

Tok

United States
Canada

(6)

Kuskokwim River

(4)

(1)

(4)

Talkeetna

Willow
Wasilla

Palmer

(1)

Glennallen

Wrangell Mts.

(2)

Whitehorse,
Yukon

(4)

ANCHORAGE

(10)

McCarthy

Lake Clark National
Park and Preserve

Kenai
Soldotna

Valdez

Wrangell–St. Elias
National Park and Preserve

(1)

(7)

(1)

Dillingham

Whittier

Cordova

Skagway

BRITISH
COLUMBIA

King
Salmon

Homer

Seward
Halibut Cove
Kenai Fjords
National Park

Prince
William
Sound

Yakutat

Haines

Seldovia

Glacier Bay National
Park and Preserve

Gustavus

★ Juneau

Admiralty Island
National Monument

Katmai National
Park and Preserve

Alaska
Marine
Highway

Gulf of Alaska

Chichagof Island

Admiralty Island

Petersburg

Kodiak

Baranof Island

Sitka

Wrangell

Kodiak Island

Prince of Wales Island

Craig
Ketchikan

Aniakchak National
Monument and Preserve

Misty Fjords
National Monument

Prince Rupert,
B.C.

To Seattle ↘

O C E A N

Unpaved Road	⌇⌇⌇
Ferry	- - -
Paved Road	——
State or Provincial Route	—①—

0 ___ 100 Mi
0 ___ 100 Km

they both really know what they're doing. Princess concentrates more on the Anchorage/Denali/Fairbanks routes, while Holland America has many itineraries that get you to the Yukon Territory's Dawson City and Whitehorse.

3 The Best Glaciers

More of Alaska—more than 100 times more—is covered by glacier ice than is settled by human beings.

- **Grand Pacific Glacier** (Glacier Bay National Park): Two vast glaciers of deep blue meet at the top of an utterly barren fjord. They rubbed and creased the gray rock below for thousands of years before just recently releasing it to the air again. Three intimidating walls of ice surround boats that pull close to the glaciers. See "Glacier Bay National Park" in chapter 5.
- **Childs Glacier** (Cordova): Out the Copper River Highway from Cordova, this is a participatory glacier-viewing experience. The glacier is cut by the Copper River, which is ¼ mile broad; standing on the opposite shore (unless you're up in the viewing tower), you have to be ready to run like hell when the creaking, popping ice gives way and a huge berg falls into the river, potentially swamping the picnic area. Even when the glacier isn't calving, you can feel the ice groaning in your gut. See "Cordova: Hidden Treasure" in chapter 7.

- **Exit Glacier** (Seward): You can drive near the glacier and walk the rest of the way on a gravel path. It towers above like a huge blue sculpture, the spires of broken ice close enough to breathe a freezer-door chill down on watchers. See "Exit Glacier" in section 6 of chapter 7.
- **Western Prince William Sound:** On a boat from Whittier, you can see a couple dozen glaciers in a day. Some of these are the amazing tidewater glaciers that dump huge, office-building-size spires of ice into the ocean, each setting off a terrific splash and outward-radiating sea wave. See "Whittier: Dock on the Sound" in chapter 7.

4 The Most Beautiful Drives & Train Rides

You'll find a description of each road in "Alaska's Highways a la Carte" on p. 358. Here are some highlights:

- **White Pass and Yukon Route Railway** (Skagway to Summit): The narrow-gauge excursion train, sometimes pulled by vintage steam engines, climbs the steep grade that was chiseled into the granite mountains by stampeders to the Klondike gold rush. The train is a sort of mechanical mountain goat, balancing on trestles and steep rock walls far above deep gorges. See p. 187.

- **Seward Highway/Alaska Railroad** (Anchorage to Seward): Just south of Anchorage, the highway and rail line have been chipped into the side of the Chugach Mountains over the surging gray water of Turnagain Arm. Above, Dall sheep and mountain goats pick their way along the cliffs, within easy sight. Below, white beluga whales chase salmon through the turbid water. Farther south, the route splits and climbs through the mountain passes of the Kenai Peninsula. See "The

Seward Highway: A Road Guide" in Chapter 7 for information on the highway, and p. 258 for information on this Alaska Railroad route.

- **Denali Highway:** Leading east-west through the Alaska Range, the highway crosses terrain that could be another Denali National Park, full of wildlife and with views so huge and grand they seem impossible. See p. 322.

- **Richardson Highway:** Just out of Valdez heading north, the Richardson Highway rises quickly from sea level to more than 2,600 feet, switching back and forth on the side of a mountain. With each turn, the drop down the impassable slope becomes more amazing. North of Glennallen, the highway rises again, bursting through the tree line between a series of mountains and tracing the edges of long alpine lakes, before descending, parallel with the silver skein of the Alaska pipeline, to Delta Junction. See "The Richardson Highway & Copper Center," in chapter 9.

- **The Roads Around Nome:** You can't drive to Nome, but 250 miles of gravel roads radiate from the Arctic community into tundra that's populated only by musk oxen, bear, reindeer, birds, and other wildlife. See p. 428.

- **The Dalton Highway:** When you're ready for an expedition—a real wilderness trip by road—the Dalton Highway leads from Fairbanks across northern Alaska to the Arctic Ocean, a mind-blowing drive through 500 miles of spectacular virgin country. See "The Dalton Highway" in chapter 9.

5 The Best Fishing

The quality of salmon fishing in Alaska isn't so much a function of place as of time. See p. 39 for information on how to find the fish when you arrive.

- **Bristol Bay:** This is the world's richest salmon fishery; lodges on the remote rivers of the region are an angler's paradise. See p. 40.

- **Copper River Delta, Cordova:** The Copper itself is silty with glacial runoff, but feeder streams and rivers are rich with trout, Dolly Varden, and salmon, with few other anglers in evidence. See p. 314.

- **The Kenai River:** The biggest king salmon—up to 98 pounds—come from the swift Kenai River. Big fish are so common in the second run of kings that there's a special, higher standard for what makes a trophy. Silvers and reds add to a mad, summer-long fishing frenzy. See p. 275.

- **Homer:** Alaska's largest charter-fishing fleet goes for halibut ranging into the hundreds of pounds. See p. 291.

- **Unalaska:** Beyond the road system, Unalaska has the biggest halibut. See p. 421.

- **Kodiak Island:** The bears are so big here because they live on an island that's crammed with spawning salmon in the summer. Kodiak has the best roadside salmon fishing in Alaska, and the remote fishing, at lodges or fly-in stream banks, is legendary. See p. 413.

6 The Best Tips for Cooking Salmon

Now that you've caught a Pacific salmon, you need to know how to cook it—or order it in a restaurant—to avoid spoiling the rich flavor. Tips for getting your fish home are on p. 292.

- **Freeze As Little As Possible:** It's a sad fact that salmon loses some of its richness and gets more "fishy" as soon as it's frozen. Eat as much as you can fresh, because it'll never be better. Ask if the salmon is fresh when you order it in a restaurant. Don't overlook smoking, the traditional Native way of preserving fish for the winter. See p. 292 for information on where to get your salmon frozen and smoked.
- **Choose the Best Fish:** The best restaurants advertise where their salmon comes from on the menu. In early summer, Copper River kings and reds are the richest in flavor; later in the summer, Yukon River salmon are best. The oil in the salmon gives it the rich, meaty flavor; the fish from the Copper and Yukon are high in oil content. King, red, and silver salmon are the only species you should find in a restaurant. Avoid farm-reared salmon, which is mushy and flavorless compared with wild Alaska salmon.
- **Keep It Simple:** When ordering salmon or halibut in a restaurant, avoid anything with cheese or heavy sauces. When salmon is fresh, it's best with light seasoning, perhaps just a little lemon, dill weed, and pepper and salt, or basted with soy sauce; or without anything on it at all, grilled over alder coals.
- **Don't Overcook It:** Salmon should be cooked just until the moment the meat changes color and becomes flaky through to the bone, or slightly before. A minute more, and some of the texture and flavor are lost. That's why those huge barbecue salmon bakes often are not as good as they should be—it's too hard to cook hundreds of pieces of fish just right and serve them all hot.
- **Fillets, Not Steaks:** Salmon is cut two ways in Alaska: lengthwise fillets or crosswise steaks. The fillet is cut with the grain of the flesh, keeping the oil and moisture in the fish. Do not remove the skin before cooking—it holds in the oils, and will fall off easily when the fish is done. If you have a large group, consider cooking the salmon bone-in (sometimes called a roast), stuffing seasonings in the body cavity. When it's done, the skin easily peels off and, after eating the first side, you can effortlessly lift out the skeleton.

7 The Best Bear Viewing

There are many places to see bears in Alaska, but if your goal is to make *sure* you see a bear—and potentially lots of bears—these are the best places:

- **Anan Wildlife Observatory:** When the fish are running, you can see many dozens of black bear feeding in a salmon stream from close at hand. Access is easiest from Wrangell. See p. 112.
- **Pack Creek** (Admiralty Island): The brown bears of the island, which is more thickly populated with them than anywhere else on earth, have learned to ignore the daily visitors who stand on the platforms at Pack Creek. Access is by air from Juneau. See p. 156.
- **Katmai National Park:** During the July and September salmon runs, dozens of giant brown bears congregate around Brooks Camp, where, from wooden platforms a few yards away, you can watch the full range of their behaviors. Flight services from Kodiak also bring guests at any time of the summer to see bears dig clams on the park's

eastern seashore. See "Katmai National Park" and "Kodiak: Wild Island" in chapter 10.

- **Kodiak Island:** The island's incredible salmon runs nourish the world's largest bears, Kodiak brown bears; pilots know where to find them week to week, landing floatplanes as near as possible. See p. 412.

- **Denali National Park:** The park offers the best and least expensive wildlife-viewing safari in the state. Passengers on the buses that drive the park road as far as the Eielson Visitor Center usually see at least some grizzlies. See chapter 8.

- **Alaska Rainforest Sanctuary** (Ketchikan): A creek south of town where black bear come to feed on salmon coming back to a hatchery has been developed with boardwalks and facilities for tour buses. It remains to be seen if the bears will stay with all those people around, but if they do, this may become Alaska's most popular bear viewing site. See p. 98.

8 The Best Marine Mammal Viewing

You've got a good chance of seeing marine mammals almost anywhere you go boating in Alaska, but in some places it's almost guaranteed.

- **Frederick Sound** (Petersburg): A humpback jumped right into the boat with whale-watchers here in 1995. Petersburg boats also see otters and baby seals sitting on icebergs floating in front of LeConte Glacier. See p. 121.

- **Icy Strait** (Gustavus) and **Bartlett Cove** (Glacier Bay National Park): Humpback whales show up off Point Adolphus, in Icy Strait, just a few miles from little Gustavus, a town of luxurious country inns, and in Bartlett Cove within Glacier Bay National Park. See "Glacier Bay National Park" and "Gustavus: Country Inns & Quiet" in chapter 5.

- **Sitka Sound:** Lots of otters and humpback whales show up in the waters near Sitka. In fall, when the town holds its Whale Fest, you can spot them from a city park built for the purpose. See "Sitka: Rich Prize of Russian Conquest" in chapter 5.

- **Kenai Fjords National Park** (near Seward): You don't have to go all the way into the park—you're pretty well assured of sea otters and sea lions in Resurrection Bay, near Seward, and humpbacks and killer whales often show up, too. See "Kenai Fjords National Park" in chapter 7.

- **Prince William Sound:** Otters, seals, and sea lions are easy—you'll see them on most trips out of Valdez, Whittier, or Cordova—but you also have a chance of spotting both humpback and killer whales in the Sound. See chapter 7.

9 The Best Encounters with Native Culture

- **Ketchikan Totem Poles:** This Tlingit homeland has three unique places to see totem poles: historic poles indoors at the Totem Heritage Center, faithful reproductions outdoors in a natural setting at Totem Bight State Park, and brand new poles as they are created in a workshop at the Saxman Native Village Totem Pole Park. See p. 96.

- **Alaska Native Heritage Center** (Anchorage): All of Alaska's Native groups joined together to build this grand living museum and gathering place, where dance and music performances, storytelling, art and craft demonstrations, and simple meetings of people happen every day. See p. 219.

- **Alutiiq Museum** (Kodiak): The Koniag people are recovering their culture from the ground and from artifacts repatriated from the world's museums. Visitors can even join in archaeological fieldwork. See p. 411.

- **Iñupiat Heritage Center** (Barrow): A living museum, this is a place to meet and enjoy performances by the Native people who built it, and to see extraordinary artifacts they have made and recovered from digs in frozen ground. See p. 436.

10 The Best Museums & Historic Sites

- **Sitka National Historic Park:** The site of the 1804 battle between the Tlingits and Russians, in a totem pole park and seaside stand of old-growth forest, allows you to really appreciate what the Native people were fighting for. Inside the visitor center, some of the best historic totem poles are on display while Native craftspeople create new ones and demonstrate other traditional arts and talk with visitors. See p. 129.

- **Alaska State Museum** (Juneau): This richly endowed museum doesn't just show off its wealth of objects—it also uses them to teach about the state. A visit will put Alaska's Native cultures and pioneer history entirely in context. See p. 143.

- **Anchorage Museum of History and Art:** Alaska's largest museum has the room and expertise to tell the story of Native and white history in Alaska, and to showcase contemporary Alaskan art and culture. See p. 217.

- **Pratt Museum** (Homer): The Pratt explains natural history (especially the life of the ocean) in an intimate and clear way you'll find nowhere else in Alaska. See p. 287.

- **UAF Museum of the North** (Fairbanks): This university museum is undergoing a spectacular renovation, with a swooping new gallery to present Alaska's art due for completion in 2005. Its existing galley contained an extraordinary natural history collection, presented with the help of some of the world's top scientists on Alaskan subjects. See p. 366.

11 The Best Winter Destinations

- **Anchorage:** Anyone can enjoy the Fur Rendezvous and Iditarod sled dog races, which keep a winter-carnival atmosphere going through much of February and March, but winter sports enthusiasts get the most out of winter here. The city has some of the best Nordic and telemark skiing anywhere, close access to three downhill skiing areas, dog mushing, and lake skating. See chapter 6.

- **Alyeska Resort** (Girdwood): Alaska's premier downhill skiing area has lots of snow over a long season, fantastic views, few lift lines, and a luxurious hotel. See "The Best Hotels," below, and p. 237.

- **Chena Hot Springs Resort:** A 90-minute ride from Fairbanks and you're out in the country, where the northern lights are clear on a starry winter afternoon and night. The resort has lots of activities to get you out into the snowy countryside, or you can just relax in the hot mineral springs. See p. 384.

- **Sitka:** Much of historic Sitka is as available in winter as at any other time of year, but with fewer crowds and lower prices. The humpback whale-watching is exceptional in the late fall and early winter, as the whales stop off here on their migration. See "Sitka: Rich Prize of Russian Conquest" in chapter 5.
- **Barrow:** Go to the shore of the frozen Arctic Ocean and you have a chance to experience the most extreme winter conditions in the world. It's dark for 65 days, when the aurora blasts across the sky. There's not much to do, but you could run into a polar bear in the street. See "Barrow: Way North" in chapter 10.

12 The Strangest Community Events

- **Cordova Ice Worm Festival** (Cordova): The truth is, ice worms do exist. Really. This winter carnival celebrates them in February. The highlight is the traditional annual march of the ice worm (a costume with dozens of feet sticking out) down the main street. See p. 310.
- **Midnight Sun Baseball Game** (Fairbanks): The semipro baseball game, played without lights, doesn't begin until 10:30pm on the longest day of the year. See p. 363.
- **Bering Sea Ice Golf Classic** (Nome): The greens are Astroturf, as the sea ice won't support a decent lawn in mid-March. Hook a drive and you could end up spending hours wandering among the pressure ridges, but you must play the ball as it lies. See p. 427.
- **Polar Bear Swim** (Nome): This swim in the frigid Bering Sea takes place in late June, but only if the sea ice has opened up sufficiently to provide enough liquid water. See p. 427.
- **Pillar Mountain Golf Classic** (Kodiak): The course is one hole, par is 70, and elevation gain is 1,400 feet. Having a spotter in the deep snow of late March is helpful, but use of two-way radios, dogs, and chain saws is prohibited. Also, there's no cutting down of power poles, and cursing tournament officials carries a $25 fine. See p. 411.
- **Tea-Making Contest** (Barrow): Part of the April Piuraagiaqt festival, the contest sets couples against each other in a race to set up a camp stove, gather a piece of ice, and brew a good cup of tea. Or the community may have come up with some other silly contest this year. See p. 435.
- **Mountain Mother Contest** (Talkeetna): In this event in the July Moose Dropping Festival, mothers compete in a test of Bush skills, including splitting wood, balancing on rocks to cross a stream, carrying water, and diapering a baby. See p. 350.

13 The Best Hotels

- **Westcoast Cape Fox Lodge** (Ketchikan; ✆ **800/325-4000**): Standing in its own little forest atop a rocky promontory that dominates downtown Ketchikan, this cleanly luxurious hotel has the feel of a mountain lodge or resort. A funicular tram carries visitors to the Creek Street boardwalks, or you can take the wooded cliff-side path. The rooms and common areas, accented with masterpieces of Tlingit art, have exceptional views of the city and Tongass Narrows through the trees. See p. 101.

- **Hotel Captain Cook** (Anchorage; © **800/843-1950**): This is the grand old hotel of downtown Anchorage, with a heavy nautical theme, teak paneling, and every possible amenity. It remains the state's standard of service and luxury. See p. 201.

- **Alyeska Prince Hotel** (Girdwood; © **800/880-3880**): The first sight of this ski resort hotel—designed in a château style and standing in an undeveloped mountain valley—will make you catch your breath. Wait till you get inside and see the starscape and polar bear diorama in the lobby atrium, or the swimming pool, with its high-beamed ceiling and windows, looking out on the mountain. A tram carries skiers and diners to the mountaintop. See p. 237.

- **Land's End Resort** (Homer; © **800/478-0400**): It's the location: right on the end of Homer Spit, five miles out in the middle of Kachemak Bay, where you can fish for salmon from the beach right in front of your room, or watch otters drifting by. The hotel itself is excellent, too, with a tremendous variety of rooms, some extraordinarily luxurious, and a complete spa. See p. 295.

- **Westmark Fairbanks Hotel & Conference Center** (Fairbanks; © **800/544-0970**): A new tower rises over the flat river city of Fairbanks, a stylish and charming new wing of the city's oldest modern hotel. The owners, the Holland America cruise line, demolished much of the original building, leaping decades from the past to just a little into the future. See p. 374.

14 The Best Websites

Many useful websites are listed throughout the book; some of the best are under "Visitor Information" near the beginning of each town section.

- **www.trollart.com**. Ketchikan artist Ray Troll has created a website that carries you deep into his mind, which is full of odd and resonant humor about the evolution of fish, man, and our common relations. His vibrantly colored art makes it an aesthetic journey.

- **www.alaska.gov/adfg**. The Alaska Department of Fish and Game posts valuable information for anyone interested in fishing, hunting, wildlife-watching, or just learning about creatures. Everyone from children to wildlife biologists will find something at his or her level.

- **www.alaska.com**. Operated by Alaska's largest newspaper, the *Anchorage Daily News,* this site is so full of information for visitors that it's a bit overwhelming. Look here for a deep mine of information from an authoritative source.

- **www.awrta.org**. The Alaska Wilderness Recreation and Tourism Association unites hundreds of small eco-tourism operators. Authentic local guides and lodges can be hard to find, but they are listed here on a comprehensive and easy to use site.

- **www.gi.alaska.edu**. The Geophysical Institute at the University of Alaska Fairbanks maintains a fascinating and cool site filled with real-time earth science information about Alaska, such as aurora predictions, volcano watches, earthquake and tsunami updates, rocketry, and space science.

- **www.wohlforth.net**. A bit of self-promotion here, but readers can get something out of it. I answer reader questions on a discussion board on my own website. Read answers to scores of other readers' questions and, if you like, ask your own. I supply answers on the entirely free service as soon as I have time. You will also find links to many of the establishments listed in this book, and some of my other writings on Alaska and other subjects.

- **Favorite Small-Town Sites:** Small-town Alaska newspapers, and people in communities too small to have a newspaper, are communicating through the Internet; visitors to these sites can vicariously experience the pleasures and pitfalls of remote living, which can be touching and hilarious. The best I've found are: Seldovia's **www.seldovia.com**; McCarthy and Kennecott's **www.mccarthy-kennicott.com/WSEN.htm**; Nome's **www.nomenugget.com**; Kotzebue's **www.cityofkotzebue.com**; and Talkeetna's **www.talkeetnanews.com**.

2

Planning Your Trip to Alaska

Planning a trip to Alaska can be a bit more complicated than getting ready to travel in the rest of the United States. Aside from the vast distances and range of climatic conditions, the best places book up quickly for the high summer season. This chapter provides general orientation information, then covers when and how to plan a trip to Alaska, including the best outdoor activities and places and the businesses to get you there. I've also included primers on fishing and shopping for Alaska Native art.

1 The Regions in Brief

SOUTHEAST ALASKA The Southeast Panhandle is the relatively narrow strip of mountains and islands lying between Canada and the Gulf of Alaska. To Alaskans, it's Southeast, but to the rest of the country, it's more like the northernmost extension of the lush Pacific Northwest. This is a land of huge rainforest trees, glacier-garbed mountains, and countless islands ranging in size from the nation's third largest to tiny, one-tree islets strewn like confetti along the channels and fjords. The water is the highway of Southeast Alaska, as the land is generally too steep and rugged to build roads, but there are lots of towns and villages reachable by the ferry system or cruise ships. Southeast contains **Juneau,** Alaska's capital and third-largest city, and **Ketchikan,** next in size to Juneau. Southeast's towns are as quaint and historic as any in Alaska, especially **Sitka,** which preserves the story of Russian America and its conflict with the indigenous Native people. Alaska Native culture—here, Tlingit and Haida—is rich and close at hand. No other region offers more opportunities for boating or seeing marine wildlife. Likewise, no other region is as crowded with tourists,

with well over half a million cruise-ship passengers jamming the little towns all summer. The weather is wet and temperate.

SOUTHCENTRAL ALASKA As a region, Southcentral is something of a catchall. The area is roughly defined by the arc of the Gulf of Alaska from the Canadian border on the east to Cook Inlet and the end of the road network to the west. It's a microcosm of the state, containing **Prince William Sound,** which is similar to the wooded island habitat of Southeast; the **Kenai Peninsula,** a fishing, boating, and outdoor mecca with roads; **Anchorage,** the state's modern, major city; and the **Matanuska and Susitna valleys,** an agricultural and suburban region of broad flatlands between steep mountains. Southcentral dominates Alaska, with most of the state's population and a more highly developed transportation system than elsewhere, including a network of highways and the Alaska Railroad. The ocean influences Southcentral's weather, keeping it from being very hot or very cold. The coastal areas are wet, while just behind the coastal mountains the weather is drier.

Alaska by the Numbers

This chart shows some comparative indicators for 17 of Alaska's most popular destinations. The third column is the best season to visit—months during at least part of which there's enough going on and weather is suitable (that includes weather that's good for winter sports). The fourth column lists modes of transportation to each community—in Alaska you can't drive everywhere.

Place	Population	Season	Transportation	Precip. (in.)	Snow (in.)
Anchorage	274,003	May–Sept Jan–Mar	Road, air, rail	15.7	71
Barrow	4,417	June–Aug	Air	4.5	30
Cordova	2,372	May–Sept	Air, ferry	93.1	119
Denali National Park	133	June–Sept	Road, rail	15.3	83
Fairbanks	82,214	May–Sept Jan–Mar	Road, air, rail	10.5	68
Glacier Bay National Park	438	May–Sept	Air, boat	70	117
Haines	1,715	May–Sept/ Nov	Road, ferry, air	48	123
Homer	4,893	May–Sept	Road, air, ferry	24.6	55
Juneau	31,283	May–Sept	Air, ferry	56.3	99
Kenai	7,125	May–Sept	Road, air	19.3	61
Ketchikan	13,548	May–Sept	Air, ferry	150.7	37
Kodiak Island	13,811	May–Sept	Air, ferry	76.3	73
Kotzebue	3,076	June–Aug	Air	9.5	50
Nome	3,448	June–Aug/ Mar	Air	16.1	61
Petersburg	3,060	May–Sept	Air, ferry	110.4	67
Seward	2,733	May–Sept	Road, rail, ferry	66.4	81
Sitka	8,891	May–Sept/ Nov	Air, ferry	86.4	39
Skagway	845	May–Sept	Road, ferry, air	26.4	50
Unalaska/ Dutch Harbour	4,388	June–Sept	Air, ferry	59.9	88
Valdez	4,060	May–Sept	Road, air, ferry	61.5	304

THE INTERIOR The vast central part of the state is crossed by highways and by rivers that act as highways. Big river valleys lie between great mountain ranges, the largest of which are the Alaska Range, which contains **Mount McKinley,** North America's tallest peak, and the Brooks Range, the northern end of the cordillera that includes the Rockies. McKinley is the centerpiece of **Denali National Park,** Alaska's premier road-accessible wildlife-viewing destination. The region's dominant city is **Fairbanks,** Alaska's second largest, which lies on the lazy Chena River, roughly in the middle of the state. The natural environment is drier and less abundant than that in Southeast or Southcentral. The Athabascans, the Interior's first people, still subsist on this sparse land in tiny villages and river fish camps. Summer days can be hot and winters very cold in the Interior, because of the distance from the ocean.

THE BUSH Bush Alaska is linked by lifestyle rather than by geography. One good definition would be that the Bush is the part of the state that's closer to the wilderness than to civilization. It's also the only part of the state where Native people outnumber whites and other relative newcomers. In many Bush villages, readily accessible to the outside world only by small plane, people still live according to age-old subsistence hunting-and-gathering traditions. The Bush region includes the majority of Alaska outside the road and ferry networks, ranging from the north end of the Canadian border all the way around the coast, out to the Aleutians, and the Alaska Peninsula and Kodiak Island, south of Anchorage. But some towns in each of the other regions also could be called "Bush villages." The Bush contains many regions, including the Arctic, Northwest, and Southwest Alaska.

2 Visitor Information

The **Alaska Travel Industry Association,** 2600 Cordova Street, Suite 201, Anchorage, AK 99503 (© **907/929-2842;** www.travelalaska.com) is the state's official visitor information agency, but you may find the Anchorage Convention and Visitor Bureau more responsive (p. 198).

For outdoor recreation, the **Alaska Public Lands Information Centers** are centralized sources of information on all government lands, which include some 85% of the state. The centers, located in Anchorage, Fairbanks, Ketchikan, and Tok, are operated cooperatively by many land agencies, including the National Park Service and U.S. Forest Service. The Anchorage center is at 605 W. 4th Ave., Suite 105, Anchorage, AK 99501 (© **907/271-2737;** www.nps.gov/aplic); the Fairbanks center is at 250 Cushman St., Suite 1A, Fairbanks, AK 99701 (© **907/456-0527**).

Tips Questions, Anyone?

If you can't find the answers you are looking for in this book, check out my personal website, at www.wohlforth.net, where I post and respond to reader questions and comments on travel experiences (specific questions please, not "what should I do on my vacation?"). Reader feedback through the site plays a decisive part in my coverage, pointing out knowledge gaps, showing preferences, and highlighting problems. You will also find some of my other writings about Alaska on the website, links to many of the businesses and agencies in the book, and information about my book, *The Whale and the Supercomputer; On the Northern Front of Climate Change* (North Point Press, $25), which is about the adventures of Eskimos and scientists dealing with the warming of the Arctic.

3 Money

Alaska is an expensive destination any way you slice it. With the exception of a few out-of-the-way spots, standard motel rooms are rarely less than $100 in the high season, and usually over $120. Airfare from Seattle to Anchorage fluctuates wildly with competition among the airlines, but a $300 round-trip, with 14-day advance purchase, is an excellent deal. (Flying is cheaper than the alternatives, driving or taking the ferry and bus.) You can easily pay twice that to fly to an Alaska Bush community. Even the train is expensive, with a one-way fare from Anchorage to Fairbanks (a 350-mile trip) costing $175 on the least luxurious of three choices of cars.

A couple ordering a good salmon dinner, appetizers, and wine will likely pay $100 in a fine restaurant, plus tip. One reason cruise ships have become such a popular way to visit Alaska is that, for the same quality level, they're less expensive on a daily basis than independent travel, and offer the chance to see remote coastal areas that can be quite costly to get to for land-based visitors. (See chapter 4 for details on cruising.)

To travel at a standard American comfort level, a couple should allow $120 per person, per day, for room and board. The cost of an activity such as flightseeing, wildlife cruises, or guided fishing typically is $75 to $250 per person. Add ground transportation: a car is the best way to see much of the state, and you won't do much better than $50 a day for an economy model from the major national firms, although you can save with an unknown company. Weekly rentals generally cost the same as renting for 5 individual days. You also may need train and ferry tickets.

You can trim your costs, however, by cutting your demands. You'll learn more about the real Alaska staying in B&B accommodations than in a standard hotel room. Expect to pay $90 to $110 for a nice room with a shared bathroom, $100 to $130 for a private bathroom (much more in a luxury B&B inn). The complimentary breakfast cuts down on food costs, too. And there are plenty of family restaurants where you can eat a modest dinner for two for $35, with a tip and a glass of beer. Traveling in that style will bring down the cost of room and board to about $90 per person, per day, for a couple.

You can save the most money by giving up a private room every night and cooking some of your own meals. Camping is a fun way to really see Alaska and costs only $10 to $15 a night in state and federal government campgrounds. Hostels are available in most towns for around $20 a night.

Don't economize, however, when it comes to activities. Unlike other destinations where relatively inexpensive museums or an interesting street scene take up much of your time, a trip to Alaska is all about getting outside and seeing nature. You can hike for nothing, but to go sea kayaking, whale-watching, or flying out to see bears or to fish in a remote stream, you have to pay. Cut those expenses and you cut much of the reason for going in the first place.

You can save on activities, however, by traveling in the shoulder season, before and after the peak summer season. Hotel and guided activity prices drop significantly, typically 25% or more. May and September are solidly in the shoulder season, and sometimes you get bargains as late as June 15 or as early as August 15. Traveling in the winter is a whole different experience, but certainly saves a lot of money—where hotels are open, you'll find their rates typically running half of their high-season levels. For other considerations on off-season and shoulder-season travel, see "When to Go," below.

Native Art: Finding the Real Thing

In a gift shop in Southeast Alaska, I watched as a woman who said she was an artist's assistant sanded a Tlingit-style carving. When I asked who made the carving, the artist said, "It's my work." At the time, that seemed like an odd way of putting it. Only later did I learn from one of the artist's former assistants that his "work" involved ordering the carvings from Southeast Asia and shipping them to Alaska, where he hired locals to pretend to be working on them in the shop. Journalists have repeatedly documented shops fraudulently removing "Made in Taiwan" stickers and the like, and replacing them with "Made in Alaska." One journalist found a whole village in Bali carving Alaska Native designs out of ivory, whalebone, and other materials sent from Alaska.

Good estimates don't exist of the amount of counterfeit Alaska Native art sold annually, but authorities put it close to $100 million. That's money taken from Alaska Bush economies where jobs in the cash economy are virtually nonexistent and prices for essentials such as fuel and housing are astronomical. Buying fake Native art is cultural and financial theft from subsistence hunters and fishermen who can least afford it. And besides, who wants to come home with an Eskimo mask made in Bali?

You can avoid being scammed if you pay attention. Ask questions before you buy. Any reputable art dealer will provide you with a biography of the artist who created an expensive work. Ask specifically if that artist actually carved the piece: Some Native artists have sold their names and designs to wholesalers who produce knockoffs. Price is another tip-off. An elaborate mask is more likely to cost $3,000 than $300. Another indicator is the choice of materials; most soapstone carvings are not made in Alaska. Even less expensive craftwork should bear the name of the person who made it, and the shop owner should be able to tell you how he or she acquired the item.

The **Alaska State Council on the Arts** (© 907/269-6610) authenticates Native arts and crafts with a **silver hand** label, which assures you it was made by the hands of an Alaska Native with Alaskan materials. But the program isn't universally used, so the absence of the label doesn't mean the work definitely isn't authentic. Other labels aren't worth much: An item could say ALASKA MADE even if only insignificant assembly work happened here. Of course, in Bush Alaska and in some urban shops, you can buy authentic work directly from craftspeople. Buying in Native-owned co-ops is also safe.

Another program covers any item made within the state, both Native and non-Native. The logo of a mother bear and cub (www.madeinalaska.org/mia) indicates that a state contractor has determined that the product was made in Alaska, when possible with Alaskan materials. Non-Natives produce Alaskan crafts of ceramics, wood, or fabric, but not plastic—if it's plastic, it probably wasn't made here. Again, price is an indicator: As with anywhere else in the United States, the cheapest products come from Asia.

Carrying your money need not be a problem, regardless of your style of travel; those from the United States don't need to make any adjustments in their usual habits. Even Bush hub communities now have ATMs. The only places that don't usually have ATMs these days are remote outdoor destinations such as lodges or parks and tiny Native villages. In the "Fast Facts" section for each town in this book, I'll tell you where to find an ATM, or if you should get cash before going.

Every business you'd expect to take credit, charge, or debit cards at home will accept them here. Even bed-and-breakfasts and greasy-spoon diners usually take cards now. Few businesses of any kind will take an out-of-state personal check. Traveler's checks are good just about anywhere, but there's no longer any reason to go through the hassle and expense.

4 When to Go

CLIMATE & SEASONS

The weather in Alaska can be extreme and unpredictable. The state is the first to get whatever Arctic Siberia or the void of the North Pacific have to throw at North America. The extremes of recorded temperatures are a high of 100°F (38°C) and low of −80°F (−62°C). At any time of year your vacation could be enlivened by weeks of unbroken sunny weather or weighed down by weeks of unbroken rain. All you can do is play the averages, hope for the best, and, if you do get bad weather, get out and have fun anyway—that's what Alaskans do. A statistical summary of weather probabilities in various Alaska places is found below in "Alaska's Climate, by Months & Regions." I've summarized the best visitor season in each destination in "Alaska By The Numbers," above.

JUNE, JULY & AUGUST Summer in Alaska is a miraculous time, when the sun refuses to set, the salmon run upriver, and people are energized by limitless daylight. The sun dips below the horizon in Anchorage for only about 4 hours on June 21, the longest day of the year, and the sky is light all night. The state fills with people coming to visit and to work in the seasonal fishing, timber, and construction industries. Weather gets warmer, although how warm depends on where you go (see the chart below).

June is the driest of the summer months, July the warmest, and August generally the rainiest month of the brief summer, but warmer than June. In most respects, June is the best summer month to make a visit, but it does have some drawbacks to consider: In the Arctic, snow can linger until mid-June; in Southcentral Alaska, trails at high elevations or in the shade may be too muddy or snowy; and not all activities or facilities at Denali National Park open until late June. It's also the worst time for mosquitoes.

Summer also is the season of high prices. Most operators in the visitor industry have only these 90 days to make their year's income, and they charge whatever the market will bear. July is the absolute peak of the tourist season, when you must book well ahead and when crowds are most prevalent. (Of course, crowding depends on where you are. With a population density of roughly one person per square mile, Alaska is never *really* crowded.) Before June 15 and after August 15, the flow of visitors relaxes, providing occasional bargains and more elbow room. Real off-season prices show up before Memorial Day and after Labor Day. But the length and intensity of the visitor season varies widely in different areas: In cruise-ship ports, it's busy from chilly early May into stormy October.

Alaska's Climate, by Months & Regions

	Jan	Feb	Mar	Apr	May	June	July	Aug	Sept	Oct	Nov	Dec
Anchorage: Southcentral Alaska												
Average high**	21/-6	26/-3	33/1	44/7	55/13	62/17	65/18	63/17	55/13	40/4	28/-2	22/-6
Average low**	8/-13	11/-12	17/-8	29/-2	39/4	47/8	51/11	49/9	41/5	28/-2	16/-9	10/-12
Hours of light*	6:53	9:41	12:22	15:20	18:00	19:22	18:00	15:15	12:19	9:29	6:46	5:27
Sunny days†	12	10	13	12	11	10	9	9	9	10	10	10
Rainy or snowy days	8	8	8	6	7	8	11	13	14	12	10	11
Precipitation‡	0.8	0.8	0.6	0.6	0.7	1.0	1.9	2.7	2.6	1.9	1.1	1.1
Barrow: Arctic Alaska												
Average high**	8/-13	-12/-24	-8/-22	6/-14	25/-4	39/4	46/8	43/6	34/1	20/-7	5/-15	-6/-21
Average low**	-20/-29	-24/-31	-21/-29	-8/-22	15/-9	30/-1	34/1	34/1	27/-3	10/-12	-6/-21	-17/-27
Hours of light*	0:00	8:05	12:33	17:43	24:00	24:00	24:00	17:34	12:30	7:46	0:00	0:00
Sunny days†	7	18	21	18	8	9	11	5	4	6	8	4
Rainy or snowy days	4	4	4	4	4	5	9	11	11	11	6	5
Precipitation‡	0.2	0.2	0.1	0.2	0.2	0.3	0.9	1.0	0.6	0.5	0.2	0.2
Cold Bay: Aleutian Archipelago												
Average high**	33/1	32/1	35/2	38/3	45/7	50/10	55/13	56/13	52/11	44/7	39/4	35/2
Average low**	24/-4	23/-5	25/-4	29/-2	35/2	41/5	46/8	47/8	43/6	35/2	30/-1	27/-3
Hours of light*	8:05	10:10	12:17	14:36	16:32	17:25	16:33	14:34	12:17	10:04	8:01	7:08
Sunny days†	8	6	8	4	3	3	3	2	4	6	6	7
Rainy or snowy days	19	17	18	16	17	16	17	20	21	23	22	21
Precipitation‡	2.8	2.5	2.3	2.0	2.5	2.3	2.4	3.7	4.3	4.2	4.2	3.3
Fairbanks: Interior Alaska												
Average high**	-2/-18	8/-13	24/-4	42/6	60/16	71/22	73/23	66/19	55/13	32/0	11/-12	1/-17
Average low**	-19/-28	-15/-26	-2/-19	20/-7	38/3	52/11	52/11	47/8	36/2	17/-8	-5/-21	-16/-27
Hours of light*	5:46	9:14	12:22	15:54	19:22	21:48	19:26	15:52	12:24	9:04	5:39	3:43
Sunny days†	15	14	17	14	16	13	12	10	10	9	12	12
Rainy or snowy days	8	7	6	5	7	11	12	12	10	11	11	9
Precipitation‡	0.6	0.4	0.4	0.2	0.6	1.4	1.8	1.8	1.1	0.8	0.7	0.8
Juneau: Southeast Alaska												
Average high**	29/-2	34/1	39/4	48/9	55/13	62/17	64/18	63/17	56/13	47/8	37/3	32/0
Average low**	18/-8	23/-5	27/-3	32/0	39/4	45/7	48/9	48/9	43/6	37/3	28/-2	23/-5
Hours of light*	7:31	9:55	12:18	14:55	17:11	18:17	17:13	14:54	12:20	9:49	7:27	6:22
Sunny days†	8	7	7	8	8	8	8	9	6	4	6	5
Rainy or snowy days	18	17	18	17	17	15	17	17	20	24	20	21
Precipitation‡	4.3	3.9	3.5	2.9	3.5	3.1	4.2	5.3	7.2	7.8	5.4	5.1
Valdez: Prince William Sound												
Average high**	27/-3	30/-1	37/3	45/7	53/12	60/16	63/17	61/16	54/12	43/6	33/1	29/-2
Average low**	18/-8	19/-7	24/-4	31/-1	39/4	45/7	48/9	46/8	41/5	33/1	23/-5	19/-7
Hours of light*	6:54	9:41	12:22	15:19	17:58	19:20	17:57	15:14	12:20	9:30	6:48	5:29
Sunny days†	9	9	11	11	9	8	8	10	8	8	10	7
Rainy or snowy days	17	14	16	14	17	15	17	17	20	20	16	18
Precipitation‡	5.7	5.5	4.7	3.2	3.2	2.8	3.6	6.5	9.3	7.9	5.7	7.6

*Hours of light is sunrise to sunset on the 21st day of each month.

**All temperatures are given in degrees Fahrenheit first, with degrees Celsius after the slash.

†Sunny days include the average observed clear and partly cloudy days per month.

‡Precipitation is the average water equivalent of rain or snow.

MAY & SEPTEMBER More and more visitors are coming to Alaska during these "shoulder months" to take advantage of the lower prices, reduced crowds, and special beauty.

May is the drier of the two months and can be as warm as summer if you're lucky, but as you travel farther north and earlier in the month, your chances of finding cold, mud, and even snow increase. In Alaska, there is no spring—the melt of snow and resultant seas of mud are called **breakup.** Flowers show up with the start of summer. Many outdoor activities aren't possible during breakup, which can extend well into May. Except in cruise-ship towns, most tourist-oriented activities and facilities are still closed before May 15, and a few don't open until Memorial Day or June 1. Where visitor facilities are open, they often have significantly lower prices. Also, the first visitors of the year usually receive an especially warm welcome. The very earliest salmon runs start in May, but for a fishing-oriented trip it's better to come later in the summer. Cruise ships begin calling May 1, and the towns they visit swing into action when they arrive.

Sometime between late August and mid-September, weather patterns change, bringing clouds, frequent rainstorms, and cooling weather, and signaling the trees and tundra to turn bright, vivid colors. For a week or two (what week it is depends on your latitude), the bright yellow birches of the boreal forest and the rich red of the heathery tundra make September the loveliest time of year. But the rain and the nip in the air, similar to late October or November in New England, mean you'll likely have to bundle up; and September is among the wettest months of the year. Most tourist-oriented businesses stay open, with lower prices, till September 15, except in the Arctic. After September 15, it's potluck. Some areas close up tight, but the silver salmon fishing is still hot on the Kenai Peninsula, and the season there stays active until the end of the month. A lucky visitor can come in September and hit a month of crisp, sunny, perfect weather, and have the state relatively to him- or herself. Or, it can be cold and rainy all month. Cruise ships continue to ply the Inside Passage well into October, while the sky dumps torrential rains: Ketchikan averages 22 inches and 24 rainy days in October.

OCTOBER, NOVEMBER & APRIL I always love Alaska, but I love it least during these transition months between winter and summer. From Southcentral Alaska northward, snow and ice arrive sometime in October; in Southeast Alaska, it is the month of cold, unending rain. Winter starts in November, but you can't count on being able to do winter sports. April is a month of waiting, as winter sports come to an end and summer activities are blocked by melt and mud. In-town activities are down in these months, too; with few visitors, many facilities are closed.

DECEMBER THROUGH MARCH Winter is the whole point of Alaska. For sightseeing, the scenery is at its best (although there are far fewer wildlife viewing opportunities). This is the time to see the aurora borealis. Communities get busy with activities such as sled dog and snow machine races, theater, music and other performing arts, ice carving competitions and winter carnivals, and all the rest of the real local culture that takes a break in the summer, when most visitors come. If you enjoy winter and its outdoor activities, an Alaska visit is paradise, with superb downhill, cross-country, and backcountry skiing; snowshoeing; snowmobiling; dog mushing; ice skating—anything that can be done on snow and ice.

By far the best time to come is late winter, from February 1 through mid-March, when the sun is up longer and winter activities hit their peak. Anchorage's Fur Rendezvous is in February, the Iditarod Sled Dog Race is in March. Visiting in late March could mean thin snow at lower elevations for cross-country skiing, but downhill skiing and skiing at backcountry locations keep going strong (at Alyeska Resort, south of Anchorage, some skiing goes on through Memorial Day).

If you come in winter, you sacrifice some popular Alaska experiences. Some tourism-oriented towns such as Skagway close down almost completely. In places on the ocean, most activities and attractions are closed for the season, but services remain open for business travelers. Inland, where winter sports are better, there is more to do. Hotel prices are often less than half of what you'd pay in the high season. Quite luxurious rooms sometimes go for the cost of a budget motel.

WHAT TO WEAR

You'll find little use for a tie or any formal attire anywhere in Alaska, but you do need to prepare for broad swings in weather.

SUMMER You're not going to the North Pole, and you don't need a down parka or winter boots weighing down your luggage. But you do need to be ready for a variety of weather, from sunny, 80°F (27°C) days to windy, rainy 50°F (10°C) outings on the water. The way Alaskans prepare for such a range is with layers. The content of the layers depends on what you'll be doing, but everyone should bring at least this: warm-weather clothes, heavy long-sleeved shirts and pants, a wool sweater or fleece equivalent, a jacket, and a waterproof raincoat and rain pants. Gloves and wool hats are a good idea, too, especially for boating trips. If you'll be camping,

add synthetic thermal long underwear and wool socks and make your jacket thick synthetic fleece. Combining these items, you'll be ready for any summer conditions. For hiking, bring sturdy shoes or cross trainers.

WINTER You can be warm and comfortable no matter how cold it is. Once you know how to dress, winter is not a time of suffering, and the world of snow opens up to you. First, what not to wear: People don't wear heavy Arctic gear in town, even in the Arctic. To make the dash from car to heated building, all you need is a greatcoat, sweater, hat, gloves, and wool socks. For outdoor pursuits, what to wear depends on how active you will be. The key to warmth and safety during vigorous outdoor activities is to wear layers of breathable clothing that will stay warm when wet, such as wool or synthetics. With the following layers, you can be ready for temperatures well below zero (at which point you won't want to ski or skate anyway): synthetic thermal long underwear, synthetic fleece pants and coat, wool sweater, wind-resistant pants and jacket, wool socks and hat, warm boots with liners or covers, and lined mittens. Remove layers for warmer temperatures. For more sedentary outdoor activities, such as watching the aurora or riding a snow machine or dog sled, you need warmer clothing. Likewise, drives on rural highways in winter require warm clothing in case of breakdowns. On guided trips or at cold weather resorts they'll tell you what to bring or provide or rent it to you. A full cold weather outfit includes synthetic thermal long underwear, the stoutest Sorel-style or Air Force bunny boots, insulated snow pants, a heavy down or fur parka with a hood, thick, insulated mittens (not gloves), a wool hat, a face-insulating mask, and ski goggles or quality sunglasses. You don't want any skin showing while riding a snow

Moments Only-in-Alaska Events

By the end of the winter, sports in Alaska can get extreme. The **Arctic Man Ski & Sno-Go Classic** (© 907/456-2626; www.arcticman.com) sounds insane just in the description: a skier goes straight down a steep 1,700-foot slope, then grabs a rope to be pulled up the next slope by a snow machine going as fast as 88 mph, then skis down the next, 1,200-foot slope. Thousands of spectators build a hard-partying city of RVs and snow machines in the remote, treeless hills of the Alaska Range near Summit Lake on the Richardson Highway. The event will be held from April 6 to 10, 2005.

Muscle-powered sports also have big late winter events, including the 50km **Tour of Anchorage** Nordic ski race (© 907/276-7609; www.tourofanchorage.com), which winds its way from one side of the city to the other, on a Sunday in early March. With as many as 1,700 racers, it has become a major community happening and draws elite skiers, kids, and grandmothers. I ski it every year. Other towns around Alaska have started their own ski marathons during the following weeks.

And don't forget the various human-powered wilderness races that cross Alaska, winter and summer. The most famous of these was the **Iditasport,** now defunct, which gave competitors the option of walking, biking, or skiing over hundreds of miles of the same Iditarod Trail used by the 1,000-mile sled dog race. The **Iditarod Trail Invitational** (www.alaskaultrasport.com) carries on the tradition with common insane distances, tough conditions, and hardy people.

machine or standing in a strong wind in below-zero (Fahrenheit) temperatures. Such a get-up costs more than $500. You can buy what you need in Anchorage at **Army Navy Store,** at 320 W. 4th Ave. (© **907/279-2401**); or in Fairbanks at **Big Ray's Store,** at 507 2nd Ave. (© **907/452-3458**).

ALASKA CALENDAR OF EVENTS

Here are some of the biggest community events of the year in Alaska's cities and towns. Because of our deadlines, many of the dates are estimates. Don't plan a vacation around them without checking for up-to-date details. I haven't listed fishing derbies, which go on in almost every coastal town in the summer and are listed in the sections on each town.

February

The **Yukon Quest International Sled Dog Race** (© 907/452-7954; www.yukonquest.org). Mushers say this rugged 1,000-mile race is even tougher than the Iditarod. It runs between Fairbanks and Whitehorse, Yukon Territory, trading the direction each year. Starts February 13, 2005, in Whitehorse.

The Anchorage Fur Rendezvous Winter Festival (© 907/274-1177; www.furrondy.net). The huge, citywide winter celebration includes all kinds of community events, fireworks, craft fairs, snowshoe softball, dog sled rides, and other fun. The main event has always been the **World Champion Sled Dog Race,** a 3-day sprint event of about 25 miles per heat. In 2005, the Rondy's end will coincide with the start of the Iditarod (see directly below). February 18 to March 6, 2005.

March

The Iditarod Trail Sled Dog Race (© 907/376-5155; www.iditarod. com). The world's most famous sled dog race starts with fanfare from **Anchorage,** then the teams are loaded into trucks for the **Iditarod Restart,** in **Wasilla,** which is the real beginning of the race. Here the historic gold rush trail becomes continuous for the dogs' 1,000-mile run to Nome. The event enlivens Wasilla at the end of a long winter. The finish in Nome is the biggest event of the year in the Arctic, drawing world media attention and turning Nome into a huge party for a few days (they even play golf out on the sea ice). The race solicits volunteers to help, which is a much better way to experience it than just watching. See p. 452 for more details on the Iditarod. In 2005 the race starts March 5.

The Nenana Ice Classic (© 907/ 832-5446; www.nenanaakiceclassic. com), Nenana. This is a betting pool on the date of spring breakup that has happened every year for the last 9 decades. The kick-off is Tripod Days, when a "four-legged tripod" that will mark the ice going out on the Tanana River is erected during the first weekend in March, with a celebration of dance performances, dog mushing, and other activities. The ticket buyer who guesses the minute the tripod will move, usually about 2 months later, wins the jackpot, typically over $300,000.

The World Ice Art Championships (© 907/451-8250; www. icealaska.com), Fairbanks. Carvers from all over the world sculpt immense chunks of clear ice cut from a Fairbanks pond. Among ice carvers, Fairbanks's ice is famous for its clarity and the great size of the chunks. Some spectacular ice sculptures stand as tall as a two-story building. Carving will be March 2 to 4 and 7 to 12 with the best viewing from March 13 to 27, 2005.

April

The Alaska Folk Festival (© 907/ 463-3316; www.alaskafolkfestival. org), Juneau. This is a community-wide celebration, drawing musicians, whether on the bill or not, from all over the state, for a week in mid-April.

May

Copper River Delta Shorebird Festival (© 907/424-7260; www. cordovachamber.com), Cordova. This festival revolves around the coming of dizzying swarms of millions of shorebirds that use the delta and beaches near the town as a migratory stopover in early May. The whole community gets involved to host bird-watchers and put on a schedule of educational and outdoor activities for 3 days.

The Kachemak Bay Shorebird Festival, (© 907/235-7740; http:// homeralaska.org/shorebird.htm), Homer. Held in early May, this festival includes guided bird-watching hikes and boat excursions, natural-history workshops, art shows, and performances, and other events.

Little Norway Festival, (© 907/ 772-4636; www.petersburg.org/ visitor/festivals.html), Petersburg. This festival celebrates the May 17, 1814, declaration of the independence of Norway from Sweden. The town has several days of community events. The festival takes place on the third full weekend in May.

Kodiak Crab Festival (© 907/ 486-5557; www.kodiak.org/crab fest.html), Kodiak. Lasting 5 days over Memorial Day weekend, this is the town's biggest event of the year and includes many fun events, the solemn blessing of the fleet, and a memorial service for lost fishermen. May 26 to May 30, 2005.

June

The Sitka Summer Music Festival (© 907/277-4852; www.sitkamusic festival.org), Sitka. Since 1972, this chamber music series has drawn musicians from all over the world for most of June. Performances take place Tuesdays and Fridays, and other events all week. June 3 to June 24, 2005.

Midnight Sun Baseball Game, Fairbanks. A summer-solstice event: The local semipro baseball team, the Fairbanks Goldpanners (© 907/ 451-0095; www.goldpanners.com) plays a game without artificial lights beginning at 10:30pm. Around June 21.

Midnight Sun Festival, Nome. Over the summer solstice, Nome gets more than 22 hours of direct sunlight, ample reason for a parade, softball tournament, raft race, and polar bear swim (so long as sea ice permits). Call © 907/443-5535 for information. June 21.

The Last Frontier Theater Conference (© 907/834-1614; www. pwscc.edu), Valdez. The conference brings playwrights and directors to the community for seminars and performances in June. Arthur Miller, Edward Albee, and other famous writers have met the public here in an intimate setting.

July

Independence Day. Most of the small towns in Alaska make a big deal of the Fourth of July. Seward always has a huge celebration, exploding with visitors, primarily from Anchorage. Besides the parade and many small-town festivities, the main attraction is the **Mount Marathon Race,** which goes from the middle of town straight up rocky Mount Marathon to its 3,022-foot peak and down again. **Seldovia, Ketchikan, Skagway,** and **Juneau** also have exceptional Fourth of July

events. See the individual town sections for more information.

August

The Southeast Alaska State Fair (© 907/766-2476; www.seakfair. org), Haines. Held for 4 days in mid-August, this is a regional small-town get-together music festival, with livestock, cooking, a logging show, a parade, and other entertainment.

The Alaska State Fair (© 907/ 745-4827; www.akstatefair.org), Palmer. The region's biggest event of the year is a typical state fair, except for the huge vegetables. The good soil and long Valley days produce cabbages the size of beanbag chairs. A mere beach ball–size cabbage wouldn't even make it into competition. Held the 12 days before Labor Day, August 27 to September 5, 2005.

October

Alaska Day Festival (© 907/747-8806), Sitka. Alaska Day, commemorating the Alaska purchase on October 18, 1867, is a big deal in this former Russian and U.S. territorial capital city.

November

Sitka WhaleFest (© 907/747-7964; www.sitkawhalefest.org), Sitka. Over a weekend in early November, during the fall and early winter period when humpback whales congregate in Sitka Sound, internationally known experts present a three-day symposium, and there are whale-watching tours, concerts, an art show, a run, and community events. The event coordinates with the Alaska Bald Eagle Festival (discussed directly below).

The Alaska Bald Eagle Festival (© 907/766-3094; www.baldeagle fest.org), Haines. Seminars and special events mark an annual congregation of 3,000 eagles near Haines. It's timed to allow visitors to also attend the WhaleFest in Sitka (see above).

The **Carrs/Safeway Great Alaska Shootout men's basketball tournament** (© 907/786-1250; www. goseawolves.com/shootout), Anchorage. The University of Alaska Anchorage hosts top-ranked college teams at the Sullivan Arena over Thanksgiving weekend.

5 Travel & Rental Car Insurance

There are three kinds of travel insurance: for **trip cancellation or interruption,** for **medical costs,** and **lost-luggage.** Insurance for trip cancellation or interruption is a must if you have paid the large cash deposits demanded by many Alaska outfitters, fishing guides, wilderness lodges, package tour operators, and cruise companies. A premium of 8% of the cost of the trip is well worth the protection against the uncertainty of Alaska weather (most deposits are lost in case of weather delays or cancellations) or unexpected crises that might prevent you from being able to depart as planned. Interruption insurance will even get you home under covered circumstances. Read the policy carefully to find out when you are covered. Think twice before buying insurance directly from the operator holding your deposit: what if they go out of business? Also, major third-party insurers such as those listed below offer policy-holders access to 24-hour phone assistance to help handle crises.

Medical insurance for travelers from outside the United States is a worthwhile investment, too, but travelers from the U.S. likely are already covered under their regular health insurance. You may want extra insurance, however, for astronomically expensive emergency medical transportation if you will spend much time on your own in remote areas; check the coverage offered by your credit cards or buy a policy just for the trip.

Insurance on your baggage is rarely advantageous. Your baggage is probably covered under your homeowners' policy or credit card benefits. If the airline loses your bags, they are usually responsible for up to $2,500 per passenger on domestic flights or, on international flights up to approximately $635 per checked bag. Expensive items such as jewelry and cameras are not included. Carry valuables with you, then insure your baggage only if the worth you are able to prove is more than the airline's responsibility and the limits on your existing policies. That's unlikely, because to prove the value of your lost clothing and such you would need bills of sale or similar documentation for each item.

Various companies sell travel insurance online, including **Access America** (© 866/807-3982; www.access america.com) and **Travel Guard International** (© 800/826-4919; www.travelguard.com). Or look for the best deal around by going to **www.insure.com** and click on the "Travel" tab. The site allows travelers to get instant quotes from many insurance companies at once by providing the dates of the trip, amount and type of coverage, and ages of the travelers.

With **rental cars** you face a whole different set of insurance considerations. Most of these are the same as renting a car anywhere, and a few simple preparations will get you through. Before you leave home, check your own auto policy for your liability coverage with a rented car (bringing proof of insurance along is a good idea), and check with your credit card issuer for coverage for damage to a rented car (make sure to use that card when you rent, too). Chances are, you are already covered and don't need to buy the unreasonably priced insurance offered by the rental car company when you rent, but if you are not

Tips **Using the Internet on the Road**

Don't take your laptop on vacation. For one thing, it's pathetic. For another, it's unnecessary. Even tiny Alaska towns have some kind of Web access these days; most have an Internet cafe, while in others you can log on at the public library. Internet access for each Alaska community is listed in the appropriate sections of the book. Typically, you can find the information you want for less than $5. Relying on this kind of access is easier than lugging a computer around, worrying about it being stolen, and trying to connect through spotty phone lines on weird hotel phone systems. While more expensive hotels oriented to business travelers often have wireless high-speed Internet or even Ethernet jacks, many others have only a dataport jack on the phone or nothing at all. Unless your Internet Service Provider has a local modem phone number in the town you are visiting, you will have to dial long distance or navigate through another system. That can be time-consuming, frustrating, and expensive.

There are three ways to check your e-mail on the Web from any computer. One: Your Internet Service Provider probably has a Web-based interface. Just find out how it works before you leave home. Two: You can open an account on a free, Web-based e-mail provider before you leave home, such as Microsoft's **Hotmail** (www.hotmail.com) or **Yahoo! Mail** (www.mail.yahoo.com). Your home ISP may be able to forward your home e-mail to the Web-based account automatically. Or, three: Use **www.mail2web.com**. This amazing free service allows you to type in your regular e-mail address and password and retrieve your e-mail from any Web browser, anywhere, so long as your home ISP hasn't blocked it with a firewall.

covered, do buy it: the potential costs you face are even larger than having a crash at home, because they include the rental company's lost business.

One special Alaska consideration: ask the reservation agent or check the rental contract for rules about driving on unpaved roads or other restrictions.

I have listed companies that rent for unpaved highways in Fairbanks and Anchorage (chapters 9 and 6, respectively) but very few others allow it. Cars do get damaged on these roads, and you may be setting yourself up for a real headache if you violate the rental contract and that happens.

6 Health & Safety

CRIME & EMERGENCY SERVICES

CRIME Sadly, crime rates are not low in Alaska's larger cities, although muggings are rare. Take the normal precautions you'd take at home. You're safe in daylight hours anywhere tourists commonly go, less so late at night leaving a bar or walking in a lonely place. Women need to be especially careful on their own, as Alaska has a disproportionately high rate of rape. Most women I know avoid walking by themselves at night, especially in wooded or out-of-the-way areas. The late-night sunlight can be deceiving—just because it's light out doesn't mean it's safe. Sexual assaults occur in towns big and small. Women should never hitchhike alone. If you are a victim of a crime, you can reach police almost anywhere by calling 911, or, if it is not an emergency, by using the numbers listed under "Fast Facts" in each community section.

MEDICAL EMERGENCIES You'll find modern, full-service hospitals in each of Alaska's larger cities, and even in some small towns that act as regional centers. There's some kind of clinic even in the smallest towns, although they often are staffed by physicians' assistants rather than medical doctors. I've listed the address and phone numbers for medical facilities in each destination under "Fast Facts." Call those numbers, too, for referrals to a dentist or other health professional. In an emergency, call 911.

If health is a particular concern, consider joining **MedicAlert** (© **888/ 633-4298;** www.medicalert.org) and wearing their engraved bracelet, which will alert emergency medical personnel of a primary preexisting medical condition and provide them with access to the organization's response center for your information on file, such as medications and physician and family contacts. The cost is $35 for the first year, then $20 a year.

OUTDOORS HEALTH & SAFETY

AVALANCHE When snow sliding down a mountain comes to a stop it hardens to a consistency that only metal tools can dig through. Avalanche survivors describe the terror of being helplessly locked in this unyielding material hoping for rescue. Understandably, survivors are in the minority. If a victim isn't found quickly (well before emergency personnel can arrive at a remote slope) they die. No one should go into the snowy backcountry without training in avalanche avoidance and recovery equipment, including locator beacons, probes, and

shovels. Go with a guide if you are unsure.

BEARS & OTHER WILDLIFE Being eaten by a bear is probably the least likely way for your vacation to end. Deaths from dog bites are much more common, for example. But it's still wise to be prepared for bears and to know how to avoid being trampled by moose, which can be fatal.

The first rule of defense is simple: *Don't attract bears.* All food and trash must be kept in airtight containers when you're camping. When car camping, the trunk of the vehicle will do. When backpacking, you can protect your food by hanging it from a long tree branch or, above tree line, storing it in a bear-resistant canister (for rent or loan in Anchorage or at Denali or Wrangell–St. Elias National Parks; see chapters 6, 8, and 9). Be careful not to spread food odors when you're cooking and cleaning up. Clean fish away from your campsite. Never keep food, pungent items, or clothing that smells like fish in your tent.

When walking through brush or thick trees, make lots of noise to avoid surprising a bear or moose. Bells you can hang on your belt are for sale at sporting-goods shops, or you can sing or carry on loud conversation. You might not scare a bear away this way, but at least you won't startle it. At all costs, avoid coming between a bear and its cubs or a bear and food (if a bear wants the fish you just caught, that's his food, too). Moose also are strongly defensive of their young. Even a moose on its own can attack if it feels you're getting too close. People are badly hurt every year trying to sneak by a moose on a trail. I see moose every day when I ski, bike, or run near my house in Anchorage; when they're in the way, I turn around and go the other way.

If you see a bear, stop, wave your arms, make noise, and, if you're with others, group together so you look larger to the bear. Don't run, tempting the bear to chase; depart by slowly backing away, at an angle if possible. If the bear follows, stop. Once in a great while, the bear may bluff a charge; even less often, it may attack. If you're attacked, fall and play dead, rolling into a ball facedown with your hands behind your neck. The bear should lose interest. In extremely rare instances, a bear may not lose interest, because it's planning to make a meal of you. If this happens, fight back for all you're worth.

Many Alaskans carry a gun for protection in bear country, but that's not practical for visitors. A good alternative is a bear-deterrent spray. These are canisters that you shoot to produce a burning fog of capsaicin pepper between you and a threatening bear. While less effective than a gun, especially in wind or rain, the sprays are legal in national parks and OK to carry across the Canadian border—two big advantages over firearms. *Note:* You can *not* bring bear-deterrent spray in your carry-on luggage. A can costs about $45 at sporting-goods stores, or order direct from **Counter Assault** (© **800/695-3394;** www. counterassault.com). Be sure to get a holster, too, as the spray is of no use buried in your backpack. If you do take a gun, it had better be a big one, such as a .300-Magnum rifle or 12-gauge shotgun loaded with slugs. No handgun is big enough for a large bear.

BOATING SAFETY Because of the cool temperatures, unpredictable weather, and cold water, going out on the ocean or floating a fast river is more hazardous in Alaska than in most other places, and you should go only with an experienced, licensed operator unless you know what you're doing. There's little margin for error if you fall into the water or capsize—you have only minutes to get out and get warm before hypothermia and death.

A life jacket will keep you afloat, but it won't keep you alive in 40°F (4°C) water. If you're sea kayaking or canoeing, stay close to shore and take plastic dry bags (also called float bags) with everything you need to quickly warm a person who gets wet (see "Hypothermia," below).

DANGEROUS PLANTS Two shrubs common in Alaska can cause skin irritation, but there is nothing as bad as poison ivy or poison oak. **Pushki,** also called cow parsnip, is a large-leafed plant growing primarily in open areas, up to shoulder height by late summer, with white flowers. The celerylike stalks break easily, and the sap has the quality of intensifying the burning power of the sun on skin. Wash it off quickly to avoid a rash. **Devil's Club,** a more obviously dangerous plant, grows on steep slopes and has ferocious spines that can pierce through clothing. Also, don't eat anything you can't positively identify, as there are deadly poisonous mushrooms and plants.

GETTING LOST Even experienced people do it. Hiking off trail or voyaging in a canoe, raft, or kayak, you quickly find that one mountain looks a lot like another. If you are unsure of your navigational skills, maps or equipment, don't go. Beyond those basics, the most important safety precautions are to go with another person and to make sure someone knows where to look for you if you don't come back. For extended trips (more than a day-hike) leave a written trip plan with a person who will call rescuers if you are late. At the very least, leave a note in your car indicating where you are bound. Cell phones sometimes work near towns and some highways, but not reliably and there is no coverage beyond populated areas.

Nowadays, it is possible to rent an Iridium satellite phone that will work outdoors anywhere on earth from

RoadPost (© **888/290-1616** or 905/ 272-5665; www.roadpost.com), starting at $89 a week plus $2 a minute; cheap if it saves your life, but not as good as knowing where you are and what you are doing. They send you the phone by overnight express. An Alaska-based firm, **Microcom** (© **907/348-0425**), offers the same service, but charges $145 a week plus $2 a minute.

HYPOTHERMIA A potentially fatal lowering of core body temperature can sneak up on you. It's most dangerous when you don't realize how cold you are, perhaps in 50°F (10°C) weather on a damp mountain hike or rainy boating trip. Dress in material (whether wool or synthetic) that keeps its warmth when wet, choosing layers to avoid chilling perspiration. (See "What to Wear," p. 24.) Eating well and avoiding exhaustion also are important. Among the symptoms of hypothermia are cold extremities, being uncommunicative, displaying poor judgment or coordination, and sleepiness. A shivering victim still has the ability to warm up if better dressed; a lack of shivering means the body has gone beyond that point and warmth must be added from the outside or from warm drinks. Get indoors, force hot liquids on the victim (except if not fully conscious, which could cause choking), and, if shelter is unavailable, apply body heat from another person, skin on skin, in a sleeping bag.

INSECT BITES The good news is that Alaska has no snakes or poisonous spiders. The bad news is that Alaska makes up for it with mosquitoes and other biting insects. West Nile virus has not arrived here at this writing so the mosquitoes are not dangerous, but they can ruin a trip. Effective insect repellent is a necessity, as is having a place where you can get away from them. We use shirts with hoods of netting when the bugs are at their worst.

Mosquitoes can bite through light fabric close to the skin, which is why people in the Bush wear heavy, baggy Carhart pants and jackets (made of canvas) even on the hottest days. Benadryl tablets or other antihistamines will often relieve swelling caused by mosquito bites.

RIVER CROSSINGS Hiking in Alaska's backcountry often requires crossing rivers without bridges. Use great caution: It's easy to get in trouble. Often, the water is glacial melt, barely above freezing and heavy with silt that makes it opaque. The silt can fill your pockets and drag you down. If in doubt, don't do it. If you do decide to cross, unbuckle your pack, keep your shoes on, face upstream, use a heavy walking stick if possible, and rig a safety line. Children should go in the eddy behind a larger person, or be carried.

SHELLFISH Don't eat mussels, clams, or scallops you pick or dig from the seashore unless you know they're safe to eat. The **Alaska Department of Environmental Conservation** maintains a hotline and Web site (© **800/731-1312;** www.alaska.gov/ dec/eh/fss/seafood/psphome.htm, or go to www.alaska.gov and search for "psp"), which explains the risks and lists beaches that have been tested and approved. These mostly are on Kachemak Bay in small inlets around oyster farms. Most of Alaska's remote beaches are not tested and so are not safe. The risk is paralytic shellfish poisoning, a potentially fatal malady caused by a naturally occurring toxin. It causes total paralysis that includes your breathing. A victim may be kept alive with mouth-to-mouth resuscitation until medical help is obtained.

WATER Unpurified river or lake water may not be safe to drink. Handheld filters available from sporting-goods stores for around $75 are the most practical way of dealing with the problem. Iodine kits and boiling also work. The danger is a protozoan cyst called *giardia lamblia,* which causes diarrhea and is present in thousands of water bodies all over the United States, even in remote areas, where it may have been carried by waterfowl. It may not show up until a couple of weeks after exposure and could become chronic. If symptoms show up after you get home, tell your doctor you may have been exposed so that you can get tested and cured.

DRIVING SAFETY

ROAD REPORTS The Alaska Department of Transportation has centralized highway reports with a handy toll-free phone and Internet system (© **511;** http://511.alaska. gov). Even in dry summer conditions, it is wise to make the call or check the site before heading on an inter-city drive, because road construction can cause long delays—at times, they will close a major highway overnight for work. In winter, checking on conditions is a basic safety essential. Here are more seasonal tips.

SUMMER Keep your headlights on all the time for safety on the highway. Drivers are required to pull over at the next pull-out whenever five or more cars are trailing them on a two-lane highway, regardless of how fast they're going. This saves the lives of people who otherwise will try to pass. When passing a truck going the other way on a gravel highway, slow down or stop and pull as far as possible to the side of the road to avoid losing your windshield to a flying rock. Always think about the path of rocks you're kicking up toward others' vehicles. Make sure you've got a good, full-size spare tire and jack if you're driving a gravel highway. For remote driving, bring along a first-aid kit, emergency food, a tow rope, and jumper cables, and keep your gas tank full.

WINTER Drivers on Alaska's highways in winter should be prepared for cold-weather emergencies far from help. Take all the items listed for rural summer driving, plus a flashlight, matches and materials to light a fire, chains, a shovel, and an ice scraper. A camp stove to make hot beverages is also a good idea. If you're driving a remote highway (such as the Alaska Hwy.) between December and March, take along gear adequate to keep you safe from the cold even if you have to wait overnight with a dead car at –40°F/–40°C (see "What to Wear," earlier in this chapter, and add blankets and sleeping bags). Never drive a road marked "Closed" or "Unmaintained in Winter." Even on maintained rural roads, other vehicles rarely come by. All Alaska roads are icy all winter. Studded tires are a necessity—nonstudded snow tires or so-called "all-weather" tires aren't adequate. Also, never leave your car's engine stopped for more than 4 hours in temperatures of –10°F (–23°C) or colder. Alaskans generally have electrical head-bolt heaters installed to keep the engine warm overnight; you'll find electrical outlets everywhere in cold, Interior Alaska areas.

7 Escorted Tour or Do-It-Yourself?

Hundreds of thousands of visitors come to Alaska each year on escorted package tours, leaving virtually all their travel arrangements in the hands of a single company that takes responsibility for ushering them through the state for a single, lump-sum fee. Many others cut the apron strings and explore Alaska on their own, in the process discovering a more relaxed, spontaneous experience. Each approach has advantages and disadvantages, of course, and which way you choose to visit depends on how you value those pros and cons. Unfortunately, some people make the choice based on expectations that aren't valid, so it's important to know what you're getting into.

An escorted package tour provides security. You'll know in advance how much everything will cost, you don't have to worry about making hotel and ground-transportation reservations, you're guaranteed to see the highlights of each town you visit, and you'll have someone telling you what you're looking at. Often, a package price saves money over traveling at the same level of comfort independently. If there are weather delays or other travel problems, it's the tour company's problem, not yours. Everything happens on schedule, and you never have to touch your baggage other than to unpack when it magically shows up in your room. If you sometimes feel like you're a member of a herd on an escorted tour, you'll also meet new people, a big advantage if you're traveling on your own. Many passengers on these trips are retired, over age 65.

If you're short on time, escorted package tours make the most of it, as they often travel at an exhausting pace. Passengers get up early and cover a lot of ground, with sights and activities scheduled solidly through the day. Stops last only long enough to get a taste of what the sight is about, not to dig in and learn about a place you're especially interested in. On an escorted trip, you'll meet few if any Alaska residents, since most tour companies hire college students from "Outside" (a term Alaskans use to refer to any place that's not in Alaska) to fill summer jobs. You'll stay in only the largest hotels and eat in the largest, tourist-oriented restaurants—no small, quaint places loaded with local character. For visiting wilderness, such as Denali National Park, the quick and superficial approach can, in my opinion, spoil the whole point of going to a destination that's about an experience, not just seeing a particular object or place.

Studies by Alaska tourism experts have found that many people choose escorted packages to avoid risks that don't really exist. Alaska may still be untamed, but that doesn't mean it's a dangerous or uncomfortable place to travel. Visitors who sign up for a tour to avoid having to spend the night in an igloo or use an outhouse may wish they'd been a bit more adventurous when they arrive and find that Alaska has the same facilities found in any other state. Except for tiny Bush villages that you're unlikely to visit anyway, you'll come across the standard American hotel room almost anywhere you go. The tourism infrastructure is well developed even in small towns—you're never far from help unless you want to be.

It's also possible for an independent traveler to obtain some of the predictability a package tour provides. You can reserve accommodations and activities and control your expenses by using a good travel agent experienced in Alaska travel. Some even offer fixed-price itineraries that allow you to travel on your own (see "Independent Travel Planning," at the end of this section). But independent travelers never have the complete security of those on group tours. Once you're on the road, you'll be on your own to take care of the details, and weather delays and other cancellations can confound the best-laid plans. If you can't relax and enjoy a trip knowing unforeseen difficulties could happen, then an escorted package tour is the way to go.

LARGE TOUR COMPANIES

Two major tour and cruise-ship companies dominate the Alaska package-tour market with "vertically integrated" operations that allow them to take care of everything you do while in Alaska with tight quality control. Each also offers tours as short as a couple of hours to independent travelers who want to combine their own exploring with a more structured experience. All can be booked through any travel agent. Other cruise lines also offer land tours, but typically only for their own passengers. If you will cruise to Alaska and want an escorted land tour, check for deals with your cruise line first.

Holland America Tours The Holland America cruise line is the giant of Alaska tourism. Holland America purchases built the business, with companies such as Gray Line and Westours to carry visitors in buses, trains, and boats, and the Westmark hotel chain to put them up for the night. Today the Alaska/Yukon operation employs more than 2,500 workers operating 184 buses, 13 railcars, and two day boats. Most clients arrive in the state on one of the company's ships (see chapter 4), but even within Alaska, chances are good that a tour you sign up for will put you on a Gray Line coach and exclusively in Westmark hotels. The quality of the Westmark chain is inconsistent; most are described in the town sections of this book. Other than the classy Baranof in Juneau, they tend to have standard to small rooms with above average amenities. On a group tour, you don't spend much time in the room, as schedules generally are tightly planned and daily departures are early. You'll find a description of the company's railcars on the Anchorage-Denali-Fairbanks run in chapter 8. Gray Line coaches are first-rate, especially several super-luxurious, extra-long vehicles that bend in the middle and have a lounge in the back. And the company goes more places than any other, with a catalog that covers just about anything in the state that could possibly be done with a group. They also have self-drive tours. Some of the tour excursions—on the Yukon River between Dawson City and Eagle, for example—are entirely unique. Prices depend on a variety of factors, but in

general a tour of a week is about $1,400 per person.

300 Elliot Ave. W, Seattle, WA 98119. ✆ **800/544-2206.** www.graylineofalaska.com or www.hollandamerica.com.

Princess Cruises and Tours Bought out by Carnival Corp., the owner of its primary competition, Holland America (see above), Princess insists it still operates and competes independently. That's important, because these two companies control the vast majority of the land tour market in Alaska. Princess built its tour operation from the ground up, surpassing Holland America with the consistently outstanding quality of its smaller list of offerings. The five Princess hotels are all among Alaska's best. Two are near Denali National Park, and one each are in Fairbanks, in Cooper Landing (on the Kenai Peninsula), and in Copper Center, near Wrangell–St. Elias National Park. Princess operates its own coaches and has superb railcars on the Alaska Railroad route to Denali. Descriptions of each hostelry can be found in the appropriate chapter. Most people on the tours come to Alaska on a cruise ship, but tours are for sale separately, too.

2815 Second Ave., Suite 400, Seattle, WA 98121-1299. ✆ **800/426-0500.** www.princesslodges.com.

INDEPENDENT TRAVEL PLANNING

With this guidebook, you can book everything yourself, but for a long trip it can get quite complicated to keep track of all the dates and deposits. If you're using a trusted travel agency to make trip arrangements, our reviews can help you make informed decisions. Read through the book, make your selections, and approach the agent with as detailed a plan as possible, derived from your own research. Then let the agent make the bookings you have chosen. Most agents who don't specialize in Alaska are aware of only the biggest attractions and best-marketed companies. Another option is to use a travel agency or trip-planner based in Alaska. They'll know much more about the place and can help you more in picking out what you want to do. I've listed a few below.

Unfortunately, there are cautions to be offered in using the agencies. They work on commission, which means they're being paid by the establishments you're buying from. A good agent will disregard the size of the commission and really look out for you, but I've encountered too many visitors on poorly planned itineraries not to advise caution. Some travel agents book visitors on trips to far-flung corners of the state in quick succession, so they wind up staying only briefly in expensive places and then zoom off somewhere else, all with little concern for the visitors' true interests. Your best defense is to do enough research so you can actively participate in the planning.

Here I've gathered the names of some agencies that book Alaska trips. Expect to pay booking fees and to have the agent collect commissions from the businesses you use. My knowledge of these agencies is limited to contacting them as a journalist, so a mention here is no guarantee; however, I do remove agencies from the list when I receive justified complaints. In 2003, one of the largest trip planners in Alaska went bankrupt, leaving many visitors with worthless vouchers for pre-paid reservations. If you pre-pay large trip expenses to a planner or a provider directly, be certain to get appropriate insurance from an independent source, such as those listed later in this chapter under "Health & Safety."

Alaska Bound This Michigan-based agency is the only one I know of in the Lower 48 that specializes in Alaska. It started as a cruise planner,

working primarily with Holland America, but now plans many independent trips, too, charging a per person fee which depends on the length of the trip ($100 per person would not be exceptional).

116 Cass St. Traverse City, MI 49684. © **888/ ALASKA-7** or 231/439-3000. www.alaskabound. com.

Alaska Tour and Travel Operated by the same folks who have the Park Connection shuttle between Denali and Kenai Fjords national parks, this agency specializes in the parks and points between, plus Wrangell–St. Elias National Park and Fairbanks. The fancy website includes pre-set itineraries for independent travelers that they will customize without additional cost.

P.O. Box 221011, Anchorage, AK 99522. © **800/ 208-0200.** www.alaskatravel.com.

All Ways Travel This is a traditional travel agency in downtown Anchorage with many years of experience which has branched out into adventure trip planning and which lists themed independent packages (fishing, native culture, etc.) on its Web site. Fees depend on the effort expended and type of bookings you need.

302 G St., Anchorage, AK 99501. © **800/676-2946** or 907/276-3644. www.alaskatripshop.com.

Fantasia Travel This agency, under the same ownership as Camp Alaska Tours (mentioned later in this chapter) gladly puts clients in B&Bs and cabins, not just the high-priced places most agents prefer to use.

290 N. Yenlo, L-2, Wasilla, AK 99654. © **800/478-2622** or 907/376-2622. www.alaskaflights.com.

Sport Fishing Alaska Choose this company to plan a fishing vacation. The owners, former guides and float, charter, and air-taxi operators Larry and Sheary Suiter, know where the fish will be week to week. They also can book the balance of your trip at

---

---

fun and interesting places. They charge a $95 upfront fee. (See "Fishing," below.)

9310 Shorecrest Dr., Anchorage, AK 99502. © **888/552-8674** or 907/344-8674. www.AlaskaTrip Planners.com.

Viking Travel An entrepreneur in the small Southeast Alaska town of Petersburg built this travel agency, initially specializing in independent outdoor trips in their own area. They plan trips for the whole state and book Alaska and B.C. ferries without surcharge. Get on their list and they will book your cabins and vehicle reservations on the first day the system makes them available.

101 N. Nordic Dr. (P.O. Box 787),, Petersburg, AK 99833 © **800/327-2571** or 907/772-3818. www.AlaskaFerry.com.

---

8 Planning an Outdoor Vacation

Most people visit Alaska to experience wilderness, so it's ironic that so many spend their time in crowded ships, buses, trains, and airplanes, the antithesis of a wilderness experience. You do need technology to get to the wilderness of Alaska, but unless you at least partly let loose of that umbilical cord, you'll never really arrive at your destination.

Every town in Alaska is a threshold to the wild. There's always a way to go hiking, biking, or sea kayaking, or to get on the bank of a stream or the deck of a boat to hook into a furiously fighting wild salmon—and end up in the evening back in a comfortable hotel room. Or take it a step further: Plan to go out overnight, perhaps with a friendly local guide at first, and then go out on your own. I've included lots of details on how to do this throughout the book. Scary? If it weren't a little scary, it would be Disneyland, and that it definitely is not. It's real, and that's why it's worth doing.

Wilderness lodges (which to me means a place you can't drive to) are listed in the following sections: section 9 in chapter 5; section 10 in chapter 7; and section 11 in chapter 8. Remote Forest Service cabins are covered in "Forest Service Cabins" in section 1 of chapter 5, and "Remote Cabins" in section 3 of chapter 7.

ACTIVITIES
BACKPACKING Alaska's best country for trail hikes is in **Chugach State Park** near Anchorage (chapter 6), on Chena Hot Springs Road and on the Steese Highway near Fairbanks (chapter 9), and in the **Chugach National Forest** on the Kenai Peninsula (chapter 7). For hiking beyond trails, go to **Denali** or the **Denali Highway** (chapter 8), **Wrangell–St. Elias National Parks** or the **Dalton Highway** (chapter 9). Alaska trail hikes require the same skills as backpacking anywhere else, plus preparation for cold and damp (see "What to Wear," earlier). Hiking beyond the trails is a glorious experience, but you need to know how to cross rivers and find your way—it's best if you have some outdoor experience. Or go with

> **Tips A Guide to Guide Gratuities**
>
> As a general rule, tip fishing guides and outfitters $10 to $20 per person per day. For outings of less than a day, adjust the tip accordingly. At wilderness lodges, which normally have all-inclusive rates, it's often best to add the tip to your final payment when you leave and let the proprietor distribute it to the staff rather than try to do it at each meal. A blanket tip of $15 per person per day is acceptable.

a guide; they're listed below. See section 9, later in this chapter, for some backcountry safety tips.

BIKING   Most every town in Alaska has a bike-rental agency. There are excellent bike routes all over the state and few restrictions on where you can ride. A bike is a great way into Denali National Park (see chapter 8); Anchorage has an extensive network of paved trails and many mountain biking routes (see chapter 6); and guided biking is available in Haines and Skagway (see chapter 5).

BIRD-WATCHING   In Alaska, birders can encounter birds in greater variety and greater numbers than they have seen before and add many new species to their life lists. Serious birders with money to spend can dedicate a trip to some of the worlds' best and most famous remote bird-watching sites. Find those tours advertised in birding magazines, such as *Bird Watcher's Digest* (www.birdwatchers digest.com) or *Birders' World* (www. birdersworld.com). Among the reputable operators coming to Alaska are Arizona-based **High Lonesome Bird-Tours** (℡ 800/743-2668; www.hi lonesome.com), priding itself on relaxed trips for small groups; and Texas-based **Victor Emanuel Nature Tours** (℡ 800/328-8368; www. ventbird.com), which counts well-known authors among its leaders.

The very best bird and wildlife destination in Alaska is probably the Pribilof Islands. You can sign up directly with the island's own residents for a tour there, described in chapter 10. Travelers with a less intense interest in bird-watching also can pursue it as part of a vacation without making birding the focus. Day tours that include exceptional bird sighting opportunities are to be had in Wrangell, Sitka, and Haines (chapter 5); at Whittier and in Kenai Fjords National Park (chapter 7); and at Unalaska (chapter 10). Community events surrounding spring migrations happen in Wrangell, Cordova (chapter 7), and Homer. Self-guided birding opportunities crop up in almost every town; I have described the best in the outdoors section on each. Among those destinations where self-guided bird-watching justifies trips in themselves are the Copper River Delta near Cordova, the Chilkat Bald Eagle Preserve near Haines, and the roads and beaches around Nome and Barrow (chapter 10).

CANOEING   Paddling a canoe on a remote Alaska lake or river is the best way to get into the wilderness without a backpack, a guide, or a great deal of expense. For beginners, it's easy to rent a canoe in Fairbanks (chapter 9) for a day trip. If you're ready to go overnight, the choices of routes are extraordinary, including the rivers of the Interior (chapter 9), the bird-watching country of the Copper River Delta near Cordova, or the supreme lake canoe routes of the Kenai National Wildlife Refuge (both in chapter 7).

CAR OR RV CAMPING Campgrounds are almost everywhere in Alaska, many in extraordinarily beautiful natural places. Public campgrounds far outnumber commercial ones. They're usually located where they are because there's something special about the place: a great view or beach, an exceptional fishing stream or trail head. Rarely will you find running water or flush toilets; most are seasonal, with hand pumps for water. (When it's time to wash up, stay at a commercial campground, which I've noted in each town section in the destination chapters throughout this book.) Alaska's public campgrounds fill up only in certain times and places (the Kenai River and Denali National Park campgrounds are among the exceptions), so campers have flexibility other travelers can't share, and are able to stop when and where they like.

Even if you don't usually consider camping, think about renting a comfortable RV for a tour. One company offers these rentals as add-ons with cruise vacations, taking care of all the details for clients (that and other rental options are under "Getting There & Getting Around," later in this chapter).

If you fly to Alaska, car camping can be a bit complicated. Carrying a camp stove on an airplane is forbidden unless there is no attached fuel canister and no odor of fuel (even in that case, keep the unit handy for inspection at check in). It may make sense to buy a new stove in Alaska and then give it away or ship it back to yourself at the end of the trip. Much car camping equipment is bulky and hard to fit into your limit of two checked bags. Consider renting some of your gear here: rental agencies are listed with large towns in this book. You can also use the mail, sending packages to yourself care of General Delivery at any post office, or simply invest in compact, backpacking equipment that you can fit in your luggage.

I've mentioned some great campgrounds throughout the book, but there are many more than I had space to cover. A map that lists all the public campgrounds is available from the Alaska Public Lands Information Centers (see "Visitor Information," earlier) for 25¢. If you are planning to camp the whole way, get a copy of *Traveler's Guide to Alaskan Camping*, by Mike and Terri Church (Rolling Homes Press; $22), which contains detailed reviews of virtually every public and commercial campground in the state.

Finally, you can join a car camping tour with a group and a guide who handles all the details. CampAlaska Tours and Alaska Wildland Adventures, described below under "Outfitters and Outdoor Package Trips," both offer these tours.

FISHING Fishing in Alaska may spoil you for fishing anywhere else. The world's largest salmon and halibut were caught here in recent years, and Pacific salmon are so plentiful that catching and processing them still provides the state's largest source of employment. Fly fishermen also come for thriving wild stocks of steelhead, cutthroat, and rainbow trout; Dolly Varden and Arctic char; and Arctic grayling.

There's no room here to tell you how to fish in Alaska—the best way is to pick it up from other anglers, most conveniently by going with a guide on your first outing. If you can afford it, a day of guided fly-in fishing to a remote stream is the ultimate (you can do it from virtually any town listed in chapters 5, 6, or 7). You can also study with a book; several are available, the best of which focus on individual areas of the state or particular fishing techniques rather than trying to cover everything.

A Salmon Primer

In Alaska, it's not so much where you wet your line, but when. The primary catch, Pacific salmon, lives in salt water but spawns in fresh water, with each fish returning to the stream of its birth during a certain, narrow window of time called a "run." When the salmon are running, fishing is hot; when they're not running, it's dead. And the runs change from day to day, typically lasting only a few weeks. (Halibut, on the other hand, are bottom-dwelling ocean fish; you can fish them from a boat every day when the tide is right.) You can fish salmon all over the state in fresh and salt water, but the closer you are to the ocean, the better the fish are. Salmon flesh softens in fresh water and the skin turns dull and red. Salmon right from salt water that haven't started their spawning cycle are called silver bright—when you see one, you'll understand why. No Pacific salmon feeds in fresh water, but kings and silvers, meat eaters at sea, strike out of habit when they reach the river.

There are five species of Pacific salmon, each preferring its own habitat, and, even when the habitat overlaps, each timing its run differently. Each species has two names.

King (or **chinook**) is the most coveted, best fighting fish, commonly growing to 30 pounds in 5 to 7 years at sea (the sport record, from the Kenai River, was 97 pounds, and the largest ever, taken by commercial fishermen near Petersburg, was 126 pounds). It takes a lot of effort to hook and land a big king, but it's the ultimate in Alaska fishing. You also need a special king stamp on your fishing license from the Alaska Department of Fish and Game which you can buy at the same time you buy your license. King runs come mostly from late May to early July.

The **silver** (or **coho**) is smaller than the king, typically 6 to 9 pounds, but it fights and jumps ferociously, making it nearly as big a prize. Silvers run mostly in the fall, beginning in August and lasting into October in some streams.

The best all-around source of information is the **Alaska Department of Fish and Game Sport Fish Division** (www.alaska.gov/adfg; click on "sport fish"). Browse the website for run timing information and hot spots updated weekly, to learn generally about fishing in Alaska, and to obtain particulars about where to wet a line in different parts of the state (click "publications" and then the region you are visiting). You can even buy a fishing license online. If you lack Internet access, the agency also produces printed guides and fields questions from the public, and they record the weekly local updates on telephone hotlines. Contact the office nearest where you will fish; I have listed the phone number for each in the town sections.

If fishing is the primary goal of your trip, think about booking time at a fishing lodge. The remote rivers of the **Bristol Bay** region have Alaska's most prolific salmon fishing, and the only way out there is to take a floatplane to a remote site. You might find a stream jammed with salmon and with few other anglers around to compete with. But you'll waste your money if you book a date that's not near the peak of the local salmon run (that does happen, as lodge owners hate to admit

Red (or **sockeye**) salmon, so named for their tasty red flesh, are the trickiest to catch. They usually weigh 4 to 8 pounds and can run in any of the summer months, depending on the region and stream. Reds feed primarily on plankton at sea, and when they strike a fly, it's out of an instinct that no one really understands; you need perfect river conditions to catch reds legally, because snagging anywhere but the mouth generally is not allowed in fresh water.

Pinks (or **humpies**) grow to only a few pounds and aren't as tasty as the other three species; their flesh lacks the fat that makes salmon so meaty in flavor and it deteriorates quickly once the fish enter fresh water. Pinks are so plentiful that Alaska anglers usually view them as a nuisance to get off the line, but visitors often enjoy catching them: There's nothing wrong with a hard-fighting 4-pound fish, especially if you use light tackle, and a sliver-bright pink salmon is tasty if cooked right.

Chum (or **dog**) salmon return plentifully to streams over much of the state but are rarely targeted by anglers. Yet a typical 5- to 10-pound chum hits and fights hard. Chums aren't prized for the table and are mostly used for subsistence by Alaska Natives, who smoke or dry the fish for winter use or freeze it to feed dog teams.

The gear you use depends on the species you are after and the regulations for the area you're fishing. You have to catch the fish in the mouth; snagging is allowed only in special circumstances. On salt water, boats troll for kings and silvers with herring bait and gear to hold it down. Lures, salmon eggs, or flies will work on silvers and kings in the rivers, but regulations vary. Flies work best with reds. Most Alaska fishermen use spinning gear on the larger salmon species—landing such a large fish is iffy with a fly rod.

slow fishing). Consequently, I've listed few river-fishing lodges in this book. (The exceptions: in sections 7 and 8 of chapter 7; and section 2 of chapter 5.) Instead, I recommend booking through **Sport Fishing Alaska,** 9310 Shorecrest Dr., Anchorage, AK 99502 (© **888/552-8674** or 907/344-8674; www.AlaskaTripPlanners.com). The business is run by a couple, Larry and Sheary Suiter, with years of experience on the Kenai River and in Southwest Alaska. After receiving a $95 advance fee, they plan a fishing vacation tailored to your budget that puts you right where fishing is hot at the time when you can travel.

FLIGHTSEEING No one should come to Alaska without seeing the scenery at least once from a small plane. The most spectacular rides of all are the Mount McKinley flights from Talkeetna (chapter 8) and the Glacier Bay National Park flights from Haines or other surrounding communities (chapter 5). But just about anywhere you go is worth seeing from the air; only then can you grasp how huge and complex the land is and how little changed it is by mankind. Fixed-wing flights give you the most time aloft for your money, with seats starting for around $100 for a half-hour flight. If you can't afford that, consider taking scheduled prop service between small communities on your itinerary for around the same price and see almost as much.

RAFTING   Letting an Alaskan river pull you through untouched wild country in a raft provides a unique perspective without the sweat and toil of backpacking. Alaska has many great rivers, virtually all undeveloped and, with few exceptions, never crowded. White-water guides operate on rivers all over the state offering day trips in many towns. Outfitters also lead trips deep into Alaska, using the rivers to visit extraordinary places that can be reached no other way. Many companies offer floats; some are listed below and still others are in the destination chapters throughout this book.

SEA KAYAKING   Just about every coastal town, from Kodiak east through Kachemak Bay, Prince William Sound, and the Southeast Panhandle has at least one kayak outfitter taking visitors on day trips or expeditions. I think it would be a shame for any fit person to come to Alaska and not take a sea-kayaking day trip. It is your best chance to get close enough to really know the wilderness and see whales, sea otters, seabirds, and marine life in an intimate way. Local guides are listed in each town section. Outfitters offering longer trips to a variety of places are listed below.

OUTFITTERS & OUTDOOR PACKAGE TRIPS

Besides the outfitters and tour guides listed below, I've noted other operators in the destination chapters covering the towns where they are based. Browse through those chapters before deciding on a trip, as a trip with a small-town guide service can be wonderful. There are many other larger operators, too; increasingly, international adventure travel companies bring groups to

Alaska, renting equipment or even hiring guides here. Although those trips may be excellent, I've listed mostly homegrown operators who know their territory intimately.

Alaska Discovery   A homegrown eco-tourism pioneer, Alaska Discovery was bought out by the famous Mountain Travel Sobek expedition company, but still keeps its local staff in Juneau and offers some of the best sea-kayaking trips in Southeast Alaska. Glacier Bay and Admiralty Island outings cater to both beginners and the truly rugged. Their inn-to-inn trips are essentially outdoor-oriented package tours, taking groups to the best spots for day activities like kayaking, rafting, or watching wildlife. Extended river trips float through the Arctic and on the Tatshenshini and Alsek rivers. They also offer outdoor packages for complete vacations. A 3-day kayak expedition near Juneau is $495 or $595, while 10 days in the Arctic is around $3,900.

5130 Glacier Hwy., Juneau, AK 99801. ✆ 800/586-1911 or 907/780-6226. www.akdiscovery.com.

Alaska Wildland Adventures This company specializes in trips for regular folks who may not have done a lot of arduous outdoor activities before. Concentrating on the Kenai Peninsula, where they operate two wilderness lodges, but also going to Denali National Park, most of the company's trips link together a series of outdoor day activities, such as rafting, hiking, or wildlife-watching, with beds and indoor plumbing in the evening. A 10-day safari is around $4,600; shorter trips, trips for families with kids, and trips with tent camping included are available, too.

P.O. Box 389, Girdwood, AK 99587. ✆ 800/334-8730 or 907/783-2928. www.alaskawildland.com.

Camp Alaska Tours   Readers have told me about the wonderful time they had with these folks, traveling in

Tips   Make Yourself Useful

You don't have to see Alaska only as an observer—you can be a participant. The **Iditarod Trail Sled Dog Race** (📞 907/376-5155; www.iditarod. com) uses hundreds of volunteers as it passes through remote villages on the 1,000-mile trek from Anchorage to Nome in March. Visitors can be part of it, and see the real Alaska along the way, contributing only their time and travel to Alaska. Find the application on the website and act early; they get more volunteers than they can use. Other races and events also use volunteers but don't have a formal program like the Iditarod's.

Some archaeological programs also use visitors to help dig Alaska Native sites and process the artifacts they find. A program that has been going on for years is called **Dig Afognak,** in Kodiak (p. 412). It costs you a bit in travel and accommodations, but it's a great opportunity to learn and do something real.

---

a van with only 12 adults and camping each night along the way. Trips last 6 days to 3 weeks, with hiking, rafting, kayaking, and an opportunity to see the outdoors with a new group of outdoors-oriented friends. Their philosophy is to keep things loose and allow people to pursue their own interests. Prices are around $125 per day, and one itinerary is available for families with children as young as age 10.

P.O. Box 872247, Wasilla, AK 99687. 📞 800/376-9438 or 907/376-9438. www.campalaska.com.

Equinox Wilderness Expeditions
Karen Jettmar, author of *The Alaska River Guide,* the standard guidebook on floating Alaska's rivers, leads challenging rafting, sea-kayaking, and hiking trips and base-camp wildlife viewing each summer in some of the wildest and most exotic places around the state. Her groups are tiny, with five to eight members, and she offers co-ed, family, and women's trips. A 10-day Arctic float trip costs around $3,500.

2440 E. Tudor Rd., Ste. 1102, Anchorage, AK 99507. 📞 604/222-1219 or 604/765-3370. www.equinox expeditions.com.

Nova   These guys started commercial rafting on Alaska's rivers in 1975, but as the industry developed, they

kept the company small, keeping their base in a tiny village on the Matanuska River, northeast of Anchorage, and primarily employing Alaskan guides. Their catalog covers longer expeditions on some of the state's wildest rivers, but also includes more affordable itineraries of 2 or 3 days. Two days on the Matanuska costs $295; 3 days on the Talkeetna, including 14-mile-long, Class IV rapids of the Talkeetna Canyon, costs $1050.

P.O. Box 1129, Chickaloon, AK 99674. 📞 800/746-5753 or 907/745-5753. www.novalaska.com.

St. Elias Alpine Guides   When you're ready for a real expedition, these are the professionals to contact. Having given up on McKinley years ago as too crowded, they specialize in trekking, climbing, and floating the deep and rugged wilderness of Wrangell–St. Elias National Park. Theirs is the only trip catalog I know of that offers first ascents as part of the product line; so far, they've taken clients to the tops of previously unclimbed mountains more than 45 times. For details, see p. 402.

P.O. Box 111241, Anchorage, AK 99511. 📞 888/933-5427 or 907/345-9048; summer 907/554-4445. www.steliasguides.com.

9 Specialized Travel Resources

FOR TRAVELERS WITH DISABILITIES

Today it is rare to find a hotel without rooms accessible for people with disabilities, and even some B&Bs have made the necessary adjustments. The results often are the best rooms in the house. Make sure to ask for the special rooms when making reservations, and question smaller establishments closely about exactly what accessible means to them.

There are several Alaska agencies for people with disabilities. **Challenge Alaska,** 3350 Commercial Dr., Suite 208, Anchorage, AK 99501 (© **907/ 344-7399;** www.challenge.ak.org), a nonprofit organization, offers therapeutic recreation and education, including outdoor adventures. They operate an adaptive ski school at their International Sports, Recreation and Education Center at Alyeska Resort in Girdwood (© **907/783-2925**). Summer outings are inexpensive: a 2-day sea-kayaking outing was only $115. Get on the mailing list for current listings.

Alaska Welcomes You! Inc., P.O. Box 91333, Anchorage, AK 99509-1333 (© or TTY **800/349-6301,** or 907/349-6301), books accessible cruises, tours in Southcentral Alaska, and extended travel packages to Denali National Park and the Kenai Peninsula, and does trip planning for independent travelers with special needs. The operator field-checks the places he books to make sure they really are accessible.

FOR SENIORS

People over age 65 get reduced-admission prices to many Alaska attractions, and some accommodations have special senior rates. National parks offer free admission and special camping rates for people over 62 with a **Golden Age Passport,** which you can obtain at any of the parks for $10 and which never expires. Also mention your age when booking your airfare; most domestic airlines offer senior discounts.

Most towns have a senior center where you'll find activities and help with any special needs. The **Anchorage Senior Center** (© **907/258-7823**) offers guidance for visitors, as well as use of the restaurant, showers, a gift shop, and fitness room. A big band plays Friday nights for dancing.

Elderhostel, 11 Avenue de Lafayette, Boston, MA 02111-1746 (© **877/426-8056;** TTY 877/426-2167; from overseas, © 978/323-4141; www.elderhostel.org), operates many weeklong Alaska learning vacations for groups of people 55 and older. The catalog of choices is on the website.

FOR GAY & LESBIAN TRAVELERS

Anchorage, Juneau, and Fairbanks have active gay and lesbian communities. In Anchorage, **Identity Inc.** (www.identityinc.org) offers referrals, publishes a newsletter called *Northview,* sponsors activities throughout the year, and operates a gay and lesbian helpline (© **907/258-4777**). The June Pridefest includes a parade and picnic, among other events. Their Gay and Lesbian Community Center of Anchorage is at 2110 E. Northern Lights, Suite A (© **907/929-4528**). Bob DeLoach is a real expert on gay and lesbian Alaska travel. His **Apollo Travel,** operating with **Whitsett Travel** (© **800/770-0661** or 907/ 274-0547), has a website with online booking at **www.apollotravelalaska. com.**

FOR STUDENTS

Many museums offer free or reduced admission for students and anyone under 18, although sometimes you have to ask. Make sure to bring a student ID card.

There are hostels in most towns in Alaska. Except for those in Anchorage, Fairbanks, and Juneau, they tend to be open in the summer only. I have described hostels in the text for each town. With just a few minor exceptions, they're not affiliated with organizations such as **Hostelling International** (© **301/495-1240;** www. hiayh.org) that provide discounts to members. For a much more comprehensive listing of hostels, go to **www.hostels.com** and navigate to Alaska by clicking on the maps.

Many students travel to Alaska for summer work. It's usually possible to get a job in a fish cannery in most coastal towns. Work on the slime line is hard and unpleasant and the pay is low, but if the season is good and you work long hours, camping to keep your expenses low (most canneries have tent cities of summer workers nearby), you can take home more money for your summer's work than you would normally earn elsewhere. Hillary Rodham Clinton worked an Alaska slime line when she was in school, and you can, too (George W. Bush worked in Alaska as a young person, as well, at a politically connected air service and construction company). Stay onshore, however, as offshore fish-processing ships are truly miserable and dangerous places to work, and if the ship doesn't get any fish, you don't make any money. Also, don't come north expecting to make fabulous wages. The stories of college students making huge crew shares on fishing boats are legends—there are experienced deckhands to take lucrative jobs before boats hire raw hands they have to train. Go that way for the adventure (and danger and hard work) but not out of greed. Jobs are always available in the tourism industry, too, although without the extreme flexibility of fish processing.

The **Alaska Department of Labor** posts a lot of useful information on its website, including job applications for seafood work and a live database of openings; start at **www.jobs.state. ak.us**.

FOR FAMILIES

When we researched our first edition of this book, my son, Robin, was 3, and my daughter, Julia, was 6 months. As I write this, Robin is 12, Julia is 9, Joseph is 5, and Becky is 3. You might run into us in a campground or on a boat dock anywhere in the state as we travel to research the next edition of "our Alaska book." Robin loves to surprise people he sees carrying the book. We also write *Frommer's Family Vacations in the National Parks* together. Yes, it's a great job, and bringing the family along is the best part.

Alaska's magnificent scenery is something even young children can understand and appreciate. Also, an Alaska vacation is largely spent outdoors, which is where kids like to be. The children never get enough ferry riding, and all four enjoy camping immensely, even Becky. Our extensive experience camping with babies, even as young as 3 months, has been entirely positive. Having everyone sleep in a tent, at baby level, is an infant's idea of vacation paradise.

There are drawbacks to Alaska as a family destination. The primary one is the expense. The airlines' half-off companion fares are inconsistently applied, and we haven't yet gotten one on the Alaska route. Activities such as flightseeing and tour-boat cruises tend to have less-than-generous children's discounts and cost too much for most families. Often, bed-and-breakfast rooms are too small for a family. Hotel rooms and restaurant meals are expensive in Alaska. Car camping solves many of those problems, with stops in a hotel every few days to get everyone cleaned up. I wouldn't take kids over the Alaska Highway, however; instead, I'd fly to Anchorage and rent a car and any bulky camping gear there (see "Car and RV Camping," in section 6 of this chapter).

Be careful in choosing your itinerary and activities with children. The highways in Alaska are long and children will require a gradual approach to covering a lot of ground. They also need time to play, explore, and rest. Frankly, children often don't enjoy activities like wildlife-watching. It takes a long time to find the animals, and when you do, they're usually off in the distance—kids younger than 8 often don't have the visual skills or patience to pick out the animals from the landscape. Don't overtax children with walks and hiking trips; we keep track of the longest hike we've managed without excessive whining, then try to extend that record just a little bit each time out. Short sea-kayaking excursions, on the other hand, are great for children who are old enough, riding in the front of a double-seat boat with a parent in back; we began with Robin at age 7, and I have friends who have done it with a 3-year-old. In practice, the age limit depends on the outfitter and your child's level of responsibility.

If you're flawed mortals like us, you'll be getting on each other's nerves after a few weeks on the road. We survive by leaving time for low-key kid activities, such as beachcombing or playing in the park, while one grown-up splits off for a museum visit,

shopping, or a special, more expensive activity. Of course, if you want to preserve your marriage, you'll have to be scrupulously fair about who gets to go flightseeing and who has to stay behind and change diapers, as you won't have my all-purpose excuse (research).

If you're interested in a package tour with your family, most of the companies listed in this chapter will take children, but research carefully to make sure you will have enough down time. A better choice would be an outdoor-oriented trip designed for children by an outfitter. **Alaska Wildland Adventures** (© 800/334-8730; www. alaskawildland.com) has various trips for kids as young as 12, and even offers a "Family Safari" for families with children ages 6 through 12 that strings together activities and hotels on the Kenai Peninsula for 8 days, including Kenai River rafting and a boat tour in Kenai Fjords National Park. It's essentially a kid-oriented escorted package tour. The cost is $3,195 for adults, $2,895 for kids, exclusive of air travel.

Alaska Discovery (© 800/586-1911; www.akdiscovery.com) takes children as young as 12 on some of its extended Southeast Alaska sea-kayaking trips, which start at $495 to $595 for 3 days and 2 nights, and welcomes younger children on its non-camping trips.

10 Getting There & Getting Around

BY PLANE
CARRIERS Anchorage is the main entry hub served by several major carriers to the rest of the United States and sometimes flights from Japan or Korea. It's also possible to fly into Fairbanks or Southeast Alaska. Most passengers come into Anchorage through Seattle, but for a bit more you can fly nonstop to Anchorage from various major cities. There are far more choices

in summer than in winter. **Alaska Airlines** (© 800/252-7522; www.alaska air.com) has more flights than all other airlines combined, with as many as 20 a day to Seattle in summer and summer nonstops to various other cities, including Chicago, Dallas/Ft. Worth, L.A., Minneapolis/St. Paul, Portland, and Vancouver. Alaska Airlines is the only jet carrier with more than token coverage anywhere in Alaska other than Anchorage and has arrangements with commuter lines that fan out from its network to smaller communities. Other major airlines serving Anchorage at this writing include **Northwest** (© **800/225-2525;** www.nwa.com), **Continental** (© **800/523-3273;** www.continental.com), **United** (© **800/864-8331;** www.ual.com), and **Delta** (© **800/221-1212;** www.delta.com). The flight line-up (and the existence of the airlines) changes too fast to keep track of here, so all of this is subject to change.

FARES Alaskans fly so much we talk about air fares the way New Yorkers talk about real estate. Fares vary wildly, so watching for sales can pay off. It's almost always cheapest to change planes in Seattle due to the competition on the Seattle-Anchorage route. The competition also makes these fares more volatile than the NASDAQ: normally a round trip is over $400, but it's not unusual to get a ticket for $300, and if you're really alert you can sometimes snag one for $200. A website maintained by an Anchorage travel consultant (www.alaskatravelgram.com/airfares) monitors the current lowest fares from many cities. Use it for a reference, but don't expect to get those rock-bottom fares without a lot of flexibility and a skilled travel agent. Summer sales sometimes hit in April. If you can make a last-minute decision, sign up for Web specials on the Alaska Airlines website and other airline sites, as there often are bargains to be had you can't get any other way.

BUSH PILOTS To fly to a roadless village, or to fly between most towns without returning to a hub, you will take a small, prop-driven plane with an Alaska bush pilot at the controls. Small air taxis also charter to fishing sites, lodges, remote cabins, or anywhere else you want to go. An authentic Alaskan adventure can be had by taking a Bush mail plane round-trip to a village and back. The ticket price is generally less than a flightseeing trip, and you'll have at least a brief chance to look around a Native village, although don't expect to find any visitor facilities without making arrangements in advance. Kodiak, Homer, Nome, Kotzebue, and Barrow are places from which you can do this with a little research.

BY SHIP

The most popular way to get to Alaska is on a **cruise ship** (chapter 4, "Cruising Alaska's Coast," provides an in-depth look at your options).

For an affordable, independent trip by sea, with a chance to stop as long as you like along the way, take the **Alaska Marine Highway System** (© **800/642-0066** or 907/486-3800; TDD 800/764-3779; www.Ferry Alaska.com). It's my favorite form of public transportation. The big blue, white, and gold ferries ply the Inside Passage from Bellingham, Washington, and Prince Rupert, B.C., to the towns of Southeast Alaska, with road links to the rest of the state at Haines and Skagway. In summer, a ferry twice a month connects from that system across the Gulf of Alaska to the central part of the state. From there, smaller ferries connect towns in Prince William Sound and the Kenai Peninsula to Kodiak Island and the Aleutian Archipelago. For a complete discussion of the system and its intricacies, see "Getting Around by Ferry: The Alaska Marine Highway" in chapter 5.

BY RAIL

You can't get to Alaska by train, but you can get close. From the west coast of the U.S. you can take **Amtrak** (© **800/USA-RAIL;** www.amtrak.com) to Bellingham, Washington; the dock for the Alaska ferry is quite close to the railroad station. From the east, it makes more sense to use Canada's **Via Rail** (© **888/VIA-RAIL;** www.

Value **The Cheapest Way to Alaska**

Flying is the cheapest and by far the simplest way to get to Alaska. Take other means only for the adventure, not for the savings. Round-trip train, ferry, and bus fare between Seattle and Anchorage costs several times as much as a good airfare between the same cities. Driving is expensive, too, when you count rooms, food, and wear and tear on your vehicle. Fuel alone for the 4,500-mile drive from Seattle to Anchorage and back would cost far more than a plane ticket. (Okay, maybe a foursome can do it cheaper if they camp every night and eat rice and beans.)

viarail.ca). The transcontinental route starts all the way back in Toronto; you change in Jasper to end up in Prince Rupert, B.C., where you can catch the Alaska ferry north.

BY CAR

A frequent question on my website (www.wohlforth.net) is how long it takes to drive between various points. You can easily calculate this for yourself. Get the mileage from the chart on p. 6, or go to www.mapquest.com, click on "Directions," and type in the two points on your route. For paved highways, you can count on averaging 50 miles per hour; simply divide the mileage by 50 to get the hours of your trip. On most roads you can go faster than 50, but you can't often drive at freeway speeds on these two-lane highways. Even when the surface is smooth (not always a given) the roads aren't designed for high speeds. Besides, you need to be on the lookout for moose; hit one of those at 75 mph and you both die.

Driving to Alaska is a great adventure, but it requires thousands of miles on the road and plenty of time. By car, Anchorage is 2,250 miles from Seattle and 3,400 miles from Los Angeles. By comparison, New York to L.A. is 2,800 miles. Traveling at an average of 50 miles per hour, few vacationers will want to cover more than 500 or 600 miles a day, and that's on a day of nothing but driving. On such a plan,

Seattle is four or five days from Anchorage without breaks.

Some of the 1,400-mile **Alaska Highway** is dull, but there are spectacular sections of the route, too, and few experiences give you a better feel for the size and personality of Alaska. Putting your car on the ferry cuts the length of the trip considerably, but raises the cost; you could rent a car for 2 weeks for the same price as carrying an economy car on the ferry one-way from Bellingham to Haines. I love riding the ferry up the Inside Passage, but I usually rent a car or bike to get around in the towns on the way. Details on the Alaska section of the Alaska Highway, and other highways, are contained in chapter 9. *The Milepost* (Morris Communications; $26) contains good maps and mile-by-mile logs of all Alaska highways and Canadian approaches; however, it's not interesting to read and is clogged with advertising that looks like editorial text.

Renting a car is the easiest way to see the Interior and Southcentral parts of the state. All the major national car-rental companies are represented in Anchorage as well as many local operators, who may have lower prices for older cars and in at least one case allow driving on gravel roads. In smaller cities and towns, there is always at least one agency; the town descriptions throughout the book provide details on firms in each town. Base rates for major rental companies are in the range of $50 a day for an economy car. Weekly rentals equate roughly to 5 day's cost.

One-way rentals between Alaska towns are an attractive way to travel, but you generally pay steep drop-off charges, so a more popular plan is to fly into and out of Anchorage and pick up and return the car there. There are two popular circular routes from Anchorage: to Denali and Fairbanks on the Parks Highway and back on the Richardson and Glenn highways, or to Valdez by ferry from Whittier and back on another part of the Richardson Highway and the Glenn Highway.

BY RV

Touring Alaska in an RV, or even driving one to the state, makes a good deal of sense. The home on wheels offers spontaneity by freeing you from hotel reservations (see "Car or RV Camping," on p. 39), and it gets you out of town and into the countryside, closer to the natural Alaska most visitors come for. At the same time, an RV is more comfortable than a tent in cool, unpredictable weather conditions.

Many retirees drive to Alaska in their motor homes, park the RV by a salmon stream, and spend the summer fishing. Sounds nice, but for most of the rest of us, with limited time, it makes more sense to rent an RV after flying to Alaska. Rental agencies are listed in Skagway (chapter 5) and Anchorage (chapter 6). The option of shipping your own RV to Alaska is also covered in the Anchorage chapter. Unless you have a large family, an RV rental saves little over traveling with a rental car, staying in hotels, and eating in restaurants (RVs rent for around

$1,400 a week, plus gas and possibly mileage charges), so you make this choice to gain advantages, not avoid costs.

Alaska Highway Cruises (© 800/ 323-5757; www.alaskarv.com) offers the unique option of traveling one way on a Holland America cruise ship then picking up an RV for a land tour. You can choose a package that ends up back at Seattle by road or by air. The tours follow set itineraries with reservations along the way—the service is designed for first-time Alaska travelers and RV drivers who don't want to worry about the details—so some spontaneity is sacrificed. You get the security and simplicity of a package without being marched around in a group or cooped up in hotels. An 11-day cruise and tour cost around $2,500 per person, double occupancy; a 3-week cruise to Alaska and drive back (or reverse) is around $3,500 per person. There are various discounts, including for third and fourth passengers.

Simple one-way RV rentals to Alaska are available, too, although they add $1,000 or more to the cost. I have listed options from Seattle and Skagway to Anchorage in chapter 6. A large national firm, **Cruise America,** 8850 Runamuck Place (© **800/327-7799** or 907/349-0499; www.cruise america.com) offers one-way rentals between Anchorage and rental centers around the country.

There is a way to do a one-way RV odyssey without spending so much. At the beginning and end of the season, the rental companies often find themselves with units in the wrong places: a clever and flexible traveler can snag a great deal by delivering an RV to where it belongs.

11 Suggested Itineraries

Many visitors to Alaska feel compelled to cover the whole state, traveling to each region and hitting each famous

wilderness park. By doing so, they spend more time and money than they should. Each of Alaska's regions, by itself, has most of what you're coming to Alaska for—wildlife, mountains, glaciers, historic sites, cute little towns—and you can have a better trip touring one or two regions than spending precious time going from region to region.

The other mistake some people make is traveling only to the largest and most famous destinations. Such a goal-oriented style of travel misses the fun, offbeat places only you can discover. Alaska's greatest sights certainly are worth your time, but visitors often tell me those were not the most memorable moments. Save time for chance encounters with wildlife or interesting local people, or simply to enjoy a peaceful moment alone in the woods.

Finally, remember why you are going to Alaska. Surely it's not to visit museums or tourist attractions, but instead to see one of the most beautiful, unspoiled places on earth. To do that, you need to get outside; there's only so much you can see and learn through glass. Take a chance on a sea kayak excursion, a day hike, or a mountain bike ride. You will never have a better chance to try these things.

To help readers understand how Alaska destinations can fit together, I've set up a series of itineraries in 1-week loops or tours. For 2- or 3-week itineraries, link a few itineraries together, spend more time in each place, or add trips to the many places I haven't included in these loops. This isn't intended as a menu, just as inspiration to create your own trip. If you're driving to Alaska, add a week to each end of your trip.

A Northern Southeast Alaska Itinerary

Day 1   Fly to Juneau, settle in.

Day 2   Take a look at the State Museum and other sights in town and Mendenhall Glacier, or take a dayhike or sea-kayaking excursion.

Day 3   Take the passenger ferry to Gustavus, with a whale-watching excursion on the way. Spend the night at one of the charming inns there.

Day 4   See Glacier Bay National Park on a boat tour.

Day 5   Fly from Gustavus to Haines on a small plane. Spending the day there seeing the eagles and totem carving studio.

Day 6   Take the passenger ferry to Skagway to see the historic sites and take the train excursion.

Day 7   Take the Alaska ferry back to Juneau and fly home.

A Southern Southeast Alaska Itinerary

Day 1   Fly to Sitka, walk around and get your bearings.

Day 2   Tour the historic sites and raptor center in Sitka.

Day 3   Take a wildlife cruise or sea kayak outing in Sitka Sound.

Day 4   Take the ferry to Petersburg.

Day 5   Go for a hike, go fishing, or go whale-watching from Petersburg.

Day 6   Take the ferry to Wrangell; explore the town or go bear viewing.

Day 7   Fly out from Wrangell.

A National Parks Itinerary: Kenai Fjords & Denali

Day 1   Fly to Anchorage. Spend time left taking in the city with a visit to the museum, zoo, or Native cultural center; or ride a bike on the coastal trail.

Day 2   Take the train or drive to Seward and take a boat ride into Kenai Fjords National Park.

Day 3   In Seward see the Alaska SeaLife Center and Exit Glacier, or take a hike or a sea kayak paddle, returning to Anchorage in the evening.

Day 4 Rent a car (if you haven't already) and drive to Denali National Park, taking an afternoon hike or raft ride in the entrance area.

Day 5 Take a shuttle bus into the park for wildlife viewing and day hiking.

Day 6 Drive back to Anchorage, with stops along the way or time for an afternoon activity in Anchorage.

Day 7 Last activities in Anchorage and fly out.

A Prince William Sound Loop

Day 1 Fly to Anchorage.

Day 2 Rent a car and drive all day to Wrangell–St. Elias National Park (take the van over the gravel road unless you are covered for your rental car). Stay at a lodge in McCarthy or Kennecott.

Day 3 See Kennecott and take a hike near the glacier.

Day 4 Drive to Valdez and see the sights in town, fish for salmon, or take a hike.

Day 5 Take a boat ride to Columbia Glacier or go sea kayaking or rafting.

Day 6 Take the car ferry from Valdez to Whittier and drive to Girdwood for a hike or tram ride and spend the night at the resort hotel there.

Day 7 Drive to Anchorage and fly home.

A Fairbanks Interior Tour

Day 1 Fly to Fairbanks and rent a car.

Day 2 Spend a day in Fairbanks exploring the city and its attractions.

Day 3 Drive the Parks Highway to Denali National Park, taking an afternoon hike or raft ride in the entrance area.

Day 4 Take a shuttle bus into the park for wildlife viewing and day hiking.

Day 5 Drive via the Denali Highway (conditions and your car permitting; otherwise simply retrace your steps on the Parks Highway) and Richardson Highway back to Fairbanks, then drive out Chena Hot Springs Road to the resort there.

Day 6 Swim at the Hot Springs and hike in the recreation area.

Day 7 Return to Fairbanks and fly out.

FAST FACTS: Alaska

Area Code All of Alaska is in area code **907**. In the Yukon Territory, the area code is **867**. When placing a toll call within the state, you must dial 1, the area code, and the number. See "Telephone," below, for important tips.

Banks & ATMs There are banks and automated teller machines in all but the tiniest towns.

Business Hours In the larger cities, major grocery stores are open until late at night and carry a wide range of products (even fishing gear) in addition to food. At a minimum, **stores** are open Monday through Friday from 10am to 6pm, are open on Saturday afternoon, and are closed on Sunday, but many are open much longer hours, especially in summer. **Banks** may close an hour earlier and, if open on Saturday, it's only in the morning. Under state law, **bars** don't have to close until 5am, but many communities have an earlier closing, generally around 2am.

Cellular Phone Coverage The most densely populated portion of the state and some of the paved highways have cellular coverage. The largest provider is an Alaska company called ACS, which posts maps of its coverage area at www.acsalaska.com (click on "wireless" then "calling areas)." AT&T has the second best network. I've found usable coverage is often less than what the companies claim, so don't bet your life on being able to make a call. In any event, if you plan to use your phone, check with your wireless provider to make sure it will work in Alaska and to find out just how badly you will be gouged on roaming charges. To be sure you are always in touch, you can rent a satellite phone (see "Getting Lost," p. 31).

Emergencies Generally, you can call ℂ **911** for medical, police, or fire emergencies. On remote highways there sometimes are gaps in 911 coverage, but dialing ℂ **0** will generally get an operator who can connect you to emergency services.

Holidays Besides the normal national holidays, banks and state and local government offices close on two state holidays: Seward's Day (the last Monday in March) and Alaska Day (October 18, or the nearest Friday or Monday if it falls on a weekend). See chapter 3 for a listing of national holidays.

Liquor Laws The minimum drinking age in Alaska is 21. Most restaurants sell beer and wine, while a minority have full bars that serve hard liquor as well. Packaged alcohol, beer, and wine are sold only in licensed stores, not in grocery stores, but these are common and are open long hours every day. More than 100 rural communities have laws prohibiting the importation and possession of alcohol (this is known as being "dry") or only the sale but not possession of alcohol (known as being "damp"). With a few exceptions, these are tiny Bush communities off the road network; urban areas are all "wet." Of the communities featured in this book, Kotzebue and Barrow are damp, and the rest are wet. Before flying into a Native village with alcohol, ask about the law—bootlegging is a serious crime (and serious bad manners), or check a list online (go to www.abc.revenue.state.ak.us and click on "Local Option Restrictions."

Maps I've noted the best trail maps in each applicable section throughout this book. For most of the popular areas, I recommend the excellent trail maps published by **Trails Illustrated,** part of National Geographic (ℂ **800/962-1643**; http://maps.nationalgeographic.com/trails). They're sold in park visitor centers, too. The maps are printed on plastic, so they don't get spoiled by rain; however, they don't cover the whole state.

Newspapers The state's dominant newspaper is the *Anchorage Daily News* (www.adn.com); it's available everywhere but is not always easy to find in Southeast Alaska. Seattle newspapers and *USA Today* are often available, and in Anchorage you can get virtually any newspaper.

Taxes At this writing there is no state sales tax, but most local governments have a sales tax and a bed tax on accommodations. The tax rates are listed in each town section throughout the book under its "Fast Facts."

Telephone I am assured that all major calling cards will work in Alaska, but this certainly hasn't been the case in the past. To make sure, contact your long-distance company, or buy a by-the-minute card.

Time Zone Although the state naturally spans five time zones, in the 1980s Alaska's middle time zone was stretched so almost the entire state would lie all in one zone, known as Alaska time. It's 1 hour earlier than the U.S. West Coast's Pacific time, 4 hours earlier than Eastern time. Crossing over the border from Alaska to Canada adds an hour and puts you at the same time as the West Coast. As with almost everywhere else in the United States, daylight saving time is in effect from 1am on the first Sunday in April (turn your clocks ahead 1 hr.) until 2am on the last Sunday in October (turn clocks back again).

3

For International Visitors

Visitors from the rest of the United States sometimes say Alaska is like a foreign country full of Americans. If you are coming from overseas, it may be doubly unfamiliar. This chapter aims to help you through the details so you can better enjoy the differences.

Information on border crossings between the United States and Canada on the Alaska Highway is contained in chapter 9.

1 Preparing for Your Trip

ENTRY REQUIREMENTS

Check at any U.S. embassy or consulate for current information and requirements. You can also obtain a visa application and other information online at the **U.S. State Department**'s website, at **www.travel.state.gov**.

DO YOU NEED A VISA? Most tourists coming to the United States do not need a visa. Canadian citizens only need proof of residence (not even a passport), and citizens of many other countries need hardly more under the U.S. State Department's **Visa Waiver Program** for visits of up to 90 days. At press time these countries included Andorra, Australia, Austria, Belgium, Brunei, Denmark, Finland, France, Germany, Iceland, Ireland, Italy, Japan, Liechtenstein, Luxembourg, Monaco, the Netherlands, New Zealand, Norway, Portugal, San Marino, Singapore, Slovenia, Spain, Sweden, Switzerland, and the United Kingdom. Citizens of these countries need only a valid passport and a round-trip air or cruise ticket in their possession upon arrival. If they first enter the United States, they may also visit Mexico, Canada, Bermuda, and/or the Caribbean islands and return to the United States without a visa. Further information is available from any U.S. embassy or consulate.

Citizens of all other countries must have (1) a valid passport that expires at least 6 months later than the scheduled end of their visit to the United States, and (2) a tourist visa, which may be obtained without charge from any U.S. consulate.

HOW TO GET A VISA To obtain a visa, the traveler must submit a completed application form (either in person or by mail) with a 1½-inch-square photo, and must demonstrate binding ties to a residence abroad. Usually you can obtain a visa at once or within 24 hours, but it may take longer during the summer rush from June through August. If you cannot go in person, contact the nearest U.S. embassy or consulate for directions on applying by mail. Your travel agent or airline office may also be able to provide you with visa applications and instructions. The U.S. consulate or embassy that issues your visa will determine whether you will be issued a multiple- or single-entry visa and any restrictions regarding the length of your stay.

MEDICAL REQUIREMENTS Unless you're arriving from an area known to be suffering from an epidemic (particularly cholera or yellow fever), inoculations or vaccinations are not required for entry into the United

States. If you have a medical condition that requires **syringe-administered medications,** carry a valid signed prescription from your physician—the Federal Aviation Administration (FAA) no longer allows airline passengers to pack syringes in their carry-on baggage without documented proof of medical need. If you have a disease that requires treatment with **narcotics,** you should also carry documented proof with you—smuggling narcotics aboard a plane is a serious offense that carries severe penalties in the U.S.

For **HIV-positive visitors,** requirements for entering the United States are somewhat vague and change frequently. According to the latest publication of *HIV and Immigrants: A Manual for AIDS Service Providers,* the Immigration and Naturalization Service (INS) doesn't require a medical exam for entry into the United States, but INS officials may stop individuals because they look sick or because they are carrying AIDS/HIV medicine.

If an HIV-positive non-citizen applies for a non-immigrant visa, the question on the application regarding communicable diseases is tricky no matter which way it's answered. If the applicant checks "no," INS may deny the visa on the grounds that the applicant committed fraud. If the applicant checks "yes" or if INS suspects the person is HIV-positive, it will deny the visa unless the applicant asks for a special waiver for visitors. This waiver is for people visiting the United States for a short time, to attend a conference, for instance, to visit close relatives, or to receive medical treatment. It can be a confusing situation. For up-to-the-minute information, contact **AIDSinfo** (*©* **800/448-0440** or 301/519-6616 outside the U.S.; www.aidsinfo.nih.gov) or the **Gay Men's Health Crisis** (*©* **212/367-1000;** www.gmhc.org).

DRIVER'S LICENSES Foreign driver's licenses are mostly recognized in the United States, although you may want to get an international driver's license if your home license is not written in English.

CUSTOMS
WHAT YOU CAN BRING IN
Personal effects, such as cameras and fishing rods, are exempt from duties. In addition, every visitor over 21 years of age may bring in the following without paying duties: (1) 1 liter of wine or hard liquor; (2) 200 cigarettes, or 100 cigars (but not from Cuba), or 3 pounds of smoking tobacco; and (3) $100 worth of gifts. To claim these exemptions you must spend at least 72 hours in the United States and cannot have claimed them within the preceding 6 months. The duty on goods exceeding these exemptions is 3% of the value on the first $1,000 (the flat rate); above that amount, it depends on the item. The flat rate applies only to items for your own use or gifts and can be used only once in 30 days. Importation of most raw food and plant material is prohibited or requires a special license. Foreign tourists may bring in or take out up to $10,000 in U.S. or foreign currency with no formalities; larger sums must be declared to U.S. Customs on entering or leaving and paperwork must be filed. For more specific information regarding U.S. Customs, contact your nearest U.S. embassy or consulate, or the **U.S. Customs** office (*©* **202/344-1770;** www.customs.ustreas.gov).

It is exceedingly complicated for foreign visitors to bring **firearms** into the United States; don't even consider it except for a hunting trip. Unless you are a U.S. citizen or permanent resident alien, you cannot bring in, buy, or even possess a gun without a permit from the **Bureau of Alcohol, Tobacco and Firearms** (*©* **202/927-8320;** www.atf.treas.gov); these take several months to acquire (the application is on the ATF website). The application must be accompanied by a valid hunting license

Tips **Exchange Money Before Leaving Home**

There are no foreign currency exchange bureaus in Alaska. A **Wells Fargo Bank** branch in the 5th Avenue Mall in Anchorage (© **907/265-2093;** www.wellsfargo.com) has a currency exchange desk, the only specialized service in the state. You can change money elsewhere, but it generally is not a good idea. Obtain U.S. dollars before you leave home or get them using your ATM card. You can pay for almost anything with a credit or charge card, with the exchange automatically made by your bank.

(there are a few narrow exceptions, such as athletes involved in shooting competitions). The **Alaska Department of Fish and Game** (© **907/465-6085;** www.alaska.gov/adfg) sells hunting licenses to non-resident aliens for $300; however, aliens can hunt only with a registered guide. First, find the guide, then let him or her help with all the paperwork, but start many months in advance and be ready to pay.

For more details on what you can and cannot bring, go to the **U.S. Customs** website at **www.customs. ustreas.gov** and click "Travel."

WHAT YOU CAN TAKE HOME WILDLIFE PRODUCTS Alaska Native art and crafts made from protected marine mammals are perfectly legal (even though possessing the raw animal pelts is not legal for non-Natives), but you do need to get permits to take these items out of the country. Permits also are required to export products made from brown or black bear, bobcat, wolf, lynx, or river otter. The best solution is to have the shop where you buy the item mail it to you insured, and have them take care of the paperwork. If you carry it with you, or buy from someone who can't handle the paperwork, you'll need to get your own permits. For Alaska wildlife products other than marine mammals, get a Personal Effects Exemption Certificate for the item by calling the **U.S. Fish and Wildlife Service** in Anchorage (© **907/271-6198**). They can handle it in a few days. To take **marine**

mammal products to another country, you need a permit from the **Fish and Wildlife Service** in Washington, D.C. (© **800/358-2104;** http://international. fws.gov). It can take a month to get these permits. There may be other regulations for bringing walrus ivory into your home country because of the international ban on elephant ivory. It's important to note that Alaska Natives have used these materials for thousands of years, and their harvest poses no threat to the species.

OTHER GOODS Rules governing what you can bring back duty-free vary from country to country, and generally are posted on the Web. For a clear summary of **Canadian** rules, request the booklet *I Declare,* issued by the **Canada Border Services Agency (CBSA)** (© **800/461-9999** in Canada, or 204/983-3500; www.cbsa-asfc.gc.ca/E/pub/cp/rc4044/). **UK** citizens should contact HM Customs & Excise at © **0845/010-9000** (from outside the U.K., 020/8929-0152), or consult their website at www.hmce.gov.uk. **Australians** can contact the Australian Customs Service (© **1300/363-263;** www.customs.gov.au). **New Zealand** citizens should contact New Zealand Customs (© **0800/428-786** or 04/473-6099; www.customs.govt.nz).

INSURANCE

Although it's not required of travelers, health insurance is a very good idea. Unlike many European countries, the United States does not generally offer free or low-cost medical care to its citizens or visitors. Doctors and hospitals are expensive and generally require that patients work out how to pay before rendering services. On the other hand, seriously ill or injured patients are cared for even if they are indigent. For peace of mind and to protect your finances, buy a travel insurance policy that covers the costs of an accident, repatriation, or death. See section 5 in chapter 2 for more information.

Packages such as **Europ Assistance's** **"Worldwide Healthcare Plan"** are sold by European automobile clubs and travel agencies at attractive rates. **Worldwide Assistance Services, Inc.** (© **800/821-2828;** www.worldwide assistance.com) is the agent for Europ Assistance in the United States.

Canadians should check with their provincial health plan offices or call **Health Canada** (© **613/957-2991;** www.hc-sc.gc.ca) to find out the extent of their coverage and what documentation and receipts they must take home in case they are treated in the United States.

I also strongly recommend trip-cancellation and interruption insurance if you place deposits on Alaska services or accommodations. Insurance providers are covered under section 5 in chapter 2. Don't buy the insurance directly from the provider, as their bankruptcy is one of the pitfalls you should insure against.

MONEY

CURRENCY The most common **bills** are the $1 (colloquially, a "buck"), $5, $10, and $20 denominations. There are also $2 bills (seldom encountered), $50 bills, and $100 bills (the last two are usually not welcome as payment for small purchases). All the paper money was recently redesigned, but the old bills are still legal tender. The common denomination **coins** are: 1¢ (1 cent, or a penny); 5¢ (5 cents, or a nickel); 10¢ (10 cents, or a dime); 25¢ (25 cents, or a quarter).

CREDIT CARDS & ATMS At least one credit card is a virtual necessity, essential to rent a car or place a deposit with many businesses. Credit cards are the most widely used form of payment in the United States. Most businesses display a sticker near their entrance to let you know which cards they accept.

SAFETY

Robberies (like muggings) are quite rare in Alaska, even in Anchorage, but the incidence of rape is high. Precautions are covered in chapter 2. Thefts can happen even in tiny towns. Keep an eye on your belongings and lock your car and hotel doors. Don't leave valuables in sight in the car. Guns are ubiquitous in Alaska. I'm not aware of a tourist ever being shot, but be aware that guns enter into violent disputes more quickly here than elsewhere.

Tips **Prepare to Be Fingerprinted**

Starting in January 2004, many international visitors traveling on visas to the United States will be photographed and fingerprinted at Customs in a new program created by the Department of Homeland Security called **US-VISIT.** Non–U.S. citizens arriving at airports and on cruise ships must undergo an instant background check as part of the government's ongoing efforts to deter terrorism by verifying the identity of incoming and outgoing visitors. Exempt from the extra scrutiny are visitors entering by land or those from 28 countries (mostly in Europe) that don't require a visa for short-term visits. For more information, go to the Homeland Security website at **www.dhs.gov/dhspublic**.

2 Getting to the United States

All but a smattering of overseas travelers to Alaska come through other domestic airports, requiring them to pass through Seattle or another major city. Canadians can drive to Alaska over the Alaska Highways, covered in chapter 9, or ride an Alaska Marine Highway System ferry from Prince Rupert, B.C., covered in chapter 5.

Getting through immigration control and Customs can take 2 or 3 hours, especially if you enter the country at a big-city airport on a busy summer day. Leave at least that much time to connect to a domestic flight. Passing between Alaska and Canada takes no time at all unless you have special complications. See chapter 9 for Canadian border requirements.

FAST FACTS: **For the International Traveler**

See "Fast Facts: Alaska" in chapter 2 for information not listed here.

Automobile Organizations Auto clubs will supply maps, suggested routes, guidebooks, accident and bail-bond insurance, and emergency road service. The **American Automobile Association (AAA)** is the major auto club in the United States. If you belong to an auto club in your home country, inquire about AAA reciprocity before you leave. You may be able to join AAA even if you're not a member of a reciprocal club; to inquire, call AAA (© **800/222-4357**). AAA is actually an organization of regional auto clubs; so look under "AAA Automobile Club" in the White Pages of the telephone directory. AAA has a nationwide **emergency** road service telephone number (© **800/AAA-HELP**).

Business Hours See p. 51.

Currency & Exchange See "Money" under "Preparing for Your Trip," above.

Drinking Laws The legal age for purchase and consumption of alcoholic beverages is 21; proof of age is required and often requested at bars, nightclubs, and restaurants, so you need ID when you go out. Open containers of alcohol are not allowed in your car or, with few exceptions, in any public place outside a bar or restaurant. Don't even think about driving while intoxicated. Alaska has mandatory jail time for this offense. See p. 52 for more information, including information on rural communities that have laws prohibiting the importation or possession of alcohol.

Electricity Like Canada, the United States uses 110 to 120 volts AC (60 cycles), compared to 220 to 240 volts AC (50 cycles) in most of Europe, Australia, and New Zealand. If your small appliances use 220 to 240 volts, you'll need a 110-volt transformer and a plug adapter with two flat parallel pins to operate them here. Downward converters that change 220–240 volts to 110–120 volts are difficult to find in the United States, so bring one with you.

Embassies & Consulates **Japan** is the only nation that has a consulate-general in Alaska. It's located at Anchorage, at 3601 C St., Suite 1300, Anchorage, AK 99503 (© **907/562-8424**). All embassies are located in Washington, D.C.; call for directory information in Washington, D.C. (© **202/555-1212**) or log on to **www.embassy.org/embassies**.

Emergencies Call © **911** to report a fire, call the police, or get an ambulance almost anywhere in the United States. This is a toll-free call (no coins are required at public telephones).

Gasoline (Petrol) Petrol is known as gasoline (or simply "gas") in the United States, and petrol stations are known as both gas stations and service stations. Gasoline costs less here than in Europe (about $2.00 per gal. at press time). Taxes are already included in the pump price. One U.S. gallon equals 3.8 liters or .85 imperial gallons.

Holidays Banks, government offices, post offices, and many stores, restaurants, and museums are closed on the following legal national holidays: January 1 (New Year's Day), the third Monday in January (Martin Luther King Jr., Day), the third Monday in February (Presidents' Day, Washington's Birthday), the last Monday in May (Memorial Day), July 4 (Independence Day), the first Monday in September (Labor Day), the second Monday in October (Columbus Day), November 11 (Veterans' Day/Armistice Day), the fourth Thursday in November (Thanksgiving Day), and December 25 (Christmas). Additionally, banks and state government offices in Alaska close on two state holidays: the last Monday in March (Seward's Day) and October 18 (Alaska Day, which is celebrated on the nearest Fri or Mon if the 18th falls on a weekend).

Legal Aid If you are "pulled over" for a minor infraction (such as speeding), never attempt to pay the fine directly to a police officer; this could be construed as attempted bribery, a much more serious crime. Pay fines by mail, or directly into the hands of the clerk of the court. If accused of a more serious offense, say and do nothing before consulting a lawyer. Here the burden is on the state to prove a person's guilt beyond a reasonable doubt, and everyone has the right to remain silent, whether he or she is suspected of a crime or actually arrested. Once arrested, a person can make one telephone call to a party of his or her choice. Call your embassy or consulate.

Mail The locations of the post offices in each town in this book are listed in the appropriate "Fast Facts" sections. You can send mail from your hotel or the post office. Mail in the United States must have a five-digit postal code (or ZIP code), after the two-letter abbreviation of the state to which the mail is addressed. You can receive mail addressed to you at "General Delivery" at the post office. At press time, domestic postage rates were 23¢ for a postcard and 37¢ for a letter. For international mail, mailing a first-class letter of up to 1 ounce costs 80¢ (60¢ to Canada and to Mexico), a first-class postcard 70¢ (50¢ to Canada and Mexico).

Measurements See the chart on the inside front cover of this book for details on converting metric measurements to U.S. equivalents.

Taxes Neither the U.S. nor the state of Alaska impose a value-added tax (VAT) or sales tax, but most Alaska communities, with the exception of Anchorage, levy their own sales taxes, and all communities impose taxes on hotel rooms and rental cars. See the individual town sections' "Fast Facts" for local tax rates.

Telephone & Fax Before using a telephone in a hotel, check for surcharges on long-distance and local calls, which can be astronomical. If so, you're better off using a **public pay telephone,** which you'll find in most public buildings and private establishments as well as in hotel lobbies and on the street. Many convenience stores sell **prepaid calling cards** in denominations up to $50; these can be the least expensive way to call home. **Local calls** made from public pay phones usually cost 25¢. In smaller Alaska communities, you may have to wait for the person you are calling to answer before quickly putting the money in the phone. Pay phones do not accept pennies or anything larger than a quarter.

Most long-distance and international calls can be dialed directly from any phone. For **long-distance calls within Alaska and the United States and to Canada,** dial 1 followed by the three-digit area code and the seven-digit number. An area code of 800, 866, 877, or 888 is toll free from anywhere.

For **international calls to places other than Canada,** dial 011 followed by the country code, city code, and telephone number of the person you are calling. U.S. area codes and international country codes are listed in the front of the White Pages telephone directory, or dial 0 to get a country code from the operator. If you're calling the **United States** from another country, the country code is 01.

For **collect, operator-assisted, and person-to-person calls,** dial 0 (the number zero) followed by the area code and number you want; an operator will then come on the line, and you should specify that you are calling collect, or person-to-person, or both. If your operator-assisted call is international, ask for the overseas operator.

For **local directory assistance** ("information"), dial 411; for long-distance information, dial 1, then the appropriate area code and 555-1212.

There are two kinds of telephone directories in the United States. The so-called **White Pages** list private households and business subscribers in alphabetical order; the **Yellow Pages** list businesses and organizations categorized by the services they provide. In Alaska, the two directories are contained in the same book in all towns except Anchorage. Look in the front of the White Pages for emergency numbers and instructions on making long-distance calls. Blue pages near the front of the White Pages directory list numbers for government agencies.

Time Most of the U.S. is divided into six time zones. From east to west, they are: Eastern, Central, Mountain, Pacific, Alaska, and Hawaii/Aleutian. For example, noon in New York City is 11am in Chicago, 10am in Denver, 9am in Los Angeles, 8am in mainland Alaska, and 7am in Honolulu and the outer Aleutian Islands. Daylight saving time is in effect from 1am on the first Sunday in April to 1am the last Sunday in October and moves the clock 1 hour ahead of standard time.

Tipping Tips make up a major part of the compensation for many service workers. To leave no tip in a restaurant is socially unacceptable and leaves your server unpaid. To leave a small tip is a powerful indication of displeasure for bad service; to leave no tip suggests you don't know any better.

In restaurants, bars, and nightclubs, tip your server 15% to 20% of the check, depending on the quality of service. Tip **bartenders** 10% to 15%, tip **checkroom attendants** $1 per garment, and tip **valet-parking attendants** $1 per vehicle. Tipping is not expected in cafeterias or fast-food restaurants where you order at a counter. In hotels, tip **bellhops** $1 per bag and tip the **housekeeper** at least $1 to $2 per day. Tip **cab drivers** 15% of the fare and tip **hairdressers** and **barbers** 15% to 20%. Do not tip gas-station attendants and ushers at movies and theaters.

See the box "A Guide to Guide Gratuities" on p. 38 for guidelines on tipping outdoor guides and outfitters.

Toilets You won't find public toilets (or "restrooms") on the streets in most U.S. cities, but they can be found in hotel lobbies, bars, restaurants, museums, department stores, railway and bus stations, or service stations.

4

Cruising Alaska's Coast

by Jerry Brown & Fran Wenograd Golden

Alaska is one of the top cruise destinations in the world, with three-quarters of a million people sailing the state's coast annually, visiting the towns and wilderness areas of the Southeast and the Gulf of Alaska by day and burrowing into their ships for effortless travel by night. This element of cruise travel—the fact that it's *easy*—is one of its main drawing cards for visitors to the Southeast, where the lack of roads between towns makes the waters of the Inside Passage the region's de facto highway. You could do the same routes on the Alaska Marine Highway System (the state ferry), but you'd have to be willing to invest more time—both for the actual traveling and for the planning—and be willing to give up the cruise ship's comforts and diversions. (On the other hand, the ferry gives you unlimited stops along the way and a chance to meet Alaskan residents; see "Exploring Southeast Alaska," in chapter 5.)

Now for the bad news: All those cruise ships aren't necessarily good for Alaska and its residents. Alaskans are known for their hospitality, but we all have our limits. The presence of too many cruise passengers has unquestionably spoiled some of Alaska's quaint places. Once-charming streets are transformed into carnival midways jammed wall-to-wall with people from simultaneous ships landings. Some communities feel that the cultural bulldozing brought by these floating cities is not worth the economic benefit, and have placed limits on the number of ships that can come in to port or levied new taxes based on the number of people the ships bring. After years of fast growth, the industry, too, has begun talk of a "carrying capacity."

As a visitor, you can avoid these problems or you can ignore them. To avoid overcrowded port calls, choose a small-ship cruise that spends less time hopping from town to town and more time enjoying the wilderness. Such vessels also call on small towns that the big ships can't get into. On the other hand, riding a megaship is a different kind of fun—the ship itself is an attraction with far more amenities than any of the towns along the way. If you need to relax and leave all stresses of life at home behind—and if seeing Alaska isn't the most important part of your trip—a big ship is the way to go. You can always travel independently after the cruise to find the real Alaska. (For more on the relative benefits of big versus small cruise ships, see "Weighing Your Cruise Options," below.)

In this chapter we'll go through the cruise options available in the state, focusing primarily on those that give a real in-depth experience. For even more information, pick up a copy of *Frommer's Alaska Cruises & Ports of Call.*

1 Weighing Your Cruise Options

Your three main questions in choosing a cruise in Alaska are, "When should I go?" "Where do I want to go?" and "How big a ship?"

WHEN TO GO?

Alaska is a seasonal, as opposed to year-round, cruise destination, with the season generally running May through September, although some smaller ships start up in April. May and September are considered the shoulder season, and lower brochure rates are offered during these months (and more aggressive discounts, as well). Cruising in May is extremely pleasant—the crowds have yet to arrive and locals are friendlier than they are later in the season, when they're pretty much ready to see the tourists go home for the winter. There is also the statistical fact that May in the Inside Passage ports is the driest month in the season. Late September, though, also offers the advantage of fewer fellow tourists clogging the ports. The warmest months are June, July, and August, with temperatures generally around 50°F to 80°F (10°C–27°C) during the day, and cooler at night. You may not need a parka, but you will need to bring along some outerwear. June 21 is the longest day of the year, with the sky lit virtually all night. June tends to be drier than July and August (we have experienced trips in July when it rained nearly every day). April and May are drier than September, although in early April you may encounter freezing rain and other vestiges of winter. If you are considering traveling in a shoulder month, keep in mind that some shops don't open until Memorial Day, and the visitor season is generally considered over on Labor Day (although cruise lines operate well into Sept).

INSIDE PASSAGE OR THE GULF OF ALASKA?

Typically, the cruise lines offer two basic weeklong itineraries. **Inside Passage cruises** generally sail round-trip from Vancouver, British Columbia, visiting three or four port towns (typically Juneau, Skagway, Ketchikan, and either Sitka, Haines, or Victoria, B.C.) along the Inside Passage, spending a day in Glacier Bay or one of the other glacier areas, and spending 2 days "at sea," meaning they just cruise along, allowing you to relax and enjoy the scenery.

Gulf of Alaska cruises generally sail north- and southbound between Vancouver and Seward (the port for Anchorage) in alternating weeks (Princess cruises go up to Whittier this year), visiting many of the same towns and attractions as the Inside Passage cruises but—since they don't have to turn around and sail back to Vancouver—also tacking on a visit to Valdez, Hubbard Glacier, College Fjord, or one or more of the other Gulf towns or natural attractions.

Though most of the major operators stick pretty closely to these two basic routes, the small-ship cruise lines tend to offer more **small-port and wilderness-oriented itineraries,** some sailing round-trip from Juneau or Sitka, some sailing between Juneau and Ketchikan, and one even sailing between Juneau and Glacier Bay. Many of these ships visit the major ports of call, but may also include visits to small ports that aren't accessible to the bigger ships, calling at towns like Petersburg, Wrangell, Gustavus, Elfin Cove, and possibly the Native village of Metlakatla. Some ships sail itineraries where passengers can explore by kayak or take hiking treks.

Cruisetours combine a cruise with a land tour, either before or after the cruise. Typical packages link the cruise with a 3- to 5-day Anchorage/Denali/Fairbanks tour, a 7-day Yukon tour (which visits Anchorage, Denali, and Fairbanks on the way), or a 5- to 7-day tour of the Canadian Rockies. Holland America, Princess, and Cruise West (a distant 3rd) are the three leaders in the cruisetour market. Even if you book with another cruise line, chances are your land tour will be through one of these operators.

BIG SHIP OR SMALL?

Imagine an elephant. Now imagine your pet pug dog, Sparky. That's about the size difference between your options in the Alaska market: behemoth modern ships and small, more exploratory coastal vessels.

BIG SHIPS   The **big ships** in the Alaska market fall generally into two categories: midsize ships and megaships. Carrying as many as 2,670 passengers, the **megaships** look and feel like floating resorts. Big on glitz, they offer loads of activities, attract many families and (especially in Alaska) seniors, offer many public rooms (including fancy casinos and fully equipped gyms), and provide a wide variety of meal and entertainment options. And though they may feature 1 or 2 formal nights per trip, the ambience is generally casual. The Alaska vessels of the Carnival, Celebrity, Princess, and Royal Caribbean fleets all fit in this category, as does Norwegian Cruise Line's *Norwegian Sky* and *Norwegian Sun*. **Midsize ships** in Alaska fall into two segments: the ultra-luxury ships of the Crystal and Radisson Seven Seas fleets; and the modern midsize *Veendam, Ryndam, Volendam, Amsterdam, Maasdam, Zaandam,* and *Statendam* of Holland America Line. In general, the sizes of these ships are less significant than the general onboard atmosphere of the company that runs them. Both the midsize ships and the megaships have a great range of facilities for passengers. Cabins on these ships range from cubbyholes to large suites, depending on the ship and the type of cabin you book. Big dining rooms and a tremendous variety of cuisines are the norm. These ships carry a lot of people and can, at times, feel crowded.

The sizes of these big ships also come with **three major drawbacks** for passengers: (1) they can't sail into narrow passages or shallow-water ports, (2) their size and inflexible schedules limit their ability to stop or even slow down when wildlife is spotted, and (3) when their passengers disembark in a town, they tend to overwhelm that town, limiting your ability to see the real Alaska.

SMALL SHIPS   Just as big cruise ships are mostly for people who want every resort amenity, **small** or **alternative ships** are best suited for people who prefer a casual, crowd-free cruise experience that gives passengers a chance to get up close and personal with Alaska's natural surroundings and wildlife. Small ships offer little in terms of amenities: they usually have small cabins, only one lounge/bar and dining room, and no exercise facilities, entertainment, or organized activities. There are no stabilizers on most of these smaller ships, and the ride can be bumpy in open water—which isn't much of a problem on Inside Passage itineraries, since most of the cruising area is protected from sea waves. They are also difficult for travelers with disabilities, as only four (Cruise West's *Spirit of '98* and *Spirit of Oceanus,* Clipper's *Clipper Odyssey,* and American West Steamboat Company's *Express of the North*) have elevators. Despite all of this, they're universally more expensive than the big ships, and offer fewer discounts. That's the minus side.

On the plus side, they can sail almost anywhere (including far into Misty Fjords, where no large ship can penetrate). These ships tend to have more flexibility in their schedules than the large ships, and will usually take time to linger if whales or other wildlife are sighted nearby. Their small size doesn't scare off wildlife as easily as the big ships, and the fact that you're at or near the waterline (rather than 10 stories up, as on the large ships) means you get a more close-up view. Many smaller cruise companies compensate for a lack of onboard activities by offering more active off-ship opportunities, such as hiking or kayaking. The alternative ships are also more likely to feature expert lectures on Alaska-specific topics, such as marine biology, history, and Native culture.

Tips Sick Ships

Every summer, hundreds of cruise-ship passengers and plenty of visitors on shore come down with vomiting and diarrhea caused by a bug now known as the norovirus. I believe I've had it, and my review is definitely negative. The miserable illness lasts a day or two; it's rarely serious, although some passengers do end up in the hospital because of dehydration. The virus is extremely contagious from the first symptoms until at least 3 days and up to 2 weeks after it clears up. Touching a contaminated handrail and then your face is enough to catch it. To minimize your chances of contracting the virus, wash hands frequently, drink bottled water and avoid eating raw food on board, especially shellfish. The Centers for Disease Control also recommended in 1998 that passengers 65 and older or those with chronic illnesses check with their doctors before taking a cruise. The CDC website (www.cdc.gov/nceh/vsp) posts sanitation inspection scores for each ship. Type "norovirus" into their search page to find a fact sheet.

Visitors aboard large ships may physically be in Alaska, but unless they're reminded of it they might never know, such is the disjunction between the glitzy modern ships and the real world outside. Visitors aboard small ships, however, get an experience that's many times more intimate, allowing them to really get in touch with the place they've come to see. For all these reasons, our advice to anyone wanting to experience Alaska rather than just get a postcard impression of it is to spend the extra money for a small-ship cruise. As with any product, you get what you pay for, and by paying extra in the short term for a more intimate cruise, you're almost guaranteed to have an Alaska experience that you'll remember your whole life.

2 The Best Cruise Experiences in Alaska

Cruise lines are in the business of giving their guests a good time, so they've all got something going for them. Here's my pick of Alaska's best, though, in a few different categories.

- **The Best Ships for Luxury:** Crystal Cruises' 940-passenger *Crystal Harmony* is the big luxury ship in the Alaska market. We're talking superb cuisine, elegant service, lovely surroundings, great cabins, and sparkling entertainment. If you want a more casual kind of luxury (a really nice ship with a no-tie-required policy), Radisson Seven Seas Cruises' *Seven Seas Mariner* offers just that, including plush all-suite cabins (most with private balconies) and excellent cuisine (plus, you get complimentary wine with dinner). And for the ultimate Alaska small ship experience, check out the yachts of *American Safari Cruises,* where soft adventure comes with luxury accouterments.
- **The Best of the Mainstream Ships:** Every line's most recent ships are beautiful, but Celebrity's *Infinity* is a stunner, as is its sister ship, *Summit.* These modern vessels, with their extensive art collections, cushy public rooms, and expanded spa areas, give Celebrity a formidable presence in Alaska in 2005.
- **The Best of the Small Ships:** Clipper Cruise Line's newest vessel, the *Clipper Odyssey,* is a really stunning little ship, offering a higher level of comfort

than most of the other small ships in this category. The most adventurous small-ship itineraries in Alaska are offered by Glacier Bay Cruiseline, whose *Wilderness Adventurer* and *Wilderness Explorer* both concentrate on kayaking, hiking, and wildlife, hardly visiting any ports at all over the course of their itineraries.

- **The Best Ships for Families:** All the major lines have well-established kids' programs. **Holland America** and **Norwegian Cruise Line** win points in Alaska for their special shore excursions for kids and teens, and **Carnival** offers special shore excursions for teens.

- **The Best Ships for Pampering:** It's a toss-up: Celebrity's *Infinity* and *Summit* offer wonderful AquaSpas complete with thalassotherapy pools and a wealth of soothing and beautifying treatments, while *Crystal Harmony* pampers all around, and the solariums on Royal Caribbean's *Vision of the Seas, Legend of the Seas,* and new *Radiance of the Seas* offer relaxing indoor pool retreats.

- **The Best Shipboard Cuisine: Radisson** and **Crystal** (in that order) are tops. Of the mainstream lines, **Celebrity** is the best, with its cuisine overseen by renowned French chef Michel Roux. And there are signs of a new and rather surprising challenger for the cuisine award: **Carnival.** Although the line had not hitherto been especially noted for its food, it has upgraded both its main dining room and buffet offerings. And the line's new *Carnival Spirit* has raised the company's standards considerably. Its intimate Nouveau Supper Club (which you can visit for a $25 fee) serves about as elegant a meal as you're likely to find anywhere.

- **The Best Ships for Onboard Activities:** The ships operated by **Carnival** and **Royal Caribbean** offer a very full roster of onboard activities, that range from the sublime (such as lectures) to the ridiculous (such as contests designed to get passengers to do or say crazy things).

- **The Best Ships for Entertainment:** Look to the big ships here. **Carnival** and **Royal Caribbean** are tops when it comes to an overall package of show productions, nightclub acts, lounge performances, and audience-participation entertainment. And **Princess** offers particularly well-done stage shows.

- **The Best Ships for Whale-Watching:** If they come close enough, you can see whales from all the ships in Alaska. Smaller ships, though, such as those operated by **Glacier Bay Cruiseline** and **Cruise West,** may actually change course to follow a whale. Get your cameras ready!

- **The Best Ships for Cruisetours: Princess** and **Holland America** are the entrenched market leaders in getting you into the Interior either before or after your cruise. They own their own hotels, deluxe motor coaches, and rail cars, and after many years in the business, they both really know what they're doing. Some of the other lines actually buy their cruisetour products from Princess or Holland America. Holland America's cruisetours' strength is its 3- and 4-night cruises combined with an Alaska/Yukon land package. Its exclusive entry into the Yukon's Kluane National Park last year proved extremely popular. Princess is arguably stronger in 7-day Gulf of Alaska cruises in conjunction with Denali/Fairbanks or Kenai Peninsula land arrangements. In 2002, Princess also introduced its fifth wilderness lodge— the Copper River Lodge, by the entry to hitherto difficult-to-access Wrangell–St. Elias National Park. Its addition gave Princess an attractive new cruisetour component, which will be even more popular this year, with growing public awareness.

- **The Best Ports: Juneau** and **Skagway** are our favorites, but we also really like **Haines.** Juneau is one of the most visually pleasing small cities anywhere and certainly the prettiest capital city in America. It's fronted by the Gastineau Channel and backed by Mount Juneau and Mount Roberts, offers the very accessible Mendenhall Glacier, and is otherwise surrounded by wilderness—and it's a really fun city to visit, too. As for Skagway, no town in Alaska is more historically significant, and the old buildings are so perfect you might think you stepped into a Disney version of what a gold-rush town should look like. If, that is, you can get over the decidedly turn-of-the-millennium Starbucks coffee vendor in the Mercantile Center and all the upscale jewelry shops that have followed cruise passengers from the Caribbean. For a more low-key Alaska experience, take the ferry from Skagway to Haines, which really reminds us of the low-key Alaska as depicted on the TV show *Northern Exposure* and is a great place to spot eagles and other wildlife. (Some ships also stop at Haines as a port of call.)
- **The Best Shore Excursions: Flightseeing** and **helicopter trips** in Alaska are really unforgettable ways to check out the scenery if you can afford them. (They're pretty pricey.) A helicopter trip to a dog sled camp at the top of a glacier (usually the priciest of the offerings) affords both incredibly pretty views and a chance to try your hand at the truly Alaskan sport of dog sledding (and earn great bragging rights with the folks back home). For a less extravagant excursion, nothing beats a ride on a clear day on the aforementioned White Pass and Yukon Route railway out of Skagway. And we also like to get active with **kayak and mountain-biking excursions** offered by most lines at most ports; in addition to affording a chance to work off those shipboard calories, these excursions typically provide optimum opportunities for spotting eagles, bears, seals, and other wildlife.
- **The Best Natural Sights Seen from On Board:** There are so many in Alaska it's hard to choose, but Glacier Bay, Hubbard Glacier, College Fjord, and Misty Fjords National Monument (into which big ships can only get a short distance) would have to appear on anyone's top-10 list.

3 Booking Your Cruise

Almost every cruise line publishes brochure prices that are the travel equivalent of a new car's sticker price: wildly inflated in the hope that someone, somewhere, might take them at face value. In reality, especially as sailings get close and it looks as if the line will get stuck with unsold space, cruise lines are almost universally willing to sell their cruises for much, much less. (The small-ship lines tend to be the exception to this rule. Since they have less space to sell and appeal to a more specific market niche, they can often get their initial asking price.)

Traditionally (meaning over the past 30 years or so) people have booked their cruises through **travel agents.** But, you may be wondering, hasn't the traditional travel agent been replaced by the **Internet,** and gone the way of typewriters and eight-track tapes? Not exactly. Travel agents are alive and kicking, though the Internet has indeed staked its claim alongside them and knocked some out of business. Some traditional agencies have also created their own websites to try and keep pace.

So which is the better way to book a cruise these days? Good question. The answer can be both. If you're computer savvy, have a good handle on all the elements that go into a cruise, and have narrowed down the choices to a few cruise lines that appeal to you, websites are a great way to trawl the seas at your own pace and check out last-minute deals, which can be dramatic. On the other hand, you'll barely get a stitch of personalized service searching for and booking a cruise online. If something goes wrong or you need help getting a refund or arranging special meals or other matters, you're on your own.

BOOKING A SMALL-SHIP CRUISE

The small-ship companies in Alaska—Glacier Bay Cruiseline, American Safari Cruises, Clipper, Cruise West, and Lindblad Expeditions—all offer real niche-oriented cruise experiences, attracting passengers who have a very good idea of the kind of experience they want (usually educational and/or adventurous, and always casual and small-scale). In many cases, a large percentage of passengers on any given cruise will have sailed with the line before. Because of all this, and because the passenger capacity of these small ships is so low (12–235), in general you're not going to find the kind of deep discounts you do with the large ships. Still, for the most part these lines rely on agents to handle their bookings, taking very few reservations directly. (Clipper is the exception to this rule, taking most of their Alaska bookings directly, rather than through agents.) All of the lines have a list of agents with whom they do considerable business and can hook you up with one or another of them if you call (or e-mail) and ask for an agent near you.

BOOKING A MAINSTREAM CRUISE

If you don't know a good travel agent already, try to find one through your friends, preferably those who have cruised before. For the most personal service, look for an agent in your local area, and for the most knowledgeable service, look for an agent who has cruising experience. It's perfectly okay to ask an agent questions about his or her personal knowledge of the product, such as whether he or she has ever cruised in Alaska or with one of the lines you're considering. The easiest way to be sure the agent is experienced in booking cruises is to work

---

Tips **Shopping for Shore Tours**

Most cruise-ship passengers sign up for onshore activities and excursions that leave from the dock when they arrive on board. It's easy and convenient, and you can be sure the outing will be timed to your port of call. On the down side, these tend to be the most superficial and highest-priced choices in town and almost always involve large groups. For outdoor activities, trooping down a trail or paddling a sea kayak in a big mob can spoil the experience. There is an alternative, however. A large part of the high shipboard price for shore tours is the cut taken by the cruise line. You can get a much better deal (as much as half off) by arranging your own activities in advance. Most guides will be happy to tailor an outing to your limited time, and you'll probably have a far more intimate experience in the bargain. And it only takes a little advance prepwork: Study your ports of call, the activities and operators there (for which this book will be an invaluable guide), and the time you will be ashore, and then make your reservations before you leave, putting down the appropriate deposits and getting directions for making transfers.

with an agent at a **cruise-only agency** (meaning that the whole agency specializes in cruises) or to find an agent who is a **cruise specialist** (meaning he or she specializes in cruises). If you are calling a full-service travel agency, ask for the **cruise desk,** which is where you'll find these specialists.

A good and easy rule of thumb to maximize your chances of finding an agent who has cruise experience and who won't rip you off is to book with agencies that are members of the **Cruise Lines International Association (CLIA)** (℡ 212/ 921-0066; www.cruising.org) or the **National Association of Cruise Oriented Agencies (NACOA)** (℡ 305/663-5626; www.nacoaonline.com). Members of both groups are cruise specialists. Membership in the **American Society of Travel Agents (ASTA)** (℡ 800/275-2782; www.astanet.com) assures the agency is monitored for ethical practices, although it does not in itself designate cruise experience.

You can tap into the Internet sites of these organizations for easy access to agents in your area.

THE COST: WHAT'S INCLUDED & WHAT'S NOT

However you arrange to buy your cruise, what you basically have in hand at the end is a contract for transportation, lodging, dining, entertainment, housekeeping, and assorted other miscellaneous services that will be provided to you over the course of your vacation. It's important, though, to remember what extras are *not* included in your cruise fare. Are you getting a price that includes port charges, taxes, fees, and insurance, or are you getting a cruise-only fare? Are airfare and airport transfers included, or do you have to book them separately (either as an add-on to the cruise fare or on your own)? Make sure you're comparing apples with apples when making price comparisons. Read the fine print!

Aside from **airfare,** which is usually not included in your cruise fare (see more on air arrangements below), the most pricey addition to your cruise fare, particularly in Alaska, will likely be **shore excursions.** Ranging from about $20 for a walking tour to $250 or more for a helicopter or seaplane flightseeing excursion, these sightseeing tours are designed to help cruise passengers make the most of their time at the ports the ship visits, but they can add a hefty sum to your vacation costs.

You'll also want to add to your calculations **tips for the ship's crew.** Tips are given at the end of the cruise, and passengers should reserve at least $9 per passenger per day ($10 on some ships) for tips for the room steward, waiter, and busperson. (In practice, we find that most people tend to give a little more.) Additional tips to other personnel, such as the head waiter or maitre d', are at your discretion. On the small ships, all tips often go into one pot, which the crew divides up after the cruise.

Most ships charge extra for **alcoholic beverages** (including wine at dinner) and for soda. Nonbubbly soft drinks, such as lemonade and iced tea, are included in your cruise fare.

MONEY-SAVING STRATEGIES

Cruise pricing is a fluid medium, and there are a number of strategies you can use to save money off the booking price.

EARLY & LATE BOOKING

The best way to save on an Alaska cruise is to **book in advance.** In a typical year, lines offer early-bird rates, usually 25% or more off the brochure rate, to those who book their Alaska cruise by mid- to late February of the year of the cruise.

If the cabins do not fill up by the cutoff date, the early-bird rate may be extended, but it may be slightly lower—say, a 15% or 20% savings.

It used to be rare to find last-minute deals on Alaska cruises due to their popularity, but over the past few years, with bigger capacity ships in the Alaska market, there has been a proliferation of discounting (with last-minute specials offering up to 60% off and in some cases even more), and that trend is likely to continue for 2005. Keep in mind, though, that last-minute deals are usually for a very limited selection of cabins. Planning your Alaska cruise vacation well in advance and taking advantage of early-booking discounts is still the best way to go.

SHOULDER SEASON DISCOUNTS

You can save by booking a cruise in the **shoulder months of May or September,** when cruise pricing is lower than during the high summer months. Typically, Alaska cruises are divided into budget, low, economy, value, standard, and peak seasons, but since these overlap quite a bit from cruise line to cruise line, we can lump them into three basic periods:

1. **Budget/Low/Economy Season:** May and September
2. **Value/Standard Season:** Early June and late August
3. **Peak Season:** Late June, July, and early to mid-August

DISCOUNTS FOR THIRD & FOURTH PASSENGERS & GROUPS

Most ships offer highly discounted rates for third and fourth passengers sharing a cabin with two full-fare passengers, even if those two have booked at a discounted rate. It may mean a tight squeeze, but it'll save you a bundle. Some lines offer **special rates for kids,** usually on a seasonal or select-sailings basis, that may include free or discounted airfare.

One of the best ways to get a cruise deal is to book as a **group** of at least 16 people in at least eight cabins. The savings include a discounted rate, and at least the cruise portion of the 16th ticket will be free. Ask your travel agent about any group deals they may offer.

SENIOR DISCOUNTS

Seniors may be able to get extra savings on their cruise. Some lines will take 5% off the top for those 55 and up, and the senior rate applies even if the second person in the cabin is younger. Membership in groups such as AARP is not required, but such membership may bring additional savings.

BOOKING AIR TRAVEL THROUGH THE CRUISE LINE

Except during special promotions, airfare to the port of embarkation is rarely included in the cruise rates, so you'll have to purchase airfare on your own or buy it as a package with your cruise through your travel agent or online cruise site. You can usually find information on these "air/sea" programs in the back of cruise line brochures, along with prices. The benefits of booking through the cruise line is that round-trip **transfers** between the airport and the ship are usually included, and as big customers of the airlines, the cruise lines tend to get decent (if not the best) discounted airfare rates. Also, the cruise line will know your airline schedule, and in the event of delayed flights and other unavoidable snafus, will be able to do more to make sure you and the other people on your flight get on the ship; if you've booked your air transportation separately, you're on your own. The only time it may pay to book your own air transportation is if you are using frequent-flier miles and can get the air for free, or if you are fussy about which carrier you fly or route you take.

CHOOSING YOUR CABIN

Cruise-ship cabins run from tiny boxes with accordion doors and bunk beds to palatial multiroom suites with hot tubs on the balcony. Which is right for you? Price will likely be a big factor here, but so should the vacation style you prefer. If, for instance, you plan to spend a lot of quiet time in your cabin, you should probably consider booking the biggest room you can afford. If, conversely, you plan to be out on deck all the time checking out the glaciers and wildlife, you might be just as happy with a smaller (and cheaper) cabin to crash in at the end of the day. Cabins are either **inside** (without a window or porthole) or **outside** (with), the latter being more expensive. On the big ships, the more deluxe outside cabins may also come with **private verandas.** The cabins are usually described by price (highest to lowest), category (suite, deluxe, superior, standard, economy, and others), and furniture configuration ("sitting area with two lower beds," for example).

SPECIAL MENU REQUESTS

The cruise line should be informed at the time you make your reservations about any special dietary requests you have. Some lines offer kosher menus, and all will have vegetarian, low-fat, low-salt, and sugar-free options available.

4 The Small-Ship Cruise Lines

Small ships allow you to see Alaska from sea level, without the kind of distractions you get aboard the big ships—no glitzy interiors, no big shows or loud music, no casinos, no spas, and no crowds, as the largest of these ships carries only 235 passengers. You're immersed in the 49th state from the minute you wake up to the minute you fall asleep, and, for the most part, you're left alone to form your own opinions. Personally, we feel that despite these ships' higher cost, they provide by far the better cruise experience for those who really want to get the feel of Alaska.

Small-ship itineraries can be categorized as **port-to-port,** meaning they mimic the larger ships in simply sailing between port towns; **soft-adventure,** meaning they provide some outdoors experiences like hiking and kayaking, while not requiring participants to be trained athletes; and **active-adventure,** meaning the hiking and kayaking will be the real focus of the trip, and may be strenuous.

On all of these types of cruises, the small-ship experience tends toward education rather than glitzy entertainment. You'll likely get **informal and informative lectures** and, sometimes, video presentations on Alaska wildlife, history, and Native culture. Meals are served in open seatings, so you can sit where and with whom you like, and time spent huddled on the outside decks scanning for whales fosters great camaraderie among passengers.

Cabins on these ships don't generally offer TVs or telephones, and they tend to be very small and sometimes spartan (see the individual reviews for exceptions). There are no stabilizers on most of these smaller ships, so the ride can be bumpy in rough seas. Alaska Sightseeing's *Spirit of '98* and *Spirit of Oceanus,* Clipper Cruise Line's *Clipper Odyssey,* and American West Steamboat Company's *Empress of the North* have elevators, but in general the small ships are not good choices for travelers who require the use of wheelchairs or have other mobility problems.

Discover Prince William Sound by Boat

Discovery Voyages is one of the few cruise companies that offers overnight trips into Prince William Sound. The 12-passenger, 65-foot *Discovery* departs from Whittier on 5-, 6-, 7- and 11-day cruises that bring you up close and personal with the area's glaciers. Naturalists and outdoor guides are on board to organize such trip activities as birding, whale and wildlife-watching, kayaking, and hiking excursions. For more information, call 🕿 **800/324-7602** or try www.discoveryvoyages.com. For more on Prince William Sound, see chapter 7.

AMERICAN SAFARI CRUISES

19101 36th Ave. W., Suite 201, Lynnwood, WA 98036. 🕿 **888/862-8881.** Fax 425/776-8889. www.am safari.com.

Directed to the slightly jaded high-end traveler, American Safari Cruises promises an intimate, all-inclusive yacht cruise to some of the more out-of-the-way stretches of the Inside Passage. The company books only 12 to 22 people per cruise, guaranteeing unparalleled flexibility and privacy. Black-bear aficionados can chug off in a Zodiac boat for a better look; active adventurers can explore the shoreline in one of the yacht's four kayaks; and lazier travelers can relax aboard ship. Another big plus: All off-ship excursions—including flightseeing and trips to boardwalked cannery villages and Tlingit villages—are included in the cruise fare, as are drinks. The price is considerable, as is the pampering.

The line offers 7-night and 8-night Inside Passage cruises.

PASSENGER PROFILE   Passengers, almost always couples, tend to be more than comfortably wealthy and range from 45 to 65 years of age. Most hope to get close to nature without sacrificing luxury. Dress is always casual, with comfort being the prime goal.

SHIPS   More private yachts than cruise ships, the 22-passenger *Safari Quest,* the 12-passenger *Safari Spirit,* and the 12-passenger *Safari Escape* look like Ferraris—all sleek, contoured lines and dark glass. Cabins are comfortable, and sitting rooms are intimate and luxurious, almost as if they had been transported whole from a spacious suburban home. A big-screen TV in the main lounge forms a natural center for impromptu lectures during the day and movie-watching at night. A shipboard chef assails guests with multiple-course meals and clever snacks, barters with nearby fishing boats for the catch of the day, and raids local markets for the freshest fruits and vegetables—say, strawberries the size of a cub's paw and potent strains of basil and cilantro. **Brochure rates per person:** Lowest-price outside cabins $3,895 for a 7-night cruise; no inside cabins or suites.

AMERICAN WEST STEAMBOAT COMPANY

2101 4th Ave., Suite 1150, Seattle, WA 98121. 🕿 **800/434-1232** or 206/292-9606. Fax 206/340-0975. www.columbiarivercruise.com.

Carrying 235 passengers, this company's ship, *Empress of the North,* belongs in a whole, new, separate category—sternwheelers. Clearly, the appeal here is the nostalgia. Pure Americana—that's what the *Empress of the North* represents. There is not much in the way of organized fun and games. A lecturer accompanies each cruise, offering insights into the passing scenery and cultures. Shore excursions are included in the price, but don't look for kayaks off the back of the vessel, or scuba diving or anything of that nature.

The line offers 11-night Inside Passage cruises.

PASSENGER PROFILE Not necessarily filthy rich, but probably comfortably off. And they are experienced cruisers.

SHIPS *Empress of the North,* built in 2003, carries 235 passengers. It has four decks, two lounges, and elevators. The cabins are large by small-ship standards, all have views of the ocean, and 105 out of 112 of the cabins have verandas. Elegance is the byword in public rooms. **Sample rates per person:** Outside $4,859 for 11-night cruise, suites $7,399 for 11-night cruise; no inside cabins.

CLIPPER CRUISE LINE

11969 Westline Industrial Dr., St. Louis, MO 63146. (℄ **800/325-0010** or 314/655-6700. Fax 314/655-6670. www.clippercruise.com.

Clipper's down-to-earth, comfortable small ships focus on offbeat ports of call, learning, and mingling with your fellow passengers. It's the ideal small-ship cruise for people who've tried Holland America or Princess but want a more intimate cruise experience. Its ships sail port-to-port itineraries. As aboard Alaska's other small-ship lines, the onboard atmosphere is casual; what lies out there beyond the ship's rail is most passengers' real focus. Throughout the cruise, onboard naturalists offer a series of informal lectures and accompany passengers on shore excursions. Organized shore excursions are offered at each port (the tours cost extra), including flightseeing, sport fishing, and city tours with commentary by local residents. No need to dress up here—everything's casual.

The ships sail 14-night Alaska Coast/Russian Far East itineraries, 13-night Gulf of Alaska/Inside Passage/British Columbia itineraries, 12-night Inside Passage/British Columbia itineraries, and 7-night Inside Passage itineraries.

PASSENGER PROFILE The majority of Clipper passengers are well-traveled, 50+ couples. Most are well-educated though not academic, casual though not sloppily so, and adventurous in the sense that they're up for a little hiking but are happy to be able to get back to their comfortable cabins or have a drink in the lounge afterwards.

SHIPS Along with Cruise West's *Spirit of Endeavor* and *Spirit of Oceanus* and Glacier Bay's *Executive Explorer,* the 120-passenger *Clipper Odyssey* and 138-passenger *Yorktown Clipper* are two of the best choices in Alaska for someone who wants small-ship intimacy and flexibility but doesn't want to skimp on comfort. Their public rooms are larger and more appealing than those aboard competing ships, and all cabins are outside. Except for those at the lowest level (which have portholes), all cabins have picture windows. Although relatively simple in ingredients and presentation, the cuisine is easily the equal of all but the best that is served aboard mainstream megaships. **Sample rates per person:** Lowest-price outside cabins on *Yorktown Clipper:* $2,450 for 7-night cruise; on *Odyssey:* $5,630 for 14-night cruise. No inside cabins on either ship.

CRUISE WEST

2401 4th Ave., Suite 700, Seattle, WA 98121. (℄ **800/426-7702** or 206/441-8687. Fax 206/441-4757. www. cruisewest.com.

Cruise West is the largest operator of small ships in Alaska, offering port-to-port itineraries in various areas of Alaska, friendly service, and a casual onboard atmosphere. As with Clipper Cruise Line, Cruise West's ships are for people who want to visit Alaska's port towns and see its wilderness areas up close and in a relaxed, small-scale environment without big-ship distractions; they're not for people who want to spend their days hiking and kayaking.

The operative words here are casual, relaxed, and friendly. The line's friendly, enthusiastic staffs are a big, big plus, making guests feel right at home. At sea, the lack of organized activities on the line's port-to-port itineraries leaves you free to scan for wildlife, peruse the natural sights, or read a book. In port, the line arranges some novel, intimate shore excursions, such as a visit with local artists at their home outside Haines or an educational walking tour led by a Native guide in Ketchikan.

A cheerful and knowledgeable **cruise coordinator** accompanies each trip to answer passengers' questions about Alaska's flora, fauna, geology, and history, and Forest Service rangers, local fishers, and Native Alaskans sometimes come aboard to teach about the culture and industry of the state.

Ships sail a 10-night Inside Passage itinerary, an 8-night "Wilderness Waterways" itinerary (a round-trip from Juneau that visits Tracy Arm, Endicott Arm, Sitka, Glacier Bay, and Icy Strait), and a 13-night Bering Sea itinerary that cruises between Nome and Anchorage.

PASSENGER PROFILE   Cruise West passengers tend to be older (typically around 60–75), financially stable, well educated, and independent-minded—folks who want to visit Alaska's ports and see its natural wonders in a relaxed, dress-down atmosphere.

SHIPS   The 96-passenger *Spirit of '98,* a replica of a 19th-century steamship, carries its Victorian flavor so well that fully two-thirds of the people we met on board thought the ship had been a private yacht at the turn of the 20th century. If you use a wheelchair or otherwise have mobility problems, note that the '98 is one of only four small ships in Alaska that has an elevator. (The line's *Spirit of Oceanus,* American West Steamboat Company's *Empress of the North,* and Clipper's *Clipper Odyssey* are the others.) The 78-passenger *Spirit of Alaska* and *Spirit of Columbia,* and 84-passenger *Spirit of Discovery* are all spartan ships designed to get passengers into small ports and allow them to see the state up close. The 102-passenger *Spirit of Endeavour,* on the other hand, offers among the highest levels of small-ship comfort of any small ship in Alaska, comparable to Clipper's *Yorktown Clipper* and Glacier Bay's *Executive Explorer.* The line's new, 114-passenger *Spirit of Oceanus,* the former *Renaissance V* of Renaissance Cruises, is the line's most luxurious ship, able to sail more far-flung itineraries. **Sample rates per person:** Lowest-price inside cabins $2,999 for 7-night cruise, lowest-price outside $3,149 for 7-night cruise.

GLACIER BAY CRUISELINE

2101 4th Ave., Suite 2200, Seattle, WA 98121. ℂ 800/451-5952 or 206/623-7110. Fax 206/623-7809. www.glacierbaycruiseline.com.

Glacier Bay Cruiseline—the only Native-owned cruise line in Alaska—offers three types of cruises: soft-adventure (aboard the *Wilderness Explorer*), active-adventure (aboard the *Wilderness Adventurer*), and port-to-port (aboard the slightly more luxurious *Executive Explorer*). The *Wilderness Discoverer* is a hybrid, sailing itineraries that mix 3 days of adventure activities with 3 days spent visiting popular ports of call.

The adventure sailings are for a particular type of traveler, one interested in exploring Alaska's wilds rather than its towns. On the *Wilderness Explorer*'s soft-adventure cruises, for example, the biggest town you're likely to encounter after departing Juneau is tiny little Elfin Cove, population around 30 to 35 (at least in the summer). Other than this, days are spent hiking in remote regions, exploring the glaciers, cruising the waterways looking for whales and other wildlife, and kayaking—the *Wilderness Adventurer, Wilderness Explorer,* and *Wilderness Discoverer* carry fleets of stable two-person sea kayaks, which are launched from dry platforms at the ships' sterns. A weeklong sailing typically includes three kayak treks. **Naturalists** sail with every cruise to point out natural features and lead off-ship expeditions, all of which are included in the cruise price. On board, the atmosphere is casual and friendly; the staff provides just enough informal attention while leaving you the space to enjoy your vacation. Entertainment facilities on all ships are minimal: board games, books, and a TV/VCR in the lounge, on which passengers can view tapes on wildlife, Alaska history, Native culture, and a few feature films. Cabins are basic and quite small.

Ships sail 5-night Glacier Bay itineraries and 7-night Inside Passage itineraries.

PASSENGER PROFILE   Passengers tend to be on the youngish side, with as many couples in their 40s and 50s as in their 60s and 70s, and a scattering of 30-somethings (and a few 80- or 90-somethings) filling out the list. Whatever their age, passengers tend to be active and interested in nature and wildlife, especially on the adventure itineraries.

SHIPS   The 49-passenger *Executive Explorer* is the line's fanciest vessel. The spartan, 74-passenger *Wilderness Adventurer* and almost identical 86-passenger *Wilderness Discoverer* are the line's soft-adventure ships, outfitted with sea kayaks and kayak dry-launch platforms in their sterns. The 36-passenger *Wilderness Explorer* is the line's most basic ship, with tiny cabins and bunk-style beds. She visits no ports, instead offering the most active cruise experience available in Alaska, with cruises structured so passengers are out kayaking and hiking most of each day and only use the vessel to eat, sleep, and get from place to place. **Sample rates per person:** Lowest-price inside cabins $2,520, lowest-price outside cabins $2,735 for a 7-night cruise; lowest-price outside cabins $1,780 (on the *Wilderness Explorer*) for a 5-night cruise.

LINDBLAD EXPEDITIONS

720 Fifth Ave., New York, NY 10019. ℭ 800/397-3348 or 212/765-7740. Fax 212/265-3770. www.expeditions. com.

Lindblad Expeditions specializes in environmentally sensitive, soft-adventure vacations that are explorative and informal in nature, designed to appeal to the intellectually curious traveler seeking a cruise that's educational as well as relaxing. Days aboard are spent learning about the Alaskan outdoors from high-caliber expedition leaders trained in botany, anthropology, biology, and geology, and observing the world around you either from the ship or during shore excursions, which are included in the cruise package. Educational films and slide presentations aboard ship precede nature hikes and quick jaunts aboard Zodiac boats. Flexibility and spontaneity are keys to the experience, as the route may be altered at any time to follow a pod of whales or school of dolphins.

The ship cruises an 11-day itinerary between Juneau and Seattle, and a 7-day "coastal wilderness" itinerary between Juneau and Sitka.

PASSENGER PROFILE   Lindblad Expeditions tends to attract well-traveled and well-educated, professional, 55+ couples who have "been there, done that" and are looking for something completely different in a cruise experience.

SHIPS   The shallow-draft, 70-passenger *Sea Lion* and *Sea Bird* are identical twins. With just two public rooms and utilitarian cabins, they're very similar to other "expedition style" small ships, such as Glacier Bay's *Wilderness Adventurer* and Cruise West's *Spirit of Alaska.* Cabins are small and functional, and public space is limited to the open sun deck and bow areas, the dining room, and an observation lounge that serves as the nerve center for activities. **Sample rates per person:** Lowest-price outside cabins $3,840 for a 7-night cruise; lowest-price outside cabins $3,980 for an 11-day cruise; no inside cabins or suites.

5 The Big-Ship Cruise Lines

The ships featured in this section vary in size, age, and offerings, but share the common thread of having more activities and entertainment options than any one person can possibly take in over the course of a cruise. You'll find swimming pools, health clubs, spas, nightclubs, movie theaters, shops, casinos, multiple restaurants, bars, and special kids' playrooms, and in some cases sports decks, virtual golf, computer rooms, martini bars, and cigar clubs, as well as quiet spaces where you can get away from it all. In most cases you'll find lots and lots of onboard activities, including games, contests, classes, and lectures, plus a variety of entertainment options and show productions, some very sophisticated.

CARNIVAL CRUISE LINES

3655 NW 87th Ave., Miami, FL 33178-2428. ✆ **800/CARNIVAL.** Fax 305/471-4740. www.carnival.com.

Translating the line's warm-weather experience to Alaska has meant combining the "24-hour orgy of good times" philosophy to include the natural wonders, so you may find yourself bellying up to the rail with a multicolored party drink to gawk at a glacier. Drinking and R-rated comedians are part of the scene, as are "hairy-chest contests" and the like.

Entertainment is among the industry's best, with each ship boasting a dozen dancers, a 12-piece orchestra, comedians, jugglers, and numerous live bands, as well as a big casino. Activity is nonstop. Cocktails begin to flow before lunch, and through the course of the day you can learn to country line-dance or ballroom dance, take cooking lessons, learn to play bridge, watch first-run movies, practice your golf swing by smashing balls into a net, or just eat, drink, shop, and then eat again. Alaska-specific naturalist lectures are delivered daily. In port, Carnival offers **nearly 100 shore excursions,** divided into categories of easy, moderate, and adventure. For kids, the line offers Camp Carnival, an expertly run children's program with activities that include Native arts and crafts sessions, lectures conducted by wildlife experts, and special shore excursions for teens.

Ships cruise the Gulf of Alaska route. In May and September, Inside Passage cruises that visit Glacier Bay are offered.

PASSENGER PROFILE Overall, Carnival has some of the youngest demographics in the industry: mostly under 50, including couples, lots and lots of singles, and a good share of families. It's the same Middle America crowd that can be found in Las Vegas and Atlantic City and at Florida's megaresorts. This is not a sedate, bird-watching crowd. They may want to see whales and icebergs, but they will also dance the Macarena on cue.

SHIPS The 2,124-passenger, 84,000-ton *Carnival Spirit* is big, new, and impressive, with four swimming pools, a wedding chapel, a conference center, and, in addition to the formal dining room and casual buffet restaurant, an alternative restaurant sitting high up by the ship's smokestack. The ship also has more of what makes Carnival tick, including a two-level oceanview gym, balconies on over half the cabins, a large children's center (complete with beepers for parents who want to stay in touch), and two consecutive decks of bars, lounges, and nightspots, one with an outdoor wraparound promenade. **Sample**

rates per person: Lowest-price inside cabins $1,579, lowest outside $1,929, lowest suite $2,929 for a 7-night cruise.

CELEBRITY CRUISES

1050 Caribbean Way, Miami, FL 33132. ✆ **800/437-3111** or 305/262-8322. Fax 800/437-5111. www. celebritycruises.com.

Celebrity Cruises offers a great combination: a classy, tasteful, and luxurious cruise experience at a moderate price—it's definitely the best in the midpriced category. The line's ships are real works of art; its cuisine—guided by Michel Roux, one of the top French chefs in Britain—is outstanding; its service first-class, friendly, and unobtrusive; and its spa facilities among the best in the business.

A typical day might offer bridge, darts, a culinary art demonstration, a trap-shooting competition, a fitness-fashion show, an art auction, a volleyball tournament, and a none-too-shabby stage show. Resident experts give lectures on the various ports of call, the Alaskan environment, glaciers, and Alaskan culture. For children, Celebrity ships employ a group of counselors who direct and supervise a camp-style children's program. Activities are geared toward different age groups. There's an impressive kids' play area and a lounge area for teens.

The company offers 7-night Inside Passage and 7-night Gulf of Alaska itineraries.

PASSENGER PROFILE   The typical Celebrity guest is one who prefers to pursue his or her R&R at a relatively relaxed pace, with a minimum of aggressively promoted group activities. The overall impression leans more toward sophistication and less to the kind of orgiastic Technicolor whoopee that you'll find, say, aboard a Carnival ship. You'll find everyone from kids to retirees.

SHIPS   Sleek, modern, and stunningly designed, both the 1,870-passenger *Mercury* and the larger, 1,950-passenger *Infinity* and *Summit* have a lot of open deck space and lots of large windows that provide access to the wide skies and the grand Alaskan vistas. All the ships (but especially *Mercury*) feature incredible spas with hydrotherapy pools, steam rooms, and saunas, plus health and beauty services and exceptionally large fitness areas. **Sample rates per person:** Lowest-price inside cabins $850, lowest outside $1,100, lowest suite $1,650 for a 7-night cruise.

CRYSTAL CRUISES

2049 Century Park E, Suite 1400, Los Angeles, CA 90067. ✆ **800/446-6620** or 310/785-9300. Fax 310/785-3891. www.crystalcruises.com.

Luxury all the way. Crystal offers all the amenities of much bigger ships, but in a more luxurious and intimate atmosphere, with only 940 passengers. Everything on the *Crystal Harmony* is first class, with fine attention paid to detail and to making guests feel comfortable. Service on the ship is nothing short of superb. The ship carries a battery of Alaska naturalists, environmentalists, and National Park Service rangers to educate and entertain passengers in the wilderness areas of the 49th state. The line's food-and-wine series presents well-known chefs and wine experts who put on food preparation demonstrations, lecture on the art of cookery, and prepare dinner one night during the cruise. A PGA-approved golf pro accompanies practically every *Harmony* cruise, conducting clinics along the way. There's dazzling show-lounge entertainment, first-run movies, and a Caesar's Palace at Sea casino.

The ship cruises a 12-night-long route through the Inside Passage.

PASSENGER PROFILE   Passengers aboard Crystal tend to be successful businesspeople who can afford to pay for the best. In years past, the average age was probably closer to 60 than 70. But that average age is dropping fast to cruisers in their 40s and 50s—probably thanks to Crystal's *incredible* shore-excursion program, its Caesar's Palace at Sea casino, and its entertainment package. Whatever their age, they tend to be people who like to dress up rather than down. "Casual night" doesn't mean the same thing to Crystal guests as it means to other people.

SHIPS   A handsome ship by any standard, the *Harmony* has one of the highest passenger-space ratios of any cruise ship. Its cabins are large, well appointed, and tastefully decorated with quality fittings and in agreeable color tones. Almost half of them have private verandas. The one small criticism is that space to hang clothes is a little tight in some of the lower cabin categories. Public rooms are classy throughout. It's our opinion that Palm Court is the prettiest public space afloat. Two alternative restaurants, Prego (Italian, mostly northern) and Kyoto (Asian/Japanese), introduce variety to the dining experience. **Sample rates per person:** Lowest-price inside cabins $3,120, lowest outside $3,190, lowest suite $9,510 for a 12-night cruise.

HOLLAND AMERICA LINE

300 Elliott Ave. W., Seattle, WA 98119. ℂ 800/426-0327 or 206/281-3535. Fax 206/286-7110. www.holland america.com.

Holland America can be summed up in one word: *tradition.* The company was formed way back in 1873 as the Netherlands-America Steamship Company, and its ships today strive to present an aura of history and dignity, like a European hotel where they never let rock stars register. And thanks to its acquisition, over the years, of numerous land-based tour operators, Holland America has positioned itself as Alaska's most experienced and comprehensive cruise company.

Though most of the line's Alaskan fleet is relatively young, the ships are designed with a decidedly "classic" feel—no flashing neon lights here. Similarly, Holland America's ships are heavy on more mature, less frenetic kinds of activities. You'll find good bridge programs and music to dance (or just listen) to in the bars and lounges, plus health spas and the other amenities found on most large ships. The line has improved its nightly show-lounge entertainment. In 2005, the line continues its Artists in Residence Program, arranged through the Alaska Native Heritage Center in Anchorage, with Alaska Native artists accompanying all 7-night cruises and demonstrating traditional art forms such as ivory and soapstone carving, basket weaving, and mask making. Club HAL is one of the industry's more creative children's programs, though the children's playrooms (often no more than a meeting room stocked with toys) are no match for what you find on the latest Princess or Celebrity megaships.

Alaska itineraries include 7-night Inside Passage cruises and 7-night Gulf of Alaska cruises.

PASSENGER PROFILE   Holland America's passenger profile used to reflect a much older crowd. Now the average age is dropping, partly thanks to an increased emphasis on its Club HAL program for children and partly due to some updating of its onboard entertainment. Still, HAL's passengers in Alaska include a large percentage of middle-aged-and-up vacationers.

SHIPS   The 1,266-passenger *Maasdam, Ryndam, Statendam,* and *Veendam* are more or less identical. All cabins have a sitting area and lots of closet and drawer space, and even the least expensive inside cabins run almost 190 square feet, quite large by industry standards. Outside doubles have either picture windows or verandas. The striking dining rooms, two-tiered showrooms, and Crow's Nest forward bar/lounges are among these ships' best features. The newer, 1,440-passenger *Volendam* and *Zaandam* are larger and fancier, with triple-decked oval atriums, 197 suites and deluxe staterooms with private verandas, five showrooms and lounges, and an alternative restaurant designed as an artist's bistro, featuring drawings and etchings. The smallest cabin is a comfortable 190 square feet. The 1,380-passenger *Amsterdam* is an attractive, midsize ship that combines classic style with innovation. Strategically located in public areas around the ship are sculptures of big ol' Alaskan grizzly bears, done by British artist Susanna Holt. Accommodations are warm, comfortable, low-key—and totally functional. The *Oosterdam,* the newest vessel in the fleet, is 85,000 tons and carries 1,848 passengers. **Sample rates per person:** Lowest-price inside cabins $1,052, lowest outside $1,857, lowest suite $2,902 for a 7-night cruise.

NORWEGIAN CRUISE LINE

7665 Corporate Center Dr., Miami, FL 33126. ℂ 800/327-7030 or 305/436-4000. Fax 305/436-4120. www.ncl.com.

Norwegian Cruise Line (NCL) offers an informal and upbeat onboard atmosphere on the *Norwegian Sun,* sailing from Vancouver, and the *Norwegian Sky* and *Norwegian Star,* both sailing from Seattle. The line excels at activities, and its recreational and fitness programs are among the best in the industry. Though the onboard food has been described as unmemorable, NCL recently inaugurated what has become a very popular casual-dining policy that allows passengers to dine when they want pretty much any time between 5:30pm and midnight, with whomever they want, dressed however they want.

In Alaska, NCL offers an Alaskan lecturer, wine tastings, art auctions, trap shooting, cooking demonstrations, craft and dance classes, an incentive fitness program, and bingo, among other activities. Passengers can choose from a good selection of soft-adventure shore excursions, including hiking, biking, and kayaking. Entertainment is generally strong, and includes Vegas-style musical productions. The top-notch kids' program includes an activity room, video games, an ice-cream bar, and guaranteed babysitting aboard, plus sessions with park rangers and escorted shore excursions.

The line offers 7-night Inside Passage cruises.

PASSENGER PROFILE In Alaska, the demographic tends more toward retirees than on the line's warmer-climate sailings, but you'll find families as well, including grandparents bringing along the grandkids.

SHIPS The 1,936-passenger *Norwegian Sun* is the first ship built with NCL's new "freestyle" dining policy in mind, as evidenced by the nine separate onboard restaurants. An airy eight-story glass atrium welcomes visitors in the lobby. More than two-thirds of the guest rooms (about 650 in all) have ocean views, and closet space is more generous than on other NCL ships. Joining the Norwegian fleet in 2003, the 1,966-passenger *Norwegian Spirit* features seven restaurants, a multi-level showroom, several spots to dance the night away, and two lounges. The 2,240-passenger *Norwegian Star* has no fewer than 11 rooms in which people can eat—depending on the time of day. The *Star* is well equipped for the sports-minded and active vacationer—in addition to the fitness center, there are three heated pools, a jogging/walking track, and a wide array of sports facilities. **Sample rates per person:** Lowest-price inside cabins $959, lowest outside $1,204, lowest suite $1,844 for a 7-night cruise.

PRINCESS CRUISES

24844 Avenue Rockefeller, Santa Clarita, CA 91355. © 800/PRINCESS (774-6237) or 661/753-4999. Fax 310/277-6175. www.princess.com.

Consistency is Princess's strength. With new ships joining its fleet like so many cars off a Detroit assembly line, you'd think that maintaining acceptable service standards could be a problem. All things considered, though, Princess accomplishes this rather well. Throughout the fleet, the service in all areas—dining room, lounge, cabin maintenance, and so on—tends to be of consistently high quality. Aboard Princess, you get a lot of bang for your buck, attractively packaged and well executed. Although its ships serve every corner of the globe, nowhere is the Princess presence more visible than in Alaska. Through its affiliate, Princess Tours, it owns wilderness lodges, motor coaches, and railcars in the 49th state, making it one of the major players in the Alaska cruise market, alongside Holland America.

Princess passengers can expect enough onboard activities to keep them going morning to night, if they've a mind to, and enough nooks and crannies to allow them to do absolutely nothing, if that's their thing. Kids are well taken care of, with especially large children's playrooms. On shore, the line's shore-excursion staffs get big points for efficiency.

Princess offers 7-night Inside Passage cruises, 7-night Gulf of Alaska cruises, and a special 10-night round-trip Inside Passage cruise that departs from San Francisco.

PASSENGER PROFILE   Typical Princess passengers are likely to be between, say, 50 and 65, and are experienced cruisers who know what they want and are prepared to pay for it. Recent additional emphasis on its youth and children's facilities has begun to attract a bigger share of the **family market.**

SHIPS   The *Dawn, Sun, Coral* and *Island Princess* ships are virtually indistinguishable from one another except for cosmetics. They all carry around 1,950 passengers, but despite their size, you'll probably never feel crowded. Decks, buffet dining areas, and lounges feel spacious. There are beautiful libraries, patisseries for pastries and cappuccino, and pizzerias for good made-to-order Italian fast food. The ships have extensive children's playrooms. As for cabins, even the smallest is a spacious 175 square feet, and more than 80% of rooms have private verandas. The 2,670-passenger *Diamond Princess* and *Sapphire Princess* are the newest Princess ships on the water. Their offerings are large and impressive, including a wide range of dining, lounge, and bar options and generously equipped spas and fitness centers. The 1,590-passenger *Regal Princess* offers spacious and tasteful cabins, and a well-equipped gym and aerobics room. **Sample rates per person:** Lowest-price inside cabins $1,309, lowest outside $1,499, lowest suite $1,939 for a 7-night cruise.

RADISSON SEVEN SEAS CRUISES

600 Corporate Dr., Suite 410, Fort Lauderdale, FL 33334. © 800/285-1835. www.rssc.com.

Radisson offers the best in food, service, and accommodations in an environment that's a little more casual and small-shiplike than Crystal's more determined luxury.

The line assumes for the most part that passengers want to entertain themselves on board, so organized activities are limited, but they do include lectures by local experts, well-known authors, and the like, plus facilities for card and board games, blackjack and Ping Pong tournaments, bingo, big screen movies with popcorn, and instruction in the fine arts of pom-pom making, juggling, and such. Bridge instructors are onboard on select sailings. The line has a no-tipping policy, and offers creative shore excursions. Room service is about the best you'll find on any ship, and the cuisine is excellent.

The *Seven Seas Mariner* (see below) sails a 7-night Gulf of Alaska itinerary.

PASSENGER PROFILE Radisson tends to attract passengers in their 50s with a household income of more than $100,000, who don't like to flaunt their wealth. The typical passenger is well educated, well traveled, and inquisitive.

SHIPS Cabins on the 700-passenger *Seven Seas Mariner* are all oceanview suites, and all have private verandas. The standard suite is a large 301 square feet; some suites can interconnect if you want to book two for additional space. The Constellation Theater is two-tiered and designed to resemble a 1930s nightclub. There are two additional lounges, plus a casino and the Connoisseur Club, a cushy venue for pre-dinner drinks and after-dinner fine brandy and cigars. The ship's spa offers Judith Jackson European spa treatments using a variety of herbal and water-based therapies. **Sample rates per person:** Lowest-price suite $2,987 for 7-night cruise; no inside or standard outside cabins.

ROYAL CARIBBEAN INTERNATIONAL

1050 Caribbean Way, Miami, FL 33132. ℂ 800/327-6700 or 305/379-4731. www.rccl.com.

Royal Caribbean sells a mass-market style of cruising that's reasonably priced and offered aboard informal, well-run ships with nearly every diversion imaginable—craft classes, horse racing, bingo, shuffleboard, deck games, line-dancing lessons, wine-and-cheese tastings, cooking demonstrations, art auctions, and the like—plus elaborate health clubs and spas, covered swimming pools, large open sun deck areas, and innumerable bars, lounges, and other entertainment centers. The Viking Crown Lounge and other glassed-in areas make excellent observation rooms from which to see the Alaska sights. Royal Caribbean spends big bucks on entertainment, which includes high-tech show productions. Headliners are often featured. Port lectures are offered on topics such as Alaska wildlife, and the line offers some 65 shore excursions. The line's children's activities are some of the most extensive afloat.

The line offers 7-night Inside Passage cruises.

PASSENGER PROFILE The crowd on Royal Caribbean ships, like the decor, rates pretty high on the party scale, though not quite at the Carnival level. Passengers represent an age mix from 30 to 60, and a good number of families are attracted by the line's well-established and fine-tuned kids' programs. In Alaska, Royal Caribbean is focusing more on international sales than the entrenched market leaders, Princess and Holland America, which has resulted in sailings populated by a good many international passengers, especially travelers from Asia and Europe.

SHIPS The 2,500-passenger *Radiance of the Seas* and *Serenade of the Seas* are slightly more upscale than the line's other vessels. They are designed to remind guests they are at sea—walls of glass everywhere you go allow you to view the passing Alaska scenery. Cabins are larger than on the *Vision*—the smallest is 170 square feet—and more come with verandas. And here's a nice touch: the pool tables have built-in self-leveling mechanisms in case waves get too high. The 2,435-passenger *Vision of the Seas* has small cabins, though nearly a quarter of them offer verandas and all have sitting areas. The ship also offers loads of fine dining, shopping, and entertainment options. **Sample rates per person:** Lowest-price inside cabins $761, lowest outside $961, lowest suite $1,611 for a 7-night cruise.

SILVERSEA CRUISES

110 E. Broward Blvd., Fort Lauderdale, FL 33301. ✆ **800/722-9955.** Fax 954/522-4499. www.silversea.com.

No argument here: Radisson Seven Seas and Crystal Cruises, the two recognized luxury operators in Alaska, have some new and very real competition resulting from Silversea's decision to offer the 49th state as a cruise destination in 2004. With the company entering its tenth year of operation, Silversea's four ships have roamed the globe, generally eschewing the mass market destinations such as the Caribbean in favor of more exotic trades—the Mediterranean, for example, Southeast Asia, South America, and the like.

The line offers 11-night round-trip cruises from San Francisco.

PASSENGER PROFILE   Silversea's guests tend toward the 60–and–up age bracket. They are well-educated, experienced cruisers with very definite ideas about the meaning of the word luxury in service, cuisine, and accommodations. And the means to pay for it!

THE SHIP   *Silver Shadow* is a 388-passenger, all-suite vessel that is the last word in elegance and service. Spacious suites, no tipping expected, free beverages (alcoholic and otherwise), friendly faces, swift and caring baggage handling—these are the hallmarks of the Silversea product. The cabins are all outside suites, all but a few of them with private verandas. The smallest suite has no veranda, but it's plenty big—278 square feet. From there, sizes get better and better. All the suites come with convertible twin-to-queen-size beds, walk-in closets, marble-appointed bathrooms with double vanity basins, full-size tubs and showers, TVs and VCRs, and refrigerator/minibars. Nothing has been left to chance. Nothing has been overlooked. The biggest suites have guest powder rooms and flat screen televisions. Get the message? The Mandara Spa offers just about everything you would want on a cruise, including a range of hydrotherapy, massage, and beauty treatments, men's and women's sauna and steam rooms, and two whirlpool baths. **Sample rates per person:** Lowest-price suites $4,036 for an 11-night cruise; the ship only has suites.

Southeast Alaska

Rich, proud people have lived in Southeast Alaska for thousands of years, fishing the region's salmon and hunting through its primeval forests, where the tree trunks grow up to 10 feet thick. In canoes, they explored the hundreds of misty, mossy, enchanted islands where animals, trees, and even ice had living spirits. The salmon lived under the sea in human form, becoming fish in the summer to swim in seething masses up the rivers and streams as a gift of food to feed their kin, the people. In return, the people treated the salmon with respect and ceremony, allowing their spirits to return to human form under the sea to live another year. So blessed, the Tlingit and Haida built great, carved houses and poles, fought wars, owned slaves, traded with faraway tribes, and held rich contests of giving called potlatches, where they passed on the stories that still help explain their mysterious world. Even for a modern non-Native walking in the grand quiet of the old-growth rainforest, it's easy to find yourself listening for the spirits of the trees speaking their mysteries.

Discovery subsists on mystery, and Southeast Alaska is still being discovered. A honeycomb of limestone caves under Prince of Wales Island wasn't found until 1987. Explorers continue to map its endless miles of caverns, finding the bones of extinct animals, the artifacts of some of North America's earliest prehistoric people, bear dens, strange eyeless shrimp that live nowhere else, and even underground streams that host spawning salmon. The caves network at every step into passages that lead straight up or down or off to either side, some only wide enough to allow a cool wind to pass through. The unfathomable intricacy is exhilarating but also a bit disquieting, like a breath of the supernatural, for it is proof of the unknowable.

Southeast Alaska unfolds like this intricate, hidden world below the tree roots. On a map, this land of ice and forest may not look as large as other parts of Alaska, but the better you know it, the bigger it becomes, until you have to surrender to its immensity. You don't need to go underground to experience the sensation—you can feel it by gazing from a boat at the fractal geometry of the endlessly folded, rocky shoreline. On a cruise through the Inside Passage, you'll marvel at all the little beaches and rocky outcroppings you pass, hundreds of inviting spots each day. If you were to stop at random on any one of those uninhabited beaches in a skiff or kayak, you'd find you could spend a day surveying just a few acres of rocks, the overhanging forest, and the tiny pools of water left behind by the tide. And if you gazed down into any one of those pools, you'd find a complex world all its own, where tiny predators and prey live out their own drama of life in the space of a few square feet. The discoveries you make in Southeast Alaska depend only on how closely you look.

The region stands apart from the rest of Alaska, and not only because most of it can't be reached by road. No other part of the state shares the mysterious, spirit-laden quality of the coastal rainforest. No other area has such mild weather, more akin to the climate of the Pacific Northwest than to the heart of Alaska. Certainly no other area in Alaska gets as much rain, nor do many other places on earth. The traditional Native people here differed from other Alaska Natives, too: They were far richer and left behind more physical artifacts. The Tlingit, Haida, and Tsimshian exploited the wealth nature gave them and amplified it by successfully trading with tribes to the south and over the mountains in today's British Columbia and Yukon Territory. In their early contact, the Tlingits even briefly defeated the Russian invaders in the Battle of Sitka, and after white dominance was established, managed to save many of their cultural artifacts and stories.

Along with its other riches and complexities, Southeast Alaska also has many charming small towns and villages that seem to have grown organically from the mountainsides bordering the fjords and channels of the islands. With economies that predate Alaska's oil boom, they developed slowly, their fishermen building houses to hand down to their children. The smaller towns remain completely exempt from the American blight of corporate sameness. Real, old-fashioned main streets are prosperous with family businesses where the proprietors know their customers by first name.

1 Exploring Southeast Alaska

A unique and inviting aspect of travel in Southeast Alaska is that no roads connect most of the communities. People are forced to get out of their speeding cars and ride on boats, where they can meet their fellow travelers and see what's passing by—slowly. The islands of the region form a protected waterway called the **Inside Passage,** along which almost all of the region's towns are arrayed. Thanks to the **Alaska Marine Highway** ferry system, it's inexpensive to travel the entire passage, hopping from town to town and spending as much time in each place as you like. And if you're short on time, air service is frequent, with jets to the major towns and commuter planes to the villages.

GETTING AROUND BY FERRY: THE ALASKA MARINE HIGHWAY

The state-run **Alaska Marine Highway System** (✆ **800/642-0066** or 907/465-3941, TDD 800/764-3779; www.ferryalaska.com), is a subsidized fleet of big, blue-hulled ferries whose mission is to connect the roadless coastal towns of Alaska for roughly the same cost you'd pay if there were roads and you were driving. Call for a free schedule or download it from the website.

PROS & CONS   The ferry system's strengths are its low cost, frequent summer sailings, inexpensive stopovers, exceptional safety, and the fact that kids love it. In the summer, Forest Service guides offer interpretive talks on board in Southeast's Inside Passage and in Prince William Sound. The system's weaknesses are crowding during the July peak season, the fact that if they're late they can be many hours late (although they're usually on time), and a shortage of cabins, which means that most people have to camp on deck or in chairs during overnight passages.

ROUTES   The system mostly serves Southeast Alaska, though it does cover most of coastal Alaska, with one sailing a month (the *Kennicott*) connecting Southeast Alaska with the Southcentral region nearer Anchorage. The smaller Southcentral ferries link communities all the way out the Aleutian chain (see chapters 7 and 10).

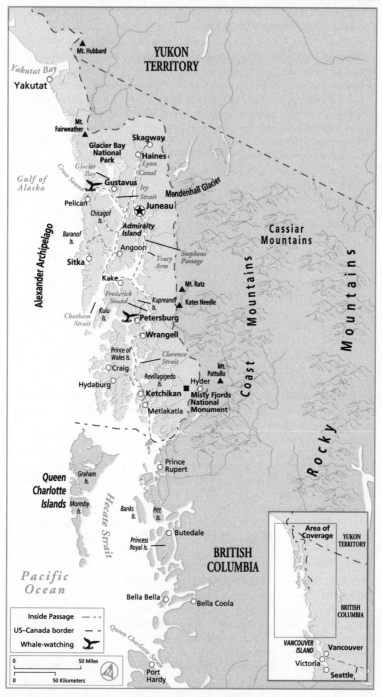

Mt. Hubbard ▲

YUKON TERRITORY

Yakutat Bay

Yakutat ○

Mt. Fairweather ▲

Skagway ○
Haines ○

Glacier Bay National Park

Glacier Bay

Gustavus ✈

Lynn Canal

Mendenhall Glacier

Gulf of Alaska

Cross Sound

Pelican ○

Icy Strait

Juneau ★

Chicagof Is.

Admiralty Island

Baranof Is.

Angoon ○

Cassiar Mountains

Sitka ○

Tracy Arm

Stephens Passage

Kake ○

Frederick Sound

Kupreanof Is.

Mt. Ratz ▲

Kates Needle ▲

Kuiu Is.

Petersburg ✈

Chatham Strait

Wrangell ○

Prince of Wales Is.

Clarence Strait

Mt. Pattullo ▲

Craig ○

Revillagigedo Is.

Hyder ■

Hydaburg ○

Ketchikan ○

Misty Fjords National Monument

Metlakatla ○

Alexander Archipelago

Coast Mountains

Rocky Mountains

Prince Rupert ○

Queen Charlotte Islands

Graham Is.

Moresby Is.

Hecate Strait

Banks Is.

Pitt Is.

Butedale ○

Princess Royal Is.

BRITISH COLUMBIA

Pacific Ocean

Bella Bella ○
Bella Coola ○

Queen Charlotte Strait

Port Hardy ○

Inside Passage — — —
US–Canada border —— ——
Whale-watching ⤴

0   50 Miles
0   50 Kilometers

Area of Coverage

YUKON TERRITORY

BRITISH COLUMBIA

VANCOUVER ISLAND

Vancouver
Victoria
Seattle

Tips Ferry System Booking

The introduction of Internet booking for **Alaska Marine Highway** ferries (www.ferryalaska.com) should simplify life for those who use it. Just be sure to make vehicle and cabin reservations as early as possible. If you need to talk to a real person for advice or to change reservations, the system has a toll-free number (✆ **800/642-0066**), but it can be understaffed, with waits of half an hour for an operator. Try instead the staff at the ferry office in Anchorage, where they have less to do, at ✆ **907/272-7116**. That office is staffed for walk-ins, too, and is located in the Alaska Public Lands Information Center, at 4th and F streets in Anchorage.

Or call **Viking Travel**, in Petersburg (✆ **800/327-2571** or 907/772-3818; www.AlaskaFerry.com), which will accept your booking before the official reservation system starts taking reservations, submitting it the first day it becomes available. They can also take care of all your air and tour connections, lodgings, activities, and so on.

You can sometimes avoid crowds on the boats with careful scheduling. Ferries are crowded northbound in June and southbound in August and both ways in July. If you're planning to fly one way and take the ferry the other, go against the flow.

In the Southeast, five large, mainline ferries serve the Inside Passage. Two begin their run in British Columbia's Prince Rupert and run about 30 hours north to Haines and Skagway. Two more start in Bellingham, Washington, travel 37 hours nonstop to Ketchikan, then continue up to Skagway and Haines. Each of these four towns is connected to the rest of the world by roads, but none of the towns in between are. In the summer, the large ships stop at least daily (although sometimes in the middle of the night) in Ketchikan, Wrangell, Petersburg, Juneau, Haines, and Skagway. Some make a side trip to Sitka on the way. Juneau is the hub, with many extra sailings north from Juneau on the Lynn Canal to Haines and Skagway. These are offered by the new fast ferry, the *Fairweather,* which travels at up to 45 mph. It cuts travel times in half, connecting Juneau with Haines five days a week, Skagway four days a week, and Sitka two days a week.

Smaller ferries connect the larger towns to tiny villages up and down the coast. They mostly take local residents back and forth to their villages, so they're rarely crowded. Those routes are definitely off the beaten track, offering the cheapest and easiest way to absorb the real wilderness of the Alaska Bush. The feeder ferries have food service but no cabins.

CONNECTING TO THE FERRY   From the south: The appeal of taking the Alaskan Marine Highway ferry to Alaska from Bellingham, Washington is obvious, but it is not cheaper than flying and it takes 2 days just to get to Ketchikan. The popular alternative is to board the ferry in Prince Rupert, B.C. You can get to Prince Rupert by rail (this is covered under "Getting There & Getting Around" in chapter 2).

Another option is riding the **BC Ferries** system, 1112 Fort St., Victoria, B.C., Canada V8V 4V2 (✆ **888/223-3779** or 250/386-3431; www.bcferries.bc.ca) to Prince Rupert, B.C. That would require you cover British Columbia's Vancouver Island by car on the way, getting on the island by ferry from the south.

BC Ferrries can carry you from the city of Vancouver to the town of Nanaimo on Vancouver Island, or you can reach Vancouver Island's city of Victoria from Port Angeles, Washington (that route is operated by **Black Ball Transport; ✆ 360/457-4491;** www.cohoferry.com). Once you're on Vancouver Island, you drive north to Port Hardy and take the B.C. ferry to Prince Rupert, where it docks right next to the Alaska ferry.

To the north: The northern end of the Inside Passage ferry system rejoins the road system in Skagway and Haines. Haines is a bit closer to the rest of the state but has just one independent car rental agency. Skagway has more transportation options, including car and RV rental and a bus that connects Skagway to Whitehorse, Yukon, where you can catch another bus onward on the Alaska Highway. See the Skagway and Haines sections, later, for details.

By air: By flying to your starting point, you can save time and reduce the chance of having to spend the night sleeping in a chair on board. Long hauls on the ferry can be uncomfortable and don't save you much money over flying, but the ferry is much less expensive and more appealing for connecting nearby towns within the Southeast region. Fly into Juneau, Sitka, or another sizable town and plan a ferry trip from there, stopping at various places before returning to catch your plane home.

STOPPING OVER   Buying ahead or booking round-trip tickets saves you nothing on the ferry, and stopovers of any length add little to the cost of your passage. Use the ferry system to explore the towns along the way, grabbing the next ferry through to continue your journey. If you travel without a vehicle, you generally don't need reservations (with the possible exceptions of the Bellingham sailings and passages across the Gulf of Alaska). Bring along a bike, or even a sea kayak, to have total freedom in exploring the Southeast. Port calls usually are not long enough to see the towns; if the boat is running late, they may not let you off at all.

WALK-ON FARES   Fares change every year so don't count on these, but they may help for planning. The adult walk-on fare from Prince Rupert to Skagway is $156. Bellingham to Ketchikan is $201, Bellingham to Skagway $306. Juneau to Sitka is $37. Fares for the fast ferry, where available, are about 10% more. Fares for children 11 and under are roughly half price, and children 2 and under ride free. Off season only, October through April, the driver of a vehicle does not need a separate walk-on ticket, and kids 4 and under ride free.

BRINGING VEHICLES   In the summer, you often need a reservation for any chance of taking your vehicle on the ferry, and reserving three to six months early is wise. The vehicle spots on the ferries from Bellingham and Prince Rupert are particularly coveted. Fares vary according to the size of the car as well as your destination; a passage from Prince Rupert to Haines for a typical 15-foot car is $316, the passage from Bellingham to Haines is $636. You also have to buy a separate ticket for each person on the ferry, including, in summer, the driver. Renting a car at your destination will probably save money and enhance your trip because you will have more flexibility in your stopovers. You can carry a kayak, canoe, or bike on the ferry (without a car) quite inexpensively.

CABIN RESERVATIONS   Sometimes you can snag a cabin from the standby list when you sail (board quickly and approach the purser immediately), but generally you must reserve ahead for the summer season. Cabins from Bellingham book many months ahead. A two-berth outside cabin (one with a window) with a bathroom is under $70 on most town-to-town hops, $150 from Prince

Rupert to Haines, and $331 from Bellingham to Haines, plus the cost of your ticket. The great majority of the cabins are small and spartan, coming in two- and four-bunk configurations, but for a premium you can reserve a more comfortable sitting-room unit on some vessels. Most cabins have tiny private bathrooms with showers. Try to get an outside cabin so that you can watch the world go by. Cabins can be stuffy, and the windowless units can be claustro- phobic as well.

DO YOU NEED A CABIN?   If you do a lot of layovers in Southeast's towns, you can arrange to do most of your ferry travel during the day, but you'll prob- ably have to sleep on board at least once (unless you make that hop by air). You can't sleep in your vehicle. One of the adventures of ferry travel is finding a chair to sleep in or setting up a tent on deck with everyone else. The patio-furniture lounge chairs on the covered outdoor solarium, on the top deck, are the best public sleeping spots on board, in part because the noise of the ship covers other sounds. If you're tenting, the best place is behind the solarium, where it's not too windy. On the *Columbia,* that space is small, so grab it early. Bring duct tape to secure your tent to the deck in case you can't find a sheltered spot, as the wind over the deck of a ship in motion blows like an endless gale. The recliner lounges are comfortable, too, but can be stuffy. Bring a pillow. If the ship looks crowded, grab your spot fast to get a choice location. **Showers** are available, although there may be lines. Lock any valuables and luggage you don't need in the **coin- operated lockers.** If all that sounds too rugged, or if you have small children and no tent, reserve a cabin. It offers a safe and private home base and a good night's rest, and there's a certain romance to having your own compartment on a public conveyance.

FERRY FOOD   If you can, bring at least some of your own food on the ferry. Ferry food can get boring after several meals in a row and, during peak season, lines are sometimes unreasonably long. We usually bring a cooler or picnic basket. Even if you're traveling light, you can pick up some bagels and deli sandwiches on a stopover or long port call.

THE BEST RUNS   Going to Sitka through **Peril Straits,** the ferry fits through extraordinarily narrow passages where no other vessel of its size ven- tures; the smooth, reflective water is lovely, and you may see deer along the shore. The **Wrangell Narrows,** between Petersburg and Wrangell, is also an incredible ride, day or night, as the ship accomplishes a slalom between shores that seem so close you could touch them, in water so shallow the schedules must be timed for high tide. **Frederick Sound,** between the Narrows and Wrangell, is prime for whale sightings. Approaching Skagway through the towering moun- tains of the **Lynn Canal** fjord also is impressive.

GETTING AROUND BY AIR & ROAD

BY AIR   Air travel is the primary link between Southeast's towns and the rest of the world. Several towns without road access have jet service, provided by **Alaska Airlines** (✆ **800/252-7522;** www.alaskaair.com), the region's only major airline. Juneau is Southeast Alaska's travel hub. Ketchikan and Sitka each have a few flights a day, while Wrangell, Petersburg, and Yakutat each have one flight going each direction daily. Gustavus is served from Juneau once daily dur- ing the summer. Some of these "milk runs" never get very far off the ground on hops between small towns: On the 31-mile Wrangell-to-Petersburg flight, the cabin attendants never have time to unbuckle. Haines and Skagway, which have

---

Tips **Seeing Southeast from Above**

If you can possibly afford it, take a **flightseeing** trip at some point during your trip. The poor man's way of doing this is to fly a small prop plane on a scheduled run between two of your destinations instead of taking the ferry. If you ask, the pilot may even go out of his or her way to show you the sights; if not, you'll still gain an appreciation for the richness and extreme topography of the region. Each flight service also offers flightseeing tours in addition to scheduled runs between destinations. Flightseeing costs as little as $100 for a brief spin. Flight services are listed in each town section.

---

highway connections, don't receive visits from jets, but all the towns and even the tiny villages have scheduled prop service.

Like the ferries, the planes can be quite late. Each of the airports in Southeast has its own challenges caused by the steep, mountainous terrain and the water. In bad weather, even jet flights are delayed or they "overhead"—they can't land at the intended destination and leave their passengers somewhere else. Your only protection against these contingencies are travel insurance, a schedule that allows plenty of slack in case you're significantly delayed, and low blood pressure.

BY ROAD Three Southeast Alaska communities are accessible by road: Haines, Skagway, and the village of Hyder, which lies on the British Columbia border east of Ketchikan and is accessible from the gravel Cassiar Highway through Canada. If you're driving the Alaska Highway, passing through Haines and Skagway adds 160 miles of very scenic driving to the trip, as well as a 15-mile ferry ride between the two towns (they're separated by 362 road miles). This ferry route is not as heavily booked as the routes heading between either town and Juneau, but it's still a good idea to reserve ahead. You also can rent a car from Haines or Skagway for travel to the rest of the state at the end of a ferry journey (Haines saves just 60 miles over Skagway); buses serve Skagway; details are listed in the sections on each of those towns. If you're driving the highway in winter, you should be prepared for weather as cold as 40°F below zero (–40°C). Alaska winter driving information is under "Health & Safety" in chapter 2.

Bikes make a lot of sense for getting around Southeast's small towns, which tend to be compact. You can rent one almost anywhere you go, or bring your own on the ferry. The networks of abandoned or little-used logging roads on some islands offer limitless routes for mountain biking. Elsewhere, Forest Service hiking trails are often open for riding.

GETTING OUTSIDE IN THE TONGASS NATIONAL FOREST

Nearly all of Southeast Alaska, stretching 500 miles from Ketchikan to Yakutat, is in Tongass National Forest. The towns sit in small pockets of private land surrounded by 17 million acres of land controlled by the U.S. Forest Service—an area nearly as large as the state of Maine, and considerably larger than any other national forest or national park in the United States. The majority of this land has never been logged and the rate of logging has dropped dramatically in recent years, preserving one of the world's great temperate rainforests in its virgin state. It's an intact ecosystem full of wildlife, and mostly free of human development.

Indeed, you quickly forget it *is* the Tongass National Forest. Since it always surrounds you when you're in this region, it's simply the land.

FOREST SERVICE CABINS

One of the best ways to get into Southeast's wilderness is by staying at one of the scores of remote Forest Service Public Recreation Cabins. These are simple cabins without electricity or running water where you can lay your sleeping bag on a bunk and sit by a warm woodstove out of the rain. You need to bring everything with you, as if camping, but it's a good deal more comfortable than a tent. And you will probably find yourself in a stunningly beautiful spot, perhaps with your own lake and a boat for fishing. Cabins are located along canoe trails, on beaches best reached by sea kayak, on high mountain lakes accessible only by floatplane, and along hiking trails. We do this with our family several times a summer by boat or canoe or on foot. I've learned three critical lessons to pass on: Do your research, pack carefully (take all the essentials, but little more), and spend at least 3 nights, preferably a week, to make all the effort pay off with real relaxation.

GETTING CABIN INFORMATION   In this chapter, I've listed a few of the cabins in the sections devoted to the town that they're closest to, but for complete information check the Tongass website (**www.fs.fed.us/r10/tongass**) or contact the visitor centers and ranger offices listed with each town section in this chapter. The main contact point for recreation information for the whole forest is the **Southeast Alaska Discovery Center,** 50 Main St., Ketchikan, AK 99901 (© **907/228-6220** or 907/288-6237 TDD; fax 907/228-6234).

You'll need a good map to figure out where the cabins are, and an idea of how to get there and how much travel will cost—generally, the cost of transportation will be many times larger than the cabin rental fee of $25 to $45 a night. Few cabins can be reached without a boat or aircraft, and for all but large groups, flying is the economical way to go. A flight service can help you choose a cabin according to your interests and how far you can afford to fly. You may be able to rent the gear you need, but you'll have to reserve that ahead, too. The solution to these puzzles is different for each town; I've listed where to find help in the town sections later in this chapter.

RESERVING A CABIN OR CAMPSITE   The cabins and some campgrounds are reserved through a national system. Don't rely on the reservations operators or website for advice or cabin information—they're in upstate New York—instead, pose your questions to the ranger station nearest where you plan to go. The rangers are friendly and have probably stayed in the cabin you're interested in.

Use the reservations system when you're ready to book; you can check cabin availability dates and reserve on the Internet, which is by far the best way to do it (**www.reserveusa.com**). By telephone, contact the **National Recreation Reservations Service (NRRS),** operated by **Reserve America,** at © **877/444-6777,** 877/833-6777 TDD, or 518/885-3639 with toll from overseas. The phone lines are open April 1 through Labor Day Monday through Friday from 8am to midnight EST, Saturday and Sunday 8am to 9pm; in winter Monday through Friday 10am to 7pm, Saturday and Sunday 10am to 5pm. They take American Express, Discover, MasterCard, and Visa, or you can reserve on the phone and then pay by certified check or money order. Cabins are available for reservation on a first-come, first-served basis, starting 180 days ahead, and campsites are available 240 days ahead. For the most popular cabins, you need to be online the minute reservations become available to have a chance.

2 Ketchikan: On the Waterfront

Had they known about it, the film noir directors of the 1950s would have chosen the Ketchikan (*ketch*-e-kan) waterfront for Humphrey Bogart to sleuth. The black-and-white montage: A pelting rain drains from the brim of his hat, suspicious figures dart through saloon doors and into the lobbies of concrete-faced hotels, a forest of workboat masts fades into the midsummer twilight along a shore where the sea and land seem to merge in miles of floating docks. Along Creek Street, salmon on their way to spawn swim under houses chaotically perched on pilings beside a narrow boardwalk; inside, men are spawning, too, in the arms of legal prostitutes. Meanwhile, the faces of totem poles gaze down on the scene disapprovingly, mute holders of their own ancient secrets.

Today, the director hoping to re-create that scene would have his work cut out for him removing the T-shirt shops and bright street-front signs that seek to draw in throngs of cruise passengers to buy plastic gewgaws. Not so long ago, Ketchikan was a rugged and exotic intersection of cultures built on the profits of logging Southeast's rainforest, but in a decade it has transformed itself into a tourist center, softening its rough edges while selling its charm to visitors. And the changes can only accelerate. More and bigger ships are coming, and Southeast Alaska's last major timber mill—the Louisiana Pacific–owned pulp plant in Ward Cove, north of town—closed in 1997 due, in part, to environmental concerns. A major portion of the mill was blown up in 1999; they sold tickets to see who would get to press the button on the explosives, but the occasion was less than festive, as former employees saw the scene of their work lives disappear into dust. A smaller, more labor-intensive operation, intended to replace the lost pulp mill jobs with jobs sawing lumber and making veneer, closed down in 2001. In the meantime, the economy had moved on.

On summer days, the white cruise ships tower above the town like huge new buildings on the dock facing Front Street, the downtown's main drag. Each morning their gangways disgorge thousands of visitors, clogging the streets and, for a few hours, transforming the town into a teeming carnival. With only a few hours to spend here, the passengers explore the closest of the twisting streets, see the museum at the Southeast Alaska Discovery Center, or take a tour to one of the totem pole parks. Then evening comes, the streets empty, and the cruise ships slide off quietly on the way to their next port.

That is when a sense of the old, misty, mysterious Ketchikan starts to return. Visitors with a little more time to spend, and the willingness to explore beyond the core tourist areas, can drink in the history and atmosphere of the place. Stay in a quaint old hotel, hike a boardwalk path through the primeval rainforest, and visit the museums, clan house replicas, and totem pole parks that make Ketchikan a center of Tlingit and Haida culture.

Ketchikan also makes a great jumping-off point for some spectacular outdoor experiences, including a trip to **Misty Fjords National Monument** (p. 104). As the state's fourth-largest city, Ketchikan is the transportation hub for the southern portion of Southeast Alaska. (The nickname "Gateway City" refers to its geographical location and transportation function.) Seaplanes based on docks along the waterfront are the taxis of the region, and a big inter-agency visitor center can get you started on your explorations of the area. Ketchikan is one of the wettest spots on earth, with rain measured in the hundreds of inches; quality rain gear is requisite for any activity, in the wilds or in the streets of town.

ESSENTIALS
GETTING THERE

BY AIR   Alaska Airlines (© 800/252-7522; www.alaskaair.com) jet service connects Ketchikan south to Seattle non-stop and north to Petersburg, Wrangell, Sitka, Juneau, and Anchorage. Commuter lines run wheeled planes and floatplanes from Ketchikan to the neighboring communities, and also offer fishing packages and flightseeing.

The airport is on Gravina Island, to which there is no bridge. A ferry runs each way every ½ hour (more frequently at peak times). Believe the airline when it tells you when to catch the ferry for your plane. The fare is $4 for adults, $2 ages 6 to 12, and free under 6. Returning the same day is free. The fare for cars is $6 each way, no matter how soon you come back. See "Getting Around," below, for how to get from the airport ferry dock to town and for a water taxi right from the airport (a fun option).

BY FERRY   The dock is 2½ miles north of downtown. **Alaska Marine Highway** ferries (© 800/642-0066; www.ferryalaska.com) run 6 hours north to Wrangell and 6 hours south to Prince Rupert, B.C. The walk-on fare from Prince Rupert is $50, from Wrangell it's $32; children under 12 go half price. Call the local terminal at © 907/225-6182 or 907/225-6181 for a recording of updated arrival and departure times.

ORIENTATION

Ketchikan is on huge **Revillagigedo Island,** popularly known as **Revilla Island.** The downtown area, pretty much taken over by tourism, is quite compact and walkable, but the whole of Ketchikan, including a second commercial area used by locals, is long, strung out between the Tongass Narrows and the mountains. A waterfront road goes under various names through town (it's Water St. on our map), becoming North Tongass Highway as it stretches about 16 miles to the north. Saxman is 2½ miles to the south of downtown on the 14-mile South Tongass Highway.

GETTING AROUND

You can spend a day seeing the downtown sights on foot, but you will need transportation to get to the totem pole parks or airport.

BY SHUTTLE OR BUS   The **Airporter Shuttle** (© 907/225-5429) meets each flight and picks up at the major hotels according to a schedule you can get at the front desk. They'll pick up anywhere else by arrangement. The $18 fare downtown includes the cost of the airport ferry, a good deal for a single passenger, but a couple would save money taking the ferry and then getting a cab. Since the shuttle drives right to the terminal, however, it's still the best way to go for a couple with a lot of luggage. The least costly way to the airport or ferry dock is the **Ketchikan Gateway Borough bus** (© 907/225-8726). To get downtown or points south from the airport costs $1.50. Buses come every half hour. Your luggage must fit under the seat

BY TAXI   The local taxis, mostly minivans, are convenient and usually easy to flag down on the single main road through town. Try **Sourdough Cab** (© 907/ 225-5544). Taking a cab to the airport terminal is costly because of time that runs up on the meter waiting for and riding the ferry to Gravina Island. Take the cab just to the airport ferry dock and walk on. If you have a lot of luggage, take the Airporter Shuttle (see above), which goes to the terminal, or take a water taxi from downtown.

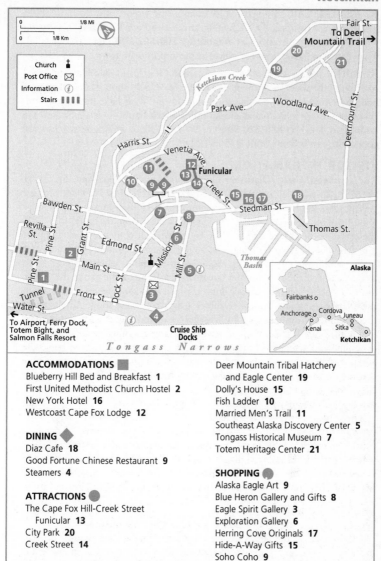

ACCOMMODATIONS ■
Blueberry Hill Bed and Breakfast **1**
First United Methodist Church Hostel **2**
New York Hotel **16**
Westcoast Cape Fox Lodge **12**

DINING ◆
Diaz Cafe **18**
Good Fortune Chinese Restaurant **9**
Steamers **4**

ATTRACTIONS ●
The Cape Fox Hill-Creek Street
  Funicular **13**
City Park **20**
Creek Street **14**

Deer Mountain Tribal Hatchery
  and Eagle Center **19**
Dolly's House **15**
Fish Ladder **10**
Married Men's Trail **11**
Southeast Alaska Discovery Center **5**
Tongass Historical Museum **7**
Totem Heritage Center **21**

SHOPPING ●
Alaska Eagle Art **9**
Blue Heron Gallery and Gifts **8**
Eagle Spirit Gallery **3**
Exploration Gallery **6**
Herring Cove Originals **17**
Hide-A-Way Gifts **15**
Soho Coho **9**

BY WATER TAXI Only in Ketchikan could you take a boat from the airport to your hotel. **Tongass Water Taxi** (ⓒ **907/209-8294**) also happens to be reasonably priced and quick. The six-passenger boat runs back and forth from near the airport ferry dock to downtown all day for $15 per person. It also crosses the same route as the airport ferry (without going on to downtown) for $4. Several hotels are right on the water, so the water taxi can take you almost to your door. The operator holds up a sign in the baggage claim area to meet arriving flights or you can call to arrange a pick-up. I hope that the operator can keep it going, but don't be surprised if this service is unavailable when you arrive.

BY RENTAL CAR **Budget** has locations at the airport or in town (© **800/ 527-0700** reservations, 907/225-6004 at the airport, 907/225-8383 in town; www.budget.com). **Alaska Car Rental** (© **800/662-0007** or 907/225-5000; www.akcarrental.com) also has offices at the airport or in town.

BY BIKE   A bike is a good way to get around Ketchikan. A 2½-mile bike trail runs along the water to Saxman, stopping a few blocks short of the totem pole park there, and another goes north 6⅓ miles to the Ward Lake Recreation Area. Bikes are for rent at the **Great Alaska Lumberjack Show,** on Main St. near the cruise ship dock (© **888/320-9049** or 907/225-9050; www.lumberjacksports. com). The cost is $8 an hour, $25 half day.

VISITOR INFORMATION

The **Southeast Alaska Discovery Center,** 50 Main St., Ketchikan, AK 99901 (© **907/228-6220** or 907/288-6237 TDD; fax 907/228-6234; www.fs.fed.us/ r10/tongass), is much more than a visitor center. Housed in a large, attractive building of big timbers and cedar, and located a block from the cruise-ship dock, the center is the best museum in the region when it comes to illustrating the interaction of the region's ecology and human society, including both traditional Native and contemporary uses. Some of the exhibits about logging seem strained, as if intended to counter potential opposition on the part of the viewer, but that doesn't spoil the overall impact, which is to show what's special about these lands. An auditorium here shows a high-tech slide show. Admission to these facilities in summer costs $5, free ages 6 and under, with a $15 family max-imum; in winter it's free. Without paying, you can get guidance about planning your time and activities in the outdoors. An information kiosk and bookstore are located near the entrance, and downstairs you'll find a luxurious book store decorated like an explorer's private den with room to relax. The center is open May through September daily from 8am to 5pm, October through April Tues-day through Saturday from 10am to 4:30pm.

The **Ketchikan Visitors Bureau,** 131 Front St., Ketchikan, AK 99901 (© **800/770-3300** or 907/225-6166; fax 907/225-4250; www.visit-ketchikan. com), stands right on the cruise-ship dock, offering town information and desks where tourism businesses sell their wares, including tickets for tours. The center is open daily in the summer from 8am to 5pm and when cruise ships are in town; weekdays only in winter.

SPECIAL EVENTS

There's a detailed **events calendar** at **www.visit-ketchikan.com**.

Celebration of the Sea, a 10-day event beginning around the first of May, includes a variety of art, music, and community events; you can get a schedule from the Ketchikan Visitors Bureau. **King Salmon Derby,** a 50-year-old tradi-tion, takes place at the end of May and the beginning of June.

The **Fourth of July** celebration is huge, with a long parade on Front Street attended by mobs of locals and cruise-ship passengers. After the parade, there's a **Timber Carnival** with an all-afternoon loggers' competition at the baseball field near City Park on Park Avenue; admission is free.

The crowd-pleasing **Great Alaskan Lumberjack Show** goes on all summer behind the Alaska Discovery Center (© **888/320-9049;** www.lumberjack sports.com). Canadian and U.S. professional teams compete three or more times daily, mostly to an audience of cruise-ship passengers. Tickets are $29 adults, half price ages 5 to 12.

The Blueberry Arts Festival, held the first weekend of August, has booths, music, and food, and is put on by the very active Ketchikan Area Arts and Humanities Council, 716 Totem Way (© **907/225-2211;** www.ketchikanarts. org). Check with the council for winter performing-arts events, too, including the **Monthly Grind** music and poetry show in the Saxman Tribal House every third Saturday from September to April, and a wearable art show in February.

FAST FACTS: Ketchikan

Banks A bank with an ATM is at 306 Main St.; grocery stores and the visitor center also have ATMs.

Hospital **General Hospital** is at 3100 Tongass Ave. (© **907/225-5171**).

Internet Access **SeaPort Cyberstations** (© **907/247-6419;** www.seaportel. com) is at the ship dock on the second floor at 5 Salmon Landing.

Police Call © **907/225-6631** for nonemergencies.

Post Office 3609 Tongass Ave.; a more convenient downtown substation is two blocks from the cruise ship dock at the Great Alaska Clothing Company, 422 Mission St.

Taxes Sales tax is 5.5%. Room taxes for accommodations total 11.5%.

EXPLORING KETCHIKAN

Pick up a copy of the **Official Historic Ketchikan Walking Tour Map,** available all over town, which has three ways through town to follow and loads of information about sites of both great and modest interest on the way.

Schoolteacher Lois Munch, of **Classic Tours** (© **907/225-3091;** www. classictours.com), makes her tours **fun:** She wears a poodle skirt to drive visitors around in her '55 Chevy. A 2-hour tour to the Saxman totem poles is $70; a 3-hour tour adds a natural history stop and costs $90. Rates are per person and include the admission to Saxman. The maximum group size is five. Other residents offer tours, too; check at the town visitor center for many more choices.

TLINGIT, HAIDA & TSIMSHIAN CULTURAL HERITAGE

The Ketchikan area has two totem pole parks and a totem pole museum, as well as a wealth of contemporary Native art displayed all over town. Notable pieces stand at Whale Park at Mission and Bawden streets and at the Westcoast Cape Fox Lodge. Most of what you see in Southeast Alaska is Tlingit—the Haida and Tsimshian generally live to the south and east in British Columbia—but Ketchikan is near the boundary between the three peoples' areas, so their similar cultures mix here.

Totem Heritage Center ★★ Located near City Park, the center contains the largest collection of original 19th-century totem poles in existence. The poles, up to 160 years old, are displayed indoors, mostly unpainted, many with the grass and moss still attached from when they were rescued from the elements in villages. Totem poles were never meant to be maintained or repainted—they generally disintegrate after about 70 years, and were constantly replaced—but these were preserved to help keep the culture alive. A high ceiling and muted lighting highlight the spirituality of the art. Well-trained guides are on hand to explain what you're looking at, and there are good interpretive signs. The gift shop, open during the summer, carries authentic Native crafts.

601 Deermount St. © **907/225-5900**. Admission $5 in summer, free in winter. Summer daily 8am–5pm; winter Mon–Fri 1–5pm.

Totem Bight State Historical Park ★★★ The park presents poles and a clan house carved beginning in 1938 by Natives working with traditional tools to copy fragments of historic poles that had mostly rotted away. The project, funded by the New Deal's Civilian Conservation Corps, helped save a Tlingit and Haida culture that had been essentially outlawed until that time. The setting, purportedly the site of a traditional fishing camp, is a peaceful spot on the edge of Tongass Narrows, at the end of a short walk through the woods, so the experience is both aesthetic and educational. The park also stands out for its excellent interpretive signs, a printed guide, and an interpretive website. There's a small park bookstore.

Ketchikan Area State Park Office, 9883 N. Tongass Hwy. © **907/247-8574**. www.alaskastateparks.org (click on "Individual Parks"). Free admission. Park always open. 10 miles out of town on N. Tongass Hwy.

Saxman Native Village Totem Pole Park ★ Saxman's park has artifacts similar to those at Totem Bight park, but with an added attraction: You can see carvers at work in the building to the right of the park. It's possible to see the studio and the poles without joining a tour, using a pamphlet that costs $1.50, but Totem Bight is better for that kind of visit—it has a more inspiring location and better interpretive materials. Cape Fox Corp., which operates the tours, caters mainly to cruise-ship passengers with its 2-hour tour, which includes entry to the clan house, a short performance of a Tlingit legend, and a demonstration of traditional dance and song by the Cape Fox Dancers. The tour schedule is different each day, depending on the ships. Buy tour tickets in the gift store on the right as you enter the park.

In Saxman, 2½ miles south of Ketchikan on the S. Tongass Hwy. © **907/225-4846** for tour times and tickets. http://capefoxtours.com. Tour $35 adults, $18 children 12 and under; unguided visits free. Park open at all times. No tours Oct–Apr.

DOWNTOWN ATTRACTIONS

Ketchikan's best downtown attractions are all within walking distance of one another. See Creek Street, then walk up Park Avenue past the Ketchikan Creek fish ladder and up to lovely **City Park,** site of the Totem Heritage Center, described above. The park is among my favorite places in Ketchikan. The creek splits into a maze of ornamental pools and streams once used as a hatchery, with footbridges, a fountain, and large trees with creeping roots.

The Creek Street boardwalk starts at the Stedman Street bridge, running over the tidal creek. It was Ketchikan's red-light district until fairly recently; now it's a quaint tourist mall. Prostitution was semi-legal in Alaska until 1952, recent enough to survive in local memories but distant enough to have made Creek Street historic and to transform the women who worked there from outcasts to

---

Tips **Avoiding the Crowds**

Ketchikan is overrun with as many as 10,000 cruise-ship passengers every day May through September, far more than the small visitor attractions or even the streets can comfortably handle. Independent travelers can avoid the crush by planning to visit popular spots in the afternoon. Spend the morning on an outdoors activity instead. Ships usually leave the town in early evening.

icons. Dolly Arthur, who started in business for herself on the creek in 1919 and died in 1975, lived through both eras, and her home became a commercial museum not long after her death. **Dolly's House** (✆ **907/225-6329**) is amusing, mildly racy, and a little sad. Admission is $4 (but possibly soon to rise); it's open from 8am to 4pm during the summer and when cruise ships are in town.

Creek Street has some interesting shops, described below, but it's also fun just to walk on the creekside boardwalk, into the forest above, and over the **Married Men's Trail**—once a discreet way for married men to reach the red-light district. The **Cape Fox Hill-Creek Street Funicular** (known as "the tram"), a sort of diagonal elevator, runs 211 feet from the boardwalk up to the Westcoast Cape Fox Lodge on top of the hill. Take it up and then enjoy the walk down through the woods. The summertime fare is $2, but if no one is around, just press the "up" button and go.

Deer Mountain Tribal Hatchery and Eagle Center ★★   This remarkable nonprofit center combines one of Alaska's best hatchery tours and a great place to see a bald eagle close up. The wooden buildings stand over Ketchikan Creek. You can see fish climbing against the current up into pools where they are sorted before being cut open to complete their biological purpose (salmon die when they spawn anyway). The hatchery tours are special for letting you get so close, right in the action, where you can feed the fry (young salmon) yourself. The hatchery produces king and silver salmon and steelhead trout. Visitors can also walk right through the eagle enclosure. Remarkably, the resident pair of injured, flightless bald eagles have mated for life and built a nest where they lay eggs each year. They hunt salmon swimming naturally through their enclosure. No glass stands between you and this activity, only a few feet away.

1158 Salmon Rd. ✆ 800/252-5158 or 907/225-6760. Admission $7.95 adults, $3.50 ages 6–12, free under 6. May–Sept daily 8am–4:30pm; winter by arrangement.

Tongass Historical Museum   This one-room museum is where Ketchikan talks back to itself, with well-executed revolving exhibits that have always held my interest. A small permanent area shows Native artifacts. In the same building, the attractive Ketchikan Public Library is a great place to recharge, especially in the children's section downstairs, where big windows look out on Ketchikan Creek's falls.

629 Dock St. ✆ 907/225-5600. Admission $2 summer; free winter. Summer daily 8am–5pm; winter Wed–Fri 1–5pm, Sat 10am–4pm, Sun 1–4pm.

SHOPPING

The Ketchikan art scene is one of Alaska's liveliest, thanks in part to the Ketchikan Arts and Humanities Council, whose helpful staff operates the **Main Stay Gallery,** near Creek Street at 716 Totem Way (www.ketchikanarts.org). Shows change monthly.

Ray Troll is Alaska's leading fish-obsessed artist. His small gallery, **Soho Coho,** at 5 Creek St., is worth a visit even if you aren't a shopper. It shows Troll's own work and that of other Ketchikan artists from the same school of surreal rainforest humor. In Troll's art, subtle ironies and silly puns coexist in a solidly decorated interior world. T-shirts are his most popular canvas; "Spawn Till You Die" is a classic. Troll's incredible art-filled website delves far into his strange mind (and sells shirts), at www.trollart.com. The gallery is open summer daily from 9am to 6pm; winter Wednesday through Saturday from noon to 5:30pm; or order at ✆ **800/888-4070.**

Adjacent to Soho Coho, **Alaska Eagle Arts** is a serious gallery featuring the bold yet traditional work of Native artist Marvin Oliver. Upstairs, don't miss **Parnassus Books,** a wonderfully cluttered browsing nirvana with broad, sophisticated collections of Alaskana, art, and women's art, among other special subject areas; the owner is a local institution. Down the boardwalk at 18 Creek St., craftspeople carve and interact with visitors at **Hide-A-Way Gifts.**

At 123 Stedman St., across the creek, **Blue Heron Gallery and Gifts** carries Alaska arts and crafts that appeal to locals as well as visitors: jewelry, stained glass, clothing, jam, prints, and so on. Just to the south, at 229 Stedman, **Herring Cove Originals** is Sharron Huffman's studio and gallery of sharp, vivid prints made using fish, plants, and other things from nature; pieces cover a broad price range.

Also nearby, at 633 Mission St., David Dossett's **Exploration Gallery** (www.explorationgallery.com) uniquely specializes in antique maps and prints, and also carries contemporary prints, pottery, and Native art, with more thoughtful selections than the sameness found in most other shops.

Moving back toward the waterfront, **Eagle Spirit Gallery of Ketchikan,** at 310 Mission St. shows some very impressive Alaska Native art, including large carved pieces from this region.

Note: Ketchikan is a shopping and art destination, but if you want something authentically Alaskan you have to be careful. For some important tips, see "Native Art: Finding the Real Thing," in chapter 2.

GETTING OUTSIDE

There's lots to do outdoors around Ketchikan, but most of it will require a boat or plane; drive-by attractions are limited. In any event, your first stop should be the trip-planning room at the Southeast Alaska Discovery Center (see "Visitor Information," earlier), for details on trails, fishing, and dozens of U.S. Forest Service cabins.

BEAR-VIEWING   Salmon returning to a fish hatchery on a creek several miles south of town have long attracted black bears, eagles, and even seals. In 2004, a group of local businessmen turned that abundance into a tourist attraction. The **Alaska Rainforest Sanctuary,** 116 Wood Road (© 907/225-5503), takes in a patch of forest and marsh along the creek. Guests are led in groups along a well-made gravel trail and long boardwalk, then through a defunct sawmill that makes an interesting and picturesque ending to the tour. Will the bears stay for the tour buses? After all the work of developing a first class attraction, one certainly hopes so. The whole thing is oriented to the cruise ships and independent visitors must join one of those groups. Call for times. The cost is $45 at the door. Bears should be present June through September and peak in July and August.

The traditional kind of bear-viewing is still going on, too: get on a float plane, soar over water and wooded islands, and land where bears are gathering at streams where the salmon are running. Depending on where the bears are, it costs $250 to $400 per person. **Promech Air** (© **800/860-3845** or 907/225-3845; www.promechair.com) and **Island Wings Air Service** (© **888/854-2444** or 907/225-2444; www.islandwings.com) offer this service; both are described in "Majestic Misty Fjords," p. 104.

CABIN TRIPS   The U.S. Forest Service maintains more than 50 **cabins** around Ketchikan; all are remote and primitive, but at $25 to $45 a night, you can't beat the price or the settings. This is a chance to be utterly alone in the wilderness; many of the lake cabins come with a boat for fishing and exploring. For details and descriptions of all the cabins, contact the **Southeast Alaska Discovery Center** (© **907/228-6220;** www.fs.fed.us/r10/tongass). The reservations system to use when you're actually ready to book a cabin is described in "Getting Outside in the Tongass National Forest" on p. 89.

If you stay in a cabin, you'll need all your camping gear except a tent, including sleeping bags, a camp stove, your own cooking outfit and food, a lantern, and so on. The easy way to handle this is to contact **Alaska Wilderness Outfitting and Camping Rentals,** 3857 Fairview St. (© **907/225-7335;** www.latitude56.com/camping/index.html), which has been supplying cabin trips for more than 15 years. They rent almost everything you need, including small outboards and life jackets for the skiffs, and deliver directly to the air taxi or water taxi.

The cabins are remote. You can hike or take a boat to some of them, but most are accessible only by floatplane (and unless you have loads of stuff, flying is probably the cheapest way to go). Expect to pay around $1,000 round-trip for three passengers. (Obviously, it makes sense only if you will stay for a while—we never go for less than three nights.) For recommended carriers, see "Majestic Misty Fjords," p. 104.

FISHING   The **Alaska Department of Fish and Game** produces a 24-page fishing guide to Ketchikan with details on where to find fish in both fresh and salt water, including a list of 17 fishing spots accessible from the roads. Get it from the local office of the **Alaska Department of Fish and Game,** at 2030 Sea Level Dr., Suite 205, Ketchikan, AK 99901(© **907/225-2859;** www.alaska.gov/adfg, click "Sport Fishing" then on the Southeast region on the map). More fishing ideas are under "Hiking" and "Cabin Trips."

Guided fishing charters can take you out on the water for salmon and halibut, and nonguided, bareboat rental also is available (generally, you pay under $200 a day for a skiff, but you need to know what you are doing). The Ketchikan Visitors Bureau can put you in contact with a charter boat operator. A daylong guided charter costs around $225 per person, ½ day about $140.

HIKING   Eight miles out the North Tongass Highway, the **Ward Lake Recreation Area** covers a lovely patch of rainforest, lake and stream habitat, and has a picnic area, several trails, and campgrounds. Ward Creek has steelhead and cutthroat trout, Dolly Varden char, and silver salmon; check current regulations before fishing. The wide, gravel **Ward Lake Nature Trail** circles the placid lake for 1⅓ miles among old-growth Sitka spruce large enough to put you in your place. For a more challenging hike, **Perseverance Lake Trail** climbs through forest with steps and boardwalks from the Three Cs Campground, across the road from Ward Lake, to a lake 2.3 miles away that can be reached no other way. There's a good bit of climbing to get there, but the trail is extraordinarily well maintained, without mud even in wet weather. To reach the recreation area, turn right off the highway on Revilla Road and follow the signs.

Deer Mountain Trail, right behind downtown, is a steep but rewarding climb through big, mossy trees up to great views. You can walk from City Park to the trailhead, half a mile and 500 feet higher on steep Fair Street and Ketchikan Lakes Road, but if you take a cab you will save energy for the trail. The first mile rises 1,000 feet to a great ocean view south of Tongass Narrows, and the next mile and 1,000 feet to another great view, this time of Ketchikan. The alpine summit, at 3,001 feet, comes near the 3-mile mark. A public shelter (a first-come, first served cabin) is a bit farther, and the trail continues to another trailhead 10 miles away. Pick up a trail guide sheet from the Forest Service at the Southeast Alaska Discovery Center (p. 94).

SEA KAYAKING The islands, coves, and channels around Ketchikan create protected waters rich with life and welcoming for exploration by kayak. **Southeast Sea Kayaks** (© 800/287-1607 or 907/225-1258; www.kayakketchikan. com), rents kayaks and guides day trips and overnights. They specialize in taking small groups of independent travelers, not big mobs from the cruise ships, and have half-day trips that start with a boat ride to real wilderness with only six paddlers along. Those are $139 per adult (no kids under 12). A 2½-hour paddle is $76 adults, $56 children as young as 6. They have multiday Misty Fjords expeditions, too.

WHERE TO STAY

In addition to the hotels and B&Bs listed below, the **Ketchikan Reservation Service,** 412 D-1 Loop Rd., Ketchikan, AK 99901 (© 800/987-5337 or phone/fax 907/247-5337; www.ketchikan-lodging.com), books many bed-and-breakfasts and outfitted apartments online.

EXPENSIVE

Best Western Landing ★★ This hotel already boasted newly furnished rooms, done in bright colors and with granite bathroom counters, when the owners announced a plan to demolish an entire wing and rebuild it with 47 brand new rooms. If all goes as planned, that work will be complete in 2005. What I was able to see prior to that work showed standards familiar to corporate travelers, with reasonable amenities provided in solidly built, perfectly clean rooms. Service is professional. The location, right across from the ferry dock, is distant from the downtown sights, so you'll need to rent a car or use the courtesy van that the hotel offers.

The **Landing Restaurant,** a fountain and grill with lots of chrome, is a local favorite. Lunch and dinner range from $7.25 to $25. You can order from that same steak and seafood menu upstairs, at **Jeremiah's** bar, which also serves sandwiches, pizza, and good pasta in a sumptuous room; the nonsmoking area is glassed off and not smoky.

3434 Tongass Ave., Ketchikan, AK 99901. © 800/428-8304 or 907/225-5166. Fax 907/225-6900. www. landinghotel.com. 76 units. High season $175 double; $185 suite. Low season $135 double; $148 suite. AE, DC, DISC, MC, V. **Amenities:** 2 restaurants; bar; exercise room; courtesy van; limited room service; laundry service; dry cleaning. *In room:* TV, dataport, high-speed Internet, fridge, coffeemaker, hair dryer, iron, microwave.

Salmon Falls Resort ★★ If fishing is your goal, a stay at this huge on-island lodge has several advantages. First, there's the incredible setting, on island-dotted Clover Pass next to a waterfall where 10,000 pink salmon spawn. Next is the cost savings of a road-accessible lodge, since you don't have to fly there. Finally, you're not trapped in the middle of nowhere if one of you doesn't want to fish—the attractions of Ketchikan are a 17-mile drive down the road. The facilities are quite good: large, up-to-date white-walled motel rooms with phones but without TVs and with small bathrooms. Those in the upper building are slightly preferable and cost the same. Some 40 lodge-operated boats tie at the dock. Inclusive fishing packages start at $950 per person, double occupancy, for a 3-day stay with 2 days on the water, self-guided. With a guide, the price is $1,350 per person. Without fishing, room and board are $650.

The **restaurant** and bar are in a massive log octagon held up in the center by a section of the Alaska pipeline, with great views and a menu of steak and seafood ranging from $18 to $29. It's worth a drive out the road for dinner, even if you aren't staying here (the restaurant doesn't open until May 30).

16707 N. Tongass Hwy. (P.O. Box 5700), Ketchikan, AK 99901. **℘ 800/247-9059** (reservations) or 907/225-2752. Fax 907/225-2710. www.salmonfallsresort.com. 52 units. See rates in description above. AE, MC, V. Closed Sept 15–May 15. **Amenities:** Restaurant; bar; inclusive guided fishing.

Westcoast Cape Fox Lodge ✦✦✦   This is Alaska's most beautiful hotel. It stands on a wooded pinnacle above downtown, reached from Creek Street by a funicular. The sheer drop-off and tall rainforest trees create the lofty feeling of a treehouse in the rooms and restaurant. Perfectly proportioned buildings are executed in extraordinarily good taste. Warm wood frames complement the stunning views out of the double-hung windows. The Cape Fox Native corporation built the hotel, and the lobby and parking area are a museum of Tlingit art masterpieces, adding to the peace and rainforest spirit. Rooms are large and airy, appointed in rich-toned wood, and all but a dozen share a view of Ketchikan and the sea and islands beyond (rooms on the opposite side are $10 less). Each room has an attractively tiled bathroom.

The **Heen Kahidi** ✦ restaurant has one of Alaska's most attractive dining rooms, a tall, narrow rectangle of windows with a fireplace. It is a beautiful, calming place to eat. I was disappointed by the service on my last visit, but the food was good. Lunch ranges from $7 to $20; dinner main courses range from $17 to $37, with most around $25. The dining room is open from 7am to 9pm daily.

800 Venetia Way, Ketchikan, AK 99901. **℘ 800/325-4000** or 907/225-8001. Fax 907/225-8286. www.west coasthotels.com. 72 units. High season $169–$179 double; low season $139–$149 double; year-round $250 suite. AE, DC, DISC, MC, V. **Amenities:** Restaurant; bar; limited room service; dry cleaning. *In room:* TV w/pay movies and Nintendo rental, dataport, coffeemaker, hair dryer, iron.

MODERATE

Blueberry Hill Bed and Breakfast ✦✦ *Finds*   This gracious 1917 house, once a residence for nuns, stands atop the rocky cliff that bounds the north side of the downtown waterfront, above the tunnel. The center of the action is just down the hill, 117 steps away on a public stairway, but up here all is peaceful in common rooms with high ceilings, stately dimensions, and fine old trim. Each of the guest rooms is large and light, with its own bathroom and phone, as well as queen beds with down comforters. The eclectic decor chosen by the current owner neatly sidesteps the too-precious feel of many historic inns but still includes the antiques, elegance, and visual interest you would expect. The B&B is currently for sale, but it has remained top-notch through a past change of ownership. Smoking is not allowed in the house.

500 Front St. (P.O. Box 9508), Ketchikan, AK 99901. **℘ 877/449-2583** or 907/247-2583. Fax 907/247-2584. www.blueberryhillbb.com. 4 units. High season $110–$145 double; low season $80–$105. Extra person $25. Rates include full breakfast and afternoon snack. DISC, MC, V.

Edgewater Bed and Breakfast ✦   Situated over the water on the coastal bike trail about 1½ miles south of town, this place is a great choice for long stays or if you want to cook for yourself. The rooms are large and light, if sparsely decorated, with big bathrooms and access to a large kitchen. Each room except one has a private entry from the wraparound deck. An upstairs suite is enormous, perfect for a family or group—the host doesn't charge extra for more people. Best of all, the ocean is at your doorstep. You can fish right from a floating dock on the property and watch wildlife from the deck. It is easy to bike here, but may want a car in case of rain.

2070 S. Tongass Hwy. (P.O. Box 9302), Ketchikan, AK 99901. © **907/247-3343.** Fax 907/225-1184. www. edgewaterbb.com. 4 units. Summer $125–$150 per room, regardless of the number of people in the room; winter rates negotiable. MC, V. **Amenities:** Free laundry machines. *In room:* TV.

The Narrows Inn 🐟   The motel buildings sit above the water, where fishing charters and floatplanes collect guests for outings. The rooms, done in an outdoors theme, are fresh and nicely decorated, with wallpaper borders. My only complaint is that they are too small—the TV is mounted on the wall. The bathrooms are large. Rooms with balconies rent for $10 more. The location is 4 miles from downtown; they have an airport shuttle, but I would rent a car if staying here.

4871 N. Tongass Hwy. (P.O. Box 8296), Ketchikan, AK 99901. © **888/686-2600** or 907/247-2600. Fax 907/ 247-2602. www.narrowsinn.com. 46 units. High season $130–$140 double; $210 suite. Low season $89–$99 double; $150 suite. Extra person $10. AE, DC, DISC, MC, V. **Amenities:** Restaurant; bar; courtesy airport shuttle; marina. *In room:* TV, fridge, coffeemaker, hair dryer, microwave.

INEXPENSIVE

Captain's Quarters Bed & Breakfast 🐟🐟 *Value*   The rooms here rival the best hotel rooms in Ketchikan (those at the Cape Fox), but cost half as much. They are large, quiet, and immaculate, with sweeping views of the city and ocean, and share a self-contained, self-service breakfast room. Little things are done right, such as each room having a private phone with its own outside line and number. A light nautical theme carries through the building. One room has a full kitchen. The setup allows as much privacy as you want—socialize with hostess Toni Bass, a gregarious school secretary, or come and go without seeing anyone. The house is perched in a mountainside neighborhood just north of the tunnel, where half the streets are stairs or wooden ramps. It's a significant but doable walk from downtown. There's no smoking in the house.

325 Lund St., Ketchikan, AK 99901. © **907/225-4912.** www.ptialaska.net/~captbnb. 3 units. High season $90 double; low season $69 double. Extra person $15. Rates include continental breakfast. MC, V. *In room:* TV, hair dryer.

New York Hotel 🐟🐟 *Value*   In the process of a name change to "Inn at Creek Street," this cozy lodge puts you right in the center of the most historic area in rooms that reflect the character of the place. The original portion is a funny little 1924 building with charming, antique-furnished rooms. It is on the National Register of Historic Places, and the owners have done a good job of adding modern comfort while keeping the essentially funky feel. Four rooms look out on a small boat harbor while five, with less street noise, face the garden. All are a great value—more attractive than other hotel rooms in town that cost much more. For the new part of the inn the owners have bought apartments above the shops on the Creek Street boardwalk and renovated them into spacious, modern suites. These units are downright luxurious, with kitchens, excellent amenities, and great privacy, and they sit on pilings over the flowing creek. The hotel offers a courtesy van to the airport, ferries, and hiking trails. The lobby is tiny and the standard rooms are not large; steep, narrow stairs to some units will be a barrier to some.

The **New York Cafe** is attached to the hotel. It's got an interesting dining room: there is an old-fashioned lunch counter and table seating and light floods in from high windows on a black, white, and red tiled floor and a large Ray Troll mural. They serve three meals a day, focusing on healthy ingredients and local seafood. At this writing, however, the cafe had just changed hands and was not ready to be reviewed.

207 Stedman St., Ketchikan, AK 99901. ✆ **866/225-0246** or 907/225-0246. Fax 907/225-1803. www.
thenewyorkhotel.com. 10 units. High season $94–$104 double, $149 suite; low season $69–$79 double, $99
suite. DISC, MC, V. **Amenities:** Restaurant; courtesy van. *In room:* TV, high speed Internet.

A HOSTEL & CAMPING

Three Forest Service campgrounds with a total of 47 sites are located at **Ward
Lake Recreation Area** (see "Hiking" on p. 99). A salmon stream runs through
the middle of the lakeside Signal Creek Campground, which, along with the
Last Chance Campground, can be reserved through the national system
described in "Getting Outside in the Tongass National Forest," in section 1 of
this chapter. The camping fee at either place is $10.

Eighteen miles out North Tongass Highway, the **Settler's Cove State Park**
includes a sandy beach (a good place to watch whales, beach-comb, or even
swim); a disabilities-accessible path to a spectacular waterfall; and a short coastal
trail. There are 14 campsites, half of which will take rigs of up to 30 feet, without hookups. Camping costs $10 a night. For information, contact the **Alaska
Division of Parks** (✆ **907/247-8574**), 9883 N. Tongass Hwy.

If you need hookups for an RV, try **Clover Pass Resort,** about 15 miles north
of the ferry terminal on North Point Higgins Road (✆ **800/410-2234** or
907/247-2234; www.cloverpassresort.com). They charge $28 a night.

First United Methodist Church   This downtown church hostel is affiliated
with HI/AYH, so you can get your member discount. Utilitarian dorms are male
and female, and guests have use of the church kitchen. Bring a sleeping bag. It
is open only June through August; office hours are from 7 to 9am and 6 to
11pm.

400 Main St. (P.O. Box 8515), Ketchikan, AK 99901. ✆ **907/225-3319.** 19 beds. $12 per person HI/AYH
member, $15 nonmembers. Closed Sept–May.

WHERE TO DINE

Besides these restaurants, see the Westcoast Cape Fox Lodge, Salmon Falls
Resort, Best Western Landing, and New York Hotel, all above, for other good
choices.

Bar Harbor Restaurant ★★ SEAFOOD/ECLECTIC   The wonderful food
and attentive service here are the result of a family's commitment to bringing a
new class of dining to Ketchikan. They know they're in a small town, so you still
find fish and chips and other basics on the menu, but the best of the seafood
selections are as good as you find anywhere in Alaska. I was especially impressed
by the crab cakes and the clam appetizer. They also do many specials, both
to allow the chef-owner to stretch and to educate their audience. Prices are
reasonable—usually around $18 for a seafood special. The restaurant operates in
an old house over the water a drive from the downtown tourist area, and the dining room consists of a series of partly connected small rooms, all decorated in a
cozy fashion with bric-a-brac and white Christmas lights. The name derives
from the boat basin that the restaurant overlooks. Given the few seats, reservations are essential.

2813 Tongass Ave. ✆ **907/225-2813.** www.barharborketchikan.com. Reservations recommended. Lunch
$7–$11, dinner $13–$30. DC, DISC, MC, V. Summer Sun–Thurs 7am–9pm, Fri–Sat 7am–10pm; Winter
Tues–Sat 8am–8pm.

Diaz Cafe ★ *Finds* FILIPINO   Many Alaskan towns have strong, cohesive Filipino communities, created over decades by large, close families drawn across the
ocean one by one for cannery work. In Ketchikan, the heartbeat of the Filipino

Majestic Misty Fjords

In **Punchbowl** Cove, south of Ketchikan in Misty Fjords National Monument, sheer cliffs rise 3,150 feet straight up from calm water, as high and smooth as those in the Yosemite Valley. Misty is well over twice Yosemite's size, but there isn't a single car here; there isn't so much as a mile of road; in fact, there are hardly any trails. It's something like a great national park before the people arrived.

Visits to the monument are by tour boat, floatplane, or, for the hardy, sea kayak. It isn't a cheap place to go, and you don't see much wildlife. By boat, you don't see glaciers, although glaciated mountains are a spectacular feature of the flights. Unlike Glacier Bay, Tracy Arm, Kenai Fjords, or Resurrection Bay—all places with more wildlife and more glaciers at sea level—the experience at Misty is pure geology: You go for the scenery.

The main tour boat operation to Misty is **Alaska Cruises,** owned by Juneau's Goldbelt Native corporation, 57 Main St., Suite 201, Ketchikan ((C) **800/228-1905** or 907/225-6044; www.goldbelttours.com). They run a high-speed, 92-passenger catamaran on daily 6½-hour trips out to Punchbowl Cove, Rudyerd Bay, and back. The fare is $150 adults, $125 children. They serve a continental breakfast on the outbound trip, and snacks and chowder on the way back.

I prefer seeing the fjords by air (and I certainly recommend that for those susceptible to sea sickness). Flying over the scenery is amazing, but it's the floatplane landing that really blows your mind, because then you get a sudden sense of the scale of everything you've seen from the air. The cliffs are magnified while you shrink to a speck. Go in the late afternoon when the light is pretty and the swarms of planes carrying cruise-ship passengers are gone.

community has beat in this bright little diner since the early 1950s as ownership passes generation to generation in the same family. The place is so well-loved among all ethnicities in Ketchikan that its current owner is unable to change the slightest detail—she even faced an insurrection when she tried to change the color of the menus—so everything remains today as it was half a century ago: the Formica, worn from wiping, the garish yellow and red walls, and the nondescript street front (which could scare you off, although the restaurant inside is immaculate). If you haven't had Filipino food, this is the place to try it. The spicy chicken *adobo,* a huge, delicious half chicken bathed in gravy with rice, is $12. Regulars order the "Large guy," a bowl of sweet-and-sour rice mixed with meat, which arrives instantly and costs $5.25. You can also get sandwiches, burgers (also served with rice), and Chinese food.

335 Stedman St. (C) **907/225-2257.** Lunch and dinner $5.25-$14. No credit cards. Tues–Sat 11:30am–2pm, 4–8pm; Sun noon–7:30pm.

Good Fortune Chinese Restaurant CHINESE   This restaurant stands on pilings in Creek Street, with small upstairs and downstairs dining rooms. The food is consistently good year after year, with a long and varied menu that allows you to choose by style of cuisine—Cantonese, Szechuan, and so on.

Several air-taxi operators in Ketchikan take flightseeing day trips to Misty Fjords or drop clients at remote cabins. **Promech Air** (© 800/860-3845 or 907/225-3845; www.promechair.com) is a large one, charging $189 for a 75-minute flight including about 10 minutes on the ground. But I like best a smaller company, **Island Wings Air Service** (© 888/854-2444 or 907/225-2444; www.islandwings.com). The owner and pilot is Michelle Madsen, and my flight with her was among the most memorable of the many I've taken around Alaska. She flew the plane with her long blond hair flowing and her little white dog Perro at her side (although she offered to leave him behind), offering a choice of CDs for the stereo as background to her impromptu commentary about the fjords. We soared with Van Morrison while Michelle told us about her favorite places down below. The landing was as long as anyone needed to soak in the awesome surroundings. It felt like an outing with old friends. Madsen charges $199 for a seat on a six-passenger DeHavilland Beaver for a 2-hour flight that includes 45 minutes on the ground at the fjords. She also flies guests to Forest Service cabins (many of them in Misty), places she knows intimately, and she will take the time to help you choose one that suits your interests and budget. Take a look at her informative website for a good start.

Visiting the fjords by kayak is a real expedition, advisable only for those who already know they enjoy this mode of travel, but I can think of few more spectacular places to paddle. **Southeast Exposure** (© 907/225-8829; www.southeastexposure.com) does guided paddles there, and has for many years, earning a good reputation. Their 6-day trip is $950 per person.

4 Creek St. © **907/225-1818.** Lunch $6.25; dinner $12–$19. DISC, MC, V. Mon–Sat 11am–9pm; Sun noon–9pm. Winter closed Mon.

Ocean View Restaurante ★ (Finds MEXICAN/ITALIAN Everyone in Ketchikan already knows how good the food is at this family restaurant, which is why the place is so lively and festive even on an off-season weeknight—in fact, the dinning room can be deafening. Few tourists know about it or make the drive a mile from downtown. The menu is long and reasonably priced, with separate columns of Mexican and Italian cuisine (and an occasional Greek item slipped into the Italian column), a page of seafood and sautéed entrees, plus chicken, veal, steak, pasta, and pizza. Variety is a common technique used by small-town restaurants to make it through the winter; the difference here is remarkably good cooking. They serve beer and wine. Smoking is not allowed. The pizza, delivered free, is the best in town.

1831 Tongass Ave. © **907/225-7566.** Reservations recommended. Lunch $7–$9; dinner $6–$16. MC, V. Daily 11am–11pm.

Steamers ★ STEAK/SEAFOOD Open only in the summer and located three floors up right on cruise ship dock, this restaurant isn't a favorite with the locals, but it's no tourist trap, either, despite the throngs of visitors who commonly descend. The menu is full of appealing, unusual choices (lots of seafood), and my meals have been surprisingly good: a blackened halibut wrap was moist and flavorful, and not so heavily seasoned as to spoil the fish, and the smoked salmon chowder was exceptional. The dining room has a very high ceiling and enormous windows looking over the water. In the evening, after the ships clear out, come here for the many beers on tap, the super-hot wings, and, Friday nights, live music.

76 Front St. ⓒ **907/225-1600.** Reservations recommended. Lunch $9–$35; dinner $15–$40. AE, DC, DISC, MC, V. Mon–Sat 11am–10pm. Closed off-season.

3 Wrangell

Wrangell, valued for its position near the mouth of the Stikine River, began as a Tlingit stronghold and trading post and became the site of a Russian fort built in 1834. The British leased the area from the Russians in 1840, and their flag flew until the U.S. purchase of Alaska in 1867. Over the balance of the 19th century, Wrangell experienced three gold rushes and the construction of a cannery and sawmill.

Then time pretty much stopped.

While the world outside changed, Wrangell stayed the same from the mid-20th century on. It even moved backward. Elsewhere, Wal-Mart and shopping malls were invented and small-town main streets deflated. Then people noticed what they had lost and tried to bring back their communities. Not out here, beyond the road system. With little incentive for anyone to visit, Wrangell stayed as it was after a 1952 fire burned the downtown: a burly, blue-collar American logging town, simple and conservative. Wrangell cut trees, processed them, and shipped them. The bars stayed busy, and no one thought of opening a health food restaurant. As long as there were trees to saw into lumber, the future was safe in the past.

Or so it seemed until environmental and economic issues closed the mill in 1994. Some feared the town would die, too. Sawing lumber had sustained the local economy for more than 100 years and a third of the paychecks in town came from that one plant. But it hasn't been so simple. The logging industry survived, off and on, and on a much smaller scale. The town grew quieter. Some trailer houses disappeared and stores closed, but the lights didn't go out. The population declined slowly, and the decline seems to continue—down to 2,113 in 2004.

But Wrangell is working to improve on its positive qualities. Residents show an endearing eagerness to please. A big new museum should be complete by 2005, and ecotourism operators offer kayaking, hiking, biking, and the like. Tour boats take guests up the wild Stikine River, out on the water for Southeast's great salmon fishing, and over to the mainland to see hordes of bears at the Anan Wildlife Observatory. The U.S. Forest Service maintains gravel roads that lead to some spectacular places. The town even built a golf course called **Muskeg Meadows** (ⓒ **907/874-GOLF**). Named for the area's hummocky swamps, it was built up on wood waste from the old mill, and there's a course rule that there's no penalty if a raven steals your ball.

The town has a nonthreatening, small-scale feel that allows a family to wander comfortably and make friends. We were invited home to dinner by another family we had just met. With so little crime there is no fear of strangers. We picnicked in a totem pole park, hiked in the rainforest, and looked at ancient art strewn across Petroglyph Beach. We were sorry to have to leave. On the ferry

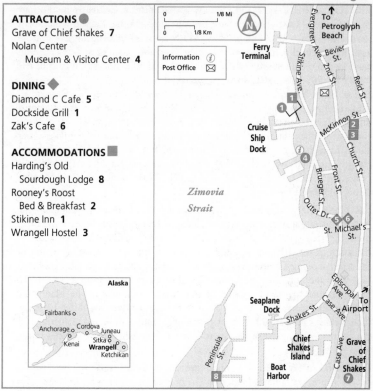

ATTRACTIONS ●
Grave of Chief Shakes **7**
Nolan Center
   Museum & Visitor Center **4**

DINING ◆
Diamond C Cafe **5**
Dockside Grill **1**
Zak's Cafe **6**

ACCOMMODATIONS ■
Harding's Old
  Sourdough Lodge **8**
Rooney's Roost
  Bed & Breakfast **2**
Stikine Inn **1**
Wrangell Hostel **3**

back to Juneau, a class of Wrangell sixth-graders sat next to us. They talked with excited innocence of all the new things they hoped to experience in the state capital, the most electrifying of which seemed to be the prospect of eating for the first time at McDonald's. Wrangell, I thought, still has a long way to go to catch up with the rest of the world, and that is a condition much to be envied.

ESSENTIALS

GETTING THERE   **Alaska Airlines** (*C* **800/252-7522;** www.alaskaair.com) serves Wrangell once daily with a jet flying 28 minutes north from Ketchikan and another 19 minutes south from Petersburg, a flight that skims treetops the entire way.

    Wrangell is on the main line of the **Alaska Marine Highway System** (*C* **800/642-0066;** www.ferryalaska.com). The voyage through the narrow, winding **Wrangell Narrows** north to Petersburg is one of the most beautiful and fascinating in Southeast Alaska. It's quite a navigational feat to watch as the 400-foot ships squeeze through a passage so slender and shallow the vessel's own displacement changes the water level onshore as it passes. The route, not taken by cruise ships, which approach through larger waterways, is also a source of delays, as the narrows are deep enough for passage only at high tide. The walk-on fare is $32 from Ketchikan, $27 from Petersburg. The terminal is downtown (*C* **907/874-3711**) a block from the Stikine Inn.

VISITOR INFORMATION   The **Wrangell Visitor Center** is in the new Nolan Center—which also contains the museum—on the water in the heart of town at 296 Outer Dr. (© **800/367-9745;** www.wrangellalaska.org). Staff from both the Wrangell Chamber of Commerce and the U.S. Forest Service are on hand to answer questions. Reach the chamber at P.O. Box 49, Wrangell, AK 99929 (© **907/874-3901;** www.wrangellchamber.org).

The Forest Service's **Wrangell Ranger District Office** is at 525 Bennett St. (P.O. Box 51), Wrangell, AK 99929 (© **907/874-2323;** www.fs.fed.us/r10/tongass), located on the hill behind town. Forest Service personnel here or at the visitor center have local knowledge of the logging roads and fishing holes, offer guides to each Forest Service cabin and path, and, for $6, sell a detailed and recently updated Wrangell Island Road Guide topographic map, which is printed on waterproof material. The office district office is open Monday through Friday from 8am to 4:30pm.

ORIENTATION   The main part of town is laid out north to south along the waterfront on the northern point of Wrangell Island. **Front Street** is the main business street, leading from the small-boat harbor and **Chief Shakes Island** at the south to the city dock and the ferry dock at the north. Most of the rest of the town is along **Church Street,** which runs parallel to Front Street a block higher up the hill. **Evergreen Avenue** and **Bennett Street** form a loop to the north that goes to the airport. The only road to the rest of the island, the **Zimovia Highway,** heads out of town to the south, paved for about 12 miles, then connects to over 100 miles of gravel logging roads built and maintained by the Forest Service, most of which are usable by two-wheel-drive vehicles in the summer.

GETTING AROUND   You can do the town on foot, but you will need wheels for the airport or Zimovia Highway. The only place to rent a car in Wrangell is **Practical Rent A Car,** at the airport (© **907/874-3975**). **Northern Lights Taxi** is at © **907/874-4646.**

Rent **bikes** from Rainwalker Expeditions (© **907/874-2549;** www.rainwalkerexpeditions.com) at the city dock, described under "Gearing Up," below.

FAST FACTS: **Wrangell**

Bank **Wells Fargo** is at 115 Front St., with an ATM. There's also an ATM across from the Stikine Inn.

Hospital **Wrangell Medical Center** is at 310 Bennett St. (© **907/874-7000**).

Internet Access At the public library on Church Street. (© **907/874-3535**).

Police For non-emergency calls, dial © **907/874-3304.**

Post Office At 105 Federal Way, near the ferry dock.

Taxes Sales tax is 7%. Rooms carry a $4 bed tax on top of that.

SPECIAL EVENTS   The **Garnet Festival,** held the third week of April, marks the arrival of the sea lions, hooligans, shorebirds, and a great concentration of bald eagles on the Stikine River Delta, a spring tornado of wildlife in the region's largest coastal marshes. Community activities take place in town while jet boat tours traverse the delta. **The Wrangell King Salmon Derby,** the last half of May and first half of June, started in 1953. Contact the Wrangell Visitor Center (see above) for details. Wrangell also puts on a classic small-town **Independence Day** celebration.

EXPLORING WRANGELL & ENVIRONS

Before white settlers arrived, the Tlingit had already warred for centuries over this strategic trading location near the mouth of the Stikine River. The first Chief Shakes was a successful conqueror who enslaved his enemies, then handed down power through the female line, in the Tlingit tradition, for seven generations. Charlie Jones was recognized as Chief Shakes VII, the last of the line, at a potlatch in 1940, but the position had long since lost most of its status. The decline began after the Alaska purchase, in 1867. Word came of the Emancipation Proclamation, which theoretically freed a third of the residents of the coast's Tlingit villages. Chief Shakes VI sent his slaves in canoes to dry halibut; they kept paddling home to Puget Sound, never looking back.

Chief Shakes Island, a tiny islet in the middle of the small-boat harbor, is the site of a Tlingit clan house and collection of totem poles constructed by Native workers, using traditional tools, in the Civilian Conservation Corps during the 1930s. Unlike some CCC clan house replicas in the region, which mix Tlingit styles, this house is an exact, scaled-down copy of the 1834 house in which Chief Shakes VI lay in state in 1916. The inside of the clan house is fascinating, both in the sense it gives of the people's ways, and for some extraordinary artifacts. Unfortunately, it takes some effort to get inside, as it is open mostly only when the cruise ships are in town, a few times a week in the summer. These times are posted around town or at the clan house. At those times, admission is $2.50. Otherwise, you can pay a $25 minimum to have someone come down and show you around. Call Nora Rinehart at ℂ **907/874-2023** (e-mail norarinehart@ yahoo.com), or, if you can't reach Nora, Margret Sturdevant at ℂ **907/874-3747.** Nora can give you the cruise ship schedule before you come, too. Even if you can't manage that, visit the island to see the rotting totem poles and the charming setting (and, with extra time, visit the overgrown grave of Chief Shakes V, on Case Ave. just across the harbor). There's a resident otter that you can often see near the island's footbridge, sometimes feeding its young.

The carved house posts in the clan house are replicas of the mid-18th-century originals protected by the local museum. These are probably the oldest and certainly the best-preserved Tlingit house posts in existence, still bearing the original fish egg and mineral paints, and a gash where, during a potlatch, a chief hacked off an image that a visitor admired and gave it to him—a gesture that demonstrated the extent of his wealth then, and still does.

The new **Nolan Center Museum,** at 296 Outer Drive (ℂ **907/874-3770** or 907/367-9745) is an impressive 15,000-square-foot building, with galleries devoted to natural history, logging and fishing, Native culture, and several others. The Wrangell museum—the predecessor—already owned many important Alaska Native pieces, and a lot of just plain old stuff telling the story of Wrangell, one of Alaska's most historic towns. Admission is $5 adults; $2 seniors and children 6 to 12; $12 families. Summer hours are Monday through Saturday 10am to 5pm; they open earlier when a big cruise ship is in town. Winter hours: 1 to 4:30pm.

The museum helped preserve an impressive set of petroglyphs that lie on the beach a mile north of town. The 50 carvings at **Wrangell Petroglyph Beach State Historic Park** probably represent the work of forgotten indigenous people pre-dating the Tlingit, and were made over a long period of time. The images, chipped into rocks, are of animals and geometric forms. Their purpose is lost to time. Walk north on Evergreen Avenue and follow the signs down to the beach (don't go within an hour of high tide). Replicas of the petroglyphs were recently carved so that visitors who want to take rubbings will not destroy the originals; also try not to step on them. The great pleasure here is simply to search for the carvings—they're just lying out there, and it takes some looking—and to wonder at their meaning and age.

GETTING OUTSIDE

ON THE ISLAND   Wrangell Island's network of gravel roads, maintained by the Forest Service, leads to places of awesome beauty rarely visited by non-Alaskans. There are a few day-hike trails, some lovely campsites, and paths to remote shelters and fishing lakes you can have to yourself. There are also a couple of calm and scenic places to start a kayak paddle.

There's only one way out of town: south on the Zimovia Highway along narrow Zimovia Strait. The Forest Service map (see "Visitor Information," above) is helpful for anything you might want to do along this route.

The place to see along the way is **City Park,** just south of town. Besides having a picnic area on the shore among big trees, it's a fine **tide-pooling** spot. Go a couple of hours before a good low tide.

Five miles out Zimovia Highway you reach the **Shoemaker Bay Recreation Area,** with a small boat harbor, campground, and picnic sites (see "A Hostel & Camping," below).

Continuing south, **Eight Mile Beach** is a good stop for a ramble, and don't miss **Nemo Point,** a high, oceanside overlook from which you can see more than 13 miles along Zimovia Strait all the way back to town. There are eight gorgeous campsites, and a boardwalk trail along the road leads down to the beach.

All the way across the island, about 45 minutes from town, **Earl West Cove** gives access to the protected wilderness waters on the Eastern Passage. There's a campsite there, too.

OFF THE ISLAND   Wrangell provides a stepping-off point for vast, rich wild lands and remote fishing, rafting, sea kayaking, or wildlife-watching. I've described two of the main off-island destinations below—the Stikine River and the Anan Wildlife Observatory—but there are many more, too many to mention. The guides I've listed can give ideas, or look into the Forest Service cabins for rent to the public, many of which provide exclusive access to exceptional fishing.

To get beyond the island, you need a boat or floatplane. You can go independently, hiring a water taxi for $120 to $150 an hour; it costs about $450 to $700, one-way, to get to a remote Forest Service cabin by boat. That service is offered by various operators (see "Gearing Up," below). If you prefer to go by air, **Sunrise Aviation** (© **800/874-2311** or 907/874-2319) is a Wrangell-based operator.

GEARING UP   For a lift over the water, a guide, or rental equipment, there are several long established businesses. **Alaska Waters,** with a desk in the Stikine Inn, 107 Stikine Ave. (© **800/347-4462** or 907/874-2378; www.alaskawaters. com) rents equipment and offers various marine services, including fishing and tours. **Alaska Vistas** (© **866/874-3006** or 907/874-3006; www.alaskavistas. com), at the cruise ship dock (the city dock) started as a sea kayaking business, but now offers water taxis and other services. You can stop in at their office on the dock for advice, books, maps, gear, and espresso. Both companies are listed below under the appropriate headings.

Marie Oboczky's **Rainwalker Expeditions** (© **907/874-2549;** www.rain
walkerexpeditions.com) rents bikes, sea kayaks, and canoes, and also leads
guided hikes and offers accommodations on a houseboat in Wrangell or afield
(all covered later in this section). Oboczky also has teamed up with other
outdoor businesses in town to offer joint booking and trip planning. She
offers advice on her website and at an office near the city dock, next door to the
Stikine Inn.

OUTDOOR ACTIVITIES NEAR WRANGELL

BIKING   A paved 6-mile bike trail along the water next to the Zimovia Highway leads all the way from town to the Shoemaker Bay Loop Road. There are
many more miles of appealing mountain-bike routes on Forest Service roads all
over the island. See "Gearing Up," above, for rental information.

FISHING   Anglers can dip a line in various streams and lakes on Wrangell
Island reachable by car or a drive and short hike. The Forest Service provides a
list, and the **Alaska Department of Fish and Game** (© **907/874-3822;** www.
alaska.gov/adfg, click "Sport Fishing" then the southeast region) publishes an
extensive *Petersburg/Wrangell Sport Fishing Guide.* May and June are the prime
months for king salmon fishing, silvers start in July, and halibut are available all
summer.

The well-run **Alaska Waters** (see "Gearing Up," above) offers a long day of
saltwater fishing for $225 per person; they're professional, knowledgeable, and
fun to go boating with. They also rent skiffs with outboard motors for self-
guided fishing. Many other charter boats are available at the harbor; ask at the
visitor center. You can often arrange to use part of the day on the boat for sightseeing and wildlife-watching, too.

HIKING   Across the road from the Shoemaker Bay Recreation Area, the
Rainbow Falls Trail climbs steeply for just under a mile (and 500 ft. in elevation gain) on a boardwalk with steps, up a ridge between two creeks, forested
with big, mossy Sitka spruce and western hemlock. The falls seem to tumble
down between the branches. From that point, you can continue another 2.6
miles and another 1,100 feet higher into open alpine terrain on the **Institute
Creek Trail** to the Shoemaker Overlook, where there are great views, a picnic
area, and a shelter. An additional section of the trail continues from there
another 8 miles across the island. **Rainwalker Expeditions** (see "Gearing Up,"
above) leads nature walks on the lower part of the trail, and longer hikes all over
the island, starting at $25 for a two-hour outing. The advantage of going with
guide Marie Oboczky is that she is a skilled naturalist and teacher and knows all
the best places to go.

The Rainbow Falls Trail is the island's busiest, especially when cruise ships are
in town. If you want to be sure you won't see anyone, take one of the less developed walks you can reach along the logging roads—the Forest Service can point
the way. One good choice is the **Salamander Ridge Trail,** which leads a mile to
subalpine terrain, where you can go off-trail hiking. The trail begins 27 miles
from Wrangell on Salamander Road, also known as Forest Road 50050. The
Long Lake Trail leads over a half-mile boardwalk to a public shelter and rowboat on the lake, on Forest Road 6271 (you'll need a map).

SEA KAYAKING   **Alaska Vistas** (see "Gearing Up," above) offers kayaking
day trip paddles starting from the boat harbor, longer day tours to lovely Earl
West Cove on the east side of the island, or guided trips of many days. A 5-day
trip starts with a jet-boat trip on the Stikine River to Shakes Lake, and then

paddles back to Wrangell with stops at the natural hot springs and other sites along the way.

THE STIKINE RIVER

The Stikine's gray, glacial waters rush all the way from the dry Interior of British Columbia to a broad, shallow delta in the rainforest a few miles from Wrangell. It's among the fastest free flowing navigable rivers in North America, and in early gold rush years was a route through the Coastal Range. Tours that sometimes go as far as Telegraph Creek, B.C., speed against the current with the roar of high-powered engines that send a jet of water out from under their shallow, metal bottoms. On still water, the jet boats can go as fast as a car on the highway.

The shallow delta is an exceptionally rich wildlife-viewing area, a habitat of grasslands, braided channels, and marshes populated by sea lions, eagles, and many other species of birds. In late April and early May, when the hooligans run, more than 1,500 bald eagles congregate, and some two million other birds rest on their West Coast migration. Later in the year, when summer's salmon are running, you can see them thrashing in their spawning pools. Farther upriver, tours encounter Sitka black-tailed deer, moose, brown and black bears, mountain goats, river otters, and beavers.

Traveling upriver, tours usually stop at the **Shakes Glacier** and **Shakes Lake,** where there are 3,000-foot cliffs and some 50 waterfalls. Bring a swimsuit for a dip in the Forest Service-owned **Chief Shakes Hot Springs,** where there's an indoor and an outdoor tub for public bathing. The temperature is adjustable up to 120°F (49°C). Alaska Waters and Alaska Vistas offer these tours (see "Gearing Up," above). Alaska Waters goes all the way to Telegraph, B.C., 160 miles upriver, bringing travelers to a remote homestead lodge. Commentary on all their trips includes natural history and Tlingit cultural traditions and legends. A 3-day, 2-night package is $820. The going rate for a 6-hour jet boat tour from Wrangell to the glacier, delta, and hot springs is $150 to $175.

Rafting the Stikine offers fast water, expansive scenery, and the potential for a remote, many-day journey. Alaska Vistas offers these guided trips, lasting about 10 days to 2 weeks, for an inclusive price of around $2,500 per person. Alaska Vistas and Alaska Waters rent rafts and other gear for floating the Stikine. A raft rents for about $100 a day. (See "Gearing Up," above.)

ANAN WILDLIFE OBSERVATORY

When the pink salmon are running in July and August (peak is mid-July to Aug 20), a population of more than 40 **black bears** and a few brown bears gather near a waterfall on Anan Creek, on the mainland southeast of Wrangell Island, often walking close to a platform where visitors stand watching. Don't visit outside the time of this salmon run, however, unless you have it on good authority that bears are actively using the creek. Forest Service interpreters are on duty during the bear months; visitors must also follow safe bear behavior (they'll brief you when you arrive; also see "Outdoors Health & Safety," in chapter 2). Most visitors will enjoy a guided day trip from Wrangell more than going on their own. Both **Alaska Waters** and **Alaska Vistas** go by boat (see "Gearing Up," above), each charging about $190 per person for the hour-long run from Wrangell and a few hours with the bears. It's also possible to go without a guide, but you will need a permit issued by the Forest Service **Wrangell Ranger District Office,** at 525 Bennett St. (P.O. Box 51), Wrangell, AK 99929 (© **907/874-2323;** fax 907/874-7595; www.fs.fed.us/r10/tongass). The system

---

Fun Fact **Why the Garnet Stands?**

In the streets of Wrangell, you sometimes encounter kids selling garnets the way children other places sell lemonade. The gems come from the Garnet Ledge, near the mouth of the Stikine River, a mine that is still productive recreationally 130 years after its discovery. A visit to the mine isn't worth the effort for most travelers, but the story is interesting. The ledge was mined commercially from 1907 to 1936 by the first all-woman corporation in the nation, a group of investors from Minneapolis. Its current ownership is unusual, too: a 1962 deed gave the mine to the Boy Scouts and all the children of Wrangell, which is interpreted to mean that only children have the right to remove the stones. You can get a water taxi out there, but take a kid along if you intend to remove garnets. Of course, it's easier simply to buy garnets from a kid at a card table in the street.

---

was new in 2004; as it stands now, 60 permits are available for each day of the peak season, with 12 held back until 3 days before the visit. They are given out first-come, first-served by mail, fax, e-mail, or in person. An application form, instructions, and calendar showing how many permits are left for each day are posted on the website. Permits cost $10. There's a Forest Service cabin for rent, too, in very high demand during the bear season. The walk to the observatory is a half mile from the shore where you land, on a good trail.

Sunrise Aviation (℃ **800/874-2311** or 907/874-2319) offers charters to Anan for prices competitive with going by boat.

WHERE TO STAY

Besides the places listed below, you will also find good, inexpensive rooms at **Grand View Bed and Breakfast,** Mile 2, Zimovia Hwy. (P.O. Box 927), Wrangell, AK 99929 (℃/fax **907/874-3225;** www.grandviewbnb.com).

Harding's Old Sourdough Lodge ☆   Mayor Bruce Harding, a large dog, and a cat run the hotel in the style of a fishing lodge, renting the rooms alone or as packages with trips to the Anan Bear Observatory, Stikine River tours, fishing, kayaking, rafting, and other outdoor activities. The attractive building with a wraparound porch is in a waterfront area about a mile from the ferry dock, but Harding will drive you there or wherever else you want to go. The lodge is decorated in an outdoors theme. Most rooms are small, without TVs, and most have only shower stalls, not tubs, but the suites are huge and have Jacuzzi tubs. Fresh seafood dinners are served nightly, family style (you eat what they cook). Dinner prices are $16 to $24 per person; nonguests by reservation only.

1104 Peninsula (P.O. Box 1062), Wrangell, AK 99929. ℃ 800/874-3613 or 907/874-3613. Fax 907/874-3455. www.akgetaway.com. 16 units. $95 double; $135 triple or quad; $150–$195 suite. Rates include continental breakfast. AE, DC, DISC, MC, V. **Amenities:** Sauna; bike rental; tour desk; courtesy car; coin-op laundry; fish freezing.

Rooney's Roost Bed & Breakfast ☆☆   Located downtown, this attractive old house with dormer windows was restored by a new generation of the family that has operated the place for years. They didn't miss a detail, adding antiques on the hardwood floors for an elegance otherwise unknown in Wrangell. The rooms, while small, are decorated according to themes (the Moose Room features outdoorsy decor, the Princess Room is all roses, and so on). All rooms have fans and four-poster beds with thick mattresses, comforters, and oversize pillows. The bathrooms attached to three of the rooms are also new; two have showers only, one has a claw-foot tub. The other rooms share bathrooms. Elaborate breakfasts with local ingredients, such as seafood or berries, are served in a sunny dining room at the guests' convenience. The rooms with private bathrooms also have TVs with VCRs.

206 McKinnon (P.O. Box 552), Wrangell, AK 99929. ✆ **907/874-2026.** Fax 907/874-4404. www.rooneys roost.com. 6 units, 3 with private bathroom. $95 double private bathroom; $75 double shared bathroom. Extra person $15. Rates include full breakfast. MC, V. **Amenities:** Courtesy car; laundry service.

Stikine Inn   The town's main hotel is close to the ferry dock and stands right on the water's edge, a center of community activity. It had fallen on hard times prior to new ownership in 2004 and a major remodel. Not enough of that was done to evaluate on our visit, but the proprietors seemed energetic and dedicated and had big plans. In any event, the waterside views were always superb. You can hear the water lapping the shore outside as you fall asleep, or watch the sunset on the ocean. Based on our visit, I cannot recommend the Dockside Grill, a family restaurant in the hotel; but it recently changed management, too, so improvements may be in store.

107 Front St. (P.O. Box 990), Wrangell, AK 99929. ✆ **888/874-3388** or 907/874-3388. Fax 907/874-3923. www.stikine.com. 34 units. High season $111–$122 double; low season $100–$111 double. Extra person over age 12 $10. AE, DC, DISC, MC, V. **Amenities:** Restaurant. *In room:* TV, dataport.

A HOSTEL & CAMPING

Wrangell Hostel is at the First Presbyterian Church, 220 Church St. (P.O. Box 438), Wrangell, AK 99929 (✆ **907/874-3534**). They're open from mid-June to Labor Day, and the rate is $18 a night.

There are several attractive campgrounds in Wrangell. I've never seen another campground in a spot like the mountaintop **Nemo Point Forest Service Campground** (see "Getting Outside," earlier in this section), but it's more than a dozen miles out of town. Five miles south of town, the **Shoemaker Bay Recreation Area** has sites by the road overlooking the boat harbor, right across from the Rainbow Falls Trail. There are free tent sites and RV sites with electric hookups for $10 a night, $6 without electric; the camping fee includes use of the town pool and its showers. Contact the **Wrangell Recreation and Parks Department** (✆ 907/874-2444) for information. They also manage **City Park,** right at the edge of town on Zimovia Highway, where camping is permitted with a 1-night limit. For a full hookup RV site, try **Alaska Waters'** small park, at 241 Berger St. (✆ **800/347-4462**). They charge $18 a night.

Rent a Houseboat

Marie Oboczky, the naturalist who owns **Rainwalker Expeditions** (✆ **907/ 874-2549;** www.rainwalkerexpeditions.com), offers a cute and cozy old wooden houseboat as a summer accommodation. Early in summer it sits in Shoemaker Harbor, then July through September Oboczky keeps it tied up in remote Bradford Canal, 35 miles from town. This is a chance to stay in relative comfort in the wilderness, and for a true bargain price: $85 a night. The boat isn't large, but a couple or family of three who enjoy the outdoors could be very content here, kayaking and enjoying the outdoors, while still able to cook and use the shower and bathroom on board. You can put the stay together with an outfitter for guided activities, too.

WHERE TO DINE

There's just one really good restaurant in Wrangell, Zak's, described below. Otherwise, the **Diamond C Cafe,** 215 Front St. (© **907/874-3677**), is a nice, clean diner open early in the morning daily in summer. **Harding's Old Sourdough Lodge** (see "Where to Stay," above) serves meals to guests, and to others by reservation. It's a family-style dinner without a menu.

Zak's Café ★★ STEAK/SEAFOOD   It's a surprising treat to find food like this in Wrangell, but there's a good explanation: the owners got tired of the lack of good dining options and decided to do something about it. For lunch they serve salads, wraps, burgers, and sandwiches, and for dinner a short but diverse menu of steak, seafood, pasta, and chicken. The stir-fry was seasoned just right, and the steak béarnaise melted in the mouth. The dining room is small, light, and spare; it doesn't live up to the food. Take the time to talk with the fascinating owners, James and Katherine, who staff the kitchen and dining room respectively.

Front St. © **907/874-3355.** Reservations recommended for dinner. Lunch $6.25–$10, dinner $13–$25. MC, V. Mon–Sat 11am–9pm.

4 Petersburg: Unvarnished Threshold to the Outdoors

Petersburg is the perfect small town, the sort of prosperous, picturesque, quirky place that used to be mythologized in Disney films. Except that Petersburg would never let Disney in the door. People here are too smart for that, and too protective of a place they know would be spoiled by too much attention. For the same reason, Petersburg is just as glad the big cruise ships can't enter their narrow harbor. The town is unspoiled by the ships' throngs of tourists and seasonal gift shops. Instead, locals spend the money that keeps Nordic Drive, the main street, thriving with family-owned grocery and hardware stores, a fish market, and other businesses. Wooden streets over Hammer Slough still serve utilitarian purposes, making them far more appealing than if they were prettied up as tourist areas. As you walk along Sing Lee Alley and check out the stylish little bookstore, you rarely see others like yourselves—instead, you see Norwegian fishermen in pickup trucks and blond-haired kids on bikes.

Because Petersburg is insular and authentic the sublime outdoor opportunities nearby remain little used. There are wonderful trails, mountain-biking routes, and secret places. On the water, the humpback whale-watching is as reliable as anywhere in Alaska and largely undiscovered. There's a glacier to visit, terrific fishing, and limitless sea-kayaking waters. The in-town attractions are few—a day is plenty for simple sightseeing—and little attempt has been made to accommodate lazy gawkers. But Alaska's best is waiting for those willing to spend the effort to look.

Petersburg is named for its founder, Peter Buschmann, who killed himself after living here for only 4 years. But that shouldn't be a reflection on the town, which is in an ideal location and has flourished since that inauspicious beginning. In 1898, or thereabouts (historians differ), Buschmann founded a cannery on Mitkof Island facing the slender, peaceful Wrangell Narrows in what was to become Petersburg. The stunning abundance of salmon and halibut and a nearby source of ice—the LeConte Glacier—made the site a natural. Buschmann had emigrated from Norway in 1891 and, as a proud old Son of Norway told me, he always hired Norwegians. Any Norwegian who came to him, he hired. In a few years, the cannery failed. Perhaps an excessive payroll? My suggestion was met with an icy glance and a change of subject. Teasing aside,

Buschmann's mistake was merging his cannery with a firm trying to challenge a monopolistic canning operation, and they went down together.

Buschmann's suicide followed his financial reverses, but the promise of Petersburg remained. The Norwegians stayed and slowly built a charming town of white clapboard houses with steeply pitched roofs, hugging the water. Their living came from the sea, as it still does. Appropriately, the downtown area doesn't stop at water's edge. Roads, boardwalks, and buildings continue over the smooth waters of Wrangell Narrows, out to the cannery buildings that survive on long wooden piers, and into the boat harbors, which branch out in a network far more extensive than the city's streets.

Today the town's economy is based on fishing and government work. The Stikine Ranger District of the Tongass National Forest is headquartered here. That makes for a wealthy, sophisticated, and stable population.

ESSENTIALS

GETTING THERE   Petersburg has the most welcoming **ferry terminal** in the system (© **907/772-3855**), with a grassy lawn and a pier from which to watch the boats and marine animals. It's about a mile to the town center. The **Alaska Marine Highway** (© **800/642-0066;** www.ferryalaska.com) connects to Juneau directly (an 8-hr. run), or by way of Sitka, far to the west (10 hr. to Sitka from Juneau, then 9 more from Sitka to Petersburg). The fare is $27 from Wrangell (3 hr.), $37 from Sitka, and $55 from Juneau.

Petersburg is served by **Alaska Airlines** jets (© **800/252-7522;** www.alaskaair.com) once north and once south each day, with the nearest stops on the puddle jumper being Juneau and Wrangell.

From the airport, call **Maine Cab** (© 907/772-6969) for a taxi into town.

VISITOR INFORMATION   The Petersburg Chamber of Commerce **Visitor Information Center,** at the corner of 1st and Fram streets (P.O. Box 649), Petersburg, AK 99833 (© **907/772-4636;** www.petersburg.org), offers guidance on outdoor opportunities, boats, and lodgings, and distributes trail guides and natural history publications. The center is open in summer Monday through Saturday from 9am to 5pm, Sunday from noon to 4pm; winter Monday through Friday from 10am to 2pm.

The full-service **Viking Travel** agency, corner of Nordic Drive and Sing Lee Alley (© **800/327-2571** or 907/772-3818; www.alaskaferry.com), also specializes in booking local guides for tours, kayaks, whale-watching, flights, fishing charters, and other activities. Owners Dave and Nancy Berg are knowledgeable and helpful.

ORIENTATION   Petersburg is on Mitkof Island, divided from the much larger Kupreanof Island by the long, slender channel of the Wrangell Narrows. There are three small-boat harbors and so many docks, boardwalks, and wooden streets that the town seems to sit on the ocean. **Nordic Drive** is the main street, running from the ferry dock through town, then becoming **Sandy Beach Road** as it rounds Hungry Point to the north. At Sandy Beach, you can circle back, past the airport, which stands above the town, to **Haugen Drive,** which meets Nordic again near **Hammer Slough,** right in town. To the south, Nordic becomes the **Mitkof Highway,** which runs to the undeveloped balance of the island.

GETTING AROUND   You can walk downtown Petersburg, but you'll need wheels or a boat to get to most outdoor activities. The **Tides Inn Motel** and **Scandia House** (see "Where to Stay," below) both rent cars, but not many are

Petersburg

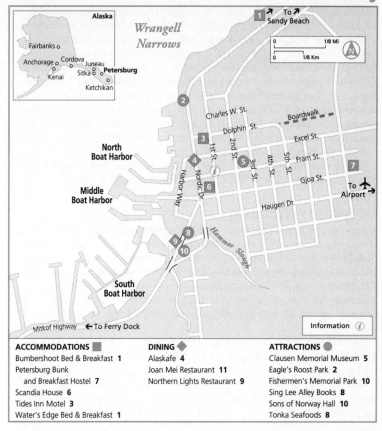

ACCOMMODATIONS ■
Bumbershoot Bed & Breakfast **1**
Petersburg Bunk
  and Breakfast Hostel **7**
Scandia House **6**
Tides Inn Motel **3**
Water's Edge Bed & Breakfast **1**

DINING ◆
Alaskafe **4**
Joan Mei Restaurant **11**
Northern Lights Restaurant **9**

ATTRACTIONS ●
Clausen Memorial Museum **5**
Eagle's Roost Park **2**
Fishermen's Memorial Park **10**
Sing Lee Alley Books **8**
Sons of Norway Hall **10**
Tonka Seafoods **8**

available in town, so book well in advance for summer. The Scandia House also rents small boats, a wonderful way to explore Wrangell Narrows and get to trails across on the other side, or to go fishing inexpensively. An 18-footer with a 40-horsepower outboard rents for $160 a day, gas included, $25 less for guests of the hotel. They don't provide fishing gear.

FAST FACTS: Petersburg

Banks There are two banks, both with ATMs, at the intersection of Nordic Drive and Fram Street.

Hospital **Petersburg Medical Center** is at 2nd and Fram streets (℃ **907/ 772-4291**).

Internet Access Free at the public library, at Nordic and Haugen drives.

Police Find them on Nordic Drive near Haugen; nonemergencies ℃ **907/ 772-3838**.

Post Office Near the airport on Haugen Street.

Taxes Sales tax is 6%. The tax on accommodations totals 10%.

SPECIAL EVENTS **The Little Norway Festival,** which celebrates the May 17, 1814 declaration of independence of Norway from Sweden, is an occasion for Petersburg to go wild. The 4-day schedule of events includes a street fair, food and craft booths, a parade, and a salmon bake on the beach. The celebration is held on the third full weekend of May. **The King Salmon Derby** offers $30,000 in prizes over Memorial Day weekend. **July 4th** is a very big deal in Petersburg. **The Canned Salmon Classic** lasts from July 1 to August 15, with a first prize of up to $4,000 going to the person who guesses how many cans of salmon will be packed in Petersburg during the season. **Julebukking,** a Norwegian tradition, happens on Christmas Eve, when merchants offer food and drink to their customers and the streets fill with people.

For information on any of the above events, contact the **Petersburg Chamber of Commerce** (© 907/772-3646; www.petersburg.org/visitor/festivals. html).

EXPLORING PETERSBURG

A walk around Petersburg should include the boardwalk streets of **Hammer Slough,** the tidal mouth of a creek that feeds into the waterfront. **Sing Lee Alley** leads from North Nordic Drive at the charming center of town, passing by several interesting little shops, including **Sing Lee Alley Books,** at no. 11 (© 907/ 772-4440), where there's a good collection on natural history and local culture. Petersburg has so many thriving little shops because of its isolation and healthy economy—so far, it's been too small to attract the predation of Wal-Mart and other chains.

Sing Lee Alley turns from solid ground to wooden dock before you reach the **Sons of Norway Hall,** a town center where a large model Viking ship used in the Little Norway Festival is often parked. Next door, also on pilings, is the **Fishermen's Memorial Park.** Plaques memorialize Petersburg mariners lost at sea under a bronze statue of Bojer Wikan, a fisherman and lifelong resident. Across the street, on the outboard side, **Tonka Seafoods** (© 888/560-3662 or 907/ 772-3662; www.tonkaseafoods.com) is a specialty fish processor with a shop and mail-order operation; they will process your sport-caught fish, too. They offer 1-hour tours for $5 during the summer at 1 and 3pm Monday through Saturday.

Continue on to Nordic Drive, then turn left, crossing back over the slough to **Birch Street,** which follows the slough's bank on pilings upstream past old, weathered houses that hang over the placid channel. Many have one door for the road and another for the water. It's a charming, authentic place. Step out of the way of cars on the one-lane dock/street.

Back down at the waterfront, stroll the harbor floats to see the frenetic activity of the huge commercial fishing fleet in the summer, then continue north on Nordic Drive to **Eagle's Roost Park,** where there is a grassy area to sit and a stairway that leads down to the water. At low tide an interesting but rugged beach walk starts here. You're almost guaranteed to see eagles, which congregate for the fish waste from the nearby cannery. Look in the tops of the trees. (In fact, you can see eagles almost anytime and anywhere along the water in Petersburg.) Another nice walk leads you on a boardwalk a third of a mile over muskeg swamp from the uphill side of the elementary school, at 4th Street.

The **Clausen Memorial Museum,** at 2nd and Fram streets (© 907/772-3598; www.clausenmuseum.alaska.net), interprets Petersburg and its history for the people who live here. It has a living, community feel. On one visit a portfolio of old photographs was on display with notes for visitors to write down the names of anyone they could identify and other memories. The office of a leading fish packer is displayed just as he left it in the 1970s, a time capsule of the ordinary that says much about the town. No doubt the local fishermen are fascinated by the obsolete fishing gear, rugged old nautical equipment, and a model fish trap, outlawed in 1959 when Alaska became a state. It's like being invited into the town's collective memory. The museum is open in summer Monday through Friday from 10am to 5pm, and Saturday from 10am to 4:30pm; call for hours in the winter. Admission is $3 for adults, free for children 12 and under.

GETTING OUTSIDE

I have listed only a few highlights from Petersburg's wealth of outdoor opportunities. For other choices, many of them just as good as those I've written about here, or for the detailed trail and backcountry information you'll need, contact the U.S. Forest Service at the **Petersburg Ranger District** offices at 12 N. Nordic Dr. (P.O. Box 1328), Petersburg, AK 99833 (© **907/772-3871;** www.fs. fed.us/r10/tongass/districts/petersburg).

Some of the best places to go around Petersburg require a boat. **Viking Travel** (see "Visitor Information," above) books most of the dozen or so small charter boats that operate from the harbor at any one time, allowing them to consolidate small groups into 6- to 15-person boatloads for whale-watching, sightseeing, or fishing.

Some operators have made a specialty of natural history and environmentally responsible tours. Barry Bracken, a marine biologist, offers these kinds of trips on his 28-foot vessel. Contact **Kaleidoscope Cruises** (© **800/TO-THE-SEA** or 907/772-3736; www.alaska.net/~bbsea).

SPECIAL PLACES

SANDY BEACH The beach is an easy bike ride or a longish walk 1½ miles up Nordic Drive, around Hungry Point at the northern tip of the island, then along Sandy Beach Road to the beach and picnic area. Return by way of the airport, coming back into town on Haugen Drive. The beach itself is coarse sand and fine gravel, and you can't swim in the frigid water, but it's a lovely spot, facing Frederick Sound on the east side of Mitkof Island.

If you go at high tide, you can beachcomb and bird-watch—a great blue heron was hanging out once when I visited—but a better plan is to time your visit at a low tide (free tide books are widely available, or ask at the visitor center). At tides of 1 foot or lower, you can see the outlines of ancient fish traps built on the beach beginning 2,000 years ago. They look like V-shaped rows of rocks, and at times you can see stakes. The indigenous people who built them knew how to create channels that would corral salmon at high tide, leaving them stranded to be gathered up when the water receded. These ancient people presumably also created the petroglyphs on rocks near the traps, which may depict the traps or could have something to do with the sun. Finding the traps and petroglyphs isn't easy—it's best if you can get someone to lead you, perhaps by joining the occasional Forest Service walks that you can ask about at the Ranger District office. But, if you have the time and inclination to explore, walk out to the left from the picnic area, to the edge of the lagoon near the house with the greenhouse. A major petroglyph is on a black bedrock face, visible when you are looking back toward the picnic area, and the traps are just offshore from there. Please be sensitive to the delicate artifacts so they can last another 2,000 years.

RAVEN TRAIL & RAVEN'S ROOST CABIN   About 4 miles up the steep but spectacular Raven Trail, which begins behind the airport off Haugen Drive roughly a mile from town, the Raven's Roost Forest Service cabin sits atop a mountain with a sweeping view of the town and surrounding waters and islands. It's the sort of place that inspires artists and poets. Allow 3 to 4 hours for the climb along a boardwalk, then up a steep muddy slope, then along a ridge, with an elevation gain of over 1,000 feet. It's possible to continue hiking over the steep, subalpine terrain of the Twin Ridge Ski Trail another 5 miles to the Twin Creek Road, and then get a ride 11 miles back to town. Check with the visitor center for trail conditions. You'll need sleeping bags, cooking gear, lights, and food. Reserve the cabin through the national system described in section 1 of this chapter, "Getting Outside in the Tongass National Forest," and check there for information sources on the other 19 cabins in the area, most of which are reached by plane or boat.

MITKOF ISLAND   The Mitkof Highway, leading south from Petersburg, opens access to most of Mitkof Island, with its king salmon fishing; views of swans, fish, and glaciers; salmon hatchery; hiking trails; lakes; and many miles of remote roads for mountain biking. The town's swimming hole and ice-skating pond are out the road, too. Anyone can enjoy a day's sightseeing drive over the island, and if you like hiking and the outdoors, you'll find days of fun. Pick up the $4 *Forest Service Mitkof Island Road Guide* map at the visitor center or ranger office; it shows what you'll find along the way.

The **Three Lakes Loop Road** intersects with the highway twice, once 10 miles from Petersburg and again 20 miles from town. From the north intersection, the one closest to town, it's 15 more miles to the level, 4.5-mile boardwalk **Three Lakes Trail,** which circles four small lakes, each of which contains trout, and three of which have Forest Service rowboats for public use. Besides the fish, it's a place of abundant wildflowers and berries, where you may see deer, beavers, bear, and many birds, including seasonal sandhill cranes.

Fourteen miles down Mitkof Highway from Petersburg, a quarter-mile wheelchair accessible boardwalk leads across the damp, hummocky ground of the rainforest muskeg to **Blind River Rapids,** a peaceful spot with a three-sided shelter where you can watch and fish for king salmon in June and silvers in September, and sometimes see eagles and bears feeding on the fish. A mile-long loop leads farther into the forest and muskeg.

At 17 miles, somewhat hidden in the trees on the right, a bird-watching blind looks out on **Blind Slough,** where trumpeter swans winter. Swans normally will be gone by mid-March.

At 18 miles, at the end of the pavement, you'll reach the **Blind Slough Recreation Area,** where locals go to swim in amber water in the summer. Water warms in the narrow slough, more than 5 miles from Wrangell Narrows. In the winter much of the town congregates here for ice-skating and bonfires.

At 20½ miles from Petersburg, the popular **Man Made Hole** picnic area and swimming pond is newly improved with foot bridges and a pathway; it is accessible to people with disabilities.

At 22 miles you reach the **Ohmer Creek campground,** with a 1-mile trail, a floating bridge over a beaver pond, and access to king salmon in June and July and trout and some salmon in late summer. The road continues from here along the south shore of Mitkof Island, with great ocean views, to its end at mile 32.

PETERSBURG CREEK   The lovely, grassy Petersburg Creek area could offer either an afternoon frolic among the meadows of wildflowers that meet the

Travel Tip: He who finds the best hotel deal has more to spend on facials involving knobbly vegetables.

Hello, the Roaming Gnome here. I've been nabbed from the garden and taken round the world. The people who took me are so terribly clever. They find the best offerings on Travelocity. For very little cha-ching. And that means I get to be pampered and exfoliated till I'm pink as a bunny's doodah.

travelocity®

1-888-TRAVELOCITY / travelocity.com / America Online Keyword: Travel

Plan your vacation

- flights, hotels, car rentals
- cruises & vacation packages
- destination guides
- fare alerts
- go to yahoo.com, click travel

DO YOU YAHOO!?

(Finds Takeout Lunch & Take-home Fish

Stop in at **Coastal Cold Storage,** at Excel Street and Nordic Drive ((C) **907/ 772-4177),** where they sell seafood from freezers and live from tanks. They'll freeze and ship seafood home for you. It's also a good shop for burgers, sandwiches, fish specials, and ice-cream cones at the counter.

---

water, or could be the start to a challenging 21-mile, multiday hike into the **Petersburg Creek-Duncan Salt Chuck Wilderness.** The fishing is exceptional. You'll need a skiff or sea kayak, or get a charter to drop you off, as the creek is on Kupreanof Island, across Wrangell Narrows from town; the state maintains a dock there. **Guided sea-kayak day trips** go up the creek (see "Sea Kayaking," below), which contains four species of salmon and two of trout. The trail is maintained by the Forest Service and has miles of boardwalks and two cabins, one at Petersburg Lake and one at East Salt Chuck, each with a boat for public use (reservations are required). Petersburg Lake has trout, and odds are good you'll see ducks, geese, loons, trumpeter swans, bald eagles, and black bears. The Kupreanof dock also provides access to the 3-mile, 3,000-foot trail that climbs Petersburg Mountain, a challenging hike that has spectacular views from the top.

ACTIVITIES

FISHING   There are many fishing streams and lakes that you can reach on the roads—several are mentioned above, under "Mitkof Island." For more choices, check at the visitor center, or contact the **Alaska Department of Fish and Game** ((C) 907/772-3801; www.alaska.gov/adfg). They produce an informative *Petersburg/Wrangell Sport Fishing Guide,* available on paper or on the website (click on "Sport Fishing," then the southeast region).

The boat harbor has a couple dozen licensed charter fishing boats, mostly six-passenger vessels. As elsewhere, halibut and salmon are usually the target. You can get a list of operators at the visitor center, or book through **Viking Travel** (see "Visitor Information," earlier). Half day salmon charters cost around $175 per person, while halibut charters or longer salmon charters are around $210.

SEA KAYAKING   The waters of Wrangell Narrows are protected and interesting, with plenty to see. On longer trips of 3 days to a week, you can get out among the glaciers, Stikine River Delta, and even the whales—there's as much variety here, among these rainforest islands, as anywhere in the region. It's possible to set up a kayak trip linking some of the Forest Service cabins, too, or to use one as a base camp for a few days of exploration. **Tongass Kayak Adventures** ((C) 907/772-4600; www.tongasskayak.com) offers guided and unguided versions of each of these adventures (they rent equipment, too). Their 4-hour paddle crosses Wrangell Narrows from the harbor and penetrates Petersburg Creek, where they stop for a snack and often see bear and deer. No experience is required; they charge $70. A 3-night base camp tour costs $790 per person; an 8-night version begins at $1,390.

WHALE-WATCHING   Most summers, **Frederick Sound** is one of the best places in the state to see humpbacks feeding. Whale-watching charters can go any day from May 15 to September 15, but the height is July and August. You may see stunning bubble-net feeding, when the whales confine a school of fish in a circle of bubbles, then lunge upward to scoop them up, bursting through the surface in a great swoosh. Whales have even been known to spy hop, poking their heads as high above the surface as possible in order to look down into the boats that are watching them. In summer 1995, a humpback jumped right into one of these boats, presumably accidentally. (No one was injured, but a few people fell into the water.) Several charter operators offer trips in small, six-passenger boats. Some, including **Kaleidoscope Cruises** (p. 119), have hydrophones on board, so you may be able to hear the whales' vocalizations while waiting for them to surface, if their feeding behavior and the water conditions are right. Book trips through Viking Travel or directly with one of the operators. Trips usually leave around 8am and stay out 6 to 10 hours, with several hours among the whales. Prices are $135 to $185 per person.

WHERE TO STAY

Bumbershoot Bed & Breakfast ★ *Finds*   The industrious Gloria Ohmer, who also owns the Tides Inn Motel (see below), has opened her extraordinary waterfront home on Frederick Sound to guests as well. The rooms are large, decorated with quilts she made. Gloria and her husband, Don Koenigs, also will share their beadwork, woodwork, sewing, stained glass, stone cutting and engraving, music room, fish-cleaning room, and deck barbecue with you. It's hard to come away without gaining a little of their enthusiasm for life. Some rooms have water views, and the water is only barely beyond your reach. For $160 a night, you can rent the entire downstairs apartment, with two rooms, a kitchen, and a large living room with a fireplace. They also lend bicycles, offer free use of the laundry machines, and arrange transportation from the ferry dock or airport.

901 Sandy Beach Rd. (P.O. Box 372), Petersburg, AK 99833. © **907/772-4683.** Fax 907/772-4627. glohmer@pobox.aptalaska.net. 4 units, 2 with shared bathroom. $80–$90 double. Rates include continental breakfast. No credit cards. **Amenities:** Free bicycle loan; courtesy car; free laundry machines. *In room:* TV/VCR, hair dryer, iron.

Scandia House ★★   Rebuilt in the town's distinctive Norwegian style, this building's solid simplicity puts it in a class by itself. White rooms with blonde-wood trim are blessed with natural light. You have a choice: front rooms with king-size beds, rooms with kitchenettes, twin-bedded rooms, or a magnificent fourth-floor suite with towering ceilings. Most rooms have only one bed and a few have shower stalls, not tubs. Book well in advance for the busy summer season. The owners offer skiff rentals and car rentals.

110 Nordic Dr. (P.O. Box 689), Petersburg, AK 99833. © **800/722-5006** or 907/772-4281. Fax 907/772-4301. scandia@alaska.net. 33 units. $90–$110 double, $130 double with kitchenette; $185 suite. Extra person over age 12 $10. Rates include continental breakfast. AE, DC, DISC, MC, V. **Amenities:** Car rental; courtesy van. *In room:* TV.

Tides Inn Motel ★ *Value*   Few hotels in Alaska have such good rooms at such affordable prices. The kitchenette rooms, which rent for the same rate as the standard rooms, are an incredible bargain. The biggest difference among the rooms is the views, as all have been recently upgraded. Those in the older part of the motel face the other building, while nonsmoking units in the front of the new section get a sweeping view. I watched bald eagles doing aerobatics less than 50 feet from my front window. The management is efficient and committed to quality, and they keep the motel in clean, attractive condition. The hotel has an Avis car-rental franchise and serves a continental breakfast in the lobby.

307 N. 1st St. (P.O. Box 1048), Petersburg, AK 99833. © 800/665-8433 or 907/772-4288. Fax 907/772-4286. tidesinn@alaska.net. $85 double. Extra person $10. Rates include continental breakfast. AE, DC, DISC, MC, V. **Amenities:** Car rental; courtesy van. *In room:* TV.

Waterfront Bed & Breakfast   This building, designed as a bed-and-breakfast as well as a family home, sits on pilings over the Wrangell Narrows near the ferry dock. Rooms are decorated with Mission-style oak furniture and down comforters; they have shower stalls, not tubs. Four of the rooms have one bed—two with a queen and two with a double—and one has two double beds. The rate is the same no matter how many people stay in the room. They'll drive guests to or from the airport or harbor with prior arrangements, or give you a lift in a boat to a hiking or fishing site. The family even cooks seafood dinners for those who make arrangements. Smoking is allowed only on the large new deck.

1004 S. Nordic Dr. (P.O. Box 1613), Petersburg, AK 99833. © 866/772-9300 or 907/772-9300. Fax 907/772-9308. www.waterfrontbedandbreakfast.com. 5 units. $95–$105 per room. Rates include full breakfast. MC, V. **Amenities:** Covered outdoor Jacuzzi; free laundry machines.

Water's Edge Bed & Breakfast ★ *(Finds)*   Barry and Kathy Bracken's house sits right on the beach on Frederick Sound, about 2 miles from town center, with a creek running next to one room. You can sit in the large common room and watch waterfowl through big windows, or borrow the canoe for a paddle along the shore. Probably the best thing to do here is to book a package combining a stay at the B&B and an excursion on Barry's 28-foot boat. A marine biologist, he leads natural history glacier- and whale-watching excursions. His knowledge of the area is deep and his enthusiasm infectious. Book well ahead, as it's a rare and popular opportunity. No smoking is permitted.

705 Sandy Beach Rd. (P.O. Box 1201), Petersburg, AK 99833. © 800/TO-THE-SEA (800/868-4373) or phone/fax 907/772-3736. www.alaska.net/~bbsea. 2 units. High season $100 double; low season $70 double. Extra person $10. 2-night minimum stay. Rates include continental breakfast. No credit cards. No children under 12. **Amenities:** Free canoe and bike loan; courtesy car; free laundry machines; kitchenette. *In room:* Hair dryer.

A HOSTEL & CAMPING

Friendly little **Petersburg Bunk and Breakfast Hostel,** at 805 Gjoa St. (© **907/772-3632** or 907/723-5340; www.bunkandbreakfast.com), has male and female dorm rooms with four beds in each. The $25 nightly rate includes a continental breakfast, room tax, and Internet access. They're open regularly from May 15 to September 15; call for the winter schedule. Check in and office hours are 8 to 10am and 5 to 8pm.

The closest natural camping is found 22 miles out the Mitkof Highway at **Ohmer Creek** (see "Special Places: Mitkof Island," above). **Twin Creek RV Park** is 7½ miles out the highway (© **907/772-3244**), charging $20 for full hookups.

WHERE TO DINE

The lack of a really good restaurant is one of Petersburg's main drawbacks. There are some acceptable family restaurants typical of a small town, but that's about the best of it. For takeout pizza or calzone, try **Papa Bear's Pizza** (© **907/772-3727**), across from the ferry terminal, open Monday through Friday 8am to 9pm, Saturday noon to 8pm, and Sunday 3 to 8pm. It is one of the better bets in town. **Alaskafe,** upstairs at 306B N. Nordic, at the corner with Excel Street (© **907/772-JAVA**), is a pleasant place for lunch, with local art exhibits and indoor and outdoor dining areas. They're open Monday through Saturday from 8am to 3pm.

Joan Mei Restaurant ☆ CHINESE This would be my first choice for dinner. The whole family works together in a large, bright dining room, serving flaky egg rolls and entrees with vegetables that remain crisp and flavorful rather than being smothered or overcooked. The American food is better than elsewhere in town, too. Locals come here for a nice dinner out, and we saw many happy faces. They also have a karaoke room.

1103 S. Nordic, across from the ferry dock. ☏ 907/772-4222. Lunch $6.25–$13; dinner $8–$22. MC, V. Mon–Tues and Thurs–Fri 11am–9pm; Sat–Sun 7am–9pm. Closed mid-Jan to mid-Feb.

Northern Lights Restaurant SEAFOOD/DINER You couldn't find a much better site for a restaurant than this one, sitting on pilings in Hammer Slough, overlooking two boat harbors. Unfortunately, it seems to change hands every few years, and the food has been inconsistent. On our last visit, the prices were quite high for the quality, but that could change again.

203 Sing Lee Alley. ☏ 907/772-2900. Lunch $7–$11; dinner $13–$24. MC, V. Daily 6am-10pm.

5 Sitka: Rich Prize of Russian Conquest

If I could visit only one Alaska town, it would probably be Sitka.

Sitka preserves the Russian look of Alaska's initial European invasion and, more deeply, the story of the cultural conflict between Alaska Natives and the newcomers, and the Natives' resistance and ultimate accommodation to the new ways. Here, 18th-century Russian conquerors who had successfully enslaved Aleuts to the west met their match in battle against the rich, powerful, and sophisticated Tlingit. A visit to Sitka reveals the story of that war, and also the cultural blending that occurred in the uneasy peace that followed under the influence of the Russian Orthodox church—an influence that remained even after the Russians sold Alaska to the U.S. in 1867 (that exchange also happened here), and that continues today.

Sitka's history is Alaska's richest, and there's more of real interest in this town than any other you might visit. The fact is, most Alaska towns haven't been on the map long enough to have accumulated much history. Those that have been around for a while often have been wiped out a time or two, leaving little to remind you of the distant past. There's usually a small museum and a few gold rush sites that can be seen in half a day. Not so in Sitka. Historic photographs bear a surprising resemblance to today's city. The National Park Service protects buildings and grounds of major historic significance—places where the pioneers spoke Russian, with ways much more European than those of the rest of the American West. Even a superficial exploration of the attractions takes a day, and that's without time for the out-of-the way points of interest or the outdoors.

In 1799, the Russians chose these protected waters on Sitka Sound, on the ocean side of Baranof Island, for a new fort as part of a strategy of pushing their sea otter hunting operations and territorial claims east and south along the west coast of North America. The Tlingit understandably considered this to be an invasion and in 1802 they attacked the Russian's redoubt and killed almost everyone inside. The Russians counterattacked in 1804 with the cannons of the ship *Neva* and a swarm of Aleut warriors, eventually forcing the Tlingit battle leader, Katlian, to withdraw. But the Russians never rested easy in their new capital, named New Archangel, and the hostility of the proud and dangerous

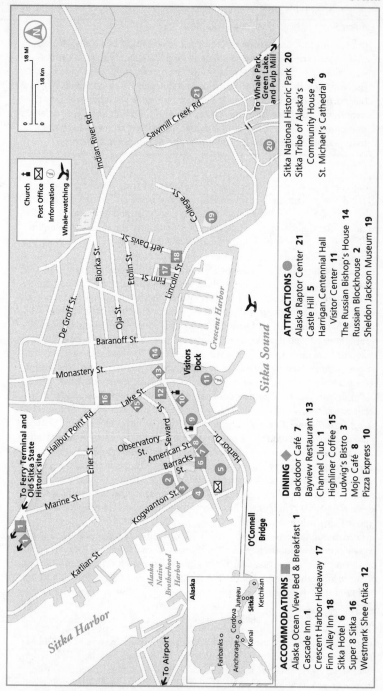

Sitka

ACCOMMODATIONS
Alaska Ocean View Bed & Breakfast **1**
Cascade Inn **1**
Crescent Harbor Hideaway **17**
Finn Alley Inn **18**
Sitka Hotel **6**
Super 8 Sitka **16**
Westmark Shee Atika **12**

DINING ◆
Backdoor Café **7**
Bayview Restaurant **13**
Channel Club **1**
Highliner Coffee **15**
Ludwig's Bistro **3**
Mojo Café **8**
Pizza Express **10**

ATTRACTIONS ●
Alaska Raptor Center **21**
Castle Hill **5**
Harrigan Centennial Hall
  Visitor Center **11**
The Russian Bishop's House **14**
Russian Blockhouse **2**
Sheldon Jackson Museum **19**

Sitka National Historic Park **20**
Sitka Tribe of Alaska's
  Community House **4**
St. Michael's Cathedral **9**

Fun Fact Thank You. No, Thank *You.*

In 1867, Russia's Czar Alexander feared that he couldn't hold the unprofitable colony of Alaska and saw a political advantage in doing his American allies the favor of selling it to them. Ironically, the Americans thought they were doing Russia a favor by buying it. Congress balked at paying the $7 million price that Secretary of State William Seward had negotiated for this worthless waste, relenting more than a year later partly out of fear of offending the czar. Americans didn't change their dim view of "Seward's Folly" until gold discoveries decades later.

Tlingit long remained. Some Russian laborers intermarried and essentially adopted Tlingit culture, but the bureaucrats and naval officers sent to run the colony for the czar tended to view Alaska as purgatory and left as soon as they could. Under their ineffective and uninterested control the Russians made surprisingly little impression on the great mass of Alaska. They failed to explore the Interior and held only tenuous control of the vast coastline.

The departing Russians rushed home, leaving only three significant towns—Unalaska, Kodiak, and Sitka—of which only Sitka retains more than a single Russian building. During their century of rule the Russians had nearly wiped out the sea otter and the culture of the Aleuts, but both would eventually bounce back. The Russian Orthodox church stood as Russia's only lasting cultural gift to Alaska. Thanks to the efforts of one extraordinary cleric, Bishop Innocent Veniaminov, Alaska Natives were able to worship in their own languages, winning for the Russian Orthodox church many villages' continuing loyalty over less tolerant Protestant churches that came under American rule.

Besides its historic significance, Sitka also is fun to visit. Somehow it has retained a friendly, authentic feel, despite the crush of thousands of visitors. Perhaps because cruise-ship travelers must ride shuttle boats to shore, or because Sitka is a slightly inconvenient, out-of-the-way stop on the Alaska Marine Highway's main-line ferry routes, the city's streets haven't been choked by solid rows of seasonal gift shops, as has occurred in Ketchikan, Skagway, and a large part of Juneau. It remains picturesque, facing Sitka Sound, which is dotted with islands and populated by feeding eagles. Tourism is important here, but Sitka's own residents remain the center of the business and cultural world. The process of being "spoiled" hasn't begun.

Even beyond the town and its rich history, Sitka is a gateway to a large, remote portion of Southeast Alaska, in the western coastal islands. This area contains some of Tongass National Forest's least-used outdoor opportunities. The ocean halibut and salmon fishing are excellent and not overexploited, and the bird- and wildlife-watching is exceptional.

ESSENTIALS

GETTING THERE Sitka sits on the west side of Baranof Island, a detour from the Inside Passage for the **Alaska Marine Highway System** (© **800/642-0066;** www.ferryalaska.com). It receives visits from some big, main-line ferries, twice weekly from the fast ferry *Fairweather,* and often from the little *LeConte,* which is like a local bus, stopping at all the little villages, and giving visitors an insight into their island lifestyle. The *Fairweather* cuts a 9-hour journey from

Juneau to less than five, but runs only twice a week. On any of the ships, the ride through narrow Peril Straits into Sitka is definitely worth the trip. The shore seems close enough to touch, and if you look closely you can sometimes see deer. The fare on the conventional ferry from either Juneau or Petersburg (10 hours away) is $37. The *Fairweather* is $41 to Juneau. The ferry dock (© **907/747-3300**) is 7 miles out of town.

Alaska Airlines (© **800/252-7522;** www.alaskaair.com) links Sitka daily to Juneau and Ketchikan with flights that then continue nonstop to Seattle and Anchorage.

To get to town from the airport or ferry dock, the **Sitka Tours bus** charges $5 one-way, $7 round-trip. No reservations are needed, just climb aboard and pay the driver.

Sitka Cab is at © **907/747-5001;** the ride from the ferry dock is around $15.

VISITOR INFORMATION   A kiosk in the city-operated **Harrigan Centennial Hall Visitor Center,** 330 Harbor Dr., next to the Crescent Boat Harbor (© **907/747-3225**), is the only walk-in information stop. It is staffed by volunteers only when cruise ships are in town, although you may be able to ask questions of hall staff other times. The hall is open Monday through Friday from 8am to 10pm, Saturday 8am to 5pm, and sometimes Sunday. The town's professional visitor organization is the **Sitka Convention and Visitors Bureau,** at P.O. Box 1226, Sitka, AK 99835 (© **907/747-5940;** fax 907/747-3739). They maintain a very useful website at **www.sitka.org.**

The **Sitka National Historic Park Visitor Center,** 106 Metlakatla St., Sitka, AK 99835 (© **907/747-0110;** www.nps.gov/sitk), run by the National Park Service, which maintains the key historic sites in Sitka, is an essential stop to gather information and learn about what happened here. The "Historic Sites of Sitka" map produced by the park service and Sitka Historical Society is an indispensable guide to the buildings and parks around town. You can easily see Sitka's history on foot with one of these maps. The center is open daily from 8am to 5pm in summer, Monday through Saturday from 8am to 5pm in winter. Also see "Exploring Sitka," below, for more on the park.

ORIENTATION   Sitka, on the west side of Baranof Island, has only a few miles of road. The **ferry terminal** is located at its north end, 7 miles out, on **Halibut Point Road;** the site of an abandoned pulp mill is at the south end, roughly the same distance out **Sawmill Creek Road.** The town faces Sitka Sound. Across Sitka Channel is **Japonski Island,** with the **airport** (don't worry, it only looks as if your plane is going to land in the water). **Lincoln Street** contains most of the tourist attractions.

GETTING AROUND   The airport has branches of **Avis** (© **800/230-4898** or 907/966-2264; www.avis.com) and **North Star Rent-a-Car** (© **800/722-6927** or 907/966-2552; www.ptialaska.net/~rfahey).

The Visitor Transit Bus operated by the **Sitka Tribe** (see "Exploring Sitka," below) makes a continuous circuit of the sites from May to September, Monday through Friday from 12:30 to 4:30pm, with added morning hours when cruise ships are in. The fare is $7 all day or $5 one-way.

Bike rental makes a good deal of sense in Sitka. **Yellow Jersey Cycles,** at 329 Harbor Dr., right across from the Centennial Hall downtown, (© **907/747-6317;** www.yellowjerseycycles.com), rents quality bikes for $25 a day.

FAST FACTS: Sitka

Banks Three banks are at the center of downtown, around 300 Lincoln St., with ATMs, which are also found at local grocery stores.

Hospital **Sitka Community** (℃ **907/747-3241**) is at 209 Moller Dr.

Internet Access Try **Highliner Coffee,** on Lake Street near Seward Street (℃ **907/747-4924**), or at the downtown post office.

Police Call ℃ **907/747-3245** for nonemergency business.

Post Office At 338 Lincoln St.; it is open Saturday.

Taxes Sales tax is 5% October through March, 6% April through September. The tax on rooms totals 11%.

SPECIAL EVENTS   The **Starring Ceremony,** January 7, marks Russian Orthodox Christmas with a procession through the streets and song and prayer at the doors of the faithful. Call St. Michael's Cathedral for information (℃ **907/747-8120** or 907/747-3560 voice message).

The **Sitka Salmon Derby** occurs at the end of May and beginning of June, when the kings are running; contact the Sitka Sportsman's Association (℃ **907/ 747-8791**) for information.

The **Sitka Summer Music Festival,** a chamber-music series that began in 1972, is one of Alaska's most important cultural events, drawing musicians from all over the world in for three weeks in early summer (June 3–24, 2005). Performances take place Tuesdays and Fridays, and other events all week. Contact the festival office for information (℃ **907/277-4852;** www.sitkamusicfestival. org).

Alaska Day, October 18, commemorating the Alaska Purchase, is a big deal in this former Russian capital city; the **Alaska Day Festival** lasts 4 days leading up to the big event. The Convention and Visitors Bureau has information. The **Sitka Grind,** a music and arts celebration at varying sites around town, takes place the third Saturday of each month from October to March.

The **Sitka WhaleFest** (℃ **907/747-7964;** www.sitkawhalefest.org) takes place over a weekend in early November, during the fall and early winter period when humpback whales congregate in Sitka Sound. Internationally known experts present a three-day symposium, and there are whale-watching tours, concerts, an art show, a run, and community events. Consider combining it with the Alaska Bald Eagle Festival in Haines, coordinated to follow (see section 9 of this chapter, on Haines).

EXPLORING SITKA

The **Sitka Tribe of Alaska**'s Community House is a good starting point, where you can watch dance performances (see below), join walking or bus tours, or sign up for kayaking or other outdoor activities, including trail hikes. A 2-hour walking tour includes the town, national historic park, and a marine science facility at Sheldon Jackson College. The house is at 200 Katlian St. (℃ **888/ 270-8687** or 907/747-7290; www.sitkatribe.org). **Sitka Tours** (℃ **907/747-8443**) also offers tours, taking more of the Russian perspective. On days when cruise ships are in town you can combine their tours with a Russian folk dance performance by the **New Archangel Dancers** (℃ **907/747-5516**) in the Harrigan Centennial Hall at 330 Harbor Dr., next to the Crescent Boat Harbor.

Prices for each choice of tour range from about $10 for a brief downtown tour to $42 for a longer town tour that includes most of the attractions and dancing; the type of dancing—Native or Russian—depends on which firm you go with.

SITKA'S TLINGIT & RUSSIAN HERITAGE

Sitka National Historical Park ★★★   In 1799, the Russian America Company, led by Alexander Baranof, landed from their base in Kodiak, established Redoubt St. Michael (today the **Old Sitka State Historic Site**, 7½ miles north of town—just a grassy picnic area with interpretive signs), and claimed the Pacific Northwest of America for Russia. The Tlingit, who were sophisticated traders and already had acquired flintlocks, attacked with knives, spears, and guns, and destroyed the redoubt in mid-June 1802, killing almost all of the Russians. The Natives immediately began building fortifications on the site now within the national historical park, anticipating a Russian counterattack, which came in 1804. Baranof returned with an attacking force of a Russian gunship and a swarm of Aleut kayaks, which towed the becalmed vessel into position to begin the bombardment. The Tlingits withstood the siege for 6 days, then vacated their fort at night after a canoe delivering gunpowder exploded, leaving them short of ammunition. The Russians founded and heavily fortified the town of New Archangel, and in 1808 it became their administrative capital. But the Tlingit name is the one that stuck: Shee Atika, since contracted to Sitka.

The historic significance of the battle site was recognized early. Pres. Benjamin Harrison, a friend of Alaska missionary Sheldon Jackson, set the land aside as a public park in 1890. In 1902 and 1905, a collection of totem poles from around Southeast was brought here, and in 1910 the site was designated a national monument. The park visitor center and grounds emphasize the Native perspective. There is no better place to learn about Tlingit art and history. A naturally lit hall with a 30-foot ceiling displays the original poles (reproductions stand outside) in startlingly good condition despite their age. The artistic power of these poles is overwhelming, and their age and critical value for the Tlingit culture only adds to the impact. Moreover, the art still lives. Extraordinary poles by current Tlingit artists stand outside, and within the building artisans of the Southeast Alaska Indian Cultural Center work in a series of windowed workshops creating traditional crafts of metal, wood, beads, textiles, and woven grass. Visitors are invited to enter the workshops and ask questions. A free 12-minute video provides a good historical overview.

The outdoor totem park and the site of the battle and of the fort also must not be missed. The totems stand tall and forbidding along a pathway through massive spruce and hemlock, where misty rain often wanders down from an unseen sky somewhere above the trees. The shoreside battle site and the nearby fort—only a grassy area now—are along the trail. While plenty of imagination is needed to place a desperate fight in this peaceful setting, it is easy to feel deep down what the Tlingits were fighting for when you stand among the trees and totems and hear the lapping sea and raven's call.

Though they lost the battle for this ground, the Tlingit won the war—they're still here. In 1996, a gathering of clans erected a major new pole in front of the center to explain their story back to mankind's arrival in North America. It took quite a bit of debate to settle the story the pole would tell. For example, the crests of the eagle and raven tribal moieties are traditionally never shown on the same pole, but they had to be to tell the whole history of the Tlingits. In 1999, another new pole rose at the site of the battle to commemorate that story. At the bottom of the pole is a carving of the raven helmet worn by Katlian, the

Tlingit's leader in the battle of Sitka. You can see the helmet itself in the Sheldon Jackson Museum (see below). Contrary to the popular phrase "low man on the totem pole," the position shows the strength with which Katlian led and supported his people.

106 Metlakatla St. © **907/747-6281**. Admission $3. Visitor center open summer daily 8am–5pm; winter Mon–Sat 8am–5pm. Park open summer daily 6am–10pm, winter daily 7am–8pm.

The Russian Bishop's House ★★★   Bishop Innocent Veniaminov, born in 1797, translated scriptures into Tlingit and other Native languages and trained deacons to carry Russian Orthodoxy back to their Native villages. Unlike most of the later Protestant missionaries led by Sitka's other historic religious figure, Sheldon Jackson, Veniaminov and his followers allowed parishioners to use their own language, a key element to saving Native cultures. When the United States bought Alaska in 1867, few Russians remained, but thanks to Veniaminov's work, the Russian Orthodox faith remains strong in Native Alaska; today there are 89 parishes, primarily in tiny Native villages. In 1977, Veniaminov was canonized as St. Innocent in the Orthodox faith.

In 1842, the Russian America Company assigned Finnish shipbuilders to construct this extraordinary house for Veniaminov as a residence, school, and chapel. It may have survived many years of neglect in part because its huge beams fit together like a ship's. In 1972, the National Park Service bought and began restoring the building, which is the best of only three surviving from all of Russian America (the others are in Kodiak and at 206 Lincoln St. in Sitka, today occupied by the Log Cache Gifts). The Bishop's House is Alaska's most interesting historic site. Downstairs is a self-guided museum; upstairs, the bishop's quarters are furnished with original and period pieces. It's an extraordinary window into an alternate stream of American history, from a time before the founding of Seattle or San Francisco when Sitka was the most important city on North America's Pacific Coast. The tour concludes with a visit to a beautiful little chapel with many of the original icons Innocent brought from Russia.

Lincoln and Monastery sts. No phone; call Sitka National Historical Park Visitor Center (© **907/747-0110**). Admission $3 per person or $15 per family (family admission covers both facilities). Summer daily 9am–5pm; by appointment in winter.

Sheldon Jackson Museum ★★   Sheldon Jackson, a Presbyterian missionary with powerful friends in Washington, was Alaska's first General Agent for Education, a paternal guardian of the welfare, schooling, and spiritual lives of Alaska's Natives. His benevolent aim was to defend Natives from exploitation and abuse and bring them into American civilization as equals. Tragically, his strategy to accomplish this goal was to erase indigenous cultures and replace them with Protestantism, causing incalculable, lasting harm to peoples over a broad swath of Alaska. As a side hobby during his travels from 1888 to 1898, Jackson gathered an omnivorous 5,000-piece collection of Native art, including cultural and everyday objects. That collection, the best in Alaska, has been displayed for more than a century in a concrete building on the college campus that bears Jackson's name. It's a jewel box; the overwhelming wealth is displayed by Alaska state museum curators in ingenious ways that avoids a feeling of clutter. Many drawers open to reveal more displays. Despite the age of many of the pieces, they appear new, as if just made. Don't miss Katlian's helmet, worn by the Kiksadi clan's war leader in the Battle of Sitka in 1804; raven-shaped, it is that rare piece of great history that's also great art. Native artists demonstrate their skill on summer days, and the gift shop contains almost exclusively authentic Native arts and crafts. Authentic Native art pieces cost more than tourist trinkets: plan to spend over $100 except for small, simple items.

104 College Dr. © 907/747-8981. www.museums.state.ak.us. Admission $4 adults, free for ages 18 and under. Mid-May to mid-Sept daily 9am–5pm; mid-Sept to mid-May Tues–Sat 10am–4pm.

St. Michael's Cathedral ★   The first Orthodox cathedral in the New World stands grandly in the middle of Sitka's principal street, where it was completed in 1848. Bishop Veniaminov (see "The Russian Bishop's House," above) designed it and oversaw construction. The cathedral contains several miraculous icons, some dating from the 17th century. The St. Michael, the farthest right of six on the front screen, was bound for Sitka aboard the *Neva* in 1813 when the ship went down some 30 miles from Sitka. Thirty days later the icon, in its crate, washed ashore undamaged and was recovered by Sitka's townspeople. The original building burned down in a 1966 fire that started elsewhere and took much of Sitka's downtown, but almost all the contents were saved by a human chain in the 30 minutes before the building was destroyed. One man lifted down the huge central chandelier, which later took six men to carry. Orthodox Christians all over the United States raised the money to rebuild the cathedral exactly as it had been, using a Russian architect who could interpret Veniaminov's original plans. It was completed in 1976. A knowledgeable guide is on hand to answer questions or give talks when large groups congregate. Sunday services are sung in English, Church Slavonic, Tlingit, Aleut, and Yupik. Right across Lincoln Street stop in at the cathedral's well-stocked Archangel Michael Icons, Books and Gift Shop for souvenirs, music CDs, books, and even children's books.

Lincoln and Cathedral sts. © **907/747-8120**. $2 donation requested. Summer Mon–Fri 9am–4pm. Call for weekend and winter hours.

Sitka Tribe Dance Performances ★   The Sheet'ka Kwaan Naā Kahidi, Sitka's community house, standing on the north side of the downtown parade ground, is a modern version of a Tlingit Clan House, with an air handling system that pulls smoke from the central fire pit straight up to the chimney. The magnificent house screen at the front of the hall, installed in 2000, is the largest in the Pacific Northwest. Performances last 30 minutes, including three dances and a story. It's entirely traditional and put on by members of the tribe. You can also sign up for tours and activities in the lobby.

200 Katlian St. © **888/270-8687** or 907/747-7290. www.sitkatribe.org. $7 adults, $5 children. Call for times.

OTHER ATTRACTIONS IN TOWN

Alaska Raptor Center ★★   This nonprofit center takes in injured birds of prey (mainly bald eagles, but also owls, hawks, and other species) for veterinary treatment and release or, if too badly injured, for placement in a zoo or as part of the collection of 25 that live on-site. Visitors get to see the impressive birds up close in a lecture setting, through the glass wall of the veterinary clinic, and in outdoor enclosures, but the highlight is an extraordinary flight-training center, built in 2003 at a cost of $3 million. This enormous aviary is where recuperating birds learn to fly again, and visitors can walk its length behind one-way glass watching them preen, feed, and take to the air in a peaceful setting simulating their natural habitat. Seeing these giant birds fly from so close is awesome. The center's grounds also include a pleasant, disabled-accessible nature trail that leads down to a river with four species of salmon, where healthy eagles sometimes can be seen feeding.

1000 Raptor Way (off Sawmill Creek Blvd.) © 800/643-9425 or 907/747-8662. www.alaskaraptor.org. $12 adults, $6 ages 12 and under. Summer daily 8am–4pm. Winter call for hours.

WALKING DOWNTOWN   The grassy park at Lincoln and Katlian was the site of the Russians' barracks and parade ground. Just north on Marine Street is a replica of a **Russian Blockhouse;** across Lincoln Street to the south and up the stairs is **Castle Hill,** a site of historic significance for the ancient Tlingits, for the Russians, and for Native Alaskans. The first American flag raised in Alaska was hoisted here in 1867. There are historic markers and cannons. As you walk east past the cathedral and Crescent Harbor, several quaint historic buildings are on the left. My favorite is **St. Peter's by-the-Sea Episcopal Church,** a lovely stone-and-timber chapel with a pipe organ, consecrated in 1899. At the east end of the harbor is a **public playground;** turn left, uphill on Jeff Davis Street (named for the first commander of the Alaska garrison, not the Confederate president) past **Sheldon Jackson College** to the Sitka National Cemetery, which has some old and interesting graves.

SHOPPING

There are some good shops and galleries in Sitka, mostly on Lincoln and Harbor streets. Several are across the street from St. Michael's Cathedral. **Fishermen's Eye Fine Art Gallery and Graphic,** at 239 Lincoln St. (www.fishermens eye.com), is owned by an artist who shows only work by Alaskans, most of it created in Sitka. **Fairweather Prints,** at 209 Lincoln St., has a fun, youthful feel; it is large and has a diverse selection, including wearable art (including T-shirts), watercolors, prints, ceramics, and cute, inexpensive crafts. Continue west on Lincoln to **Baranov's Russian and American Store** on the right, and, on the left, **Log Cache Gifts,** a typical gift store housed in an 1835 Russian cabin. **Old Harbor Books,** at 201 Lincoln St., is a good browsing store with an excellent selection of Alaska books. Back in the other direction, near the Crescent Harbor dock, the **Sitka Rose Gallery** occupies a Victorian house at 419 Lincoln St., featuring higher-end work, mostly local: sculpture, original paintings, engraving, and jewelry. The **Sheldon Jackson Museum Gift Shop,** 104 College Dr., is an excellent place to buy Alaska Native arts and crafts with assurance of their authenticity.

GETTING OUTSIDE: ON THE WATER

The little islands and rocks that dot Sitka Sound are an invitation to the sea otter in all of us; you must get out on the water.

SIGHTSEEING & WILDLIFE TOURS

When conditions allow, tour boats visit **St. Lazaria Island,** a bird rookery where you can expect to see tufted puffins, murres, rhinoceros auklets, and other pelagic birds. Storm petrels show up by the hundreds of thousands at dawn and dusk for those who charter a boat to stay overnight at the rookery. The volcanic rock drops straight down into deep water, so even big boats can come close, but in rough weather even they won't go to the exposed location of the island. Even then, there's plenty to see. Humpback whales show up in large groups in the fall and are often seen by the half dozen in the summer. There are so many bald eagles that you're pretty well guaranteed to see them even from shore. But the lowly sea otter is the most common and, in my experience, most amusing and endearing of marine mammals, and you'll certainly see them from a tour boat. The public tubs at **Goddard Hot Springs,** 17 miles south of town, are another possible stop for charters.

The **Sitka Wildlife Quest,** operated by Allen Marine Tours (© **888/747-8101** or 907/747-8100; www.allenmarinetours.com), runs a popular marine tour with well-trained naturalists to explain the wildlife. You have a good chance of encountering humpback whales and sea otters and tours visit St. Lazaria Island when sea conditions permit. A 2-hour cruise Tuesday and Thursday at 6pm costs $59 adults, $30 children. A 3-hour cruise Saturday and Sunday at 8:30am costs $79 adults, $40 children. The boat leaves from the Crescent Harbor Visitors Dock late May through early September. Buy tickets on board. These are different excursions from the ones offered cruise-ship passengers. Allen Marine is a remarkable home-grown success story, a Sitka boat building company that has grown to the point that they are now building new passenger ferries for use in New York Harbor.

For $100 per person, you can charter a six-passenger boat for a 3½-hour tour to St. Lazaria Island, for whale-watching, and to learn about the Sound with a married couple who are both former wildlife biologists, Kent Hall and Beverly Minn, at **Sitka's Secrets** (© **907/747-5089**; www.sitkasecret.com). They do fishing charters, too.

Sea Life Discovery Tours (© **877/966-2301** or 907/966-2301; www.sealife discoverytours.com) offers a chance to see the rich underwater life of Sitka Sound from an extraordinary boat with big windows 4 feet below the waterline; it's really cool. They charge $79 for a two-hour tour; call for times.

SALTWATER FISHING
Many charter boats are available for salmon or halibut. The Sitka Convention and Visitors Bureau (see "Visitor Information," earlier) keeps a detailed charter boat list, including rates, that goes on for pages.

Alaska Adventures Unlimited (© **907/747-5576**; akfish@gci.net.) is a booking agent handling more than half the charter boats in the harbor. They have been offering charters for more than 20 years.

If you can handle your own boat, skiffs rent for $85 half day and up from **Sitka Ocean Adventures** (© **907/747-6375**; www.ssoceanadventures.com).

SEA KAYAKING
Sitka's protected waters and intricate shorelines are perfect for sea kayaking. You're almost sure to see sea otters, seals, sea lions, and eagles, and could see whales. **Baidarka Boats** is a good place for serious kayakers to know about. Their well-stocked shop for sales, rentals, and guided tours is at 320 Seward St. (© **907/747-8996**; www.kayaksite.com). Their shortest guided paddle is a half day, allowing time for beachcombing, tide pooling, and snacks. The competitive rates depend on the size of your group.

GETTING OUTSIDE: ONSHORE
FRESHWATER FISHING
Anglers should pick up the *Sitka Area Sport Fishing Guide,* which has lots of tips on streams, lakes, and fishing methods in the area, which you can download from **Alaska Department of Fish and Game** at www.alaska.gov/adfg (click "Sport Fishing," then the southeast region). The site also has weekly fishing updates. The local Fish and Game office is at 304 Lake St., Room 103, Sitka, AK 99835 (© **907/747-5355**).

FOREST SERVICE CABINS
The **Sitka Ranger District,** 204 Siginaka Way, Sitka, AK 99835 (© **907/747-4220**; www.fs.fed.us/r10/tongass), maintains two dozen wilderness cabins on

Baranof, Chichagof, and Kruzof islands, in sea kayaking coves and on remote fishing lakes, where rowing skiffs generally are provided. The cabins and their facilities are described in a Forest Service handout or on their website.

You will need camping gear and a boat or floatplane to get there, a much greater cost than the nightly rental of $35 to $45. For cabins on salt water within 40 miles of Sitka, the most affordable way is via **Sitka Sound Water Taxi** (© **907/738-5970;** www.sitkawatertaxi.com). **Harris Aircraft Services,** 400 Airport Rd. (© **877/966-3050** Alaska only, or 907/966-3050; www.harrisair craft.com) offers floatplane charters to cabins or anywhere else. Either way, allow time in your schedule in case bad weather prevents backcountry travel. Information on researching and reserving a cabin is under "Getting Outside in the Tongass National Forest," in section 1 of this chapter. Another remote cabin option is the Camp Cougan Bay Hideaway, listed below, under "Rent A Floathouse."

HIKING

Already a great hiking area, Sitka is busily building more trails to thread all over the mountains behind the town. There are a dozen U.S. Forest Service hiking trails accessible from the roads around Sitka and another 20 rough trails you can get to by plane or boat. A handy map, the *Outdoor Recreation Guide,* shows all the road-accessible trails, including easy walks from downtown. Get it and advice from the ranger district (see the preceding paragraph).

From downtown, the 4-mile (one-way) **Indian River Trail** is a relaxing rain-forest walk rising gradually up the river valley to a small waterfall. Take Indian River Road off Sawmill Creek Road just east of the downtown. For a steeper mountain-climbing trail to alpine terrain and great views, the **Gavan Hill-Harbor Mountain Trail** is near the end of Baranof Street, which starts near the Russian Bishop's House. It gains 2,500 feet over 3 miles to the peak of Gavan Hill, then continues another 3 miles along a ridge to meet Harbor Mountain Road. The **Sitka Cross Trail** connects these trails and neighborhood streets, allowing you to start almost anywhere.

At the north end of Halibut Point Road, 7½ miles from downtown, several wonderful trails loop through the **Starrigavan Recreation Area.** On the right, the **Estuary Life Trail** and **Forest Muskeg Trail,** totaling about a mile, are exquisitely developed and accessible to anyone, circling a grassy estuary rich with birds and fish. The well-built **Mosquito Cove Trail,** starting from the far end of the campground loop on the left, loops 1.25 miles along the shore to the secluded gravel beach of the cove, returning over boardwalk steps through the old-growth forest. Camping here is covered below.

TIDE POOLING & SHORE WALKS

Halibut Point State Recreation Area, 4½ miles north of town on Halibut Point Road, is a great place for a picnic, shore ramble, and tide pooling. The Mosquito Cove Trail (above) is also promising. To find the best low tides, check a tide book, available all over town. It's best to go at the lowest tide possible, arriving on the shore an hour before the low. To identify the little creatures you'll see, buy a plastic-covered field guide at the National Park Service visitor center at the historical park (p. 129).

WHALE-WATCHING

Humpback whales stop to feed in Sitka Sound on their way south in the winter migration. During October, November, December, and March, you can watch from shore—the local government has even built a special park for the purpose.

At **Whale Park,** just south of town on Sawmill Creek Road, spotting scopes are mounted on platforms along a boardwalk and at the end of staircases that descend the dramatic, wooded cliffs. Excellent interpretive signs, located near surfacing concrete whales in the parking lot, explain the whales. The Sitka WhaleFest, in November (see "Special Events," earlier), is the best time for whale enthusiasts, as then you can watch whales in the company of cetacean scientists.

WHERE TO STAY

In addition to the places below, you'll find super-clean rooms with many amenities in a quiet building downtown at the **Super 8 Sitka,** 404 Sawmill Creek Blvd. (© **800/800-8000** for reservations, or 907/747-8804; www.super8.com). A nice single-unit B&B, **Finn Alley Inn** (© **907/747-3655;** www.ptialaska. net/~seakdist/finn.htm), is at 711 Lincoln St. Also, the **Sitka Convention and Visitors Bureau** (© **907/747-5940;** www.sitka.org) has links to many B&Bs on its website, and can send you a printed list as well.

Alaska Ocean View Bed & Breakfast ★★★ Ebullient Carole Denkinger and her husband, Bill, have a passion for making their bed-and-breakfast one you'll remember. They've thought of everything—the covered outdoor Jacuzzi where you can watch the eagles, toys and games for the kids, thick robes and slippers, an open snack counter, a big and delicious full breakfast, and even wildflower seeds to take home. Rooms are soft and plush and guests are pampered with unique extras such as DVD players and a media library, wireless Internet with the free loan of the card needed for your laptop, and HEPA air cleaners in each room for people with allergies. The hospitality is exceptional, too. For example, Carole has stocked her kitchen with Atkins-approved food for low-carb dieters and cooks special meals for those sensitive to gluten or lactose. The B&B is on a residential street with a view of the water about a mile from the historic district. No smoking is permitted.

1101 Edgecumbe Dr., Sitka, AK 99835. © 888/811-6870 or 907/747-8310. Fax 907/747-3440. www.sitka-alaska-lodging.com. 3 units. High season $119–$189 double, extra person $10–$30; low season $79–$129 double, extra person up to $30. Rates include full breakfast. AE, DC, DISC, MC, V. **Amenities:** Outdoor Jacuzzi; business center. In room: TV/VCR and DVD, dataport, fridge, coffeemaker, hair dryer, iron, microwave, CD player, free media library.

Cascade Inn ★ Two and a half miles from downtown, this family-operated waterfront hotel puts you in a trim standard room with a balcony over Sitka Sound and a spectacular view. The red building is fronted by gas pumps and a convenience store, but don't let that fool you. The rooms, although small, are an oasis of ocean light where you can fall asleep to the sound of the sea. Each has one or two queen-size beds, and some include handy kitchenette units, which cost $15 more. You can acquire food to cook or movies to watch at the convenience store. The sauna has a glass front to take advantage of the view. *Note:* Stay elsewhere if you have trouble with stairs, and plan on having wheels to get around.

2035 Halibut Point Rd., Sitka, AK 99835. © 800/532-0908 or 907/747-6804. www.cascadeinnsitka.com. 10 units. High season $115–$140 double, low season $85–$105 double. Extra person beyond 2 or 4 (depending on room) $10 each. AE, DISC, MC, V. **Amenities:** Sauna; coin-op laundry. In room: TV/VCR, coffeemaker, hair dryer, iron.

Crescent Harbor Hideaway ★ *Finds* This stately 1897 house, one of Sitka's oldest, stands across a quiet street from Crescent Harbor and the lovely park at the harbor's edge, with a glassed-in porch to watch the world go by. One unit is a large, one-bedroom apartment with a full kitchen, stocked with food and a private patio and phone line; it's the best unit I've seen in Sitka, cheery, bright, and utterly comfortable. The other unit nestles adorably under the eaves. The style is simple elegance, with antiques and colonial reproductions, Berber carpet, and attractive bathrooms. Everything is clean and fresh. Hostess Susan Stanford is an artist and makes friends of her guests, sometimes serving cookies in the afternoon. If you're very lucky, you might get to see her blow glass. The common areas are shared with an Australian shepherd named Lacy. No smoking is permitted, even outside.

709 Lincoln St., Sitka, AK 99835. ℂ/fax 907/747-4900. www.sitkabedandbreakfast.com. 2 units. High season $120–$150 double; low season $85–$115 double. Extra person $25. Rates include continental breakfast. No credit cards. *In room:* TV/VCR, kitchenette in 1 room, hair dryer.

Sitka Hotel *Value* This is a family-owned budget hotel. Each year the proprietors take on another improvement project in the 1939 building: on my last visit, they had installed free wireless Internet throughout and had a computer work station in a booth off the lobby. The small rooms will never be luxurious, and some were slightly faded, but the hotel has many comfortable, quirky units and the owners keep them quite clean. The location is prime, right across from the Russian parade grounds. Some rooms have shared bathrooms rather than private bathrooms, but there are only about four people to a shared bathroom and the facilities are in good shape. On one of our stays they were unable to reduce the heat in a top floor room, while other units were reportedly too cold—perhaps the price that is sometimes paid for staying in an old building with low room rates.

Victoria's Restaurant, with about a dozen tables in the storefront downstairs, tries, like the hotel, for a high Victorian feel, but in actuality it's more of a friendly small-town diner, with hearty breakfasts and lunches in winter and an inexpensive fine-dining dinner menu added in the summer.

118 Lincoln St., Sitka, AK 99835. ℂ 907/747-3288. Fax 907/747-8499. www.sitkahotel.com. 60 units, 45 with private bathroom. $60 double with shared bathroom, $80 double with private bathroom. Extra person $7. AE, MC, V. **Amenities:** Restaurant; bar; coin-op laundry. *In room:* TV.

Westmark Shee Atiká ★★ The community's main upscale hotel, above Crescent Harbor in the heart of the historic district, contains many comfortable rooms with sweeping views of Sitka Sound (you pay $10 more to be on the water side). The lobby suggests the building style of Northwest Native Americans, but the more anonymous rooms will be familiar to any business traveler, with furniture of warm wood and all the expected amenities. Service likewise comes with a professionalism you won't find elsewhere in town.

The **Raven Dining Room** restaurant shares the hotel's view and is one of the best places in town for an evening meal. It's quiet and somewhat refined and my service was careful and respectful. There's a long menu of seafood and beef in the evening and even the more challenging entrees are expertly prepared.

330 Seward St., Sitka, AK 99835-7523. ℂ 800/544-0970 for reservations, or 907/747-6241. Fax 907/747-5486. www.westmarkhotels.com. 101 units. High season $149–$159 double; low season $139–$149 double. Extra person over age 13 $15. AE, DC, DISC, MC, V. **Amenities:** Restaurant; bar; summer tour desk. *In room:* TV, high-speed Internet, coffeemaker, hair dryer, iron.

A HOSTEL & CAMPING

Hostelling International—Sitka is located at 303 Kimsham St., in the United Methodist Church (P.O. Box 2645, Sitka, AK 99835; ℂ **907/747-8661**), more than a mile from downtown. The 18 beds are $13 per night for members, $16

Finds **Rent a Floathouse**

Southeast Alaska has a unique kind of dwelling called a floathouse, a house on a barge, permanently anchored in some quiet, forgotten cove. There have even been float-towns, with houses, schools, and other buildings tied together, usually at remote logging sites. **Camp Coogan Bay Hideaway** (© 907/747-6375; www.ssoceanadventures. com) is a floathouse you can rent. It floats in a narrow, placid bay out of a wilderness fantasy, 20 minutes from Sitka by boat (it's also the best place in the area to see bears). A charming, peeling old bunkhouse from town was stuck on a 1940s barge and anchored here, with a rain-water system, a woodstove for heat, propane appliances, and a diesel generator if you want light. A wood-fired sauna and a gas barbecue are out on deck. Don't expect the Hilton: It's primitive and a little grubby. You'll want to rent a boat or sea kayaks for mobility; owners John and Barbara DeLong offer those services too, and have two other floathouses for rent.

---

for non-members. Guests need to bring their own sleeping bags. It's open June through August; office hours and dorm access are from 8 to 10am and 6 to 10pm. Reservations are required, but advance payment is not accepted: simply call or write to tell them when you will need a bed.

The Forest Service's **Starrigavan Campground,** at the north end of Halibut Point Road, 7½ miles from town and ½ mile from the ferry dock, is one of the loveliest in Alaska. There are three loops. The Backpackers' Loop has six hike-in sites. The Estuary Loop (which joins the Estuary Life Trail), on the right, has sites for RVs or tents, which are widely separated under huge trees. The Bayside Loop, at the water's edge, is the last left on the highway. Three of its sites are situated next to the Starrigavan Bay, creating the feeling that you're way out in the wilderness. Fees are $12 to $16 a night. Fourteen sites are available on a first-come, first-served basis, but all the rest must be reserved on the national system (see "Reserving a Cabin or Campsite," p. 90). The campground is open all year, but vehicle access is restricted in the winter. May through mid-September, access gates are locked from 10pm to 7am.

There are two RV parks, each with water and electric hookups only and each charging under $22: city-run **Sealing Cove RV Park** (© 907/747-3439) is near the airport, and **Sitka Sportsman's Association RV Park** (© 907/747-6033) is near the ferry dock.

WHERE TO DINE

See other good restaurant choices at the Westmark Shee Atika and Sitka Hotel above, under "Where to Stay." A Subway sandwich shop is at Seward and Lake streets, behind the Westmark.

Bayview Restaurant ☆ BURGERS/PASTA/SEAFOOD The view of the boat harbor and good food make this small second-story restaurant popular year-round, although it's sometimes noisy and slightly cramped. Everything I've tried from the extensive menu has been well prepared and quickly served by friendly staff. Most recently, I was quite satisfied with a lunch of a tasty Cajun halibut taco, which came with a salad and the always wonderful clam chowder for $9.75. Dinner prices also are competitive with other places in Sitka, and even then you have the option of simple fare or fancier seafood selections. It's a great spot for breakfast, too.

407 Lincoln St. ⒸⒸ **907/747-5440**. Main courses $6–$28. AE, DISC, MC, V. High season Mon–Sat 6am–9pm, Sun 6am–3pm; winter Mon–Sat 7am–8pm, Sun 7am–3pm.

Channel Club ★ STEAK/SEAFOOD   Occupying one big room where the cigarette smoke floats freely, the restaurant is like a manly club for fish slayers to let loose, laughing loud and drinking after a day on the water. A swordfish decorates one wall, the grill is on the other, and the dress code seems to be T-shirts and baseball caps. They grill a good steak here, and the salad bar, which comes with every meal, is something like a potluck dinner all by itself, with a wide and wonderful array of unfamiliar flavors. The service is as casual as in the greasiest greasy-spoon diner: guests are just expected to know that they should load up a plate from the salad bar before someone comes by to ask what kind of steak they want from the list up on the wall—there is no menu. Channel Club is several miles out Halibut Point Road, but a courtesy van will come get you and take you home at the end of the evening. They have a full bar, which stays open an hour after the restaurant closes (hours below are just for the restaurant).

2906 Halibut Point Rd. Ⓒ **907/747-9916**. Reservations recommended. Main courses $12–$42. AE, DC, DISC, MC, V. Sun–Thurs 5–10pm, Fri–Sat 5–11pm.

Ludwig's Bistro ★★ MEDITERRANEAN   This tiny dining room and its young proprietors offer Sitka's only first-rate cuisine, and it's a very pleasant place for a meal. They've taken a formerly grungy concrete space and filled it with charm and warmth, with Mediterranean colors, wine bottles, and nice clutter. They can only serve 40 to 60 meals a night here, so each one is carefully crafted, coming from a changing menu intended to stretch the chef and introduce the small-town clientele to new tastes. A recent menu included grilled marinated lamb chops, a wild mushroom ragu, and calamari, among other selections. The lunch menu is simpler, but still finds room for items such as steamed clams in a wine broth with Spanish ham. Best of all, they're not

---

⌐ **Tips**   **Hip Eats & Coffee in Sitka**

The same cool couple owns two of the coolest hangouts in town: **Mojo Café**, at 203 Lincoln St. (Ⓒ **907/747-0667**), and **The Backdoor Café,** in the back half of Old Harbor Books at 104 Barracks St. (Ⓒ **907/747-8856**). The two addresses are nearly next door. These are the kinds of places that develop a following among local poets, musicians, and the like. Mojo is open Monday through Saturday from 6:30am to 3pm and Sunday 9am to 3pm, serving fresh pastries for breakfast and a single special for lunch (which can run out). The Backdoor is a coffee place and also offers the owners' own homemade bagels. It's open Monday through Saturday from 7am to 5pm. Neither place takes credit cards.

   Highliner Coffee, on Lake Street just above Seward Street (Ⓒ **907/747-4924**), is a fancier place, with Internet access ($5.25 for the first ½ hr.). A "highliner" is a top commercial fisherman; the name here is a bit of a boast for its fisherpeople owners, who hope to educate customers about their way of life as well as roasting Sitka's coffee. It's open Monday through Saturday from 5:30am to 5pm, Sunday from 8am to 4pm.

pretentious. The owners, Colette and Lisa, create a sense of friendship with diners; at times the whole place feels like a big dinner party.

256 Katlian St. (C) **907/966-3663.** Reservations recommended. Lunch $5–$15, dinner main courses $17–$27. AE, MC, V. Tues–Sat noon–9pm.

Pizza Express *(Value* MEXICAN/PIZZA   Come here when you want a filling, inexpensive meal in a light, pleasant dining room. The owners and most of the menu are Mexican, but they also serve and deliver good pizza.

236 Lincoln St., Ste. 106. (C) **907/966-2428.** Main courses $7–$13. MC, V. Mon–Sat 11am–10pm, Sun noon–1pm; closes at 9pm on Sundays in winter.

6 Juneau: Forest Capital

Juneau (*June*-oh) hustles and bustles like no other city in Alaska. The steep downtown streets echo with the mad shopping sprees of cruise-ship passengers in the summer tourist season and the whispered intrigues of politicians during the winter legislative session. Miners, loggers, and eco-tourism operators come to lobby for their share of Southeast's forest. Lunch hour arrives, and well-to-do state and federal bureaucrats burst from the office buildings to try the latest restaurant or brown-bag on one of the waterfront wharves, the sparkling water before them and gift store malls behind. The center of town becomes an ad hoc pedestrian mall as the crush of people forces cars to creep.

My Juneau is close at hand, but very different. As a child, at a magical age, I lived here with my family in a house on the side of the mountains above downtown. My Juneau is up the 99 steps that lead from the cemetery to the bottom of Pine Street—the way I walked home from school—and then to the top of residential Evergreen Avenue, where the pavement gives way to a forest trail among fiddlehead ferns and massive rainforest spruces. That trail leads to the flume (a wooden aqueduct that used to bring water down from the mountains), upon which we would walk into the land of bears and salmon, the rumbling water at our feet. It's still a short walk from the rackety downtown streets to a misty forest quiet, where you can listen for the voices of trees.

Juneau is Alaska's third-largest city (Anchorage and Fairbanks are larger), with a population of 30,000, but it feels like a small town that's just been stuffed with people. Splattered on the sides of Mount Juneau and Mount Roberts along Gastineau Channel, where there isn't room for much of a town, its setting is picturesque but impractical. Further development up the mountains is hemmed in by avalanche danger; beyond is the 1,500-square-mile **Juneau Icefield,** an impenetrable barrier. Gold-mine tailings dumped into the Gastineau created the flat land near the water where much of the downtown area now stands. The Native village that originally stood on the waterfront is today a little pocket of mobile homes several blocks from the shore. There's no road to the outside world, and the terrain discourages building one. Jets are the main way in and out, threading down through the mountains to the airport.

Gold was responsible for the location; it was found here in 1880 by Joe Juneau and Richard Harris, assisted by the Tlingit chief Kowee, who told them where to look. All three men are buried in the Evergreen Cemetery. Their find started Alaska's development. The territory's first significant roads and bridges and its first electrical plant were built in the mountains here, which were carved with miles of hard rock tunnels well before the Klondike gold rush began. In a few years these mines removed more gold than the United States paid for all of Alaska, as attested to by a photograph in the State Museum showing comparative piles. There's plenty of gold left, but mining died out with World War II; efforts to start again are stymied by environmental controls and low gold prices. There are several interesting gold mining sites to visit.

In 1900, Congress moved the territorial capital here from Sitka, which had fallen behind in the flurry of gold rush development. Alaskans have been fighting over whether or not to keep it here for many decades since, but Juneau's economy is heavily dependent on government jobs, and it has successfully fought off a series of challenges to its capital status. In 2002 voters turned down a petition initiative to move the legislature by a two-to-one margin. The closest the issue came was in the 1970s, when voters approved moving the capital, but then balked at the cost of building a whole new city to house it—a necessity since neither Anchorage nor Fairbanks, which have their own rivalry, would support the move if it meant the other city got to have the capital nearby.

There's plenty to see in Juneau, and it's a good town to visit because the population of government workers supports restaurants and amenities of a quality not found elsewhere in Southeast. Alaska's most accessible glacier, the Mendenhall, is in Juneau, and many businesses have set up tours, including visits to the fish hatchery, the brewery, and an abandoned mine. Juneau is also a starting point and travel hub for outdoor activities all over the northern Panhandle: you'll likely pass through on your way to Glacier Bay or virtually anywhere else in the region. The outdoors is always close at hand in Juneau. You can start from the capitol building for a hike to the top of Mount Juneau or Mount Roberts, or up the Perseverance Trail that leads in between. Sea-kayaking and whale-watching excursions are nearby, as well as some of Alaska's most scenic tide pooling and beach walking.

Downtown, the crush of visitors can be overwhelming when many cruise ships are in port at once. The streets around the docks have been entirely taken over by shops and other touristy businesses. Many of these are owned by people from outside Alaska who come to the state for the summer to sell gifts made outside Alaska. But only a few blocks away are quiet mountainside neighborhoods of houses with mossy roofs, and only a few blocks farther are the woods and the mountains, populated by bear, eagles, and salmon.

ESSENTIALS
GETTING THERE
BY AIR   Jet service is available only from **Alaska Airlines** (© 800/252-7522; www.alaskaair.com), with several daily nonstop flights from Seattle and Anchorage and from the smaller Southeast Alaska towns. Many of the region's commuter and air-taxi operators also maintain desks at the airport and have flights out of Juneau. Among the best, with many flights to surrounding communities and an active flightseeing operation, is **Wings of Alaska** (© 907/789-0790; www.wingsofalaska.com).

BY FERRY   All the main-line ferries of Southeast's **Alaska Marine Highway System** (© 800/642-0066; www.ferryalaska.com) stop at the terminal in Auke Bay (© 907/789-7453 or 907/465-3940 recording), 14 miles from downtown, and the new fast ferry, *Fairweather,* is based here, too. It cuts the running time to Haines (4½ hr.) in half and runs there five days a week. The passenger fare on the conventional ferries is $32 to Haines, $42 to Skagway; on the *Fairweather,* it is $35 and $46.

GETTING INTO TOWN FROM THE AIRPORT & FERRY TERMINAL
Airport shuttle businesses have been starting up and going out of business

Tips Flying to Juneau

Juneau's mist-shrouded airport, wedged between ocean and mountain, has a special verb: *to overhead*. That means that when you try to fly to Juneau on a foggy day, you could end up somewhere else instead (although this now happens less frequently thanks to new navigational technology). Planes overhead other Southeast towns, too, but more do it more often in Juneau, since it is the region's travel hub, with many flights a day. The airline will put you on the next flight back to Juneau when the weather clears, but they won't pay for hotel rooms or give you a refund. Your only protection is travel insurance and a loose itinerary. This situation is such an ingrained part of Juneau's way of life that a channel on the cable TV system broadcasts the view from the airport 24 hours a day, showing the weather over the Gastineau Channel (it's called the Channel Channel, 23 on the dial). Residents know the view so well they can tell from the silent image if they'll get out that day.

regularly for several years; rather than list a number here that may change, I recommend you ask at the visitor desk in the baggage claim area. An express **Capital Transit city bus** (© 907/789-6901) comes to the airport at 11 minutes past the hour on weekdays from 7:11am to 5:11pm and costs $1.50; your luggage has to fit under your seat or at your feet. Ask the driver for the stop closest to your hotel; you may need a short cab ride from there. Shuttles sometimes operate from the ferry dock downtown in the summer, but the arrangements are changeable. Ask when you arrive, or call ahead to the visitor center (below). A cab downtown from the airport will cost you $20, from the ferry dock $28. One taxi company is **Capital Cab** (© 907/586-2772 or 907/789-2772), which also offers tours for $55 an hr).

ORIENTATION
Juneau has three main parts: downtown, the Mendenhall Valley, and Douglas. Downtown Juneau is a numbered grid of streets overlying the uneven topography like a patterned quilt over a pile of pillows. As you look at Juneau from the water, Mount Juneau is on the left and Mount Roberts on the right; Mount Roberts is a few hundred feet taller, at 3,819 feet. **Franklin Street** extends south of town 5½ miles to good hiking trails and the hamlet of Thane. When the city outgrew its original site downtown, housing spread to the suburban **Mendenhall Valley,** about a dozen miles north out the Egan Expressway or the parallel, two-lane Glacier Highway. The glacial valley also contains the Juneau International Airport, University of Alaska Southeast, and **Auke Bay** area, where the ferry terminal is located. The road continues 40 miles to a place known as **"The End of the Road."** Across a bridge over the Gastineau Channel from downtown Juneau is Douglas Island. Turn left for the town of **Douglas,** mostly a bedroom community for Juneau, and turn right for the North Douglas Highway, which leads to the ski area and some beautiful rocky beaches.

GETTING AROUND
BY RENTAL CAR   A car is a hindrance in compact downtown Juneau, but if you're going to the Mendenhall Glacier or to any of the attractions out the road or on Douglas Island, renting a car for a day or two is a good idea. Hertz, Avis, Budget, Alamo, and National are based at the airport.

BY BIKE If you can handle hills, bikes make good sense in Juneau, where separated paths parallel many of the main roads and downtown traffic is slow. The 24-mile round-trip to Mendenhall Glacier keeps you on a bike path almost all the way. Bikes are for rent at the **Driftwood Lodge,** 435 Willoughby Ave. (✆ **800/544-2239** or 907/586-2280; www.driftwoodalaska.com) for $25 a day, $15 for a half day.

VISITOR INFORMATION

The **Visitor Information Center** is in the Centennial Hall at 101 Egan Dr., near the State Museum (✆ **888/581-2201** or 907/586-2201; fax 907/586-6304; www.traveljuneau.com). Operated by the Juneau Convention and Visitors Bureau, the center distributes a *Juneau Travel Planner,* online or on paper, that contains exhaustive listings of hotels and B&Bs, charter boats, tours, and other services. The center is open in summer Monday through Friday from 8:30am to 5pm, and Saturday and Sunday from 9am to 5pm; in winter Monday through Friday from 9am to 4pm. A ticket desk for the Alaska Marine Highway System is staffed by an agent Monday through Friday year-round. Visitors bureau volunteers also operate **information desks** at the airport, near the door in the baggage-claim area, and at the Auke Bay ferry terminal. During the summer, centers are staffed at the cruise ship terminal and at Marine Park.

The **Tongass National Forest Juneau Ranger District** is near the airport at 8465 Old Dairy Rd., Juneau, AK 99801 (✆ **907/586-8800,** TTY 907/790-7444; fax 907/586-8808; www.fs.fed.us/r10/tongass).

FAST FACTS: Juneau

Banks **Wells Fargo,** at 123 Seward St. (✆ **907/586-3324**), is one of the many banks and stores that have ATMs.

Hospital **Bartlett Regional,** at 3260 Hospital Dr. (✆ **907/796-8900**), is 3 miles out the Glacier Highway from downtown.

Internet Access Computers are easy to find downtown at coffee houses and businesses such as **Copy Express,** at 233 Seward St. (✆ **907/586-2174**). In the Mendenhall Valley, try **Electronic Adventures,** 9105 Mendenhall Mall Rd. (✆ **907/790-3658**).

Police The police station is at 6255 Alaway Ave. (✆ **907/586-0600** for non-emergencies).

Post Office Downtown in the federal building, 709 W. 9th St.; and in the Mendenhall Valley at 9491 Vintage Blvd., by Carr's supermarket. A postal contract station handy to the cruise ship dock is at 127 S. Franklin St.

Taxes Sales tax is 5%. You pay 12% tax on rooms.

SPECIAL EVENTS

An exhaustive event calendar is posted on the visitors' bureau website: www. traveljuneau.com/discover.

The **Alaska Folk Festival** (✆ **907/463-3316;** www.alaskafolkfestival.org) is the state's biggest annual coming together of musicians, at Centennial Hall, over a week in mid-April. Musicians take over the town and can be found jamming in every bar, coffee house, or wherever a crowd gathers.

Tips **The Cruise Ship Dock: Where Do You Get Off?**

Cruise-ship passengers disembark in Juneau's attractive **Marine Park** waterfront area, where a kiosk dispenses information and tour operators sell their services. Downtown shops and attractions are close by. Among the most popular sights is one right at the dock, the statue of a small dog facing the ships as they come in. This is *Patsy Ann,* a bull terrier that in the 1930s always seemed to know when a steamer was arriving and faithfully stationed herself on the dock to meet the disembarking passengers. There's also a spotting scope in the park for watching mountain goats on Mt. Juneau. For a quiet break, visit the beautiful library at the top of the parking garage at the south end of the dock.

The **Juneau Jazz & Classics Festival** (C 907/463-3378; www.jazzand classics.org), in late May, includes nine days of concerts and workshops in many styles of music at various venues, even on a boat, and at many prices—free to $60 a ticket. Most evening performances are around $20.

Gold Rush Days (C 907/790-1998; www.juneaugoldrush.com) includes logging and mining events and competitions that anyone can join. The date in 2005 is up in the air at this writing, but will be posted on the website.

The **Golden North Salmon Derby** (C 907/463-3830; www.salmonderby. org), held annually since 1947, targets kings and silvers August 5-7, 2005. Unlike some other such fishing contests around the state, this isn't just a tourist thing—it brings out as many as 3,000 local fishermen and is even covered live on the radio.

EXPLORING DOWNTOWN

Alaska-Gastineau Mill and Gold Mine Tour ⋆ A half-day tour visits the ruins of a hard-rock gold operation that operated from 1915 to 1921, then goes 360 feet into one tunnel for a mining demonstration. Guests also get to pan for gold from the mine's tailings. Although Princess Tours provides the buses and sells the tickets, the tour is the work of people who came to Juneau to reopen the A.J. mine (of which this was a part), and stayed to turn it into a tourist attraction when that project failed; their fascination is infectious. The mine site is south of town, but buses pick up visitors at the state museum downtown. The tour is quite in-depth; those without interest in mining history or mechanical matters may get bored. Dress warmly.

Book though Princess Tours, 151 Mill St. C 907/463-3900. $59 adults, $30 children 12 and under. Daily departures during summer; call ahead to reserve.

Alaska State Museum ⋆⋆⋆ The museum contains a large collection of art and historical artifacts, but it doesn't seem like a storehouse at all because the objects' presentation is based on their meaning, not their value. Come here to put the rest of your visit in context. A clan house in the Alaska Native Gallery contains authentic art in the functional places where it would have been used in a memorial potlatch. The Lincoln Totem Pole is here, carved by an artist who used a picture of the president as his model to represent his clan's first encounter with whites. Superb artifacts from Native cultures from around the state are presented to illustrate the lifestyle of those who made them. The ramp to the second floor wraps around the natural history display, with an eagle in a tree, and at the top a state history gallery uses significant pieces to tell Alaska's story. The children's area is exceptionally fun, with a ship—Captain Cook's *Discovery*—that the kids can play in. Allow at least two hours for the museum; half a day would not be out of line. The shop off the lobby is also well worth a look. Although small, it carries lots of quality Alaska Native art, books, and no junk at all.

395 Whittier St. © 907/465-2901. www.museums.state.ak.us. Admission mid-May to mid-Sept $5 adults, free for ages 18 and under; mid-Sept to mid-May $3 adults, free for ages 18 and under. Mid-May to mid-Sept daily 8:30am–5:30pm; mid-Sept to mid-May Tues–Sat 10am–4pm.

The Juneau-Douglas City Museum ★   This fun little museum displays artifacts and photographs from the city's pioneer and mining history and Tlingit culture with special exhibits that change annually. It's quite well done and holds real interest. There are gorgeous stained-glass windows and a large topographical model of the Juneau area. A 26-minute video on Juneau's gold mining history shows each half hour. The tiny bookshop is stocked with handy information for your visit to Juneau, including the historic hike guide booklet, free historic walking-tour map, and maps of the Evergreen Cemetery and the old Treadwell Mine. The plaza in front is where the 49-star U.S. flag was first raised in 1959—they didn't make many of those, as Hawaii was admitted as the 50th within a year, but you'll still find one flying here.

At the corner of 4th and Main sts. © 907/586-3572. www.juneau.org/parksrec/museum. Admission $3 adults ($2 in winter), free for ages 18 and under. Summer Mon–Fri 9am–5pm, Sat–Sun 10am–5pm. Winter Tues–Sat noon–4pm.

The Last Chance Mining Museum and Historic Park ★ *Finds*   On the site on forested Gold Creek where gold was first discovered in Juneau, the museum preserves old mining buildings and some of their original equipment, including an immense 1912 air compressor and a layered glass map of the tunnels. This was once a nerve center for one of the world's biggest hard-rock mines. The highlight is its energetic and learned guide, Renee Hughes, who lives above the compressor with her husband Gary Gillette. Both are leaders of the Gastineau Channel Historical Society. Ask Renee about the cave-in of the Treadwell Mine to hear her riveting storytelling. The entrance to the site—which contains relics and buildings spread over several acres—is a bridge over the creek, which leads to a steep trail up to the buildings.

1001 Basin Rd. © 907/586-5338. Admission $4. Daily 9:30am–12:30pm and 3:30–6:30pm. Closed Oct to mid-May. From downtown, take Gold St. up the hill to it's end, then join Basin Rd., continuing 1½ miles up the valley to the end of the road.

Mount Roberts Tramway ★   The tram takes only 6 minutes to whisk passengers from tourist-clogged Franklin Street to the clear air and overwhelming views at the tree line (1,760 ft.), a destination that used to require a day of huffing and puffing to witness. The tram can be crowded; it's once you're up there that the beauty hits you. The Alaska Native owners seem to understand that, and they have done a good job of building a network of paths that take advantage of the views as you pass through a fascinating alpine ecosystem; the owners have even carved clan crests into the living trunks of some of the trees. If you're energetic, you can start a 6-mile round-trip to Mount Roberts's summit (at 3,819 ft.), or you can hike the 2.5 miles back to downtown. There's an auditorium at the top tram station showing a film on the Tlingit culture, a shop where Native artisans are often at work, and a bald eagle enclosure. The bar and grill serves lunch and dinner. I would choose something else to do on a day when fog or low overcast obscures the view, especially considering the price; however, I am told it is sometimes sunny up top while rainy down on Franklin Street—it can't hurt to ask.

490 S. Franklin St., at the waterfront near the cruise-ship dock. (C) **888/461-8726** or 907/463-3412. www.goldbelttours.com. Full-day pass $22 adults, $13 children 12 and under, tax included. May–Sept daily 9am–9pm. Closed Oct–Apr.

A JUNEAU WALKING TOUR

Start& Finish: Alaska State Capitol, 4th and Seward streets.
Time: 1 to 1½ hours for standard tour; 2½ hours for the extended tour, with
                    minimal stops.

❶ The Alaska State Capitol

This structure fills the block between 4th and 5th and Main and Seward streets. Except for the marble portico on the 4th Street side, it is a nondescript brick box, probably the least impressive state capitol in the most beautiful setting in the nation. The federal government built the structure in 1931, when Alaska was still a territory. Inside, some of the old-fashioned woodwork and decorative details are interesting, and the public is free to walk through. During the summer, free tours start every half hour Monday through Friday from 9am to 4:30pm; other times, pick up a self-guided tour brochure in the lobby. Call (C) **907/465-3800** for information. The legislature is in session from January to early May.

Across 4th is the:

❷ State Courthouse

The statue of a bear in front defines Alaskan taste in art: It replaced a hated abstract steel sculpture called *Nimbus* that was removed by an act of the legislature and that finally came to rest in front of the state museum a few blocks away.

On the opposite, northwest corner is the:

❸ Juneau-Douglas City Museum

Stop in here now to buy the Evergreen Cemetery map if you plan to include that in your walk, or get the *Historic Downtown Juneau Guide* to learn more on the whole walk.

On the southwest corner of Main and 4th is the:

❹ State Office Building

This building is built into the edge of a cliff that forms a major barrier through the downtown area; if you're headed for the lower land, where the State Museum and Centennial Hall are located, you can avoid eight flights of steps in between by taking the building's elevator down. In any event, visit the towering atrium, with its great views and a 1928 movie theater pipe organ that's played on Fridays at noon. The state library historical collections off the lobby contain historic photographs and artifacts, some of which are often on exhibit. On sunny days, the patio off the atrium is a warm place for a picnic, with a fabulous view.

Leaving again through the door that you entered, turn left and follow Calhoun Street around the curve. An outdoor staircase here leads down to the flat area of town below (but you know about taking the elevator). Continue on Calhoun; the governor uses the pedestrian overpass (which we walk under) to cross Calhoun to get to the Capitol from the white, neoclassical:

❺ Governor's Mansion

Located on the left, the mansion was built by the federal government in 1912 for $40,000. It isn't normally open for public tours. Gov. Frank Murkowski, a Republican, became the eighth to hold the office when he was sworn in on December 2, 2002, returning from 22 years as a U.S.

Senator. He then appointed his own daughter, Lisa Murkowski, to fill out his term in the Senate.

Shortcut: If you don't mind missing the next stop (Gold Creek), you can save yourself some hill-climbing by continuing on Calhoun, turning right on Goldbelt Street, climbing past some beautiful houses to 7th, then picking up the tour at the Wickersham House.

Otherwise, continuing down Calhoun, you'll come to:

⑥ Gold Creek

Juneau's founders made their gold strike in this stream in 1880. Trace it upstream through peaceful **Cope Park,** past the playground and tennis courts to the unique ball-field, which is bounded by the stream's forested canyon walls. (To continue this walk to Evergreen Cemetery and up to the top of the town and through the woods on the flume—a long, strenuous walk—return to Calhoun Street and continue in the direction you were going. That route is covered below under "The Extended Walk.")

Go all the way to the right side (your right) of the baseball diamond to find a lovely path and public stairway through the woods steeply up to 7th Street. Seventh runs along a narrow ridge between downtown Juneau and the creek. Across the street from the top of the stairway is:

⑦ The Wickersham House State Historic Site

This white, 1898 frame house, at 213 7th St. (© **907/586-9001;** www. alaskastateparks.org, click "Individual Parks"), was the retirement home of Judge James Wickersham, who was revered by Alaskans for bringing law to the gold rush in Eagle, Nome, and Fairbanks; for exploring the Denali area and helping to make it a national park; for convincing the federal government to build the Alaska railroad and found the state university; and for winning Alaska's right to make its own laws when he represented the territory

in Congress. The house was in the family from 1928 until the state bought it in 1984, so it still contains Wickersham's belongings, including an Edison cylinder gramophone he took to Fairbanks, and his assignment to go to Alaska, which is signed by Theodore Roosevelt. The house badly needs work and a renovation project funded in part by the National Park Service is in the works. Chances are good that it will be closed in 2005. If not, do join the delightful and well-informed live-in guide for a tour. She requests a $2 donation. During normal operations, the house has been open from mid-May to the end of September from 10am to noon and 1 to 5pm, winter by appointment.

Continue on Seventh to Gold Street, turn right and follow it downhill to Fifth, site of the:

⑧ St. Nicholas Orthodox Church

This small structure is a significant architectural and historic landmark. The octagonal chapel was built in 1893–94 by Slavic miners and Tlingits. Many Tlingits chose the Russian Orthodox faith in the late 19th century when government-sponsored Protestant missionaries arrived with authority to force Christianity on Alaska Natives. The Protestants' civilizing program entailed wiping out Native languages and culture, but the Orthodox allowed people to worship in Tlingit and to continue more of their own customs. Bishop Innocent Veniaminov had translated sacred texts into Tlingit 50 years earlier when the Russians were still in Sitka. Today, Alaska Natives make up the bulk of Russian Orthodox congregations in Alaska, and St. Nicholas still has an active Tlingit parish. Lengthy services are sung in English, Tlingit, and Church Slavonic for Saturday vespers at 6pm and on Sunday morning at 9am; the congregation stands throughout the service. Otherwise, the church

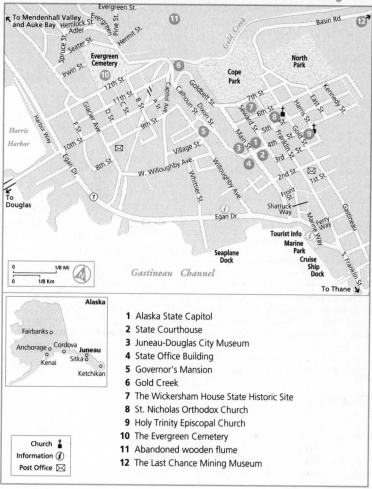

Evergreen St.

To Mendenhall Valley and Auke Bay

Basin Rd.

Alaska

Fairbanks o

Anchorage o Cordova o
Kenai o   **Juneau**
           Sitka o
                Ketchikan o

1 Alaska State Capitol
2 State Courthouse
3 Juneau-Douglas City Museum
4 State Office Building
5 Governor's Mansion
6 Gold Creek
7 The Wickersham House State Historic Site
8 St. Nicholas Orthodox Church
9 Holy Trinity Episcopal Church
10 The Evergreen Cemetery
11 Abandoned wooden flume
12 The Last Chance Mining Museum

Church †
Information ⓘ
Post Office ✉

is open for visitors during the tourist season Monday through Friday from 9am to 5pm, Saturday 10am to 1pm, and Sunday 1 to 5pm. Admission is $2.

One block down, on Gold and 4th, is:

⑨ Holy Trinity Episcopal Church
This church is worth a stop for its peaceful turn-of-the-20th-century sanctuary of dark wood under a steeply pitched roof; it's unlocked all day. The church was built in 1896 by Alaska's first Episcopal bishop, when he established the denomination's first mission in Juneau. A little-known piece of church history: As an under-size acolyte at age 8, I almost smashed the stained glass in the back of the church when I lost control of the heavy crucifix and had to run down the aisle to keep up with it.

Turn right and walk 2 blocks to the start/ finish point.

THE EXTENDED WALK
This walk of roughly 3 miles includes some steep stairways and streets. Follow the walking tour until you reach Gold Creek (see number 6, above).

Cross the creek and stay on the same road (which goes under various names), bearing right as it becomes Martin Street. On the left is:

⑩ The Evergreen Cemetery

The cemetery slopes toward the ocean, opening a wonderful vista over the clear green lawn. One reason the view is so broad and open is that the markers are flush with the ground. The old Alaska Native graves are in the wooded portion on the far side. Joe Juneau and Richard Harris, the city's founders, are buried near the cross at the top end of the cemetery, near where you arrive on the walk. Across the road from the cross, Hermit Street reaches a little way into the mountainside.

Follow the steep public stairs next to house no. 430 up to the bottom of Pine Street. This is the walk I described in the introduction. The views get better and better as you rise to the top of Pine Street then go right on Evergreen Street, following the road to where it dissipates into a trail among shadowy spruce and western hemlock. Continue on the peaceful forest trail among the ferns and evergreens up the valley, coming to the:

⑪ Abandoned wooden flume

Once the town's aqueduct, the flume now is maintained as a boardwalk into the forest. Since it carried water, it's nearly level, but watch your step in wet weather, as it crosses some high trestles over gullies.

At the end of the flume, cross over the valley to Basin Road. Stop here to see:

⑫ The Last Chance Mining Museum

The museum is described on p. 144. To the left is the Perseverance Trail, described below, which continues up between the mountains; the Perseverance also leads to the trail head for a challenging hike up Mount Juneau (both hikes are covered below).

To get back to town, follow Basin Road 1½ miles back down the valley. Taking the first right will put you at the top of Gold Street. Descend a block to 7th and pick up the walking tour at stop seven (the Wickersham House is a block down 7th) or continue down Gold to St. Nicholas Orthodox Church, stop eight on the tour.

SHOPPING

The shops near the dock cater primarily to cruise-ship passengers. After the last of more than 500 port calls each summer, many close their doors. The year-round community and more local shops tend to be farther up the hill. If you're looking for authentic Alaska Native arts and crafts, be warned that counterfeiting is widespread. For buying tips, read "Native Art: Finding the Real Thing" in chapter 2.

The Raven's Journey, 435 S. Franklin (© **907/463-4686**), shows Tlingit and other Northwest Indian carvings and masks, and whalebone, ivory, basketry, and fossil ivory carvings and jewelry from the Yup'ik and Iñupiat of western and northern Alaska. Works are displayed with biographical placards of the artists.

Juneau Artists Gallery, in the Senate Building at 175 S. Franklin (© **907/586-9891;** www.juneauartistsgallery.com), is staffed by a co-op of local artists and shows only the members' work: paintings, etchings, photography, jewelry, fabrics, ceramics, and other media. Much of it is good and inexpensive, and the way it is displayed creates a panorama of artistic visions.

Juneau's Rie Muñoz is one of Alaskans' favorite artists for her simple, graphic, generally cheerful watercolors of coastal Alaskan communities and Native people. Her prints and tapestries are shown downtown at the **Decker Gallery,** 233 S. Franklin (© **907/463-5536**), and in the Mendenhall Valley at the **Rie Muñoz Gallery,** at 2101 Jordan Ave. (© **800/247-3151** or 907/789-7449; www.riemunoz.com).

For gifts, try **Annie Kaill's** fine arts and crafts gallery at 244 Front St. It's a little out of the cruise-ship shopping area and gets business from locals. The shop has a rich, homey feeling, with local work at various price levels. The long-established **Ad Lib,** at 231 S. Franklin St., also is reliable and oriented to authentic items made in Alaska.

Galligaskins, 219 S. Franklin St. (www.galligaskins.com), essentially just a gift store, has a rich feel, but it is a home-grown place that started with clothing on Alaska-themed designs.

Hearthside Books (www.hearthsidebooks.com) is a cubbyhole of a bookstore at the corner of Franklin and Front streets, but has a good selection for its size, especially of Alaskan books. (A larger branch, with a good toy department, is in the Mendenhall Valley's Nugget Mall, at 8745 Glacier Hwy.)

The Observatory, at 200 N. Franklin St. (© **907/586-9676;** www.observatorybooks.com), a browser's paradise, specializes in rare maps and books about Alaska, and is owned by a real expert, a member of the Royal Geographical Society.

Bill Spear sells his own brightly colored enamel pins and zipper pulls from his studio upstairs at 174 S. Franklin (© **907/586-2209;** www.wmspear.com). Alaskans collect the vividly executed fish, birds, airplanes, dinosaurs, vegetables, and many other witty, provocative, or beautiful pins, which cost from $4 to $20 each.

Taku Store, at 550 S. Franklin, across the parking lot from the tram station (© **800/582-5122** or 907/463-3474; www.takustore.com), is worth a stop if you're nearby, even if you're not in the market for the pricey seafood in the case: It's interesting to watch workers fillet, smoke, and pack salmon through large windows, and to read the explanatory signs about what they're doing. They'll ship fish anywhere in the U.S.

ATTRACTIONS BEYOND WALKING DISTANCE

Mendenhall Glacier Transport (© 907/789-5460; www.mightygreattrips.com) does a 2½-hour town and Mendenhall Glacier tour for $20, or you can ride their "Blue Bus Express" to the glacier for only $5. Generally, it runs on the hour from the waterfront visitor center daily 9am to 6pm in summer, and on the half hour from the glacier back downtown.

Otherwise, take a rented car or, for vigorous people, bike 24 miles out to the Mendenhall Glacier and back. I've listed these sites by distance from downtown with directions starting from there.

Alaskan Brewing Company   Beer lovers and aspiring capitalists will enjoy the tour of Alaska's most popular craft brewery. Now too big to be called "micro," the brewery started small in 1986 when Geoff and Marcy Larson had the idea of bringing a local gold rush–era brew back to life. It worked, and now Alaskan Amber and several other brews are everywhere in Alaska and in much of the Northwest, and the brewery has won a long list of national and international awards for its brews. The short, free tour, which starts every ½ hour, is fairly interesting, with views of the brewing equipment behind glass, but it's the tasting that makes it fun. They serve free samples of half a dozen beers, often creating an impromptu party in the lobby.

5429 Shaune Dr. © 907/780-5866. www.alaskanbeer.com. May–Sept daily 11am–4:30pm; Oct–Apr Thurs–Sat 11am–4pm. Turn right from Egan Dr. on Vanderbilt Hill Rd., which becomes Glacier Hwy., then right on Anka St., and right again on Shaune Dr.

Glacier Gardens This is the place to see the rainforest if you have mobility problems. The heart of the hour-long tour is a ride in vehicles similar to golf carts up a steep mountainside, past a stream and pools, to a platform with a view of the Gastineau Channel. They cater to the cruise ships, but the staff will take groups of just a few visitors for a ride, explaining the forest flora in as much detail as you wish. Gardeners will especially enjoy the extraordinary hanging baskets and other bright and ingenious plantings in the lower area—weddings of cruise ship passengers are held here almost every day in the summer. The gardens' trademark is upside-down trees whose roots, way up in the air, are planted with trailing flowers. All good—but if you're planning a hike in the area, the ride will hold less interest, and, as much as I like the place, I have to point out it is priced as a guided tour, not a botanical garden. More vigorous visitors, who don't want to ride in the golf carts, may find the admission price too high.

7600 Glacier Hwy. ℭ **907/790-3377.** www.glaciergardens.com. Admission $18 adults, $13 ages 6–12, free under 6. Summer daily 9am–6pm. Closed Oct–Apr. Near the Fred Meyer store about 1 mile from the airport.

Macaulay Salmon Hatchery ✸ The hatchery, known by locals as DIPAC (Douglas Island Pink and Chum, Inc.), was ingeniously designed to allow visitors to watch the whole process of harvesting and fertilizing eggs from outdoor decks. From mid-June to October, salmon swim up a 450-foot fish ladder, visible through a window, into a sorting mechanism, then are "unzipped" by workers who remove the eggs. Guides and exhibits explain what's happening. During that period you can often see seals and other wildlife feeding on the returning salmon just offshore from the hatchery. Inside, large and realistic saltwater aquariums show off the area's marine life as it looks in the natural environment. The tour is less impressive in May and June, before the fish are running. At that time visitors see the immature salmon before their release and sometimes get to feed them. The tours don't take long; allow 45 minutes for your entire visit.

2697 Channel Dr. 3 miles from downtown, turn left at the 1st group of buildings on Egan Dr. ℭ **877/ 463-2486** or 907/463-5114. www.dipac.net. Admission $3.25 adults, $1.75 children ages 12 and under. Summer Mon–Fri 10am–6pm, Sat–Sun 10am–5pm; off season call ahead.

Mendenhall Glacier ✸✸ At the head of Mendenhall Valley, the Mendenhall Glacier glows bluish white, looming above the suburbs like an Ice Age monster that missed the general extinction. Besides being a truly impressive sight, Mendenhall is the most easily accessible glacier in Alaska and the state's third most visited attraction. The parking and an adjacent shelter have a great view across the lake to the glacier's face, and a wheelchair-accessible trail leads to the water's edge. The land near the parking lot shows signs of the glacier's recent passage, with little topsoil, stunted vegetation, and, in many places bare rock that shows the scratch marks of the glacier's movement. Atop a bedrock hill, reached by stairs, a ramp, or an elevator, the Forest Service visitor center contains a glacier museum with excellent explanatory models, computerized displays, spotting scopes, and ranger talks. Admission is $3 for adults, free for children under 12. In late summer, you can watch red and silver salmon spawning in **Steep Creek,** just short of the visitor center on the road.

There are several trails at the glacier, ranging from a half-mile nature trail loop to two fairly steep, 3.5-mile hikes approaching each side of the glacier. At the visitor center and a booth near the parking lot, the Forest Service distributes a brochure, "Mendenhall Glacier: Carver of a Landscape," which includes a trail map. The **East Glacier Loop Trail** is a beautiful day hike leading through the

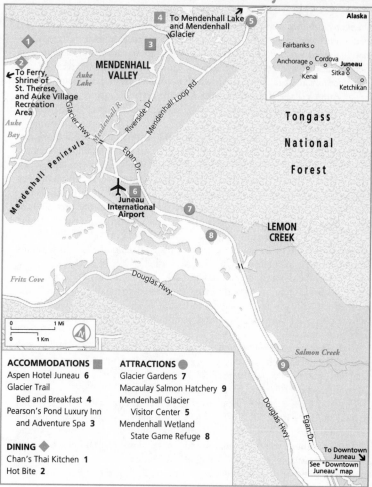

Alaska

Fairbanks

Anchorage   Cordova   **Juneau**
          Kenai   Sitka
                        Ketchikan

To Mendenhall Lake
and Mendenhall
Glacier

MENDENHALL
VALLEY

Auke
Lake

To Ferry,
Shrine of
St. Therese,
and Auke Village
Recreation
Area

Auke
Bay

Glacier Hwy.

Mendenhall R.

Riverside Dr.

Mendenhall Loop Rd.

Egan Dr.

Mendenhall Peninsula

Juneau
International
Airport

Tongass

National

Forest

LEMON
CREEK

Fritz Cove

Douglas Hwy.

Salmon Creek

Douglas Hwy.

Egan Dr.

To Downtown
Juneau
See "Downtown
Juneau" map

0   1 Mi
0   1 Km

ACCOMMODATIONS
Aspen Hotel Juneau **6**
Glacier Trail
    Bed and Breakfast **4**
Pearson's Pond Luxury Inn
    and Adventure Spa **3**

DINING
Chan's Thai Kitchen **1**
Hot Bite **2**

ATTRACTIONS
Glacier Gardens **7**
Macaulay Salmon Hatchery **9**
Mendenhall Glacier
    Visitor Center **5**
Mendenhall Wetland
    State Game Refuge **8**

forest to a waterfall near the glacier's face and parts of an abandoned rail tram
and an abandoned dam on Nugget Creek; the trail has steep parts but is doable
for school-age children. You can park at the visitor center and start from there.
The **West Glacier Trail** is more challenging, leaving from 300 yards beyond the
Skater's Cabin and following the edge of the lake and glacier, providing access
to the ice itself for experienced climbers with the right equipment. You will need
wheels to get to the trailhead. Take the Mendenhall Loop Road to Montana
Creek Road, turn right, and then turn right again on Skater's Cabin Road.

The Skater's Cabin is also the starting point for a groomed cross-country-ski
loop on Mendenhall Lake in front of the glacier. Don't go beyond the orange
safety markers near the glacier's face. Other trails weave through the pothole
lakes across from the glacier.

At the head of Glacier Spur Rd. Visitor center (© 907/789-0097) open daily in summer 8am–6pm; winter
Thurs–Fri 10am–4pm, Sat–Sun 9am–4pm. Right from Egan Dr. on Mendenhall Loop to Glacier Spurs.

WHAT TO SEE & DO "OUT THE ROAD"

On sunny summer weekends, Juneau families get in the car and drive "out the road" (northwest along the Glacier Hwy., as it's officially known). The views of island-stippled water from the paved two-lane highway are worth the trip, and there are also several good places to stop. To use this road guide, set your trip odometer to zero at the ferry dock (which is 14 miles from downtown Juneau).

The **Auke Village Recreation Area** is a mile beyond the ferry dock and is a good place for picnics and beach walks. Less than a mile farther is a Forest Service campground.

The **Shrine of St. Therese** ✹ (𝄋 **907/780-6112;** www.shrineofsaint therese.org), 9 miles beyond the ferry dock, rests on a tiny island reached by a foot-trail causeway. The wonderfully simple chapel of rounded beach stones, circled by markers of the 15 stations of the cross, stands peaceful and mysterious amid trees, rock, water, and the cries of the raven and eagle. It is the most spiritual place I know. The vaguely Gothic structure was built in the late 1930s of stone picked up from these shores and dedicated by Alaska's first Catholic bishop to St. Therese of Lisieux, who died in 1897 at the age of 24. Sunday liturgy services are held from June to September at 1:30pm. The shrine is part of a large retreat maintained by the Juneau Catholic Diocese, which includes a log lodge on the shore facing the island as well as several cabins for rent as lodgings. The shrine's island is a good vantage from which to look upon **Lynn Canal** for marine mammals or, at low tide, to go tide pooling among the rocks. The website covers the shrine's history and gives information on the facilities, gardens, and trails.

Eagle Beach, 14 miles beyond the ferry dock, makes a good picnic area in nice weather, when you can walk among the tall beach grass or out on the sandy tidal flats, watch the eagles, or go north along the beach to look for fossils in the rock outcroppings.

The road turns to gravel, then comes to **Point Bridget State Park,** 24 miles beyond the ferry dock (𝄋 **907/465-4563;** www.alaskastateparks.org, click on "Individual Parks"). A flat 3.5-mile path leads through forest, meadow, and marsh to the shore, where you may see sea lions and possibly humpback whales. Two public-use cabins rent for $35 a night. See "State Parks Cabin Reservations," on p. 244. The road ends 26 miles from the ferry dock at pretty **Echo Cove.**

GETTING OUTSIDE: ONSHORE

BIRD-WATCHING   Bald eagles are as common as pigeons in Juneau. Years ago, one of them made off with a tourist's Chihuahua, starting a statewide debate about whether it was funny or horrible. Eagles are most common on the shoreline, especially where fish are plentiful, such as at the hatchery.

For more variety, visit the **Mendenhall Wetlands State Game Refuge,** which encompasses 4,000 acres of tidal estuaries in the Gastineau Channel near the airport. Some 140 species of birds use the refuge, mainly during the April and May migrations. Access points are on either side of the channel, including a viewing platform on the downtown-bound side of Egan Drive, at mile six.

FRESHWATER FISHING   Juneau isn't known particularly for its stream fishing, but there are a few places on the roads where you can put in a line. The advice you need is in the free printed **Juneau Sportfishing Guide** available from the Alaska Department of Fish and Game, 802 3rd St. (P.O. Box 240020), Douglas, AK 99824 (𝄋 **907/465-4270;** www.alaska.gov/adfg, click on "Sport Fishing," then on the Southeast region on the map).

For a remote fly-in experience with fly or spinning gear, contact **Alaska Fly 'n' Fish Charters,** 9604 Kelly Court (✆ **907/790-2120;** www.alaskabyair.com). A guided 4½-hour trip is $400 per person, with a two-person minimum. The same reputable guy (Butch Laughlin) also does flightseeing and bear viewing flights.

HIKING   I've mentioned several good hikes at Mendenhall Glacier and out the road, above. More than two dozen are described in a nicely made book with detailed topographic maps of each, *Juneau Trails* (www.alaskanha.org, $8), which you can find at visitor centers. *In the Miner's Footsteps,* a guide to the history behind 14 Juneau trails, is available for a nominal price from the Juneau-Douglas City Museum. The Juneau city **Department of Parks and Recreation** (✆ **907/586-5226;** www.juneau.org/parksrec) leads hikes (and other activities) through the year; check the website or call the 24-hour hike line at ✆ **907/586-0428.**

The **Perseverance Trail** climbs up the valley behind Juneau and into the mining history of the area it accesses. It can be busy in summer. The trail head is about 1½ miles from town on Basin Road. The trail is 4 miles of easy walking on the mountainside above Gold Creek to the Perseverance Mine, at the Silverbow Basin, a mining community from 1885 to 1921. Use caution on icy patches, as there are steep drop-offs. A well-documented historic pamphlet is for sale at the Juneau–Douglas City Museum.

Two trails start from points along the Perseverance Trail. The challenging **Mount Juneau Trail** rises more than 3,500 feet over about 2 miles from a point 1 mile along from the Perseverance trailhead. Go only in dry weather to avoid disastrous falls. The **Granite Creek Trail,** starting 2 miles in on the Perseverance Trail, climbs 1,200 feet over 1.5 miles to an alpine basin. Both are quieter than the Perseverance Trail.

Another hike right from downtown climbs **Mount Roberts**—just follow the stairway from the top of 6th Street in a neighborhood called Star Hill. The summit is 4.5 miles and 3,819 vertical feet away, but you don't have to go all the way to the top for incredible views and alpine terrain. At the 1,760-foot level, you come to the restaurant at the top of the Mount Roberts tram, mentioned on p. 144. Of course, it's easier to take the tram up and hike down, or start from the tram stop to hike to the summit.

The **Treadwell Mine Historic Trail,** on Douglas Island, is a fascinating hour's stroll through the ruins of a massive hard-rock mine complex that once employed and housed 2,000 men. Since its abandonment in 1922 big trees have grown up through the foundations, intertwining their roots through rails and machinery and adding to the site's exceptional power over the imagination. A well-written guide to numbered posts on the trail is available from the Juneau–Douglas City Museum. This is a great hike for kids. To find the trailhead, take 3rd Street in Douglas, bearing left at the Y onto Savikko Street, which leads to Savikko Park, also known as Sandy Beach Park. The trail starts at the far end of the park.

Another great family outing is to the **Outer Point Trail,** 1.3 miles on a forest boardwalk to a beach with good tide pooling, lots of eagles, and possible whale sightings. Nowhere else I know do so many different kinds of lovely spots present themselves in such a short walk: the mossy rainforest, the stunted muskeg swamp, a glassy little creek, and the pebbled beach and bedrock ocean pools. From there, on the western point of Douglas Island—the opposite side from Juneau—you can see Auke Bay to the east, Admiralty Island to the west, and the tiny islands of Stephens Passage before you. The trail's only drawback is crowding, especially when tour groups tromp through; avoid them by going early or late. To get there, drive over the bridge to Douglas, then right on North Douglas Highway 11½ miles to the trailhead.

RAFTING   The Mendenhall River isn't a wild or scary ride, so the guides on the Native-owned **Auk Ta Shaa Discovery,** 76 Egan Dr. (© **800/820-2628** or 907/586-8687; www.goldbelttours.com), offer commentary on Native legends and natural history. The 4-hour rides cost $99 for adults, $66 ages 16 and under (no kids under 50 lb. allowed). Transportation from downtown is included in the price, but even with that considered the cost is higher than similar rafting outings at other Alaska destinations.

SKIING   For **downhill skiing,** the city-owned **Eaglecrest Ski Area** (© **907/ 790-2000;** www.skijuneau.com) is the large, steep home hill of Olympic silver medalist Hillary Lindh, Juneau's favorite daughter (her father helped choose the site in the 1970s). A chair goes almost to the top of Douglas Island, with expansive views and 640 acres of skiing terrain. The 3 lifts serve 31 runs with a total vertical drop of 1,400 feet, rated 40% expert, 40% intermediate, and 20% novice. It's only 12 miles from downtown on North Douglas Highway. An all-day lift ticket is $26 for adults. Even among Alaskans, Eaglecrest is little known, despite being second in size and ski lift development only to Alyeska Resort, near Anchorage.

Eaglecrest has 5 miles of **cross-country-skiing** trail. But, generally, Juneau's warm, damp winters don't provide enough snow for good cross-country skiing at lower elevations. Many of the hiking trails into the mountains become winter backcountry routes, however, and snow does stick up there. Before going out, always check with the Forest Service (see "Visitor Information," earlier) for advice on your route and on avalanche conditions. Several of the Forest Service cabins also serve as winter warm-up houses during the day, and make good skiing destinations. If conditions permit, a network of trails is set around the Mendenhall Glacier (see above).

GETTING OUTSIDE: OFFSHORE

DIVING   The **Channel Dive Center,** 8365 Old Dairy Rd. (© **907/790-4665;** www.channeldive.com), offers instruction and rentals, and guides dry-suit diving. Guided dives include historic shipwrecks near town. From fall to spring, you can dive among sea lions. Diving is not as good in the summer, when plankton blooms tend to cloud the water.

SALTWATER FISHING & WHALE-WATCHING   The closest I ever came to a humpback whale—I almost touched it—was on the way back from king salmon fishing out of Juneau on a friend's boat. More than two dozen companies offer charters from Juneau and Auke Bay; you can go to **watch whales** or fish, or both. Juneau is well protected behind layers of islands, so the water generally is calm. A lot of companies offer trips. The Juneau Convention and Visitors Bureau maintains a list of businesses and their website has links to each. **Juneau Sportfishing and Sightseeing,** 2 Marine Way, Suite 230 (© **907/586-1887;** www.juneausportfishing.com), is one of the largest operators, and their rates are typical: $215 per person for a full day fishing for salmon, $240 for halibut; or $135 for 4 hours fishing salmon. They charge $95 for a 2½-hour whale-watching trip.

SEA KAYAKING The protected waters around Juneau appeal to sea kayakers, and the city is a popular hub for trips on the water farther afield. Besides the sublime scenery, you'll almost certainly see eagles, sea birds, and seals, and possibly humpback whales.

There are many operators offering sea-kayaking excursions, but the area's most established ecotourism operator is **Alaska Discovery,** 5310 Glacier Hwy. (✆ **800/586-1911** or 907/780-6226; www.akdiscovery.com), with trips all over Southeast and beyond. Part of the company's ethic and reason for being is to build support for protecting Alaska's wild places. A multiday kayak trip is your chance to really know the Alaska wilderness. Alaska Discovery will even custom-design a trip for your group. If you haven't spent much time in the outdoors but would like to see real Alaska wilderness, I couldn't recommend a better introductory trip than the Coastal Escape, a 3-day, 2-night camping trip to Berner's Bay, on Lynn Canal north of the end of the road. Besides paddling, groups spend plenty of time exploring the beaches and rainforest shorelines. Fit beginners will do fine, with teens as young as 14 normally invited; some trips may include kids as young as 10. No whiners, however: There's a good chance of rain, you'll sleep in a two-person tent, and paddling is work. The cost is $495 to $595 per person. Alaska Discovery's other trips range up to 12 days and go to some truly incredible places, including Glacier Bay National Park; they'll take fit beginners, but I recommend some sea-kayaking experience before heading out on an expedition.

If you don't have that kind of time, **Alaska Travel Adventures** (✆ **800/ 791-2673** outside Alaska or 800/478-0052 in Alaska; www.alaskaadventures. com), offers 3½-hour kayak trips from an unspoiled spot on north Douglas Island for $79 adults, $53 children 6 to 12. The tour includes orientation for beginners, transportation from downtown, and a snack.

A business that rents and delivers kayaks is listed under "Gearing Up for Juneau's Outdoors" (p. 156).

GETTING OUTSIDE: ON THE ICE

More than 36 major glaciers around Juneau flow from a single ocean of ice behind the mountains, the 1,500-square-mile **Juneau Icefield.** You can land on it in a helicopter just to touch the ice or to take a nature hike or dog sled ride. It's expensive, but there are few other places to see, let alone explore, the kind of ice sheet that carved North America in the last ice age. From the air, glaciers look unreal, like creations by a graphic artist, their sinuous lines of blue and white ice striped with darker gray gravel debris. Only standing on the ice, which on closer inspection resembles the crusty compressed snow of springtime snow berms, do you get a clear sense of this entirely unfamiliar kind of terrain.

It's worth noting that these tours have had some major mishaps. While the accidents represent a tiny fraction of all the safe flights, they're a reminder that flying a helicopter to a glacier is not like flying an airliner.

Era Helicopters (✆ **800/843-1947** or 907/586-2030; www.flightseeing tours.com) is among Alaska's oldest and most respected operators. Their 1-hour flight over four glaciers with a 15-minute landing on Norris Glacier costs $225 per person. They also offer a program of **dog sled rides** on the ice, a chance to try a winter sport in the summer. That excursion includes the 4-glacier overflight and adds about an hour at a sled dog camp on a glacier with a ride behind the dogs. It costs $389 per person. One caveat: Poor or even overcast weather makes it difficult to see the ice clearly, but if you wait for a sunny morning all seats will

---

Tips Gearing Up for Juneau's Outdoors

You can rent the gear you need for outings on the water or to equip Forest Service cabin visits from **Alaska Boat and Kayak,** at the Auke Bay Harbor (© 907/586-8220 or 907/789-6886; www.juneaukayak.com). They rent sea kayaks ($45 a day for a single, $60 double), camping gear, and skiffs with outboard motors ($130–$300 a day) that you can use for fishing or exploring, and they offer guidance in planning where and how to go. They will deliver sea kayaks anywhere on Juneau's road system or to Admiralty Island. See "Getting Around," earlier in this section, for bike rentals.

---

likely be booked. They have a 48-hour cancellation policy, so you have to gamble to some extent on good viewing conditions. Of course, they don't fly in unsafe conditions.

NorthStar Trekking (© **907/790-4530;** www.glaciertrekking.com), another company with its own helicopters, specializes in hiking and teaching about glaciers. Their small groups (a maximum of 11, with two guides) go on ice hiking excursions of up to a few miles, with the speed determined by the group. The 4-hour trip, which includes 2 hours on the ice and half an hour in the air (the balance is getting to the helicopter and gearing up), costs $329 per person. They have more expensive overnight options and less expensive options, too.

Wings of Alaska (© **907/789-0790;** www.wingsofalaska.com) offers glacier overflights by floatplane and flightseeing tours to the remote Taku Lodge, where they land for salmon for brunch, lunch, or dinner.

GETTING OUTSIDE: ON ADMIRALTY ISLAND

Beyond Douglas Island from Juneau, near the entrance to Gastineau Channel, is 900,000-acre Admiralty Island, one of the largest virgin blocks of old-growth forest in the country. The vast majority of the island is the protected **Kootznoowoo Wilderness.** Kootznoowoo, Tlingit for "fortress of bears," is said to have the highest concentration of brown bears on earth. Despite the town of Angoon on the western side of the island, there are more bears than people on Admiralty. The island's **Pack Creek Bear Viewing Area** is the most famous and surefire place to see bears in Southeast. The area has been managed for bear viewing since the 1930s, when hunting was outlawed. There's a platform for watching the bears up close as they feed on salmon spawning in the creek in July and August. Peak viewing occurs in the middle of that period. The bears generally pay no attention to the people watching them from a safe viewing platform.

Only 25 miles from Juneau, Pack Creek is so popular that the Forest Service uses a permit system to keep it from being overrun during the day (from 9pm to 9am, no humans are allowed). The great majority of people go for only a few hours. There are no facilities in this wilderness area and you can't even camp without some kind of water craft to get to a permitted area. The easiest way to go is with a tour operator who has permits. The Forest Service District Ranger Office can give you a list of guides. **Alaska Discovery,** 5310 Glacier Hwy. (© **800/586-1911** or 907/780-6226; www.akdiscovery.com), has many permits for Pack Creek sea kayak trips. Their 1-day excursion flies out and then paddles to the creek; no experience is necessary, but you must be physically capable of hiking and paddling. It costs $550 per person. A 2-night campout and sea kayak near the creek offers more time to see the bears and appreciate the scenery. It costs $1050 per person. **Alaska Fly 'n' Fish Charters,** 9604 Kelly Court (© **907/790-2120;** www.alaskabyair.com), also has permits for its naturalist-guided 5½-hour fly-in Pack Creek visits, which cost $475 per person, with everything you need included.

Twelve permits per day go to the commercial operators and 12 to people who go without any guide (and you aren't allowed to hire a guide after getting the permit); 8 of those 12 can be booked in advance with the Forest Service, and the other four are distributed 3 days before the date on which they're good, or the previous Friday for Tuesday and Wednesday, at 9am at the Juneau Ranger District Office. In the peak season, July 5 to August 25, permits cost $50 for adults, $25 for those ages 16 or under or 62 and over. Lower prices and easier availability prevail outside the peak, but then you might not see any bears. After you have the permit, you'll still need a way to get there, plus your own gear (including rubber boots and binoculars). The Forest Service lists air taxi operators on its Web site (www.fs.fed.us/r10/tongass/districts/admiralty).

Among the best is **Alaska Fly 'n' Fish Charters,** which charges $250 per person, round-trip, to drop off customers with their own permits; the price drops to $175 per person for groups of three or more.

Protected **Seymour Canal,** on the east side of the island, is good for canoeing and kayaking, and has two other sites besides Pack Creek where bears often show up: Swan Cove and Windfall Harbor. Outfitters are listed above, under "Gearing Up for Juneau's Outdoors."

For information on the island, its 15 Forest Service cabins, and an excellent $4 map, contact the **Admiralty Island National Monument,** 8461 Old Dairy Rd., Juneau (© **907/586-8790;** www.fs.fed.us/r10/tongass/districts/admiralty).

Finds **Remote Cabins on Foot**

Five U.S. Forest Service cabins and two Alaska State Parks cabins are accessible by hikes of less than a day on trails connected to Juneau's road system. That means that you can get to these cabins without an expensive plane or boat charter, and that's a rarity. The two Alaska State Parks cabins are at Point Bridget State Park (see "What to See & Do 'Out the Road,'" earlier in this chapter). The Forest Service cabins include: **Peterson Lake,** with lake and stream fishing for Dolly Varden char and cutthroat trout; **John Muir,** on a 1,500-foot ridge top above Auke Bay, up the Auk Nu Trail; **Dan Moller,** on Douglas Island right across from town; **Eagle Glacier,** overlooking the glacier upriver from Eagle Beach and reached by the Amalga Trail; and beautiful **Windfall Lake,** with fishing. Each cabin rents for $35 a night, and generally there's a 2-night maximum stay. All are popular and must be reserved well in advance. If you can afford a charter, or if you are an expert sea kayaker, there are many more choices farther afield, especially on Admiralty Island (see above). You'll need camping gear to stay at these primitive cabins (see "Gearing Up for Juneau's Outdoors," p. 156). Get information on cabins from the Ranger District (see "Visitor Information," p. 142), then reserve through the national system described in "Getting Outside in the Tongass National Forest" on p. 89.

WHERE TO STAY

Hotel rooms can be tight in the summer, so book ahead. Bed-and-breakfasts are a good way to get a better room and have more fun. The **Juneau Convention and Visitors Bureau**'s *Juneau Travel Planner* and website contain listings of the hotels and B&Bs with links (© **888/581-2201;** www.traveljuneau.com).

You also can find a B&B in Juneau, or anywhere in Southeast Alaska, through **www.accommodations-alaska.com**, a site created co-operatively by B&Bs. For contact with a real person associated with the site call **Ketchikan Reservation Service** (© **800/987-5337** or 907/247-5337).

EXPENSIVE

Besides the lodgings listed in full below, Juneau has a first-rate business hotel downtown: **Goldbelt Hotel Juneau,** 51 W. Egan Dr., (© **888/478-6909** or 907/586-6900; www.goldbelttours.com). The large bedrooms, with either two full-size or one king bed, are nicely furnished and noticeably quiet and immaculate. The views are good, and there is wireless Internet throughout. Summer rates are $169 to $179 double.

Alaska's Capital Inn ★★★   This scrupulously restored 1906 mansion offers constant surprises in its fascinating detail: the shining potbellied stove and 1879 pump organ in the parlor, the Alaskan artwork and Persian rugs, the original (electrified) gas lamps, period wallpaper, and even those old-fashioned push-button light switches. It took owners Linda Wendeborn and Mark Thorson 2½ years to bring the house back to this former glory, and they never would have done it without a driving vision, for they poured effort and expense into making details authentic that no one will ever notice. Fortunately, the house was worth it, with many large rooms with high ceilings, good views, fireplaces, claw foot tubs, and real elegance. The best asset of all, however, may be the warmth and fun of the inn. The common rooms are conducive to socializing and the hosts love to connect with guests and strive to accommodate their needs. For this reason, and the location just steps from the state Capitol Building, the inn fills with the best-connected lobbyists in the winter: people who could stay anywhere stay here. There are some lower-priced rooms, allowing those on mid-range budgets to enjoy the ambience, but the real showplaces carry luxury rates. An adorable scottie dog named Riley patrols the place. An elaborate breakfast is served at 8:30am. Smoking is not allowed, and they don't take children under 11.

113 W. 5th St., Juneau, AK 99801. © **888/588-6507** or 907/586-6507. Fax 907/586-6508. www.alaska capitalinn.com. 7 units. High season $124–$275 double; low season $99–$225 double. Extra person $15. Rates include full breakfast. AE, DC, DISC, MC, V. Children under 11 are not permitted. **Amenities:** Jacuzzi; shared computer with Internet access. *In room:* TV/VCR, dataport.

Baranof Hotel ★★   The Baranof is the only lodging in Alaska with the pedigree and style to pull off the role of the old-fashioned grand hotel. Built of concrete in 1939, it served for decades as an informal branch of the state capitol. Legislators and lobbyists still confer amid the overstuffed furniture and dark wood of the opulent lobby. The structure itself constrains modernization—the bathrooms and many rooms tend to be small—but features such as glass doorknobs and pressed-tin ceilings remain to show that it comes by its faults honestly. The management appreciates the building's ambience, and they have kept the style intact while lightening and updating rooms over the years. The upper-floor rooms have great views on the water side, while lower rooms were redone most recently. There are many appealing suites.

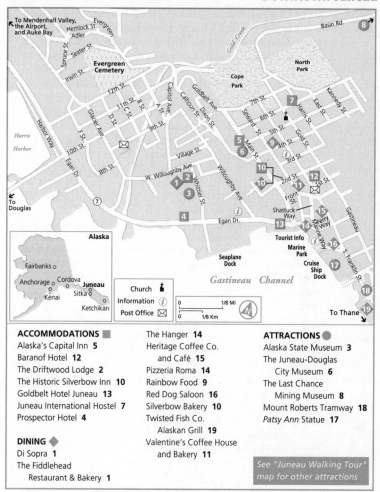

ACCOMMODATIONS
Alaska's Capital Inn **5**
Baranof Hotel **12**
The Driftwood Lodge **2**
The Historic Silverbow Inn **10**
Goldbelt Hotel Juneau **13**
Juneau International Hostel **7**
Prospector Hotel **4**

DINING
Di Sopra **1**
The Fiddlehead
    Restaurant & Bakery **1**

The Hanger **14**
Heritage Coffee Co.
    and Café **15**
Pizzeria Roma **14**
Rainbow Food **9**
Red Dog Saloon **16**
Silverbow Bakery **10**
Twisted Fish Co.
    Alaskan Grill **19**
Valentine's Coffee House
    and Bakery **11**

ATTRACTIONS
Alaska State Museum **3**
The Juneau-Douglas
    City Museum **6**
The Last Chance
    Mining Museum **8**
Mount Roberts Tramway **18**
Patsy Ann Statue **17**

See "Juneau Walking Tour" map for other attractions

The Art Deco **Gold Room** ✦ restaurant is Juneau's most traditional fine-dining establishment. The dining room combines intimacy and grandeur in a real showplace of shining brass, frosted glass, and rich wood. The food varies greatly in quality year to year. Most entrees are $20 to $25.

127 N. Franklin St., Juneau, AK 99801. ☎ **800/544-0970** or 907/586-2660. Fax 907/586-8315. www.westmarkhotels.com. 196 units. High season $149–$169 double, low season $129–$139 double. Extra person over age 12 $15. AE, DC, DISC, MC, V. **Amenities:** 2 restaurants; bar; tour desk; salon; limited room service; laundry service; dry cleaning. *In room:* TV, dataport, high-speed Internet, kitchenettes in some rooms, hair dryer, iron.

Pearson's Pond Luxury Inn and Adventure Spa ✦✦✦   Diane Pearson found a vocation when she opened her bed and breakfast years ago in a suburban house near the Mendenhall Glacier, and she pursued it with a zeal that's still startling to encounter after all the years I have known her. The result is an extraordinary, sensual retreat of superbly appointed rooms, packed with every conceivable amenity, in a building and on grounds that create the illusion of being in a fairyland somewhere in the Alaska wilderness—there's even a private pond with a rowboat. Diane herself remains the wizard behind the curtain, putting out her husband's freshly baked bread with the wine that greets new guests. On overhearing visitors wish they could have fish for dinner she has been known to grab her rod, ride her bike down to the Mendenhall River, catch a salmon, and light the barbecue in time for the evening meal. As the place has grown, she has added well-trained staff, so you can get a massage or join twice-daily yoga classes, and of course the palaces (I mean rooms) are always immaculate. She hosts business travelers—there's a well-stocked snack room and all units have Ethernet ports and access to a wireless LAN (and she'll lend you a laptop, too)— but it's really a place for couples. Diane is a wedding planner and commissioner; some rooms have wonderful bathing facilities, and all are heavily sound-proofed for nights of passion. She also plans custom tour packages, if you want her to set up your whole vacation (see the sample itineraries on the website), and has more conventional condo-like lodgings downtown.

4541 Sawa Circle, Juneau, AK 99801. © **888/658-6328** or 907/789-3772. Fax 907/790-1965. www.pearsons pond.com. 5 units. High season $169–$299 double; low season $79–$179 double. Extra person $30. AE, DISC, DC, MC, V. **Amenities:** Health club; 2 outdoor Jacuzzis; free loan of rowboat, paddleboat, fishing gear, bike or laptop computer; concierge; business center; massage; free laundry service. *In room:* TV/VCR and DVD, high-speed Internet port and wireless Internet, kitchenette, coffeemaker, hair dryer, iron, CD player.

Prospector Hotel ⭐   If you want a standard American hotel room, this place is a very good choice. Situated just across the road from the water, it has nice views and close proximity to the state museum and other attractions. Parking is easy, too. The rooms are spacious and well furnished with two queen-sized beds each; one I saw had sleigh beds, while another had Shaker-style pieces in gorgeous wood. Colors are rich but calming, and the housekeeping seemed to be flawless. The standard room upstairs had a walk-in closet and facilities for snacks. But rooms are not all the same: those on upper floors and facing the water are the best (the water view carries a $6 premium), but there is noticeable road noise on that side. The elevator runs only from the lobby level upward (floors 2-5); an entire floor of rooms below (floor 1) is half-basement and can be reached only by stairs. The attached restaurant, **TK McGuire's,** is comfortable and consistent.

375 Whittier St., Juneau, AK 99801-1781. © **800/331-2711** outside Alaska, 800/478-5866 inside Alaska, or 907/586-3737. Fax 907/586-1204. www.prospectorhotel.com. 63 units. High season $149–$155 double; low season $129–$135 double. AE, DC, DISC, MC, V. **Amenities:** Restaurant; bar; limited room service; laundry service; dry cleaning. *In room:* TV, dataport, fridge, coffeemaker, hair dryer.

MODERATE

Glacier Trail Bed & Breakfast ⭐⭐ *Finds*   You wake up to an expansive view of the Mendenhall Glacier filling a picture window in a big, quiet, tastefully decorated room. Luke and Connie Nelson built the house with this moment in mind. Before beginning construction, they researched B&Bs all over the country, finding ideas for the amenities in the rooms and gaining inspiration for how to put the rooms together—not just as bedrooms with a lot of stuff in them, but as a cohesive, calming whole. A family apartment downstairs is perfect for large groups and has a kitchen. All rooms have Jacuzzi tubs. The Nelsons are fascinating, literate people with varied interests and a lifetime of experience with Alaska's outdoors. Luke's family owns a lodge on Admiralty Island, and with them he does Pack Creek tours (see "Getting Outside: On Admiralty Island," above). You'll need to rent a car if you stay here. The Nelsons also rent kayaks for outings on nearby Mendenhall Lake.

A Day Trip to Tracy Arm

Readers gush to me about the **boat tours to Tracy Arm,** south of Juneau. One reason, I suspect, is that the fjords of the Tracy Arm–Fords Terror Wilderness (part of Tongass National Forest) are relatively unknown outside the area, but the scenery and wildlife viewing easily rival those of Glacier Bay National Park, which was rated the best national park to visit by the readers of *Consumer Reports.* For those not riding a cruise ship, Tracy Arm has a significant advantage over Glacier Bay: it costs less than half as much and is easier to get to. A Tracy Arm tour takes about 8 hours; going to Glacier Bay from Juneau is an exhausting day trip—it's wiser to overnight there, though that adds more to the cost.

The Tracy Arm fjord is a long, narrow, twisting passageway into the coastal mountains, with peaks up to a mile high that jut straight out of the water, waterfalls tumbling down thousands of feet down their sides. At its head, Sawyer Glacier and South Sawyer Glacier calve ice into the water with a rumble and a splash. Whales and other wildlife usually show up along the way. And, as at Glacier Bay, John Muir paid a visit. No second-best here!

The largest operator is the Native-owned **Auk Nu Tours** (part of Goldbelt, which owns many of the big tourism businesses in town), 76 Egan Dr., Juneau (① **800/820-2628** or 907/586-8687; www.auknutours. com). They offer daylong trips every day of the week, with the exact destination somewhat contingent on tides: at times they go to Fords Terror and Dawes Glacier. Tours start at 8:45am in the summer (check for schedule changes). A naturalist provides commentary on the high-speed catamaran. A light meal and the use of binoculars are included in the adult price of $119, $70 children.

Other large boats compete with Auk Nu, and you can shop around. **Adventure Bound Alaska,** at 215 Ferry Way, Juneau (① **800/228-3875** or 907/463-2509; www.adventureboundalaska.com), is a family business operating a 56-foot single-hull boat with deck space all the way around. They charge $105 adults, $65 ages 17 and younger.

Another way to go to Tracy Arm is to charter your own boat. Although it may cost twice as much or more per person, you can decide when and where to linger with the animals or ice. Check with the visitor center for a referral, or with **Juneau Sportfishing and Sight-seeing** (① **907/586-1887**), listed in this section under "Saltwater Fishing & Whale-Watching."

1081 Arctic Circle, Juneau, AK 99801. ① **907/789-5646.** Fax 907/789-5697. www.juneaulodging.com. 3 units. High season $128–$153 double; low season $93–$108 double. Extra person $20. Rates include full breakfast. AE, MC, V. **Amenities:** Bike loan; coin-op laundry. *In room:* TV/VCR, kitchen/kitchenette, fridge, coffeemaker, hair dryer, iron, microwave.

The Historic Silverbow Inn ✦ There is an oddly pleasing style to this quirky little downtown hotel. The 1914 building, with wood floors, bare brick, and stained glass, is decorated with family pictures and weird postcards, mismatched furniture, and varied fabrics. The cozy little rooms come with extras such as lollypops and popcorn, among the original and considerate touches that show up repeatedly—for example, the shelf of supplies you may have forgotten, the answering machines on the direct-line phones, and the sack breakfast if you have to leave too early for the free breakfast in the bakery. The youthful proprietors and staff and the scene they have created with their popular **Silverbow Bakery** and their cinema give the whole place a communal feel. With the small rooms and bathrooms it's more reminiscent of a European pension than a standard hotel. The on-site cinema is an opportunity to watch independent and classic movies while tossing down a few pints of beer and scarfing up free popcorn. The restaurant, Silverbow Bakery, is described below.

120 2nd St., Juneau, AK 99801. ℂ 800/586-4146 or 907/586-4146. Fax 907/586-4242. www.silverbowinn. com. 6 units. High season $138 double; low season $88 double. Extra person $15. $10 surcharge for 1-night stays in high season. Rates include continental breakfast. AE, DISC, MC, V. **Amenities:** Restaurant; cinema. *In room:* TV, hair dryer.

INEXPENSIVE

The Driftwood Lodge *Value*   This downtown motel, next door to the State Museum, is popular with families, and houses legislators and aides in the winter in its apartmentlike kitchenette suites. Although the building can't hide its cinderblock construction and old-fashioned motel exterior, small bathrooms, or lack of elevators, the rooms are remarkably comfortable and well kept. The management has held prices low while making continuous improvements, so for the price of a budget room elsewhere ($115), you can put four people in a two-bedroom suite with a full kitchen. The round-the-clock courtesy van saves big money to the airport or ferry and the rental bikes will cover your transportation needs downtown.

435 Willoughby Ave., Juneau, AK 99801. ℂ 800/544-2239 or 907/586-2280. Fax 907/586-1034. www. driftwoodalaska.com. 63 units. High season $85 double, $93–$115 suite; low season $62 double, $89 suite. Extra person $7. AE, DC, DISC, MC, V. **Amenities:** Bike rental; courtesy van; coin-op laundry. *In room:* TV, coffeemaker.

A HOSTEL

Juneau International Hostel *Finds*   The historic yellow house among the downtown sights is a showplace of custom cabinetry and big, light common rooms. The shared kitchen was squeaky-clean when I visited (everyone has to pitch in with a chore). Men and women sleep in a number of small separate dorm rooms, and there is one private family room, which is in high demand. Office hours are from 7 to 9am and 5pm to midnight in the summer, 8 to 9am and 5 to 10:30pm in the winter, with lockout during the day. There's a coin-op laundry, free Internet access, lockers, and free local calls. Reservations must be prepaid by mail or phone for a 3-night maximum stay; if there is space available, you can stay up to 7 days. Alcohol, drugs, and pets are not allowed and shoes are removed at the door.

614 Harris St., Juneau, AK 99801. ℂ 907/586-9559. www.juneauhostel.org. 47 beds. $10 per adult; $5 children ages 6–17 with adult, free 5 and under. $1.50 premium for credit card payment. MC, V. Closed 2 weeks during winter holidays. **Amenities:** Free Internet access, coin-op laundry.

CAMPING

Juneau has two exceptional Forest Service campgrounds open from mid-May to mid-September. For information, call the **Juneau Ranger District** at ℂ 907/ 586-8800 or contact them at www.fs.fed.us/r10/tongass; neither takes reservations. The **Mendenhall Glacier Campground,** overlooking the lake and glacier

---

Finds **Quick Bites in Juneau**

The **Silverbow Bakery,** at 120 2nd St. (© **907/586-4146;** www.silverbow inn.com), is a happening spot for bagels or hearty sandwiches.

You can pick up a tasty picnic at the deli at the **Rainbow Food** health-food grocery at the corner of 224 4th Street (© **907/586-6476**).

Hot Bite, a stand at the Auke Bay boat harbor, is a local secret, serving charcoal-broiled burgers and mind-blowing milkshakes.

Downtown Juneau's young, professional population supports several good coffeehouses. **Valentine's Coffee House and Bakery,** 111 Seward St. (© **907/463-5144**), serves light hot meals in an authentic old-fashioned storefront.

Heritage Coffee Co. and Café, at 174 S. Franklin St. (© **907/586-1087;** www.heritagecoffee.com) and 216 2nd St. (© **907/586-1752**) has two trendy, comfortable coffee houses good for watching people or using the Internet, either wireless or on their terminals. They also roast famous coffee.

---

and next to the Mendenhall River, is the most-improved public campground in the state, with granite block construction. The bathrooms have showers and flush toilets and there is a half-mile disabled-accessible nature trail. The 69 sites are huge and broadly separated; nine have full RV hookups and another nine have electricity and water. Tents and RVs are segregated. To get there, turn right on Montana Creek Road from Mendenhall Loop Road. Tent sites are $10, RV sites $24 and $26. The 12-site **Auke Village Campground,** 1¾ miles north of the ferry dock, is in an extraordinary place, with sites among large trees along an ocean beach, looking out on the islands of Auke Bay. The campground has pit toilets and running water. Sites are $8 per night.

Spruce Meadow RV Park, at 10200 Mendenhall Loop Rd. (© **907/789-1990;** www.juneaurv.com), has full hookups in a natural setting with many amenities. Full hookups are $26, plus $2.50 for cable.

WHERE TO DINE

Besides these restaurants, see the **Gold Room** in the Baranof Hotel, and **TK McGuire's** in the Prospector Hotel, above. Unless otherwise stated, reservations are accepted.

EXPENSIVE

DiSopra ★★★ MEDITERRANEAN   I had a perfect meal here recently. The dining room was quiet and airy—there is a wall of windows, a huge mural, and plenty of space—the service was friendly but highly professional, and the food was both flawless in every detail and memorably delicious and interesting. Selections change frequently, but the common theme of the cuisine is adventurous flavor and texture. Before the meal, olives and bread on a plate with oil and vinegar; next I had the antipasto, with wonderful marinated grilled vegetables, shrimp, and firm, moist smoked salmon. Even the potatoes with my venison were delicious. The deserts, baked in-house, are beautiful and delicious. The wine list is nice and simple but well selected and reasonably priced. Of course there is an owner-chef behind all this, Kirk Stagg, and he clearly is on a mission.

429 W. Willoughby Ave. © 907/586-3150. Reservations recommended. Dinner main courses $16–$28. AE, DISC, MC, V. Summer daily 5–10pm; winter Tues–Sat 5:30–9pm.

MODERATE

The Fiddlehead Restaurant and Bakery ☆ SANDWICHES/ECLECTIC
This is a healthy, relaxed place with a long pedigree. It began, as the name suggests, as a ferny 1970s whole foods restaurant, and the knotty pine paneling and stained glass remain. But new owners updated the food, and now they serve from a long menu of flavorful choices, with a great variety of ethnic influences and delicacies made into sandwiches on bread baked in the restaurant. You can have lunch or dinner here for around $10 and get something memorable. One of the best fine restaurants in Alaska, DiSopra, is upstairs, under the same ownership.

429 W. Willoughby Ave. ⓒ 907/586-3150. Lunch $8–$11; dinner $8–$24. AE, DISC, MC, V. Summer daily 7am–10pm; winter daily 7am–9pm.

The Hangar ☆ STEAK/SEAFOOD/PASTA   Situated in a converted airplane hangar on a wooden pier with large windows, this bar and grill has great views and a fun atmosphere; even off-season, it's packed. It's a fine place to drink beer (with 24 brews on tap), listen to live music, or play at one of the three pool tables. What's surprising is that the food is good, too. The seared ahi sashimi appetizer, raw inside, had a pleasant texture and taste, and the jambalaya, a huge portion for $12, was spicy but balanced—the shrimp didn't get smothered, as they often do.

2 Marine Way. ⓒ 907/586-5018. Reservations recommended. Main courses $12–$25. AE, MC, V. Daily 11am–10pm.

Twisted Fish Co. Alaskan Grill ☆ SEAFOOD/PIZZA/BURGERS   Overlooking the water at the cruise ship dock, in the same building as Taku Smokeries, the dining room is magnificent, with high ceilings and an entire wall of windows on the Gastineau Channel, a fireplace of beach rock, lots of hardwood and, to keep it from being too grand, cartoon-like fish hanging down. The quality and range of the food brings locals to a tourist zone they would otherwise avoid: items like salmon on a cedar plank or in pastry, halibut or salmon tacos, and also little pizzas, burgers, and terrific deserts. The service is fast and attentive, but the dining room makes you want to stay long after you are done eating.

550 S. Franklin St. ⓒ 907/463-5033. Reservations recommended. Lunch $7–$15; dinner main courses $12–$30. AE, DISC, MC, V. Summer daily 11am–10pm. Closed Oct–Apr.

INEXPENSIVE

Chan's Thai Kitchen ☆☆ *Finds* THAI   The small, over-lit dining room in a half-basement sees few tourists, but locals brag to each other about how long they were willing to stand in the small entrance area to get a table. When I went I became a believer, too—the authentic Thai food is that good and the atmosphere, if lacking in polish, is conducive to a good time. You will need a car, as the location is 20 minutes from town across from the Auke Bay boat harbor. Reservations are not accepted and they do not have a liquor license.

11820 Glacier Hwy. ⓒ 907/789-9777. Reservations not accepted. Main courses $9–$13. MC, V. Tues–Fri 11:30am–2pm and 4:30–8:30pm, Sat 4:30–8:30pm, Sun 4:30–8pm.

Pizzeria Roma ☆ PIZZA   The pizza here is fantastic—the best in Southeast Alaska. They also serve tasty calzones, pasta, many foccacia sandwiches, and terrific salads and have a good wine list. The dining room is small, can be hot, and gets quite crowded, but it's a good place if you can slip in. The location is on the water, across the hall from the Hanger.

Tips **Lodging at the Airport**

The **Aspen Hotel Juneau** (📞 **888/559-9846** or 907/790-6435; www.aspen hotelsak.com) is nearer to your gate than the check-in desk at most airports, and it's also among Juneau's best hotels, with large, elegantly decorated rooms with high ceilings and every amenity, including a continental breakfast that is included in the price of the room. The hotel has a small pool. A room for two people is $139 summer, $89 winter.

---

2 Marine Way (In the Wharf Building). 📞 907/723-4658. Reservations not accepted. All items $7–$15. AE, DISC, MC, V. Summer daily 11am–10pm; winter daily 11am-9:30pm.

NIGHTLIFE

Alaska Travel Adventures has offered its **Gold Creek Salmon Bake** for more than 30 years. It's touristy, yes, but fun, with marshmallow roasting, music, and other entertainment—great for families. (I'd avoid it in the rain, however.) The cost is $29 for adults, $19 for children. Call 📞 **907/789-0052** to arrange pickup by van.

For more substantial performances, try to catch a show by Juneau's non-profit **Perseverance Theatre,** Alaska's largest professional theater. The winter season, starting in September and lasting until early June, includes Alaska's best cutting-edge drama, including serious homegrown work. Paula Vogel was here when she wrote "How I Learned to Drive," which later won the Pulitzer Prize. Summer offerings are limited to youth theater and workshops. To find out what's playing, contact the theater's office at 914 3rd St., Douglas (📞 **907/364-2421**), or check the website at www.perseverancetheatre.org.

A political scandal or two put a damper on some of the infamous legislative partying that once occurred in Juneau, far away from home districts, but good places to go out drinking and dancing still exist. The **Red Dog Saloon,** at 278 S. Franklin St., is the town's most famous bar, with a sawdust-strewn floor, a slightly contrived but nonetheless infectious frontier atmosphere, and walls covered with Alaska memorabilia. Locals hang across the street, at **The Alaskan Bar,** 167 S. Franklin, which occupies an authentic gold rush hotel with a two-story Victorian bar room. Boisterous parties and music go on there all year. **The Hangar,** listed above under "Where to Dine," is the place for beer drinkers. They have a big-screen TV and live music Friday and Saturday nights, as well as pool and darts.

7 Glacier Bay National Park

Glacier Bay is a work in progress; the boat ride to its head is a chance to see creation unfolding. The bay John Muir discovered in a canoe in 1879 didn't exist a century earlier. Eighteenth-century explorers had found instead a wall of ice a mile thick where the entrance to the branching, 65-mile-long fjord now opens to the sea. Receding faster than any other glacier on earth, the ice melted into the ocean and opened a spectacular and still-unfinished land. The land itself is rising 1½ inches a year as it rebounds from the weight of now-melted glaciers. As your vessel retraces Muir's path—and then probes northward in deep water where ice stood in his day—the story of this new world unravels in reverse. The trees on the shore get smaller, then disappear, then all vegetation disappears, and finally, at the head of the bay, the ice stands at the water's edge surrounded by barren rock, rounded and scored by the passage of the ice but not yet marked by the waterfalls cascading from the clouds above. And there, still doing their landscape-shaping work, are the great, blue glaciers, the largest among them the awesome Grand Pacific Glacier.

Glacier Bay, first set aside as a national monument by Calvin Coolidge in 1925, is managed by the National Park Service, which has the difficult job of protecting the wilderness, the whales, and the other wildlife while serving the huge public visiting the park. This rugged land the size of Connecticut cannot be seen by car, only by boat or plane, and the presence of too many boats threatens the wilderness experience and may disturb the wildlife. The whales appear to be sensitive to the noise of vessels and, since the 1970s, when only a single whale returned one year, the park service has used a permit system to limit the number of ships that can enter the bay. Any boat sees several other ships on a day's journey up the bay, but how much the vessels bother the whales and other wildlife is difficult to measure precisely, and political pressure always pushes for more huge ships. In response to legislation pushed through by Alaska's pro-development Congressional delegation, the park service increased the number of cruise ships entering the bay, but in 2001 environmentalists won a court ruling that briefly reduced the number and held off a further increase pending study. In 2003, the Park Service completed an Environmental Impact Statement on the issue. It allows an increase from 139 cruise ships a year to 184 per year, but only if recommended by a science advisory board. To read more about the park's vessel management plan, go to www.nps.gov/glba.

On my longest visit, I saw humpback whales breaching (leaping all the way out of the water) every day. I saw orcas, too. One day, while fishing for halibut from a small boat in foggy Icy Strait, just outside the park, I heard a sound like thunder not far off. Like thunder, the sound was repeated, growing closer, but its source remained hidden behind the white circle of fog that surrounded us. Then the smooth water suddenly bulged and a huge, barnacled creature shot upward and crashed down with a sharp clap and a splash that rocked the boat. And then it happened again. The whale went on performing for most of an hour. A day later, I encountered the same spectacle while sea kayaking in the park's Bartlett Cove.

Leaping whales and falling glaciers are hard to beat. But the park also has major drawbacks to consider. Sightings aren't guaranteed, so there's a risk that you'll spend a lot of money and not see any whales. And even though this is a huge wilderness, the ways to see it are limited, so most people never get away from crowds. The lone concessionaire-operated tour boat into the bay costs $159 per person and is usually full of people. The large cruise ships that bring most visitors to the park view the scenery without getting up close to the shore or wildlife and miss the shore-based attractions. Smaller ships see more, with smaller groups and more chances to get outdoors. Independent travelers can spend a few days in some of Alaska's most attractive remote accommodations, in Gustavus, with great fishing, hiking, sea kayaking, and tour boat rides into the park. But the only way to see the heart of the park in true solitude is on a boat you charter for yourself (out of range of most budgets) or on a rugged overnight sea-kayaking adventure.

As an alternative, consider the other places to see Alaska's glaciers and whales that are easier and less expensive to visit. If you're in Juneau, consider a day trip to Tracy Arm instead. In Southcentral Alaska, plan a day trip from Whittier to see the glaciers of western Prince William Sound or from Seward to see Kenai

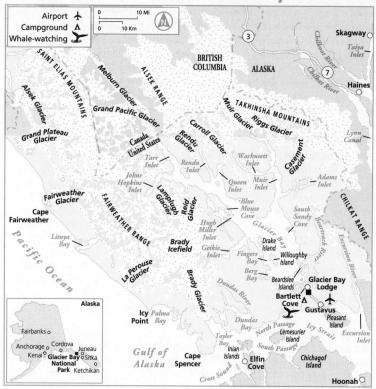

Airport ✈
Campground ▲
Whale-watching ⟋

0 ——— 10 Mi
0 ——— 10 Km

BRITISH COLUMBIA
ALASKA

Skagway
Taiya Inlet
Haines

SAINT ELIAS MOUNTAINS
Melburn Glacier
ALSEK RANGE
Chilkoot River
Chilkat River
TAKHINSHA MOUNTAINS
Riggs Glacier
Muir Glacier
Lynn Canal

Alsek Glacier
Grand Pacific Glacier
Carroll Glacier
Rendu Glacier
Wachusett Inlet
Casement Glacier

Grand Plateau Glacier
Canada United States
Tarr Inlet
Rendu Inlet
Queen Inlet
Muir Inlet
Adams Inlet
CHILKAT RANGE

Fairweather Glacier
Johns Hopkins Inlet
Lamplugh Glacier
Reid Glacier
Blue Mouse Cove
South Sandy Cove

Cape Fairweather
FAIRWEATHER RANGE
Hugh Miller Inlet
Glacier Bay
Bearroach River
Excursion River

Lituya Bay
Brady Icefield
Geikie Inlet
Fingers Bay
Drake Island
Willoughby Island

Pacific Ocean
La Perouse Glacier
Berg Bay
Beardslee Islands
Glacier Bay Lodge

Brady Glacier
Dundas River
Bartlett Cove
Gustavus
Pleasant Island

Icy Point
Palma Bay
Dundas Bay
Lemesurier Island
Icy Strait
Excursion Inlet

Gulf of Alaska
Taylor Bay
Inian Islands
North Passage
South Passage
Cape Spencer
Elfin Cove
Chichagof Island

Cross Sound
Hoonah

Alaska
Fairbanks
Anchorage Cordova Juneau
Kenai Glacier Bay Sitka
National Park Ketchikan

Fjords National Park. There are other places in Southeast rich with marine wildlife, as well. Still, Glacier Bay beats them all—and just about anyplace on earth—for the combination of lots of whales and lots of big glaciers.

ESSENTIALS
GETTING THERE

Gustavus, covered in the next section of this chapter, is the gateway to Glacier Bay. Unless you're on a cruise ship passing through the bay without landing, you probably will pass through Gustavus, either by air or on the Glacier Bay Ferry. To avoid duplication, I have covered the ferry in the Gustavus section on p. 171. Vans to the park headquarters at Bartlett Cove meet planes and boats and charge $12 to make the 10-mile trip to the park, plus $2 for baggage. It's free if you are traveling with a package tour; also, most of the inns and lodges in Gustavus offer free transfers to the park.

BY TOUR BOAT   A day boat is the main way for independent travelers to see the park. It is operated by park concessionaire, a joint venture of ARAMARK and Huna Totem, with offices at 241 W. Ship Creek Ave., Anchorage, AK 99501 (© **888/229-8687** or 907/276-7234; fax 907/258-3668; www.visit glacierbay.com), or, locally, in the summer only, at P.O. Box 179, Gustavus, AK 99826 (© **907/697-4000;** fax 907/697-4001). The boat leaves from the dock in Bartlett Cove and sails to the fjords' very head and the Grand Pacific Glacier. The 8-hour voyage is too long for many children. There's a snack bar, and a simple lunch is provided. Bring good rain gear and layers of warm clothing. Binoculars, a necessity, are provided. A park service ranger does the commentary, so you can count on accuracy and a didactic approach missing from most commercial tours. The fare is $165 for adults, $83 for children.

The company offers a same-day trip from Juneau, Haines, or Skagway, but it makes for too long a day, and the schedule leaves no shore time in Glacier Bay or Gustavus or time for whale-watching in Icy Strait (covered in the Gustavus section). A better choice is to book one of their multiday packages, which may save money over separate transportation and room rates, and include all the transfers and details.

BY SMALL CRUISE SHIP   If your budget allows, there may be no better way to see Glacier Bay than on a small cruise ship on an excursion of a couple of days or more. **Glacier Bay Cruiselines** has developed a whole small-ship cruise fleet around this idea, and visitors come back overjoyed. Three vessels, the *Wilderness Explorer* and the larger *Wilderness Adventurer* and *Wilderness Discoverer,* carry racks of sea kayaks. **Cruise West** also offers small-ship itineraries including Glacier Bay. See chapter 4 for complete reviews of each.

Local family operators based in Gustavus also do these trips. If you have a large group, you can have a boat and guide to yourself. Mike Nigro, a former backcountry ranger and longtime resident, takes groups of four to six for $1,600 per day on a 42-foot yacht. His **Gustavus Marine Charters** can be reached at ✆ **907/697-2233** or www.gustavusmarinecharters.com.

VISITOR INFORMATION
Contact the **Glacier Bay National Park and Preserve** at P.O. Box 140, Gustavus, AK 99826 (✆ **907/697-2230;** www.nps.gov/glba). The park service interprets the park mainly by placing well-prepared rangers on board most cruise and tour vessels entering the bay. The park also maintains a modest visitor center with displays on the park on the second floor of the lodge at wooded Bartlett Cove. Pick up the park map and handy guide, *The Fairweather.* Nearby are the park's offices, a free campground, a backcountry office, a few short hiking trails, a dock, sea kayak rental, and other park facilities. Rangers lead daily nature walks and present an evening slide show.

ACTIVITIES AT THE PARK
HIKING AT BARTLETT COVE   There are three short hiking trails through the rainforest of Sitka spruce and western hemlock at Bartlett Cove. Each weaves through the cool, damp quiet created by these huge trees and the moss on the forest floor. Wet spots are often crossed by boardwalks with railings. A free trail guide is available at the visitor center.

The **Forest Loop** is an easy trail about 1 mile long, beginning at the lodge and passing through the woods and past some park buildings to the cove's pebble beach. The **Bartlett River Trail** is a 4-mile round-trip leading to the Bartlett River Estuary, a good bird-watching spot, especially during migrations. The **Bartlett Lake Trail** branches off the Bartlett River Trail after about ¼ mile for a 3.75-mile one-way forest hike to the lake.

KAYAKING IN THE PARK   You won't forget seeing a breaching humpback whale from a sea kayak, sitting just inches off the water. It happens around here. When we breathlessly told our innkeepers about the experience, they smiled politely. They hear the same descriptions all the time.

Inexperienced paddlers should choose a guided trip. **Alaska Discovery,** 5310 Glacier Hwy., Juneau (✆ **800/586-1911** or 907/780-6226; www.ak discovery.com), is Alaska's best large sea-kayak guide organization. They offer paddles ranging from 6 hours to 8 days in Glacier Bay. A 6-hour guided paddle from Bartlett Cove is the best choice for beginners. Although the trip goes nowhere near the glaciers, the paddlers stand a good chance of seeing whales, sometimes quite close up. The guides are well trained and know how to teach and make the trip an adventure. Any fit person can enjoy the trip. It costs $125, including a tasty lunch and a ride from your lodgings or the airport. The longer tours also are well guided and outfitted, but I wouldn't recommend a week of sea kayaking to anyone who hasn't tried it before (what if you find out the first day that you don't like kayaking?). If you're up to it, however, this is the most intimate and authentic way to experience this wilderness, with almost unlimited time to see the glaciers and wildlife. A 5-day trip to the bay's more visited west arm, geared to novices, is $1,895; a more strenuous 8 days in the spectacular but forgotten east arm is $2,495. The company also has a simple bed-and-breakfast in Gustavus, for 1- or 2-night stays at the beginning or end of a sea-kayaking excursion.

It's also possible to paddle around Bartlett Cove or near Gustavus without a guide. Raw beginners can try it, but a safer course is to take a guided outing first. **Glacier Bay Sea Kayaks,** based in Gustavus (✆ **907/697-2257;** www.glacier bayseakayaks.com), is the park service rental concessionaire, operating from May 1 to September 30. They offer day rentals, which begin with an instructional briefing, for $60 a day. Getting dropped off in the wilderness up the bay, near the glaciers, costs $190 round-trip. You will need a backcountry permit from the park service to make such a self-guided expedition, and you'll have to attend a briefing by a ranger. Permits are readily available at the park headquarters, but research what to bring before you leave for the park.

WHALE-WATCHING   It's sometimes possible to see whales from the lodge at Bartlett Cove and they often show up for passengers on the day boat cruise that is the main way into the park, but there is another option with whale sightings essentially guaranteed: the Glacier Bay Ferry, which takes off from the Bartlett Cove Dock four afternoons a week for whale-watching in Icy Strait, outside the park. See p. 171.

FLIGHTSEEING   One way to get into the park is by flightseeing. Gustavus-based **Air Excursions** (✆ **907/697-2375**) offers air tours, as do other operators from various towns, Haines and Skagway being the closest (see section 10). You'll see the incredible rivers of ice that flow down into the bay, and you may even see wildlife. What you give up is the sense of scale from ground level.

WHERE TO STAY, CAMP & DINE

Glacier Bay Lodge ✮   Operated by a new park concessionaire in 2004, this is the only place to stay in the park (although Gustavus, 10 miles down the road, has some of the most attractive accommodations in Alaska; see the next section). The lodge rooms were in the process of being upgraded at this writing; previously, they were comfortable but behind the times. The buildings are set amid the soothing quiet of large rainforest trees and are reached from the main lodge by boardwalks and steps.

The **restaurant** has huge windows looking onto Bartlett Cove, where you can sometimes see whales. Again, everything was under revision at this writing and not ready to be reviewed. The new menu includes a wider variety of dishes, including more fresh fish. I have always enjoyed dining on the deck and watching for whales. The restaurant serves breakfast as early as 5:30am and dinner as late as 10pm. Drinks are served in the restaurant or on the deck over the cove from 4 to 10pm; on rainy days, visitors congregate around the fire in the comfortable lobby. Laundry facilities and bike rentals are available.

The area's least expensive lodgings are the bunks in men's and women's dorms with six beds each. The lodge also provides public showers for the free park service **campground.** About ¼ mile from the dock, the campground lacks running water but has a warming hut, firewood, and bear-resistant food caches. You have to cook in a fire ring in the intertidal zone and observe other bear avoidance rules the rangers will explain. Get a camping permit at the ranger station when you arrive; the campground is almost never full.

Bartlett Cove (P.O. Box 179), Gustavus, AK 99826. ✆ **888/229-8687** or 907/697-4000. Fax 907/258-3668 or 907/697-4001. www.visitglacierbay.com. 56 units. $189 double. Extra person $10. Hostel bunks $35 per person. AE, DC, DISC, MC, V. Closed mid-Sept to mid-May. **Amenities:** Restaurant; bike rental; coin-op laundry.

8 Gustavus: Country Inns & Quiet

The unincorporated town of Gustavus (gus-*tave*-us) remains an undiscovered treasure—or at least it succeeds in making itself feel that way. It's wonderfully remote, accessible only by air or a small passenger ferry, but has a selection of comfortable and even luxurious inns and lodges, plus several days' worth of outdoor activities, excellent salmon and halibut fishing, nearly surefire whale-watching, close access to sea kayaking and other activities at Glacier Bay National Park, and places for casual hiking and bicycle outings. Neither large cruise ships nor the Alaska state ferry land here, leaving the roads free of their throngs of shoppers. Miraculously, the 400 townspeople have been smart enough to value what they've got and build on it. Even the gas station is a work of art. Walking, biking, or driving down the quiet roads, everyone you pass—every single person—waves to you.

The buildings, mostly clapboard houses and log cabins, are scattered widely across an oceanfront alluvial plain. Several of the founding homesteads were farms, and the broad clearings of sandy soil wave with hay and wildflowers. The setting is unique in Alaska, and when I had a choice to go anywhere in the state for a 4-day trip with extended family, this is the place I chose. Each of us took something lasting from the trip. My older son, then 8, learned what it was like to be able to bike anywhere at will, making discoveries in the woods and friends on the quiet lanes without his parents reining him in. My parents, in their 60s, glowed when they returned from kayaking among the breaching humpback whales in the park's Bartlett Cove. I often reminisce about a day at the beach when I built dams and sand castles with the children, looking up to see a family of orcas romping just offshore. My cousin won't forget the huge platters of Dungeness crab that came for dinner one night at the inn.

Tips Be Prepared before Arriving in Gustavus

Gustavus isn't formally a town; it has no bank or ATM and few other businesses. Bring cash, as credit cards aren't always accepted, and don't count on being able to buy incidentals. Reserve all accommodations before you come.

The problem with Gustavus is the expense (and the dampness, but you get used to that). The best outdoor activities involve charters or rentals, which can add more than $200 a day per person to the cost of your trip. Most accommodations have all-inclusive plans, which include great meals but come with price tags of at least $150 per person per night. Less expensive B&Bs exist, but the choice of restaurants for dinner is limited.

ESSENTIALS

GETTING THERE   The **Glacier Bay Ferry,** a privately-operated foot passenger vessel (© **800/820-2628** or 907/586-8687; www.goldbelttours.com), travels from Juneau to the national park headquarters in Bartlett Cove four days a week June through August. The schedule seems to change every year, but at present the boat leaves Monday, Wednesday, Friday, and Saturday at 10am from a dock in Auke Bay near the state ferry terminal. It arrives at Bartlett Cove at 1pm. Next the boat goes on a 2½ hour whale-watching cruise in Icy Strait, ending up at the Gustavus Dock (vans carry passengers who want to return to Bartlett Cove). At 5:30pm the boat leaves Gustavus and arrives back at Auke Bay at 8:30pm. The one-way fare from Juneau to Gustavus/Glacier Bay is $69 adults, $35 children. A transfer from downtown Juneau to the Auke Bay dock is $15, from the Juneau airport $10. The whale watch alone costs $79 for adults and $49 for children. The combined round-trip and whale watch costs $195. The ferry will carry kayaks, bikes, and other cargo for an added fee, and they serve light meals.

During the summer, **Alaska Airlines** (© **800/252-7522;** www.alaskaair. com) flies a jet once a day from Juneau to Gustavus and back in the early evening. The fare is around $130, round-trip. For more frequent service by prop from Juneau to Gustavus, at roughly the same fare as Alaska Airlines, use **Wings of Alaska** (© **907/789-0790** reservations, or 907/697-2201 in Gustavus; www. wingsofalaska.com).

VISITOR INFORMATION   The traditional way to plan a trip to Gustavus is to contact a lodge and, once you're comfortable with them, allow them to advise you and book your activities. The **Gustavus Visitors Association** (www.gustavusalaska.org) operates a website with links to each of the lodges and other accommodations, and lots of other community information, but there is still no staffed visitor center. Reach them by mail at P.O. Box 167, Gustavus, AK 99826. A local travel agency, **Alaska's Glacier Bay Travel** (© **907/697-2475;** www.glacierbaytravel.com), run by the same folks as the TLC Taxi (see below), also can help with choices and reservations. Be certain to reserve a place to stay before showing up in Gustavus.

GETTING AROUND   There are just a few roads. The main one starts at the airport and runs about 10 miles to **Bartlett Cove,** the Glacier Bay National Park base of operations. **Dock Road** branches off to the left, at the gas station, and leads to the ocean dock. There's a map and list of businesses posted near the gas station and most businesses will give you one to take along for exploration by bicycle. Many inns and B&Bs have courtesy vans and free bicycles; ask about transportation when you reserve. **TLC Taxi** (© **907/697-2239;** tlctaxi@glacier baytravel.com) offers transportation between the airport, ferry, and Bartlett Cove. Reserve ahead. The fare depends on the number of travelers. A van can accommodate groups, gear, and kayaks. **Bud's Rent a Car** is at © **907/697-2403.**

EXPLORING GUSTAVUS

Everything to do in Gustavus involves the outdoors. I've listed the activities here in priority order.

WHALE-WATCHING & FISHING   Whales keep their own schedule, but you're almost certain to see them on a whale-watching excursion here, where the swirling current of Icy Strait creates such a rich feeding ground that humpbacks come back every summer without fail. Whale-watching trips aboard the comfortable Glacier Bay Ferry (see "Getting There," above) leave Bartlett Cove Monday, Wednesday, Friday, and Saturday at 2pm, returning to the Gustavus Dock at 4:30pm. A good, light meal is included in the price. The fare is $79 adults, $60 children, and you get your money back if you don't see whales—which virtually never happens.

Other, smaller operators will provide a more intimate experience on smaller boats, usually getting you closer to the whales. They'll also combine the trip with superb halibut and salmon fishing (if salmon are running). The waters are protected and seasickness generally is not a concern. Your inn host in Gustavus can make the arrangements. A boat typically charters for $200 or more per person for a full day, plus the cost of having your fish professionally packed and shipped home to you.

SEA KAYAKING   Alaska Discovery, 5310 Glacier Hwy., Juneau (© 800/586-1911 or 907/780-6226; www.akdiscovery.com), offers an easy 3-day, 2-night kayaking expedition among the whales for $850 per person. They take a boat to a base camp, then kayak among the whales from there. The outing is suitable for fit beginners and older children.

Gustavus-based **Spirit Walker Expeditions** (© 800/KAYAKER or 907/697-2266; www.seakayakalaska.com) has a good reputation locally. They lead guided 1- to 7-day trips to the whale-watching grounds and beyond.

Sea Otter Kayak Glacier Bay (© 907/697-3007; www.he.net/~seaotter) rents kayaks and gear and provides basic training (although beginners should go with a guide) on Dock Road for Gustavus or Glacier Bay waters. They also help with trip planning.

HIKING & BICYCLING   There are few cars in Gustavus—they have to be hauled here on a barge or plane—but most inns provide bikes. The roads are fun to explore, and the sandy beaches, accessed from the town dock, are great for a walk and a picnic, to watch eagles and other birds and wildlife. You can go many miles, if you are of a mind for a run or long walk, but we saw little reason to go far before stopping to play and picnic on a broad sand beach undisturbed by any other human footprint.

WHERE TO STAY & DINE

Gustavus contains some of Alaska's best remote accommodations, more than I have room to describe here. In addition to the accommodations detailed below, another of the best is the **Glacier Bay Country Inn,** Tong Road (© 800/628-0912 or 907/697-2288; www.glacierbayalaska.com).

Most accommodations are "Gustavus style," which means they charge a daily per-person price for rooms, breakfast and dinner served family style, brown-bag lunches, bicycles, and some other outdoor equipment and transfers, and they book and charge for fishing, sea kayaking, hiking, and Glacier Bay tours. It's expensive, but it's a carefree way to visit. Another set of accommodations charges less, but leaves you on your own for lunch and dinner.

If you choose the less costly, a la carte approach, you'll likely take your evening meals at the inns anyway, as Gustavus is short on restaurants. You'll have to make prior arrangements; you can't just show up and eat. The Glacier Bay Lodge serves three meals a day—but it's 10 miles away at the park's Bartlett Cove headquarters. A country store on Dock Road sells basics for picnics or cooking yourself.

One free-standing restaurant that's been going strong for years is **A Bear's Nest Cafe,** less than half a mile from the main intersection on Wilson Road (② **907/697-2440;** www.gustavus.com/bearsnest), where the often braided Lynne Morrow serves organic dishes, homemade bread, local seafood, soup, sandwiches, and dessert in a homey dining room with baskets hanging from the open beam ceiling. It is open in summer daily 11am to 8pm. She accepts Discover, MasterCard, and Visa and has a couple of cabins for rent, too.

Except as noted, rooms in Gustavus don't have phones. Some of the inns do not have licenses to serve alcohol; if that's a consideration, be sure to ask before you book your stay.

Blue Heron Bed and Breakfast at Glacier Bay ⭐   Stay here if your budget doesn't allow a pricey all-inclusive package, and you'll still get many of the same comforts in fresh, attractive rooms with features such as VCRs, comforters, and superior linens. The hosts, longtime residents, are enthusiastic about their guests and serve large breakfasts. If you rent one of the cottages, you can cook your own evening meal; even the rooms have limited cooking facilities. The location is among the wildflowers and marshland near the Gustavus waterfront.

Off Dock Rd. (P.O. Box 77), Gustavus, AK 99826. ② **907/697-2337.** Fax 907/697-2293. www.blueheron bnb.net. 2 units, 2 cabins. $130 double, $160 double cottage. Extra adult $60–$70; discounts for children. No credit cards. **Amenities:** Free bike loan; courtesy van; massage; laundry machines ($6 per load). *In room:* TV/VCR.

Glacier Bay's Bear Track Inn ⭐⭐⭐   Six miles from Gustavus, this extraordinary log building faces its own field of wildflowers, which, if you walk half a mile across it, leads to the sea. You look out on this scene from a lobby with a huge fireplace, a ceiling 28 feet high, and a wall of windows. The immense logs of the walls and the isolation give the place the feeling of a wilderness lodge, but the rooms are as good as those of any upscale hotel, and have the advantage of large dormer windows with sweeping views. Objectively, it's the best place in Gustavus, and one of the best remote lodges in Alaska, but which place you prefer depends on your taste: what the Bear Track gains from perfection it loses in the funky, quaint atmosphere I like about the area. One major advantage over the other lodges and inns: meals here are cooked to order from a varied menu. Those not staying here can buy dinner, too. The inn serves beer and wine. It also offers car rental.

255 Rink Rd., Gustavus, AK 99826. ② **888/697-2284** or 907/697-3017. Fax 907/697-2284. www.beartrack inn.com. 14 units. $454 per person, double occupancy; discounts for additional nights. Rates include roundtrip air from Juneau, transfers, and all meals. DISC, MC, V. Closed Oct–Apr. **Amenities:** Restaurant; free bike loan; children's programs; concierge; tour desk; car rental; business center; limited room service; massage; babysitting; laundry service. *In room:* Hair dryer.

Gustavus Inn at Glacier Bay ⭐⭐⭐   This is the original and still my favorite of the Gustavus full-service inns. By objective standards of modern luxury, imitators have surpassed the old homestead farmhouse, but no one could duplicate the extraordinary hospitality of the Lesh family, honed over 35 years of running the inn. They know how to make guests feel immediately a part of the place. The site is unsurpassed, too, standing at the center of the community amid blowing grass and with a huge vegetable garden that provides much of the dining room's wonderful food. Dave, the chef, has published a cookbook. The seasonings he uses on seafood are a real revelation. He serves big, inexhaustible platters in the dining room, where there's also a beer and wine bar and sushi appetizers. Before going, talk over what you want to do with Dave or his father, Jack, and let them book everything.

1 Gustavus Rd. (P.O. Box 60), Gustavus, AK 99826. © **800/649-5220** or 907/697-2254. Fax 907/697-2255. www.gustavusinn.com. 11 units. $160 per person per night based on double or triple occupancy. Half price for children under 12. Rates include all meals. AE, MC, V. Closed Sept 16–May 15. **Amenities:** Restaurant; fishing rods (bring your own tackle); bike loan; courtesy car; laundry service.

9 Haines: Eagles & the Unexpected

For years we always just passed through Haines on the way from the ferry up the highway. I didn't know what I was missing until I stopped and took a couple of days to really investigate. Now Haines is one of my favorite Alaska towns.

Haines is casual, happy, and slightly odd. It waits for you to find it, but once found, it unveils wonderful charms. If you're looking for the mythical town of Cicely from television's *Northern Exposure,* you'll get closer in Haines than anyplace else I know (in fact, the producers scouted here before choosing to shoot in Roslyn, Washington). As I walked down a sidewalk, I saw a sign in a storefront that said to look in the big tree across the street. I looked, and there was an eagle peering back at me. At the Alaska Indian Arts Native cultural center, seeking an office or a ticket window or someone in charge, I wandered into a totem pole studio where a carver was completing a major commission. He gladly stopped to talk. It turned out there wasn't anyone in charge. Issues that are a big deal in some other towns just aren't in Haines.

Haines's dominant feature, the 1904 **Fort William H. Seward,** gives the town a pastoral atmosphere. The fort is a collection of grand white-clapboard buildings arranged around a 9-acre parade ground, in the middle of which stands a Tlingit clan house—out of place, yes, but wonderfully symbolic of Haines. The town is a friendly, accessible center of Tlingit culture as well as a retired outpost of seemingly pointless military activity.

And Haines has **bald eagles**—always plenty of bald eagles, and in the fall, a ridiculous number of bald eagles. More, in fact, than anywhere else on earth. The chance to see the birds draws people into the outdoors here. There are well-established guides for any activity you might want to pursue, all cooperating and located together. There are some excellent hiking trails right from town, as well as protected sea-kayaking waters. Also, it's worth noting that because of its location in the flow of weather, adjacent to the drier Interior, Haines is not quite as rainy as towns father south.

ESSENTIALS
GETTING THERE The **Alaska Marine Highway System,** 1591 Glacier Ave., Juneau, AK 99801-1427 (© **800/642-0066** or 907/766-2111 locally; www.ferryalaska.com), is how most people get to Haines, and the cruise on the Lynn Canal fjord from Juneau or Skagway is among the most beautiful in the Inside Passage. The conventional ferry takes about 5 hours from Juneau and costs $32 (the fast ferry takes half the time and costs $35). The trip to Skagway takes an hour and the fare is $26. The dock is 5 miles north of town.

If you're just going to or from Skagway without a car, a good alternative is the Haines-Skagway Fast Ferry, operated by **Chilkat Cruises and Tours** (© **888/766-2103** or 907/766-2100; www.chilkatcruises.com). The company's

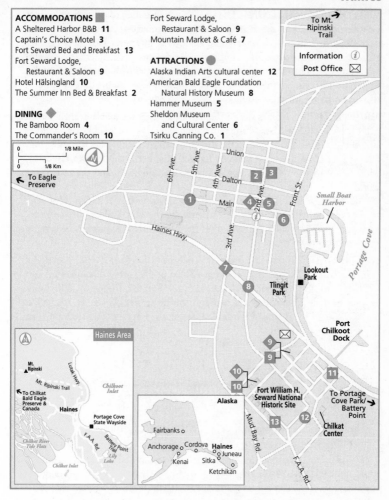

ACCOMMODATIONS ■
A Sheltered Harbor B&B **11**
Captain's Choice Motel **3**
Fort Seward Bed and Breakfast **13**
Fort Seward Lodge,
   Restaurant & Saloon **9**
Hotel Hälsingland **10**
The Summer Inn Bed & Breakfast **2**

DINING ◆
The Bamboo Room **4**
The Commander's Room **10**

Fort Seward Lodge,
   Restaurant & Saloon **9**
Mountain Market & Café **7**

ATTRACTIONS ●
Alaska Indian Arts cultural center **12**
American Bald Eagle Foundation
   Natural History Museum **8**
Hammer Museum **5**
Sheldon Museum
   and Cultural Center **6**
Tsirku Canning Co. **1**

Information ⓘ
Post Office ✉

To Mt.
Ripinski
Trail

Fairweather Express, a 150-passenger catamaran, makes at least three 35-minute round-trip runs a day. The catamaran leaves from the Port Chilkoot dock, below Fort William Seward. Adult round-trips are $45, one-way $25; children 12 and under pay half price.

If you're driving, the **Haines Highway** leads 155 miles to Haines Junction, Yukon Territory, an intersection with the Alaska Highway (you must pass through Canadian Customs—see section 5, "The Alaska Highway," in chapter 9 for rules). The road runs along the Chilkat River and the bald eagle preserve, then climbs into spectacular alpine terrain. Anchorage is 760 driving miles from Haines and Fairbanks is 644.

Several air services offer scheduled prop service, air taxis, and flightseeing tours to surrounding communities from Haines. **Wings of Alaska** (☎ **907/ 789-0790** reservations, or 907/766-2030 in Haines; www.wingsofalaska.com) has plenty of flights, charging $160 round trip from Juneau.

VISITOR INFORMATION   The small but well-staffed and -stocked **Haines Convention and Visitors Bureau Visitor Information Center,** 2nd Avenue near Willard (P.O. Box 530), Haines, AK 99827 (© **800/458-3579** or 907/ 766-2234; www.haines.ak.us), is operated by the city government, which also sends out a vacation-planning packet. It's open summer Monday through Friday from 8am to 7pm, Saturday from 9am to 5pm, Sunday from 11am to 5pm; in winter, hours are Monday through Friday from 8am to 5pm.

ORIENTATION   Haines sits on the narrow Chilkat Peninsula near the north end of the Southeast Alaska Panhandle. Highways run north and east on either side of the peninsula; the one on the east side goes to the ferry dock, 5 miles out, and ends after 11 miles at **Chilkoot Lake.** The other is the **Haines Highway,** which leads to the Canadian border, the Alaska Highway, and the rest of the world.

The town has two parts: the sparsely built downtown grid and, a short walk to the west down Front Street or 2nd Avenue, the Fort William Seward area. Vans and buses that meet the ferry offer free or inexpensive transfers, seeking to take you on a town tour.

GETTING AROUND   Bikes are available from **Sockeye Cycle,** just uphill from the Port Chilkoot Dock on Portage Street in the Fort William Seward area (© **907/766-2869;** www.cyclealaska.com), for $12 for 2 hours or $30 a day. **Haines Shuttle and Tours** is a taxi and shuttle service. It can be reached at © **907/766-3138.** Rent at **Affordable Cars,** in the Captain's Choice Motel (see "Where to Stay," below).

FAST FACTS: **Haines**

Bank **First National Bank of Alaska,** which has an ATM, is at Main Street and 2nd Avenue.

Hospital The **Haines Medical Clinic** (© **907/766-2521**) is on 1st Avenue, near the visitor center.

Internet Access **Mountain Market,** at 3rd Avenue and the Haines Highway (© **907/766-3340**), charges $8 an hour. Nearby, at the gorgeous **Haines Borough Library,** 111 3rd Ave. S. (© **907/766-2545;** www.haines library.org), you can log on for free.

Police Reach city police in non-emergencies at © **907/766-2121.** Outside city limits, call the **Alaska State Troopers** at © **907/766-2552.**

Post Office At 55 Haines Hwy., just west of Fort Seward.

Taxes The local sales tax is 5.5%.

SPECIAL EVENTS   The 160-mile **Kluane to Chilkat International Bike Relay** (© **907/766-2202;** www.kcibr.org) is held the third Saturday in June, heading steeply down the Haines Highway from Haines Junction, with more than 1,000 entrants riding in teams of two, four, or eight.

The **Southeast Alaska State Fair and Bald Eagle Music Festival** (© **907/ 766-2476;** www.seakfair.org) is the biggest event of the summer, held for 4 days in mid-August; it's a regional small-town get-together, with livestock, cooking, a logging show, a parade, music, and other entertainment. Buildings constructed for the filming of the movie *White Fang* in 1990 were donated to the fair, and now form the nucleus of a retail area here. One stop of interest here, at any time, is the local microbrewery, Haines Brewing Co., which offers samples and informal tours.

The **Alaska Bald Eagle Festival** (© **907/766-3094;** www.baldeaglefest.org) offers seminars and special events to mark the annual eagle congregation. Held over 4 days the second weekend in November, it is timed to allow visitors to also attend the WhaleFest in Sitka.

EXPLORING HAINES

It seems that each year Haines further cements its position as Alaska's center of odd or unusual museums. In the spirit of this distinction, I've described these attractions in the order of their creation, beginning with the Tlingit art center in an old military hospital and ending with the newest addition, a collection of more than 1,000 hammers.

You can't miss **Fort William H. Seward National Historic Site,** the collection of large, white, wood-frame buildings around sloping parade grounds overlooking the magnificent Lynn Canal fjord. (Get the informative History Walking Tour brochure of the National Historic Site from the Haines Convention and Visitors Bureau to learn about each building.)

The fort led a peaceful life, for a military installation. By the time the U.S. Army built it, in 1904, the Klondike gold rush was over, and there's no evidence it ever deterred any attack on this little peninsula at the north end of the Inside Passage. It was deactivated at the end of World War II, when it was used for training.

In 1947 a group of five veterans from the Lower 48 bought the fort as surplus with the idea of forming a planned community. That idea didn't quite work out, but one of the new white families helped spark a Chilkat Tlingit cultural renaissance in the 1950s. The Heinmillers, who still own a majority of the shares in the fort, were looking for something to do with all that property when someone suggested a Tlingit tribal house on the parade grounds. The project, led by a pair of elders, took on a life of its own, and the **Alaska Indian Arts** cultural center followed. Lee Heinmiller, a member of the family's second generation, still manages the arts center, where you can see totem carving and silversmithing practiced. It is open from 9am to 5pm Monday through Friday and evenings when cruise ships are in town. It occupies the old fort hospital on the south side of the parade grounds.

In the downtown area, the **Sheldon Museum and Cultural Center,** 11 Main St. (© **907/766-2366;** www.sheldonmuseum.org), contains an upstairs gallery of well-presented Tlingit art and cultural artifacts; downstairs is a collection on the white history of the town. There's a uniquely personal feel to the Tlingit objects, some of which are displayed with pictures of the artisans who made them and the history of their relationship with the Sheldons, for whom the museum is named. It's open in summer Monday through Friday 11am to 6pm, Saturday and Sunday 2 to 6pm; in winter, it's open Monday through Friday from 1 to 4pm. Admission is $3 for adults, free for children under 12.

The entirely unique **American Bald Eagle Foundation Natural History Museum,** at 2nd Avenue and Haines Highway (© **907/766-3094;** www.baldeagles.org), is essentially a huge, hair-raising diorama of more than 180 eagles and other animal mounts. Dave Olerud often sits in a wheelchair behind the desk and will talk your ear off about the museum if you want him to—he worked on it for 18 years and was paralyzed in a fall during construction. Admission is $3 adults, $1 ages 8 to 12; children need to be with an adult. It's open summer Monday through Friday from 9am to 6pm, Saturday and Sunday from 1 to 4pm; closed during the winter.

The **Tsirku Canning Co.,** at 5th Avenue and Main Street (© **907/766-3474;** www.cannerytour.com), is a museum of Alaska salmon canning, full of 80-year-old machinery salvaged from abandoned canneries around the state, including a 120-foot line that goes through the process of canning imaginary fish, including making the can. The fishing industry remains the state's largest employer, and was long its largest industry by any measure. In 1929, 157 canneries stood all along the coast, teeming with summer workers and served by frequent steamer service, many in places where nothing remains today but broken dock pilings. Haines had nine. The hour-long museum tour, including a 10-minute video, costs $10 adults, free ages 12 and under. Call for a recorded message of the time of the next tour, which is changeable.

The newest addition to Haines' line-up of the unusual is the **Hammer Museum,** at 108 Main St., across from the bank (© **907/766-2374**). Longshoreman Dave Pahl created his collection of hammers over a couple of decades of building a homestead. He found the prize of his collection, an 800-year-old Tlingit war hammer, while digging up the foundation of the museum itself. More than 1,000 hammers from all over the world, old and new, exotic and ordinary, fill a tiny space. The fun part is guessing what each is for. It is open summer Monday through Friday 10am to 5pm, closed off season. Admission is $3 adults, free for children 12 and under.

GETTING OUTSIDE

EAGLE VIEWING   Haines is probably the best place on earth to see bald eagles. The **Chilkat Bald Eagle Preserve** protects 48,000 acres of river bottom along the Chilkat River. From October to mid-December, peaking around Thanksgiving, up to 3,000 eagles gather in the cottonwood trees (also known as western poplar) on a small section of the river, a phenomenon known as the Fall Congregation. (A healthy 200–400 are resident the rest of the year.) The eagles come for easy winter food: A very late salmon run spawns here into December in a 5-mile stretch of open water known as the Council Grounds. During the Congregation, dozens of eagles stand in each of the gnarled, leafless cottonwoods on the riverbanks, occasionally diving for a fish. The best places to see them are pull-outs, paths, and viewing areas along the Haines Highway from miles 18 to 21. Don't walk on the flats, as that disturbs the eagles. The preserve is managed by **Alaska State Parks** (www.alaskastateparks.org, click on "Individual Parks"). Contact the local ranger at © **907/766-2292;** the headquarters is at 400 Willoughby, 3rd Floor, Juneau, AK 99801.

Local guides offer trips to see the eagles by raft, bicycle, or bus—mostly in the summer, when the eagles are fewer but visitors more numerous. **Chilkat Guides,** based at Mile 1 Haines Hwy. along Sawmill Road (© **907/766-2491;** www.raftalaska.com), does a rafting trip several times a day during the summer down the Chilkat to watch the eagles. The water is gentle—if it's too low, there's a chance you'll be asked to get out and push—and you'll see lots of eagles, mostly at a distance. The company is run by young people who create a sense of fellowship with their clients. The 4-hour trip, with a snack, costs $79 for adults, $62 for children ages 7 to 12. **Sockeye Cycle** (see "Biking," below) has guided bike tours to see eagles and Fort Seward on a 90-minute trip that costs $42. Serious bird watchers and others who want an in-depth tour should join **Alaska Nature Tours** (© **907/766-2876;** www.alaskanaturetours.net), which leads 3-hour wildlife viewing tours by bus for $55 year round. The company also offers longer tours, such as all-day guided hikes, for $100, and cross-country skiing in and around the preserve.

BIKING   **Sockeye Cycle,** at 24 Portage St., near the dock (© **907/766-2869;** www.cyclealaska.com), leads a variety of guided trips—a couple of hours, half or full day, or even a 9-day trek along gold rush routes. A 3-hour ride along Chilkoot Lake costs $85. Or you can rent your own bicycle for $30 a day. The area is quite conducive to biking.

FISHING   There are several charter operators in Haines for halibut and salmon fishing, and guided freshwater fishing for silver or sockeye salmon, Dolly Varden, and cutthroat trout. The **Haines Convention and Visitors Bureau,** 2nd Street near Willard (P.O. Box 530), Haines, AK 99827 (© **800/458-3579** or 907/766-2234; www.haines.ak.us) can help you find a guide or fishing lodge through the links on their website or the list of operators they keep at the office. For self-guided fishing advice and weekly updates of what's running, contact the local office of the Alaska Department of Fish and Game (© **907/766-2625;** www.alaska.gov/adfg, click on "Sport Fishing," then "Region 1"). See "Sea Kayaking and Boating," below, for self-guided boat rental.

FLIGHTSEEING   This is one of Alaska's best places to go flightseeing. The Inside Passage is beautiful, and one mountain away is Glacier Bay National Park; the icefield and the glaciers spilling through to the sea are a sight you won't forget. It's possible to land on an immense glacial icefield and see the sun slicing between the craggy peaks. **Alaska Mountain Flying and Travel,** 132 2nd Ave. (© **800/954-8747** or 907/766-3007; www.flyglacierbay.com), offers these flights—or, as owner Paul Swanstrom says, adventures. He is known for his glacier and beach landings. Prices range from $115 to $259 per person, and reservations are recommended. Other flight services offer these tours, too; ask at the visitor center.

HIKING   There are several good trails near Haines, ranging from an easy beach walk to a 10-mile, 3,650-foot climb of **Mount Ripinsky,** north of town (it starts at the top of Young Street). Get the *Haines Is for Hikers* trail guide from the visitors' bureau. The easiest for families is the 2-mile **Battery Point Trail,** which goes along a beach decorated with wild iris. The trail starts at the end of Beach Road, which leads southeast from the Port Chilkoot cruise-ship dock. **Mount Riley** is south of town, with three trail routes to a 1,760-foot summit that features great views and feels much higher than it is; get the trail guide or ask directions to one of the trail heads. **Seduction Point Trail** is 7 miles long, starting at Chilkat State Park at the end of Mud Bay Road south of town and leading to the end of the Chilkat Peninsula. It's a beach walk, so check the tides; they'll give you a tide table at the visitors bureau.

SEA KAYAKING & BOATING   **Deishu Expeditions,** 425 Beach Rd. (© **800/552-9257** or 907/766-2427; www.seakayaks.com), offers instruction, short guided trips, longer expeditions, and rentals ($45 a day for a single, plus $25 for drop-off and pickup anywhere on the Haines Rd. system; or paddle right from the shop). A half-day guided paddle is $85, including a snack; a full day, including lunch, is $125. They also offer rental of top-quality welded aluminum boats for self-guided sightseeing, fishing, or remote sea kayaking. You can take these well-equipped, heavy-duty skiffs out on your own, allowing the least-fit family member to explore places that only experienced kayakers could normally reach. This freedom is a unique feeling. The boats are 23 feet long and rent for $300 for 8 hours, with fishing gear available (and they have good stuff, including fish finders and down riggers); it's a good deal. They also rent from Skagway. For this line of Deishu's Expeditions' business, the website is www. alaskaboatrentals.com.

WHERE TO STAY

Besides the hotels I've listed below, you'll find good economy rooms at these other places: **A Sheltered Harbor B&B,** 57 Beach Rd. (© **907/766-2741;** www.geocities.com/asheltered); and **Fort Seward Lodge, Restaurant & Saloon,** in the old fort exchange (© **800/478-7772** or 907/766-2009; www. ftsewardlodge.com);

Captain's Choice Motel ★   Many towns have a lot of chainlike hotels and only one or two unique places with character. In Haines, the situation is reversed, and these trim, red-roofed buildings are the one exception to the general eccentricity. The standard rooms contain all the anticipated amenities, yet the motel still has a certain amount of charm, making it—objectively, anyway—probably the best hotel in town. The room decor is on the dark side, with paneling, and is somewhat out-of-date, but it's quite clean, and many of the rooms have good views on a large sun deck.

108 2nd St. N. at Dalton St. (P.O. Box 392), Haines, AK 99827. © **800/478-2345** or 907/766-3111. Fax 907/766-3332. www.capchoice.com. 39 units. High season $113 double; low season $80 double. Year round $128–$168 suite. Extra person $5. Rates include continental breakfast. AE, DC, DISC, MC, V. **Amenities:** Tour desk; car rental; courtesy van; limited room service; coin-op laundry. *In room:* TV, dataport, fridge, coffeemaker, hair dryer.

Fort Seward Bed and Breakfast ★ *(Finds)*   The fort surgeon's quarters overlook the parade grounds and the Lynn Canal with a big wraparound porch. The inn has an unspoiled historic feel. Norm Smith has lived in this house most of his life and in 1981 started the B&B with his wife, Suzanne, a gifted hostess who instantly makes you feel like an old friend. The rooms have high ceilings, fireplaces, wonderful cabinetry—all kinds of authentic charm. It's a social place, with a barbecue on the porch, and guests are welcome to use the kitchen, where Norm produces a fine full breakfast of sourdough pancakes. Smoking is not allowed.

1 Fort Seward Dr. (P.O. Box 5), Haines, AK 99827. © **800/615-NORM(6676)** or phone/fax 907/766-2856. www.fortsewardbnb.com. 7 units, 4 with private bathroom. High season $90–$128 double; low season $78 double. Extra person $25. Rates include full breakfast. AE, DISC, MC, V. Closed Oct 15–Easter. **Amenities:** Bike loan; kayak rental; courtesy car. *In room:* TV/VCR.

Hotel Hälsingland ★   This grandly rambling hotel fell on hard times after more than 50 years in the same family until new owners, Jeff and Shannon Butcher, took over in 2002 and started putting in a lot of work, as well as new carpeting, furniture, drapes, paint, and beds. The hotel has always been the most interesting place in town to stay. The group of buildings, designated a National Historic Landmark, served as the Commanding Officer's Quarters for Fort William Seward during both World Wars. You can almost hear well-shined boots on the wood floors, echoing off high ceilings and old-fashioned woodwork. Rooms vary widely, so it's a good idea to take a look before checking in. Some with private bathrooms have only shower stalls while others have claw-footed tubs. The hotel also books tours and has an RV park out back.

The remodeled **Commander's Room** restaurant offers a short menu of expertly prepared dishes, with prices for main courses in the $13 to $30 range. It's open for dinner and breakfast. The small bar has craft brews on tap. This is a friendly, low-key place in the evening.

Fort William Seward parade grounds (P.O. Box 1649), Haines, AK 99827. © **800/542-6363** or 907/766-2000. Fax 907/766-2060. www.hotelhalsingland.com. 50 units, 45 with private bathroom. $69 double without bathroom, $89–$109 double with private bathroom. AE, DISC, MC, V. Closed mid-Nov to mid-Mar. **Amenities:** Restaurant; bar; tour desk; courtesy van; coin-op laundry. *In room:* TV.

The Summer Inn Bed & Breakfast *Value*   This lovely old clapboard house downtown has a big porch and a living room decorated in whites and pale, lacy fabrics, like Grandma's house. The five rooms are cozy but small, and share three bathrooms among them (bathrooms were immaculate when we visited). The house was built by a reputed former member of Soapy Smith's gang in 1912 (see Skagway section for more on Soapy) and the great big claw foot tub is said to be the first in the history of Haines upstairs bathtubs. No smoking or drinking allowed.

117 2nd Ave. (P.O. Box 1198), Haines, AK 99827. ©/fax **907/766-2970.** www.summerinnbnb.com. 5 units, none with private bathroom. High season $80 double, $100 suite; low season $70 double, $90 suite. Extra person $15. Rates include full breakfast. MC, V.

WHERE TO DINE

Haines doesn't have a great restaurant, but you can eat well at the Hotel Hälsingland (see "Where to Stay," above) during the summer, and there are lots of places for a burger or a slice of pizza. Among the best lunch places is the **Mountain Market & Café** ⚘, a natural food and grocery store at 3rd Avenue and the Haines Highway (© **907/766-3340**). The main town hangout and the best espresso stop, it serves hearty and reasonably priced sandwiches, tortilla wraps, and soups, and many fresh baked goods. Pick up a picnic, or stop by for coffee, roasted in-house, or breakfast.

The Bamboo Room ⚘ DINER/SEAFOOD   This small restaurant, in the same family for 50 years, was rescued from being a smoky adjunct to the bar. It has been divided off by attractive etched glass and made into a first-class diner serving burgers, salads, pasta, and lots of seafood. Many light and healthful items are on the menu along with the solid fried foods. The building started as a French restaurant during the gold rush era and then became a brothel and speakeasy before the Tengs family got it in 1953. The history is on the back of the menu. Get the halibut and chips.

2nd Ave. near Main St. © **907/766-2800.** www.bambooroom.net. Lunch $6–$13; dinner $6–$23. AE, DISC, DC, MC, V. Summer daily 6am–midnight; winter daily 6am–8pm.

Fort Seward Lodge, Restaurant & Saloon ⚘ STEAK/SEAFOOD   A favorite of the locals, the restaurant resides in a tall room in the old Post Exchange of the historic fort, where patrons have long speared dollar bills to the

---

Tips **A Quick Side Trip to Juneau from Haines or Skagway**

Without changing your lodgings, you can travel from Skagway and Haines for a tour of Juneau's highlights and a sightseeing day cruise of the Lynn Canal. **Alaska Fjordlines'** high-speed catamaran (© **800/320-0146**; www.alaskafjordlines.com) carries passengers to spend half a day in Juneau, with wildlife sightings on the way. The boat fare all by itself is $109; for $20 more, add a narrated bus tour of Juneau and Mendenhall Glacier. The whole excursion is about 12 hours.

ceiling, which is now papered with money. This is a fun place, with a friendly and gregarious staff and a partying tradition (although the bar is in a separate room). The food—simple seafood, meat, and vegetables—is among the best in town. The prime rib is especially famous, and in midsummer there is all-you-can-eat Dungeness crab. The full bar has Alaska microbrews on tap.

Mile 0 Haines Hwy., in Fort William Seward. © 907/766-2009. www.ftsewardlodge.com. Dinner $8–$25. DISC, MC, V. Summer daily 5–10pm; winter daily 5:30–9pm.

10 Skagway: After the Gold Rush

It's only been 100 years since white civilization came to Alaska. There were a few scattered towns in Southeast before that—Juneau, Sitka, and Wrangell, for example—but until the Klondike Gold Rush, the great mass of Alaska was populated only by Natives who had never seen a white face. Then, in a single year, 1898, the population exploded. It still stands as the greatest event in Alaska's short but eventful history, for the flow of people in a few short years set the patterns of development ever since.

In the rush years of 1897 and 1898, Skagway and its ghost-town twin city of Dyea were the logical places to get off the boat to head off on the trek to the gold fields near the new city of Dawson City, Yukon Territories (see "Dawson City & Eagle: Detour Into History," p. 391.) Skagway instantly grew from a single homestead to a population of between 15,000 and 25,000. No one knows exactly how many—in part because the people were flowing through so fast and also because there was no civil authority to count them. This was a wide-open boomtown, a true Wild West outpost that in its biggest years was completely without law other than the survival of the meanest. Then, almost as quickly as it started, the rush ended and the town deflated.

But Skagway survived by showing off where it all happened. In 1896 there was a single log cabin in Skagway, in 1897 the word of the Klondike strike made it to the outside world, and in 1898 Skagway was a huge gold rush boomtown. In 1899 the gold rush was ending, and in 1903, 300 tourists arrived in a single day to see where the gold rush happened. By 1908, local businessmen had started developing tourist attractions, moving picturesque gold rush buildings to Broadway, the main street, to create a more unified image when visitors arrived on the steamers. By 1920, tourism had become an important part of the economy. By 1933, historic preservation efforts had started. Today, more money and more than 20 times as many visitors come through in a year as made the trip to the Klondike during the gold rush.

With 862 residents and about half a million visitors annually, the "real" town has all but disappeared, and most of the people you'll meet are either fellow visitors or summer workers brought north to serve them. Most of the tourists are from cruise ships—it's not unusual for several ships to hit town in a single morning, unleashing waves of people up the wharf and into the one historic street. There are plenty of highway and ferry travelers, too, and outdoor enthusiasts come to do the Chilkoot Trail, just as the stampeders did.

Is it worth all those visits? Skagway, spared from fire and recognized so long ago for its history, may be the best-preserved gold rush town in the United States. What happened here in a 2-year period was certainly extraordinary, even if the phenomenon the town celebrates is one of mass insanity based on greed, inhumanity, thuggery, prostitution, waste, and, for most, abject failure. While Canada was well policed by the Mounties, Skagway was truly lawless—a hell on

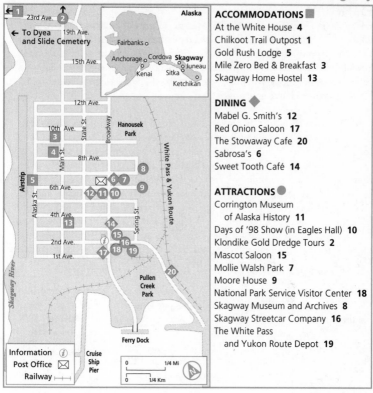

earth, as one Mountie described it. Soapy Smith ruled this scam-pire with a team of con artists and toughs who milked the suckers for every dollar available. Half of the stories about Soapy are probably lies, but this one is too good not to repeat: he set up a telegraph office for suckers to wire their money home, but with no telegraph line. Such was his influence and high repute in the newspapers he controlled that the governor offered to put Smith officially in charge as a territorial marshal and rode with him in the 1898 Independence Day parade. Four days later, Smith was shot dead in a gunfight with Frank Reid, who led a vigilante committee upset over one of Smith's thefts. Reid died of wounds sustained in the shootout, too, but Soapy Smith's gang was broken. Of course, the gold rush was about to end anyway.

In 1976 the National Park Service began buying many of Skagway's best old buildings for the **Klondike Gold Rush National Historic District,** and now it owns about 15, having completed restoration in 1999. Broadway is a prosperous, freshly painted 6-block strip of gold rush era buildings. A few that look like real businesses turn out to be displays showing how it was back then. Other buildings restored by the park service are under lease to gift shops and such. Sadly, those historic businesses not preserved by the Park Service have been lost to the onslaught of cruise ship oriented shopping: a curio shop operating since the gold rush was converted a few years ago, and in 2003 the longest operating hotel in Alaska, which dated from the earliest days, became a T-shirt shop.

ESSENTIALS

GETTING THERE   The **Alaska Marine Highway System** (© 800/642-
0066, or 907/983-2941 locally; www.ferryalaska.com) connects Skagway daily
with Haines and Juneau. The fare is $26 from Haines, $42 from Juneau; on the
fast ferry, the Juneau-Skagway fare is $41. If you're headed to Haines without a
vehicle, consider the private passenger ferry listed under "Getting There" in the
Haines section. Haines is 15 miles away by boat but more than 350 miles by
road.

Since 1978, **Klondike Highway 2** has traced the route of the stampeders
through the White Pass into Canada, a parallel route to the Chilkoot Trail. The
road runs 99 miles, then meets the Alaska Highway a dozen miles southeast of
the Yukon capital of Whitehorse. The border is at the top of the pass, 14 miles
from Skagway. (Information on Customs is in chapter 9 in the Alaska Highway
section.) This is one of the most spectacular drives anywhere in Alaska, and the
road is a well-maintained two-lane highway with wide shoulders. The views are
basically equivalent to those from the White Pass and Yukon Route railway, but
a lot cheaper. Do it in clear weather, if possible, as in cloudy weather all you'll
see is whiteout. Car rentals in Skagway are available from **Avis,** in the Westmark
Hotel at 3rd and Spring streets (© **800/230-4898** or 907/983-2247; www.
avis.com).

Riding the ferry or a cruise ship to Skagway and then heading inland in a
rented RV is an attractive option. Expect to pay around $200 a day, plus many
required extras (it's not a cheap option). **Alaska Motorhome Rentals** (© 800/
323-5757; www.alaskarv.com) also rents RVs one-way to Anchorage with a
$495 drop-off fee, plus the cost of the rental, mileage, and gas. The same com-
pany, under a different name, also offers structured RV tours from Skagway as
add-ons to cruise vacations; that's covered in chapter 2 under "Getting There &
Getting Around."

It takes 2 days to travel by bus between Skagway and Anchorage or Fairbanks;
you have to spend the night and change buses in Whitehorse, Yukon. **Alaska
Direct Bus Line** (© **800/770-6652** or 907/277-6652) operates year-round
from the ferry terminal, charging $230 one-way to Anchorage, $200 to Fairbanks. Call ahead to learn the frequency of service and departure times at the
time you plan to travel.

Several air taxi operators serve Skagway. A round trip from Juneau costs $182
on **Wings of Alaska** (© **907/789-0790** reservations, or 907/983-2442 in Skagway; www.wingsofalaska.com).

VISITOR INFORMATION   Located in the restored railroad depot, the
National Park Service Visitor Center, 2nd Avenue and Broadway (P.O. Box
517), Skagway, AK 99840 (© **907/983-2921;** www.nps.gov/klgo), is the focal
point for activities in Skagway. Rangers answer questions, give lectures, and
show films, and five times a day lead an excellent guided walking tour. The
building houses a small museum that lays the groundwork for the rest of what
you'll see. The park service's programs are free. The visitor center is open early
May through late September daily from 8am to 6pm, the rest of the year the
museum is open Monday through Friday from 8am to 5pm.

The **Skagway Convention and Visitors Bureau Center,** 245 Broadway
(P.O. Box 1029), Skagway, AK 99840 (© **907/983-2854,** fax 907/983-3854;
www.skagway.com), occupies the historic Arctic Brotherhood Hall, the building
with the driftwood facade. The website contains links to lodgings and activities,
or you can request the same information on paper (order at © 888/762-1898).

Stop in especially for the handy and informative **Skagway Walking Tour Map** of historic sites. The center is open daily from 8am to 6pm in the summer, Monday through Friday from 8am to 5pm in the winter.

GETTING AROUND   Skagway is laid out on a simple grid, with streets branching off from Broadway. The main sights can be reached on foot. If you want to go to Dyea (2 miles along Klondike Hwy. 2, then 8 miles on a gravel road) or the gold rush cemetery, a bike is a fun way to do it. **Sockeye Cycle,** on 5th Avenue off Broadway ((C) **907/983-2851;** www.cyclealaska.com), rents good mountain bikes for $12 for 2 hours and leads guided day trips (see "Getting Outside," below).

FAST FACTS: Skagway

Bank   **Wells Fargo,** at Broadway at 6th Avenue, has an ATM.

Hospital   The **Skagway Medical Clinic,** staffed by a physician's assistant, can be reached at (C) **907/983-2255** during business hours.

Internet Access   There are three choices, including **Alaska Cruiseship Services,** charging $6 an hour, at 2nd Avenue and State Street ((C) **907/983-3398).**

Police   For nonemergency business, call (C) **907/983-2232.** The station is located at State Street, just south of First Avenue.

Post Office   On Broadway between 6th and 7th avenues.

Taxes   Sales tax is 4%. The bed tax totals 8%.

SPECIAL EVENTS   **Skagway's July 4th Parade and Celebration,** organized by the chamber of commerce and featuring lots of small-town events, has been a big deal since Soapy Smith led the parade in 1898. **The Klondike Road Relay,** a 110-mile overnight footrace over the pass, brings hundreds of runners in teams of 10 from all over the state. It's held in early September. Call the visitor center for information.

EXPLORING SKAGWAY

You can see most of Skagway on foot, and everything by bike. Many companies also offer car, van, or bus tours, too. No one goes to greater lengths to give visitors a unique experience than the **Skagway Streetcar Company,** 270 2nd Ave. ((C) **907/983-2908;** www.skagwaystreetcar.com), which uses antique touring vehicles and costumed guides performing "theater without walls." The very personal and amusing 2-hour streetcar tour, based on a tour originally given to President Harding in 1923, is $40 for adults and $20 for children 12 and under. The company operates out of a big gift shop with an espresso counter and a theater, where the tour finishes. Book the tour at least 2 weeks in advance, as they're always sold out.

TOURING THE HISTORIC PARK

The main thing to do in Skagway is to see the old buildings and historic gold rush places. Do it with the *Skagway Walking Tour Map* or join a fascinating National Park Service guided walking tour (see "Visitor Information," above).

Start with a visit to the **museum** at the National Park Service Visitor Center and in the building next door. It helps put everything else in context. Of greatest interest is a collection of food and gear similar to the ton of supplies each prospector was required to carry over the pass in order to gain entry into Canada, a requirement that prevented famine among the stampeders, but made the job of getting to Dawson City an epic struggle.

While they prepared to go over the pass, gold rush greenhorns spent their time in Skagway drinking and getting fleeced in the many gambling dens and brothels. Nothing was against the law in the town's heyday because there was no civil authority. It's hard to picture at times, because everything looks so orderly now, but the park service has tried. For example, the **Mascot Saloon,** at Broadway and 3rd Avenue, has statues bellying up to the bar. It's open daily from 8am to 6pm; admission is free.

The Park Service offers free tours of the 1897 **Moore House,** near 5th Avenue and Spring Street, from 10am to 5pm during the summer. Ten years before the gold rush happened, Capt. William Moore brilliantly predicted it and homesteaded the land that would become Skagway, knowing that this would be a key staging area. He built a cabin in 1887, which stands nearby. But when the rush hit, the stampeders simply ignored his property claims and built the city on his land without offering compensation. Years later, he won in court.

A block east, on 6th Avenue, is **Mollie Walsh Park,** with a good children's play area, public restrooms, and phones. A sign tells the sad story of one of Skagway's first respectable women, a lady who chose to marry the wrong man among two suitors and was killed by him in a drunken rage. The other suitor—who'd previously killed another rival for her affections—commissioned the bust of Walsh that stands at the park.

The **Gold Rush Cemetery** is 1½ miles from town, up State Street. Used until 1908, it's small and overgrown with spruce trees, but some of the charm and mystery of the place is lost because of the number of visitors and the shiny new paint and maintenance of the wooden markers. The graves of Soapy Smith and Frank Reid are the big attractions, but don't miss the short walk up to Reid Falls. The closely spaced dates on many of the markers attest to the epidemics that swept through mobs of stampeders living in squalid conditions. Remember, there was little sanitation for the tens of thousands who passed this way in 1898.

About 9 miles north of Skagway is the ghost town of **Dyea,** where stampeders started climbing the Chilkoot Trail. It's a lovely coastal drive or bike ride: From Skagway, go 2 miles up Klondike Highway 2 and then turn left, continuing 8 miles on gravel road. Dyea is a lot more ghost than town. All that remains are a few boards, broken dock pilings, and miscellaneous iron trash. On a sunny day, however, the protected historical site is a perfect place for a picnic, among beach grasses, fields of wild iris, and the occasional reminder that a city once stood here. The National Park Service leads an interesting guided history and nature walk here daily, usually at 2pm; check at the visitor center. (See "Getting Outside," below, for more on going to Dyea.)

The little-visited **Slide Cemetery,** in the woods near Dyea, is the last resting place of many of the 60 to 70 who died in an avalanche on the Chilkoot Trail on Palm Sunday, April 3, 1898. No one knows how many are here, or exactly who died, or how accurate the wooden markers are. In 1960, when the state reopened the Chilkoot Trail, the cemetery had been completely overgrown and the markers were replaced. But somehow the mystery and forgetting make it an even more ghostly place, and the sense of anonymous, hopeless hardship and death it conveys is as authentic a gold rush souvenir as anything in Skagway.

MUSEUMS & ATTRACTIONS

The White Pass and Yukon Route ★★ A narrow-gauge railroad line that originally ran to Whitehorse, the White Pass was completed after only 2 years in 1900. It's an engineering marvel and a fun way to see spectacular, historic scenery. The excursion begins at a depot with the spine-tingling whistle of a working steam engine. The steamer pulls the train a couple of miles, then diesels take the cars—some of them originals more than 100 years old—up steep tracks that were chipped out of the side of the mountains. They "recommend" you don't get out of your seat, but it's a long ride on a slow train, and most people get up and socialize; however, you cannot move from car to car while the train is moving. The trick is to go in clear weather. When the pass is socked in all you see is white clouds. Tickets are expensive, however, and you have to reserve ahead. Take the gamble: Cancellation carries only a 10% penalty and you can change dates for no charge. Also, try to go on a weekend, when fewer cruise ships are in town taking up all the seats; weekend trains can be booked as little as a week ahead, while midweek excursions can book up months ahead. The summit excursion—which travels 20 miles with an elevation gain of 2,865 feet, then turns back—takes about 3 hours and costs $89 for adults. All fares are half price for ages 3 to 12 (except for Chilkoot Pass hiker's fares; p. 188).

The biggest treats for train lovers are the steam-powered trips. An all-day round-trip to Lake Bennett, where the stampeders launched their boats for the trip to Dawson City, leaves each Saturday morning June through August. The fare is $160 including lunch and a walking tour at Lake Bennett. (The train is pulled by a diesel on Friday and costs $135.) These days, the line operates only as a tourist attraction, May through September.

2nd Ave. depot (P.O. Box 435, Dept. B), Skagway, AK 99840. © **800/343-7373** or 907/983-2217. www.wpyr. com. For the entire fare schedule, see the website.

Skagway Museum and Archives ★ The museum contains a fine collection of gold rush artifacts and other items reflecting Skagway's colorful history. The building is the town's most impressive, and one of the state's most dignified architectural landmarks, with crisp granite walls and high pitched roof standing among tall shade trees on the edge of town. It began life as a short-lived gold rush-era college and later became a federal courthouse and jail. The city hall and museum, in the building since 1961, moved back in when renovations were completed in 2000.

7th and Spring sts. © **907/983-2420.** Admission $2 adults, $1 students, free for children 12 and under. Summer Mon–Fri 9am–5pm, Sat–Sun 1–5pm. Winter hours vary, call ahead.

Corrington Museum of Alaska History The eclectic exhibit that leads into the gift shop is well worth a brief stop. Alaska's history is told in 32 tusks of walrus scrimshaw. Besides owning some interesting items, they've done a good job of putting it all together in an understandable way.

Fifth Ave. and Broadway, in Corrington's gift shop. © **907/983-2580.** Free admission. Mid-May to mid-Sept 9am–7pm. Closed winter.

Klondike Gold Dredge Tours Gold mining never happened in Skagway; it was only a transit point. But more gold rush tourists come here than anywhere else, so promoters brought a dredge to where the people are. The 1937 rig, weighing 350 tons, dug up and sorted gravel to remove gold first in Idaho, then near Dawson City, and finally near the border on the Top of the World Highway. A 2-hour visit includes a 10-minute video, costumed guides who spice up the tour with humor, and gold panning in heated water. If you will visit

Dawson City or Fairbanks, you can see larger dredges in authentic historic settings for less money, but if not, this stop can satisfy your mechanical curiosity and fever to pan for gold.

Mile 1.7 Klondike Hwy. (🕿 907/983-3175. www.klondikegolddredge.com. $34 adults, $24 under age 12. Add $5 for transfer from Skagway. Summer daily 8:30am–4:30pm; full tours 8:30am, 9:30am, 1:30pm, 2pm and 2:30pm.

GETTING OUTSIDE

The **Mountain Shop,** 355 4th Ave. (🕿 **907/983-2544;** www.packerexpeditions. com), rents and sells the equipment you need for backpacking or other outdoor activities in Skagway. The owner, who is also the mayor, leads guided day hikes, backpacking trips, and float trips under the name Packer Expeditions, at the same address.

BACKPACKING The National Park Service and Parks Canada jointly manage the famous **Chilkoot Pass Trail,** publishing a trail guide and offering information at their offices in Skagway and Whitehorse. Some 20,000 stampeders used the trail to get from Dyea—9 miles from Skagway—to Lake Bennett, 33 miles away, where they could build and launch boats bound for Dawson City. Today about 3,000 people a year make the challenging hike, taking 3 to 5 days. The Chilkoot is not so much a wilderness trail as an outdoor museum, but don't underestimate its difficulty, as so many did during the gold rush.

To control the numbers, **Parks Canada,** 205-300 Main St., Whitehorse, Yukon Y1A 2B5 Canada (🕿 **867/667-3910,** fax 867/393-6701; www.pc.gc.ca/ chilkoot), allows only 50 hikers with permits per day to cross the summit. To buy the permits, call with a Visa, American Express, or MasterCard, the date you plan to start, and the campsites you will use each night. Permits are C$50 for adults, C$25 ages 6 to 16, plus a C$10 per person reservation fee. You pick up the permit at the Trail Centre in Skagway; that's also where 8 of the 50 daily permits are held for walk-ins, to be distributed along with any no-shows.

Once over the pass, you're on Lake Bennett, on the rail line 8 miles short of the road. You can walk to the road, or get back to Skagway on the White Pass and Yukon Route railway (p. 187), which runs Monday through Saturday at 1pm for most of the summer. The one-way fare to Frasier, B.C., is $35 and the scenic 3-hour ride to Skagway is $65. There is a $15 surcharge per person if you buy your tickets at Bennett. Saturday trains cost more and don't run in the late season. Be sure to make your reservations well in advance.

There are two **U.S. Forest Service cabins** near Skagway, and official access to both is by the White Pass and Yukon Route railway. Both are on trails described in the *Skagway Trail Map,* mentioned below. The **Denver Caboose** is an old, red White Pass caboose parked next to the tracks 6 miles up the line at the trail head for the 4.5-mile **Denver Glacier Trail.** Another cabin is 1½ miles off the track, 14 miles up on the spectacular **Laughton Glacier Trail.** For either, you need a $35 cabin permit (see "Getting Outside in the Tongass National Forest," in section 1 of this chapter, for reservations information) and a train ticket from the railroad. For details, contact the National Park Service visitor center (see above), or the **Juneau Ranger District,** 8465 Old Dairy Rd., Juneau, AK 99801 (🕿 **907/586-8800;** www.fs.fed.us/r10/tongass).

BIKING **Sockeye Cycle,** on 5th Avenue off Broadway (🕿 **907/983-2851;** www.cyclealaska.com), leads bike tours, including one that takes clients to the top of the White Pass in a van and lets them coast down on bikes; the 2½-hour trip is $72. Going up on White Pass and Yukon Route railroad and riding back down brings the price to $152. Riders must be at least 14 years old. The company also leads a tour of the quiet ghost town site of Dyea for the same price, going over in a van. I rode to Dyea from Skagway on my own over the hilly, 10-mile coastal road, one of the most pleasant, scenic rides I can remember.

FLIGHTSEEING   Skagway, like Haines, is a good place to choose for a flightseeing trip, as Glacier Bay National Park is just to the west. The flightseeing operators listed in the Haines section offer flights from Skagway, too (p. 179). **Temsco Helicopters** (© **907/983-2900;** www.temscoair.com) takes 55-minute tours near Skagway with a 25-minute landing on a glacier (not in Glacier Bay); those flights cost $199. A helicopter and dog sled tour on Denver Glacier is $359.

HIKING   A *Skagway Trail Map* is available from the visitor center, listing 11 hikes around Skagway. An easy evening walk starts at the footbridge at the west end of the airport parking lot, crossing the Skagway River to **Yakutania Point Park,** where pine trees grow from cracks in the rounded granite of the shoreline. Across the park is a shortcut taking a couple of miles off the trip to Dyea and to the **Skyline Trail and A.B. Mountain,** a strenuous climb to a 3,500-foot summit with great views. On the southeast side of town, across the railroad tracks, a network of trails heads up from Spring Street between 3rd and 4th avenues to a series of mountain lakes, the closest of which is **Lower Dewey Lake,** less than a mile up the trail.

WHERE TO STAY

The accommodations in Skagway are within close walking distance of the historic district, except as noted.

At The White House ★   The Tronrud family essentially rebuilt a burned 1902 gable-roofed inn, which has dormer and bow windows and two porticos with small Doric columns. They made the rooms comfortable and modern while retaining the authentic gold rush style of the original owner, Lee Guthrie, a successful gambler and saloon owner of the early years. The inn has hardwood floors and fine woodwork. Bedrooms vary in size, but all have quilts and other nice touches, including ceiling fans.

Corner of 8th and Main sts. (P.O. Box 41), Skagway, AK 99840-0041. © **907/983-9000.** Fax 907/983-9010. www.atthewhitehouse.com. 10 units. High season $115 double; low season $75 double. Extra person $10. Rates include continental breakfast. AE, DISC, MC, V. **Amenities:** Courtesy van. *In room:* TV.

Chilkoot Trail Outpost ★   These beautifully crafted log cabins built in 2002 by long-time residents contain comfortable, modern lodgings with carpeted floors and log interior walls, some in the form of two-room suites, with many amenities (but no phones). Two rooms in a duplex with bunkbeds rent for $80 double, plus $40 for each additional person, including breakfast but without linens. The location, in Dyea near the Chilkoot Trail and Taiya River, puts you in quiet, natural surroundings away from the carnival atmosphere created by the crush of tourists in Skagway proper. In good weather, the hosts have a nightly campfire and provide supplies for s'mores. You can also cook your own food at a barbecue and sink in a screened gazebo. Breakfast, served in a remarkable log building with a vaulted ceiling, consists of a buffet with various choices, including one hot selection, such as eggs or pancakes. They pick up guests in Skagway, if necessary, and lend bikes.

8.5 Mile Dyea Rd. (P.O. Box 286), Skagway, AK 99840. (© **907/983-3799**. Fax 907/983-3599. www.chilkoot trailoutpost.com. 10 units. $35 per person double in duplex, $140 cabin for 2. Extra adult $25, extra child 2–11 years $13. DISC, MC, V. Rates include full breakfast. **Amenities:** Bike loan; courtesy car. *In room:* TV/VCR, fridge, coffeemaker, microwave.

Gold Rush Lodge ★ *Value*   This is a clean, comfortable motel by the airstrip, 3 blocks from the historic district, with a grassy picnic area out back. The rooms are on the small side but are modern and attractively decorated in light colors and have many amenities, including fans. Bathrooms have shower stalls, no tubs. The hosts provide fruit, coffee, and a cookie jar in the lobby, and write the guests' names and hometowns on an erasable board so they can get to know each other. Smoking is not allowed.

6th Ave. and Alaska St. (P.O. Box 514), Skagway, AK 99840. (© **877/983-3509** or 907/983-2831. Fax 907/ 983-2742. www.goldrushlodge.com. 12 units. High season $80–$115 double; low season $65–$85 double. Extra person $10. Ask about discounts. AE, DISC, MC, V. **Amenities:** Courtesy car. *In room:* TV/VCR, dataport, fridge, coffeemaker, hair dryer, microwave.

Mile Zero Bed & Breakfast ★   This building was designed to be a B&B and it shows in details such as the soundproofing and the back doors to every room—guests can access the common rooms through one door or go outside through French doors leading to the porch. The idea is to offer the privacy and convenience of a motel and the warmth and character of a B&B, and it works. The site is a few blocks from the historic area. Smoking is not allowed. There are barbecue facilities on-site.

9th Ave. and Main St. (P.O. Box 165), Skagway, AK 99840. (© **907/983-3045**. Fax 907/983-3046. www.mile-zero.com. 7 units. High season $125 double; low season $75 double. Extra person $25. Rates include continental breakfast. DISC, MC, V.

A HOSTEL & CAMPING

A primitive **National Park Service Dyea Campground** has 22 well-separated sites near the water; with a $5 fee. There are several RV parks. The **Pullen Creek RV Park** (© **800/936-3731** or 907/983-2768) is near the small-boat harbor, with coin-operated showers. RV sites with power, water, and dump station use are $25, car camping sites are $18, tenting with no vehicle $14.

Skagway Home Hostel   Frank Wasmer and Nancy Schave open up their historic home to hostellers, sharing their meals, refrigerator, bathrooms, laundry machines, bicycles, and hospitality side by side with guests. The atmosphere is like off-campus shared housing at college, except the house is nicer and better kept. Bunks are in separate male and female dorm rooms except for the single private room. To reserve, use the Web site, as they don't return long-distance calls. In winter, reservations are required, as Frank and Nancy might otherwise not be there. Summer registration hours are 5:30 to 10:30pm. No pets, alcohol, or smoking.

3rd Ave. near Main St. (P.O. Box 231), Skagway, AK 99840. (© **907/983-2131**. www.skagwayhostel.com. 1 private room, 3 dorms. $15 per bunk, $40 double private room. No credit cards. **Amenities:** Bike loan; laundry machines $3.

WHERE TO DINE

Restaurants go out of business and open up faster in Skagway's entirely seasonal economy than anywhere else I know, so you may need to ask around for a current recommendation. Stop off for espresso and baked goods at **Mabel G. Smith's** (© **907/983-2609**), a bakery, card, gift, and coffee shop on 5th Avenue off Broadway. Also, the **Sweet Tooth Café**, at 315 Broadway (© **907/983-2405**), is a good, year-round diner, open for breakfast and lunch.

Sabrosa's ★ *Finds* DELI/MEXICAN/VEGETARIAN This tiny sidewalk cafe down an alley across from the post office feeds locals. Seating is either indoors or in a pleasant fenced area, a sort of patio arrangement. It's an island of intimacy out of the stream of the tourist rush. Our halibut, pasta salad, and vegetarian sandwich were tasty, wholesome, filling, and inexpensive, a rare combination in Skagway. They also serve Mexican specials and fresh baked goods, beer, wine, and homemade sangria. Service is quick and friendly.

6th and Broadway. ✆ **907/983-2469.** Lunch $3.50–$9, dinner $8–$15. No credit cards. Summer daily 8am–8pm. Closed off-season.

The Stowaway Cafe ★★ SEAFOOD/CAJUN Housed in a small, gray clapboard house overlooking the boat harbor, a 5-minute walk from the historic sites, Jim and Kim Long's little restaurant is a labor of love—they met here when he worked the kitchen part-time when it first opened, a decade ago. Jim is still back in the kitchen, cooking the grilled and blackened salmon and halibut that anchor the menu; there's also beef, pasta, and all the usual waterfront restaurant items. Kim handles the front (and the paperwork). Service is fast. The tiny dining room is decorated with a miscellaneous collection of knickknacks that will keep your attention almost as well as the harbor view. They have a beer and wine license and serve inexpensive lunches from a walk-up window.

End of Congress Way near the small boat harbor. ✆ **907/983-3463.** Reservations recommended. Dinner $13–$29. V. Summer daily 11am–10pm. Closed winter.

NIGHTLIFE

Incredibly, the ***Days of '98 Show*** has been playing since 1927 in the Fraternal Order of Eagles Hall No. 25, at 6th Avenue and Broadway (✆ **907/983-2545**). Jim Richards carries on the tradition each summer with actors imported from all over the United States, doing three shows a day (10:30am, 2:30pm and 7pm). The evening shows begin with an hour of mock gambling at a casino run by the actors. The actual performance, which lasts 1 hour, includes singing, cancan dancing, a Robert Service reading, and the story of the shooting of Soapy Smith. Matinees are $14 and evening shows are $16. Children 15 and under are charged half price.

The **Red Onion Saloon,** at 2nd Avenue and Broadway, is an authentic-feeling old bar that often has terrific live jazz and other styles of music, but the players sometimes jump up suddenly and leave—they're cruise-ship musicians who enjoy coming here to stretch out and jam, and they can't afford to miss the boat. It was a brothel originally—what wasn't in this town?—and a mock madam is on hand offering tours of the upstairs. The bar closes in winter.

Moe's Frontier Bar, at 5th Avenue and Broadway, is more of a gritty local hangout, open year-round.

6

Anchorage & Environs

As teenagers living in Anchorage, my cousin and I got a job from a family friend painting his lake cabin. He flew us out on his floatplane and left us there, with paint, food, and a little beer. A creek that ran past the lake was so full of salmon that we caught one on every cast until we got bored and started thinking of ways to make it more difficult. We cooked the salmon over a fire, then floated in a boat on the lake under the endless sunshine of a summer night, talking and diving naked into the clear, green water. We met some guys building another cabin one day, but otherwise we saw no other human beings. When the week was over, the cabin was painted—it didn't take long—and the floatplane came back to get us. As we lifted off and cleared the trees, Anchorage opened in front of us, barely 10 minutes away.

The state's largest city, Anchorage—where 40% of Alaska's population resides—is accused crushingly of being just like a city "Outside," not really part of Alaska at all. It's true that the closer you get to Anchorage, the more the human development reminds you of the outskirts of Anytown, USA, with fast-food franchises, occasional traffic jams, and the ugly big-box retail development inflicted everywhere by relentless corporate logic. You often hear the joke, "Anchorage isn't Alaska, but you can see it from there," and writers piously warn visitors to land in Anchorage but move on as soon as possible, as if it's catching.

When I hear that advice, I think of the many great experiences I've had here—like painting that cabin, years ago. Anyone in Anchorage with a few hundred dollars for a floatplane can be on a lake or river with the bears and salmon in a matter of minutes, in wilderness deeper than any you could find in the Lower 48. **Chugach State Park** is largely within the city limits, but it's the size of Rocky Mountain National Park and has similar alpine terrain, with the critical difference that most of it is virtually never visited. Yet you can be climbing those mountains in half an hour's journey from your downtown hotel. **Chugach National Forest,** the nation's second largest, is less than an hour down the road. In downtown's **Ship Creek,** people catch 40-pound salmon from under a freeway bridge. Even within the city, you can bike dozens of miles along the coast or through wooded greenbelts, or ski in one of the nation's best Nordic skiing parks.

Anchorage is indeed a big American city, with big-city problems of crime and pollution, but it's also entirely unique for being surrounded by pristine and spectacular wild lands. Anywhere else, Anchorage would be known not for its shortcomings, but as one of America's greatest cities for outdoor enthusiasts.

ANCHORAGE YESTERDAY & TODAY

Anchorage isn't old enough to have a sharp identity as a city. The first mayor to be born here was elected only in 2003 (and he's barely 40). The city started as a tent camp for workers mobilized to build the Alaska Railroad in 1915. A few houses and businesses went up to serve the federal employees who were building and later running the railroad, as Steve McCutcheon's father was. McCutcheon, who died in 1998, remembered a remote, sleepy railroad town enlivened by a couple of large World War II military bases, but never more than strictly functional. As one visitor who came in the early 1940s wrote, the entire town looked like it was built on the wrong side of the tracks.

McCutcheon looked out the picture window from his living room on a placid lake surrounded by huge, half-million-dollar houses, each with a floatplane pulled up on the green front lawn, and he recalled the year people started to take Anchorage seriously. It was the year, he said, when they started thinking it would be a permanent city, not just an encampment where you went for a few years to make money before moving on—the year they started building Anchorage to last. That year was 1957. Oil was discovered on the Kenai Peninsula's Swanson River, south of here. It was around that time that McCutcheon built his own house all by itself on a lake, far out in the country. At that time, you could homestead in the Anchorage bowl. Those who had the opportunity but chose not to—my wife's family, for example—gave it a pass only because it seemed too improbable that the flat, wet acreage way out of town would ever be worth anything.

Oil fueled Anchorage's growth like nitrogen fertilizer poured on a shooting weed. Those homesteads that went begging in the 1950s and early 1960s now have shopping malls and high-rise office buildings on them. Fortunes came fast, development was haphazard, and a lot was built that we'd all soon regret. I had the bizarre experience of coming home from college to the town I'd grown up in and getting completely lost in a large area of the city that had been nothing but moose browse the last time I'd seen it. Visitors found a city full of life but empty of charm.

In the last 20 years, that has started to change. Anchorage is slowly outgrowing its gawky adolescence. It's still young, prosperous, and vibrant—and exhausting when the summer sun refuses to set—but now it also has some excellent restaurants, a good museum, a large Native cultural center, a nice little zoo, and culture in the evening besides the tourist melodramas you'll find in every Alaska town. People still complain that Anchorage isn't really Alaska—in Fairbanks, they call it "Los Anchorage" (and in Anchorage, Fairbanks is known as "Squarebanks")—yet the great wilderness around the city remains intertwined with its streets. Along with a quarter million people, Anchorage is full of moose—so many, they're considered pests and wintertime hazards, inspiring debate about hunting them within the city limits. Bears and bald eagles also show up regularly on the system of greenbelts and bike trails that brings the woods into almost every neighborhood.

Anchorage stands on broad, flat sediment between the Chugach Mountains and the silt-laden waters of upper Cook Inlet. At water's edge, mud flats not yet made into land stretch far offshore when the tide is at its low point, up to 38 vertical feet below high water. There's a **downtown area** of about 8 by 20 blocks, near Ship Creek where it all started, but most of the city lies on long commercial strips. Like many urban centers built since the arrival of the automobile, the

Anchorage

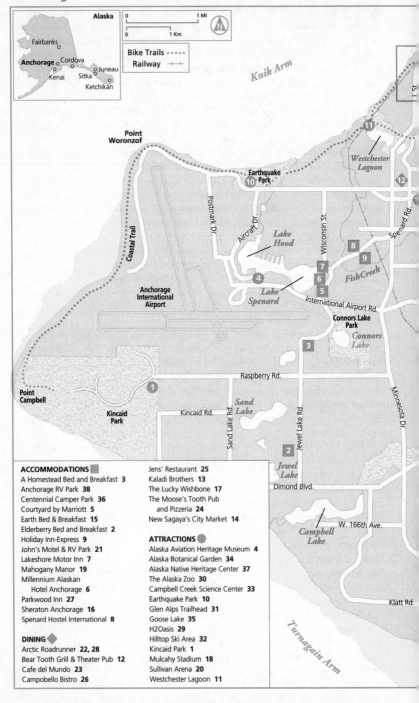

Alaska

Fairbanks

Anchorage ○ Cordova
Kenai ○ ○ Sitka ○ Juneau
Ketchikan

0   1 Mi
0   1 Km

Bike Trails ·····
Railway ┼─┼─┼

Knik Arm

Point
Woronzof

Earthquake
Park **10**

*Westchester
Lagoon* **11**

12

Postmark Dr.

Aircraft Dr.

Wisconsin St.

Spenard Rd.

*Lake
Hood*

8

7

9

Coastal Trail

4

6

5

Fish Creek

Anchorage
International
Airport

*Lake
Spenard*

International Airport Rd.

**Connors Lake
Park**

*Connors
Lake*

3

Raspberry Rd.

**Point
Campbell**

1

*Sand
Lake*

**Kincaid
Park**

Kincaid Rd.

Sand Lake Rd.

Jewel Lake Rd.

Minnesota Dr.

2

*Jewel
Lake*

Dimond Blvd.

*Campbell
Lake*

W. 166th Ave.

Klatt Rd.

Turnagain Arm

ACCOMMODATIONS ▪
A Homestead Bed and Breakfast **3**
Anchorage RV Park **38**
Centennial Camper Park **36**
Courtyard by Marriott **5**
Earth Bed & Breakfast **15**
Elderberry Bed and Breakfast **2**
Holiday Inn-Express **9**
John's Motel & RV Park **21**
Lakeshore Motor Inn **7**
Mahogany Manor **19**
Millennium Alaskan
    Hotel Anchorage **6**
Parkwood Inn **27**
Sheraton Anchorage **16**
Spenard Hostel International **8**

DINING ◆
Arctic Roadrunner **22, 28**
Bear Tooth Grill & Theater Pub **12**
Cafe del Mundo **23**
Campobello Bistro **26**

Jens' Restaurant **25**
Kaladi Brothers **13**
The Lucky Wishbone **17**
The Moose's Tooth Pub
    and Pizzeria **24**
New Sagaya's City Market **14**

ATTRACTIONS ●
Alaska Aviation Heritage Museum **4**
Alaska Botanical Garden **34**
Alaska Native Heritage Center **37**
The Alaska Zoo **30**
Campbell Creek Science Center **33**
Earthquake Park **10**
Glen Alps Trailhead **31**
Goose Lake **35**
H2Oasis **29**
Hilltop Ski Area **32**
Kincaid Park **1**
Mulcahy Stadium **18**
Sullivan Arena **20**
Westchester Lagoon **11**

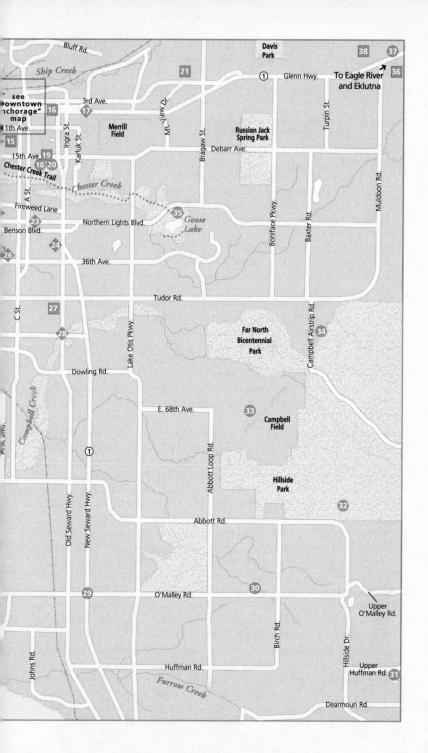

layout is not particularly conducive to any other form of transportation. But the roads go only so far. Just beyond, wilds beckon in the Chugach, along the trails of Turnagain Arm, at Alyeska Ski Resort in Girdwood, in Prince William Sound, and in the Matanuska and Susitna valleys. You'll find ways to that wilderness, and the urban pleasures by its side, throughout this chapter.

1 Essentials

GETTING THERE

BY PLANE   You'll probably get to Anchorage at the start of your trip by air, as it has by far the most flights linking Alaska to the rest of the world on many airlines. The **Ted Stevens Anchorage International Airport** is a major hub. Seattle has the most frequent flights connecting to Anchorage, with numerous domestic carriers flying nonstop all day. (See "Getting There & Getting Around," in chapter 2 for more details.) Within Alaska, most flights route through here, even for communities that are much closer to each other than they are to Anchorage. **Alaska Airlines** (✆ 800/252-7522; www.alaskaair.com) is the dominant carrier for Alaska destinations, and the only jet operator to most Alaska cities. Various commuter carriers link Anchorage to rural destinations not served by jet. **Era Aviation** (✆ 800/866-8394 or 907/266-8394; www.FlyEra. com) is one of the largest for Southcentral Alaska destinations and can be booked directly or through Alaska Airlines.

Unless your hotel has a courtesy van or you rent a car, a taxi is probably the best way to get downtown from the airport. A **taxi ride** downtown from the airport runs about $15. Try **Alaska Cab** (✆ 907/563-5353). Various shuttle vans operate, but they have not been consistent enough to merit mention here. The People Mover city bus also serves the airport on a seasonal basis; see "Getting Around," below.

BY CAR   There's only one road to the rest of the world: the Glenn Highway. It leads through the Mat-Su Valley area and Glennallen to Tok, and to the Alaska Highway, 330 miles from Anchorage. Thirty miles out of town the Glenn meets the Parks Highway, which leads to Denali National Park and Fairbanks. The other road out of town, the Seward Highway, leads south to the Kenai Peninsula. See "Alaska's Highways a la Carte," in chapter 9. For more on driving to Alaska, see chapter 2.

BY BUS   **Alaska Trails** (✆ 888/600-6001; www.AlaskaShuttle.com), a van and bus service, runs between Anchorage and Fairbanks, with stops in Talkeetna and Denali National Park. From Fairbanks, they run to Valdez and Dawson City, and anyplace on the way. In Anchorage they stop at the downtown Hostelling International, Anchorage, at 700 H St. A ticket from Denali is $66, Fairbanks $86. Various other van and bus services offer transportation to and from Seward, Homer, Talkeetna, Fairbanks, and Denali National Park; see the sections on each of those places for details.

BY RV   A recreational vehicle is a popular way to explore the region. Renting an RV in Anchorage for a tour is covered below under "Getting Around." Driving an RV to Alaska is covered in chapter 2. It's also possible to come to Alaska with your own RV without making the time-consuming round trip by shipping your RV either way (or both ways) between Anchorage and Tacoma, Washington. **Totem Ocean Trailer Express** (✆ 800/234-8683 in Anchorage, ✆ 800/426-0074 in the Lower 48; www.totemocean.com) offers this service.

In addition, several firms offer one-way rentals between Anchorage and Skagway (the ferry terminus) or cities around the U.S. **Alaska Motorhome Rentals** (© 800/323-5757; www.alaskarv.com) offers Skagway one-way rentals to Anchorage with a $495 drop-off fee, Seattle for $795, plus the cost of the rental, $179 to $199 a day in the high season, plus mileage (or pay $25 a day for unlimited mileage), and gas (budget generously). The same company has another operation, **Alaska Motorhome & Cruise Vacations** (© 800/323-5757), who provides packages to cruise one way, tour Alaska in an RV, and fly home. For more on that option and on one-way rentals from the balance of the Lower 48, see chapter 2.

BY RAIL The **Alaska Railroad** (© 800/544-0552, 907/265-2494, or 907/265-2620 TDD; www.alaskarailroad.com) connects Anchorage with Seward and Whittier to the south and Fairbanks and Denali National Park to the north. It's a fun way to travel, with expert commentary in the summer, good food, and clean, comfortable cars. However, the train is priced as a tourism excursion and costs much more than ordinary transportation. For example, the spectacular Seward run, only about 120 miles, costs $98 round-trip. Most trains run only in the summer, but a snowy 12-hour odyssey to Fairbanks runs once a week all winter (the summer fare is $175 one-way, the winter fare is $125 one-way, $100 for Alaska residents). See chapter 8 on Denali National Park, and sections on other destinations for fares and service details.

ORIENTATION

Many visitors never make it beyond the **downtown** area, the old-fashioned grid of streets at the northwest corner of town where the large hotels and gift shops are located. Street numbers and letters work on a simple pattern, and navigation is easy. Beyond downtown, most of Anchorage is oriented to commercial strips, and you'll need a map to find your way. The map on p. 194 will suffice for major thoroughfares, but to find anything on smaller streets, pick up a detailed map at the visitor centers, at a grocery store, or on the Internet. Some parts of greater Anchorage are in distinct communities outside the bowl formed by the Chugach Mountains, including **Eagle River** and **Eklutna,** out the Glenn Highway to the northeast, and **Girdwood** and **Portage,** on the Seward Highway, to the south. The suburban **Matanuska and Susitna valleys** (known as Mat-Su) lie north of the city on the Glenn and Parks highways.

GETTING AROUND

BY RENTAL CAR Driving is the most practical way for most independent travelers to tour the main part of Alaska, and the location of Anchorage at the hub of transportation networks makes it the handiest place to start. A car improves a visit to Anchorage, too, as the city is spread out and public transportation and taxi service are poor. Most major car-rental companies operate in Anchorage, largely from desks at the airport in a tunnel off the domestic baggage-claim area. A compact car for $50 a day, with unlimited mileage, is a fair deal. The airport adds a 10% concession fee, which you can avoid by renting off-site from **Avis,** at 5th Avenue and B Street (© **800/230-4898** or 907/277-4567; www.avis.com) or several other firms. The city charges an 8% rental car tax and the state adds an additional 10% tax. Including the airport fee, that's a total tax of 28%. Sorry about that! Cars can sell out in summer, so reserve ahead.

Tips Car Wheels on Gravel Roads

One Anchorage company, **Affordable New Car Rental,** 4707 Spenard Rd. (© **800/248-3765** or 907/243-3370; www.ancr.com), allows clients to drive its vehicles on the unpaved Denali Highway (p. 322) and McCarthy Road (p. 400). Others do not. Of course, you assume the risk for damage; or, for $7 a day, they'll cover the tires and windshield. You can't take these cars on the Dalton Highway, but two Fairbanks firms that do allow that are on p. 369 under "Equipped for the Back Roads."

BY RENTAL RV Several large RV rental agencies operate in Anchorage (see "Getting There," above). High-season rates are around $1,400 a week, plus the large amount of fuel you use. **ABC Motorhome Rentals,** 3875 W. International Airport Rd. (© **800/421-7456** or 907/279-2000; www.abcmotorhome.com), charges no mileage fee. See "Getting There and Getting Around," in chapter 2, for more on this option.

BY BUS It takes a long time to go far using the **People Mover** bus system (© **907/343-6543;** www.peoplemover.org), but if you have the time it's inexpensive and covers most of the city. Bus fares all over town are $1.50 for adults, 75¢ for ages 5 to 18, 35¢ over age 60. The transit center bus depot is at 6th Avenue and G Street. Buses generally come every half hour but are less frequent on weekends.

BY BIKE The network of bike trails is a great way to see the best side of Anchorage, but not a practical means of point-to-point transportation for most people. The **Tony Knowles Coastal Trail** starts right downtown (see "Getting Outside," later in this chapter). Good street bikes are usually for rent near Elderberry Park downtown, at the start of the Coastal Trail, from the **Copper Whale Inn,** at the corner of 5th Avenue and L (© **866/258-7999** or 907/258-7999). They charge $15 for a half day, $25 for 24 hours. Midtown, **The Bicycle Shop** at 1035 W. Northern Lights Blvd. (© **907/272-5219**), rents and services a wide selection of bikes, charging $20 half day, $30 the first full day, $20 for each additional day.

VISITOR INFORMATION

The **Anchorage Convention and Visitor Bureau,** 524 W. 4th Ave., Anchorage, AK 99501-2212 (© **907/276-4118;** fax 907/278-5559; www.anchorage.net), offers information on the whole state at its centers and extensive website. The main location is the **Log Cabin Visitor Information Center,** downtown at 4th Avenue and F Street (© **907/274-3531;** open daily June–Aug 7:30am–7pm, May and Sept 8am–6pm, Oct–Apr 9am–4pm). If it's crowded, go to the storefront office right behind it. You'll also find visitor information desks at the airport: one in the baggage-claim area in the domestic terminal and two in the international terminal (in the lobby and the secured transit area).

The **Alaska Public Lands Information Center,** located at 605 W. 4th Ave. (across the intersection from the log cabin at 4th and F), Suite 105, Anchorage, AK 99501 (© **907/271-2737** or 907/271-2738 TTY; www.nps.gov/aplic; open daily 9am–5pm in summer, Mon–Fri 10am–5pm in winter), can help anyone planning to spend time outdoors anywhere in Alaska, and has exhibits of interest even for those who aren't. The center occupies a grand room with high ceilings in the 1930s post office and federal courthouse. All the land agencies are represented by rangers whose advice is based on personal experience. You can buy ferry tickets for the Alaska Marine Highway System, and at the bookstore pick from an excellent selection of trail and field guides.

SPECIAL EVENTS

For an extensive event listing, with something almost every day of the year, check www.anchorage.net; also see "The Performing Arts," later in this chapter.

The **Anchorage Folk Festival** (© 907/566-2334; www.anchoragefolkfesti-val.org), over the weekends of January 21 and 28, 2005, imports musicians and shows off local talent in free concerts and jam sessions. They have other events through the year, including a Novemberfest; check the website.

The **Fur Rendezvous Winter Festival** (© 907/274-1177; www.furrondy. net; Feb 18–Mar 6, 2005) is the city's big winter celebration, with many community events, fireworks, craft fairs, snowshoe softball, dog sled rides, and other fun. The Rondy's traditional centerpiece is the **World Champion Sled Dog Race,** a 3-day sprint event of about 25 miles per heat. In addition, at the end of the festival comes the start of the **Iditarod Trail Sled Dog Race** (© 907/ 376-5155; www.iditarod.com). The Iditarod usually begins from Anchorage the first Saturday in March (Mar 5 in '05) and then proceeds in trucks to the restart the next day in Wasilla for the 1,000-mile run to Nome (see the section on Nome in chapter 10 for more details).

The **Native Youth Olympics** (© 907/297-1700), held in late April at the University of Alaska Anchorage Sports Center, is a tough competition in traditional Alaska Native sports such as the seal hop (done on the knuckles) and the spectacular high kick, which can reach more than nine feet off the floor.

The **Saturday Market** is a big street fair and farmer's market held every Saturday from mid-May through mid-September at 3rd Avenue and E Street (© 907/272-5634; www.anchoragemarkets.com).

The **Ship Creek Salmon Derby,** for 10 days in early June and again in early August, offers a chance to win cash and benefit charity by catching big salmon in downtown Anchorage (© 907/276-6472; www.anchoragederbies.com).

The **Blues on the Green** music festival in mid-June takes place under the sky in the natural amphitheater at Kincaid Park. It is an all-day, all-evening blues concert. Headliners in the past have included Taj Mahal, Bo Diddley, and Buddy Guy. Tickets are sold through tickets.com or at Carrs grocery stores.

The U.S. Air Force puts on the **Arctic Thunder Air Show** (© 907/552-SHOW; www.elmendorf.af.mil) over a weekend in late June, allowing the public on Elmendorf Air Force Base to see warplanes on the ground and performing aerobatics in the sky. The crowd at the event has at times topped 145,000 (this in a town of 260,000 people). Admission is free.

The **Alaska State Fair** (© 907/745-4827; www.alaskastatefair.org), which culminates a 12-day run on Labor Day each year, is the biggest event in the area. It takes place in Palmer, 40 miles north of Anchorage on the Glenn Highway. In most ways, it's a typical state fair, with rides, booths, exhibits, contests, fireworks, and live music. Not typical are the vegetables. The good soil and long days in the Matanuska Valley around Palmer boost their growth to massive size, the stuff of childhood nightmares. Cabbages are the size of bean-bag chairs. A mere beach-ball sized cabbage would be laughed off the stage. And it's not just the 100-pound cabbages. Imagine a 19-pound carrot, 35-pound broccoli,

42-pound beet, or 75-pound rutabaga (all world records from the fair, among others). The flower gardens are amazing too, although not in the same way.

The **Carrs/Safeway Great Alaska Shootout men's basketball tournament** (© **907/786-1250;** www.goseawolves.com/shootout), hosted by the University of Alaska Anchorage, brings top-ranked college teams to the Sullivan Arena over Thanksgiving weekend.

FAST FACTS: Anchorage

Banks A bank is rarely far away, and all grocery stores and gas stations also have **ATMs.** Downtown, **Wells Fargo** (© **907/263-2501**) has a branch in the 5th Avenue Mall (5th Ave. and D St.), with a foreign exchange desk and wire transfer services.

Hospitals **Alaska Regional Hospital** is at 2801 DeBarr Rd. (© **907/276-1131;** www.alaskaregional.com), and **Providence Alaska Medical Center** is at 3200 Providence Dr. (© **907/562-2211;** www.providence.org).

Internet Access & Business Services Downtown, the **UPS Store,** at 645 G St., next to City Hall (© **907/276-7888**), has three public computers with DSL connections. **Kaladi Brothers Coffee Co.** has computers at its 1360 W. Northern Lights location (© **907/277-5127;** www.kaladi.com), a shopping center that also contains the REI sporting goods store and a huge used book store. They charge 11 cents an hour. The **Z. J. Loussac Library,** midtown at 3600 Denali St. (© **907/343-2975;** lexicon.ci.anchorage.ak.us), offers free Internet access.

Police The **Anchorage Police Department** has main offices at 4501 S. Bragaw Rd., south of Tudor Road; for a nonemergency call © **907/786-8500.** For nonemergency police business outside the city, call the **Alaska State Troopers,** 5700 E. Tudor Rd. (© **907/269-5511**).

Post Office Downtown, it's downstairs in the brown building at 4th Avenue and D Street.

Taxes There's no sales tax in Anchorage. The bed tax is 8%.

---

2 Where to Stay

Hotel rooms are overpriced in Anchorage, so this is a good place to choose a B&B or small inn. I've searched for such places, choosing those with character and reasonable prices. There are hundreds more, many of them just as good. About 60 B&Bs link through a website maintained by the cooperative **Anchorage Alaska Bed and Breakfast Association** (www.anchorage-bnb.com). Rates, amenities, and location are listed in a grid with links to each business's own website. Without a computer, call their hotline (© **888/584-5147** or 907/272-5909), which is answered by hosts at member properties to offer referrals to places that meet callers' requirements.

DOWNTOWN
VERY EXPENSIVE

Besides the Hotel Captain Cook, described in full below, three other high-rise hotels downtown offer a similar level of service without as much character or quite as many amenities. The large, recently remodeled **Hilton Anchorage,** 500

Downtown Anchorage

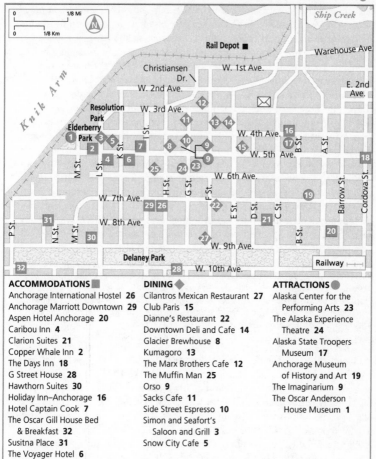

W. 3rd Ave. (© **800/HILTONS** or 907/272-7411; www.hilton.com), is right at the center of downtown activities. The **Sheraton Anchorage,** 401 E. 6th Ave. (© **800/325-3535** or 907/276-8700; www.sheratonanchorage.com), is comparable to the Hilton, but in a slightly less attractive area a few blocks away. The newer **Anchorage Marriott Downtown,** 820 W. 7th Ave. (© **888/236-2427** or 907/279-8000; www.marriotthotels.com), has a nice pool and fabulous views from rooms with wall-size picture windows.

Hotel Captain Cook ★★★   This is Alaska's great, grand hotel, where royalty and rock stars stay. Former governor Wally Hickel built the first of the three towers after the 1964 earthquake, and now the hotel fills a city block and anchors the city skyline. Inside, the brown decor has a fully realized (maybe a little excessive) nautical theme, with art memorializing Cook's voyages and enough teak to build a square-rigger. The regularly renewed rooms are decorated in a rich, sumptuous style using exquisite fabrics, unique pieces of custom-built furniture, and lots of varnished trim. The hotel never abandoned the deep colors that are now returning to fashion—not a scrap of pale wood or generic beige ever came in. Rooms are comfortable in size, but not as large as those in modern upscale chains, and all have a choice only of a king or two twin beds. Lots of custom tile and mirrors make up for the relatively small size of the bathrooms. There are great views from all sides and you don't pay more to be on a higher floor. The pool, in the below-ground lower lobby, is one of the best in town.

Sophisticated Continental food and elaborately formal service justify the high prices at **The Crow's Nest** ★★★, the city's most traditional fine-dining restaurant, on the hotel's top floor. Pheasant, quail, bison, and venison show up on the changing menu, as well as the usual seafood, beef, and lamb. Our meals have been expertly prepared. All tables have stupendous views, and high-backed booths lend intimacy for a romantic dinner. The deliberate service requires that you set aside a full evening for a special meal—dinner unfolds gradually, with almost theatrical formality. Main courses range from $26 to $50. **Fletcher's,** off the lobby, is an English pub serving good Italian-style pizza, pasta, and sandwiches. **The Pantry** is far better than the typical hotel cafe, with excellent service and interesting entrees mixed in with more predictable choices. The **Whale's Tail** serves light meals, coffee, and cocktails amid overstuffed chairs and big TVs. It's a place for a drink without feeling like you're in a bar.

4th Ave. and K St. (P.O. Box 102280), Anchorage, AK 99510-2280. © 800/843-1950 or 907/276-6000. Fax 907/343-2298. www.captaincook.com. 547 units. High season $240–$250 double; $260–$1,500 suite. Low season $135–$145 double; $150–$1,500 suite. Extra person $20. AE, DISC, MC, V. **Amenities:** 3 restaurants; 3 bars; indoor pool; health club with racquetball, Jacuzzi, and sauna; concierge; car-rental desk; business center; shopping arcade; salon; 24-hr. room service; massage; dry cleaning; concierge-level rooms. *In room:* TV w/pay movies, dual-line dataport, hair dryer, iron, Web TV.

EXPENSIVE

Here are a few chain-hotel options downtown for those who prefer national brands: The **Days Inn,** 321 E. 5th Ave. (© 800/DAYS INN or 907/276-7226; www.daysinnalaska.com), which has a courtesy van to the airport and rail depot; the **Holiday Inn Anchorage-Downtown,** 239 W. 4th Ave. (© 800/HOLIDAY or 907/793-5500; www.holiday-inn.com), which has a pool; the **Clarion Suites,** 325 W. 8th Ave. (© 877/424-6423 or 907/274-1000; www.clarionsuites.com), an all-suite building across from the Federal Building, with a small pool; and the **Hawthorn Suites,** 1110 W. 8th Ave. (© 800/527-1133 or 907/222-5005; www.hawthorn.com), with similar facilities as the Clarion Suites, plus a Benihana Restaurant on-site.

Aspen Hotel Anchorage ★★ *Kids*   The rooms in this new hotel, right across from the museum and federal building, attain a level of luxury such that it is hard to think of anything else they could have added. The ceilings are high and the colors bold, the furniture mostly stylish antique or Shaker reproductions, and the amenities, such as speaker phones, WiFi, and microwave ovens, leave out nothing. Some suites have cooking facilities and others, for families, have a separate kids' room with bunkbeds, a PlayStation, and their own DVD player. The hotel's exterior and faux brick courtyard present it as a Disney version of something from a French village, a theme which continues throughout even to the small indoor pool and large spa, which have a deck of attractive tile. Rates include a large continental breakfast in the lobby from 6 to 10am.

108 E. 8th Ave., Anchorage, AK 99501. © 907/868-1605. Fax 907/868-3520. www.aspenhotelsak.com. 89 units. High season $169 double, $199 suite; low season $79 double, $99 suite. Extra person over age 17 $10. AE, DC, DISC, MC, V. **Amenities:** Pool; exercise room; spa; business center; coin-op laundry. *In room:* A/C, TV/DVD, fridge, coffeemaker, hairdryer, iron/ironing board, microwave, wireless Internet.

Copper Whale Inn ⭐ A pair of clapboard houses overlook the water and Elderberry Park right on the Coastal Trail downtown, with charming rooms of various shapes and sizes. There's a wonderfully casual feeling to the place, with a host who serves a full breakfast and befriends guests. My favorite rooms are two with wonderful views, funny angles, and cozy decoration that share a couple of bathrooms on the second floor of the older building, which also has the entrance and common rooms. The rooms in the newer building, lower on the hill, have cherry wood furniture, high ceilings on the upper level, and are generally larger. None are very large, however, especially considering the high rates; you stay here not for luxury but for the style and for the location, which is the best in town. Rooms don't have TVs, but you can get one hooked up by request. High-speed Internet is available in the lobby.

440 L St., Anchorage, AK 99501. © 866/258-7999 or 907/258-7999. Fax 888/WHALE-IN or 907/258-6213. www.copperwhale.com. 18 units, 16 with private bathroom. High season $145 double with shared bathroom, $165–$195 double with private bathroom; low season $69 double with shared bathroom, $110 double with private bathroom. Extra person $10. Rates include full breakfast. AE, DISC, MC, V. **Amenities:** Access to health club; bike rental; concierge. *In room:* TV upon request, dataport, iron.

The Voyager Hotel ⭐⭐ Thanks to its exacting proprietor, Stan Williams, The Voyager is just right, from the warm, professional hospitality to the high quality of the linen. The size is small, the location central, the rooms large and light, all with well-designed kitchenettes, and the housekeeping is exceptional. The desks have speaker phones, high-speed or dial-up dataports, and extra electrical outlets. A recently remodeled lobby updates that part of the building,

---

⌒Finds **Three Exceptional Downtown B&Bs**

These houses and the warm and hospitable people who live there offer some of the most authentic and comfortable lodgings in Alaska.

G Street House, 1032 G St. (© **907/276-3284;** www.gstreethouse.com), is an elegant home within easy walking distance of the downtown sights. The classy rooms go for only $95 for a double with a private bath, a real bargain. The hosts, Pam and Allan Tesche, are energetic and interesting: he's on the city assembly and she's an expert on local history and a community volunteer. You can book through the Web site.

Earth Bed and Breakfast, just a block further from downtown than G Street House, at 1001 W. 12th Ave. (© **907/279-9907;** www.AlaskaOne. com/earthbb), is the vocation of Margriet van Laake, whose mission is to share a light and pleasant house with guests from all over the world. She is fluent in Dutch, German, French, Spanish, Italian, and English. The communal feel of the house makes it popular with mountain climbers. Rooms with shared bath are $99 in summer, with private bath $109.

Near the Mulcahy Park baseball stadium, a 15-minute walk to the downtown sights, **Mahogany Manor,** 204 E. 15th Ave. (© **888/777-0346** or 907/278-1111; www.mahoganymanor.com), feels like it is out in the country, with big windows that look out on treetops. The house was a grand mansion of the 1950s and the Alaskana atmosphere is preserved with redwood plank paneling, indoor waterfalls, and an extraordinary collection of Alaskan art and crafts. The rooms and property are packed with luxury amenities; summer rates range from $219 for a simple bedroom to $319 for a family-sized three-bedroom suite.

although room furnishings remain a little behind the times. There's nothing ostentatious or outwardly remarkable about the hotel, yet the most experienced travelers rave about it the loudest. Smoking is not permitted on the property.

501 K St., Anchorage, AK 99501. ℂ **800/247-9070** or 907/277-9501. Fax 907/274-0333. www.voyager hotel.com. 40 units. High season $169 (up to 3 people per room); low season $89 (up to 3 people per room). Extra person $10. AE, DC, DISC, MC, V. No smoking. **Amenities:** Restaurant; access to nearby health club with $7.50 day pass; dry cleaning. *In room:* A/C, TV, broadband dataport, kitchenette, coffeemaker, hair dryer.

INEXPENSIVE

Caribou Inn *(Value* A big old wood frame house stands incongruously on a corner in the very best part of downtown Anchorage. Instead of luxurious rooms you would expect on such valuable property, there are budget accommodations inside—rooms decorated with as much country style as could be managed with older furniture and limited funds. It's got some charm, it's clean, and the management has made a major effort to cater to visitors who simply want good value for their money rather than people who can't afford to go anywhere else. You'll meet others like yourselves. That's important, because the rates here are so far below the market—the best room in the house, a large unit with dormers and a kitchenette, costs what you normally pay for a depressing little compartment on the edge of downtown. Add the hot breakfast served from 6 to 9am, airport transfer, and free parking pass, and you are getting an amazing deal. If you don't need polish, you can save more than $50 a night here.

501 L St., Anchorage, AK 99501. ℂ **800/272-5878** or 907/272-0444. Fax 907/274-4828. www.caribou bnb.com. 14 units, 9 with private bathroom. Summer $99 double with shared bathroom, $109 double with private bathroom; winter $49 double with shared bathroom, $59 double with private bathroom. Extra person $25. Rates include full breakfast. AE, DISC, MC, V. **Amenities:** Courtesy van. *In room:* TV w/digital cable, fridge.

The Oscar Gill House Bed & Breakfast ★★ On the Delaney Park strip, just a few blocks from downtown, this is truly the oldest house in Anchorage— it was built in 1913, in Knik, before Anchorage was founded, and moved here on a barge a few years later. Oscar Gill was an early civic leader. The house was to be torn down in 1982 but was moved to storage by a historic preservation group; Mark and Susan Lutz saved it in 1994, transferring it to its present location and, with their own labor, restoring it authentically as a cozy bed-and-breakfast. Now it's on the National Historic Register. Appropriate antiques sit on plank floors in rooms sized in those more modest times. With the period decoration it's like visiting your grandmother's house when it was brand new. The Lutzes are the kind of hosts who enjoy their guests. Book early, as they fill; you can check availability and even select a room on their website.

1344 W. 10th Ave., Anchorage, AK 99501. ℂ/fax **907/279-1344**. www.oscargill.com. 3 units, 1 with private bathroom. High season $95 double with shared bathroom, $120 double with private bathroom; low season $65 double with shared bathroom, $75 double with private bathroom. Extra person $20. Rates include full breakfast. AE, MC, V. **Amenities:** Bike loan; babysitting. *In room:* TV, dataport, hair dryer, iron.

Susitna Place ★ *(Value* Just a few blocks from the downtown core, where a narrow residential street reaches a quiet end, a nondescript door under a car port leads into a rambling house of rooms ranging from comfortable and inexpensive to grand. It turns out the street side is really the back of the house, which sits at the top of a high bluff facing an unobstructed view of Cook Inlet and Mount Susitna beyond, a view so unlike most urban vistas it is easy to forget you are right in town. The suite is luxurious, but the four rooms that share bathrooms are the rarer find: cozy and very clean, sharing this prime location, they allow travelers to save money without compromise. The hosts, successful journalists, are hospitable Alaskans.

727 N St., Anchorage, AK 99501. © 907/274-3344. Fax 907/272-4141. www.susitnaplace.com. 8 units, 3 with private bath. High season $90–$95 double with shared bath, $115–$125 private bath, $145–$175 suite; low season $55–$60 shared bath, $70–$75 private bath, $90–$110 suite. Additional person in room $15. Rates include continental breakfast. AE, DISC, MC, V. **Amenities:** Free covered parking. *In room:* TV.

A HOSTEL

Anchorage International Hostel, 700 H St. (© 907/276-3635; www. anchorageinternationalhostel.org), is a 95-bed hostel right downtown, with an urban feel. A coin-op laundry, kitchen, and baggage storage are available, and they have Internet access in the lobby, a courtesy phone, and bike rental. Dorm rooms are small, with just a few bunks each. Members pay $16, nonmembers $20; private rooms are $50 double, $10 each additional person. Dorms close between 10am and 5pm daily and the curfew is 1am. A homier hostel outside the downtown area is detailed below.

BEYOND DOWNTOWN
VERY EXPENSIVE

Millennium Alaskan Hotel Anchorage ★★   Next to the float plane base at Lake Spenard, near the airport, the hotel might by a huge fishing and hunting lodge judging by the large lobby, with its warm colors and fly rods and animal mounts on display. There's a big patio to catch the sun and watch the planes. The rooms are exceptional, decorated in deep, bold colors and a light Alaska Native motif, and packed with thoughtful details. They're a delight to the eye and an invitation to relaxation. All have king-size or two queen beds and are wired for either dial-up or high speed wireless Internet. A courtesy van runs a regular schedule downtown, but this is an airport hotel, and for convenience you really need to rent a car if you stay in this area.

4800 Spenard Rd., Anchorage, AK 99517-3236. © 866/866-8086 or 907/243-2300. Fax 907/243-8815. www.millenniumhotels.com. 248 units. High season $270–$285 double, $325–$600 suite; low season $165–$185 double, $250–$400 suite. AE, DC, DISC, MC, V. **Amenities:** 2 restaurants; health club; Jacuzzi; sauna; seasonal concierge and tour desk; 24-hr. room service; laundry service; dry cleaning. *In room:* AC, TV w/Nintendo, dataport, fridge, coffeemaker, hair dryer, iron, high-speed Internet.

MODERATE

Parkwood Inn ★ *Finds*   This is where our family probably would stay if we were visitors to Anchorage and we somehow happened upon it, because with all our children we like getting a large unit similar to an apartment, with real cooking facilities, but without the suspicious odors or odd neighbors renting by the week who sometimes inhabit such places. Here they have turned apartments into trim standard hotel rooms and keep them fresh and clean. The whole place has a cheerful, professional atmosphere. Every unit has a full kitchen and a private balcony, and even the least expensive rooms have large sitting areas and dining room tables. The two bedroom suites are big enough for a large group. The site is at the intersection of two large arterials—New Seward Highway and Tudor Road—but extensive landscaping shields the inn, both visually and from the noise. There's a computer for guest use in the lobby.

4445 Juneau St., Anchorage, AK 99503. © 800/478-3590 or 907/563-3590. Fax 907/563-5560. www.park woodinn.net. 48 units. High season $130–$140 double ($10 each additional person over age 12), $210 suite (any number of guests); low season $69–$79 double, $120 suite. AE, DC, DISC, MC, V. *In room:* TV, kitchens.

> ⌒ *Tips*   **Affordable Rooms Near the Airport**
>
> Good, inexpensive standard motel rooms near the airport are rare to the vanishing point, although luxurious rooms (like those at the Millennium Alaskan Hotel Anchorage) and B&Bs are readily available. The lowest priced, consistently acceptable standard hotel rooms I could find were $139 a night double, at peak season, at the **Lakeshore Motor Inn** (ⓒ **800/ 770-3000** or 907/248-3485; www.lakeshoremotorinn.com). They have a 24-hour courtesy van. If you enjoy staying with a family, **Elderberry Bed and Breakfast** (ⓒ **907/243-6968**; www.elderberrybb.com) has three rooms with private bathrooms for $75 to $95 double. The hosts enjoy socializing and telling about their Alaska experiences and serving quick, airport overnights. I also recommend A Homestead Bed and Breakfast, below. Two good chain hotels stand near the airport, with higher rates: **Courtyard by Marriott** (ⓒ **800/321-2211** or 907/245-0322; http:// courtyard.com/ANCCY), with many amenities and a pool, at $179 double in summer; and the **Holiday Inn Express** (ⓒ **800/HOLIDAY** or 907/248- 8848; www.hiexpress.com), at $109 to $199 (normally nearer the high end of that range in the summer).

INEXPENSIVE

A Homestead Bed and Breakfast *(Finds)*   This is a real 1930s homestead house built of logs, once remote but now a few minutes from the airport and Kincaid Park. Frank and Patricia Jasper have lived here more than 40 years, and they've kept it as an authentic slice of Alaska (like themselves). One of the rooms is a charming log cabin with plank floors, the other is a many-room upstairs suite with four beds, an outside entrance, and many odd corners and pieces of furniture. Both rooms have cooking facilities. It's a great deal. (Beware, an entirely different place on Spenard Road has an almost identical name.)

6141 Jewel Lake Rd., Anchorage, AK 99502. ⓒ **907/243-5678**. Fax 907/248-6184. jasper@chugach.net. 2 units. Summer $95 double; winter $65 double. Extra person $20. Rates include full breakfast in summer, continental in winter. MC, V (5% surcharge for credit cards). No smoking. *In room:* TV/VCR, kitchenette, coffeemaker.

John's Motel and RV Park *(Value)*   If your only objective is to find a decent room for the least possible money, this may be the place for you. The location, in the Mountain View area east of downtown, is one of the roughest in Anchorage, and the motel is situated between a tattoo parlor and a pawn shop. But the room I saw was clean, well kept, and up to date. The RV park dominates the grounds, and the exterior has seen better days.

3542 Mountain View Drive, Anchorage, AK 99508. ⓒ **800/478-4332** or 907/277-4332. Fax 907/272-0739. www.johnsmotel.com. 20 units. Summer $60 double, winter $55 double. RV park $25. DC, MC, V. **Amenities:** Coin-op laundry. *In room:* TV.

A HOSTEL

Spenard Hostel International, 2845 W. 42nd Place (ⓒ **907/248-5036;** www. AlaskaHostel.org), is a friendly hostel near the airport, with free phones, inexpensive bike and storage rental, Internet access, laundry machines, and a black Lab, Skeeter. There are three lounges for different activities and three kitchens. You can come and go 24 hours a day. It feels more like communal housing than an impersonal hostel. The office is open daily from 9am to 1pm and from 7 to

11pm in summer, 7 to 11pm winter. Beds are $18 by cash or check, a dollar more if you use a credit card (AE, DISC, MC, V), with off-season discounts.

CAMPING

Anchorage is a big city, but you can find natural camping right on the urban outskirts. The municipally owned **Centennial Park** is on Boundary Road at the Muldoon Road exit from the Glenn Highway (© **907/343-6986** or 907/343-4475 off season; www.muni.org/parks/camping.cfm), just as you enter town from the north. Although it is near Muldoon's run-down commercial strip, many of the 83 sites are nicely wooded. The campground has a dump station and free showers and charges $17 a night.

There are several RV parks within the Anchorage bowl, of which the best is the wooded and landscaped **Anchorage RV Park,** 1200 N. Muldoon Rd. (© **800/400-7275** or 907/338-7275; www.anchrvpark.com), near Centennial Park and the Alaska Native Heritage Center. It has full services and excellent facilities, including instant phone hookups. Each of the 195 sites costs $30 to $39 per night. Reserve ahead. They don't take tenters.

The two closest state park campgrounds to Anchorage are at Bird Creek, to the south of town, and Eagle River, just to the north. The **Bird Creek Campground** is one of my favorites. It sits next to Turnagain Arm and the salmon-filled creek. A paved pathway passes by under the large spruce trees. There are 28 sites and the fee is $10 per night. From Anchorage drive 25 miles south on the Seward Highway to milepost 101.

The 57-site **Eagle River Campground** sits in a thickly wooded riverside spot, and it's well developed with paved roads and large sites with lots of privacy. It costs $15 a night and sites can be reserved in advance. Book up to a year ahead (© **800/952-8624** or 907/694-7982; fax 907/746-4644; www.lifetimeadventures.net). The hosts also book rafting on the Eagle River. Take the Glenn Highway 12 miles north from Anchorage and exit at Hiland Road.

3 Where to Dine

DOWNTOWN

EXPENSIVE

Club Paris ★★ STEAK/SEAFOOD   Coming from a bright spring afternoon into midnight darkness, under a neon Eiffel Tower and past the bar, I sat down at a secretive booth for two, and felt as if I should lean across the table and plot a shady 1950s oil deal with my companion. And I would probably not have been the first. In contrast to Sullivan's Steakhouse, across the street, which contrives a masculine, retro feel, Club Paris is the real thing, decorated with mounted swordfish and other cocktail-era decor. The club is the essence of old Anchorage boomtown years, when the streets were dusty and an oil man needed a classy joint in which to do business. Steak, of course, is what to order, and rare really means rare. It's consistently voted the best in town. Ask for the blue cheese stuffing; the stuffed filet is worth the years it probably takes off your coronary arteries. They have a full bar.

417 W. 5th Ave. © 907/277-6332. www.clubparisrestaurant.com. Reservations recommended. Lunch $5.75–$15; dinner $14–$44. AE, DC, DISC, MC, V. Mon–Sat 11:30am–2:30pm and 5–11pm; Sun 5–10pm.

The Marx Brothers Cafe ★★★ ECLECTIC/REGIONAL   A restaurant started by three friends back when gourmet food was an exotic hobby in Anchorage is now a standard of excellence in the state. Treatments of Alaska seafood that started here as cutting-edge creative cuisine now turn up in many of the best restaurants. Chef Jack Amon still presides in the kitchen of the cottage downtown, one of the city's first houses. Maître d' Van Hale still presides out front, preparing his famous Caesar salad at tableside, a ritual that allows him to schmooze with anyone he chooses in the tiny dining rooms. His attitude mirrors the casual elegance of the entire evening, where those wearing ties are in the minority. The cuisine is varied and creative, ranging from Asian to Italian, and is always turned out flawlessly, often with subtle surprises. A meal is an experience that takes much of the evening and most entrees are over $30. Waiting in the small entryway can be uncomfortable if your table isn't ready. The wine cellar is famous with a list the size of a dictionary, but wine prices are not unreasonable.

627 W. 3rd Ave. © 907/278-2133. www.marxcafe.com. Reservations required. Main courses $18–$36. AE, DC, MC, V. Summer Tues–Sat 5:30–10pm; winter Tues-Thus 6pm–9:30pm, Fri–Sat 5:30–10pm.

Orso ★★ ITALIAN/MEDITERRANEAN This restaurant is unique in Anchorage for serving interesting food even though it is large and oriented to the downtown tourist trade. Formerly a rather pompous place, they've lightened up the ornate dining room with big modern paintings and amped up the cuisine with bold flavors and a long menu full of surprises. The mushroom ravioli, with a generous dose of smoked salmon, was rich and strongly flavored. The rice that came with my (nicely seared) scallops had to be passed around and started a conversation—I'm still not sure exactly what made it taste so good. The antipasto plate looked great and was generously endowed. Service is professional but not stuffy, and the food comes fast enough not to use up the entire evening. Generally, the prices are reasonable for this kind of food, but to save money, dine in the still somewhat grandiose bar.

737 W. 5th Ave. © 907/222-3232. www.orsoalaska.com. Reservations recommended. Lunch $8–$18; dinner pasta or main course $12–$33. AE, DC, DISC, MC, V. Summer Mon–Fri 11:30am–4pm and 5–11pm, Sat–Sun 5–11pm; winter Sun–Mon 5–9:30pm, Tues–Thurs 5–10pm, Fri–Sat 5–11pm.

Sacks Cafe ★★★ CREATIVE/ECLECTIC This is the most fashionable restaurant in town, and also one of the best. The storefront dining room, in warm Southwest colors and sharp angles, resembles a showcase for the food and

---

Finds **The Best Takeout in Town**

Anchorage has great takeout food (as my family's continued survival attests). Downtown, **The Muffin Man,** at 817 W. 6th Ave. (© **907/279-6836**), produces some of the best meals eaten at desks in Anchorage, including the memorably delicious smoked red salmon and cream cheese sandwich. You can eat in the sunny, tiled dining room, too. The best, most original burgers are at **Arctic Roadrunner,** with locations on Arctic Boulevard at Fireweed Lane and on Old Seward Highway at International Airport Road. Try the Kodiak Islander, which has peppers, ham, onion rings, and God knows what else on top. We get carry-out Chinese from **New Sagaya's City Market** (© **907/274-6173**; www.newsagaya.com) at the corner of 13th and I streets. It's also a wonderful gourmet grocery and community meeting place, and has a good deli and Italian-style brick-oven pizza. Pack a picnic here, or eat in the enclosed or sidewalk dining areas.

diners, who can sit at tables or at a tapas bar. The cuisine defies categorization, but is consistently interesting and creative, frequently with Thai influences. The menu changes, but one recent offering was chicken with scallops, shiitake mushrooms, snow peas, udon noodles, ginger cream sauce, and black bean salsa. Vegetarians do as well as meat eaters. For lunch, the sandwiches are unforgettable, with choices such as shrimp and avocado with herb cream cheese on sourdough. The beer and wine list is extensive and reasonably priced. They serve brunch Saturday and Sunday.

328 G St. ℂ 907/274-4022. www.sackscafe.com. Reservations recommended. Lunch $5.25–$13; dinner main courses $18–$28. AE, MC, V. Daily 11am–2:30pm and 5–9:30pm; Fri and Sat till 10:30pm.

Simon and Seafort's Saloon and Grill ★★ STEAK/SEAFOOD   Simon's, as it's known, is the most fun fine-dining place in town, a jolly beef and seafood grill where voices boom off the high ceilings. On sunny summer evenings, the rooms, fitted with brass turn-of-the-20th-century saloon decor, fill with light off Cook Inlet, down below the bluff; the views are magnificent. The food is consistently very good. A long list of nightly specials includes items as exotic as a tasty crab- and macadamia-stuffed halibut, but most of the cuisine is simpler. The service, too, stands out: warm and professional, and quick enough to allow time for other evening activities. Children are treated well. To enjoy the place on a budget, order a sandwich and soup for lunch in the well-stocked bar.

420 L St. ℂ 907/274-3502. Reservations recommended (make dinner reservations a couple of days in advance in summer). Lunch $7–$15; dinner main courses $16–$40. AE, MC, V. Summer Mon–Fri 11:15am–3:30pm and 4:30–10pm, Sat–Sun 4:30–10pm; winter Mon–Fri 11:15am–3:30pm and 5–10pm, Sat–Sun 5–10pm.

MODERATE

Glacier Brewhouse ★ GRILL/SEAFOOD/PIZZA   An eclectic and ever-changing menu is served in a large dining room with lodge decor, where the pleasant scent of the wood-fired grill hangs in the air. It's a lively place to see others and be seen. There are lots of agreeable if trendy touches: the glass wall showing off the brewing equipment, which produces eight or more hearty beers, and also turns out spent grain for bread that's then set out on the tables with olive oil. An advantage for travelers is the wide price range—a pizza with feta cheese, sundried tomatoes, pesto, and garlic is $10; crab legs are $37. The food is usually quite good. Choose this place for a boisterous meal with quick, casual service that will get you out in time to do something else with the evening. Do reserve ahead, however, as waits can be long.

737 W. 5th Ave. ℂ 907/274-BREW. www.glacierbrewhouse.com. Reservations recommended for dinner. Lunch $8–$15; dinner $9–$34. AE, DISC, DC, MC, V. High season daily 11am–11pm; low season Mon 11am–9:30pm, Tues–Thurs 11am–10pm, Fri–Sat 11am–11pm, Sun 4–9:30pm.

Kumagoro ★ JAPANESE   Anchorage has several good, authentic Japanese restaurants, but this one, right on the main tourist street downtown, has the most convenient location. Among my favorite lunches anywhere is their box lunch ($14), a large sampler of many dishes, including sushi, sashimi, and other tasty things I couldn't identify. The dining room is pleasantly low-key, with tables in rows, so you may have the opportunity to meet those seated next to you. The restaurant has a beer and wine license.

533 W. 4th Ave. ℂ 907/272-9905. Lunch $6.50–$14; dinner main courses $14–$39. AE, DISC, DC, MC, V. Summer daily 11am–10:45pm; winter daily 11am–9:45pm.

INEXPENSIVE

Cilantros Mexican Restaurant *(Finds* MEXICAN   Authentic, inexpensive Mexican food is served in a little house on the park strip in cheery but sparsely decorated dining rooms large enough for only a few tables. The service is quick rather than friendly or polished, but it's tough to complain when the food is this good and this cheap. Each of my meals has been just right. They serve from the entire, very long menu all day, including breakfast: The huevos rancheros are great. When you want to save time and money on dinner, this is the place.

611 W. 9th Ave. 🕐 **907/279-8226.** Breakfast $6–$8; lunch and dinner $7–$14. MC, V. Mon–Fri 11am–10pm; Sat 4–10pm. Closed Sun.

Dianne's Restaurant *(Value* SOUP/SANDWICH   This is my first choice for a quick, healthful, inexpensive lunch downtown. Located off the lobby of a tall, glass office building, Dianne's cafeteria line fills with well-dressed folk seeking the hearty freshly baked bread, soups, sandwiches, and specials turned out for the lunch hour. The atmosphere is bright and casual and you don't waste your day eating. The restaurant does not have a liquor license.

550 W. 7th Ave., Ste. 110. 🕐 **907/279-7243.** Main courses $4.25–$9. AE, DISC, MC, V. Mon–Fri 7am–4pm.

Downtown Deli and Cafe DELI   Now mostly serving visitors, this was once a hot place for local politicos to meet. In 1994 President Clinton came for dinner. Knowing his appetite, I hope he ordered some side dishes, for much of the food here is served strictly a la carte. Best choices are the omelets for breakfast, the quiche of the day for lunch, and the salmon dinner. Prices are reasonable, especially at dinnertime, when downtown is short on inexpensive sit-down places, and kids are treated well. Service can suffer on summer mornings when the place is overrun with tourists. They serve beer and wine.

525 W. 4th Ave. 🕐 **907/276-7116.** All items $6.25–$12. AE, DC, DISC, MC, V. Summer daily 6am–10pm; winter Sun 9am–4pm, Mon–Thurs 7am–4pm, Fri–Sat 7am–9pm.

Snow City Cafe ☆ VEGETARIAN/HOME STYLE   This is a meeting place for a young, environmentally conscious crowd, and also a good restaurant. The food, served by a friendly, committed staff in a daylight-filled storefront dining room, is laced with interesting flavors and styles of preparation, including many vegetarian dishes. For lunch, the sandwiches are filling and varied, but breakfast is the main event. On weekend mornings the cafe fills with people for eggs Benedict, salmon cakes, homemade granola, and such, which are served all day. They're open Wednesday nights for an Irish music jam. Monthly art shows begin with artist receptions every first Friday, a pattern shared with all the downtown galleries. They serve beer and wine.

1034 W. 4th Ave. 🕐 **907/272-CITY.** www.snowcitycafe.com. Breakfast and lunch $5–$10. AE, DISC, MC, V. Daily 7am–4pm.

BEYOND DOWNTOWN
EXPENSIVE

Jens' Restaurant ☆☆☆ INTERNATIONAL   Chef Jens Hansen is truly gifted. His restaurant is for the kind of diner who loves exciting food, surprises, and beautiful plates of new tastes and textures; the meals are about the food, sharing bites, and saying "Wow," and "How did he do that?" I won't call it experimental, because I've never had a meal here that wasn't perfect, but the cuisine is highly eclectic and there's often only one item on the changing menu that isn't unusual or challenging: the superb pepper steak. Like everything, even that dish has a sauce, and it is complex and memorable. The wine list is exceptional

Coffeehouses

There are coffeehouses all over the city, where people go for a cup of java and a pastry, and to meet people and engage in conversation. My favorite is **Side Street Espresso,** on G Street between 4th and 5th, a gathering place for artists, activists, and anyone who wants to trade ideas, often with live acoustic music in the evening. **Cafe del Mundo,** at Northern Lights and Denali midtown, gathers an older crowd of businesspeople, yuppies, stay-at-home parents, and those looking for a comfortable meeting spot. **Kaladi Brothers,** in the shopping center on Northern Lights Boulevard between Arctic and Minnesota, is a busy place sharing space with a huge used book store. It's just down from the essential REI sporting goods store and has computers with Internet access.

and reasonably priced, and you can sip your selection while dining inexpensively on appetizers in a pleasant bar area; try the incredible spinach ravioli with Gorgonzola, for example. Desserts are sublime. The dining room is light and clean, decorated with modern art. Service is highly professional, with each formally attired waiter assigned to just a few tables.

701 W. 36th Ave. ✆ 907/561-5367. www.jensrestaurant.com. Reservations recommended. Lunch $9–$22; dinner main courses $18–$34. AE, DC, DISC, MC, V. Mon–Fri 11:30am–2pm, Tues–Sat 6–10pm. Closed Jan.

MODERATE

Bear Tooth Grill ★ *Value* SOUTHWESTERN You can't find food of this quality for prices this low anywhere else in Anchorage. Dishes such as the soy grilled halibut are sophisticated and nicely done, but take up only a small part of a menu that goes on and on with Mexican choices, sandwiches, and other selections inexpensive enough to make the restaurant fit for an after-work impulse—most main courses are under $11. The young partners who own the restaurant started in business by making beer and then opened a pizzeria to sell the beer (see the Moose's Tooth, below); next they opened a threater-pub (see "Anchorage Nightlife," later); the grill, in the same building, was the final addition. Eat tacos and wraps watching a movie or in the movie theater lobby, a loud, free-flowing setting good for kids. The grill is in a separate, calmer, and more confined dining room, best for couples and parties of four or less. The food comes more slowly, as befits the atmosphere. Tables are more comfortable than booths, but at peak times you have to take what you can get, often with a wait, so try to dine here early or late. Besides the beer, they have a full bar serving many margaritas.

1230 W. 27th Ave. ✆ 907/276-4200. Reservations not accpeted. All items $6–$20. AE, DC, DISC, MC, V. Summer Sun–Thus 4–11:30pm, Fri–Sat 4pm–12:30am; winter Sun–Thus 4–10:30pm, Fri–Sat 4pm–midnight.

Campobello Bistro ★★ NORTHERN ITALIAN/BISTRO This quiet little midtown restaurant is amazingly like stepping into northern Italy, except for the Alaska seafood. Even the service has the quality of jocular professionalism I remember from Italy. Unlike most of Anchorage's best restaurants, the bistro doesn't try to reinvent the cookbook. Most of the menu consists of recognizable dishes, such as veal Marsala or Italian sausage and polenta. Meals are bold, highly flavored, and entirely satisfying. The seafood crepe is fantastic. Those seeking the bland tomatoes and cheese of a typical Italian family restaurant should go elsewhere (Sorrento's and Romano's, both on Fireweed Lane, each do that tried-and-true formula well). The wine and food are reasonably priced.

601 W. 36th, Ste. 10. ℂ 907/563-2040. Lunch $8–$13; dinner main courses $13–$25. DC, MC, V. Mon–Fri 11am–2:30pm, Mon–Sat 5–9pm.

INEXPENSIVE

The Lucky Wishbone ★ (Finds) DINER   This Anchorage institution (in high school we called it "The Bone") is where the real pioneer Alaska meets families out for a delicious, not-too-greasy fried chicken dinner and famous milkshakes (try the hot fudge) and other delights from the fountain. It is our children's favorite. One section of the counter is reserved for discussion of aviation and golf. When the beloved owners outlawed smoking years ago, it made the front page of the newspaper. You'll see few other tourists, as the location, among the car dealerships at the extreme east end of downtown, is too far to walk to from the hotels, but I ran into Alaska's powerful senior U.S. senator, Ted Stevens. They have a drive-in.

1033 E. 5th Ave. ℂ 907/272-3454. All items $3–$9.25. MC, V. Summer daily 10am–11pm; winter daily 10am–10pm.

The Moose's Tooth Pub and Pizzeria ★★ (Kids) PIZZA   The best pizza and beer in Anchorage undoubtedly come from this fun and friendly place. The microbrewery came first, but the pizza really is the greater accomplishment. It has a soft, light crust like Italian pizza but the oomph of American pizza. They offer many ingenious toppings, but not just to dump on: the combinations really work. Dine inside (perhaps in the "hippie pad"), or at picnic tables outside in a tent that's open year-round. That's the best place in town to take kids for dinner. The only drawback is the restaurant's popularity, which can make for long waits at peak times.

3300 Old Seward Hwy. ℂ 907/258-2537. www.moosestooth.net. Large pizza $13–$25. AE, DC, DISC, MC, V. Summer Sun noon–midnight, Mon–Thurs 11am–midnight, Fri–Sat 11am–1am; winter Sun noon–11pm, Mon 11am–11pm, Tues–Thurs 11am–midnight, Fri–Sat 11am–1am.

4 What to See & Do

I've arranged this section starting with a self-guided walking tour through downtown Anchorage, followed by details on the downtown museums and then attractions that are farther afield.

The best **guided walking tour** of the historic downtown area is by **Anchorage Historic Properties,** 645 W. 3rd Ave. (ℂ 907/274-3600; www.Anchorage Historic.org), a city-endowed historic preservation group, offering 2-hour, 2-mile walks from June to August, Monday through Friday at 1pm. The volunteer guides are fun and knowledgeable. Meet at the lobby of Old City Hall, 524 W. 4th Ave., next door to the Log Cabin Visitor Information Center. Tickets cost $5 for adults, $1 for children.

Motorized city tours can get you beyond downtown to see what more of the town looks like. A couple of firms offer 1-hour tours for $10 in buses made up

---

⟮*Tips* **Helper Bees**

The people you see downtown on bikes and on foot in bright yellow-and-black outfits are the Anchorage Downtown Partnership Security Ambassadors, sometimes known as the "bumblebees" for their color scheme. They are funded by a self-imposed levy on downtown property owners in part to help visitors. Stop one to ask a question or report a problem.

like trolleys from the tourist core. Catch them along 4th Avenue between F and G streets. For something in greater depth, **Gray Line of Alaska City Tour** (© **800/544-2206;** www.graylineofalaska.com) offers a 3-hour tour with a visit to the Ship Creek area below downtown and the Alaska Native Heritage Center. It spends an hour at the center, not as long as I like to stay. The tour costs $45 for adults, $23 children, including admission to the center.

Start & Finish: 4th Avenue and F Street.
Time: 2 hours (use the shortcuts noted for a briefer tour).

Start at the **Log Cabin Visitor Information Center** at 4th Avenue and F Street. Outside is a sign that shows the distance to various cities and a 5,114-pound jade boulder put on display by Stewart's Photo Shop, an Anchorage institution that is just across the street.

Walk east, toward the mountains, to:
❶ **Old City Hall (1936)**
The building is on the right of 4th Avenue as you approach E Street. The lobby contains a fun and illuminating free display on city history, including dioramas of the early streetscape, old photographs, and the fire bell and fire pole that once were used in this building.

Crossing E Street, notice on the left side of 4th Avenue that all the buildings are modern—everything on that side from E Street east for several blocks collapsed in the 1964 earthquake. The street split in half, lengthwise, with the left side ending up a dozen feet lower than the right. That land was later reinforced with a gravel buttress by the U.S. Army Corps of Engineers and the slope below forever set aside as open space because of the earthquake risk. This stretch of 4th Avenue is where the **Iditarod Trail Sled Dog Race** and the **Anchorage Fur Rendezvous World Championship Sled Dog Race** start each year in March and February, respectively.

Continue walking east. At 4th Avenue and D Street is the:
❷ **Wendler Building (1915)**
The old Club 25 is among the oldest buildings in Anchorage. The bronze

statue of the dog commemorates the sled-dog races that start here. Across D Street is a mural that depicts a map of coastal Alaska and British Columbia, with the Iditarod Trail dimly marked.

Turn right, walking a block south through:
❸ **The culture of D Street**
This one-block street contains two of the city's most interesting cultural outlets. First on the left, at 4th and D, is **Cyrano's Off-Center Playhouse** (© **907/274-2599;** www.cyranos.org), home to the Eccentric Theater Company. They really are good; the tiny theater can cause quite a stir in town and has won many awards. They also have jazz performances, poetry readings, and the like, and you can stop in the cozy little cafe and small bookstore any time. A little farther on the left, the **International Gallery of Contemporary Art** (www.igcaalaska.org) is the community's non-profit forum for the art that is happening right now. Typically, the gallery is given over to a single artist or theme. Hours are on p. 229.

Cross 5th Avenue at the end of D Street and enter:
❹ **The 5th Avenue Mall**
This grand, four-story shopping center is Alaska's fanciest mall, with

Nordstrom and JCPenney as its anchor stores. A large, airy food court is on the top floor. Take a look, or walk straight through to the doors on the opposite side. (Just a block east are the Anchorage Museum of History and Art and the Alaska State Troopers Museum, described below.)

Cross the mall to the doors opposite, exiting onto 6th Avenue, turn right and walk a block and cross E Street to:

⑤ Town Square

The community raised money for improvements to the square by collecting donations of $40 each for the granite bricks, with an inscription of the contributor's choosing. There are 13,344 (bet you can't find mine). On the east side of the square, behind you, the huge whale mural was painted freehand by Wyland in 1994. He painted similar whale murals in cities all along the West Coast. The building on the northeast corner of the square is one of the city's oldest and was saved from demolition when the park was created; it contains a charming gift and candy shop owned by the Mayor's wife.

On the west side of the square is the massive, highly decorated, dominating:

⑥ Alaska Center for the Performing Arts

The center was completed in 1988 amid controversy about cost overruns and a design that's either clever and bold or garish and busy—you decide. The lobby is usually open, and whatever your opinion of the decor, a look inside will spark a discussion. Alaskans have gotten used to it, and now we think of the building mostly as a focal point of our cultural life. Tours are held Wednesday at 1pm; a $1 donation is requested (reach the center's administrative offices at ℃ **907/263-2900;** www.alaskapac.org). Thespians believe the building is haunted by the ghost of painter Sydney Laurence, who makes lighting mysteriously vary

and elevators go up and down with no one in them. An auditorium demolished to make room for the center was named for Laurence. Check the box office for current performances in the three theaters, Alaska's premier performance venues (and see "The Performing Arts," later).

TAKE A BREAK
From the performing arts center, cross 6th Avenue at the F Street light and turn right (west) to **Humpy's,** a popular tavern on the south side of 6th with a huge selection of microbrews, live music, and good casual meals, including halibut tacos.

The square green office building next door to Humpy's is:

⑦ City Hall

Turn left through the pedestrian walkway between Humpy's and City Hall. A large mural showing a timeline of the history of Anchorage faces the parking lot. An artistically superior mural, by Duke Russell, is on the wall in Humpy's outdoor seating area on the near side of the parking lot.

Walk west through the city hall parking lot to G Street, turn right, and proceed to 6th Avenue and G. On the northeast corner of 6th Avenue and G Street, in the corner of the Performing Arts Center, is the:

⑧ The Center for Contemporary Visual Art of Alaska

A unique gallery in Alaska, because the father-daughter owners are purely dedicated to fine art. They mount invitational shows of the state's best artists in a cool, uncluttered space. You're not likely to buy anything on a casual walk, but do stop in for a refreshing and enlightening visit to what is essentially a free museum.

Walk a block north to Fifth Avenue. The west side of G Street between Fourth and Fifth avenues contains some of the downtown's best:

Downtown Anchorage Walking Tour

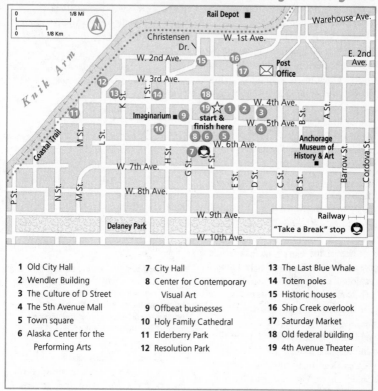

1 Old City Hall
2 Wendler Building
3 The Culture of D Street
4 The 5th Avenue Mall
5 Town square
6 Alaska Center for the
   Performing Arts
7 City Hall
8 Center for Contemporary
   Visual Art
9 Offbeat businesses
10 Holy Family Cathedral
11 Elderberry Park
12 Resolution Park
13 The Last Blue Whale
14 Totem poles
15 Historic houses
16 Ship Creek overlook
17 Saturday Market
18 Old federal building
19 4th Avenue Theater

⑨ Offbeat businesses

First comes **Aurora Fine Arts,** an attractively cluttered arts and craft shop with plenty to see. Next are: **Darwin's Theory,** a friendly, old-fashioned bar with character that shows up in an Indigo Girls song; **Suzi's Woollies** (www.suziswoollies. com), a Celtic shop carrying imported sweaters, jewelry, and CDs, and with live Irish music Saturday afternoons; **Denali Wear,** which is Tracy Anna Bader's studio and shop of bright, graphic, wearable art; and **Side Street Espresso,** where you can get into a lively discussion on art or politics and make contact with thinking people. On the opposite side of the street, at 423 G Street, the **Alaska Glass Gallery** (www.alaskaglassgallery.com)

shows fanciful and dramatic glass sculptures by Alaskan Cynthia England and other artists she selects in a light-filled storefront.

   Shortcut: You can cut an hour off the tour here by continuing north on G Street to 4th, then turning right and walking 1 block to the starting point at F Street.

Backtrack to 5th and G, then proceed west (away from the mountains) on 5th. The Imaginarium, described under "Downtown Museums," below, is on the right. Continuing west on 5th Avenue and crossing H Street, you'll see the:

⑩ Holy Family Cathedral

This concrete Art Deco church is the seat of the Roman Catholic archbishop. The interior is unremarkable.

Keep going toward the water, crossing L Street and going down the hill to:

⑪ Elderberry Park

The yellow-and-brown house is the **Oscar Anderson House,** described under "Downtown Museums," below. Besides the good playground equipment, the park offers the easiest access point to the **Coastal Trail** (see "Walking & Biking," later). The trail tunnels under the Alaska Railroad tracks from the bottom of the park.

Now hike back up the hill to L Street and turn left. At 3rd Avenue is:

⑫ Resolution Park

The bronze **Captain Cook Monument** stands on a large wooden deck, but he's gazing out to sea—the opposite of the way he was facing when he explored Cook Inlet in 1778 aboard HMS *Resolution*. Cook didn't personally come as far as Anchorage, instead sending a boat with his ship's master, William Bligh (later the Captain Bligh who inspired mutiny aboard the HMS *Bounty*). Failing to find the Northwest Passage here, Cook considered his 2 weeks in Cook Inlet a waste of time, grousing in his journal, "Nothing but a trifling point in geography has been determined." The park's informative signs, powerful mounted binoculars, and commanding vantage point make this a rewarding stop for gazing out at the water and the mountains beyond. The waters you see are ferocious and wild, with whirlpool currents and a tidal range of almost 40 vertical feet. The shore across the inlet, about 2 miles away, is virtually uninhabited.

Follow 3rd Avenue east (back toward the mountains) 1 block and turn right on K Street. On the right is:

⑬ The Last Blue Whale

Joseph Princiotti's huge 1973 bronze of combat between a whale and whalers in small boats shows the whale's point of view.

Cross K Street to walk through the plaza toward the opposite Nesbett State Courthouse. The sinuous shapes of the concrete are supposed to suggest both the flow of people through the court system and a braided glacial river. At the courthouse, at 4th Avenue and I Street, take a look at the two:

⑭ Totem poles

Carved of red cedar by Lee Wallace, of Ketchikan, and erected in 1997, they represent the eagle and raven moieties of the Tlingit people, intended to symbolize the balance of justice. A Tlingit creation story tells of how raven stole the moon and stars and brought them to mankind; here, the moon and stars are the stars of the Alaska flag.

Walk around past the courthouse on 4th Avenue and turn left onto H Street. Follow H as it crosses 3rd Avenue and becomes Christensen Drive. Descend the hill on Christensen and turn right on 2nd Avenue, toward the mountains. Look around at the:

⑮ Historic houses

The old wooden houses along 2nd are mostly attorneys' offices now, but once this was one of the better residential areas in town. Several houses are marked and a kiosk at 2nd and F relates some town history. If you imagine houses like this over much of downtown, you'll know what Anchorage looked like before oil.

Continue east on 2nd Avenue to E Street, where you will find:

⑯ A Ship Creek overlook with a monument to President Eisenhower

The bust commemorates Alaska's 1959 admission to the Union (in fact, Eisenhower was a major barrier to statehood). More interesting is the overlook. You can see the Alaska Railroad yards from here, and part of the port of Anchorage and the neighborhood of Government Hill across the Ship Creek river bottom. This is where the tent city of Knik Anchorage, later shortened to Anchorage, was set up in 1914. An informative set of signs on the overlook explains the history. The Alaska Railroad, which helped build Anchorage, still has its headquarters in a modern brick building that stands by the creek. The nearer concrete building is the railroad's stately depot. The restored steam engine on the pedestal in front was used on construction of the Panama Canal, then worked in the yard here as a switch engine. The creek itself is full of salmon in June and August (see "Fishing," later), and a walkway that crosses a dam just upstream from here is a good place to watch the fish and to feed ducks. But the walk down the stairs to the river bottom and back is strenuous.

Walk up the hill on E Street to 3rd Avenue. The extensively landscaped parking lot on the left becomes the:

⑰ Saturday Market

This street fair, held every Saturday from mid-May to mid-September, draws hundreds of vendors and thousands of shoppers. You can buy everything from local vegetables to handmade crafts to tourist junk. There are food booths and music, too.

Turn right on 3rd Avenue, then left on F Street. F Street Station, on the left, is a fun bar with an after-work crowd. Proceed to 4th Avenue, and you're back at the Log Cabin Visitor Information Center, but don't stop. Turn right on 4th Avenue. On the right side is the:

⑱ Old federal building

This grand, white, Depression-era structure now contains the Alaska Public Lands Information Center, with interesting displays and lots of information about the outdoors.

Across the street is Anchorage's most attractive historic building, the restored:

⑲ 4th Avenue Theater

The theater was built by Cap Lathrop, Alaska's first business magnate, who created it as a monument to the territory and the permanence of its new society. Today it's a gift store and dinner theater. Don't miss going in and looking at the bas-relief murals and the blinking Big Dipper on the ceiling, which during many a movie over the years was more entertaining than whatever was on the screen.

DOWNTOWN MUSEUMS

Alaska State Troopers Museum   This charming little museum has more than one way into the heart, but it is certainly not an essential stop. For law enforcement people, the appeal is obvious. Others may also enjoy perusing a trove of law enforcement insignia, equipment, a 1952 Hudson Hornet patrol car, photographs, and other memorabilia, that all conveys the positive spirit of pioneer Alaska and the troopers' obvious pride.

245 W. 5th Ave. ℂ **800/770-5050** or 907/279-5050. www.alaskatroopermuseum.com. Admission free. Open year-round Mon–Fri 10am–4pm, Sat noon–4pm.

Anchorage Museum of History and Art ★★★   The state's largest museum doesn't have its largest collection, but it has the room and staff to teach and to serve as a center of contemporary culture for this part of the world. Most visitors tour the large Alaska Gallery, an informative and enjoyable walk through the history and some of the anthropology of the state. In the art galleries, you can see what's happening in art in Alaska today; Alaskan art isn't all scenery and walrus ivory, but the grandeur of the state does influence almost every work. The Anchorage museum also gets the best touring and temporary exhibits. Depending on your interest, you could spend most of a day there. The restaurant, operated by the excellent Marx Brothers Cafe (p. 207), serves some of the best lunches to be had downtown. Call for information on the lectures, openings, and jazz happenings staged many summer evenings.

121 W. 7th Ave. ℂ 907/343-4326. www.anchoragemuseum.org. Admission $6.50 adults, $6 seniors 65 and older, free for children 17 and under. May 15–Sept 15 Fri–Wed 9am–6pm, Thurs 9am–9pm; Sept 16–May 14 Weds–Sat 10am–6pm, Sun noon–5pm.

The Imaginarium ✦ *Kids*   This science museum is one of my kids' favorite places. It's geared to children, with not many words and lots of fun learning experiences, and stuff to just play with that has nothing to do with science. The highlight is the saltwater touch tank, which is like an indoor tide pool where you can learn to identify sea creatures. There's a strong Alaska theme to most of the displays. On the other hand, the museum is small and not as professionally put together as similar places found in big cities, so don't expect too much.

737 W. 5th Ave., Ste. G. ℂ 907/276-3179. www.imaginarium.org. Admission $5.50 ages 13–64, $5 ages 2–12 and 65 and older. Mon–Sat 10am–6pm; Sun noon–5pm.

The Oscar Anderson House Museum   This house museum, moved to a beautiful site in Elderberry Park over the water, shows how an early Swedish butcher and entrepreneur lived. Although far from grand, the house is quaint, surrounded by a lovely little garden, and dates from the city's founding in 1915. The 45-minute guided tour provides a good explanation of Anchorage's short history. Anderson died in 1974, and the house contains many of the family's original belongings, including a working 1909 player piano around which the structure was built. If you come at Christmas, don't miss the Swedish Christmas tours, the first 2 weekends in December.

420 M St. ℂ 907/274-2336. www.anchoragehistoric.org. Admission $3 adults, $1 children 5–12. Summer Mon–Fri noon–5pm. Closed in winter.

SIGHTS BEYOND DOWNTOWN

Besides the attractions listed in detail below, Anchorage is the home of the **Alaska Aviation Heritage Museum,** on Lake Hood at the airport at 4721 Aircraft Dr. (ℂ **907/248-5325;** www.alaskaairmuseum.com). The museum has a wonderful topic, an impressive collection, and large buildings. If you have any

---

Big State, Big Movies

Two downtown theaters show films aimed at visitors. **The Alaska Experience Theatre** (ℂ 877/276-3030 or 907/276-3730; www.alaskaexperience theatre.com) is on the northwest corner of Sixth Avenue and G Street, partly in a dome tent. A 40-minute Omnivision wraparound movie about Alaska costs $8 for adults, $4 for children, showing hourly. It's certainly spectacular—too much so for some people, who get motion sickness. Sit toward the center at the back. An Alaska Earthquake display that really shakes is $6 for adults and $4 for children ages 5 to 12. Combination tickets are discounted. The film shows in summer daily from 9am to 9pm; in winter noon to 6pm. The earthquake demonstration has slightly longer hours. In the summer, the **Alaska Center for the Performing Arts** usually has a presentation for visitors, too. Recently they've shown *Aurora: Alaska's Great Northern Lights,* photographer Dave Parkhurst's incredible 25-year collection of auroral images (www.thealaskacollection.com), set to an original musical score. Admission is **$8.75** and showings, which last 40 minutes, take place hourly from 9am to 9pm.

---

interest in aviation or Alaska history, there is something here for you. Unfortunately, the museum is perennially short on money and has sometimes closed unpredictably. At this writing, summer hours were daily except Tuesday, 10am to 6pm, winter Friday and Saturday 10am to 4pm and Sunday noon to 4pm. Call ahead to be sure.

Alaska Botanical Garden *(Finds* The garden is young, and the volunteer staff has filled only 4 acres of its wooded, 110-acre site, but already this is a restful place to learn about native flora and hundreds of perennials that grow in Alaska, while enjoying peaceful shade and watching birds and squirrels. I don't know of many other botanical gardens where you're warned to watch out for moose and bear. A fine 1-mile nature trail with explanatory signs leaves from the garden and proceeds down to Campbell Creek, where you may see salmon swimming.

Campbell Airstrip Rd. (off Tudor Rd.). ℂ 907/770-3692. www.alaskabg.org. Donation requested. Summer daily 9am–9pm. From downtown, drive out New Seward Hwy. (Gambell St.) to Tudor Rd., exit to the east (left), turn right off Tudor onto Campbell Airstrip Rd., and park at the Benny Benson School. It's 20 min. from downtown.

Alaska Native Heritage Center *★★★* Alaska Natives built this extraordinary center to bring their cultures to visitors. It's Alaska's best Native cultural attraction. What makes it so is not the graceful building or the professional and informative displays, but the Native people themselves, real village people who often create a personal connection with visitors and rarely come across as practiced or distant. The three main parts of the center take much of a day to absorb. First, there's a hall where storytellers, dancers, and Native athletes perform, with three 30-minute programs rotating through the day. Second, there's a 10-minute film and a gallery of educational displays and a series of workshops, where artisans practice and show off traditional crafts and sometimes teach crafts to visitors. Finally, there's a pond surrounded by five traditional Native dwellings representing each cultural group, each hosted by a member of that group. There's a snack bar for soup and sandwiches and a gift shop where inexpensive items are mixed in with real Native art and crafts for sale by the center or on consignment from Native artisans. Getting to the center requires wheels, and the center is currently offering a free shuttle from various points downtown. Call for details on where and when to catch it.

8800 Heritage Center Dr. From the Glenn Hwy. take the North Muldoon exit. ℂ 800/315-6608 or 907/ 330-8000. www.alaskanative.net. Admission $21 adults, $19 seniors and military, $16 children 7–16, free under 6; Alaska residents $9 adult, $6 children, free under 6. Summer daily 9am–6pm. Winter at least Sat 10am–5pm; call for additional hours and winter discounts.

The Alaska Zoo *★★* *(Kids* Don't expect the variety of a big-city zoo, but what the Alaska Zoo lacks in size it makes up with a charm all its own. Anchorage residents have developed personal relationships with the animals, many of which are named. Watch Ahpun the polar bear play and swim underwater (you can check that out on a webcam, too). Gravel paths meander through the woods past large enclosures with natural flora for bears, seals and otters, musk oxen, Dall sheep, moose, caribou, waterfowl—all the animals you were supposed to see in Alaska but may have missed. (Don't get the elephant, Siberian tigers, yaks, snow leopards, or Bactrian camels in your snapshots—they'll blow your story.) You can easily spend half a day here. In the summer, 2-hour naturalist tours take place every day at 2:30pm, and include some backstage stops; that's $25 adults, plus $10 for a lift from downtown (half prices ages 2–17). A snack bar serves basic meals and there is a large gift shop.

4731 O'Malley Rd. ℂ 907/346-2133. www.alaskazoo.org. Admission $9 adults, $8 seniors, $5 children 12–17, $4 children 3–12, free under 3. MC, V. May–Aug daily 9am–6pm, till 9pm Tues and Fri Memorial Day to Labor Day; summer educational programs most Tues at 7pm, live music most Fridays at 7pm. Off-season open daily at 10am, closing time varies depending on the time of sunset. Drive out the New Seward Hwy. to O'Malley Rd., then turn left and go 2 miles; it's 20 min. from downtown, without traffic.

Earthquake Park   The 1964 Good Friday earthquake was the biggest ever in North America, registering at 9.2 on the Richter Scale, killing 131 people, and flattening much of the region. Downtown Anchorage and the Turnagain residential area, near the park, suffered enormous slides that turned neighborhoods into chaotic ruins. A sculpture and excellent interpretive signs commemorate and explain the event, but you can't see much through the trees that have grown up since the quake. If you are up to a walk in the woods, however, descend into the park on the paved coastal trail, then explore the dirt paths that branch from it. Those quiet ways climb over the strange topography of hummocks and small ponds created when the ground went liquid. This also is a good access point to the Coastal Trail and a likely place to see birds and moose.

West end of Northern Lights Blvd. No admission. Always open. From downtown, take L St. (it becomes Minnesota Dr.) to Northern Lights Blvd. and turn right. The park is on your right after you cross Lakeshore Dr.

Eklutna Historical Park ★   The Native village of Eklutna has a fascinating old cemetery, still in use, in which each grave is enclosed by a highly decorated spirit house the size of a large dollhouse. These little shelters excite the imagination in a way no ordinary marker would. The unique practice evolved from the melding of Athabascan and Russian Orthodox beliefs. There are two small Russian Orthodox churches on the site, including the **St. Nicholas Orthodox Church.** Built north of here of logs sometime before 1870, it is among the oldest buildings in the Southcentral region. Walk through the church and grounds by yourself or take an informative 30-minute tour for the same price. Visitors are not allowed inside the low picket fence around the cemetery, but you can see well enough and you can enter the church. Wear mosquito repellent. If you come out this far, don't miss the Thunderbird Falls, described below under "Hiking & Mountain Biking."

About 25 miles out the Glenn Hwy. ℂ 907/688-6026. www.eklutna.com. Admission $6 adult, $3 ages 6–17, free under 6. Summer Mon–Sat 10am–6pm. Take the Glenn Hwy. 26 miles to the Eklutna exit, then go left over the overpass.

SPECTATOR SPORTS

Most big events in Anchorage happen at the **Sullivan Arena,** at 16th Avenue and Gambell Street. The ticket agency is **Ticketmaster** (ℂ 907/562-4800; www.ticketmaster.com), which also sells through local Fred Meyer grocery stores.

BASEBALL   Anchorage has two semipro baseball teams—the **Anchorage Glacier Pilots** (ℂ 907/274-3627; www.glacierpilots.com) and the **Anchorage Bucs** (ℂ 907/561-2827; www.anchoragebucs.com)—with college athletes playing in a six-team Alaska league during June and July. Cool summer nights under the natural light at Mulcahy Stadium are among our family's favorite outings. You hear, smell, and feel the rhythm of the game when you sit so close in the tiny park. The quality may be uneven, but exceptional players grow up here: Among famed alumni are Mark McGwire, Rick Aguilera, Tom Seaver, Dave Winfield, Barry Bonds, Wally Joyner, and Randy Johnson. Check the *Anchorage Daily News* or the websites above for game times. Mulcahy is at 16th Avenue and A Street, a long walk or a short drive from downtown. Tickets are around $5.

Dress warmly for evening games; a blanket is rarely out of order. A weekend day game is warmer, but then you won't get to see baseball played at night without lights.

BASKETBALL The University of Alaska Anchorage basketball teams (www.goseawolves.com) host a major Division I preseason tournament, the **Great Alaska Shootout,** in late November. The noted men's tournament takes place over Thanksgiving weekend. The women's tournament is held on the days prior to Thanksgiving weekend. The Seawolves play the regular season at the Sullivan Arena and at the University Sports Center, on campus on Providence Drive.

HOCKEY The **Alaska Aces** (© 907/258-2237; www.alaskaaces.com) compete at the Sullivan Arena in national AA league hockey; the western division that Anchorage faces regularly includes cities such Las Vegas and San Diego. The **University of Alaska Anchorage** (www.goseawolves.com) plays NCAA Division I hockey and is the city's most ardently followed home team.

5 Getting Outside

Anchorage is unique in Alaska (and anywhere else I know) for the number of places right near town to hike, bike, ski, and otherwise get into the wild. I've broken the options down by activities below. In town, the city's bike trails connect through greenbelts that span the noisy, asphalt urban core with soothing creekside woods. Kincaid Park and Far North Bicentennial Park are both on the trail system within the city, and encompass scores of miles of trails for Nordic skiing, mountain biking, and horseback riding. The Chugach Mountains, which form the backdrop to the town, offer tundra hiking, backpacking, mountain biking, and climbs that range from easy to technical. More trails and streams, only slightly farther afield, are covered in the "Out from Anchorage" sections later in this chapter. Many cruises, tours, fishing charters, and sea-kayaking trips leave from nearby **Whittier,** easily managed as a day trip; see section 4 of chapter 7 for details.

INFORMATION The **Alaska Public Lands Information Center** (p. 198; © 907/271-2737; www.nps.gov/aplic) offers guidance for all these recreation areas and more throughout Alaska. For information on the bike trails, Nordic skiing parks, swimming, and other city recreation, contact **Anchorage Parks & Recreation** at © 907/343-4355 (www.muni.org/parks). Get information specific to **Chugach State Park** from the public lands center, or directly from the park at © 907/345-5014 (www.alaskastateparks.org; click on "Individual Parks"). Chugach National Forest can be reached at © 907/743-9500 or www.fs.fed.us/r10/chugach. The best trail guide to the entire region is Helen fNienhueser and John Wolfe Jr.'s *55 Ways to the Wilderness,* (The Mountaineers, $17) available in any bookstore in the area. The best trail map is the Chugach State Park topographic trail map published in 2000 by Imus Geographics and sold at either of the sporting-goods stores mentioned below.

EQUIPMENT You can rent most anything you need for outdoor activities. For bike rentals, see p. 198. Get advice and rent sea kayaks, cross-country skis, snowshoes, bear-proof containers, and mountaineering equipment at **Alaska Mountaineering and Hiking,** at 2633 Spenard Rd. (© 907/272-1811). It's a small shop where the staff takes the time to help you plan a trip. A block away, at 1200 W. Northern Lights Blvd., **REI** has a large store (© 907/272-4565; www.rei.com) that rents a wide range of gear, including lightweight canoes with car-top carriers, camping gear, packs, sleeping bags, and cross-country skis (but not bikes or ice climbing gear). It is the best stocked place in town to buy outdoor athletic clothing as well. (For Arctic cold weather gear and where to buy it, see "What to Wear" on p. 24.)

WALKING & BIKING

Anchorage has an award-winning network of paved **bike trails** spanning the city along wooded greenbelts. You rarely see a building and almost always cross roads and rail lines through tunnels and over bridges, so you're never in traffic. Here are two of the best.

TONY KNOWLES COASTAL TRAIL ★★★   Leading 10 miles from the western end of 2nd Avenue along the shore to **Kincaid Park,** the coastal trail is among my favorite things about Anchorage. It's a unique pathway to the natural environment from the heart of downtown. I've ridden parallel to beluga whales swimming along the trail at high tide and encountered as many as six moose on a single ride. (Don't approach moose or bear or try to slip by; wait at a safe distance for them to go their own way.) The most popular entrance is at **Elderberry Park,** at the western end of 5th Avenue. **Westchester Lagoon** (a pond) is 10 blocks south of Elderberry Park. From downtown, the lagoon is a good destination for a lovely stroll and a fine place to picnic and feed the ducks, which nest on small islands.

LANIE FLEISCHER CHESTER CREEK TRAIL ★   Starting at an intersection with the Coastal Trail at Westchester Lagoon, this trail runs about 4 miles east along the greenbelt to **Goose Lake,** where you can swim or paddle a rented boat in a cool woodland pond at the end of a hot bike ride and buy ice cream or other snacks from a little cafe—still, improbably enough, in the middle of the city. South from the lake, a wooded trail leads partway through the university campus. The paved bike trails, including the Fleischer, stay well back in the trees, so you rarely see a building, and tunnels and bridges span all road and railroad crossings, so you're never in traffic.

HIKING & MOUNTAIN BIKING

KINCAID PARK ★★   Covered in more detail below, Kincaid Park is an idyllic summer setting for mountain biking and day hikes. Moose sightings are a common daily occurrence on wide dirt trails that snake for about 40 miles through the birch and white spruce of the park's hilly 1,500 acres of boreal forest, often with views of the sea and mountains beyond, including McKinley. Trails open to bikes around June 1, or as soon as they dry, and a mountain bike race series runs through the summer. On the busiest summer day, however, there is plenty of room for relaxed, solitary rambling or cycling. Within the park, wooded Little Campbell Lake is a picturesque spot for family canoeing and fishing for stocked trout; there is no lifeguard. Note, the park gates are locked at 10pm, so get your car out before then.

FAR NORTH BICENTENNIAL PARK ★   The 4,000-acre park, on the east side of town, is a unique patch of urban wilderness, a habitat for bears, moose, and spawning salmon. People use it for dog mushing and skiing in winter, and for exceptional mountain biking and day hiking in summer. The Alaska Botanical Garden, listed above, and the Hilltop Ski Area, below, are both within the park's boundaries. A good place to start a hike or ride through the woods is the **Campbell Creek Science Center** (© **907/267-1247;** www.ak.blm.gov/ado/ccscentr.html), an educational facility operated by the Bureau of Land

Management. Staff are often on hand to answer questions and you can consult books and maps and look at an aquarium of native fish. To get to the science center from downtown, take Gambell Street (it becomes New Seward Hwy.) south to Dowling Road, go east (toward the mountains), turn right on Lake Otis Road, turn left on 68th Avenue, and follow 68th to its end. The park entrance is just across Abbott Road.

FLATTOP MOUNTAIN & THE GLEN ALPS TRAILHEAD ★★★   There are many ways to reach the alpine tundra, intoxicating fresh air, and cinematic views in the Chugach Mountains behind Anchorage, but the easiest and best developed portal is the Chugach State Park Glen Alps Trailhead. Even those who aren't up to hiking should go for the drive and a walk on a short, paved loop with incredible views and interpretive signs. If you are ready for a hike, you can start at the trailhead for trips of up to several days, following the network of trails or taking off across dry, alpine tundra by yourself, but usually within cell-phone range. Camping is permitted anywhere off the trails.

Flattop Mountain is the most popular hike from Glen Alps and a great family climb, if a bit crowded on weekends. It's a steep afternoon hike, easy for fit adults and doable by school-age children. There's a bit of a scramble at the top, easiest if you stick to the painted markers on the rocks. Dress warmly and don't go in the rain, when slick rocks at the top could cause a fall.

For a longer or less steep hike or a mountain-biking trip, follow the broad gravel trail that leads up the valley from the Glen Alps Trailhead to several other great routes. Trails lead all the way over the mountains to Indian or Bird Creek, on Turnagain Arm, up some of the mountains along the way or to round alpine lakes in high, rocky valleys. You're always above the tree line, so you don't need to follow a trail if you have a good map. This is wonderful backpacking country.

To get to the trail head, take New Seward Highway to O'Malley Road, head east toward the mountains, then turn right on Hillside Drive and left onto Upper Huffman Road. Finally, turn right on the narrow, twisting Toilsome Hill Drive. Don't forget to bring cash or a check for the self-service day-use fee of $5 (not required if you are going only to the overlook and park in the designated spaces).

EAGLE RIVER VALLEY & CROW PASS ★★   The **Eagle River Nature Center,** at the end of Eagle River Road, 12 miles up Eagle River Valley from the Glenn Highway exit (© **907/694-2108;** www.ernc.org), resembles a public wilderness lodge, with hands-on nature displays about the area and guided walks or talks daily in the summer and weekends year-round (2pm weekends, call for other times). Operated by a nonprofit concessionaire for Chugach State Park, it's open June through August Sunday through Thursday from 10am to 5pm, Friday and Saturday from 10am to 7pm; May and September from 10am to 5pm except Monday; October through April Friday through Sunday from 10am to 5pm. There's a $5 parking fee.

The .75-mile **Rodak Nature Trail,** with interpretive signs, leads to a viewing platform over a beaver pond. The **Albert Loop Trail** is a 3-mile route; a geology guide from the center matches with numbered posts on the way. Both trails have good bird- and wildlife-watching. The 25-mile **Crow Pass Trail,** a portion of the historic Iditarod Trail, continues up the valley into the mountains along the river. You can make a day-hike loop of 6 miles or less by returning on the new **Dew Mound Trail.** Continuing, the Crow Pass Trail eventually surmounts the Chugach in alpine terrain and passes near Raven Glacier before descending into Girdwood (see "Out from Anchorage: Turnagain Arm & Portage Glacier," later in this chapter). There are campsites with fire rings along the way, and a mile up the trail the center rents out a public-use cabin for $65 a night. A yurt on the Crow Pass Trail and another on the Albert Loop rent for the same price. Reserve well ahead for weekends. Availability is shown on the website.

THUNDERBIRD FALLS & EKLUTNA LAKE ★★ The hike to Thunderbird Falls is an easy, 1-mile forest walk with a good reward at the end; you can see the falls without the steep final descent to their foot. Take the Glenn Highway north to the Thunderbird Falls exit, 25 miles from Anchorage. Continuing 10 miles up the Eklutna Lake Road, you come to an appealing state parks campground ($10 a night, $5 day-use fee) and the glacial lake for canoeing, hiking, and exceptional mountain biking. The Lakeside Trail leads 14 miles to Eklutna Glacier; you can camp on the way, stay at the state park's Yuditna Creek Cabin at 3 miles or stay in the communal Serenity Falls hut at 13 miles (advance reservations are required for the cabin or hut, and, for the hut can be made only in person at a state parks office, not by phone or fax—see "State Parks Cabin Reservations," in section 1 of chapter 7). Rental bikes, kayaks, and other equipment, and guided kayak tours, are offered by **Lifetime Adventures,** with a booth at the trailhead of the Lakeside Trail (© **800/952-8624** or 907/694-7982; fax 907/ 746-4644; www.lifetimeadventures.net). For $70 you can kayak 8 miles to the other end of the lake and pick up a bike there to ride back.

BIRD-WATCHING

The Anchorage bowl contains varied bird habitat that is easily accessed and close at hand: lakes, streams, lagoons, freshwater and salt marshes, seashore, woodlands, and so on. Visiting birders can see species they don't encounter at home (Pacific loons, Hudsonian godwits, boreal chickadees) and familiar birds in breeding plumage unique to these northern latitudes (a red-necked grebe with a red neck, for example). Local birders have recorded more than 225 species in the city. Bird self-guided with the help of a rental car or at least a bike. Potter Marsh is a superb fresh water birding area (see section 8 later in this chapter). Salt marshes lie along the Tony Knowles Coastal Trail near Kincaid Park (see above). Right downtown, Ship Creek provides a river habitat. You can join field trips and network with local birders through the **Anchorage Audubon Society** (www.anchorageaudubon.org). The site contains an updated log of unusual sightings, which you can also check on a recorded hotline at (© **907/338-BIRD**).

FISHING

There are hatchery salmon in many of Anchorage's streams, and stocked trout, salmon, or char in 28 lakes, so you need not leave town to catch a fish. The **Alaska Department of Fish and Game,** 333 Raspberry Rd., Anchorage, AK 99518-1599 (© **907/267-2218;** www.adfg.state.ak.us, click on "Sport Fishing," then navigate by using the maps), publishes informative booklets on the Web and on paper and a fishing report updated weekly online. There's also a recorded information line (© **907/267-2503**) with what's hot and lots of other advice. See chapter 2 for general guidance and license information, and information for planning a fishing vacation, and see chapter 7 for the famous fishing opportunities on the Kenai Peninsula.

ROADSIDE FISHING Although the setting (under a highway bridge in an industrial area) might not be the wilderness experience you've dreamed about, the 40-pound king salmon you pull from **Ship Creek** may make up for it. From downtown, just walk down the hill to the railroad yard. A couple of shacks sell and rent gear in the summer. Fishing for kings is best in June and for silvers in August and September. Fish only on the rising tide, when the fish come into the creek. Fishing near the end of the rising tide will mean crossing less mud, but one successful angler I know insists it's the start of the tide that's best. Either way, you'll need rubber boots, preferably neoprene chest waders, for the muddy banks, but don't go too far out, as the mud flats are dangerous and several times every summer the fire department has to rescue stuck fishermen.

Bird Creek, 25 miles south of Anchorage on the Seward Highway (see "Out from Anchorage: Turnagain Arm & Portage Glacier" later in this chapter), is known for hot silver salmon fishing in the late summer and fall. A huge construction project for safer parking and access to the creek has disrupted fishing, but that is expected to be over for the August 2005 silver season. Pinks run from late June to early August. Other creeks along the Arm have similar but smaller runs.

FLY-IN FISHING ★★★ Serious anglers will use Anchorage as a base from which to fly to a remote lake or river with more fish and fewer people. Such a flight can be an unforgettable experience for those who are less than enthusiastic about fishing, too. The plane lifts off from Anchorage's Lake Hood floatplane base and within half an hour smoothly lands on a lake or river, often all alone. You climb out and watch as the plane lifts off and disappears, leaving behind the kind of silence unique to true wilderness. It's on these trips that avid anglers are made—or spoiled. I've heard people complain of how sore their arms got from pulling in too many salmon.

Several companies offer fly-in trips; among the best established is **Rust's Flying Service** (© **800/544-2299** or 907/243-1595; www.flyrusts.com). They can take you out guided or on your own, for the day or for a longer stay in a cabin or lodge. If you fly to a lake, they'll provide a boat. They can't make fish appear if none are running, but they will try to take you to the hot spots. You can bring your own gear, or they can provide it. Prices for an unguided day trip start at around $250 per person, with a two-person minimum.

OTHER SUMMER ACTIVITIES

FLIGHTSEEING Small planes are the blood cells of Alaska's circulatory system, and Anchorage its heart. There are several busy airports in Anchorage, and Lake Hood is the world's busiest floatplane base. More than two dozen operators want to take you on a flightseeing tour. If you will travel to Talkeetna, Denali National Park, Juneau, Glacier Bay National Park, or Ketchikan, it might be wise to save your flightseeing splurge for those extraordinary places. Likewise, for bear viewing flights, Katmai National Park, Homer, Kodiak, Juneau, and Wrangell are closer to the action. (All those places are covered in this guide with the details for flights; check the table of contents or index.) On the other hand, if time is short, you can see some very impressive scenery and even, for a price, get to bears from Anchorage. Rust's Flying Service (see "Fly-In Fishing," directly above) is a reliable operator and can get you in the air for as little as $89. A flight to Mount McKinley is $259 and takes 3 hours; for another $90 you can land on the mountain (well worth the added cost).

RAFTING There are several white-water rivers within a 90-minute drive of Anchorage. **Nova Raft and Adventure Tours** (© **800/746-5753** or 907/745-5753; http://novalaska.com) has more than 30 years of experience offering multiday trips all over the state, and five different half-day floats in the Anchorage area. Various rafting trips are available, ranging from relatively easygoing Matanuska and Kings river to the Class IV and V white water of Six-Mile Creek, for which you may be required to prove your swimming ability before you can get in the boat. That wild white water is about an hour south of Anchorage on the Seward Highway. White-water rafting always entails risk, but Nova's schedule allows you to calibrate how wild you want to get, and the company offers add-ons for self-paddling, helicopter flightseeing, or glacier hiking. The half-day trips range in price from $70 to $250. Children 5 to 11 can go on the calmer Matanuska River float for $35. Other trips are suitable only for older children and adults. You'll need your own transportation to the river and may need to bring your own lunch. **Chugach Outdoor Center** (© **866/277-RAFT** or 907/277-RAFT; www.chugachoutdoorcenter.com) also offers Six-Mile Creek rides and sea kayaking on Kenai Lake.

If you want to go rafting without traveling to the Matanuska River or Six-Mile Creek, you can save time and money by taking a shorter, somewhat less dramatic ride closer to town on the Eagle River, which runs past the Anchorage suburb of the same name. A whitewater ride is as little as $30 with **Lifetime Adventures** (© **800/952-8624** or 907/694-7982; fax 907/746-4644; www.lifetimeadventures.net) and they have longer floats that also include more smooth water. The rides go several times a day every day of the summer.

SEA KAYAKING Except at Eklutna Lake (see above), kayaking day trips from Anchorage go through Whittier, on Prince William Sound (see section 4 of chapter 7 for complete details).

SWIMMING I'm betting that most visitors from warmer climes won't be interested in chilly lake swimming in Anchorage (the best spot is Goose Lake, off Northern Lights Boulevard east of Lake Otis Road). If you have children and need to burn off some energy, however, you won't find a better spot than an indoor waterpark called **H2Oasis** (© **888/H2OASIS** or 907/522-4420; www.h2oasiswaterpark.com), near the intersection of O'Malley Road and the New Seward Highway. A big wave pool and a 500-foot "watercoaster" are the top attractions. Adults should bring earplugs, as the noise is unbearable, and a full wallet, as admission is $20 for ages 13 and older, $15 ages 3 to 12, free under age 3.

WINTER ACTIVITIES

ICE SKATING **Westchester Lagoon,** just 10 blocks from downtown (see "Walking & Biking," earlier), is a skating paradise in the winter. When the ice gets thick enough, usually by mid-December, the city clears a large rink and over a mile of wide paths that wind across the pond, mopping the ice regularly for a smooth surface. Skaters gather around burn barrels, well stocked with firewood, to socialize and warm their hands, and on weekends vendors often sell hot chocolate and coffee. Ice skates are for rent for $5 a day at **Champions Choice,** in the University Center Mall at Old Seward Highway and 36th Avenue (© **907/563-3503**). Not all sizes are available, so you may want to call ahead.

SKIING **Kincaid Park** is one of the best **cross-country skiing** areas in the country, with the first World Cup–certified trails in the U.S. About 65km of trails are geared to every ability level, but mostly intermediate and expert. Besides the superb trails, it's a beautiful place to ski, through rolling hills of open birch and spruce, with views of the mountains and ocean. Most trails are expertly groomed for skating and classical techniques, with two loops reserved for classical only. Sixteen kilometers are lighted, an important feature on short winter days. The **Kincaid Park Outdoor Center** (© 907/343-6397) is open Saturday and Sunday from 10am to 9:45pm, Monday and Wednesday through Friday from 2 to 9:45pm, but closed Tuesday. The gate closes at 10pm, so park outside it if you will be skiing later. Skiing usually lasts well into March and sometimes into April. Big races come in late February and early March (see "Special Events," earlier). **Far North Bicentennial Park** also has some excellent trails—32km total, 7km lighted—and a slightly longer season because of a hillside location. Start at Hilltop Ski Area. Many other parks and the bike trails have lengthy skiing routes, too, some lighted. See "Equipment," on p. 221 for information on where to rent skis.

Anchorage has several **downhill ski areas.** The best, **Alyeska Resort,** is described in section 9, later in this chapter. **Hilltop Ski Area,** in Bicentennial Park in town, is a great place to learn to ski, with one long beginner slope, at 7015 Abbott Rd. (© 907/346-2167; www.hilltopskiarea.org).

Anchorage also is a great starting point for **backcountry skiing.** Non-experts should go with a guide (you can find one through Alyeska Resort). Experts can get ideas from some of the folks mentioned under "Gearing Up," p. 368. The key safety consideration is, of course, avalanche awareness and preparation. I've described that on p. 30, but if you are turning to this book to learn how, you are not ready to go without a guide. An **avalanche hotline** is available for the Chugach National Forest near Anchorage (© 907/754-2369 or www.fs.fed.us/r10/chugach/glacier/snow.html).

SNOWMOBILING **Alaska Snow Safaris** (© 907/783-7669; www.snowmobile-alaska.com), offers snowmobile tours in the flat Placer Valley or on a nearby glacier or mountain pass. Raw beginners are welcome and everything is provided, but it's not the hand-holding experience you expect from a commercial tour: Guests are soon flying off through the snow in exciting style, using their own judgment. The guides are professional and the machines powerful. November through January their three-hour trips are $149; February through May they take 5-hour tours to the Placer Glacier, for $199. Longer outings and overnights are available, too, as are rentals, although going unguided is advisable only if you have some experience and knowledge of where you can safely ride. They are located at the Alaska Wildlife Conservation Center (p. 233), about 45 minutes south of Anchorage on the Seward Highway.

6 Shopping

Some of the most interesting shops are mentioned earlier, in the walking tour of downtown, where most galleries and gift shops are located.

NATIVE ARTS & CRAFTS A few shops in Anchorage carry Native Alaskan arts and crafts, but the city doesn't have a large gallery of such work, or the low prices you can find in the Bush. Before making major purchases, know what you're buying (see "Native Art: Finding the Real Thing," in chapter 2).

Nowhere else will you find another business like the **Oomingmak Musk Ox Producers' Co-operative** (© **888/360-9665** outside Alaska or 907/272-9225; www.qiviut.com), located in the house with the musk ox on the side at 6th Avenue and H Street. Owned by 250 Alaska Native women from villages across the state, the co-op sells only scarves and other items they knit of *qiviut* (*ki*-vee-ute), the light, warm, silky underhair of the musk ox, which is collected from shedding animals. Each village has its own knitting pattern. They're expensive—adult caps are $130 to $180—but the quality is extraordinary. The website contains the women's fascinating correspondence and links to two of the rural knitters' own pages.

As an aside, if you are driving north from Anchorage, you may also want to stop at the **Musk Ox Farm** (© **907/745-4151;** www.muskoxfarm.org) just north of Palmer on the Glenn Highway, where you can see the strange-looking creatures close up (open summer 10am–6pm daily; admission $8.50 adults, $7 seniors and ages 13–18, $5.50 ages 6–12). Musk oxen also are at the Alaska Zoo (covered earlier in this chapter) and are easy to see in the wild near Nome (see section 6 in chapter 10).

Anchorage has several small shops and local secret places to find authentic Native artwork. In the downtown area, **The Rusty Harpoon,** at 411 W. 4th Ave., has authentic Native items, Alaskan jewelry, less expensive crafts, and reliable, longtime proprietors who only buy direct from Native artists they know. This is where locals shop. Likewise, the **Yankee Whaler,** in the lobby of the Hotel Captain Cook, at 5th Avenue and I Street, is a small but well-regarded shop carrying Native arts. At the **Anchorage Museum of History and Art** at 7th and A streets (p. 217), check out the gift shop for a small but tastefully selected and beautifully displayed array of Alaska Native art.

If you can shop beyond the downtown area, you have two more good choices. The shop at the **Alaska Native Heritage Center** (p. 219) has a good selection and you can have confidence in their claims of authenticity. You may even be able to buy a piece made by one of the artisans you see working at the center. They also have mass-produced gifts. Probably the best place for Native crafts in Anchorage is the **Hospital Auxiliary Craft Shop** in the Alaska Native Medical Center, off Tudor east of Bragaw (© **907/729-1122**), where everything is made by those eligible to use the hospital. The work you find here is all authentic and entirely traditional. The shop is open Monday through Friday from 10am to 2pm and the first and third Saturday of each month from 11am to 2pm. They don't accept credit cards. There's exceptional Native art to see on the walls of the hospital, too.

FURS   If you're in the market for a fur, Anchorage has a wide selection and no sales tax. **David Green Master Furrier,** at 130 W. 4th Ave. (© **907/277-9595;** www.davidgreenfurs.com), is an Anchorage institution. Others are nearby.

GIFTS   There are lots of places to buy both mass-produced and inexpensive handmade crafts other than Alaska Native items. If you can be in town on a Saturday during the summer, be sure to visit the **Saturday Market** street fair, in the parking lot at 3rd Avenue and E Street, with food, music, and hundreds of miscellaneous crafts booths. You won't have any trouble finding gift shops on 4th. Our favorite is the relatively classy **Cabin Fever,** at 650 W. 4th. The **Kobuk Coffee Company,** at 5th Avenue and E Street, next to the town square, occupies one of Anchorage's earliest commercial buildings; it's a cozy candy, coffee, and collectibles shop. Midtown, on International Airport Road between the Old and New Seward highways, **Alaska Wild Berry Products** is a fun store to visit.

There's a chocolate waterfall and a big window where you can watch the candy factory at work. The chocolate-covered berry jellies are simultaneously addictive and rich enough to make you dizzy if you eat more than a few.

FINE ART   Downtown has several galleries. Openings are coordinated to happen on the first Friday of each month, allowing for an evening of free party hopping and art shopping. The **International Gallery of Contemporary Art,** 427 D St., is a non-profit space dedicated to artists. Come here for an in-depth look at just a few artists' work and to meet people who really care about art. Since it is run on contributions by volunteers, hours are short: Wednesday through Friday 10am to 2pm, Saturday and Sunday noon to 4pm, and Tuesday 5:30pm to 8:30pm, closed Monday. **The Center for Contemporary Visual Art of Alaska,** 621 W. 6th Ave., is not supposed to be non-profit, but one of the owners tells me it really is, since they make no compromises—no prints, no tourist junk—everything in the place is one of a kind. There is only one priority here: showing Alaska's best and most challenging art in a museum-like setting. (Check it out before they go out of business!) **Artique,** 2 blocks north at 314 G St., is Anchorage's oldest gallery and has a much larger selection for ordinary shoppers. Half of the gallery is given over to big oils and other gorgeous originals; the other half is chock-full of prints, less-expensive ceramics, and some mass-produced and/or corny stuff. At 5th and G, **Aurora Fine Arts** carries pottery, prints, and gifts. Directly across G is a gallery showing only glass sculpture.

7 Anchorage Nightlife
THE PERFORMING ARTS

The primary arts season begins in October and ends in April, but in the summer you can catch traveling performers, music festivals, and live music at the nightclubs and coffee houses. To find out what's happening, pick up the free weekly *Anchorage Press,* which is given away in racks all over town. Their exhaustive event and music scene calendar is online, too, at www.anchoragepress.com. Friday's edition of the *Anchorage Daily News* has a section called "8" that includes reviews and listing information in grid format (www.adn.com/weekend). See "Special Events" earlier for some major happenings and another online calendar.

There are two ticket agencies in Anchorage, and they are jockeying for position with various venues, so the line-up described here could change. Currently, **Ticketmaster** (© 907/562-4800; www.ticketmaster.com) handles the Sullivan Arena and Egan Civic and Convention Center, and sells tickets at Fred Meyer grocery stores. **Tickets.com** (© 800/478-7328) is the ticket agency for the Alaska Center for the Performing Arts and for some events elsewhere. They have ticket counters at Carrs grocery stores under the name CarrsTix and operate the box office at the Alaska Center for Performing Arts, at 631 W. 6th Ave. (www.alaskapac.org), which is open Monday to Saturday, noon to 4pm. The phone number there is © **907/297-2982,** but the company prefers callers to use the toll free number above.

The **Anchorage Concert Association** (© 907/272-1471; www.anchorage concerts.org) offers a September-through-May schedule of classical music, theater, dance, and other performing arts. **Whistling Swan Productions** (www.whistlingswan.net) promotes folk and acoustic alternative performers in intimate venues. The **Anchorage Symphony** (© 907/274-8668; www. anchoragesymphony.org) performs during the winter season. Anchorage also has lots of community theater and opera, and limited professional theater, including the experimental **Out North Contemporary Art House** (© **907/279-8200;**

www.outnorth.org), which produces local shows and imports avant-garde performers. Downtown, **Cyrano's Off Center Playhouse** (© 907/274-2599; www.cyranos.org), at 4th Avenue and D Street, is a tiny theater with its own semiprofessional repertory company.

NIGHTCLUBS & BARS

For a fun, funny night out, nothing in town compares to **Mr. Whitekeys' Fly By Night Club,** on Spenard Road south of Northern Lights Boulevard (© 907/279-SPAM). The goateed proprietor, a consummate vulgarian, ridicules Anchorage in his crude, political, local-humor musical comedy shows, in which he costars with a fallen former Miss Anchorage. If you can laugh at dog poop, you'll love it. The summer show is at 8pm Tuesday through Saturday; live music follows on Friday and Saturday. Tickets are $13 to $20, and reservations are necessary well in advance. The club is smoke-free. They serve good food, too—dine at the show, not before. (Believe me, I wrote this long before they started using a piece of my writing in one of their shows.)

Blues Central/Chef's Inn, 825 W. Northern Lights Blvd. (© 907/272-1341), is dedicated to showcasing the best blues performers available, virtually every night. Major names come through on a regular basis. Shows start at 9:30pm. They're also known for their beef.

The most famous bar in Anchorage is the huge **Chilkoot Charlie's,** at Spenard Road and Fireweed Lane (© 907/272-1010; www.koots.com). It has two stages for rock and one for swing and many bars on different themes. The place is huge and full of entertainment, like an adult Disneyland, but can be claustrophobic when crowded, with low ceilings and a dark, roadhouse atmosphere. Moreover, recent well-publicized violence suggests that it is a good place to avoid conflict.

THE MOVIES

The most fun place to see a movie is the **Bear Tooth TheatrePub,** at 1230 W. 27th Ave. (© 907/276-4200; www.beartooththeatre.net), where you can watch art films and second-run movies while sipping craft brews and eating gourmet tacos, pizzas, and the like. Arrive early, as they often sell out and parking is terrible. They also put on concerts monthly: check the website.

There are several multiplexes in Anchorage playing all the current Hollywood output; check the sources at the beginning of this section for listings and reviews. Theaters closest to downtown are the **Century 16,** 301 E. 36th Ave. (© 907/929-3456; www.centurytheatres.com) and the **Fireweed 7 Theater,** 661 E. Fireweed Lane (© 907/566-3328; www.regalcinemas.com).

8 Out from Anchorage: Turnagain Arm & Portage Glacier

One of the world's great drives starts in Anchorage and leads roughly 50 miles south on the Seward Highway to Portage Glacier. It's the trip, not the destination, that makes it worthwhile. The two-lane highway along Turnagain Arm, chipped from the foot of the rocky Chugach Mountains, provides a platform to see a magnificent, ever-changing, mostly untouched landscape full of wildlife. I've listed the sights in the style of a highway log, for there are interesting stops all the way along the road. It will take at least half a day round-trip, and there's plenty to do for an all-day excursion. Use your headlights for safety even in daylight and be patient if you get stuck behind a summertime line of cars—if you pass, you'll just come up behind another line ahead. Mileage markers count down from Anchorage. Car rental is covered in "Getting Around," earlier in this chapter.

Many bus tours follow the route and visit Portage Glacier (see "Getting There: By Bus" under "Essentials," earlier). **Gray Line of Alaska** (© **800/544-2206** or 907/277-5581; www.graylineofalaska.com) offers a 7-hour trip that includes a stop in Girdwood and a boat ride on Portage Lake for $65 adults, $33 ages 2 through 11, twice daily in summer.

POTTER MARSH (Mile 117)   Heading south from Anchorage, the Seward Highway descends a bluff to cross a broad marsh formed by water impounded behind the tracks of the Alaska Railroad. The marsh has a boardwalk from which you can watch a huge variety of birds. Salad-green grasses grow from sparkling, pond-green water.

POTTER SECTION HOUSE (Mile 115)   Located at the south end of Potter Marsh, the section house was an early maintenance station for the Alaska Railroad. Today it contains the offices of Chugach State Park, open during normal business hours, and, outside, a few old train cars and interpretive displays. Just across the road is the trail head for the **Turnagain Arm Trail.** It's a mostly level path running down the arm well above the highway with great views breaking now and then through the trees. Hike as far as you like and then backtrack to your car, or continue 9 miles to Windy Corner (if you can have a vehicle waiting for you there), or break off where the trail meets the McHugh Creek picnic area and trailhead, about 4 miles out.

McHUGH CREEK (Mile 111)   Four miles south of Potter is an excellent state park picnic area and a challenging day hike with a 3,000-foot elevation gain to Rabbit Lake, which sits in a tundra mountain bowl, or to the top of 4,301-foot McHugh Peak. You don't have to climb all the way; there are spectacular views within an hour of the road. From this point onward, most of the stops are on the right or ocean side of the road; plan your stops on the outbound trip, not on the return when you would have to make left turns across traffic.

BELUGA POINT (Mile 110)   The state highway department probably didn't need to put up scenic overlook signs on this pull-out, 1½ miles south of McHugh Creek—you would have figured it out on your own. The terrain is simply awesome, as the highway traces the edge of Turnagain Arm, below the towering cliffs of the Chugach Mountains. If the tide and salmon runs are right, you may see beluga whales, which chase the fish toward fresh water. Sometimes they overextend and strand themselves by the dozens in the receding tide, farther along, but they usually aren't harmed. The pull-out has spotting scopes to improve the viewing. The further right-hand pull-outs over the next few miles have interpretive signs about the 1895 gold rush in this area and other topics.

WINDY POINT (Mile 106)   Be on the lookout on the mountain side of the road for Dall sheep picking their way along the cliffs. It's a unique spot, for the sheep get much closer to people here than is usual in the wild; apparently, they know they're safe. Windy Point is the prime spot, but you also have a good chance of seeing sheep virtually anywhere along this stretch of road. If cars are stopped, that's probably why; get well off the road and pay attention to traffic, which will still be passing at high speeds.

You may also see windsurfers in the gray, silty waters of the Arm. They're crazy. The water is a mixture of glacial runoff and the near-freezing ocean. Besides, the movement of water that creates the huge tides causes riverlike currents, with standing waves like rapids.

Tidal Wave

Tides in Turnagain Arm rise and fall over a greater range than anywhere else in the United States, with a difference between an extreme high and low of more than 41 feet. When the tide is rising, the water can grow deeper by as much as 7 feet an hour, or a foot of water every 8½ minutes. If your foot gets stuck in the mud, it takes less than an hour to drown (yes, that has really happened). Amazing as that speed is, the tide here can go even faster. A breathtaking wall of water up to 6 feet tall called a bore tide can roar up Turnagain Arm twice a day. To see the ocean do such a thing is so unfamiliar it looks almost like science fiction as the wide arc of foam rushes ahead of a noticeably deeper sea. You can (theoretically) predict the bore tide: it happens just after the time of low tide at the town of Sunrise (1 hr., 12 min. after low tide in Anchorage), which you can look up in a tide book or at http://co-ops.nos.noaa.gov (click "Prediction" then "Alaska" then "Kenai Peninsula and Cook Inlet)." The wave moves faster than 10 miles per hour, but even at that speed it takes hours to make it all the way up the Arm, so to figure when it will pass your location requires knowing your distance from the mouth of the Arm as well as the time of the tide change. A set of signs at the Bird Point pull-out (below) explain the tides.

INDIAN VALLEY (Mile 104)   Up the road by the Turnagain House restaurant is the **Indian Valley** trail head, a gold rush–era trail that ultimately leads 24 miles to the other side of the mountains. The path, while often muddy, rises less steeply than other trails along the Arm.

BIRD RIDGE TRAIL (Mile 102) This is a lung-busting climb of 3,000 vertical feet in a little over a mile. It starts with an easy, accessible trail, then rises steeply to views that start at impressive and get more amazing as you climb. With the southern exposure, it's dry early in the year.

BIRD CREEK (Mile 100)   The excellent state campground on the right side of the highway, over the water, is described on p. 255, and the productive salmon fishing in the creek is described on p. 255. Anglers should park at the new wayside on the left before the creek. There is also a short trail, interpretive signs, an overlook, and a platform that makes fishing easier for people with disabilities. Pink salmon run from late June to mid-August, silver salmon mostly in August.

BIRD POINT (Mile 96)   The remarkable wayside here is not to be missed. A paved pathway rises up to a bedrock outcropping with a simply wonderful view—all the severity of the Turnagain Arm, but framed by the soft green of a freshwater wetland with a beaver lodge. Take a look at the fascinating interpretive signs on many subjects.

THE FLATS (Miles 96–90)   At Bird Point the highway descends from the mountainside to the mud flats. A fragment of bike trail parallels the highway on the mountain for this 6 miles with picnic sites along the way and great views.

Several pull-outs on the right side of the highway have interpretive signs. At high tide, water comes right up to the road. At low tide, the whole Arm narrows to a thin, winding channel through the mud. The Arm is not practically navigable and navigational charts are not even available. Few have ever tried to navigate it other than gold prospectors in rowboats a century ago or today's occasional death-defying canoeist or kayaker. The first to try was Capt. James Cook, in 1778, as he was searching for the Northwest Passage on his final, fatal voyage of discovery (he was killed by Hawaiians later that year). He named this branch of Cook Inlet Turnagain Arm because the strength of the currents and shoals forced the boat he sent to keep turning around.

TURNOFF TO GIRDWOOD (Mile 90)   The attractions of Girdwood, covered below, are worth a visit, but the shopping center here at the intersection is not chief among them. Stop for a simple meal or a restroom break, or to fill your gas tank for the last time for many a mile.

OLD PORTAGE (Mile 80)   All along the flats at the head of Turnagain Arm are large marshes full of what looks like standing driftwood. These are trees killed by salt water that flowed in when the 1964 quake lowered the land as much as 10 feet. On the right, 9 miles beyond the turnoff for Girdwood, across from the former rail depot, a few ruins of the abandoned town of Portage are still visible, 40 years after the great earthquake. There is good bird-watching from the turnouts, but venturing out on Turnagain Arm's tidal mud carries the real risk of getting stuck in quicksandlike mud and drowning in the tide. Don't do it.

ALASKA WILDLIFE CONSERVATION CENTER (Mile 79)   Originally conceived as a tourist attraction (formerly it was called "Big Game Alaska"), the center has become a non-profit organization giving homes to injured and orphaned deer, moose, owls, elk, bison, musk ox, bear, fox, and caribou (© **907/ 783-2025**). Visitors can drive a short course on the 140-acre compound to see the animals in fenced enclosures as large as 18 acres—at times, some animals are not visible among the natural vegetation. You can usually get closer to the animals at the Alaska Zoo and see a larger variety (p. 219), but these large enclosures are more natural. A large log gift shop and outdoor snack bar is at the end of the tour. Admission is $7.50 for adults; $5 for military, seniors, and children 4 to 12, with a maximum of $25 per vehicle. In summer, it's open daily from 8am to 8pm; in winter, daily from 10am to 5pm.

Gone But Not Forgotten

The **Begich-Boggs Visitor Center** at Portage Glacier is named for Hale Boggs, who was U.S. House majority leader, and Rep. Nick Begich, then Alaska's lone congressmen, who disappeared together in a small plane during Begich's 1972 reelection bid. The most likely theory is that the small plane iced up in Portage Pass and then crashed into Prince William Sound near here. No trace was ever found, as with many other Alaskan planes that have simply flown off into oblivion. Begich was reelected anyway. His opponent, Republican Don Young, later won a special election and continues to serve as Alaska's only congressman. Boggs' wife, Lindy, went on to serve out his term and eight more. Boggs' daughter, Cokie Roberts, is the famous broadcast journalist.

PORTAGE GLACIER (Take the 5½-mile spur road at Mile 78)   The named attraction has largely melted, receding out of sight of the visitor center. (The glacier you can see is Burns.) When the center was built in 1985, it was predicted that Portage Glacier would keep floating on its 800-foot-deep lake until 2020. Instead, it withdrew to the far edge of the lake in 1995. Today the exhibits in the lakeside **Begich–Boggs Visitor Center** focus on the Chugach National Forest as a whole, rather than just the glacier, and they're worth an hour or two to become oriented to the area's nature, history, and lifestyles. Children and adults find much to hold their interest here. To see Portage Glacier itself, take the road toward Whittier that branches to the left just before the visitor center and stop at a pullout beyond the first (toll-free) tunnel; or take the boat mentioned below.

Several short trails start near the center. Rangers lead nature walks on the quarter-mile, paved Moraine Trail up to six times a day. Another trail leads less than a mile to Byron Glacier, in case you're interested in getting up close to some ice. Always dress warmly, as cold winds are the rule in this funnel-like valley.

A **day boat** operated by **Gray Line of Alaska** (© **800/478-6388,** 907/277-5581 for reservations, or 907/783-2983 at the lake; www.graylineofalaska.com) traverses the lake right up to Portage Glacier on hour-long tours, ice conditions permitting. It costs $25 adults, $13 ages 2 to 12, and goes five times daily in summer, every 90 minutes starting at 10:30am. If this is your only chance to see a glacier in Alaska, it's probably a good choice, but if your itinerary includes any of the great glaciers in Prince William Sound, Kenai Fjords National Park, or the like, you won't be as impressed by Portage.

Sandwiches and other simple meals are sold at a cafeteria near the visitor center called the **Portage Glacier Lodge** (© **907/783-3117**). There are no lodgings in Portage, but two **Forest Service campgrounds** are on the road to the visitor center, with 72 sites between them (more details are in the Chugach National Forest section in chapter 7). At the Williwaw Campground, there's also a place to watch red salmon spawning in mid-August, but no fishing.

9 Out from Anchorage: Girdwood & Mount Alyeska

Girdwood, 37 miles south of Anchorage, is proof that a charming little town can coexist with a major ski resort, as long as the resort goes undiscovered by the world's skiers. Girdwood still has a sleepy, offbeat character. Retired hippies, ski bums, a U.S. senator, and a few old-timers live in the houses and cabins among the big spruce trees in the valley below the Mount Alyeska lifts. They all expected a development explosion to follow the construction of an international resort here a few years ago, but it hasn't happened. That may not be good news for the Japanese investors in the resort, but it is for skiers and other visitors who discover this paradise. They find varied, uncrowded skiing through long winters, superb accommodations, and an authentically funky community.

The primary summer attractions are the hiking trails, the tram to the top of Mount Alyeska, and the Crow Creek Mine, described below. In winter, it's skiing. Mount Alyeska doesn't have the size of the famous resorts in the Rockies, but it's more than large and steep enough. Better still, it's uncrowded, half the mountain is above the tree line, and the snow lasts a long time. Olympian Tommy Moe trained here and the Alpine national championships raced down these slopes in 2004. Skiers used to tamer, busier slopes rave about the skiing here, with long, challenging downhills, few lift lines, and stunning views of the Chugach Mountains and glistening Turnagain Arm below.

ESSENTIALS   A **rental car** is the most practical means for getting to Gird-wood. If you will only ski, however, you may be able to take a shuttle; call the resort before you come, as these arrangements change frequently. The **Gird-wood Chamber of Commerce** maintains an extensive website at **www. girdwoodalaska.com**. For more general visitor information, check the Anchor-age visitor information listed in section 1 of this chapter.

EXPLORING GIRDWOOD

Crow Creek Mine ✪   This mine, opened in 1898, is still operated in a small way by the Toohey family, but mostly they use the paths and eight small origi-nal buildings as a charming tourist attraction. You can see the frontier lifestyle and watch rabbits and ducks wandering around. A bag of dirt, guaranteed to have some gold in it, is provided for gold panning, and you can dig and pan to get more if you have the patience for it. Crow Creek Road, off the Alyeska Highway, is quite rough and muddy in the spring. Camping is $5 a night, with portable toilets.

Crow Creek Rd. (off the Alyeska Hwy.), Girdwood, AK 99587. 📞 **907/278-8060.** $3 adults, free for children 11 and under. Gold panning $5 adults, $4 children 11 and under. May 15–Sept 15 daily 9am–6pm.

Mt. Alyeska Tram ✪   The tram isn't cheap, but I think it's worth it for any-one who otherwise might not make it to high alpine tundra during an Alaska trip. (In winter ride on your lift ticket; in summer ride free with a meal at the Seven Glaciers Restaurant at the top; p. 237.) The tram takes 7 minutes in sum-mer to get to the 2,300-foot level, where it stops at a station containing both the Seven Glaciers Restaurant and an attractive but overpriced cafeteria. Whether or not you eat here, the tram presents an opportunity for everyone, no matter how young, old, or infirm, to experience the pure light, limitless views, and crys-talline quiet of an Alaskan mountaintop. Take the opportunity to walk around and enjoy it. Dress very warmly.

At the Alyeska Prince Hotel (see below). $16 adults ($13 Alaska residents), $15 ages 55 and older, $12 ages 8–17, $7 ages 7 and under. Summer daily 10am–9:30pm; winter, when lifts operate (call to check as hours vary).

ACTIVITIES

Here I have covered activities right in Girdwood. In nearby Whittier (p. 252) you can go ocean fishing, sea kayaking, or take a glacier and wildlife cruise. The Turnagain Arm and Portage area (p. 230) offers sightseeing along Turnagain Arm, hiking, and other summer activities. Snowmobiling in that area is covered under Anchorage winter activities (p. 227).

SKIING   Mount Alyeska, at 3,939 feet, has 1,000 acres of skiing, beginning from a base elevation of only 250 feet and rising 2,500 feet. The normal season is from early November to April, and it's an exceptional year when there isn't plenty of snow all winter. Skiing on the upper mountain often lasts through Memorial Day weekend. The average snowfall is 721 inches, or 61 feet. Because it's near the water, the weather is rarely very cold. Light is more of an issue, with short days in midwinter. There are 27 lighted trails covering 2,000 vertical feet on Friday and Saturday evenings from mid-December to mid-March, but the best Alaska skiing is when the days get longer and warmer in the spring.

Alyeska has nine lifts, including the tram. Two chairs serve beginners, with a vertical drop of around 300 feet. The other 89% of the mountain is geared to intermediate to expert skiers. The biggest drawback for less experienced skiers is a lack of runs in the low-intermediate ability range. After graduating from the

Tips **Ski Conditions**

The rainforest of Girdwood and the dry Anchorage bowl often have different weather, despite being within the same municipality. Before heading down the road for a day of skiing check out the conditions. Call ℂ **907/SKI-SNOW** for snow, weather, and visibility conditions, or check that information online at www.alyeskaresort.com, where you can also view a live webcam at the top tram station. For visibility from below, check out the cam at www.chairfive.com.

primary beginners' lift, Chair 3, skiers must jump to significantly more challenging slopes. That explains the long lines in busy periods on Chair 3 (it is the only lift on the mountain with any lines). More confident skiers like the mountain best. Most of it is steep and the expert slopes are extreme. Helicopter skiing goes right from the resort's hotel as well.

An all-day lift ticket costs $48 for adults ($42 for Alaska resident, $38 for hotel guests), $32 for ages 14 to 17, $24 for ages 8 to 13 or 60 to 69, and $10 for ages 7 and under or over 70. Discounts apply for families or for skiing the beginner lifts only. Private and group instruction are available and you can save a lot by buying your lessons, lift ticket, and equipment rental at the same time. The day lodge rents basic gear and the hotel rents high performance gear. A basic rental package costs $24 a day for adults, $13 for ages 13 and under or over 60; high performance $29 and $21 respectively. There are groomed **cross-country trails** as well, and gear for rent, but the best Nordic skiing is in Anchorage.

A center operated by **Challenge Alaska** (ℂ **907/783-2925** or 907/344-7399) with the resort allows skiers with disabilities to use the mountain, skiing down to the lift to start and back to the center at day's end. They rent the latest adaptive ski equipment, too.

A utilitarian **day lodge** with snack and rental counters is located at the front of the mountain, as is the **Sitzmark Bar,** a more comfortable place for a meal (burgers are around $8). The Alyeska Prince Hotel (below) is on the other side of the mountain, connected to the front by the tram to the top and beginner-level chair 7 (you can ski right from the door). It makes a quieter and more genteel starting point for day-trippers as well as guests, as it has its own day lockers and an equipment rental counter with higher quality equipment (and higher rates) than the day lodge. There are several dining choices here and at the top of the tram (see "Where to Stay," below).

HIKING   There are a couple of great trails starting in Girdwood. The Winner Creek Trail runs 5 miles through forest from behind the Alyeska Prince Hotel to a roaring gorge where Winner Creek and Glacier Creek meet; it's muddy and snowy in the spring. The winter ski trail takes a separate route, through a series of meadows, to the same destination. The Crow Pass Trail rises into the mountains and continues all the way over to Eagle River, after a 26-mile hike that you can do in a couple of days. But you can make a long day hike of it going just to the pass, where you can see the glaciers, wildflower meadows, and old mining equipment. The trail head is up Crow Creek Road, off the Alyeska Highway.

WHERE TO STAY

Besides the resort hotel, there are plenty of condos and B&Bs in town. **Alyeska Accommodations,** on Olympic Circle (ℂ **888/783-2001** or 907/783-2000;

www.alyeskaaccommodations.com), offers condos, cabins, and luxurious houses.

Alyeska Prince Hotel ★★★ The Alyeska Resort's hotel is among Alaska's best. The beauty of the building alone separates it from the competition, as does its location in an unspoiled mountain valley among huge spruce trees. Studded with dormers and turrets, it impresses on first sight. Inside, sumptuous cherry wood and rich colors unite the welcoming common rooms and elegant guest rooms. Although not large, rooms have every convenience, and the maintenance and housekeeping are exceptional. The salt water swimming pool is magnificent, with a cathedral ceiling and windows by the spa overlooking the mountain. The location and activities alone make the hotel worth visiting. A few days spent here skiing and swimming make the rest of life seem too drab. Now for the bad news. On weekends and school holidays in the winter the hotel is overrun by partying families from Anchorage who overtax the facilities and destroy the peaceful ambience. Children run wild, the pool becomes impossibly crowded, and service deteriorates to an unacceptable level. If coming for a skiing vacation, avoid these times.

Four restaurants vie for attention. **The Seven Glaciers Restaurant,** 2,300 feet above the lobby by tram on Mount Alyeska, serves trendy and beautifully presented dinners in a sumptuous dining room floating above the clouds. Service is warm and highly professional. Meals are expensive, especially since the small servings make it desirable to order several courses. The restaurant opens only on the weekends in the winter. A mountaintop cafeteria is right next door (great views, limited choices). At the base level, the Japanese cuisine at the Katsura Teppanyaki has developed a good reputation. The Pond Cafe is good when not jammed on the weekends and has a nice view.

1000 Arlberg Ave. (P.O. Box 249), Girdwood, AK 99587. ℂ **800/880-3880** or 907/754-1111. Fax 907/754-2200. www.alyeskaresort.com. 307 units. Summer and Christmas $195–$375 double, $750–$1,500 suite; winter $145–$280 double, $600–$1,200 suite. Extra adult $25; children stay free in parents' room. AE, DC, MC, V. **Amenities:** 4 restaurants; 2 bars; indoor pool; health club; spa; bike rental; children's programs; concierge; tour desk; business center; shopping arcade; limited room service; massage; babysitting. *In room:* TV w/pay movies, dataport, fridge, coffeemaker, hair dryer, iron, safe.

WHERE TO DINE

Also see the second paragraph of the Alyeska Prince Hotel review, under "Where to Stay," for more restaurant options.

Chair 5 Restaurant ★ *Kids* SEAFOOD/BURGERS/PIZZA This is where Girdwood locals meet their friends and take their families for dinner, and it's also one of our favorites after skiing. One afternoon, Bob Dylan music accompanied a friendly game of pool while men with ponytails and beards sipped microbrews. Another evening, a guy in the entryway entertained the children with magic tricks and the waitress asked them to draw pictures to enter into a contest. The menu offers choices pleasing to each family member, including pizza, burgers, fresh fish, and steaks.

5 Lindblad Ave., in the New Girdwood Town Square. ℂ **907/783-2500.** www.chairfive.com. All meals $8–$20; large pizza $16–$20. AE, DC, DISC, MC, V. Daily 11am–11pm.

Double Musky Inn ★★ CAJUN The ski-bum-casual atmosphere and rambling, cluttered dining room among the trees match the wonderful Cajun and New Orleans food in a way that couldn't have been contrived—it's at once too improbable and too authentic. Service is relaxed to a fault, and food takes a long time to arrive, but when it does it's flawless. The steaks are famous, and I love the jambalaya. The place isn't to everyone's taste, however; your senses can feel raw after the extreme noise, highly spiced food, and crowds, and parking can be difficult. Loud groups will enjoy it more than couples, and families don't really fit. They have a full bar.

Mile 3, Crow Creek Rd., Girdwood. © 907/783-2822. www.doublemuskyinn.com. Main courses $18–$37. AE, DC, DISC, MC, V. Tues–Thurs 5–10pm; Fri–Sun 4:30–10pm. Closed Nov.

10 Out from Anchorage: The Matanuska & Susitna Valleys

On a longer visit to Anchorage, you may want to spend a day or two in the sub-urbs to the north, known as the Mat-Su Valley. Reached by the Glenn Highway about 40 miles from Anchorage, the area is both a bedroom community for the city and a former frontier farming region with its own quirky identity. If you are driving anywhere north from the city you will pass through this area and there are some interesting places to stop if you have the time. In this summary I've covered a few highlights in the central area (the whole thing is the size of West Virginia). Some of the best attractions are covered in other parts of the book. **The Alaska State Fair,** held before Labor Day, is covered under "Special Events," near the beginning of this chapter. **The Musk Ox Farm** is under "Shopping," above. Funky Talkeetna, a gateway to Denali National Park, is in chapter 8. The Matanuska Glacier area (on the Glenn Highway), with its great canyon views and late-season cross-country skiing and snowmobiling, is in chapter 9. You can learn more about the hiking, fishing, and skiing all over the Mat-Su Valley from the **Mat-Su Visitors Center,** Mile 35.5 Parks Hwy., HC 01 Box 6166J21, Palmer, AK 99645 (© **907/746-5000;** www.alaskavisit.com).

THROUGH HATCHER PASS

If you're headed north to Denali National Park or Fairbanks, the rough, wind-ing gravel road through Hatcher Pass to Willow makes a glorious alpine detour around the least attractive part of your drive. Past the mine and skiing area, the road is open only in summer and is not suitable for large RVs. Just after the Parks Highway branches from the Glenn Highway, exit to the right on the Trunk Road and keep going north on Fishhook Road, which becomes Hatcher Pass Road. From the Glenn Highway near Palmer, take Palmer Fishhook just north of town.

Even if you're not headed north, a trip to Hatcher Pass combines one of the area's most beautiful drives, access to great hiking and Nordic skiing, and interesting old buildings to look at. The **Independence Mine State Historical Park** ★★ (© **907/745-2827** or 907/745-3975; www.alaskastateparks.org, click on "Individual Parks") takes in the remains of a hard-rock gold mine operation that closed down in 1951. Some buildings have been restored, including an assay office that's a museum and the manager's house that's a welcoming visitor center, while a big old mill, towering on the hillside, sags and leans as a picturesque ruin. A visit is interesting even if you don't go inside, using the interpretive pan-els and map on a self-guided tour. The setting, in a bowl of rock and alpine tundra, is spectacular. The day use fee is $5 per vehicle. A guided tour is an addi-tional $5 per person ($2 seniors, free under 10) and leaves at 1:30 and 3:30pm weekdays, plus 4:30pm weekends. The visitor center is open from 10am to 7pm daily in the summer, closed off-season.

Leave some time for a summer ramble in the heather if you visit the mine. In the winter, the Nordic or telemark skiing is exceptional, with a few kilometers of groomed trail and miles of open country to explore. (See the Hatcher Pass

Lodge, below, for more details.) There are four hiking trails and two mountain-biking routes in the area—ask at the visitor center. One great hike is the 8-mile **Gold Mint Trail,** which starts across the road from the Motherlode Lodge on Hatcher Pass Road and ends at the Mint Glacier, where you have to turn around to hike back.

ON THE PARKS HIGHWAY

The Museum of Alaska Transportation and Industry ⊛, off the Parks Highway at Mile 47, west of Wasilla (© **907/376-1211**), is a paradise for gearheads and tinkerers. The volunteers have gathered every conceivable machine and conveyance—13 fire trucks, seven locomotives, and two steam cranes, for example—and fixed up to running order as many as they can. An indoor museum displays their finished masterpieces, while the 20 acres outside are crammed with future projects—trains, aircraft, tractors, fishing boats, and mining equipment—all grist for memories and imagination. It's open May 1 to September 30 from 9am to 6pm daily, winter Saturday from 10am to 5pm, or by appointment. Admission is $8 for adults, $5 for students and seniors, $18 for families.

WHERE TO STAY & DINE

Three good places to eat in the Valley are at the three accommodations I have described below. In addition, there are unlimited fast food spots and roadhouse burger places. Here are two more choices, in Wasilla on your way to Denali or back to Anchorage.

Evangelo's Restaurant, at Mile 40 of the Parks Highway as you pass through town (© **907/376-1212**), is a big, free-standing restaurant that's quiet and comfortable and serves familiar Italian food.

A more memorable place is the **Valley Bistro,** at 405 E. Herning Ave., near the intersection of the Parks Highway and Main St. in Wasilla (© **907/357-5633**), which occupies the town's primary historic building, the old Teeland's country store. The dining room is pleasing with antiques, wood floors, and high ceilings, and the menu, although short, provides adequate choices of beef, chicken, and salads.

HATCHER PASS

Hatcher Pass Lodge ⊛ *(Finds)*   A charming family presides at this tiny mountain lodge in the treeless alpine bowl that also contains the Independence Mine State Historic Park, 3,000 feet above the sea, which glistens in the grand vista down below. Out on the open snowfield in winter, or the heather in summer, the nine cabins and A-frame lodge seem far more remote than they really are, just 90 minutes from Anchorage. There is a phone in the main lodge for emergencies but no TV. Our family went for a glorious Nordic skiing vacation there, and the 12 of us, aged 2 through 75, all had a great time. A place with nothing to divert you but snow, a warm cabin and good meals brings a family closer. The cabins are clean and nicely set up, with no rustic edge except chemical toilets and the lack of running water. Showers and meals come from the main lodge restaurant and bar, where the family produces surprisingly professional meals in a warm, cozy environment. Stay in summer for a taste of the real Alaska with doorstep access to wonderful alpine hiking.

P.O. Box 763, Palmer, AK 99645. © **907/745-5897**. www.hatcherpasslodge.com. 9 cabins, 3 lodge rooms. $95 lodge rooms, $115–$125 cabin for 2. Extra person $15. AE, DC, DISC, MC, V. **Amenities:** Restaurant; bar; sauna.

WASILLA

Best Western Lake Lucille Inn ★   This well-run, attractive lakeside hotel in Wasilla has the best standard rooms in the valley. They're large and well appointed, and those facing the lake have balconies and a grand, peaceful view. Flightseeing trips take off from the dock below the lawn. The **restaurant** is one of the best in the area, with a light, quiet dining room looking out on the water. It's open for dinner only. The beef and seafood menu ranges from $15 to $38.

1300 W. Lake Lucille Dr., Wasilla, AK 99654. ☎ **800/780-7234** for reservations, or 907/373-1776. Fax 907/ 376-6199. www.bestwestern.com/lakelucilleinn. 54 units. High season $149 double, $219 suite; low season $89 double, $175 suite. Extra person $10. AE, DC, DISC, MC, V. **Amenities:** Restaurant; exercise room; Jacuzzi; sauna; coin-op laundry. *In room:* TV, free high speed Internet, coffeemaker, hair dryer, iron.

PALMER

Colony Inn ★ *(Finds)*   This classic country inn occupies a restored teacher's dormitory from the New Deal Colony Project, right in the middle of Palmer. The rooms are attractively old-fashioned, although a little worn in spots, with rockers and comforters but also Jacuzzi bathtubs and big TVs with VCRs. A large sitting room and a dining room downstairs are decorated with historic photographs that help tell the building's story. Meals are served here during the summer at the **Inn Cafe** (☎ **907/746-6118**). Guests check in at the comparatively down-scale Valley Hotel, at 606 S. Alaska Street, and there often is no innkeeper on-site to let you in or help with problems.

325 E. Elmwood, Palmer, AK 99645. ☎ **907/745-3330**. Fax 907/746-3330. 12 units. $90 double, $162 suite. Extra person $5. AE, DISC, MC, V. **Amenities:** Restaurant; laundry machines. *In room:* TV/VCR, dataport.

The Kenai Peninsula & Prince William Sound

The Gulf of Alaska arcs at its northern edge, forming the rounded northern shore of the Pacific Ocean, a zone of great collisions. This is where the earth's tectonic plates collide, spewing forth froths of hot lava from dozens of volcanoes and fracturing and folding the earth with titanic earthquakes. Here the ocean's wildest weather hits mountains jutting miles high from the sea, growing immense prehistoric ice sheets and glaciers that carve the rock into long, deep, intricate fjords. The sea proffers prodigious biological wealth on these shores, including the salmon it unleashes into the rivers in furious swarms of life that climb over the mountains and into the Interior to spawn. Nature seems giant and super-abundant along this magnificent arc of land and water.

Geography endowed this one stretch of coast with several of the world's great natural places. On the east, near Cordova, the **Copper River**'s immense, entirely unspoiled delta is the largest contiguous wetlands in the Western Hemisphere. On a day trip, you're immediately alone with flocks of rare, graceful waterfowl that congregate on shallow ponds surrounded by miles of waving grass. **Prince William Sound** is a vast protected sea of wooded mountains and mammoth glaciers. This is our family's favorite place on earth, where we go each summer to camp among the otters and eagles on tiny islands out of contact with the rest of mankind. **Kenai**

Fjords National Park takes in bays off the open ocean where the mountains soar a mile straight up from the water. Boats travel here among humpback, gray, and orca whales; spot otters, seals, and sea lions; and visit swarming colonies of puffins and other seabirds. The **Kenai River** harbors the world's biggest salmon, on the western side of the Kenai Peninsula; and on its southern tip, **Kachemak Bay** is like a miniature Prince William Sound, but with people. The bay's shores are dotted by tiny towns with lodges, art galleries on pilings, and some of Alaska's best restaurants.

The whole region is exceptionally accessible, by Alaska standards. The Kenai (*keen*-eye) Peninsula, in particular, is easy to get to without the expense and exhausting travel that can make much of the state difficult. Most of what you're looking for in Alaska lies along a few hundred miles of blacktop, within reach of a rental car and perhaps a tour boat ticket: glaciers, whales, legendary sport fishing, spectacular hiking trails, interesting little fishing towns, bears, moose, and high mountains.

People from Anchorage go to the peninsula for the weekend to fish, hike, dig clams, paddle kayaks, and so on, and certain places can get crowded. There's a special phrase for what happens when the red salmon are running in July on the Kenai and Russian rivers: *combat fishing*. At hot times in certain places, anglers stand elbow to elbow on the bank, each casting into his or her own yard-wide slice of river, and still catch plenty of hefty salmon. The peninsula also exerts a powerful magnetic force on RVs, those road-whales that you find at the head of lines of cars on the two-lane highways. During the summer, the fishing rivers, creeks, and beaches on the west side of the peninsula and the end of the Homer Spit can become sheet-metal cities of hundreds of Winnebagos and Itascas parked side by side. Often some local entrepreneur will be selling doughnuts or newspapers door-to-door.

Yet the decision is yours as to whether you spend time in the company of tourists. If the roadside fishing is hairy, hiking a little farther down the bank usually means you can be by yourself. In this chapter, I'll describe some towns of unspoiled charm, where you can kayak virtually from your room. Being alone is easy. You can paddle among otters in Resurrection Bay; tramp over the heather in Turnagain Pass; hike, bike, or ski one of the many maintained trails in Chugach National Forest. And, when you're ready to come back to the comforts of civilization, you'll find that some of the state's best restaurants and most interesting lodgings are here, too.

1 Exploring the Kenai Peninsula & Prince William Sound

The towns of the Kenai Peninsula are like beads strung along the laces of the highways; everything else is wilderness. You can find all the activities and isolation you seek here, yet the presence of the towns means that comfort is closer at hand than in other parts of Alaska.

Seward, on the east side, is the charming gateway to Kenai Fjords National Park, which protects the outer edge and ice cap of the Kenai Peninsula's southern side. The park is incomparable in its remoteness, stark beauty, and abundance of marine wildlife.

Kenai, on Cook Inlet on the west side of the Kenai Peninsula, is the largest town in the region. Ten miles up the Kenai River, **Soldotna** is Kenai's twin, and together they form a unit with about a fourth of the Kenai Peninsula's population of 50,000. Famous for Kenai River salmon fishing, they're also the least interesting of the peninsula's communities. **Kenai National Wildlife Refuge** has Alaska's most accessible wilderness lake and river canoeing as well as extraordinary fishing, with access from roads near Soldotna.

Homer, at the southern end of the peninsula, has wonderful art and character and lots of ways to get out on the water. It is the gateway for **Kachemak Bay State Park,** with superb sea-kayaking waters and wilderness hiking not connected to any road. Homer also is headquarters of the **Alaska Maritime National Wildlife Refuge,** which protects the wildlife habitat of remote islands and seashores around the state.

There are three towns on Prince William Sound. **Valdez** is an oil town at the southern terminus of the trans-Alaska pipeline where tankers are loaded. **Cordova** is more attractive, a historic community on the eastern side of the Sound, with outdoor activities close at hand. **Whittier** is a grim former military outpost, but a convenient gateway to the protected fjords and glaciers of the western Sound.

Chugach National Forest takes in all of Prince William Sound and most of the eastern Kenai Peninsula. At 5.3 million acres, it's more than double the size of Yellowstone National Park. Anywhere else but Alaska it would be a national

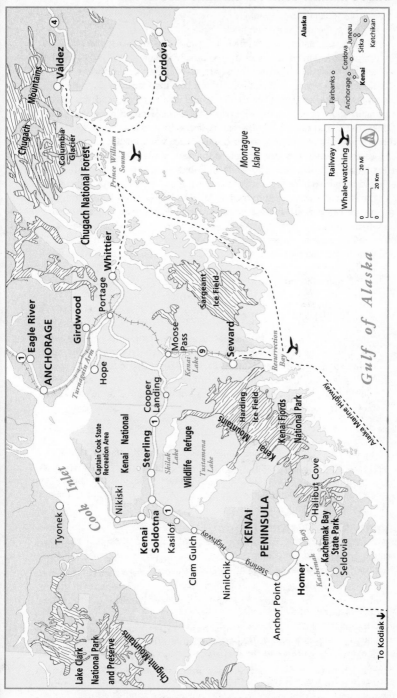

The Kenai Peninsula & Prince William Sound

Tips **State Parks Cabin Reservations**

Alaska's state parks rent remote public cabins like the famous Forest Service cabins (see section 3), but they're usually newer, larger, and easier to get to. Most are in Southcentral Alaska—in this chapter, they're mentioned near Homer, Seward, and Valdez. Like the Forest Service cabins, it takes a hike, boat ride, or air taxi to get to the cabins, and you need cabin equipment, such as a cooking stove and sleeping bags, but once there you can experience the real Alaska all by yourself.

Some of these cabins are so popular they book up the minute they become available, 6 months before the date of the stay. If your reservation arrives early, the office staff will hold it until the appropriate day and then hold a lottery if more than one applicant wants that date. You can reserve only in person, by mail, or by fax (you can ask questions by phone, but not apply). For fax reservations, you will need to use a Visa or MasterCard. The staff is friendly and will guide you around the system, and help you find a cabin where you can get a permit, even if it's not your first choice. A long-planned online reservation capability still is not in place at this writing.

The main information and reservations desk is the **Department of Natural Resources Public Information Center—Anchorage,** 550 W. 7th Ave., Suite 1260, Anchorage, AK 99501-3557 (© **907/269-8400** or 907/269-8411 TDD; fax 907/269-8901; www.alaskastateparks.org). The website is the best source of information about the cabins, with a picture and description of each, a reservation form, and a real-time availability calendar. The center is open Monday through Friday 10am to 5pm; if your application isn't there by 10 on the dot, you have no chance at a cabin sought by more than one applicant. Cabins rent for $25 to $65 a night. Most of the seaside cabins are $65.

---

park, and one of the largest and most spectacular, with some of the best sea kayaking, hiking, backpacking, wildlife-watching, and scenery anywhere. General information, camping, and ideas on remote areas in the Chugach are covered in section 3, while details about National Forest areas near towns are in the appropriate town sections.

VISITOR INFORMATION

For information on the peninsula as a whole, contact the **Kenai Peninsula Tourism Marketing Council,** 35477 Kenai Spur Hwy., Suite 205, Soldotna, AK 99611 (© **800/535-3524** or 907/262-3624; www.KenaiPeninsula.org), which distributes a vacation planner with information on businesses in the area (order through the website). The staff will answer inquiries during normal business hours.

The region's best and most central place to get outdoor information is the **Alaska Public Lands Information Center,** 605 W. 4th Ave., Suite 105, Anchorage, AK 99501 (© **907/271-2737** or 907/271-2738 TTY; www.nps. gov/aplic). You'll be able to ask guidance from residents who have spent time in the places you'll be visiting, and there are exhibits on the wildlife and outdoor opportunities in the region—even maps showing where to find various species of fish. Land agencies present information on the whole state. Pick up books and maps here and buy tickets for the ferries. Summer hours are daily from 9am to 5pm, winter Monday through Friday from 10am to 5pm. Visitor centers for particular areas are covered in the appropriate sections.

2 The Seward Highway: A Road Guide

The Kenai Peninsula's main lifeline is the road down from Anchorage, a 127-mile drive to Seward on a good two-lane highway, most of it through public land without development or services. Highway 1, commonly known as the Seward Highway, is more than scenic—it's really a wonderful attraction in itself, designated a National Scenic Byway. There are excellent campgrounds and hiking trails all along the way in the Chugach National Forest, which I've covered in section 3 of this chapter.

The mileposts start in Seward. Here we count backward, since you'll likely start from Anchorage.

MILE 127–79   The highway begins at the south end of Anchorage, the only way out of town in that direction, and runs along Turnagain Arm 48 miles to the Portage Glacier. I've written about that spectacular portion of the drive in chapter 6 under section 8, "Out From Anchorage: Turnagain Arm & Portage Glacier."

MILE 79–75   Beyond the Portage Glacier turnoff, the road traverses the salt marshes to the south side of the Arm. These wetlands are good bird-watching grounds. The dead trees on the flats are left over from before the 1964 earthquake. The area was inundated in the quake, when the entire region—the Kenai Peninsula and Prince William Sound—sank 7 feet and moved several feet

---

Why All the Dead Trees?

Whole mountainsides on the Kenai Peninsula and in Anchorage have turned brown. Thousands of dead trees topple in each windstorm. Fire danger is extreme. The spruce bark beetle is to blame. Although a natural part of the forest system, the beetles' population exploded in the last 2 decades and swept across Southcentral Alaska, wiping out four million acres of white and Sitka spruce, the biggest single insect kill of trees ever in North America. The beetles bore under the outer bark layer to eat the trees' phloem, the soft inner bark that carries food manufactured in the needles down to the roots. The beetles reproduce in the tree, sending the next generation in flight in May and June in search of more victims. Today, the blight has stopped spreading, largely because susceptible trees are already dead.

Scientists believe global climate change, which is especially pronounced in Alaska, allowed short, spotty beetle outbreaks to become a long, wide plague. Cool, damp springs usually stop the beetles in a year or two, but since 1987 the state has had a solid string of exceptionally warm, dry seasons. Ecologists also have noticed shrinking ponds, a rising tree line, and many other indicators of a changing climate on the Kenai Peninsula. In places, the ecological make-up in the forest appears to be transformed, but it will be decades before we learn if natural succession leads back to a new spruce forest, or if large tracts become grassy parklike areas. In the meantime, be careful with fire. (You can learn more on my website at www.wohlforth.net/SpruceBarkBeetles.htm.)

laterally. Besides being the second strongest earthquake ever recorded, the '64 quake moved more land than any other. People who were here tell of their surprise when the tide came far higher than they had ever seen it before in the days after the earthquake, until finally they realized that the land itself had sunk. Large parts of Homer, Hope, and Seldovia disappeared under the waves at high tide. Seward, Whittier, Valdez, and Kodiak were swept by destructive tsunami waves.

MILE 75–69   The highway steeply climbs through the spruce forest to the fresh, towering alpine terrain of the 1,000-foot-elevation **Turnagain Pass.** The vistas here are stupendous year-round.

MILE 69   If you find the meadow and tundra hard to resist for a walk, go ahead. Park at the pull-out with the toilets on the right side at the pass summit and amble off into the wildflowers (assuming the ground is dry when you're there). In the winter and spring, this is a backcountry skiing and snowmobiling paradise. Skiers go on the left side of the road and snowmobilers on the right. Always check the Chugach National Forest **avalanche hotline** first: ⓒ 907/ 754-2369 or www.fs.fed.us/r10/chugach/glacier/snow.html. An avalanche near here killed five riders in spring 1999.

MILE 69–57   The pass forms a divide; crossing it, Granite Creek flows down toward the south. The road follows, falling back below the tree line of stunted spruce and then popping back up into sweeping views. Arcing to the northwest after the Granite Creek Campground, the highway follows another north-flowing river, Six-Mile Creek.

MILE 57 & HOPE HIGHWAY   The Hope Highway divides off to the north and west along Sixmile Creek while the Seward Highway continues south. Rafting companies based in Anchorage use this wild stretch of water for some of their most challenging rides (see chapter 6).

A Side Trip to Hope   If you take this detour, you'll find **Hope** at the end of the 17-mile Hope Highway. It's a charming gold rush–era village with a wonderful campground and the starting point for some great hikes (see the Resurrection Pass Trail, p. 248, and Porcupine Campground, p. 251). A few white frame buildings remain from the days when Hope was a gold-mining boomtown after a strike in 1894. Before the 1964 earthquake, the rest of the town used to stand where the creek gives way to a tidal meadow. Wandering the gravel roads, you'll find more quaint spots. Today, Hope's year-round population is about 150. For information, contact the **Hope–Sunrise Community Library** (ⓒ 907/782-3121), which is open daily in summer from 11am to 4pm, when volunteer manpower allows.

The **Hope and Sunrise Historical and Mining Museum** (ⓒ 907/782-3740) is a one-room log cabin displaying historic objects and photographs, a barn, blacksmith's shop and miner's bunkhouse. They're trying to open the old school building by 2005. Volunteers try to keep the museum open Memorial Day to Labor Day daily noon to 4pm.

The best place to eat in town is the **Discovery Cafe** (ⓒ 907/782-3274), the community's hub and a place to get a generous burger and meet the beloved proprietor. The cafe burned to the ground in 1999 and was rebuilt almost entirely by volunteer labor, reopening in the summer of 2001.

MILE 57–46   The Seward Highway climbs steeply from the Hope Highway intersection, up the canyon of Canyon Creek, before leveling out above the tree line at about 1,400 feet elevation. Next come a series of alpine lakes in a narrow mountain valley.

MILE 46   The first business since the Portage Glacier, and the last for many miles, is on lovely Summit Lake, the **Summit Lake Lodge,** at Mile 45.5 (© **907/244-2031**). It's a traditional log roadhouse that's been updated to house a comfortable and modern restaurant. The food is generally good, but service can suffer badly when weekend highway travelers overwhelm the staff. There's an ice cream counter in the log gift shop by the lake and they rent six motel rooms with private bathrooms, but without TVs or phones.

MILE 46–38   The highway continues through similar mountain terrain before descending into the trees again and branching at **Tern Lake.** There's a bird-watching platform with interpretive signs on the lake and, on the west end, a picnic area. This is a stirringly beautiful spot year-round, and a good place to get out and taste the fresh mountain air. To the right at the intersection, the Sterling Highway leads to Cooper Landing, Soldotna, Kenai and Homer.

MILE 33–18   Trail Lake Fish Hatchery, on Upper Trail Lake, is on the first of a string of sparkling mountain lakes that the road follows for the next 15 miles.

MILE 30   The community of Moose Pass, with a population of about 200, sits on the shore of Upper Trail Lake.

MILE 18–0   Down among the big spruces of the coastal forest, the highway comes to Seward.

3 Chugach National Forest: Do-It-Yourself Wilderness

I've lived near the Chugach National Forest all my life, but it wasn't until well into adulthood that I had seen all its parts and appreciated its vastness and variety. Still, I doubt I'll ever really know this seemingly infinite land.

Prince William Sound, just one of the National Forest's three parts, has 3,500 miles of shoreline among its folded islands and deeply penetrating fjords and passages. It would take a lifetime to really know all those cove beaches, climb all the island mountains, and explore to the head of every narrow bay under big rainforest trees. The **Copper River Delta** is another world entirely. Unlike the musty secrets of the Sound's obscure passages, the delta opens to the sky like a heavenly plain of wind and light, its waving green colors splashed by the airiest brushstrokes. It's another huge area: Just driving across the delta and back from Cordova takes most of a day. Finally, there's the western part of the national forest, on the **Kenai Peninsula.** This is largely an alpine realm. The mountains are steep, their timber quickly giving way to rock, tundra, and wildflowers up above. It's got remote, unclimbed peaks, but also many miles of family hiking trails, accessible fishing streams, and superb campgrounds. This is where you go in Alaska for multiday trail hikes.

The Chugach is managed primarily for recreation and conservation, although there is some logging, too. Visitors today may see large tracts of dead spruce and sometimes areas of cut timber, but these mostly are caused by blight, the spruce bark beetle. The trees are cut in the forest and on private land to prevent fires in the standing deadwood. Logging in Prince William Sound was slowed by the *Exxon Valdez* oil spill, when conservationists recognized the need to prevent further environmental damage to support recovery from the disaster. When Exxon was forced to pay $1 billion to a recovery fund, government trustees spent much of the money to buy back timber rights in the Sound and beyond to protect the trees. They bought 1,419 miles of coastline and almost as much land as is in all of Yosemite National Park. Still, that was only a sixth of the area the Chugach already encompassed.

ESSENTIALS

GETTING THERE & GETTING AROUND   There are many ways to the Chugach National Forest. For Prince William Sound, use Whittier, Valdez, or Cordova as gateways; for the Copper River Delta, go through Cordova. Trails and campgrounds on the Kenai Peninsula generally meet the Seward or Sterling highways, or spur roads from the highways. The individual town listings later in this chapter provide details on how to get there and into that part of the national forest. Section 2, above, describes the Seward Highway.

VISITOR INFORMATION   The most central place for information on the national forest is the Alaska Public Lands Information Center in Anchorage, which is listed in full in section 1 of this chapter. For general forest inquiries, you can also contact the **forest headquarters,** 3301 C St., Suite 300, Anchorage, AK 99503 (© **907/743-9500;** www.fs.fed.us/r10/chugach). The national forest also has three ranger district offices, where you can get up-to-date local information and personal advice: **Glacier Ranger District,** on Monarch Mine Road, near the Seward Highway off Alyeska Road, in Girdwood (© **907/783-3242**); **Seward Ranger District,** 4th Avenue and Jefferson Street, in Seward (© **907/224-3374**); and **Cordova Ranger District,** 2nd and Browning streets, in Cordova (© **907/424-7661**). You can't reserve campground sites and remote cabins through these local offices—for that you must use the national system listed below under "Where to Stay"—but you can call them with questions.

GETTING OUTSIDE
HIKING, MOUNTAIN BIKING & BACKPACKING

Alaska's best long trails lead through the mountain passes of Chugach National Forest, including historic gold rush trails and portions of the original Iditarod trail (the dogsled race doesn't use these southern portions). The Forest Service maintains **public cabins** on many of these trails, and in other remote spots reachable only with a boat or small plane. If the nights you need are available, you can use the cabins instead of a tent on a backpacking trip. Or make a cabin your destination and spend a few days there hiking or fishing.

I've covered trails near Cordova in section 12 of this chapter, and some shorter hikes are mentioned below with the campgrounds under "Where to Stay." The best trail guide covering the peninsula is *55 Ways to the Wilderness* by Helen Nienhueser and John Wolfe (The Mountaineers, $17). **Trails Illustrated** publishes excellent plastic maps of the region (see "Fast Facts: Alaska," in chapter 2).

RESURRECTION PASS TRAIL   This gold rush trail begins 4 miles above the town of Hope (mentioned above in the preceding section on the Seward Hwy.) and runs over the top of the Kenai Peninsula to Cooper Landing (covered in section 7 of this chapter). It's a beautiful, remote, yet well-used trail for hiking, mountain biking, Nordic skiing, or snowshoeing; it rises through forest, crosses the alpine pass, and then descends again to a highway trail head where you'll need to have transportation waiting. The 39-mile trail has eight public-use cabins, available for $35 to $45 a night. (See "Where to Stay," below, for reservation information.) The cabins are well spaced to cover the trail in an easy 5 days, and those on lakes have boats for fishing. Cabins book up well ahead winter and summer, but there are lots of good camping spots, too. The **Devil's Pass and Summit Lake trails** cut off from the Resurrection to the Seward Highway south of Summit Lake, shortening the route. The difficulty of doing the whole trail, by any of the entrances, is that you either need two cars or someone willing to drive you back to your starting point.

RUSSIAN LAKES TRAIL   This trail begins in Cooper Landing (covered in section 7 of this chapter), near the end of the Resurrection Pass Trail, and leads to three remote cabins and a series of lakes. There's excellent fishing and wildlife viewing (bears are common). It's less than 3 miles with little elevation gain to Lower Russian Lake and the cabin there, or you can make a backpacking trip over the entire 21 miles.

JOHNSON PASS TRAIL   The 23-mile trail climbs to a pair of lakes above the tree line at the 1,450-foot Johnson Creek Summit, tracing impressively narrow mountain valleys. The route, part of the Iditarod National Historic Trail, leads from near the Trail Lake Fish Hatchery, at mile 32 of the Seward Highway, to near the Granite Creek Campground, on the highway at mile 63. Plan to do the trail as an overnight and have transportation ready at each end.

LOST LAKE TRAIL & PRIMROSE TRAIL   With their fields of alpine wildflowers and small lakes, these connected trails offer one of the most beautiful hikes in the area. Snow lasts until late in the season up at the top. The upper, northern trail head is at the 10-site Primrose Campground, on vast Kenai Lake, 17 miles from Seward off the Seward Highway on Primrose Road. The trail rises through hemlock past a waterfall about 2 miles up (look for the spur to the right when you hear water), past an old mining cabin, and then through ever smaller trees and above the tree line. A Forest Service cabin is on a 2-mile spur about 11 miles along the 16-mile route. Strong hikers can do the whole trail in a long day, but it makes more sense to hike in and out on the upper end, or to spend the night along the way. The lower, Lost Lake trailhead is in a subdivision near Seward; ask for directions at one of the visitor centers to find it.

FISHING

The national forest contains some of the most famous, and crowded, fishing banks in Alaska, including the **Russian River,** near Cooper Landing, with its incredible run of red salmon in July and good fishing lasting into September. Easiest access is at the Russian River Campground, just west of the village. There are plenty of other roadside salmon streams and remote fishing rivers and lakes in the national forest where you can lose sight of other anglers. Some remote lakes have Forest Service cabins for rent on their shores, with rowboats. The Forest Service publishes information on these opportunities. See chapter 2 for other information sources.

SEA KAYAKING & BOATING

A variety of Prince William Sound tour boats are listed in the Whittier, Valdez, and Cordova sections of this chapter. Whittier offers the greatest number of boats and the most impressive scenery, with big glaciers that come right to the water.

All three communities also have operators offering sea-kayak rentals and guided outings of various lengths. The best sea kayaking is east of Whittier, an area of long fjords, calving glaciers, narrow passages, and Forest Service cabins, but to get out there you need a boat ride first—the waters right around Whittier aren't as interesting—and that is expensive. The local sea-kayaking operators can help you arrange drop-off service. Cordova has more interesting waters right near town, so you can paddle from the boat harbor. Those who haven't done much sea kayaking should consider only a guided trip; if it's your first time, start with a guided day trip rather than an overnight.

For those who aren't up to paddling but don't want to ride a big tour boat, renting a skiff or chartering a small boat is a great alternative. Boat rental operators in the Valdez and Cordova harbors offer skiffs with fishing gear, and small-boat natural history tours go from Whittier. Exploring the Sound in a small boat is our family's favorite activity.

WHERE TO STAY
REMOTE CABINS

There is no more authentic Alaska accommodation than a pioneer cabin with a woodstove—a place to give you a better feel for the soul of a wild place. Chugach National Forest maintains more than 40 remote recreation cabins for rent to the public. This is simple shelter: Cabins don't have electricity or plumbing; you bring your own sleeping bags, cooking equipment, and other gear; and the cabin is only as clean as the last user left it. But no other room you can rent has a better location or greater privacy. Some cabins are along hiking and skiing trails, others on shores where boats and kayaks can pull up, and others on remote fishing lakes accessible only by floatplane. You can stay up to a week in most, with a summer limit of 3 days in the Resurrection Trail cabins.

The Forest Service prints a free listing of the cabins with short descriptions of each. The maps are rudimentary, so you will need a detailed map such as the Trails Illustrated plastic map mentioned on p. 53, which shows cabin locations and names. Cabins rent for $35 or $45 a night, with most priced at $45 a night. Typically, the price of the cabin itself is not your major expense: You'll need a way to get there, either by plane, by boat, or by having a vehicle to drive to a trailhead and then hiking. If you're flying, contact flight services in the nearest town (listed in the sections later in this chapter) to find out the cost *before* you book the cabin. Flight time is several hundred dollars an hour. You can rent the camping equipment you'll need at the businesses listed in the Anchorage chapter on page 221, but you should talk to a ranger first to get details about access and what to take. And start planning early. For summer dates, many cabins book up the second they become available on the reservation system, 6 months prior. This is not an exaggeration.

The National Recreation Reservation Service (NRRS), operated by **Reserve America,** a company in upstate New York, handles the reservation system. Use them to book a cabin, but contact the ranger stations first (p. 248) to choose a cabin that is right for you and to find out what to expect.

The easiest way to reserve a cabin is online at **www.reserveusa.com**, because you use its interactive maps and availability calendars to shop for open days at various cabins. To reserve by phone, call © **877/444-6777,** 877/833-6777 TDD, or 518/885-3639 with toll from overseas. The phone lines are open April 1 through Labor Day Monday through Friday from 8am to midnight EST, Saturday and Sunday 8am to 9pm; in winter Monday through Friday 10am to 7pm, Saturday and Sunday 10am to 5pm. The website takes reservations only during those hours, as well. They accept American Express, Discover, Master-Card, and Visa, or you can reserve on the phone and then pay by certified check or money order. Campsites can be reserved starting 240 days ahead, cabins 180 days ahead.

CAMPGROUNDS

Forest Service campgrounds mostly have pit toilets and water from hand pumps, and roads usually are not paved. But some of these places are truly spectacular. I've listed them in order of distance from Anchorage, counting in reverse direction on the Seward Highway mileposts. For information on campgrounds below mile 60, call the Seward Ranger District; for the others, call the Glacier Ranger District, in Girdwood (p. 248 for phone numbers). Sites in a few of the following campgrounds, as noted, take reservations through the national system explained above. RVs and cars can access and park at all of the campgrounds, but Williwaw is the only campground intended primarily for RVs.

Williwaw & Black Bear   These two campgrounds are next to each other near Portage Glacier, along a creek where you can watch spawning red salmon in mid-August (no fishing is allowed). Williwaw is one of the better-developed campgrounds in the national forest, with paved roads and pumped water, and is intended primarily for RVs.

Mile 4, Portage Glacier Rd. (turn at mile 78.9, Seward Hwy.). Williwaw: 60 sites. $10 per night. Reservations accepted with additional fee. Black Bear: 12 sites. $9 per night.

Bertha Creek   This one's in the high country.

Mile 65.5, Seward Hwy. 12 sites. $10 per night.

Granite Creek   Near the Johnson Pass trailhead.

Mile 63, Seward Hwy. 19 sites. $10 per night.

Porcupine   This campground near the gold rush village of Hope is among the most beautiful in the Chugach National Forest. The sites are on a mountainside overlooking Turnagain Arm, five with sweeping ocean views. The thick trees make for privacy, but also mosquitoes, so bring repellent. Two good day hikes leave from the campground: The level 5-mile trail to **Gull Rock** makes a good family ramble, and with some effort you can scramble down to remote beaches along the way, where we've enjoyed a picnic. The **Hope Point Trail** is a stiff climb that rises 3,600 feet to expansive views.

At the end of the Hope Hwy. 24 sites. $10 per night.

Tenderfoot Creek   This pleasant campground lies across Summit Lake from the Seward Highway as it passes through a narrow mountain valley above the tree line. Campsites look out on the water from a peaceful, sunny hillside. The nearby Summit Lake Lodge, described on p. 247, offers good meals and is the only business on the Seward Highway for many a mile.

Mile 46, Seward Hwy. 27 sites. $10 per night.

Ptarmigan Creek & Trail River   Near the tiny towns of Moose Pass and Crown Point, the Ptarmigan Creek campground is at the trail head for the trail to Ptarmigan Lake, 4 miles away with only 500 feet in elevation gain—a good place for a picnic or fishing for Dolly Varden char and rainbow trout. Trail River campground is a mile away and on the other side of the highway.

Mile 23, Seward Hwy. 16 and 63 sites, respectively. Reservations accepted, with additional fee. $10 per night.

Primrose   Another favorite, this lovely campground lies on the edge of Kenai Lake and at the base of the Primrose Trail to Lost Lake, one of the area's most beautiful (see "Getting Outside," above). This campground is the closest to Seward that has a sense of natural isolation.

Mile 17, Seward Hwy. 10 sites. $10 per night.

Russian River   This large, well-developed campground mainly serves fishermen pursuing red salmon on the river. When the fishing is good, the campground overflows and can be noisy. Overnight parking is $6. Reserve ahead.

Mile 52, Sterling Hwy., just west of Cooper Landing. Reservations accepted, with additional fee. 84 sites. 3-day limit. Flush toilets. $13 per night.

Cooper Creek   The campground has two halves bisected by the highway right in Cooper Landing. Ten sites are on the Kenai River and the balance across the road and somewhat better screened and separated.

Mile 50.7, Sterling Hwy. Reservations accepted. 26 sites. $10 per night.

Quartz Creek   Thickly wooded sites stand well separated a bit off the highway, many right on Kenai Lake and others with good mountain views. There is a boat ramp in the campground and a lodge nearby.

Quartz Creek Rd., at mile 45 Sterling Hwy. 45 sites. Reservations accepted. Flush toilets, boat launch. $13 per night.

Crescent Creek   This campground is quieter and more secluded than others near Cooper Landing, at the Crescent Lake trail head. The 6.5-mile trail leads to the Crescent Lake Forest Service Cabin, where renters have a boat for grayling fishing.

Mile 3 Quartz Creek Rd., at mile 45 Sterling Hwy. 9 sites. $10 per night.

4 Whittier: Dock on the Sound

Whittier is Anchorage's portal to Prince William Sound. Although Anchorage itself is on Upper Cook Inlet, that muddy, fast-moving water is little used for recreational boating. Whittier, on the other hand, stands on the edge of a long fjord in the northwest corner of the Sound, whose clear waters are full of salmon, orcas, and otters, and bounded by rocky shores, rainforests, and glaciers. In the past, getting to Whittier meant riding through a mountain by train. Now the railway tunnel is paved, creating North America's longest highway tunnel and, in theory, putting Whittier only an hour away from the city. But only in theory, because the tunnel is also among the most inconvenient to use in North America. It has only one lane, and that lane must be shared by traffic and trains in both directions, and in between trips the tunnel often must be aired out. A wait is almost assured.

Whittier certainly has major advantages for visitors seeking to get out on the water. The water is calmer here than on excursions to Kenai Fjords National Park, so seasickness is rare, and the glaciers are even more numerous. One company's selling point is a "26-glacier cruise," all done in a day trip from Anchorage by rail and large tour boat (see below). Prince William Sound boats also see otters and sometimes whales; Kenai Fjords tours, on the other hand, more often see whales and see more birds. Sea kayakers also have great places to go from Whittier. Almost all of Prince William Sound is in Chugach National Forest, with its public-use cabins in lovely, remote spots on the shores (see the previous section).

There's little other reason to go to Whittier, unless you're on a quest to find the oddest towns in America. Most of the roughly 180 townspeople live in a single 14-story concrete building with dark, narrow hallways. The grocery store is on the first floor and the medical clinic on the third. The rest of the people live in one other building. **The Begich Towers,** as the dominant structure is called, was built during the 1940s, when Whittier's strategic location on the Alaska Railroad and at the head of a deep Prince William Sound fjord made it a key port in the defense of Alaska. Today, with its barren gravel ground and

---

Tips **Be Prepared**

An **ATM** is located at the liquor store near the boat harbor, but Whittier lacks a bank and other services, so bring what you need.

---

ramshackle warehouses and boat sheds, the town maintains a stark military-industrial character. The pass above the town is a funnel for frequent whipping winds, it always seems to rain, and the glaciers above the town keep it cool even in summer. As one young town ambassador told me once when I was on a visit, "You're thinking, 'Thank God I don't live here,' right?" The official boosters look more on the bright side: Having everyone live in one building saves on snow removal in a place that gets an average of 20 feet per winter. Kids don't even have to go outside to get to school—a tunnel leads from the tower to the school.

ESSENTIALS

GETTING THERE   By Car   Take the Seward Highway to the Portage Glacier Road, at mile 78.9 (48 miles from Anchorage). The road through the 2¾-mile long World War II rail tunnel to Whittier is only one lane and also accommodates trains, so you'll have to wait your turn. Get the schedule through the tunnel's website (go to www.dot.state.ak.us and click "Traveler Information"), through its phone recording (© **877/611-2586** or 907/566-2244), or by tuning to 1610AM in Portage or 530AM in Whittier. Checking the schedule helps you avoid a wait of an hour or more if you miss the opening, but you can also wait if you arrive just on time, especially at 6pm during peak periods, when there may be too many vehicles in line to get through during one open period. Here's a valuable tip: Choose the shortest line, not the line marked with the lowest number, as each line gets equal time for driving through. The tunnel closes altogether at night. In summer the first opening from Whittier is at 6am and the last to Whittier is at 10:30pm. Winter hours are shorter and changeable, so check ahead. The toll is $12 for cars; $20 for RVs, cars with trailers, or large vans. It is charged only going toward Whittier. Special permits are required for really huge vehicles (over 14 ft. high or 10 ft. wide). Parking in Whittier is $5 a day. As I mentioned in the introduction, Whittier really isn't worth the trouble unless you are going out on the water.

By Train   If you plan to take a day trip on the Sound from a base in Anchorage—the way most people use Whittier—you can leave the car behind and take the train straight from the Anchorage depot. The large tour operators will book it for you when you buy your boat ticket. The **Alaska Railroad** (© **800/544-0552** or 907/265-2494; www.alaskarailroad.com) runs a daily train timed to match the schedules of Prince William Sound tour boats. Unless you have planned an activity or tour on the water, however, you'll find the 6-hour stay in Whittier is too long to just hang around. The round-trip fare is $59, one-way $49, half price ages 2 to 11. The train ride is scenic and fun, but if there is more than one of you along, a rental car will save you money.

By Bus   Boat tour operators have buses that can save time and money over the train. Reserve when you buy your boat cruise ticket.

By Ferry   Ferries of the **Alaska Marine Highway System** (© **800/642-0066,** or 800/764-3779 TDD; www.ferryalaska.com) connect Whittier, Valdez, and

Cordova. The journey takes roughly 7 hours on each side of the triangle, but the state plans to launch a new fast ferry in 2005 that would cut travel times in half and, of course, remake the schedule. Of course, big projects such as this one don't always happen on time. Currently, the fare from Whittier to Valdez is $85 for a car up to 15 feet long plus $74 for the driver or adult passenger, with ages 2 to 11 roughly half price. With the fast ferry the fares will undoubtedly rise. The Whittier-Valdez run creates the opportunity for a wonderful loop tour of a couple days or more: drive Anchorage to Whittier, take the ferry to Valdez, then return to Anchorage via the Glenn Highway or continue up the Richardson Highway to Fairbanks and drive back to Anchorage on the Parks Highway. A Chugach National Forest ranger interprets the scenery for passengers on the Prince William Sound ferry.

VISITOR INFORMATION   There is no visitor center, but you can contact the city offices at ✆ **907/472-2327,** extension 101 (admin@ci.whittier.ak.us). The chamber of commerce plans a website, not up yet, at www.whittieralaska. com. The people at the harbormaster's office are helpful and maintain public toilets and showers; it's the two-story building at the harbor (✆ **907/472-2327,** extension 110 or 115).

GETTING OUT ON THE SOUND
Whittier is the entrance to western Prince William Sound, at the end of one of many long, deep fjords where marine mammals and eagles are common. Glaciers at the heads of many of the fjords dump ice in the water for the tour boats that cruise from Whittier.

LARGE TOUR BOATS
Several companies with offices in Anchorage compete for your business for day-trip tours to the Sound's western glaciers. Besides having incredible scenery, the water is calm, making seasickness unlikely—for the queasy, this is a much better choice than Kenai Fjords National Park. Each operator times departures to coordinate with the daily Alaska Railroad train from Anchorage, described above, which means they have up to 6 hours for the trip. Some try to see as much as possible, while others take it slower to savor the scenery and wildlife sightings. Between the train and boat fare, expect to spend $190 per person for this day's outing, leaving Anchorage at 10am and returning at 9:30pm. You can save $10 to $15 a person and up to 3 hours by taking a bus the tour boat arranges instead of the train. If you have two or more people, you can save by renting a car and driving. You will be able to buy meals on board or one will be provided.

Major Marine Tours   This company operates a 149-passenger vessel at a slower pace than Phillips—they hit a mere 10 glaciers, but spend more time waiting for them to calve. The route goes up Blackstone Bay. The boat is comfortable, with reserved table seating. They also put more emphasis on their food, which costs extra; the salmon and prime rib buffet is $12 for adults, $6 for children. It's quite good. Time on the water is 5 hours.

411 W. 4th Ave., Anchorage, AK 99501. ✆ 800/764-7300 or 907/274-7300. www.majormarine.com. $99 adults, $49 children ages 11 and under.

Phillips' Cruises and Tours   The 26-glacier cruise travels the Sound on a fast three-deck catamaran, counting the glaciers as they go. The boat ride is 4½ hours, so if you use their bus you cut the total time from Anchorage to under 8½ hours. The boat has a snack bar, and lunch is provided with the fare.

519 W. 4th Ave., Anchorage, AK 99501. ℂ 800/544-0529 or 907/276-8023. www.26glaciers.com. $129 adults, $69 children under 12.

SMALL BOAT TOURS

Instead of getting on a giant tour boat with a mob of people, you can go on a small boat with a local whom you'll get to know as he shows off favorite places and lands on beaches to picnic and walk. If you see a whale or other point of interest, you stay as long or as short a time as you like. What you give up is the comfort of a large, tour bus-like vessel, you pay more, and most small boats have a four-person minimum.

Honey Charters   A family runs three sturdy aluminum boats built for these waters, specializing in personal tours, water transportation, and kayaker drop-offs. They operate with a minimum of four passengers; by paying the four-person minimum, you can have a boat to yourself. For larger groups, their *Qayaq Chief* can carry 18 kayakers or 22 passengers on a sightseeing cruise. Bring your own food.

On the Whittier waterfront (P.O. Box 708), Whittier, AK 99693. ℂ 888/477-2493 or 907/472-2493. www. honeycharters.com. 3-hr. cruise $89 per person, 6 hr. $139 per person, 11 hr. $189 person.

Sound Eco Adventures   Gerry Sanger is a retired wildlife biologist who spent years researching the waterfowl and ecology of Prince William Sound. Now he carries up to six passengers at a time on wildlife, whale, and glacier tours and does kayak drop-offs from his 30-foot aluminum boat, which has a landing-craft-like ramp perfect for pulling up on gravel beaches, and suitable for wheelchairs. Finding whales in the Sound takes skill and requires covering a lot of water; Gerry's success rate is better than 90% since 1999, and he has gone years without missing once. Prices listed are examples; you can customize and arrange discounts in certain circumstances. Fares include lunch and snacks.

P.O. Box 707, Whittier, AK 99693. ℂ 888/471-2312 or 907/472-2312. www.SoundEcoAdventure.com. 8-hr. whale and wildlife cruise $200 per person, 8-hr. sightseeing $170, or charter the whole boat for $125–$150/hr.

FISHING

About 30 charter fishing boats operate out of Whittier, the closest saltwater fishing to Anchorage, mostly targeting halibut but also getting salmon at certain times. The **Whittier Harbormaster** can give you a list of operators (ℂ 907/ 472-2337, extension 110 or 115). **Bread N Butter Charters** (ℂ 888/472-2396 or 907/472-2396; www.breadnbuttercharters.com) has been around for many years. They charge $195 per person for a day of halibut fishing and have an office on the waterfront. Honey Charters, listed above under "Small Boat Tours," has a similar service. You can also rent your own boat for fishing or camping in the Sound from **Whittier Boat & Tackle Rentals** (ℂ 866/ 667-2628 or 907/632-1188). The company carries top quality equipment, including boats suitable for an extended camping or cabin trip. Full-day rentals range from $250 to $450.

SEA KAYAKING

Whittier is a popular starting point for kayak trips to beautiful and protected western Prince William Sound. Day trips for beginners paddle along the shore near Whittier, often visiting a bird rookery, or take a boat 5 miles from the harbor to Shotgun Cove and paddle back. Longer multiday trips go by boat to even more interesting waters where you can visit glaciated fjords and paddle narrow passages. Several businesses compete in Whittier.

Alaska Sea-Kayakers (© 877/472-2534 or 907/472-2534; www.alaskasea kayakers.com) offers 3- and 5-hour day trips, for $79 to $175; paddles at Blackstone Glacier that begin and end with a charter boat ride, for $300; and extended trips. Guides are well trained and they occasionally offer weekend instructional clinics (check the website for times). Offices are at each end of Whittier Harbor. They rent to experienced paddlers, too.

The **Prince William Sound Kayak Center** (© 877/472-2452 or 907/472-2452; www.pwskayakcenter.com) offers guided half-day trips starting at $55 as well as full days and other options, and rents kayaks. They've been in business since 1981.

Most self-guided kayakers charter a boat to drop them off among the islands beyond the long, deep fjord in which Whittier is located. Honey Charters, listed above under "Small Boat Tours," offers a drop-off service. There are six Forest Service cabins in this idyllic area, which must be reserved 6 months ahead. Flat sites suitable for a tent are not plentiful on these rocky shores, which dropped in the 1964 earthquake, so do some research with the Forest Service or Alaska Public Lands Information Center in Anchorage before you go. For information and cabin reservations, see section 3, "Chugach National Forest: Do-It-Yourself Wilderness."

WHERE TO STAY & DINE

Most meals served in Whittier are for people grabbing a sandwich while waiting for a boat or otherwise passing through. Several such restaurants are in the triangle at the east end of the harbor, including a good Chinese place, the Korean-owned **China Sea** (© 907/472-2222). Lunch there is $8 or $9, dinner $12 to $19, and in the summer they serve specials such as kung pao halibut. Hours are 11am to 10pm daily.

June's Whittier Bed and Breakfast Condo Suites   Nine of these condo units are in the top two floors of the Begich Towers, the concrete building that dominates Whittier, allowing guests to live as Whittier people do, with great views and hummingbirds feeding at the high-rise windows (one is on the first floor). All have full kitchens. The friendly hostess, June Miller, and her husband, Ken, also have a fishing charter and sightseeing business, Bread N Butter Charters, listed above; you check in at their harborside office.

P.O. Box 715, Whittier, AK 99693. © 888/472-2396 or 907/472-2396. Fax 907/472-2503. www.breadn buttercharters.com. 10 units. $98–$225 double. Extra person over age 5 $15. AE, MC, V. **Amenities:** Harbor shuttle; coin-op laundry. *In room:* TV/VCR, kitchen.

5 Seward: Gateway to Resurrection Bay & Kenai Fjords

The main reason to go to Seward has always been Resurrection Bay. This agreeable little town started life as a place to fish and to get off boats arriving in Alaska, then continued as a place for Alaskans and visitors to get *on* boats and see the bay and Kenai Fjords National Park (described in section 6 of this chapter). With the growth of the cruise industry, Seward again is a place to get off the boat. Most cruises that cross the Gulf of Alaska start or end here, with their passengers taking a bus to or from the airport in Anchorage. That flow of people has brought a lot of tourist development to town, mostly of a quality that hasn't damaged the town's character.

Located by the broad fjord of Resurrection Bay, Seward is a mountainside grid of streets lined with old wood-frame houses and newer fishermen's residences. It has long been the sort of place where pedestrians casually wander across the

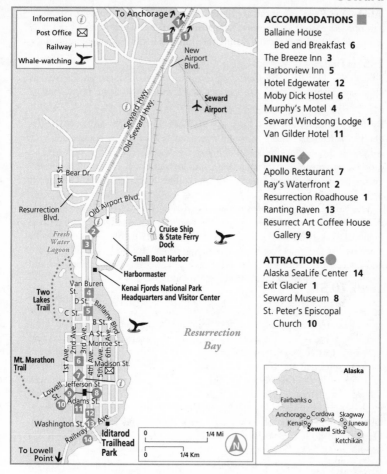

Information ⓘ
Post Office ✉
Railway ├──┤
Whale-watching 🐋

To Anchorage ↗

New Airport Blvd.

Seward HWY.
Old Seward HWY.

Seward Airport

1st St.
Bear Dr.

Resurrection Blvd.

Old Airport Blvd.

Fresh Water Lagoon

Cruise Ship & State Ferry Dock

Small Boat Harbor

Harbormaster

Kenai Fjords National Park Headquarters and Visitor Center

Two Lakes Trail

Van Buren St.
D St.
C St.
B St.
A St.
Monroe St.
Madison St.
Jefferson St.
Adams St.
Washington St.

Ballaine Blvd.
1st Ave.
2nd Ave.
3rd Ave.
4th Ave.
5th Ave.
6th Ave.

Mt. Marathon Trail

Lowell St.

Railway
Iditarod Trailhead Park

To Lowell Point ↓

Resurrection Bay

ACCOMMODATIONS ■
Ballaine House Bed and Breakfast **6**
The Breeze Inn **3**
Harborview Inn **5**
Hotel Edgewater **12**
Moby Dick Hostel **6**
Murphy's Motel **4**
Seward Windsong Lodge **1**
Van Gilder Hotel **11**

DINING ◆
Apollo Restaurant **7**
Ray's Waterfront **2**
Resurrection Roadhouse **1**
Ranting Raven **13**
Resurrect Art Coffee House Gallery **9**

ATTRACTIONS ●
Alaska SeaLife Center **14**
Exit Glacier **1**
Seward Museum **8**
St. Peter's Episcopal Church **10**

Alaska

Fairbanks ○
Anchorage ○ Cordova ○ Skagway ○
Kenai ○○   ○ Juneau
Seward ○ Sitka
Ketchikan ○

0   1/4 Mi
0   1/4 Km
N

road, hardly glancing for cars, for there likely won't be any, or, if there are, they'll be ready to stop. The growing tourism industry is bringing more traffic, but most of what's new has been good for the town. The largest addition, the Alaska SeaLife Center, is a research aquarium that's also open to the public. Combined with Seward's excellent ocean fishing, the national park, the wonderful hiking trails, and the unique and attractive town itself, the new center helps make Seward well worth a 2-day visit.

Seward's history is among the oldest in Alaska. The great Russian governor Alexander Baranof stopped here in 1793, named Resurrection Bay, and built a ship, which later sank, probably because Baranof's workers didn't have proper materials. Gold prospectors blazed trails from here to finds on Turnagain Arm starting in 1891, and in 1907 the army linked those trails with others all the way to Nome, finishing the Iditarod Trail. Today that route is discontinuous south of Anchorage, but you can follow it through Seward and hike a portion of it on the Johnson Pass Trail north of town (p. 249).

More relevant for current visitors and the local economy, the federal government took over a failed railroad-building effort in 1915, finishing the line to

Fairbanks in 1923. Until the age of jet travel, most people coming to the main part of Alaska arrived by steamer in Seward and then traveled north by rail. The train ride to Anchorage, daily during the summer, is still supremely beautiful.

ESSENTIALS

GETTING THERE   By Car   See section 2 of this chapter, on the Seward Highway, for how to make the spectacular 127-mile drive down from Anchorage. All major car-rental agencies are represented in Anchorage.

By Bus   The **Seward Bus Line** (℃ **907/224-3608** in Seward or 907/563-0800 in Anchorage) makes a round trip from Seward to Anchorage and back daily, year-round; the fare is $40 one-way, $75 round trip. They'll pick up and drop off passengers anywhere en route and, for an extra $5, take you to the airport. They share a ticket office with the Homer Stage Line in Anchorage, at 3335 Fairbanks St.

   The Park Connection Motorcoach Service (℃ **800/266-8625** or 907/245-0200; www.alaskacoach.com) connects Seward with Anchorage and Denali National Park twice daily in summer in each direction with big, comfortable coaches. The fare is $49 between Seward and Anchorage, $118 between Seward and Denali, half price for kids under age 12. Passengers between Seward and Anchorage get a pass to the Anchorage Museum of History and Art.

By Train   The train ride between Anchorage and Seward is one of miraculous beauty. The **Alaska Railroad** (℃ **800/544-0552** or 907/265-2494; www.alaska railroad.com) offers passenger service from Anchorage and back daily in summer. The route is even prettier than the highway, passing close by glaciers and following a ledge halfway up the narrow, vertical Placer River gorge, where it ducks into tunnels and pops out at bends in the river. The landscape looks just as it did when the first person beheld it. The railroad's young guides are well trained. The fare is $59 one-way, $98 round-trip; children ages 2 to 11 half price. A rental car will almost always be cheaper, but the train ride is unforgettable. The railroad also offers packages with lodging and activities in Seward. Don't try to do it in one day from Anchorage—the 16-hour marathon is too much.

By Ferry   The ferry *Tustumena,* of the Alaska Marine Highway System (℃ **800/642-0066,** Seward terminal at 907/224-5485; www.ferryalaska.com), calls on Seward a few times a month bound for Valdez to the east or Kodiak to the west. The adult walk-on fare to Valdez is $74, to Kodiak $70. Every two weeks in summer the *Kennicott* travels from Juneau across the Gulf of Alaska to Valdez and then to Seward. The fare from Juneau is $186 for an adult and the trip takes 48 hours. The terminal is at the cruise ship dock, on the outside of the small boat harbor.

GETTING AROUND   You can easily cover downtown Seward on foot, although a little help is handy to get back and forth from the boat harbor. If it's not raining, a bike may be the best way. **Seward Bike Shop** (℃ **907/224-2448**), in a railcar near the depot at the harbor, rents high-performance mountain bikes and models good for just getting around town, plus accessory equipment. A cruiser is $12 half day, $19 full day. **PJ's Taxi** (℃ **907/224-5555**) is one of the cab companies in Seward.

VISITOR INFORMATION   The **Seward Chamber of Commerce,** P.O. Box 749, Seward, AK 99664 (℃ **907/224-8051;** www.sewardak.org), has three visitor centers. The one on the right side of the Seward Highway as you enter town is open year-round (summer Mon–Fri 8am–6pm, Sat–Sun 9am–4pm; winter Mon–Fri 9am–5pm). Summer-only centers are at the small boat harbor and in a kiosk on the cruise-ship dock. They can give business information and last-minute help in finding a room. In addition to these town information sources, the **Kenai Fjords National Park Visitor Center** is covered in section 6, later in this chapter. For contacts for the Chugach National Forest, see section 3.

SPECIAL EVENTS   The **Fourth of July** is the biggest day of the year in Seward, when the whole town explodes with visitors, primarily from Anchorage. Besides the parade and many small-town festivities, the main attraction is the **Mount Marathon Race,** run every year since it started as a bar bet in 1915. The racers go from the middle of town straight up rocky Mount Marathon to its 3,022-foot peak, then tumble down again, arriving muddy and bloody at the finish line in town. Strong binoculars allow you to see the whole thing from town, including the pratfalls of the runners on their way down.

The **Silver Salmon Derby** starts the second Saturday of August, although the peak of silver season comes later. The chamber of commerce visitor centers can provide information.

FAST FACTS: Seward

Bank   Wells Fargo is at 908 3rd Ave. ((C) **907/224-5283**), with an ATM.

Hospital   Providence Seward Medical Center is at 417 1st Ave. ((C) **907/224-5205**).

Internet Access   Free at the Seward Public Library, 5th and Adams.

Police   For nonemergency situations, call the Seward Police Department ((C) **907/224-3338**) or, outside the city limits, the Alaska State Troopers ((C) **907/224-3346**).

Post Office   At 5th Avenue and Madison St.

Taxes   Sales tax is 5%. The room tax totals 9%.

GETTING OUTSIDE

Here I've described things to do out of Seward other than visiting the national park, which includes the fjords and Exit Glacier. See section 6, "Kenai Fjords National Park," later in this chapter, for that information.

BOATING & SEA KAYAKING

Miller's Landing, at Lowell Point, 3 miles south of town ((C) **866-541-5739** or 907/224-5739; www.millerslandingak.com) is a good place to know about if you intend to spend any time outdoors around Seward, especially if you like to do things on your own. They have a campground and cabins (described later in this chapter), a boat launch with skiffs, sea kayaks for rent, and fishing charters with experienced skippers. Skiffs rent for $65 for 4 hours; kayaks are $40 a day single, $50 double (they offer reasonably priced guided outings, too). Fishermen hang around the shop trading lies and advice (5¢, with a money-back guarantee). The staff will teach you how to fish for salmon and send you out on your own or on a guided charter. The water-taxi operation, a landing craft with a bow ramp, charges flat rates to take travelers to remote beaches and public cabins around the bay or to the national park—great for sea kayakers or those who just want to get off on their own ($30 one-way to Caines Head, $250 round-trip to the park service cabin in Aialik Bay; half price children under 10). They offer many other services, too, including booking full Seward visits.

For guided sea kayaking, **Sunny Cove Sea Kayaking** (© **800/770-9119** for reservations, or 907/224-8810; www.sunnycove.com) offers day trips suitable for beginners as part of the Kenai Fjords Tours trips to its Fox Island lodge, and day trips and multiday trips into the fjords themselves (see the Kenai Fjords National Park section later in this chapter). They've earned a good reputation. On a budget, you can take one of their tours right from Seward. They launch from Lowell Point, following the shore toward Caines Head State Recreation Area, where you can see sea otters, seabirds, intertidal creatures, and the salmon in Tonsina Creek. Three-hour paddles are $59; 8-hour trips are $99. A trip to Fox Island is more expensive but comes with a fjords boat tour and salmon bake, so the cost of the kayaking comes out roughly the same.

FISHING

Seward is renowned for its saltwater silver salmon fishing. The silvers start showing up in the bay in mid-July and last through September. You can catch the fish from shore, from Lowell Point south of town, or even near the boat harbor, but your chances of success are far greater from a boat. I prefer small, six-passenger boats because you can get to know the skipper better and can learn more about fishing. If your party has the whole boat, you can control where it goes, perhaps adding whale-watching or sightseeing to the day. Larger boats add more comfort and stability in the waves. The going rate for a guided charter, with everything provided, is around $170 per person, or $225 to go for salmon and halibut on the same day. Andrew Mezirow, a marine biologist and diver for the SeaLife Center, operates two boats, including a fancy new twelve-passenger vessel. Besides day fishing, he takes guests on multiday fishing expeditions to extremely remote and beautiful places. His business is **Crackerjack Sportfishing Charters** (© **877/224-2606** or 907/224-2606; www.crackerjackcharters.com). The office is on the boardwalk at the top of the harbor ramps.

There are many other fishing charter companies, mostly booked through central charter agencies, which make life simpler for visitors. **The Fish House** is the largest charter booker in Seward, located at the small boat harbor. The store also sells and rents ocean-fishing and spin-casting gear, and carries some fly-fishing supplies. For charters, reserve ahead at P.O. Box 1209, Seward, AK 99664 (© **800/257-7760** or 907/224-3674; www.thefishhouse.net). If you want a small boat, ask to be put on a "six pack," as vessels licensed for six or fewer passengers are known. See "Boating & Sea Kayaking," above, for details on the less expensive option of renting your own skiff and fishing without a guide, and for another charter booking agency, Miller's Landing.

HIKING

There are several excellent hiking trails near Seward. You can get a complete list and directions at the Kenai Fjords National Park Visitor Center (see section 6).

The **Mount Marathon Trail** is a tough hike to the top of a 3,022-foot mountain. The route of the famous Mount Marathon footrace is the more strenuous choice, basically going straight up from the end of Jefferson Street; the hikers' route starts at the corner of 1st Avenue and Monroe Street. Either trail rises steeply to the top of the rocky pinnacle and the incredible views there. Allow all day, unless you're a racer; in that case, expect to do it in under 45 minutes.

The **Caines Head State Recreation Area** (www.alaskastateparks.org, click on "Individual Parks") has a 7-mile coastal trail south of town. Parts of the trail are accessible only at low tide, so it's best done either as an overnight or with some-one picking you up or dropping you off in a boat beyond the beach portion—the Miller's Landing water taxi (p. 259) offers this service for $30 adults one-way, kids half price. The trail has some gorgeous views, rocky shores, and a fascinating destination at the end, a towering promontory with the concrete remains of Fort McGilvray, a World War II defensive emplacement. Take flash-lights and you can poke around in the spooky, pitch dark underground corridors and rooms and imagine what each was used for (going in without lights would be foolhardy). We've rarely enjoyed a hike more. Three campsites are at Tonsina Point, about 2 miles in, and a state park public-use cabin is 2 miles farther (see "Where to Stay," below; and "State Parks Cabin Reservations," p. 244). At North Beach, 4½ miles from the trail head, are two camping shelters, a ranger station, and the trails to the fort and South Beach. For an easy 2-mile hike to Fort McGilvray, start with a boat ride to North Beach. The main trail head is south of town on Lowell Point Road; pull off in the lot right after the sewage plant, then cross the road through the gate and follow the dirt road a bit until it becomes the actual trail. Before venturing out on a hike, stop at the Kenai Fjords National Park Visitor Center at the boat harbor for tide conditions and advice.

DOG MUSHING

When Mitch Seavey won the Iditarod Trail Sled Dog Race in 2004, many agreed it couldn't have happened to a nicer guy. He had made a lot of friends over the years offering rides with his dogs. It's a family business, including the four boys (one is a Junior Iditarod champ), making use of their kennel on Old Exit Gla-cier Road off Herman Leirer Road. They offer summer rides in Seward and in winter in Sterling (near Soldotna). The summer ride uses a wheeled sled and a full, 12-dog team—not the real thing (no snow), but you'll get a feeling for the dogs' power and intelligence. The 90-minute tour costs $44 for adults, $22 for children 11 and under. Husky puppies are available for cuddling, too. They call their company **IdidaRide** (© **800/478-3139** or 907/224-8607; www.ididaride.com).

Those with eight times as much to spend should consider mushing on snow at the height of summer by joining a helicopter tour to Godwin Glacier from the Seward Airport with **Godwin Glacier Dog Sled Tours** (© **888/989-8239** or 907-224-8239; http://alaskadogsled.com). A chopper lands at a camp of 80 dogs, where guests take a ride in the sled (the company also offers glacier treks and overnight camping on the ice). They charge $360 adult, $325 children.

Era Helicopters (© **800/843-1947;** www.flightseeingtours.com) offers dogsled tours on Godwin Glacier for $390, and they also offer sightseeing flights and glacier walks from the Seward Airport.

EXPLORING THE TOWN

Besides the Alaska SeaLife Center (see below), most of Seward's attractions are of the modest, small-town variety. The **Iditarod Trailhead,** on the water just east of the SeaLife Center, is where pioneers entered Alaska. The broken con-crete and twisted metal you see on the beach walking north are the last ruins of the Seward waterfront, which was destroyed by a tsunami wave in the 1964 earthquake. Sometimes you can see sea otters swimming just offshore. During silver salmon season, in August and September, it's possible to catch them by casting from shore here, although your chances are far better from a boat (see "Fishing," above).

The **Seward Museum,** at 3rd and Jefferson (© 907/224-3902), is a charming grandma's attic of a place, with clippings, memorabilia, and curiosities recalling town history, painter Rockwell Kent, and the ways of the past. Admission is $3 for adults, 50¢ under age 18. It's open during the summer daily from 9am to 5pm, in winter usually weekends (call ahead).

The steep-roofed **St. Peter's Episcopal Church** is a delightful little chapel under the mountains at 1st Avenue and Adams Street. Go inside to see the mural in the front of the church, which shows what the Resurrection would have looked like if it had happened in front of Seward locals in the 1930s.

Alaska SeaLife Center ★★★ The center is a serious research institution and an interesting aquarium of creatures from the nearby Alaska waters. You may have seen puffins diving into the water from a tour boat; here you can see what they look like flying *under* the water. Seabirds, harbor seals, and sea lions reside in three large exhibits that you can see from above or below. There are some smaller tanks with fish, crab, and other creatures, a touch tank where you can handle starfish and other tide-pool animals, and exhibits on changes in the Bering Sea and on jellyfish. Another exhibit updates the status of *Exxon Valdez* spill damage to birds and marine mammals; Exxon settlement money made the center possible. The center is not as large as a big-city aquarium, however, and you're not likely to spend more than an hour or two here. Programs for kids and adults happen all day: To make the most of the admission price call ahead so you can catch one that interests you, such as a behind the scenes tour or session on ocean research.

301 Railway Ave. (P.O. Box 1329), Seward, AK 99664. © **800/224-2525** or 907/224-6300. www.alaskasea life.org. $13 adults, $10 children 7–12, free for children 6 and under. May–Aug daily 8am–8pm; Oct–Mar daily 10am–5pm; Sept and Apr daily 9am–6pm.

SHOPPING

Stop at the **Resurrect Art Coffee House Gallery,** at 320 3rd Ave., in an old church. It's a coffeehouse and gathering place that shows local fine art; it's also conducive to hanging out and meeting people. The **Bardarson Studio,** 1317 Fourth Ave., at the boat harbor (www.bardarsonstudio.com), is a large gallery specializing in watercolor prints by Dot Bardarson and many other Alaska artists and has a welcoming attitude and lots to look at. There's a children's cave under the stairs and an elephant for them to ride, and places to sit outside or upstairs, and a public bathroom.

WHERE TO STAY

Alaska's Point of View Reservation Service (© 907/224-2323; www.alaskas view.com) is a Seward lodging and tour booking agency. The website has an impressive search function for B&B lodgings. You can get a list of B&Bs from the various chamber of commerce visitor centers (see p. 258).

Seward has several hotels beyond those I can list here; in fact, I'm not aware of a bad hotel in Seward. The **Hotel Edgewater,** 200 5th Ave. (© 888/793-6800; www.hoteledgewater.com) stands right across the street from the ocean and the SeaLife Center and many of the upscale rooms have excellent views. **Murphy's Motel** (© 800/686-8191; www.murphysmotel.com), near the boat harbor, has very good rooms with views in a new building for reasonable rates and budget rooms in an older building.

Ballaine House Bed and Breakfast *(Finds)*   This 1905 house near the downtown is a classic B&B, with its wooden floors, large living room, and tall, double-hung windows. It's on the National Historic Register and the town walking tour. The hostess, Marilee Koszewski, is accommodating and fun. She has decorated the house with antiques and handmade quilts and provides raincoats, binoculars, and other gear for outings, cooks breakfast to order, and will even do laundry. Guests can use the kitchen or the barbecue and the freezer for their fish. She also books activities and boats in Seward and some other towns, giving back the commission to guests; she doesn't make anything on it, but they save up to 20%. Rooms are not large, and all bathrooms are shared, but Marilee will often cut deals on additional rooms to make a family or group comfortable. Smoking is not allowed.

437 3rd Ave. (P.O. Box 2051), Seward, AK 99664-2051. © 907/224-2362. www.superpage.com/ballaine. 6 units, none with private bathroom. $92 double. Rates include full breakfast cooked to order. No credit cards. No children under 8. **Amenities:** Tour booking; laundry service; shared Internet access. *In room:* TV/VCR.

The Breeze Inn *(★)*   Located right at the busy boat harbor, this large, three-story, motel-style building offers good standard accommodations with the most convenient location in town for a fishing or Kenai Fjords boat trip. Rooms are frequently renovated. An annex building has excellent upscale rooms, some overlooking the harbor.

1306 Seward Hwy. (P.O. Box 2147), Seward, AK 99664-2147. © 888/224-5237 or 907/224-5238. Fax 907 /224-7024. www.breezeinn.com. 100 units. Summer $139–$199 double; winter $49 double. Extra person $10. AE, DC, DISC, MC, V. **Amenities:** Restaurant; bar; courtesy van. *In room:* A/C, TV, fridge, coffeemaker, hair dryer, iron.

Harborview Inn *(★★)*   The inn grew from Jerry and Jolene King's bed-and-breakfast operation and still shows the taste and attention to detail that made it such a success. The rooms are among the most attractive in town, with lots of light, Mission-style furniture, and Tlingit art based on Jolene's tribal crest. The rates are good by Seward standards, and the location, midway between the small boat harbor and downtown, puts both within long walking distance. Two two-bedroom apartments on the beach along Ballaine Avenue are perfect for families, and reasonably priced at $159 a night. There are two other attractive apartments in the inn, including one with four bedrooms.

804 3rd Ave. (P.O. Box 1305), Seward, AK 99664. © 888/324-3217 or 907/224-3217. Fax 907/224-3218. www.SewardHotel.com. 35 units, 4 apt. High season $139 double, $149-$189 apartment. Low season $59 double, $89-$149 apartment. Extra person $10. AE, DISC, MC, V. *In room:* TV, dataport, coffeemaker, hair dryer.

Seward Windsong Lodge *(★★)*   This hotel is the only one at Kenai Fjords National Park with a national park atmosphere. The big lobby, with its high ceiling, huge wood beams, fireplace and cedar shingles could be at Yellowstone. Moreover, the posh, solidly finished quality of the place puts it in first place among Seward's hotels. The location is out of town, among spruce trees on the broad, unspoiled valley of the Resurrection River, and the collection of buildings goes on and on. Rooms are in separate lodges with entry from exterior porches. They have a crisp feel, all with two queen beds and rustic-style furniture and good amenities. The hotel restaurant, the Resurrection Roadhouse, is reviewed below, under "Where to Dine."

½ mile, Exit Glacier Rd., also known as Herman Leirer Rd. (Mailing address: 2525 C St., Ste 405, Anchorage, AK 99503). © 888/959-9590 or 907/265-4500 in Anchorage, or 907/224-7116 in Seward. www.seward windsong.com. 108 units. High season $189 double; low season $129 double. Extra person over age 11 $15. AE, DISC, MC, V. Closed Oct–Apr. **Amenities:** Restaurant; tour desk; courtesy van. *In room:* TV/VCR, coffeemaker.

Van Gilder Hotel ★ (Value) This historic building, restored and decorated with the wallpaper of a century ago, has small and oddly shaped rooms, but the style of the place and the quality of the management more than make up for it. Even the tiny bathrooms, mostly with shower stalls, not tubs, are tiled in an old-fashioned style and immaculately clean. Two rooms share a bathroom and one has its own but down the hall. Many rooms have queen beds and fold-down Murphy beds; a group of three could save a lot staying here. The location, right downtown, is prime. The hotel has a community kitchen for guests to prepare their own light meals.

308 Adams St. (P.O. Box 609), Seward, AK 99664. © 800/204-6835 or 907/224-3079. Fax 907/224-3689. www.vangilderhotel.com. 24 units. High season $109 double shared bath, $149–$169 private bath, $219 suite. Low season $55 double shared bath, $65–$85 private bath, $125 suite. $10 each additional person. AE, DC, DISC, MC, V. *In room:* TV.

A HOSTEL, CAMPING & CABINS

A friendly family runs the **Moby Dick Hostel,** at 432 3rd Ave. (© **907/ 224-7072;** www.mobydickhostel.com). They charge $17 for a bunk, $50 for private hostel rooms, and $60 for kitchenette rooms. The place is nicely renovated.

The best campgrounds near Seward are those in Chugach National Forest, described above in section 3. The only campground in Kenai Fjords National Park is near Seward, the **Exit Glacier Campground** at mile 8.5 of Herman Leirer Rd. (aka Exit Glacier Road). The campground is on willow-covered, gravel ground that plants haven't yet reclaimed from the retreating ice. Sites are far apart and almost completely private, but lack any amenities—no picnic tables, fire grates, or anything. Use the food lockers and central cooking to keep bears away. Snow lingers into early June. There is no fee for the 10 sites, and reservations are not taken. It's open for tents only and has pit toilets and hand-pump water.

In the town of Seward itself, the seaside Waterfront Park on Ballaine Boulevard is acceptable for RV camping, but the tent sites are too noisy and exposed for my liking. Seward has tried to crack down on drinking and rowdiness in its campgrounds with partial success. The fee is $8 for tents, $12 for RVs plus $25 for a site with utilities, and showers are $2. It's operated by the city parks and recreation department (© **907/224-4055**). A quieter town campground is **Forest Acres Park,** among the spruce trees at Hemlock and Sealion Boulevard, just off Seward Highway near the Army Recreation Center. Fees are the same. Neither campground accepts reservations. RVs are welcome, but there are no hook-ups.

More appealing is **Miller's Landing,** a homestead on Lowell Point Road south of town (© **866/541-5739** or 907/224-5739; www.millerslandingak. com). Sites are along the beach or among large spruce trees. Electric hookups are $25 to $28 a night, tent sites are $20; rustic sleeping-bag cabins start at $45; and cabins with kitchens and bathrooms run $65 to $100. They also reserve the other lodgings, including along the beach at Lowell Point. There's lots to do here; see "Boating & Sea Kayaking," earlier in this chapter.

The Department of Natural Resources maintains two state park cabins for rent in the **Caines Head State Recreation Area,** south of town, and two in **Thumb Cove State Marine Park,** across the bay from Caines Head. These cabins are in high demand and usually must be reserved six months ahead for the summer months. For details on that system see "State Parks Cabin Reservations," in section 1 of this chapter. It's possible to hike to the Caines Head cabins (see "Hiking," above), but to get to Thumb Cove you need a boat. Water taxi service is offered for $40 round-trip by Miller's Landing (see "Boating & Sea Kayaking," earlier in this chapter). The Thumb Cove cabins lie in an impossibly steep bowl of mountains, a grand and lovely setting that, along with the excellent salmon fishing nearby, makes them popular and tough to reserve. However, camping is permitted along the same beach, with plenty of space and an outhouse for campers' use. Cabins in Chugach National Forest and Kenai Fjords National Park are mentioned in those sections.

WHERE TO DINE

There are various places at the harbor to grab a sandwich or other quick meal on the way out to sea; they change too frequently for me to include here. Downtown, the **Ranting Raven,** at 228 Fourth Ave. (© **907/224-2228**), is a great little gift and coffee shop serving pastries, sandwiches, and soup, open April through Christmas.

Apollo Restaurant ⚜ MEDITERRANEAN/SEAFOOD   This is a surprisingly good small-town restaurant. Seward families come back for a menu that includes anything they might want: Greek and southern Italian cuisine, seafood, pizza, and much more. But the food is far more sophisticated and expertly turned out than you expect in such a place, especially the seafood dishes, and the service is fast and professional. The dining room, with many booths, takes the Greek theme as far as it will go—I especially enjoyed the miniature Doric columns. The same folks own Apollo II, selling pizza, sandwiches and the like at the north end of the boat harbor.

229 Fourth Ave. © **907/224-3092**. Main courses $10–$18. MC, V. Daily 11am–11pm.

Ray's Waterfront ⚜ STEAK/SEAFOOD   The lively, noisy dining room looks out from big windows across the small boat harbor, with tables on terraces so everyone can see. The atmosphere is fun and the consistently good food is just right after a day on the water. While not perfect, it's more nuanced than the typical harborside place; the seafood chowder is great. Most important, they don't overcook the fresh local fish—and that's really all you can ask. On a busy summer weekend, however, the place can be overrun, with long waits and harried servers. They have a full bar.

At the small boat harbor. © **907/224-5606**. Lunch $6–$15; dinner main courses $16–$30. AE, DISC, MC, V. 18% gratuity added for parties of 6 or more. Daily 11am–11pm. Closed Oct to mid-Mar.

Resurrection Roadhouse ⚜ ALASKAN SPECIALTIES/PIZZA   This place sometimes sees an annual shift in quality typical of seasonal restaurants, but I've had wonderful food here. The menu includes fish, venison, and ribs smoked in-house. They also serve hand-thrown gourmet pizzas. The view of the mountain is great and there's plenty of space. It's a relaxing alternative to noisy Ray's. The bar's collection of Alaska craft brews on tap is exhaustive.

⅔ mile Exit Glacier Rd. © **907/224-7116**. Lunch $9–$13; dinner main courses $9–$24. AE, DISC, MC, V. Daily 7am–2:30pm and 5–10pm. Closed mid-Oct to mid-Apr.

6 Kenai Fjords National Park

Kenai Fjords is all about remote rocks, mountains, and ice that meet the ocean, and the animals that live there. The park comprises 670,000 acres of the south coast and interior landmass of the Kenai Peninsula. The shore here is exposed to the Gulf of Alaska, whose wild, recurrent storms beat against the mountainous shore unbuffered by any landmass from the vast expanse of the Pacific to the south. Wildlife thrives, but humans have never made a mark.

The geological events that formed this landscape are vast and ongoing. The steep, coastal mountains amount to a dent in the earth's crust where the north-ward-moving Pacific tectonic plate is colliding and adding land to the southern edge of Alaska. As the Pacific plate pushes under Alaska, it slams islands onto the Alaska coast, then pulls them under into the molten layer down below. These mountains are shrinking measurably as the earth swallows them up. The 1964 earthquake dropped them by 6 to 8 feet. As your boat passes the park's small, sharp, bedrock islands, now populated by seabirds and marine mammals, you are seeing the tips of ancient peaks that once stood far above the shore like today's coastal mountains.

The park's history has barely started. The fjords became a park only in 1980. In 1976, when the National Park Service explored more than 650 miles of coast-line, including the park area, they didn't find a single human being. The same was true when geologists came in 1909. British explorer Capt. James Cook made the first maps of the fjords area in 1778, but the coast was too rugged and rocky for him to land. We don't know much about Native Americans who lived in the fjords. Scientists have found some areas where people lived, or at least had camps, but no one knows exactly who they were or what they were doing here. The earth, through earthquakes or glacial action, has erased most remains. Anthropologists call these people *Unegkurmiut,* and believe they were Alutiiq, Eskimos who lived on the Pacific coast, closely related to the Chugach people of Prince William Sound and the Koniag from Kodiak Island to the south. Those groups are still around; scientists are studying the Unegkurmiut and what hap-pened to them from the little evidence they can find on the fjord's beaches.

The Natives probably never ventured inland over the impossibly rugged inte-rior of the Kenai Peninsula, leaving its heart to be discovered in 1968, when the first mountain climbers crossed the Harding Ice Field, which covers most of the national park. **Exit Glacier** and all the glaciers of Kenai Fjords flow from this ice age leftover, which may be a mile thick. The ice field lies in a high bowl of mountains that jut straight out of the ocean to heights of 3,000 to 5,000 feet. When moisture-laden ocean clouds hit those mountains, they drop lots of rain and snow—up on the ice field 40 to 80 feet of snow fall each winter, with a water-equivalent of 17 feet. Summer weather isn't warm enough to melt the snow at that elevation, so it packs down ever deeper until it turns into the hard, heavy ice of glaciers and flows downward to the sea.

The area's history finally got an ugly start in 1989, when the tanker *Exxon Valdez* crashed into a rock about 150 miles northeast of the park in Prince William Sound and spilled almost 11 million gallons of oil. Exxon did a poor job of catching the oil before it spread, and by the end of the summer the sticky, brownish-black muck had soiled beaches in the western Sound, across the fjords, and all the way to Kodiak Island and the Alaska Peninsula. More than 1,000 miles of shoreline were oiled to some degree, 30 miles in the park. Hundreds of sea otters and hundreds of thousands of seabirds were killed in the Sound and on the islands near the fjords. Nature scrubbed the oil off the rocks again, and you will see no evidence of it in the park today; but government scientists say many of the affected species of birds and animals haven't come back completely. Nonetheless, you'll still see more wildlife on a boat ride here than anywhere else I know.

Most of the park is remote and difficult to reach. A large vessel, such as a tour boat operating out of Seward, is the only practical way for most people to see the marine portion of the park. That's not cheap or quick, and there are better destinations for people subject to seasickness. The inland portion is accessible only at Exit Glacier, near Seward.

ESSENTIALS

GETTING THERE   Seward is the threshold to the park. Exit Glacier is 13 miles from the town by road; the Kenai Fjords National Park Visitor Center is at the Seward small boat harbor; and the tour boats that visit the park leave from Seward.

Many visitors try to see the park in a day, coming from Anchorage by train or road, touring the park by boat, then returning that evening. I do not recommend this. To really get to the park, you need to be on an all-day boat trip—most half-day trips barely leave Resurrection Bay and hardly see the park proper. More important, a lot of the visitors I saw riding the train back to Anchorage after a 16-hour marathon to Kenai Fjords were so tired they couldn't keep their eyes open for the extraordinary scenery passing by. A better plan is to spend at least one night in Seward and take in the full Kenai Fjords boat trip and Exit Glacier.

VISITOR INFORMATION   At the **Kenai Fjords National Park Visitor Center,** Seward small boat harbor (P.O. Box 1727), Seward, AK 99664 (© **907/ 224-7500;** www.nps.gov/kefj), you will find rangers to answer questions about the park and provide information on the all-important tour boats, and a small but handy bookstore. Call or drop by here for advice on park service cabins for rent in the fjords, guidance on a sea-kayaking expedition there, or information on places in the area to hike and on trail conditions. They're open May through Labor Day daily from 9am to 6pm, off-season Monday through Friday from 9am to 5pm.

ACCOMMODATIONS & CAMPING   There are no hotels in the park; it's best to base yourself in Seward (see my recommendations earlier in this chapter). The **Exit Glacier Campground,** the only campground in the park, also is listed on p. 264. In the heart of the park you can camp anywhere if you observe correct backcountry precautions. A free park service map shows the location of food lockers and hanging cables to keep your stuff away from bears in the kayaking waters of Aialik Bay and Northwestern Fjord. The Park Service gives voluntary permits to record your itinerary and an emergency contact phone number in case you don't return. Send away for a packet of information from the park. They also rent out four **public-use cabins,** three in the fjords, reachable only by boat or floatplane. One is a mile from Exit Glacier, but is open only during the winter when the road is closed. It's accessible by ski, dog sled, or snow machine. Contact the park headquarters for a $35-a-day cabin permit, open for reservations starting January 2 each year.

SEEING THE PARK
SIGHTSEEING & WILDLIFE CRUISES

Kenai Fjords is essentially a marine park. On a boat tour, you'll see its mountains, glaciers, and wildlife. On any of the tours you're sure to see sea otters and sea lions, and you have a good chance of seeing humpback whales, orcas, mountain goats, and black bears. I saw all those on one trip to Aialik Bay. Gray whales come in the early spring and huge fin whales show sometimes, too (but are hard to see). Bird-watchers will see bald eagles, puffins (both tufted and horned),

Tips **It's Not Easy Being Green**

An important factor in choosing your boat tour is your susceptibility to **seasickness.** To reach the heart of the park, vessels must venture into the unprotected waters of the North Pacific. Large, rolling waves are inevitable on the passage from Resurrection Bay to the fjords themselves, although once you're in the fjords the water is calm. On a rough day, most boats will turn back for the comfort of the passengers and change the full-day trip into a Resurrection Bay cruise, refunding the difference in fare. Of course, they'd rather not do that, and the decision may not be made until the vessel is out there, often after many of the passengers are already vomiting over the side. If you get seasick easily, my advice is to stick to the Resurrection Bay cruise, or take a boat tour in protected Prince William Sound out of Whittier (see section 4 in this chapter), where the water is smooth. In any event, ask about the tour company's policy on turning back and refunds, and take Dramamine *before* you leave the dock (once you're underway, it's probably too late to do any good).

murrelets (marbled and Kittletz's), cormorants (red faced, pelagic, and double breasted), murres (common and thick billed), auklets (rhinoceros and parakeet), and various other sea ducks, alcids, and gulls.

The farther you go into the park, the more you'll see. If you really want to see Kenai Fjords National Park and glaciers that drop ice into the water, the boat has to go at least into Aialik Bay to Holgate Glacier. Northwestern Glacier is even deeper in the park. Half-day Resurrection Bay cruises offer plenty of impressive scenery but pass only one glacier, and that at a distance. They have less chance of seeing whales, and see fewer puffins and other birds. The longest trips into the heart of the park proper encounter the greatest variety and number of birds and animals. If you're lucky with the weather, you can make it to the exposed Chiswell Islands, which have some of the greatest bird rookeries in Alaska, supporting more than 50,000 seabirds of 18 species. I've seen clouds of puffins swarm here. The day-long trips also allow you more time to linger and really see the behavior of the wildlife. Whatever your choice, binoculars are a necessity, but if you didn't bring your own you can often rent them on board.

Prices are around $150 to go to Northwestern Glacier in Northwestern Fjord off Harris Bay, a 10-hour trip; $120 to go to Holgate Glacier in Holgate Arm off Aialik Bay, which takes 6 to 8 hours (the most common destination); and $60 to $80 for a 3- to 4-hour Resurrection Bay tour, which doesn't go to the national park at all. Children's prices are around half off. I have seen a lot of misleading publicity material from the tour operators, so ask exactly where the boat goes or get a map of the route. They sometimes brag about going to Bear Glacier, but that's a let-down because boats can't get close to it. You have to go at least to Holgate Glacier for a noteworthy glacier encounter.

Fares with each operator differ little, although you can sometimes get early season or Web specials; instead shop for the destination, length of trip, food service, interpretation, and size or intimacy of the boat. Ask how much deck space there is outside so you can really see. What is the seating arrangement inside? How many passengers will be on board and how many crew members to answer questions? Is lunch provided, and what does it consist of? Another important point of comparison is whether you have a ranger doing the commentary, or the captain—some of these captains don't know when to shut up, and they can give inaccurate information.

Try to schedule loosely so that if the weather is bad on the day you choose for your boat trip you can wait and go the next day. If the weather's bad, you'll be uncomfortable and the animals and birds won't be as evident, or the boat may not go out of the bay at all. If you pay up front to hold a reservation on a boat—probably a good idea in the busiest months—find out the company's refund and rescheduling policy.

Most operators offer packages with the Alaska Railroad and the SeaLife Center, or even with a local hotel, which may save money, but make sure you have enough time to do everything you want to do in Seward. All have offices at the small boat harbor in Seward. In addition to the large operators listed in full below, **Renown Charters and Tours** (© **800/665-3806** or 907/272-1961; www.renowncharters.com) has smaller vessels that carry up to 70 passengers and offers some lower-priced cruises and year-round operations for off-season travelers. A 4-hour whale watch is as low as $49 adults, $25 children.

Kenai Fjords Tours   This is the dominant tour operator, with the most daily sailings and choices of destination. The main part of the operation uses 90- to 150-passenger vessels, some of which have forward-facing seats, like an airplane's. They're professionally staffed, but when the ships are crowded, the experience can be impersonal. The captain provides the commentary instead of a ranger. However, the same company also owns **Mariah Tours,** which operates 16-passenger vessels. Their trips are more spontaneous and go farther; the downside is that the smaller boats are less stable in the waves.

Most of the large Kenai Fjords vessels call on a lodge the company owns on Fox Island, in Resurrection Bay. It sits on the long cobble beach of Sunny Cove, where painter Rockwell Kent lived in seclusion with his son in 1918 and 1919 and produced the art that made him famous, as well as his classic book *Wilderness: A Journal of Quiet Adventure in Alaska* (Wesleyan University Press). It is an inspiring spot. The lodge itself stands on a narrow strip of land between the beach and a pond, which visitors overlook from large wooden decks. Boats stop for lunch of grilled salmon or a family-style dinner, and some passengers spend the night. An overnight package on the island costs $329 per person, with the day cruise and meals included. Half-day sea-kayaking paddles from the island are offered for day-trippers or overnight guests: $79 to $89 per person as an add-on for overnighters; or $149 to $169, including a Resurrection Bay tour boat ride, for day-trippers.

At the Seward small boat harbor. © **800/478-8068** or 907/224-8068 in Seward, or 907/276-6249 in Anchorage. www.kenaifjords.com.

Major Marine Tours   This company pioneered first-class onboard dining and, at this writing, is the only cruise that brings along a park ranger to assure high-quality commentary, a decisive advantage in my judgment (after all, you're here for the park). Their boats are slower than some of the competitors', so they don't make the long trip to Northwest Glacier; they either head into Aialik Bay to see Holgate Glacier or tour Resurrection Bay around Seward. Instead of bringing sandwiches or stopping for a meal, they serve a buffet of salmon and prime rib on board for $12 per person, $6 for children. The food is surprisingly good. While I like their table-seating arrangement with forward-facing seats, it can be an uncomfortable crush when the boat is crowded. Your seat is assigned, so there's no need to rush aboard or try to stake out your spot.

411 W. Fourth Ave., Anchorage. © **800/764-7300** or 907/274-7300 in Anchorage, or 907/224-8030 in Seward. www.majormarine.com.

SEA KAYAKING

The fjords are calm yet rugged, intricate, and full of wildlife and soaring vistas. It's hard to imagine a better place for a sea-kayaking expedition. They also are extremely remote and very rainy, however, so a trip there is a poor choice for your very first outing. Experienced cold water paddlers can rent kayaks and explore on their own, using the park service cabins for shelter (see above under "Accommodations & Camping"). **Sunny Cove Sea Kayaking** (p. 260) offers a kayaking day trip to Aialik Bay. They take guests out on a small charter boat for a wildlife tour then let them launch and paddle in front of the glacier while the boat stands by. The price for the day trip is $325; expensive, but it is the best of the best. For a visit with time to get more of a feel for the place, spend a couple of days. Sunny Cove's 2-day, 3-night glacier trip costs $849.

EXIT GLACIER

When I visited Italy years ago, I got to the point where I thought I'd scream if I saw another painting of the Madonna. If your trip to Alaska is long, you may start to feel the same way about glaciers. But, although relatively small, Exit Glacier really is unique, and my family—even as jaded lifelong Alaskans—still enjoys visits there. (And I've probably seen even more glaciers than Madonnas.)

You can walk close to Exit Glacier, see its brittle texture, and feel the cold, dense spires of ice looming over you. Cold air breathes down on you like air from an open freezer door. Approaching the glacier, you can see the pattern of vegetation reclaiming the land that the melting ice has uncovered, a process well explained by interpretive signs and a nature trail. The National Park Service opened a new nature center here in 2004, adding to the comfort and educational content of a visit (the building is also interesting technically, as it is powered by a hydrogen fuel cell). You can easily spend a couple of hours on a casual, pleasant visit to the glacier (longer if you do a hike). *A safety note:* Big chunks fall off the glacier ever more frequently as Alaska's climate warms. Stay behind the signs or you stand a good chance of being crushed.

The easiest way to get to the glacier is to drive. The clearly marked 9-mile road splits from the Seward Highway 3⅔ miles north of town. In winter, the road is closed to vehicles. If you don't have a car, van service is usually available; check with the park visitor center (p. 267) to see who is currently offering service.

Following the road along the broad bed of the wandering Resurrection River, you'll see in reverse order the succession of vegetation, from mature Sitka spruce and cottonwood trees down to smaller alders and shrubs. It takes time for nature to replace the soil on sterile ground left behind by a receding glacier. As you get closer, watch for signs with dates starting a couple of centuries in the past; they mark the retreat of the glacier through time.

At the end of the road an entrance booth charges a user fee of $5 per vehicle. The new nature center here is open Memorial Day through Labor Day daily 9am to 6pm. Ranger-led nature walks start daily 11am and 3pm on the short trail to the glacier. At the glacier, the trail splits: The steep route goes up along the side of the glacier, and the easy route runs on the flat gravel at its face.

One of the glacier's striking features is a high berm of gravel that fits around its leading edge like a necklace. This is a moraine, the glacier's refuse pile. The glacier gouges out the mountains with its immense, moving weight as new ice flows down from the ice field above and melts here. It carries along the rock and gravel torn from the mountain like a conveyor belt. This moraine is where the conveyor belt ends and the melting ice leaves the debris behind in a big pile. Probably without knowing it, you've seen hundreds of moraines all over North America, where the glaciers of the last ice age piled debris into hills, but this is the most obvious moraine I've ever seen, and it helps you understand how they work.

An all-day hike, 7 miles round-trip, climbs along the right side of the glacier to the Harding Icefield—the glacier gets its name for being an exit from that massive sheet. It's a challenging walk with a 3,000-foot elevation gain, but it's the easiest access I'm aware of to visit an ice field on foot. Because of snow, the trail doesn't open until late June or early July. The ice field itself is cold and dangerous, and there's an emergency shelter maintained by the park service. Don't trek out on the ice unless you know what you're doing. The park service leads hikes up the trail Saturdays in July and August, meeting at 9am in the new nature center.

The Resurrection River Trail, in Chugach National Forest, begins from the road just short of the last bridge to the glacier. It's a pleasant day hike, with lots of wildflowers in the fall, or the start of a long hike deep into the mountains.

7 Cooper Landing: Road Meets River

The little roadside community of Cooper Landing, in a wooded mountain valley along Kenai Lake and the Kenai River, begins about 8 miles west of Tern Lake, where the Sterling Highway splits from the Seward Highway, and continues sporadically along the highway for about 7 miles. (The Sterling runs generally west until Soldotna, where it heads south again.) The frothing upper **Kenai River** is the community's lifeline, each summer bringing the salmon that in turn draw visitors, who fill hotels, restaurants, and the date books of fishing guides. The **Russian River** meets the Kenai at the western edge of the community, where a mad fishing frenzy for the July red salmon season occurs. A ferry takes anglers across the river from the highway. For information on how to fish the Kenai, see "Fishing" in section 8 of this chapter; there's additional information in chapter 2.

If you're not an angler, there's not much here—a couple of operators do rafting trips, some trails start here, and some of the accommodations are suitable for a romantic mountain retreat. Cooper Landing is the starting or ending point for backpacking trips in the Chugach National Forest, described in section 3 of this chapter. Look there also for descriptions of several campgrounds for tents or RVs (there are also RV hookups at the Kenai Princess Lodge, reviewed below).

Cooper Landing has a post office, service stations, and small stores selling fishing gear and essentials, but it's not a real center of commerce. For banking or anything else not directly related to catching a salmon, you'll have to drive to Sterling, 30 miles away to the west, or Soldotna, 14 miles beyond that.

VISITOR INFORMATON   A visitor information booth is at the day use area and boat ramp, known as the landing, on the right side of the highway just after it crosses the source of the Kenai River at Kenai Lake. The area is a good place to stop anyway, with a pleasant boardwalk trail to stretch your legs (a $5 day use fee applies) and a tackle shop and booking service nearby. The information booth is operated by the **Cooper Landing Chamber of Commerce** (© **907/ 595-8888;** www.cooperlandingchamber.com), and is open summer only.

FISHING LODGES

The three lodges below can take care of everything, so you can set up your fishing and other activities with a single phone call. If all you need is a simple but comfortable, inexpensive room, try **The Hutch Bed and Breakfast,** Mile 48.5, Sterling Highway (© **907/595-1270;** www.arctic.net/~hutch).

Gwin's Lodge   This is the town's old original log roadhouse. Standing just a mile east of the Resurrection trail head and the Russian River Campground, Gwin's is convenient and has loads of character. The owner, a dynamic former F-15 fighter pilot, keeps it open 24 hours a day all summer long as the nerve center for the 24-hour fishing on the Russian River. It includes an extensive tackle shop, liquor store, and clothing shops, and the lodge books fishing, rafting, and other activities. Most of the cabins are trailer-sized units with kitchenettes, mock log exteriors, and sleeping lofts with tiny dormers; they're only a few years old. All have shower stalls, not tubs. The least expensive cabins are old log structures and not as plush, but have new carpet and bathroom fixtures.

For over 50 years, the **restaurant** has welcomed many a tired angler or backpacker for a hearty meal; after an exhausting day spent outdoors, it's hard for anyone, including me, to be objective about food. Choices in the seven-table dining room range from burgers to steaks and seafood. Meals generally are well above the greasy spoon tradition of such places. Both the restaurant and bar are open around the clock in summer.

14865 (Mile 52) Sterling Hwy., Cooper Landing, AK 99572. © **907/595-1266.** Fax 907/595-1681. www. gwinslodge.com. 13 cabins. High season $114–$174 double; low season $59–$89 per unit; $10 each additional person age 3 or older. DISC, MC, V. **Amenities:** Restaurant; bar; fishing rentals; activity desk. *In room:* Coffeemaker, free wireless Internet.

Kenai Princess Lodge ★★★   This is one of the best in the region. Each room in the red-roofed buildings feels like a remote cabin—with balconies overlooking the wooded valley, woodstoves stocked with firewood, and many unique details—yet they're luxurious hotel rooms at a resort with a spa and fine restaurant. There are three classes of rooms with a $15 price difference between each. The middle, premium class, is halfway up the hill, with rooms separated by a divider into two parts, like a real cabin. At the top level the deluxe rooms, highest on the hill, have more of a clean, elegant feel. Bathrooms are surprisingly small in all the rooms. Currently closed off-season, most rooms fill in the summer with Princess cruise ship passengers. The cycle of the ships determines if there are rooms open for independent travelers. The lodge books guided fishing, horseback riding, tours, and other activities, and there are hiking trails nearby. An attractive 35-space RV park with full hookups is on-site, with access to the facilities.

The **Eagle's Crest Restaurant** has a varied and sophisticated menu, with good use of Alaskan seafood, and a light dining room that follows the hotel's generally rustic theme. Dinner main courses are $20 to $30; the lunch menu has the expected items, plus choices such as calamari and some unusual salads, generally under $10. Even if you have no reason to stay in Cooper Landing, consider planning your drive to include a meal here that will be several steps up from highway fare due to the good food and relaxing ambiance of the lodge.

Up Bean Creek Rd. above Cooper Landing (P.O. Box 676), Cooper Landing, AK 99572. © **800/426-0500** or 907/595-1425. Fax 907/595-1424. www.princesslodges.com. 86 units. High season $239–$269 double; low season $159–$189 double. RV sites $30. AE, DC, DISC, MC, V. **Amenities:** Restaurant; bar; exercise room; Jacuzzi; tour desk; coin-op laundry. *In room:* TV, dataport, coffeemaker. Closed Oct–Apr.

Floating the Kenai River

The Kenai is more famous for fishing than rafting, but the area is beautiful and the Kenai Canyon, below Cooper Landing and above Skilak Lake, has frothy water between vertical canyon walls. **Alaska Wildland Adventures**, at the Kenai Riverside Lodge ((C) **800/478-4100** or 907/595-1279), is the most established operator and has a great reputation. They offer a 7-hour float through the canyon for $125 adults, $95 children; and a placid 2½-hour float down the upper Kenai for $49 adults, $29 children. Their guided fishing is $200 for a full day, including lunch.

Alaska Rivers Co., Mile 50, Cooper Landing ((C) **888/595-1226** or 907/595-1226; www.alaskariverscompany.com), also has been around a while. They offer scenic rafting ($46, children half price), canyon floats ($100), and guided fishing ($160 all day). They rent cabins, too.

Kenai River Sportfishing Lodge/Kenai Riverside Lodge ★★ The compound lies between the highway and the river, but down among the trees it feels like a remote lodge. I'd call the cabins faux rustic—I've never seen real Bush cabins with smooth walls, wainscoting, and bright rag rugs, but these trim places still feel like the outdoorsy real thing, with no TVs or phones. The plumbing is in a central bathhouse. The location is the real advantage: Whitewater rafting rides and fishing floats leave right from the riverfront. The lodge also possesses a scarce resource in its coveted guide permits for the hot fishing river section that runs through the Kenai National Wildlife Refuge.

Everything is covered by one price: transportation from Anchorage, meals in a central lodge building, guided salmon fishing or fly-fishing for rainbow trout in drift or power boats, and, on longer visits, halibut fishing (done from boats in salt water). You provide your own booze and fishing license and pay the tip. Many visitors come as part of a "safari" package that takes them to various outdoor activities and sites, such as the Alaska Wildland Adventures safari that's described in chapter 2 on page 42.

Alaska Wildland Adventures, Mile 50.1 Sterling Hwy. (P.O. Box 389), Girdwood, AK 99587-0389. (C) **800/478-4100** or 907/783-2928. www.alaskasportfish.com. 16 cabins. 3-day, 4-night inclusive package $1,850. MC, V. **Amenities:** Restaurant (family style); sauna; river equipment included.

8 Kenai/Soldotna & Sterling: Giant Salmon

These towns resemble the highway frontage development of shopping malls and fast-food franchises on the outskirts of any western U.S. town, but do have a claim to fame: The largest sport-caught king salmon in the world, almost 100 pounds, came from the Kenai River. The Kenai's kings run so large there's a different trophy class for the river—everywhere else in the state, the Alaska Department of Fish and Game will certify a 50-pounder as a trophy, but on the Kenai it has to be at least 75 pounds. That's because kings in the 60-pound class—with enough wild muscle to fight ferociously for hours—are just too common here. Anglers prepared to pay for a charter will be in their element on the river when the fish are running hot. Catching a big king is not easy or quick, however, and success rates vary greatly year-to-year and week-to-week.

Those not interested in fishing will find less than a day's sightseeing in these towns. Instead, use the towns as a base for the outdoors. Kenai has a strangely beautiful ocean beach and the Kenai River mouth, with exceptional bird-watching during migrations. Beyond the towns, you'll find a wealth of out-door activities, primarily in the lake-dotted **Kenai National Wildlife Refuge,** which has its headquarters in Soldotna. The refuge is covered in the next section.

Kenai came into being with the arrival of the Russians at the mouth of the Kenai River more than 200 years ago, but it came into its own only with the dis-covery of oil on the peninsula in 1957. Today its economy relies on oil, com-mercial fishing, and, to a smaller extent, tourism. Soldotna, a smaller, newer, and less attractive town, is the borough seat and the primary destination for anglers. Sterling is just a wide place in the road—incredibly wide, as a matter of fact (no one is quite able to explain why such a small town needs such a big road).

ESSENTIALS

GETTING THERE   From Anchorage, the drive on the Seward and Sterling highways to Soldotna is 147 miles. Allow 3 hours, without stops: In summer, traffic will slow you down; in winter, speeds are limited by ice and the fear of hitting moose. Kenai is 11 miles from Soldotna on the Kenai Spur Highway, the first major right as you enter Soldotna from the north on the Sterling Highway.

The **Homer Stage Line** (© **907/235-7009** or 907/399-1847; www.homer stageline.com) connects Anchorage, Homer, Seward, and points between with van service. In summer they run to Homer daily from Anchorage and six times a week from Seward, less frequently in winter. The fare from Anchorage to Soldotna is $45 one-way, $85 round-trip. Tickets are for sale in Soldotna at the **Thompson's Corner gift store** at 44224 Sterling Highway (© **907/262-9071**) or in Anchorage at the **Seward Bus Line ticket office** at 3335 Fairbanks St. (© **907/868-3914**).

Kenai receives very frequent flights from Anchorage from **Era Aviation** (© **800/866-8394** or 907/835-2636; www.FlyEra.com).

GETTING AROUND   The area is so spread out that walking most places really isn't possible, and there's no public transportation. Everyone drives. Four car rental companies operate at the Kenai airport: **Hertz, Avis, Budget,** and **Payless.** If you plan only to fish, however, you may not need a car, instead get-ting rides from your guide, your host, or a taxicab. Ask about transportation options when you reserve your rooms. There are several cab companies; try **Alaska Cab** (© **907/283-6000** in Kenai or **907/262-1555** in Soldotna).

VISITOR INFORMATION   The **Soldotna Visitor Information Center,** 44790 Sterling Hwy., Soldotna, AK 99669 (© **907/262-9814** or 907/262-1337; www.SoldotnaChamber.com), is located on the south side of town; drive through the commercial strip and turn right after the Kenai River Bridge. It's open daily in summer from 9am to 7pm; in winter, Monday through Friday from 9am to 5pm. Besides the usual brochures and free maps, they maintain notebooks full of comparative information about lodgings, camping, and other services, and will help you find a room or charter. Anglers should stop in to see the world-record 97-pound King salmon and a 20-pound rainbow trout.

In Kenai, the **Kenai Visitors and Cultural Center** at 11471 Kenai Spur Hwy., Kenai, AK 99611 (© **907/283-1991;** www.visitkenai.com) is an attrac-tion in itself. A museum does a good job of using artifacts to explain the cultures that passed through the Kenai: the Natives, the Russians who settled in 1791, and the later pioneers and oil workers. Look for the "King of Snags," an immense conglomeration of lost fishing lures, rods, and sticks from the bottom of the river. Superb temporary art exhibitions are mounted, too (see below). To get there, follow the Spur Highway past Main Street and look for the large, landscaped building on your left. In summer, admission to the museum portion is $3, free for students through high school; off season, admission is free. They are open summer Monday through Friday from 9am to 7pm, Saturday and Sunday from 10am to 6pm; and off season Monday through Friday from 9am to 5pm.

SPECIAL EVENTS   The Kenai Visitors and Cultural Center (see above) hosts **invitational art shows** each summer, often with a collection of paintings on a single theme, such as wildlife art. Admission is $3 adults, free for minors. **The Kenai River Festival** (✆ 907/260-5449), over the second weekend of June, has food, music, crafts, and games. The **KDLL Art and Music Festival** (✆ 907/283-8433) is a 12-hour outdoor concert around Summer Solstice (June 18, 2005).

In Soldotna, the **Tustumena 200 Sled Dog Race** (✆ 907/262-3270), held in late January, helps kick off the mushing season. **Progress Days** (✆ 907/262-9814), in late July, offers a parade, rodeo, car shows, and other festival events commemorating the completion of a gas pipeline in 1960—that's the area in a nutshell.

In Ninilchik, the **Kenai Peninsula State Fair** (✆ 907/567-3670), south at mile 136 on the Sterling Highway, is Aug 19–21, 2005. There will be a rodeo, music, crafts, games, agricultural and craft exhibits, and other country attractions, plus a few kids' rides. Admission is $7 adults, $5 seniors, $4 children ages 6 to 12.

FAST FACTS: **Kenai & Soldotna**

Banks You will find them on the Kenai Spur Highway in the middle of town; and in Soldotna, on the Sterling Highway commercial strip. In addition, ATMs are in grocery stores all over the area.

Hospital **Central Peninsula General** is in Soldotna at 250 Hospital Place (✆ 907/262-4404); from the Sterling Highway, take Binkley Street to Marydale Avenue.

Internet Access Connect to the Web for free at the **Kenai public library,** 163 Main St. Loop (✆ 907/283-4378), or at the **Soldotna public library,** 235 Binkley St. (✆ 907/262-4227).

Police For nonemergencies in Kenai, call the Kenai Police Department (✆ 907/283-7879); in Soldotna, call the Soldotna Police Department (✆ 907/262-4455); outside city limits, call the Alaska State Troopers (✆ 907/262-4453).

Taxes There's a 5% sales tax in Kenai and Soldotna, and 2% outside city limits.

FISHING

Fishing the Kenai River is the whole point of coming to the area for most visitors. Check at the Soldotna Visitor Information Center (p. 274) for information and regulation booklets. Or contact the **Alaska Department of Fish and Game,** 43961 Kalifornsky Beach Rd., Suite B, Soldotna, AK 99669 (✆ 907/262-9368, or 907/262-2737 for a recorded fishing report; www.alaska.gov/adfg). Serious anglers shouldn't miss that website, which includes daily sonar counts of salmon in the river and information on biology and fishing techniques; navigate through "Sport Fishing" and click on the southcentral region. Licenses are for sale on the site and in virtually any sporting-goods store. Also, read "A Salmon Primer" and "Fishing" in chapter 2.

There are more than two dozen public access points over the 80 miles of the Kenai River. A **guide brochure** with a map is available from the state **Division of Parks,** P.O. Box 1247, Soldotna, AK 99669-1247 (© **907/262-5581;** www .alaskastateparks.org); you also can pick up a copy at one of the visitor centers.

For anglers interested in less competition and more of a wilderness experience, Kenai is a gateway for vast wild lands accessible by air on the west side of Cook Inlet. There you may be able to fish a stream packed with salmon with little competition. Among others, **High Adventure Air** (© **907/262-5237;** www.highadventureair.com) offers guided day trips for $250 to $335 per person.

KINGS   King salmon, the monsters of the river, come in two runs. The early run, which sometimes has been limited to catch-and-release, comes from mid-May to the end of June, peaking in mid-June. On average less plentiful and smaller, in the 20- to 40-pound range, the run did also produce the sport-caught world's record (97 pounds, 4 oz.). The second run comes during the month of July and includes more of the massive fish. Most people fish kings from a boat, fishing specific holes. Boats hold stationary or back slowly down the river; or fishermen drift down river. Your chances from the bank are low; on average, with or without a boat, it takes 29 hours of fishing time to land a king (you'll likely get at least a dozen strikes for every fish that makes it into the boat). With a guide, the average time to land a fish is cut in half, but that still means that if you fish for only one day, chances are good that you'll get skunked. A boat of three anglers on a half-day guided charter has roughly a 50% chance of landing a king between them.

A guided charter averages $125 to $150 for a 6 1/2-hour day trip, $225 to $250 full day. There are dozens of guides. Contact the visitor center in Kenai or Soldotna (p. 274) to get in touch with a guide; also, many hotels and lodges have their own. It's possible to rent a boat, but this is advisable only if you are experienced in boats and stay out of the hazardous, faster flowing parts of the river. The **Sports Den,** at 44176 Sterling Hwy. in Soldotna (© **907/262-7491;** http://alaskasportsden.com), is one charter operator, with river and ocean trips for salmon or halibut, fly-in fishing and hunting, and they also offer lodging packages with large units. I've found them friendly and helpful over the years.

REDS   The area really goes crazy when the red (or sockeye) salmon join the kings in the river, from mid-July to early August. You can fish reds from the bank or from a boat. Reds are plankton eaters; some say they won't strike a lure, some say they do. In the most popular fishing areas, near the confluence of the Russian River or Moose River with the Kenai, regulations allow only the use of flies. Most people around here cast the flies with spinning gear, weighting the line 18 inches from the fly so it bounces along the bottom. Cast upstream from shore and allow the fly to drift down, keeping near the bank. While waiting for a strike, debate whether the fish really attack the flies, or if they get caught when they instinctively move their mouths in an eating motion, which they do in quick-moving water.

SILVERS   Silvers come in two runs. The first, heavier run is from late July through August, and the lighter run arrives in September. They're easiest to catch anchored in a boat, but you can also do well from shore. Lures work well, as does bait of salmon eggs.

OTHER SPECIES Trophy-size rainbow trout and Dolly Varden char also come out of the river. Anglers using light tackle may also enjoy catching pink salmon, which are plentiful in the Kenai during even-numbered years. Most Alaskans turn up their nose at this easy-to-catch 4-pound fish; just smile and keep hauling them in. Fresh, bright pinks taste great over a campfire.

EXPLORING THE TOWNS

Kenai's historic sites, beach walking, and bird-watching can occupy you for much of a day. Start at the visitor and cultural center mentioned above and get a copy of the *Old Town Kenai Walking Map;* follow the numbered markers. Not many of the simple, weathered buildings remain from Kenai's life before oil, but those that do are interesting and lie only a few blocks down Main Street from the center, along the Cook Inlet and Kenai River bluff. There's a cozy coffee shop on the way for a break.

The **Holy Assumption of the Virgin Mary Russian Orthodox Church** is the area's most significant building. The parish was founded in 1845 and the present church was built in 1895. It's a quaint, onion-domed church, brightly kept but with old icons. A donation is requested. Several nearby buildings are interesting for their interlocking log construction and weathered exteriors.

Stop in at **Veronica's Coffeehouse,** in one of the charming old buildings across from the church. It's a good place for a light meal—a vegetarian dish, or a daily special—or to hear a local folk musician.

The bluff nearby overlooks the broad, sandy ocean beach. A dirt path runs down from Alaska Avenue between the apartment building and the houses that contain professional offices (please don't park near here, as an excess of tourists' cars has caused a problem for the apartment building). To drive down, return to the Kenai Spur Highway, turn to the northwest (left), then turn left on South Spruce Street. There's a big parking lot with a $5 fee, which seems strange on the deserted beach until dip-netting season begins—then you will understand why. At a certain point in the summer salmon run, Alaska residents can fish from this beach by scooping up passing fish with long-handled dip-nets. That's also when you can see white beluga whales chasing salmon upriver, sometimes in great numbers. If you just want to watch, the viewpoint from the top of the bluff at Erik Hansen Scout Park, at Cook and Mission avenues, is a prime spot. However, the beach also is a lovely place for a walk. It's easy to imagine the Russians' first arrival. On a calm day the beach sand, the mud flats, and the Inlet's gray, glacial water seem to meld together into one vast shimmering plain. The water is far too cold for swimming.

The mouth of the river and the wetlands of its delta make for fine **bird-watching,** especially during spring and fall migrations. One of the best places to get to the tidal Kenai River Flats is along Bridge Access Road, which branches from the Spur Highway. The state of Alaska has developed viewing areas at each end of the bridge.

A family looking for something to do while one parent is off fishing may enjoy the magnificent **North Peninsula Recreation Area Nikiski Pool** (© **907/776-8472**), 10 miles north of Kenai on the Kenai Spur Road. The facility occupies a large dome and has a 136-foot water slide, mushroom fountains of water, and a raised hot tub from which parents can watch their children play in the pool below. The water slide is open Tuesday through Sunday from 1 to 5pm and from 6 to 9pm in the summer (swimming without the slide opens those days at 7am); the winter hours are complicated, so call for details. Pool admission is $3, or $6 to use the slide and pool. Weekends can be crowded.

WHERE TO STAY

Rates at many hotels are on seasonal schedules with three, four, or even more levels linked to the salmon runs. I've listed the highest and lowest.

Aspen Hotel Soldotna ★★ This small chain of hotels was built in recent years by Alaska businesspeople who found a niche in certain towns for accommodations with high-end amenities in an up-to-date corporate style. In Soldotna, they produced the best rooms in town in a building with high ceilings and a solid feeling of quality, if not much personality. It has the only hotel swimming pool on the whole Kenai Peninsula (small, but with a large spa beside it). Room choices include family suites with bunk beds, privacy between parents and kids, and Playstation video games. Suites with cooking facilities are available, too. All rooms are decked out with lots of amenities, including DVD players and speaker phones. The hotel is behind Arby's on the commercial strip, but the view out the back is of a settling pond and the river.

326 Binkley Cir., Soldotna, AK 99669. ✆ **888/308-7848** or 907/260-7736. Fax 907/260-7786. www.aspen hotelsak.com. 63 units. High season $169 double, $199 suite. Low season $79 double, $99 suite. $10 each additional person over age 17. Rates include continental breakfast. AE, DC, DISC, MC, V. **Amenities:** Pool; exercise room; spa; business center with computers; laundry room. *In room:* TV/DVD, dataport, fridge, coffeemaker, hair dryer, iron, microwave.

Daniels Lake Lodge Bed and Breakfast ★ *Finds* Located on peaceful and sparsely built Daniels Lake, this lovely, relaxing place has a boat and canoe you can rent for trout fishing right out the back door, among the resident ducks. Rooms are comfortable and thoughtfully decorated, with access to a shared kitchen, and the cabins, with kitchens, are remarkable—just right for these 9 acres of woods, with choices for couples or big groups. The gregarious hosts, Jim and Karen Burris, share their Christian faith with guests, and, along with their dog and rabbits, eagerly make friends. It's not a 1-night stopover, but a place to stay for a couple of days of relaxation, closer to the Nikiski Pool and the outlet of the Swanson River Canoe route of the Kenai National Wildlife Refuge than to any town. Smoking is not allowed.

21 miles north of Kenai (P.O. Box 1444), Kenai, AK 99611. ✆ **800/774-5578** or 907/776-5578. www.Daniels LakeLodge.com. 4 units, 4 cabins. High season $95–$130 double, $150–$280 cabin. Extra adult or teen $20, extra child under age 12 $10. 2-night minimum in cabins. Low season $50–$120 any unit. Extra person $15. AE, DISC, MC, V. Deposits by check only. **Amenities:** Jacuzzi; boat or canoe rental; high speed Internet; babysitting; free laundry machines. *In room:* TV.

Great Alaska Adventure Lodge ★★ For anglers, it's the location that counts, and for that this lodge is hard to top, with a third of a mile of river frontage where the Moose and Kenai rivers converge, a hot fishing spot since time immemorial, as an ancient Native site attests. In the evening, the lodge keeps a guide and campfire on the beach so you can keep casting in the midnight sun. The newly remodeled lodge rooms overlooking the river are spacious and have gas fireplaces and private bathrooms. Unfortunately, the site suffers from vehicle noise from the adjacent Sterling Highway. For guests interested in seeing wildlife and the glorious wilderness of the Kenai National Wildlife Refuge, the lodge offers trips to cushy backcountry tent camps. They also arrange day trips and overnights to a camp across Cook Inlet to watch resident brown bear engaging in natural behavior. Check the lodge's website for information on the many tours and wilderness safaris that they offer.

Moose River, 33881 Sterling Hwy., Sterling, AK 99672 (in winter, P.O. Box 2670, Poulsbo, WA 98370). ✆ **800/544-2261** or 907/262-4515. Fax 907/262-8797 in summer, 360/697-7850 in winter. www.greatalaska.com.

25 units. Rates from $175–$249 for a day trip without lodging to $3,795 for a 7-day package. Rates include all meals, guide service, transfers and travel from Anchorage. AE, MC, V. Closed Oct-mid-May.

Harborside Cottages Bed and Breakfast ✦   On a grassy compound at the top of the bluff over the mouth of the Kenai River in Old Town, these little white cottages make the most of a perfect site. The view and quiet can keep you in a peaceful reverie all day. Inside, the cottages are as immaculate as if brand new, each with its own light country decoration. They have either king-size beds or pairs of twin beds. There are no tubs, just shower stalls. The hostess stocks a self-serve breakfast the night before. Outside is a patio with a picnic table and gas barbecue.

813 Riverview Dr. (P.O. Box 942), Kenai, AK 99611. ℂ 888/283-6162 or 907/283-6162. www.harborside cottages.com. 5 cottages. High season $150 double; low season $125 double. Rates include continental breakfast. AE, DISC, MC, V. Closed winter. *In room:* TV, fridge, coffeemaker, iron, microwave.

Log Cabin Inn ✦   Ted and Carol Titus built this log house specifically to be a B&B, but with its huge common room—with a fireplace and towering cathedral ceiling—it feels more like a wilderness lodge. Located off Kalifornsky Beach Road a little south of the bridge in Kenai, the house stands over an active beaver pond with a deck and lots of windows to watch the beavers. The upstairs rooms, which cost $10 more, are well worth it—they're large and airy. A room on the main floor has French doors to a deck over the pond. Several other rooms, in the half basement, are cute but smaller, with country decoration. If you like to stay up late or rise early, the strict 10pm to 7am quiet hours in the house could make the cabins an attractive choice. They are large and comfortable, but authentic, with plank floors, rag rugs, and rough-cut wood walls. Carol serves a full breakfast.

49860 Eider Rd. (P.O. Box 2886), Kenai, AK 99611. ℂ/fax 907/283-3653. www.acsalaska.net/~ted.titus. 9 units, 3 cabins. High season $100–$110 double; low season $80–$100 double. Extra adult $25; extra child under 12 $10. Rates include full breakfast. AE, DISC, MC, V. **Amenities:** Jacuzzi.

CAMPING

Soldotna's appealing **Centennial Park Campground** extends along a long section of the Kenai River bluff among thick spruce and birch trees with ramps down to fishing spots on the river. Although natural in its setting, it has a coffee stand and newspaper vending machine and is next door to the visitor center and close to stores. Turn right on Kalifornsky Beach Road just after the bridge on the Sterling Highway. Camping fees are $11 a night and day use is $5, payable at a manned entrance booth. The park is open May 1 to October 1. There's a dump station, usable for a $10 fee. **Swiftwater Park** is a similar city-operated riverside campground near the Fred Meyer grocery store and Taco Bell as you enter town from the north.

   RV parks are scattered about. The best spot is **Beluga Lookout Lodge and RV Park,** 929 Mission Ave. (ℂ 907/283-5999; belugarv@ptialaska.net) in Kenai's Old Town, at bluff's edge over the inlet and the river's mouth. Full hookups are $20 to $35 a night. They offer bike rentals and charters for salmon and halibut fishing, bear- or beluga-watching.

WHERE TO DINE

Franchise fast-food and burger-steak-seafood places dominate in Kenai and Soldotna. **Paradisos,** at Main Street and Kenai Spur Highway in Kenai (ℂ 907/ 283-2222), is a good multiethnic family restaurant. **Louie's,** in the Uptown Motel at 47 Spur View Dr. (ℂ 907/283-3660), serves good, solid food in a

dining room and bar room that call to mind the den of a maniacal sportsman—
if the animal mounts came to life, you'd be crushed in a stampede.

Charlotte's Bakery, Café, Espresso ★ SANDWICHES   Rich-textured
bread from the bakery anchors the sandwiches, and lettuce from a nearby garden completes the large, filling salads, but the motherly owner doesn't make a
point of that—hers is not a trendy or gimmicky place. Locals fill the big wooden
chairs in the bright dining room because the food is wonderfully flavored, the
service sweetly attentive, and the prices reasonable.

115 S. Willow, Kenai. ℂ 907/283-2777. All items $5–$9. MC, V. Mon–Fri 7am–4pm.

Mykel's ★★STEAK/SEAFOOD   This is a traditional, dark, fine dining
restaurant for a date or an especially relaxing evening. Located in the Soldotna
Inn, near the intersection of the Sterling and Kenai Spur highways, the dining
room, with high-backed booths, is well kept but dated. On my last visit, the
easy-listening violin music got on my nerves, but the food left nothing to be
desired and the service was professional and more than friendly—indeed it was
in a different class than anything else in the area. The dinner menu contains
many familiar beef and chicken dishes, but the restaurant also does local seafood
in creative ways and several nightly specials attempt more adventurous flavors.
Servings are large, so one course is plenty. The lounge has 18 wines by the glass
and many microbrews. At lunchtime there are lots of salads to choose from
besides the expected sandwiches.

35041 Kenai Spur Hwy., Soldotna. ℂ 907/262-4305. Reservations recommended. Lunch $8–$13, dinner
$18–$28. V. High season daily 11am–10pm; low season Tues–Thurs and Sun 11am–9pm, Fri–Sat 11am–10pm,
closed Mon.

Sal's Klondike Diner DINER   It certainly looks corny and touristy from the
outside, but Sal's turns out to be a classic Western highway diner, with huge portions, fast service, and nothing fancy that doesn't have to be. Our sandwiches,
burgers, and halibut fish and chips were just what we wanted for a quick lunch,
and our coffee cups stayed full. The children's menu is good and cheap.

44619 Sterling Hwy., Soldotna. ℂ 907/262-2220. Lunch $4.50–$9; dinner main courses $7–$10. AE, MC, V.
Daily 24 hr.

9 Kenai National Wildlife Refuge

Floating through the Kenai National Wildlife Refuge in a canoe narrows the
world into a circle of green water, spruce, and birch. You can paddle and hike
for days without encountering more than a few other people, your only expense
the cost of your canoe and the vehicle that carried you to the trail head. Out
there with my older son, I once noticed that, other than his voice, the only
sounds I had heard in 2 days were the gurgling of the water and the wind shush-
ing in the birch leaves. You rely on yourself, but your greatest tests are not overly
taxing. Trail a line behind the canoe, and, when you catch a rainbow trout, land
it and make a fire to cook it. Launch your body into the clear, frigid water to
rinse off the sweat on a warm day. Float slowly, watching eagles circle the treetops and puffy clouds drift like ships past your little world.

Most of the western half of the Kenai Peninsula lies within the two million
acres of the refuge—it's almost as large as Yellowstone National Park—and much
of that land is impossibly remote and truly dedicated to the wildlife. The Kenai
River flows through part of the refuge, but the refuge is just a name to the
anglers who pursue its salmon. (Information about fishing and rafting the river

is above, in the Kenai/Soldotna and Cooper Landing sections.) Canoeists will be more interested in the lowlands on the west side, west of the Sterling Highway and north of Kenai and Soldotna. The lakes there are as numerous as the speckles on a trout's back, or at least that's how they appear from the air. From the ground, the region is a maze of lakes connected by trails—more than 70 lakes you can reach on canoe routes stretching more than 150 miles. It's the easiest way to real Alaska wilderness I know.

ESSENTIALS

GETTING THERE   The refuge surrounds much of the land from Cooper Landing at the north to Homer at the south and Cook Inlet to the west. The Sterling Highway and roads that branch from it are the main ways to the lakes, trails, and rivers, and there is no practical way there without a vehicle.

VISITOR INFORMATION   Stop in at the **Kenai National Wildlife Refuge Visitor Center,** Ski Hill Road (P.O. Box 2139), Soldotna, AK 99669 (© **907/ 262-7021;** http://kenai.fws.gov), for guidance before plunging into the wilderness. The U.S. Fish and Wildlife Service, which manages the refuge, exhibits natural history displays here, shows a film each hour in the afternoon in the summer, and maintains a three-mile nature trail. The staff offers advice and sells books and maps that you'll definitely need for a successful backcountry trip. To find the center, turn left just south of the Kenai River Bridge, taking the unpaved road uphill from the building-supply store. It's open in summer Monday through Friday from 8am to 5pm, Saturday and Sunday from 9am to 6pm; winter, Monday through Friday from 8am to 4:30pm, Saturday and Sunday from 10am to 5pm. The website also contains detailed trip-planning information for the canoe routes.

GETTING OUTSIDE
CANOEING

Once known as the Kenai National Moose Range, the refuge's brushy wetlands—rich in willow and birch shoots and pondweeds—are paradise for moose. Moose like to dine while wading. Waterfowl and other birds, beavers, muskrats, and other aquatic animals are common on the lakes. People also must be partly aquatic to explore the lakes, paddling canoes across their surfaces, pushing through lily pad passages between lakes, and frequently hiking in rubber boots between lakes while carrying the canoe and camping gear.

There are two main canoe routes, both reached from Swanson River and Swan Lake roads, north of the Sterling Highway from the town of Sterling. The **Swan Lake Canoe Route** is a 60-mile network of 30 connected lakes. It meets Swan Lake Road twice, allowing a loop of several days, and in between adventurers can penetrate many lakes deep into the wilderness, visiting remote lakes they'll have all to themselves. It's also possible to canoe through to the Moose River and ride its current 17 miles over a long day back to the Sterling Highway.

Getting anywhere requires frequent portages of a quarter mile or so, and more ambitious routes have mile-long portages. You can skip all the portaging, however, by floating 2 days down the **Swanson River** to its mouth, at the Captain Cook State Recreation Area (see below), joining the river at a landing at mile 17.5 of Swanson River Road. The water is slow and easy all the way.

The most challenging of the routes is the **Swanson River Canoe Route,** which connects to the river's headwaters through a series of lakes and longer portages. The route covers 80 miles, including 40 lakes and the river float. Both routes have many dozens of remote campsites—just lakeside areas of cleared ground with fire rings—and most of the portages are well marked and maintained with wooden planking over the wet areas.

You can rent canoes and everything else you need for a wilderness trip near the intersection of Swanson River Road and the Sterling Highway in Sterling, where the Finch family operates **Alaska Canoe & Campground** (© **907/262-2331;** www.alaskacanoetrips.com). Coleman canoes rent for $40 for 24 hours and lighter, fiberglass canoes for a little more. They offer a shuttle service to carry canoeists from one entrance to another so you don't have to double back on your trip and they can give valuable expert advice. They also rent a lot of other outdoor stuff: kayaks, mountain bikes, rafts, etc. Call ahead to check on equipment and to reserve. Their campground is fully equipped, too, a good base where you can return for showers and laundry.

If you go, among your most important tools will be the book *The Kenai Canoe Trails,* by Daniel L. Quick, (Northlite Publishing, $19). This extraordinary guide contains super-detailed maps and directions, and advice on how to plan your trip and fish and camp on your way—I've never seen a trail guide like it.

Guided paddles on the Kenai Canoe routes are available from **Blue Moose Lakeside Lodge** (© **877/256-6673** or 907/262-0669; www.blue-moose.com), but you don't need a guide if you know how to canoe and are prepared for wilderness. I haven't provided detailed driving instructions because you'll need detailed maps to go at all. **Trails Illustrated** produces a good detailed map of the whole area, printed on plastic (see "Fast Facts: Alaska," in chapter 2 for details). A serviceable free map is distributed by the refuge visitor center. There's much more to do in the refuge too, including several upland hiking trails. The refuge visitor center provides guidance and maps.

CAMPING

For car camping away from all the fishing mayhem, the **Captain Cook State Recreation Area** is a lovely and underused 3,460-acre seaside area on Cook Inlet, 25 miles north of Kenai on the North Kenai Road, at the mouth of the Swanson River. There are lots of attractive sites among large birches, trails, beach walking, a canoe landing at the end of the Swanson River Canoe Route, and lake swimming. The State Parks camping fee is $10. **Daniels Lake Lodge,** listed above in section 8 (on Kenai/Soldotna) of this chapter, is nearby.

There are many campgrounds within the refuge, too, some of them lovely, quiet spots on the edge of uninhabited lakes, such as the small **Rainbow Lake** and **Dolly Varden Lake campgrounds,** on Swanson River Road near the start of the canoe routes, and the **Watson Lake** and **Kelly-Peterson Lake campgrounds** on the Sterling Highway between Sterling and Cooper Landing. Get a complete listing from the visitor center. Generally, there is no camping fee.

<hr>

10 Homer & Kachemak Bay: Cosmic Hamlet by the Sea

Homer's leading mystic, the late Brother Asaiah Bates, always maintained that a confluence of metaphysical forces causes a focus of powerful creative energy on this little seaside town. It's hard to argue. Homer is full of creative people: artists, eccentrics, and those who simply contribute to a quirky community in a beautiful place. Indeed, Brother Asaiah may have been the quintessential Homeroid, although perhaps an extreme example, with his gray ponytail, extraordinary openness and generosity, and flowery rhetoric about "the cosmic wheel of life." Homer is full of outspoken, unusual, and even odd individualists—people who

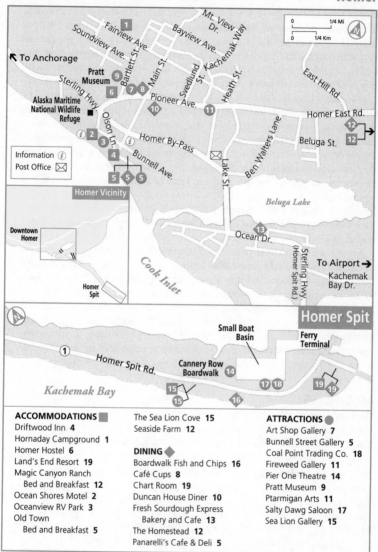

make living in the town almost an act of belief. I can say this because I'm a former Homeroid myself.

The geography of Homer—physical as well as metaphysical—has gathered certain people here the way currents gather driftwood on the town's pebble beaches. Homer is at the end of the road; the nation's paved highway system comes to an abrupt conclusion at the tip of the Homer Spit, almost 5 miles out in the middle of Kachemak Bay, and believers of one kind or another have washed up here for decades. There were the "barefooters," a communal group that eschewed shoes, even in the Alaska winter (Brother Asaiah came with them in the early 1950s). There are the Russian Old Believers, who organize their strictly traditional communities around their objection to Russian Orthodox church reforms made by Peter the Great. There are the former hippies who have become successful commercial fishermen after flocking here in the late 1960s to camp as "spit rats" on the Homer Spit beach. And there are even the current migrants—artists and retired people, fundamentalist preachers and New Age healers, wealthy North Slope oil workers and land-poor settlers with no visible means of support—all people who live here simply because they choose to.

The choice is understandable. Homer lies on the north side of Kachemak Bay, a branch of lower Cook Inlet of extraordinary biological productivity. The halibut fishing, especially, is exceptional. The town has a breathtaking setting on the spit and on a wildflower-covered bench high above the bay. The outdoors, especially on the water and across the bay, contains wonderful opportunities. And the arts community has developed into an attraction of its own. There are several exceptional galleries and the Pratt Museum, which has a national reputation.

You'll be disappointed, however, if you expect a charming little fishing town. Poor community planning has created a town that doesn't live up to its setting— indeed, highway sprawl is in the process of ruining some of it. Homer Spit in summer is a traffic-choked jumble of cheap tourist development and RVs.

Homer began to take its modern form after two events: In the 1950s the Sterling Highway connected it to the rest of the world, and in 1964 the Good Friday earthquake sank the spit, narrowing a much larger piece of land with a small forest into the tendril that now barely stands above the water. If not for constant reinforcement by the federal government, the spit long since would have become an island, and Homer would hardly exist. As long as it survives, however, the town makes the most of that unique finger into the sea. Whether or not it is a cosmic focal point, it certainly is an exceptional launching point to one of the world's great marine recreation areas.

ESSENTIALS

GETTING THERE **By Car** At about 235 miles, Homer is roughly 4½ hours from Anchorage by car, if you don't stop at any of the interesting or beautiful places along the way. It's a scenic drive. If you take a rental car, drive it both ways, as the drop-off fees from Anchorage to Homer are high.

By Bus **Homer Stage Line** (© **907/235-7009** or 907/399-1847; www. homerstageline.com) runs to Anchorage and back daily during the summer, less frequently the rest of the year, and six times weekly to Seward. The Anchorage-Homer fare is $55 one-way, $100 round-trip. Tickets are for sale at **Quicky Mart,** 1242 Ocean Dr., in Homer (© **907/235-2252**). In Anchorage, buy tickets at **Seward Bus Line,** 3335 Fairbanks St. (© **907/868-3914**).

By Air **Era Aviation** (© **800/866-8394** or 907/835-2636; www.FlyEra.com) serves Homer from Anchorage several times a day. Small air-taxi operators use Homer as a hub for outlying villages and the outdoors.

By Ferry The **Alaska Marine Highway System** (© **800/642-0066;** www.FerryAlaska.com) connects Homer to Seldovia, Kodiak, and points west along the Alaska Peninsula and Aleutian Archipelago, and to Seward and Valdez to the east, with the ferry *Tustumena.* The run to Kodiak takes 9½ hours and costs $63 for an adult walk-on passenger (children half off). It's a long trip, but a memorable one. A U.S. Fish and Wildlife Service naturalist rides the ferry to present programs and answer questions.

VISITOR INFORMATION The **Homer Chamber of Commerce Visitor Information Center,** 201 Sterling Hwy. (P.O. Box 541), Homer, AK 99603

(*©* **907/235-7740;** www.homeralaska.org), is on the right as you enter town. In summer, staff is on hand Monday through Friday from 9am to 7pm, Saturday and Sunday 10am to 6pm. Besides answering questions and handing out brochures on local businesses and public lands they sell tickets for the halibut derby (p. 286). Winter hours are Monday through Friday from 9am to 5pm.

On the highway as you arrive in town, the **Islands and Oceans Visitor Center** (*©* **907/235-6961;** http://islandsandoceans.org) is the place to stop for information if you plan to go outdoors anywhere in the area, and worth a look even if you don't. The grand new building is a joint project of the Alaska Maritime National Wildlife Refuge and the Kachemak Bay Research Reserve. It has a theater showing a film about the refuge and exhibits about its wildlife and history and is said to be among the three largest refuge visitor centers in the nation. Hours are summer daily from 9am to 6pm, winter Tuesday through Saturday 10am to 4pm. The refuge itself consists of islands off Alaska from the Arctic to near British Columbia. The U.S. Fish and Wildlife Service manages these lands for the benefit of birds and marine mammals, and people rarely set foot on their shores, but rangers in Homer offer bird and beach walks frequently in the summer, and give programs at the center. Call for times.

In season, call the **Kachemak Bay Bird Alert Information Line** (*©* **907/ 235-7337**) to find out about recent sightings and upcoming birder events, and to leave news of your own observations. It is operated by the wildlife refuge.

The **Kachemak Bay State Park District Office,** mile 168.5 on the Sterling Hwy., 4 miles from town (*©* **907/235-7024;** www.alaskastateparks.org), can help answer questions about planning a trip to the trails and beaches across Kachemak Bay from Homer and give advice on renting remote cabins (although you make the reservation through the Anchorage office—see "State Parks Cabin Reservations," in section 1 of this chapter). Depending on staffing, the office should be open Monday through Friday from 9am to 5pm.

GETTING AROUND   The best way to get to and around Homer is by car. If you didn't bring one, you can rent a car at the airport from **Hertz** (*©* **800/ 654-3131** or 907/235-0734; www.hertz.com) or one of three local firms. Taxis are available from **CHUX Cab** (*©* **907/235-CHUX**), among others.

For strong riders, a bike is a good way around town. You do have to dodge traffic in places downtown, but a trail parallels the road for the 5 miles of the spit. Some excellent mountain-biking routes are mentioned below. **Homer Saw and Cycle,** 1532 Ocean Dr. (*©* **907/235-8406;** homersaw@xyz.net), rents mountain bikes, street bikes, kid's bikes, and trailers. Bike rentals start at $15 for a half day. The shop keeps track of trail conditions and is a good source of advice. It is open Monday through Friday from 9am to 5:30pm, Saturday from 11am to 5pm. They rent as well from Land's End Resort at the end of the spit, open every day. It's wise to reserve bikes a day or two ahead, especially if an outing depends on getting one.

SPECIAL EVENTS   Homer's **Winter Carnival** (*©* **907/235-7740**), in mid-February, is a big community event, a small-town celebration with a beer-making contest, parade, and snow-sculpture competition, among other highlights.

The **Kachemak Bay Shorebird Festival** (*©* **907/235-7740;** http://homer alaska.org/shorebird.htm), held in early May, includes guided bird-watching hikes and boat excursions, natural history workshops, art shows and performances, and other events. It's organized by Alaska Maritime National Wildlife Refuge and the Homer Chamber of Commerce to mark the return of the annual migration. **The Kachemak Bay Wooden Boat Festival,** which takes place at the same time as the Shorebird Festival, displays handmade boats from around the region and presents workshops and films. **Kachemak Kayak Fest** (© 907/235-7740; www.kachemakkayakfest.com) is a 10-day schedule of events, instruction and paddles in late May.

Concert on the Lawn, usually held the last Sunday in July by KBBI public radio (© 907/235-7721), is a day-long outdoor music, craft, and food festival that brings together the whole town.

The **Jackpot Halibut Derby** (© 907/235-7740; http://homerhalibutderby.com), lasting the whole summer, has a top prize that has reached over $48,000 for the biggest fish of the summer, and smaller monthly prizes and tagged fish prizes. Grand prize fish are usually 300 pounds or more. Of course, you must buy your $10 ticket before you fish.

FAST FACTS: **Homer**

Bank Three banks with ATMs, including **Wells Fargo,** are on the Sterling Highway near Heath Street.

Hospital **South Peninsula Hospital** is at the top of Bartlett Street, off Pioneer Avenue. (© 907/235-8101).

Internet Access **Tech Connect Computer Sales and Services,** 432 E. Pioneer Ave., (© 907/235-5248), offers broadband access for $5 an hour.

Police For nonemergencies within the city limits, call the **Homer Police Department** (© 907/235-3150); outside the city, phone the **Alaska State Troopers** (© 907/235-8239). Both have offices located across Pioneer Avenue from the intersection with Heath Street.

Post Office Sterling Highway at Heath Street.

Taxes Sales tax in Homer is 5.5%. Outside the city, you pay 2%.

EXPLORING THE TOWN

The best activities are on the beaches, in the hilltop meadows, and on Kachemak Bay, and the best man-made attractions all somehow relate to that setting. The art inspired by Homer's environment shows in more than a dozen galleries and studios in town, not including those across the bay in Halibut Cove (see below). New shows open all over town on the first Friday of the month, when restaurants hold special evenings and the entire community comes out for an evening of gallery hopping.

A widely distributed brochure lists most of the galleries in town, with a map. Most are close together on Pioneer Avenue. You'll mostly find photography, prints, pottery, fabric, woodwork, and other crafts, since these are small businesses owned by local people trying to make a living. But there is some expensive fine art, too. Among my favorites galleries are **Ptarmigan Arts,** at 471 E. Pioneer Ave. (© 907/235-5345), an artists' co-op showing a cross-section of what the area offers; the **Fireweed Gallery** (© 907/235-3411; www.xyz.net/~homerart), next door to Ptarmigan, with true fine art in an elegant, airy space; and the large, friendly, and well-stocked **Art Shop Gallery** (© 907/235-7076), in the octagonal, cedar-sided building at 202 W. Pioneer Ave.

There are galleries on Homer Spit, too, among the gift shops, food stands, and fishing charters. My favorite there is Gary Lyon's **Sea Lion Gallery,** on the

Central Charters Boardwalk at 4241 Homer Spit Rd. (© **907/235-3400;** www. sealiongallery.com). Lyon's work captures Alaska wildlife in spectacular detail but also transforms his subjects with a distinctively dreamy vision. His gallery is a tiny jewel box of valuable works.

Bunnell Street Gallery ★★   This nonprofit gallery, located in a perfect space in an old hardware store near Bishop's Beach at the lower end of Main Street, is my favorite in Alaska. Unlike most other Alaska galleries, which double as tourist gift shops, Bunnell was made by and for artists, and the experience is noncommercial and often challenging. You may be tempted to become a member of the nonprofit corporation that runs it, for membership comes with a one-of-a-kind plate made by one of the artists. As with all Homer art, the themes of the work tend to be fishy, and the medium and style can be anything. Invitational or juried art shows from beyond the community are mounted every May. The gallery also puts on summer folk and classical music concerts, poetry readings, and films.

106 W. Bunnell Ave. © **907/235-2662.** www.bunnellstreetgallery.org. Summer daily 10am–6pm; winter, Mon–Sat 10am–6pm. Closed Jan.

Norman Lowell Studio & Gallery ★ *Finds*   Lowell built his own huge gallery on his homestead to show his life's work. The immense oils of Alaska landscapes, which are not for sale, hang in a building that counts as one of Alaska's larger art museums. Admission is free, and Lowell or his wife, Libby, often host guests who walk through. Their original 1958 homestead cabin also is a museum, showing pioneer life in Alaska as it was when they settled here. The studio/ gallery sells some of Lowell's paintings, with prices ranging from $750 to $30,000; prints start at $100. They don't take credit cards.

Norman Lowell Dr. © **907/235-7344.** May Mon–Sat 9am–5pm; June–Aug Mon–Sat 9am–7pm, Sun 1–5pm; Sept Mon–Sat 10am–5pm. Closed Oct through Apr. Turn from Sterling Hwy. at mile 160.9 (4½ miles from Anchor Point, about 12 miles from Homer).

Pratt Museum ★★★   The Homer Society of Natural History's museum is as good as any you'll find in a town of this size, and it has achieved a well-deserved national reputation. The Pratt displays art and explains local history, too, but it is strongest in natural history. It helped pioneered technology that allows visitors to watch birds on Gull Island; you can operate the controls in the museum. There is a saltwater aquarium housing local marine life, and if you're curious about all the fishing boats down in the harbor, you can find out about the different types of gear as well as the fish they catch. In the small botanical garden outside you can learn to identify all the local wildflowers, and a forest trail teaches about the area's ecology. There's much more to see, too, including a good gift shop.

3779 Bartlett St. (at Pioneer Ave.). © **907/235-8635.** www.prattmuseum.org. Admission $6 adults, $5.50 seniors, $3 children ages 6–18, $20 family rate. High season daily 10am–6pm; low season Tues–Sun noon–5pm. Closed Jan.

GETTING OUTSIDE

The best **map of the Kachemak Bay area** is produced by Alaska Road and Recreation Maps. Available all over town, it costs around $5, depending on where you buy it.

ON THE HOMER SIDE OF KACHEMAK BAY

TIDE POOLING   Exploring Kachemak Bay's tide pools is the best way to really get to know the sea and meet the strange and wonderful animals that live in it, and it doesn't cost anything but the price of a pair of rubber boots. First, check a tide book, available for free in virtually any local store, or ask a local to check one for you. You need a low tide of -2 or lower, meaning that low water will be at least 2 feet below the normal low, some 25 feet below the high. Extra-low tides expose more of the lower intertidal zone that contains the most interesting creatures. At a -5 tide, you could find octopus and other oddities. Also, the lower the tide, the more time you'll have to look. Keep track of the time: The tide will come in faster than you imagine, and you could get stranded and drown in the cold water.

The best place to go tide pooling right in town is reached from Bishop's Beach Park, near the lower end of Main Street. Walk west on the beach toward the opening of the bay to Cook Inlet. It's at least a half-hour brisk walk to the Coal Point area, where the sand and boulders end. This is where you'll find pools of water left behind by the receding tide, many full of life. Explore patiently and gently—look at the animals and touch them, but always put them back as they were and try not to crush them underfoot. Marine invertebrate identification keys and many other field guides are sold at the Islands and Ocean Visitor Center, above under "Visitor Information," where rangers happily give advice. If you want to keep going, there's usually a sea otter raft offshore about 3 miles down the beach. Just continue walking, keeping your eyes on the water. As always with watching wildlife, binoculars will improve the experience.

HIKING   There are trails on the bench of land above Homer as well as across the bay at Kachemak Bay State Park (see below). The 7-mile **Homestead Trail** is an old wagon road used by Homer's early settlers. The largely informal trail is lovely and peaceful, tunneling through alders, crossing fields of wildflowers, and passing old homestead cabins. From a hilltop meadow you can see all the way to the inlet and the volcanoes beyond. A trail head is at the reservoir on Skyline Drive—drive up West Hill Road from the Sterling Highway, turn right, and follow Skyline, turning left before the pond. A map and guide produced by the Kachemak Heritage Land Trust is available at the visitor center.

DRIVING OR MOUNTAIN BIKING   Several gravel roads around Homer make for exquisite drives or bike rides. Mountain bikers can use the Homestead Trail, too (it is described under "Hiking"). A lovely drive leads out **East End Road,** through seaside pastures, a forest, and the village of Fritz Creek, then follows the bluff line through meadows toward the head of the bay. When the road gets too rough, explore onward on a mountain bike. **Skyline Drive** has extraordinary views of high canyons and Kachemak Bay; drive up East Hill Road just east of Homer. **Homer Saw and Cycle,** the bike shop listed above, under

---

⌢Tips Walk with an Expert

The **Wynn Nature Center,** operated by the nonprofit **Alaska Center for Coastal Studies** (℅ **907-235-6667;** www.akcoastalstudies.org) offers a chance to learn about the ecology of the area and see its birds and wildflowers on an easy walk. The center encompasses 140 acres of spruce forest and wildflower meadow off Skyline Drive, with an 800-foot boardwalk accessible to people with disabilities. It is open daily from 10am to 6pm from mid-June to Labor Day for self-guided walks; guided walks are every 2 hours. Fees are adults $5, seniors $4, under age 18 $3. Call about the weekly programs, including family programs and naturalist lectures.

"Getting Around," can give you many more ideas. The great mountain biking across the bay is described below.

HORSEBACK RIDING   Ranchers have worked around Kachemak Bay for decades. Drive east of town on East End Road and you can see pastures full of cattle overlooking views that anywhere else would be used for resort hotels. Mark Marette guides half-day trail rides here to the head of Kachemak Bay, leading every group himself, as he has since 1986. His business is **Trails End Horse Adventures** (© **907/235-6393**), 11 miles out East End. He charges $20 per hour and he takes all ages and raw beginners.

ON & ACROSS KACHEMAK BAY

Along the south side of the Kachemak Bay, glaciers, fjords, and little wooded islands are arrayed like a smorgasbord before Homer. A quick boat ride puts you there for sea kayaking, mountain biking on unconnected dirt roads, hiking in the mountains, or eating sushi in a top-flight restaurant on pilings. Or gallery hopping, or resting at a remote lodge, or studying at a nature center, or walking the streets of a forgotten fishing village. The far side of the bay has no road link to import the mundane, mass-produced world, but it does have people, and they make the landscape even richer and more enchanting than it would be alone. And underneath the water, there's a wealth of halibut and salmon.

PLANNING AN OUTING   Central Charters, 4241 Homer Spit Rd., Homer, AK 99603, (© **800/478-7847** or 907/235-7847; Fax: 907/235-2895; www.centralcharter.com), is a long-established booking agent that represents businesses for many of the most popular activities, including halibut fishing, water taxis, boat tours to Seldovia and Halibut Cove, and even local theater. They have a ticket office on the right side of the spit as you drive out.

TRANSPORTATION ACROSS THE WATER   Many water taxis operate from Homer to wilderness cabins, kayaking waters, hiking trails, and mountain biking roads accessible from the Jakolof Bay Dock, Seldovia, Halibut Cove, Kachemak Bay State Park, and other remote points. Rates vary little; it's around $55 to get to Kachemak Bay State Park, for example. Water taxis can be booked through Central Charters, mentioned above. **Mako's Water Taxi** (© **907/235-9055;** www.makoswatertaxi.com) has experience and a good reputation. Mako Haggerty also rents sea kayaks and drops them off; with his advice, you can plan a one-way paddle, with the water taxi providing a lift at each end. Karl Stolzfus's **Bay Excursions Water Taxi and Tours** (© **907/235-7525;** www.bayexcursions. com) offers simple transportation, too, but specializes in hosting serious birders. He rents sea kayaks, too.

KACHEMAK BAY STATE PARK   The park comprises much of the land across the water that makes all those views from Homer so spectacular. For around $55 you can be dropped off there after breakfast, walk the beach, hike in those woods, climb the mountains, then meet your boat in time to be back in Homer for dinner and the first other people you've seen all day. This is heaven, as far as I'm concerned.

The park's main office is at the ranger station listed on p. 285. Its center is the summer-only **ranger station** in Halibut Cove Lagoon, where there's a dock and mooring buoys for public use, three public rental cabins over the water, a campsite, and excellent king salmon fishing in mid-June.

The park has about 80 miles of trails, mostly linking at the ranger station; a free trail guide is available there, but you're well advised to get a good map before you leave Homer. The trails generally start at tidewater amid a lush, mossy forest and rise into the craggy mountains—up sharp peaks to a glacier, or, if you don't want to climb, over the hills to the next secluded beach. Bring mosquito repellent and review bear avoidance skills (see "Outdoors Health & Safety," in chapter 2). You can hike to a public rental cabin on secluded China Poot Lake less than 3 miles from the Halibut Cove dock. The park's fifth cabin is on Tutka Bay, off the Halibut Cove trail network. You can also use one of these places as a base for self-guided sea kayaking. Cabin permits are $65 a night and usually must be reserved 6 months in advance (see "State Parks Cabin Reservations," in section 1 of this chapter).

SELDOVIA   This historic fishing village is like Homer without all the cars and people: just a lot of quiet, the lovely ocean waters, and some nice places to stay. It belongs in this outdoor section only because there's nothing at all to do there other than bike, paddle, or fish (you can do nothing there very well, too).

The trip across Kachemak Bay to Seldovia is one of the best parts of going there. For most people, the **Rainbow Tours** (© 907/235-7272; www.rainbow tours.net) daily round-trip is the practical alternative. They leave Homer Harbor at 9am and return from Seldovia Harbor at 5pm. After subtracting the time on the boat, you have 6 hours free in the village—plenty of time for lunch, a bike ride, a kayak tour, or seeing the town. While visitors are in Seldovia, the boat continues on for whale-watching (see "Whale-Watching," below). Round-trip fares to Seldovia are $35 adults, $30 seniors, $20 children; one-way $20 for everyone.

Go sea kayaking in Seldovia with **Kayak'atak** (© 907/234-7425; www.alaska.net/~kayaks). The couple doing the tours, longtime Seldovia residents, take pride in showing off the wildlife and beauty of this little-used area. They charge $120 for a 5-hour tour, including lunch. They also rent kayaks and offer overnight trips.

King salmon are stocked in Seldovia Slough, right in the middle of the town. The run peaks in mid-June, and you can fish from shore. Seldovia also has an edge for halibut anglers, because you start out an hour closer to the **halibut** grounds than anglers at Homer, potentially giving you more time to actually fish. You can find a charter through the **Seldovia Chamber of Commerce** (© 907/234-7803; www.xyz.net/~seldovia).

JAKOLOF BAY   A state-maintained dock opens an area of gentle shorelines and abandoned roads to visitors who seek the wilderness without paying to stay at a wilderness lodge. West of Kachemak Bay State Park and east of Seldovia, the lands have roads, but the roads aren't connected to anything and are used as much by mountain bikers as by anyone else. You can take a water taxi straight to the Jakolof dock. Lodgings are nearby at Across the Bay Tent and Breakfast (p. 297).

There's plenty to do in the area. The waters of Jakolof, Little Jakolof, Kasitsna, and Little Tutka bays, and the tiny Herring Islands, are appealing and protected for sea kayaking. Supreme mountain biking trails lead along the shore and right across the peninsula through forest and meadows for berry picking. The Red Mountain and Rocky River roads are prime routes, different each year depending on wash-outs and intermittent maintenance—that's part of the adventure. A maintained 10-mile road west leads to the charming village of Seldovia, described below.

GULL ISLAND   The island is a rock across the bay from Homer Spit that is a busy bird colony in the summer. It's easy to get to and boats can edge close, as the water is deep all around. You can usually see tufted and horned puffins,

A Day Trip to Halibut Cove

The artists' colony of Halibut Cove sits on either side of a narrow, peaceful channel between a small island and the mainland; the water in this channel is the road. Boardwalks connect the buildings, and stairs reach down to the water from houses perched on pilings over the shore. The post office is on a floating dock. Visitors arrive each afternoon to walk the boardwalks, visit the galleries, and eat at the restaurant, the Saltry. That's a place to sit back on the deck and sip microbrews and eat fresh baked bread, mussels, sushi, and locally grown salads, followed by fresh fish grilled over charcoal.

The classic wooden boat *Danny J* (book through Central Charters at C 800/478-7847 or 907/235-7847; www.centralcharter.com) leaves Homer daily in the summer at noon, brings back day-trippers, and takes over guests to the Saltry Restaurant at 5pm, then brings back the diners later in the evening. The noon trip includes bird-watching at Gull Island. Seating is mostly outdoors, and I wouldn't take the trip in the rain. You also take the *Danny J* if you're spending the night in Halibut Cove. The noon trip is $47 for adults, $40 seniors, $25 children; the dinner trip is $25 for everyone, regardless of age, but to go you must have a dinner reservation at the Saltry (also made at Central Charters). When not everyone will fit on the *Danny J,* the steel *Storm Bird* goes, too. Reservations and fares are identical to those of the *Danny J.*

On an afternoon trip, you can bring lunch or eat at the Saltry, described below, and then explore the **boardwalk** that runs from the restaurant along Ismailof Island past the galleries, boat shops, and houses. There's also a barnyard perched on a flat patch above the water along the boardwalk. Kids, who already will be in heaven, can look at rabbits, pigs, chickens, ponies, and other animals. The summer-only **Halibut Cove's Experience Fine Art Gallery** (C 907/296-2215) is the first building past the farm on the boardwalk, on pilings above the water. The airy room contains works by Halibut Cove artists only.

Farther on, Diana Tillion, who, with her husband, Clem, pioneered the community, opens her **Cove Gallery** (C 907/269-2207) and studio to guests year round. Since the 1950s, she has worked almost exclusively in octopus ink, painstakingly extracted with a hypodermic needle. Trails branch from the boardwalk across the island to broad views of the bay or to the quiet opposite end of the island.

---

black-legged kittiwakes, common murres, red-faced and pelagic cormorants, pigeon guillemots, and glaucous-winged gulls. Tour boats to Halibut Cove or Seldovia may cruise by the island, and if you are taking a water taxi to Halibut Cove Lagoon, ask to take a look on your way.

ACTIVITIES

FISHING   Homer is known for **halibut,** those huge, flat bottom fish, and the harbor is full of charter boats that will take you out for the day for around $180 per person in the high season. Every day, a few people catch fish that are larger than they are, and halibut over 50 pounds are common. Getting out to where the fish are plentiful requires an early start and a long ride to unprotected waters. People who get seasick easily shouldn't go, as the boat wallows on the waves

Tips   Getting Your Fish Home

A typical angler comes back from a halibut charter with around 60 pounds of fish that, when cleaned, will yield 30 pounds of filets. A large serving is less than a pound of halibut. Eat as much fresh as you can, as it will never be better, but be prepared for how you will deal with the rest of your bounty. The typical 30 pounds is worth more than $250 in the grocery store (it's illegal to sell sport-caught fish). If it is properly and quickly frozen, it will retain much of its quality well into the winter; if not, you waste this superb food. If you're lucky enough to catch that much salmon, the problem is even more immediate, as salmon is more sensitive to proper handling. Most fishing towns have a sport processor who can vacuum-pack and flash-freeze your catch for around $1 a pound. The best way to get it home is as checked baggage; the processor can provide sturdy fish boxes and cold packs. If you aren't leaving right away, processors will hold the fish, and many hotels have freezer facilities. If you have to ship it, use an overnight service (expensive) and make sure someone is there to put it in the freezer on the other end. Above all, keep the fish _hard frozen;_ if it thaws, even only partially, refreezing will ruin it (especially salmon). Consider having some of your salmon smoked, making it a ready-to-eat delicacy very welcome as a homecoming gift. Halibut can be smoked, too, but because of its low fat content and delicate flavor and texture it doesn't smoke as well as salmon. In Homer, **Coal Point Trading Co.,** 4306 Homer Spit (© **907/235-3877;** www.welovefish.com), will process, pack, and ship your catch as ordered (including smoking). Ask your charter captain—if you don't want to, you don't ever have touch your fish until you're ready to eat it back home.

during fishing. (Take Dramamine _before_ you set out; if you wait, it probably won't do any good.) Using gear and lines that look strong enough to pick up the boat, you jig the bait (chunks of herring or cod) up and down on the bottom. Halibut aren't wily or acrobatic, and fighting one can be like pulling up a sunken Buick. One good, large operator is **Silver Fox Charters** (© **800/478-8792** or 907/235-8792; www.silverfoxcharters.com).

Half-day charters have less chance of getting way out to the biggest fish, but cost a lot less: $85 on the big boats operated by **Rainbow Tours** (© **907/235-7272;** www.rainbowtours.net). This makes good sense if you are not a fishing fanatic, as a full day halibut fishing is exhausting and can be tedious.

Other charter boats can be booked through Central Charters, listed above under "Planning An Outing," or you can find one on the **Homer Charter Association** website, which has a list and links to many boats, at www.homer charterassociation.com.

Salmon feed in Cook Inlet year-round, not only when they're running in the streams, and Homer anglers pursue them with trolling gear even in the dead of winter. The town has a Winter King Salmon Tournament in March (check with the chamber of commerce). But that's for the hardy and the lucky. Most people fish salmon in summer. Although without as many great road-accessible, streamside fishing spots as found further north, the bay does have some good spots. A small lagoon called the Fishing Hole on the Spit is stocked with terminal run king and silver salmon by the Alaska Department of Fish and Game. Kings are in the lagoon from late May to the end of June. Silvers arrive in mid to late July, peaking in early August and finishing by mid-month. These salmon have nowhere to spawn, so all must be caught (some anglers scorn such "fish-in-a-barrel" fishing). At the end of the runs, snagging is permitted, which is something like mugging salmon and can be a lot of fun, if not something you'll brag about later at the Rod and Gun Club. For salmon fishing in a more natural setting, you can surf cast for silvers from the end of the spit; head over to Halibut Cove Lagoon (see Kachemak Bay State Park, above) or Seldovia, or drive back up the Sterling Highway to the Anchor River, an excellent steelhead trout stream (catch-and-release only), and the other rivers that flow west into Cook Inlet. The **Alaska Department of Fish and Game** maintains a fishing hotline at ℂ **907/ 235-6930.** They're located at 3298 Douglas Place (ℂ **907/235-8191**).

NATURAL HISTORY TOURS   The nonprofit **Center for Alaska Coastal Studies** (ℂ **907/235-6667;** www.akcoastalstudies.org) is dedicated to educating the public about the shore, and interpreting Kachemak Bay for visitors on daily explorations of the Peterson Bay and China Poot Bay area. At low tide they lead guests on a fascinating guided tide-pool walk. The center also has access to lovely woodlands where nature walks visit a Native American archaeological site. Saltwater tanks at the lodge contain creatures from the intertidal zone and microscopes to inspect your finds. It's a relaxed and truly Alaskan outing. They also offer sea kayaking with hiking and overnights. Reserve by calling the center at the number above, or by e-mail to cacs@xyz.net. The day tour is $90 adults, $60 ages 3 to 11. Pack your own lunch or buy a light lunch there; bring footwear suitable for hiking and beach walks and warm clothing for the boat ride.

SEA KAYAKING   Silence fell as the boat pulled away from the beach, leaving us behind with the kayaks and our guide. For the rest of the day my son and I absorbed the water-reflected sunlight and glided past fancifully shaped rocks and resident sea otters around Yukon Island. We explored beaches, picnicked, raced, and discovered tiny bays too small for any other craft. At the end of the day, we had a new friend in our quietly cheerful guide, Alison O'Hara, and discovered that she'd imperceptibly taught us a lot about sea kayaking. O'Hara runs **True North Kayak Adventures** (ℂ **907/235-0708;** www.truenorthkayak.com). Her 8-hour beginner day trips cost $135, including lunch and passage across the bay. Most kayaking day trips in Alaska towns barely get out of the small boat harbor. This trip doesn't feel so tame—it's more like a mini-expedition. They also offer more challenging overnight and multiday trips to remote waters in the area, and a $285 package that includes the day tour, a night in the attractive Hesketh Island Cabins, and a second day of hiking.

Various others offer Kachemak Bay kayak trips. You can choose through Central Charters (p. 291). The protected waters, tiny islands, and remote settlements are fascinating paddling no matter who you go with, or, for experienced paddlers, if you go on your own. Kayakers can take a water taxi across and explore at will, camping or staying in cabins over much of the bay. Check with Kachemak Bay State Park for guidance. **Mako's Water Taxi** (ℂ **907/235-9055;** www.makoswatertaxi.com) offers rides and rents and delivers kayaks. True North Kayak (see the previous paragraph) also rents to experienced paddlers, and rents camping gear. For kayaks expect to pay $65 a day for a double, $45 single.

FLIGHTSEEING & BEAR-VIEWING   There are several good air taxis in Homer, providing access to the very remote areas of the southern Kenai Penin-sula and lower Cook Inlet that you can't easily reach by boat, but **Kachemak Bay Flying Service** (© 907/235-8924; www.alaskaseaplanes.com) is really spe-cial. It offers spectacular scenic flights over the bay and glaciers starting at $130 per person. The personable Bill de Creeft, flying out of Homer since 1967, is experienced enough to qualify as a pioneer aviator, but the real old-timer is his favorite plane, a restored 1929 Travel Air S-6000-B, one of only six remaining examples of the executive aircraft, with mahogany trim and wicker seats. He'll also fly you into backcountry lakes.

Emerald Air Service (© 907/235-6993; www.emeraldairservice.com), oper-ated by de Creeft alumni Ken and Chris Day, specializes in bear-viewing flights using float planes, landing on fresh or salt water and then taking naturalist-guided hikes to see the wildlife. The couple pride themselves on their knowledge and care for the environment. They helped the National Wildlife Federation film an IMAX movie called "Bears," and starred in it along with the title char-acters. The trips last most of a day and cost $450 to $530 per person.

WHALE-WATCHING   Whales can't be counted on to come into Kachemak Bay, but a long-established tour boat operator, **Rainbow Tours** (© 907/235-7272; www.rainbowtours.net), found a few years ago they could be found reli-ably in the waters at the entrance of Cook Inlet and in the Barren Islands. That's a long ride and the waves can be large, so these trips are not a good idea for those who get seasick, but the trip is a good chance to see humpback and orca whales and sometimes minke and fin whales. The trip takes all day, from 9am to 6pm, and includes lunch on board a comfortable, 100-passenger vessel, the *Rainbow Connection,* which also serves the town of Seldovia as a passenger ferry. The fare is $125 adults, $110 seniors, and $85 children.

WHERE TO STAY

Homer has many good B&Bs. The Homer Chamber of Commerce (www.homeralaska.org) has links to a prodigious number of them. In addition to the places I've listed in detail, **The Sea Lion Cove,** above the Sea Lion Gallery on Homer Spit (© 907/235-3400 in summer or 907/235-8767 in winter; www.sealiongallery.com), has two comfortable rooms with kitchens and a deck right over the beach where you can hear the waves roll in at night. **Cranes' Crest Bed and Breakfast,** 59830 Sanford Dr. (© 800/338-2969 or 907/235-2969; www.akms.com/cranes), 5 miles out atop the hillside behind the town, has nest-ing sandhill cranes that wander around like lawn ornaments, and sweeping, cin-ematic views you can sit and watch all day. Up the hill on the other side of town, **A Memorable Experience Bed and Breakfast** (© 800/720-9275 ext. 7374 or 907/235-7374; www.amemorableexperience.com) offers huge rooms done up in extreme cuteness with country decor and teddy bears, and a large cabin, all with a spectacular view and garden setting. The owners also run the Fresh Sourdough Express restaurant and give guests a voucher to eat there.

If you just want good, simple lodgings downtown, you'll find an extraordi-nary value at the clean and friendly **Pioneer Inn,** 244 W. Pioneer Ave. (© 800/782-9655 or 907/235-5670; www.xyz.net/~abc), which offers big, apartment-style units for $99 in summer ($109 in July) with up to four people in the room. Rooms with two twins or a queen bed are $79–$89 in summer.

Driftwood Inn *(Value*   The historic building a block from Bishop's Beach and across from the Bunnell Gallery resembles a lodge or B&B with its large fireplace of rounded beach rock, the hot coffeepot and inexpensive self-serve breakfast in the lobby, and a friendly attitude. There's a cozy feel that's somehow enhanced by sloping floors and old fixtures. Most of the rooms are like Pullman compartments in size and configuration, but they are cute and clean and have some real style. And they're inexpensive. Nine bedrooms share two bathrooms. Larger rooms have more amenities, but not as much charm. The walls are thin, so there's a no-noise policy during evening hours. There's also an appealing 22-site RV park. The inn offers a fish cleaning and freezing facility. Smoking is not allowed.

135 W. Bunnell Ave., Homer, AK 99603. (C) 800-478-8019 or (C)/fax 907/235-8019. www.thedriftwoodinn. com. 20 units, 11 with private bathroom. High season $65–$140 double; low season $45–$78 double. RV sites $26–$29, full hookup. Extra person $10. DISC, MC, V. No smoking. **Amenities:** Coin-op laundry. *In room:* TV.

Land's End Resort ★★★   Traditionally *the* place to stay in Homer, Land's End would be popular no matter what it was like inside because of its location at the tip of Homer Spit, the best spot in Homer and possibly the best spot for a hotel in all of Alaska. It's composed of a line of weathered buildings that fittingly straggle along the beach crest like driftwood logs. Inside, the local owners keep high standards in rooms and public areas decorated with town history and old photographs, nautical memorabilia, and bold colors. The place has a lot of intentional charm. Rooms range from cute ship-like compartments with fold-down Murphy beds to big, two-story affairs. The resort attractions include a real spa in a calming space with a professional massage staff called the Raven's Nest, a tiny moving-water lap pool, bike rentals, and an activities desk. The hotel is near the boat harbor, and you can fish right from the beach in front. The front desk also rents a series of privately owned townhouse condos next door; for groups or couples on extended visits, these are the best accommodations in the region, with stylish furniture, lots of space and light, and a beachfront location second to none. The condos rent for $250 to $350 a night.

The **Chart Room restaurant** makes good use of its wonderful location, looking out over the beach and bay from big windows. There's a casual, relaxing atmosphere in the long, wood-trimmed dining room. The deck outside has glass windshields, making it a warm, satisfying place to sit over coffee on a sunny day. You can watch otters, eagles, and fishing boats while you eat. I've had simply prepared fresh seafood there that couldn't have been better. The extensive appetizer and bar menus offer an inexpensive way to enjoy the atmosphere. Main courses are $16 to $38.

4786 Homer Spit Rd., Homer, AK 99603. (C) 800/478-0400 or 907/235-0400. Fax 907/235-0420. www.lands-end-resort.com. 80 units. High season $125–$192 double; low season $69–$99 double. Extra person $10. AE, DC, DISC, MC, V. **Amenities:** Restaurant; bar; indoor lap pool; exercise room; spa; outdoor Jacuzzi; sauna; tour desk. *In room:* TV, coffeemaker.

Magic Canyon Ranch Bed and Breakfast ★   At the top of a canyon road off East End Road, the Webb family shares its charming home, 74 unspoiled acres, a tree house, and sweeping views with guests, a cat, and a herd of retired llamas. The air is mountain clear and quiet between the high canyon walls—you start to relax as soon as you get out of the car. The Webbs serve sherry in the evening and a full breakfast in the morning. The four rooms, some nestled cozily under the eaves, are decorated in country and Victorian style, with lots of nice details and some family antiques. The house isn't historic by any means, but it feels like it is.

40015 Waterman Rd., Homer, AK 99603. ⓒ/fax **907/235-6077**. http://magiccanyonranch.com. 4 units, 2 with private bathroom. High season $90–$105 double; low season $60–$75 double. Extra adult $25; extra child 12 and under $20. Rates include full breakfast. MC, V. Closed Winter.

Ocean Shores Motel ★ Buildings on a grassy compound overlook Kachemak Bay, with a path leading down to Bishop's Beach, yet the location is right off the Sterling Highway as you enter town, within walking distance of downtown Homer. Rooms are fresh and bright, most with private balconies, refrigerators, and microwaves; four have full kitchens (one rents for only $99). The less expensive rooms lack the views and are older, but are still modern and have cute touches. The place is decorated with photographs and art collected over a family's five generations in Alaska. Smoking is not allowed.

451 Sterling Hwy. no. 1, Homer, AK 99603 ⓒ **800/770-7775** or 907/235-7775. Fax 907/235-8639. www.oceanshoresalaska.com. 32 units. High season $99–$159 double; low season $59–$75 double. Extra person $5. AE, DISC, MC, V. *In room:* TV, dataport, coffeemaker.

Old Town Bed and Breakfast ★ *(Finds* These rooms combine the artiness of the excellent Bunnell Street Gallery downstairs (see "Exploring the Town," earlier) and the funky, historic feel of the old trading post/hardware store that the building used to house. The wood floors undulate with age and settling, and the tall, double-hung windows, looking out at Bishop's Beach, are slightly cockeyed. The antiques, handmade quilts, and wonderful original art fit in as if they have always been there, yet the rooms are comfortable, fresh, and very clean. The rates include a hot breakfast at a charming little cafe downstairs called Panarelli's. The B&B is not a good choice for people who have trouble with stairs.

106–D W. Bunnell, Homer, AK 99603. ⓒ **907/235-7558**. Fax 907/235-9427. www.oldtownbedandbreakfast. com. 3 units, 1 with private bathroom. High season $85 double shared bathroom, $100 private bathroom. Low season $60 double shared bathroom, $75 double private bathroom. Extra person $15. Rates include full breakfast. MC, V. **Amenities:** Self-serve laundry.

Seaside Farm *(Finds* Take a step back in time—all the way to the 1960s. Mairis Kilcher's farm is populated by Morgan horses, cows, chickens, latter-day hippies, and international backpackers, many of whom do chores in exchange for lodging (when chores are needed): 2 hours of work equals a night in the hostel bunks, and 1 hour earns a campsite in the pasture above the bay. Campers have use of an outdoor cooking and washing area, fire pit and barbecue, and autumn raspberry picking. Some of the quaint, unpolished cabins sit in lovely, quiet places; two are right on the water. The farm, its meadows dotted with cottonwood trees, slopes spectacularly to Kachemak Bay. Homer's pioneering and beloved Kilcher family spawned the singer Jewel (rarely seen hereabouts any longer).

40904 Seaside Farm Rd. (5 miles from downtown off East End Rd.), Homer, AK 99603. ⓒ **907/235-7850**. www.xyz.net/~seaside. 4 units, 4 cabins, 12 hostel beds (co-dorms). $50–$65 cabin for 2; $45–$55 private room with shared bathroom; $15 per person hostel bunk; $6 campsite. Extra adult or teen in room or cabin $15, free under age 12. MC, V. No dogs allowed.

CAMPING & HOSTELS

The most popular place to camp in Homer is out on the spit, amid the sand and pebbles. It can be windy and crowded, and toilet facilities are minimal; but waking up on a bright, pebbled beach makes up for much. The fee is $6 for tents, $10 for RVs, payable at a small log cabin on the spit across the road from the fishing hole. The city also operates the more protected **Hornaday Campground** near the hospital: from Pioneer Avenue, take Bartlett Street uphill; turn left on Fairview and right on Campground Road. For information call **Homer Public**

Works at (C) **907/235-3170** (http://publicworks.ci.homer.ak.us/ and click "Parks and Recreation"). Tent campers will find a natural, pastoral setting at Seaside Farm, mentioned above, which also has hostel beds.

More conveniently located hostel rooms are at **Homer Hostel,** 304 W. Pioneer Ave. ((C) **907/235-1463;** www.homerhostel.com), charging $21 a night for beds in gender-separated or co-ed dorms with four to six bunks each, or $46 for private rooms. It's a nice old house with a shared full kitchen, but common areas are small. They also rent bikes and fishing rods and have a grill on the porch guests can use.

If you want hookups for your RV, there are plenty of places to go off the spit, including the Driftwood Inn, above. **Oceanview RV Park,** 455 Sterling Hwy. ((C) **907/235-3951;** www.oceanview-RV.com), has 100 spaces near the downtown area overlooking the water with a trail to the beach. Rates are $29 a night for full hookups, including cable TV and showers.

LODGINGS ACROSS THE BAY

These places to stay are all based across Kachemak Bay from Homer, each in its own remote cove, bay, or village, and each in its own market niche, from family lodgings to luxurious accommodations. It's wise to reserve rooms at any of these places months in advance (the preceding winter isn't too soon). I regret I can't include many more that are also deserving, but you can find more than a dozen listed with links at www.homeralaska.org/lodging.htm, and here are some other standouts: **Sadie Cove Wilderness Lodge** ((C) **888/283-7234** or 907/235-2350; www.sadiecove.com), a *Swiss Family Robinson* collection of weathered wood and boats on the side of a steep fjord with personable hosts offering great food and a sense of adventure and remoteness; the beautiful **Alaska Center for Creative Renewal,** in Halibut Cove ((C) **907/296-2283;** www.centerforcreativerenewal. com), which offers art and spiritual workshops and individual retreats with a commitment to "provide an optimal nurturing atmosphere to inspire personal discoveries"; and, in Seldovia, **Alaska Dancing Eagles B&B and Cabin Rental** ((C) **907/234-7627** in summer or 907/278-0288 in winter; www.dancingeagles. com) a picturesque and relaxing house on the town's historic boardwalk overlooking calm water and, usually, a sea otter.

Across the Bay Tent and Breakfast (C) *Value*   Tony and Mary Jane Lastufka created this unique place, a spot where families can afford to live for a few days in a backwoods paradise, beachcombing by day and feasting on Tony's grilled seafood in the evening. It looks like a summer camp, with large canvas tents on wooden platforms that stand off by themselves on a steep hillside among towering spruce trees. There's a central house for relaxation, evening games, or conversation, an organic garden to produce the food, two outhouses with stained-glass windows, a bathhouse with plumbing, and a forest volleyball court. A long beachfront faces placid Kasitsna Bay—that's where water taxis drop off visitors and where guided sea-kayaking excursions depart ($75 half day, $95 full day per person). Up the stairs to the road, mountain bikes are for rent ($15 half day, $25 full day) to explore the area's network of abandoned logging roads or to pedal to Seldovia. The tents have beds, but you sleep in your own bag. You can save further by cooking your own meals.

On Kasitsna Bay (P.O. Box 81), Seldovia, AK 99663). (C) **907/235-3633.** (winter P.O. Box 112054, Anchorage, AK 99511; (C) **907/345-2571**). www.tentandbreakfastalaska.com. 6 tents. $63 per person with breakfast, $95 with all meals. Half price for children 6–11, free for children 5 and under. MC, V. Closed mid-Sept to Memorial Day.

Kachemak Bay Wilderness Lodge ★★★ I can think of no more idyllic way to become acquainted with Alaska's marine wilderness than by staying at this intimate, luxurious lodge, run for more than 25 years by hospitable and generous Mike and Diane McBride. I only wish it were affordable for more people, because it's a place of unforgettable experiences. The McBrides' meals are legendary, and their four cabins manage to seem rustic while having every comfort; it's easy to pretend you're the only guest. But their site, on China Poot Bay, is what's really special. The lodge sits on an isthmus, a peaceful and lovely setting with excellent tide pooling, kayaking, and good hiking trails nearby. Expert, environmentally conscious guides lead just a few guests at a time for sea kayaking, hiking, wildlife-watching, and learning about nature; guests set the agenda, and everything is included. With a 3-day add-on a lucky few can visit the remote Loonsong Mountain Camp, where Mike and Diane personally guide and cook for just two couples or one family of four at a time in a lodge on its own mountain lake reached by float plane.

China Poot Bay (P.O. Box 956), Homer, AK 99603. ℂ 907/235-8910. Fax 907/235-8911. www.alaska wildernesslodge.com. 5 cabins. $2,800 per person for a 5-day stay. $1,800 Loonsong 3-day add-on. Rates all-inclusive. Mon–Fri package only. No credit cards; checks accepted. Closed Oct 15–May 1. **Amenities:** Hot tub and sauna; boating, kayaking, and all guiding included.

Tutka Bay Wilderness Lodge ★★★ Jon and Nelda Osgood's personalities are reflected in the amazing place they've built—open and enthusiastic, perfectionist and safety conscious, clean-cut but truly Alaskan. On pilings and on a narrow, grassy isthmus by the green water of the Tutka Bay fjord, they've put together what amounts to an upscale hotel in the wilderness, with cabins connected by long boardwalks, a deck large enough for a helicopter to land on, and a kitchen capable of producing gourmet meals. It's quite a feat—the water system alone is a wonder. There's plenty to do: guided tide-pool and forest walks, bird-watching, hiking, berry picking, rowing, fishing from the dock, and other activities around the lodge; you can pay extra for guided fishing or kayaking, bear-viewing flights, and other outdoor experiences that go farther afield.

P.O. Box 960, Homer, AK 99603. ℂ 800/606-3909 or 907/235-3905. Fax 907/235-3909. www.tutkabay lodge.com. 5 cabins. $350–$375 per person per night. Rates include all meals. 2-night minimum stay. MC, V. Closed Oct–Apr. **Amenities:** Sauna; hot tub. *In room:* TV/VCR, stocked fridge, coffeemaker, hair dryer.

WHERE TO DINE

Besides those places listed here, don't miss the **Chart Room** at Land's End, described under "Where to Stay," above. Also, I've heard many good things about a new place I haven't yet had a chance to try: **Fat Olives,** at 27 Olson Lane and the Sterling Highway, next to the visitor center (ℂ **907/235-8488**); it has a wood-fired Italian brick oven for gourmet pizza and sandwiches, and at dinnertime also serves local seafood, beef, and the like. It's under the same ownership as the Homestead, described below, which is a very good sign. Hours are Monday through Saturday 11am to 10pm.

For good local halibut and cod, burgers, and milkshakes in an attractive beachfront dining room, try **Boardwalk Fish and Chips** (ℂ **907/235-7749**), on the boardwalk across from the harbormaster's office on the spit. It's relaxed fast food, but the place is clean and grown-up and serves local beer. **Duncan House Diner** (ℂ **907/235-5344**) downtown at 125 E. Pioneer Ave., is a good, traditional place where you can eat at a counter or in booths. It is open daily 6am to 2pm. **Panarelli's Cafe & Deli,** next to the Bunnell Gallery at 106 W. Bunnell St. (ℂ **907/235-1555**), produces tasty sandwiches, baked goods, and coffee. It is open daily in summer 7am to 6pm and doesn't take credit cards.

Café Cups ★★ SEAFOOD/SANDWICHES   The facade of the yellow house on Pioneer Avenue is unmistakable with its elaborate bas-relief sculpture. The small dining room is a work of art, too, a masterpiece of wood, light, and space. Jennifer Olsen seats guests, and her husband, David, is the chef. As the owners, they've combined a love for good food with small-town practicality: the menu contains many mainstream and inexpensive dishes as well as the more ambitious specials and thoughtfully seasoned seafood. Most of the flavors I experienced were familiar, not experimental, and the portions large. Beer and wine are served.

162 W. Pioneer Ave. ℭ 907/235-8330. Reservations recommended. Lunch $6–$10; dinner main courses $16–$23. MC, V. High season Mon–Sat 11am–10pm; low season Mon–Sat 11am–9pm.

Fresh Sourdough Express Bakery and Cafe *Kids* ★★ BAKERY/CAFE Ebullient Donna and Kevin Maltz's organic eatery is quintessential Homer, starting with its motto: "Food for people and the planet." But there's no New Age dogma here. The Sourdough Express is fun and tasty, even as it grinds its own grain and recycles everything in sight. An inexpensive lunch menu includes many vegetarian choices as well as hearty sandwiches. The evening menu includes many specials, elaborate dishes, including huge portions of local seafood with rich sauces, and, perhaps more remarkably, simple, solid choices, too, for those who don't want to spend a lot (in fact, all the prices are reasonable). This is a great place for a family, as the atmosphere is relaxed and the service warm, and there is a big sandbox and an old van out front where they can play while you wait for your meal. Stop by on the way to a day on the water for a hearty breakfast or to pick up the brown bag lunch you will need for a charter fishing trip. Don't miss dessert from the made-from-scratch bakery.

1316 Ocean Dr. ℭ 907/235-7571. www.freshsourdoughexpress.com. Breakfast $4–$8, lunch $5.50–$10; dinner main courses $7.50–$20. MC, V. High season daily 7am–9pm; Spring and fall daily 8am–3pm. Closed Oct–Mar.

The Homestead ★★★ STEAK/SEAFOOD   The ambience is that of an old-fashioned Alaska roadhouse, in a large log building decorated with contemporary art and lots of summer light. The food is wonderfully satisfying. The seafood is done simply but right, often just grilled to a turn, which is a good call with this wonderfully fresh Alaskan fish. The salads and the side dishes let the chef show more sophistication, and we were impressed. The seafood portions are generous, and if you want a big piece of rare prime rib, go no further. After a day outdoors, it's a warm, exuberant place for dinner, but with polished edges: white table linens, and professional service. The wine list is well selected but not intimidating and mostly in the $22–$28 range. They also have a full bar with local beers on tap.

Mile 8.2, East End Rd. ℭ 907/235-8723. Reservations recommended. Main courses $21–$39. AE, MC, V. Jun–Aug daily 5–10pm; March–May and Sept–Dec Wed–Sat 5–9pm. Closed Jan–Feb.

HOMER NIGHTLIFE

The **Pier One Theatre** (ℭ **907/235-7333;** www.pieronetheatre.org) is a strong community theater group housed in a small, corrugated-metal building on the spit, between the fishing hole and the small boat harbor. Instead of the ubiquitous gold rush melodrama and Robert Service readings, Pier One often presents serious drama, musicals, and comedy—not just schlock. They also produce dance, classical music, and youth theater events during the summer. There's generally something playing Thursday through Sunday nights in the summer. Check the *Homer News* or the website for current listings. They strongly

Hermits on the Homestead

Late in October, the snow was holding back in the clouds like a strong emotion. This was the one time of year when, with a stout four-wheel-drive truck, you could drive in to Ben's cabin. It stood on a small rise amid his hundreds of acres of swampy ground, the only spot where trees could get out of the dampness and grow. The heavy, lovingly peeled logs of the house lay horizontally amid big birch and white spruce trees. Ben had dragged these huge tree trunks from far afield, by himself, when he started his homestead nearly 40 years earlier, so he could keep living trees nearer to his house.

Ben was a private guy. He generously invited us in, offered coffee from the percolator on top of the soapstone woodstove, but it was clear that he wasn't quite sure he remembered how to talk to people—where to look, for example—and he kept mumbling and looking at my feet or the sky. He showed us around the huge rocks he'd dragged in to build a foundation, the cellar where he stored his food. Food tended to walk by each fall—he never had to go far to get his moose, and he shot one of the biggest right on the doorstep. Everything about his home was exactly the way he wanted it, the product of immense effort to make it all with his own hands. I could see how he'd spent his days all these years. But I could only imagine what his nights must have been like—the piles of *Reader's Digest* and *National Geographic* magazines, the insistent silence.

I finally asked Ben why he'd spent his whole adult life so far from other people. Well, he said, he did work construction in the summer for cash. But I knew that was an evasion. How, I asked, did he first end up out here, in the middle of nowhere? What made him want to be off by himself so long ago? Pause—check the shoes, check the sky—well, he said, it seems there was a woman. She chose the other guy.

Years ago, *U.S. News & World Report* did an article about a homesteader on the Kenai Peninsula who was a Vietnam veteran—just one of the many mad hermits from the war who had hidden in the Alaska woods, populating the wilderness with human time bombs. The subject of the story, a well-respected member of his little homesteading community, resented the characterization, and the magazine later paid him to settle his libel suit and printed a retraction. Everyone in the area knew the article was a bunch of baloney; Alaska homesteaders are as varied as people in the city. They aren't all crazed veterans any more than they're all victims of unrequited love, although those make the best stories. What they do have in common is a willingness to invest hard physical labor every day of their lives into the things the rest of us obtain effortlessly by turning a thermostat or a faucet handle.

Alaska's homesteaders came in waves. There were the prospectors from the gold rush who stayed. Then, after World War II, GIs with families looking for broad new opportunities came north and settled more land. The counterculture movement of the 1960s brought yet another group. Federal homesteading laws written to open the Great Plains to agriculture in the 19th century made getting land difficult and required Alaska homesteaders to do a lot of anachronistic, absurd work, such as clearing large tracts for farming that could never occur. The homesteaders had to survey the land, live on it, clear much of it, and then answer any challenges about their accomplishments at a hearing. If they passed the test, they received a patent to up to 160 acres.

The laws allowing homesteading on federal lands in Alaska were all repealed by 1986, but the state government still sometimes provides land to its citizens. The parcels are very remote and smaller than the old federal homesteads, and the rules still don't make it easy—for a homestead, you have to live at least 25 months on the land in a 5-year period, for example. Many families try, only to give up when they learn firsthand of the hardship, privations, and cold.

I know from experience that I want never again to live in a home where the heating is by wood or the water is in jugs. Homesteading isn't like camping. Outdoor skills won't help unless you also know how to repair engines below zero, build houses without power tools, carry all your own water and firewood, and live poor, largely without an income or any of the things money can buy. You have to be willing to bathe rarely, be cold in winter, be eaten alive by mosquitoes in summer, and end up with land that isn't really worth anything.

Many successful homesteading experiences end with growing children. A couple may make it in the wilderness before having children, and kids don't care if they can take a bath, so long as the parents don't mind washing diapers by hand and being far from medical care. But when children get to a certain age, they need to go to school and be around other children. The families often expect to go back to the homestead someday, but they rarely do. Areas that were thriving little communities of neighbors in the 1950s or 1960s now are deserted, perhaps with one hermit left—like my friend Ben. Only about 160,000 acres of Alaska today—out of a total landmass of 365 million acres—show any signs of human habitation. Less than 1% is in private ownership.

My wife's parents homesteaded in the 1950s and 1960s. Her father was a World War II veteran. Today the family still has some acreage, and a treasure trove of great stories—among them the tales of my late father-in-law's feats of strength and endurance, and my wife's memory of playing with dolls as a girl, then looking up to meet the eyes of a bear that had been watching her.

But my favorite is the story of Rose and her lover. They lived in the same area in Northern California where my wife Barbara's parents grew up. Everyone in town knew the story of the red-headed beauty who had an affair with an older man. Rose's parents refused to let her marry him and decreed that the couple couldn't see each other anymore. She entered a convent, and he disappeared, never to be seen in the town again. Many years later, after moving to Alaska, Barbara's parents were boating in Kachemak Bay when they got caught by bad weather on the opposite side of the bay from Homer. On their own in an open boat and looking for shelter, they found a cabin on a remote beach of an otherwise uninhabited island. They were taken in and befriended by the hermit who'd homesteaded there for years. After warming up with coffee, they got to talking about where they'd come from and how they'd ended up in Alaska. When it came time for their host to tell his story, it was about a beautiful young woman he'd loved, named Rose.

recommend making reservations by phone; they can be changed or canceled if necessary. Tickets may also be available at the door.

The landmark **Salty Dawg Saloon** is a small log cabin on the spit with a lighthouse on top. It's the place to swap fish stories after a day on the water.

11 Valdez

Big events have shaped Valdez (val-*deez*). The deepwater port, at the head of a long, dramatic fjord, first developed with the 1898 Klondike gold rush and an ill-fated attempt to establish an alternative route to the gold fields from here. Later, the port and the Richardson Highway, which connected Valdez to the rest of the state, served a key role in supplying materials during World War II. On Good Friday, March 27, 1964, all of that was erased when North America's greatest recorded earthquake occurred under Miners Lake, west of town off a northern fjord of Prince William Sound. It set off an underwater landslide that caused a huge wave to sweep over the waterfront and kill 32 people. The U.S. Army Corps of Engineers moved the town, rebuilding a drab replacement in a safer location that slowly filled with nondescript modern buildings. A printed walking tour available from the visitor center provides the locations of a few buildings that were moved.

The construction of the trans-Alaska pipeline, completed in 1977, brought a new economic boom to Valdez and enduring economic prosperity as tankers came to fill with the oil. Then, on March 24, 1989, on Good Friday 25 years after the earthquake, the tanker *Exxon Valdez,* on its way south, hit the clearly marked Bligh Reef, causing the largest and most environmentally costly oil spill ever in North America. The spill cleanup added another economic boom. More than a decade later, some wildlife populations have recovered and some have not, although visible signs of the spill are difficult to find.

Today, Valdez is a middle American town, driven by industry but turning to the vast resources of Prince William Sound for outdoor recreation. In town you can tour two small museums and take a hike or a river float. The town has made major strides in improving its appearance, especially on the waterfront, but it isn't the sort of historic or charming fishing village that justifies a trip all by itself. Instead, come for the setting—the wildlife, fishing, and sightseeing in the Sound, and the spectacular drive down the Richardson Highway.

Because Valdez lies at the end of a funnel of steep mountains that catches moisture off the ocean, the weather tends to be overcast and rainy in summer and extremely snowy in winter.

ESSENTIALS

GETTING THERE   By Car   The **Richardson Highway** (see section 7 in chapter 9) dramatically crosses Thompson Pass and descends into the narrow valley where Valdez lies. Try to do the trip in daylight, in clear weather, and stop at the Worthington Glacier. This is the only road to Valdez. The drive from Anchorage is 6 hours without stops.

By Bus   Alaska Trails (© **888/600-6001;** www.AlaskaShuttle.com) connects Valdez to Fairbanks in the summer for $94 one-way. Reservations are required, as they won't go without enough people.

By Ferry   The **Alaska Marine Highway System** (© **800/642-0066** or 907/835-4436; www.FerryAlaska.com) connects Valdez, Whittier, and Cordova by ferry. One time-tested way to see the Sound is to put your vehicle on the ferry

Valdez

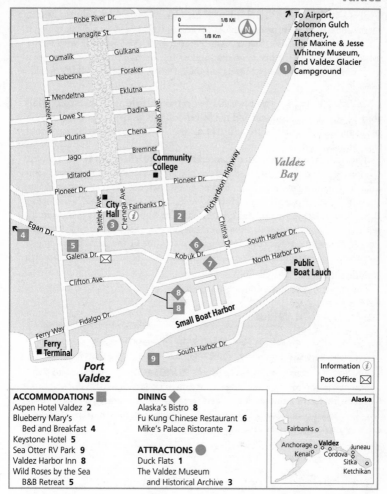

in Whittier for the run to Valdez, then drive north on the Richardson Highway. A forest ranger rides on board to present programs. The current fare is $85 for a car up to 15 feet long and $74 for an adult passenger (children half price). The *Tustumena* comes from Seward roughly once a week. The *Kennicott* runs across the Gulf of Alaska between Valdez and Juneau twice a month in the summer. The 40-hour run costs $114 for adults, $100 to $190 for a cabin. See section 1 in chapter 5 for information about the system.

By Air   **Era Aviation** (© 800/866-8394 or 907/835-2636; www.flyera.com) flies two or three times a day each way between Anchorage and Valdez.

GETTING AROUND   The main part of the town and boat harbor are compact enough to walk, but you will need wheels for the airport, the attractions on Dayville Road, or most of the hiking trails. Rental cars are available at the airport from **Valdez-U-Drive** (© 907/835-4402; www.valdezudrive.com). Taxis are available from **Valdez Yellow Cab** (© 907/835-2500).

VISITOR INFORMATION   The Valdez Convention and Visitors Bureau maintains a **Visitor Information Center** at 200 Fairbanks Dr., a block off Egan Drive (P.O. Box 1603), Valdez, AK 99686 (© **907/835-4636;** www.valdez alaska.org). Pick up the free town map and useful *Vacation Planner.* They're open in summer daily and winter Monday through Friday; the center couldn't provide exact hours.

SPECIAL EVENTS   The town has two **summer fishing derbies.** The **Halibut Derby** runs all summer and the **Silver Salmon Derby** is the entire month of August. Derby tickets are available all over town, including at the harbor boat-rental booth.

The **Last Frontier Theater Conference** (© **907/834-1614;** www.pwscc. edu) brings major playwrights, directors, and actors to the community for seminars and performances in June. Recent guests included writers Arthur Miller, Edward Albee, August Wilson, Horton Foote, and Terrence McNally and actors Anne Meara, Patricia Neal, and John Heard. The public encounters these luminaries in intimate settings; asking questions one-on-one is easy. In more than a decade of operation, the conference has become one of the most important of its kind, and those interested in literature and theater will find it well worth arranging a trip around the event.

FAST FACTS: Valdez

Banks   Two **banks** are on Egan Drive, both with ATMs.

Hospital   **Valdez Community** (© **907/835-2249**) is at 911 Meals Ave.

Internet Access   An **Internet Café** (© **907/835-9000**) is at 321 Egan Dr. You can go online free at **Valdez Consortium Library** (© **907/835-4632**) at 260 Fairbanks St., but you may need to call ahead to reserve a time.

Police   For nonemergencies phone the **Valdez Police Department** at © **907/835-4560,** at 212 Chenega Ave.

Post Office   Galena Drive and Tatitlek Street, 1 block back from Egan Drive.

Taxes   Valdez has no sales tax but does charge a 6% bed tax.

GETTING OUTSIDE
SIGHTSEEING & WILDLIFE TOURS

For most visitors, a daylong ride on a tour boat into the Sound is likely to be the most memorable part of a visit to Valdez. The main tour boat company in town is **Stan Stephens Glacier and Wildlife Cruises** (© **866/867-1297** or 907/835-4731; www.stanstephenscruises.com). The office is on the dock at the end of the small boat harbor near the Valdez Harbor Inn. Stephens has been showing off the Sound and defending it from pollution for decades. After passing through the long fjord of Port Valdez, boats enter an ice-choked bay in front of **Columbia Glacier** on a 6-hour tour that often encounters seals, sea otters, and sea lions, and sometimes whales, for $80 adults. A light lunch is served. Going on to Meares Glacier, farther west, adds four hours to the round trip, but brings you to a glacier you can get a better look at and that may drop ice into the water. That cruise is $119 and includes a lunch of seafood pasta. Prices for children 2 to 11 are half-price on either trip.

SEA KAYAKING & SAILING

Raven Charters, Slip C-25, Valdez Boat Harbor (© **907/835-5863;** www.
alaska.net/~ravenchr), is run by a family who shares its home on a 50-foot boat
with clients to sail and explore the Sound. The wind tends to be light and
changeable, but a sailboat makes a comfortable base for discovering interesting,
isolated places. All-inclusive prices for the whole boat start at $750 per night for
up to four passengers, or $600 for a day charter, with discounts for longer trips.

Right around Valdez, short sea kayaking day trips see wildlife on the Duck
Flats, but that's hardly wilderness, as it's also reached by road and is within sight
of the oil facilities. Day trips to Shoup or Columbia glaciers get you into more
of the beautiful, remote country that makes Prince William Sound so exceptional. **Pangaea Adventures** (© **800/660-9637** or 907/835-8442; www.alaska
summer.com) offers guided sea kayaking from Valdez, or rentals for experienced
paddlers (for whom the Sound is a paradise). They also offer multiday guided
camping trips deeper into the Sound, or, for those who prefer a bed, lodge, and
"mother ship" expeditions, wherein clients paddle by day and stay on board or
in a lodge at night. Check out Pangaea's website for many other options, including "multi-sport" treks in the Sound and Wrangell–St. Elias National park.

FISHING & BOATING

The ocean waters around Valdez are rich in salmon and halibut. It's possible to
fish for salmon from shore. Popular spots include Dayville Road west of the fish
hatchery, the city dock near the ferry dock in town, or even the harbor floats.
Except at the hatchery, you're hoping a fish swims by your lure or bait at the
right moment: there isn't a fresh water destination to concentrate the fish.
Chances and the fishing experience are improved if you get out on the water.
Many small fishing charter boats are available in the boat harbor, or you can rent
your own boat and gear; book either through **Fish Central** (© **888/835-5002**
or 907/835-5002; www.fishcentral.net).

HIKING & MOUNTAIN BIKING

Valdez has a broad selection of good day hikes and an overnight. The visitor center can advise you on choices beyond those I list here. The easiest hike is a pleasant forest and shore walk to **Dock Point,** starting at the east side of the boat
harbor, at the end of North Harbor Drive. It's a peaceful, natural walk close to
town, with boardwalks and overlooks and berries along the way in season.

For a longer hike and perhaps an overnight, the **Shoup Glacier Trail** runs 12
miles west from town along the shore of Port Valdez to a lagoon in front of the
glacier's face. The going is generally flat and there are many places to get down
to the beach, with wild iris and many other flowers. Cool yourself in a waterfall.
Camping is unrestricted, but be sure to bring mosquito repellent and review
bear avoidance techniques (see "Outdoors Health & Safety," p. 30). If you plan
to go all the way, reserve one of the three state parks cabins near the glacier (see
"State Parks Cabin Reservations," in section 1 of this chapter). The trail starts at
the end of West Egan Drive.

The **Solomon Gulch Trail** starts across from the fish hatchery on Dayville
Road (see below) and goes steeply up to Solomon Lake, where locals swim. Be
prepared for bears. Trails off **Mineral Creek Road,** above town off Hanagita
Street, are great for walking, mountain biking, or berry picking, and in winter
there is a fine cross-country skiing trail network. The new **Valdez Goat Trail**
runs from the spectacular Bridal Veil Falls at mile 13.8 of the Richardson Highway for a distance of 2.5 miles on an abandoned roadbed, past some great views.

RAFTING

Keystone Raft and Kayak Adventures (© **800/328-8460** or 907/835-2606; www.alaskawhitewater.com) takes five trips a day 4½ miles down the amazing Keystone Canyon, a virtual corridor of rock with a floor of frothing water, past the crashing tumult of the 900-foot Bridal Veil Falls. The whitewater is rated Class III, meaning it is not too wild for most people, but rafting is not without risk—serious mishaps do sometimes occur. They charge $40 per person. The company also has numerous longer trips, ranging from a day to 10 days, on many of the region's rivers.

HELI-SKIING

Valdez is a magnet for backcountry alpine and extreme skiing and snowboarding thanks to its prodigious snow and limitless steep mountains. A bunch of guide companies offer these trips, operating by helicopter from mid-February to mid-May. One established operator is **Valdez Heli-Ski Guides** (© **907/835-4528;** www.valdezheliskiguides.com). Expect to pay around $750 a day.

EXPLORING THE TOWN

The community college's **Maxine & Jesse Whitney Museum,** at the airport (© **907/834-1615;** www.pwscc.edu), contains a large collection of Alaska Native arts and crafts and animal mounts accumulated by the couple over 50 years. It is open from May to mid-September Monday through Friday from 9am to 6pm; admission is $5.

The Solomon Gulch Hatchery ★   When the pink salmon return from late June to early August, they swarm on the hatchery in a blizzard of fish. The hatchery releases more than 200 million pinks and 2 million silvers (or coho) each year. There is no stream for the salmon to return to, so they try to get back into the hatchery, crowding together in a solid sea of fighting muscle. Seals and birds come in to feed, and you can stand on shore and watch (and smell) the spectacle. Surefire fishing is allowed up the shore on Dayville Road. A construction project has kept the self-guided walking tour off limits; call or ask at the visitor center to find out if they're open when you visit.

On Dayville Rd. on the way to the tanker terminal. © 907/835-1329. Free self-guided tours. Summer daily 9am–9pm.

The Valdez Museum and Historical Archive ★★   The museum contains an exceptional history display that follows the story of the area from early white exploration through the oil spill. Among the most popular exhibits are the shiny old fire engines, dating back to 1886, and the annual summer show of local quilting and fiber crafts. An annex contains a remarkable ⅟₂₀-scale model of how Valdez looked at its old site, before the 1964 earthquake forced the town to move. Using photographs, records, and oldtimers' memories, they have brought that lost city back to life in 400 miniature buildings. It is at 436 S. Hazelet Ave. Admission covers both buildings. Sunday hours were expected to change, but had not been decided at this writing.

217 Egan Dr. © 907/835-2764. www.alaska.net/~vldzmuse. $5 adults, $4.50 over age 65, $4 ages 14–17, free for children under 14. Main museum summer Mon–Sat 9am–6pm, Sun 8am–5pm; winter Mon–Fri 1–5pm, Sat noon–4pm. Annex summer only daily 9am–4pm.

WHERE TO STAY

Aspen Hotel Valdez ★★   Stay here for standard rooms at the quality level you would find in a corporate travel hotel. The home-grown Aspen chain took an old building, gutted and remodeled it, then added rooms and major amenities, including the town's only hotel swimming pool. The Aspen has wide halls and spacious rooms decorated in burgundy, hunter green, and dark wood, with lots of extras, large TVs, and mirrors. A continental breakfast is included in the rate. Ask about discounts you may qualify for.

100 Meals Ave., Valdez, AK 99686. © **800/483-7848** or 907/835-4445. Fax 907/835-2437. www.aspen hotelsak.com. 104 units. High season $129–$149 double; low season $99 double. AE, DISC, DC, MC, V. **Amenities:** Indoor pool; exercise room; spa; business center (computer, printer, copier, dataport); coin-op laundry. *In room:* TV/VCR, dataport, fridge, coffeemaker, hair dryer, iron, microwave.

Best Western Valdez Harbor Inn ★ This newly remodeled hotel commands the best location in town, right on the harbor near the tour boats, although few rooms have views. The rooms are well equipped, set up to make snacks or breakfast, and with DVD players connected to the big TVs to play movies rented at the front desk. A good restaurant on site is described below (Alaska's Bistro) and the lobby contains a barbershop.

100 Harbor Dr. (P.O. Box 468), Valdez, AK 99686. © **888/222-3440** or 907/835-3434. Fax 907/835-2308. www.valdezharborinn.com. 88 units. High season $129–$139 double. Low season $69–$79. Additional person age 12 or older $15. AE, DISC, MC, V. **Amenities:** Restaurant; exercise room; limited room service; coin-op laundry. *In room:* A/C, TV/DVD, dataport, fridge, coffee maker, hairdryer, iron, microwave, Internet access in common room.

Blueberry Mary's Bed and Breakfast ★ *Value* A lucky few get to sleep under Mary Mehlberg's handmade quilts on her feather beds, gaze at the ocean views, bake in the sauna, and breakfast on her blueberry waffles made from wild berries that grow just outside the house. She only takes parties of two or less and sometimes closes for breaks. Those who do stay here get a terrific deal on immaculate, handcrafted rooms at a prime location.

Blueberry Hill Rd., off W. Egan Dr. (P.O. Box 1244), Valdez, AK 99686. © **907/835-5015.** http://home.gci. net/~blueberrymary. 2 units. $90–$100 double, including tax. Rates include full breakfast. No credit cards. Closed Oct–May. **Amenities:** Sauna. *In room:* TV/VCR w/free movies, fridge, coffeemaker, hair dryer, iron, microwave.

Keystone Hotel *Value* This basic budget hotel, made of modular units, was built by Exxon to serve as its offices for the oil-spill cleanup operation but wasn't completed until late summer 1989, so the company occupied it for only about a month. It stood vacant for 5 years before a new owner remodeled it into a hotel, with small rooms that mostly have two twin beds or one double bed, though some have two doubles. Select a room when you check in, as they vary in decor; some have dark paneling, some are more modern.

401 W. Egan Dr. (P.O. Box 2148), Valdez, AK 99686. © **888/835-0665** or 907/835-3851. Fax 907/835-5322. www.alaskan.com/keystonehotel. 104 units. $95 double. Extra person over age 12 $10. Rates include continental breakfast. AE, MC, V. Closed in winter. **Amenities:** Restaurant (outdoor salmon bake); coin-op laundry. *In room:* TV.

Wild Roses by the Sea B&B Retreat ★★ Light pours from bay windows that overlook the water and surrounding woods into large, elegantly appointed rooms with high ceilings, decorated with Asian and contemporary art, and finished in light colors, wood floors, and Berber-style carpets. Best of all is the spacious and private "Ocean View Guesthouse," a downstairs suite with a kitchen, living room, and VCR. The hostess, Rose Fong, prepares elaborate breakfasts in the summer and feeds guests snacks and beverages all day.

620 Fiddlehead Lane (P.O. Box 3396), Valdez, AK 99686. © **907/835-2930.** Fax 907/835-4966. www.alaska bytheseabnb.com. 3 units. Summer $128–$165 double, including full breakfast. Winter $89 double, including continental breakfast. Extra adult $20, child $15. MC, V. *In room:* TV, dataport, hair dryer, iron.

CAMPING

The **Sea Otter RV Park,** P.O. Box 947, Valdez, AK 99686 (© **907/835-2787**), sits on the outside of the boat harbor breakwater, a mosquito-free spot with views and beachfront where you can fish for salmon or watch the harbor sea otters. The RV park has a laundry and other facilities, and charges $25 for full hookups.

The town's **Valdez Glacier Campground** (© **907/835-2282**; www.valdez campgrounds.com) has 101 well-separated sites among alder and cottonwood trees near the airport, but the trees also make it a mosquito haven. They have pit toilets; water comes from a big container. The fee is $10 a night. To get there, take the Richardson Highway to Airport Road.

The best campground in the area is the state's **Blueberry Lake Campground,** 24 miles out of town on the Richardson Highway, just below Thompson Pass. The campground is above the tree line, with mountaintop views and access to limitless alpine hiking. It can be windy and cold. The small lake is stocked with trout. Fifteen well-screened sites are $12 on a self-serve system. There are pit toilets. RVs are welcome, but there are no hook-ups.

WHERE TO DINE

Alaska's Bistro ✸ MEDITERRANEAN/PIZZA   A harborside dining room with big windows creates a proper setting for a restaurant with fine dining aspirations. The food includes lots of local seafood prepared in Northern Italian and similar styles; the chicken, pork, and beef also get more than the typical small town treatment, although you can also get a simple grilled steak. The pizza is European, too, with toppings such as pesto, sun-dried tomatoes, and feta cheese. It's obviously the work of a single mind: at this writing, the chef was even contributing the paintings on the walls as well as his special paella. They have a full bar.

102 N. Harbor Dr. © 907/835-5688. Reservations recommended. Lunch $9–$15, dinner courses $10–$30. AE, MC, V. Daily 11am–1pm and 5–10pm.

Fu Kung Chinese Restaurant ✸ CHINESE   This long-established family restaurant near the harbor serves some of the best meals in town; in Valdez, that's not a huge claim to fame, but this place is good. The interior is clean and pleasant, with a fish tank, warm colors, and plenty of room. The food is plentiful and tasty, especially the gingery bean curd with vegetables, the hot and sour soup, and the kung pao chicken. They feature local seafood in Chinese dishes. The sushi is good, too. Service is fast and attentive. In winter, they often close earlier than the hours listed below.

207 Kobuk Dr. (1 block from the boat harbor). © 907/835-5255. Lunch $6.75–$8.75; dinner main courses $11–$16. MC, V. Daily 11am–11pm.

Mike's Palace Ristorante PIZZA/STEAK/SEAFOOD   This is a good family pizza restaurant, a place where Valdez residents come for a casual evening out. The calzone is good, the service skilled, and everything consistent. It's a warm, cheerful place, perfect after a day on the water—the boat harbor is right across the street. Mike's also has a place in history: Capt. Joseph Hazelwood was waiting for a take-out pizza here when he slipped next door to the Club Bar for his last drink before starting the fateful voyage of the *Exxon Valdez* that hit Bligh Reef. Mike also serves his national Greek cuisine and has a beer and wine license.

201 N. Harbor Dr. © 907/835-2365. Lunch $5–$9; dinner main courses $9–$25. MC, V. Daily 11am–11pm.

12 Cordova: Hidden Treasure

The first time I ever went to Cordova, my companion and I arrived at the Mud-hole Smith Airport in a small plane and happened upon an old guy with a pickup truck who offered to let us ride in back with some boards for the 10 miles to town. The highway led out onto a broad, wetland plain—the largest contiguous wetland in the Western Hemisphere, as it happens. Our guide's voice, studded with profanity, boomed through the back window as he told us proudly about the diversity of the wildlife to be found out there. Then, absolutely bursting with enthusiasm, he leaned on the horn and bellowed, "Look at them f---ing swans!" We looked; trumpeters paddling in the marsh looked back. He would have invited them along to the bar, too, if he'd known how.

Every time I've been to Cordova since, I've been taken under the wings of new friends. Although they usually don't express themselves the same way that first gentleman did, they are just as enthusiastic to show off the amazing natural riches of their little kingdom. Tourists are still something of a novelty here, for Cordova isn't just off the beaten track—it's not on the track at all. There's no road to the rest of the world, and the town is an afterthought on the ferry system. Boosters call their town "Alaska's Hidden Treasure." For once, they're right.

Our family has had some of our happiest times in Cordova, visiting the Childs Glacier and seeing the swans and geese on the delta; hiking into the mountains behind town; boating on the Sound to meet the sea otters, sea lions, eagles, and spawning salmon; hiking and canoeing at a remote lake cabin—and meeting no other people at all. In town, we made new friends whenever we turned around, and received hearty greetings from old friends from previous visits. Leaving on the ferry for Valdez, I've watched Cordova shrinking behind us with a wistful hope that it would never change.

So far, I've gotten my wish. You can feel a bit like an anthropologist discovering a tribe lost to time, for Cordova has the qualities small towns are supposed to have had but lost long ago in America. Walking down First Street, you pass an old-fashioned independent grocery store, the fishermen's union hall, and Steen's gift shop, run by the same family since 1909—no chains or franchises. People leave their keys in the car and their doors unlocked at night. When a friend of mine bought one of the quaint, moss-roofed hillside houses, he didn't receive a key—the simple reason was that the front door didn't have a lock.

The commercial fishermen who power the economy have fought to protect Cordova from change. They pushed for the oil industry to improve its shipping practices years before the 1989 oil spill and then, after the disaster (which hurt Cordova worst of all), lobbied for the money won from Exxon to be spent on the Sound's environment. They have resisted building a road to Cordova, as well. Another faction in town, the merchants and tourism workers, want a road. The debate is hot, and several local elections between the two camps have been decided by a single vote.

This controversy has been going on for 60 years. The town's heyday was in 1911, when the Copper River and Northwestern Railroad opened, carrying copper ore down from the mine at Kennecott; it hit a low when the mine closed in 1938. Since then, boosters have been trying to get a road built on the old rail line, north along the Copper River to Chitina (that fascinating area is covered in chapter 9, under "Wrangell–St. Elias National Park & Kennecott"). The road builders have made it only about 50 miles out of town so far. From Cordova, the

Copper River Highway provides access to the best bird-watching and, in my judgment, the most impressive glacier in Alaska, as well as trails and magnificent vistas and areas to see wildlife. In town, the small boat harbor is a doorway to Prince William Sound.

ESSENTIALS
GETTING THERE By Ferry Cordova is served by ferry from Valdez and Whittier by the **Alaska Marine Highway System** (© **800/642-0066** or 907/424-7333 local dock; www.FerryAlaska.com). It's a spectacular ride, with a good chance of seeing wildlife. The schedule has been inconvenient for visitors, but introduction of a new fast ferry in 2005 should make it easier. At present (prior to the new ferry) the passenger fare from Valdez is $41, while the trip from Whittier is $74; children pay half. It may pay to bring a car, depending on how much time you want to spend out on the road, on the delta, and at the glacier. Taking a vehicle under 15 feet one-way from Valdez to Cordova is $76. See section 1 of chapter 5 for information about the system.

By Air Alaska Airlines (© **800/426-0333**; www.alaskaair.com) flies daily each direction, from Anchorage to the west and Yakutat, Juneau, and Seattle to the southeast, with more flights from Anchorage operated by **Era Aviation** (© **800/866-8394** or 907/835-2636; www.FlyEra.com).

GETTING AROUND You can easily walk around downtown Cordova, but that's not where the most interesting sights are. To get out on the Copper River Highway, you'll need a car, bus, or, if you're vigorous, a bike. Cars are for rent from the **Northern Nights Inn** (p. 315). Taxis are available from **Cordova Taxi** (© **907/424-5151**).

Water taxi and rental of bikes, kayaks, skiffs, canoes, and fishing and camping gear are available at **Cordova Coastal Outfitters,** at the boat harbor below the fishermen's memorial (© **800/357-5145** or 907/424-7424; www.cdvcoastal.com). They're described in full below. To get to remote cabins and fly-in fishing, try **Fishing and Flying** (© **907/424-3324**), located at the airport; or **Cordova Air** (© **907/424-3289**), based on Eyak Lake.

VISITOR INFORMATION A **Cordova Chamber of Commerce Visitor Center** (© **907/424-7260;** www.cordovachamber.com) is at 404 First St., north of Council Avenue (P.O. Box 99, Cordova, AK 99574). They're open Monday through Saturday from 10am to 3pm; summer hours are longer, but vary. Besides the usual information, the center has a 60-minute recorded walking tour that you can listen to as it guides you around town.

The **Cordova Ranger District** of the Chugach National Forest, upstairs in the old white courthouse at 2nd Street and Browning (P.O. Box 280), Cordova, AK 99574 (© **907/424-7661;** www.fs.fed.us/r10/chugach), has displays and provides maps and guide information that's indispensable for planning outdoor activities. The staff will sit down and help you figure out what you want to do.

SPECIAL EVENTS The Cordova Ice Worm Festival is a winter carnival the first full weekend in February; the big ice worm—or, to be precise, ice centipede—marches in a parade. The **Copper River Delta Shorebird Festival** (**907/424-7260;** www.cordovachamber.com) revolves around the coming of dizzying swarms of millions of shorebirds that use the delta and beaches near the town as a migratory stopover in early May. The whole community gets involved to host bird-watchers and put on a full schedule of educational and outdoor activities that lasts 3 days.

Cordova

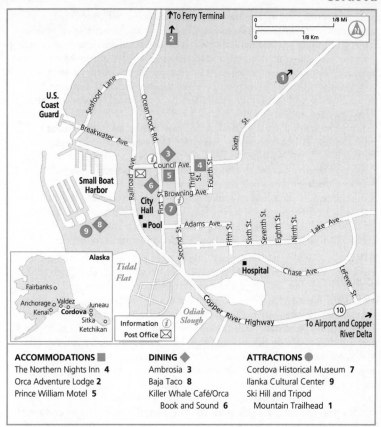

ACCOMMODATIONS ■
The Northern Nights Inn **4**
Orca Adventure Lodge **2**
Prince William Motel **5**

DINING ◆
Ambrosia **3**
Baja Taco **8**
Killer Whale Café/Orca
Book and Sound **6**

ATTRACTIONS ●
Cordova Historical Museum **7**
Ilanka Cultural Center **9**
Ski Hill and Tripod
Mountain Trailhead **1**

FAST FACTS: Cordova

Banks There are two banks on First Street., with **ATMs**.

Hospital **Cordova Community Medical Center** is on Chase Street. (℃ 907/424-8000), off the Copper River Highway near the slough.

Internet Access Find it at the **Cordova Public Library** (℃ 907/424-6667) and at **Laura's Liquor Shoppe** (℃ 907/424-3144), both on First Street.

Police For nonemergency calls, call ℃ 907/424-6100.

Post Office At Railroad Avenue and Council.

Taxes Sales tax is 6%; rooms and car rentals carry an additional 6%.

EXPLORING THE TOWN & HIKING NEAR TOWN

ATTRACTIONS   Cordova mostly is for outdoor activities (covered below), but save some time to wander around town, make discoveries, and meet people, possibly with the help of the **historic walking tour booklet** produced by the historical society, available from the chamber of commerce.

The **Cordova Historical Museum,** at 622 First St. (© **907/424-6665;** www.cordovamuseum.org), is a well-presented one-room display with some valuable artifacts reflecting Cordova's eventful past and a collection of classic Alaskan art. There's a historic lighthouse lens, a Linotype machine, the interior of a fishing boat, and photographs of fishing and historic scenes. The museum is open summer Monday through Saturday from 10am to 6pm, Sunday from 2 to 4pm; winter Tuesday through Friday from 10am to 5pm, Saturday from 1 to 5pm. Recommended donation is $1.

A new museum opened in 2004, after I was able to see it, the **Ilanka Cultural Center,** 110 Nicholoff Way (near the Fishermen's Memorial at the small boat harbor; © **907/424-7903**). The Eyak people set out to create the museum to present their collection of artifacts, photographs, and oral histories, and a fully reconstructed orca whale skeleton, as well as space for artists to work and demonstrate their skills, and a gift shop. Cordova is a center for the Eyak, a small but distinct Native group whose language now has only one speaker left. Hours are summer Monday through Saturday 10am to 4pm, winter Monday through Friday 10am to 4pm. Admission is free, but donations are encouraged.

HIKING   Cordova has more good hiking trails per capita than any place I know. The Cordova Ranger Station can provide you with a free trail-guide booklet with lots of ideas and maps. There are three hikes close to town and more on the Copper River Delta, covered later in the section on the Delta, and at Hartney Bay (ask at the ranger station).

The **Tripod Mountain Trail** begins right from town and climbs 1,255 feet over less than a mile up the first mountain back from the shore, a half-day hike with views that present the Sound and Cordova like a map below you. The trail begins at the foot of the town ski lift, on Sixth Street—take Browning up the hill.

Partway up Tripod Mountain, near the middle drop-off of the ski lift, a 1-mile trail links to the **Crater Lake Trail,** which eventually joins the **Power Creek Trail** on a loop of 12 miles. An easier start for that route is the Power Creek Road—drive it along the north side of Eyak Lake to the end, 7 miles from town. The creek has spawning red salmon in July and attracts a lot of bears; watch, but don't get out of your car if you come upon one. The trail follows the creek through dramatic scenery 4.25 miles to the Power Creek Forest Service cabin, with a great view (reserve through the system described on p. 250).

THE COPPER RIVER DELTA

The delta and its star attraction, the **Childs Glacier,** make an unforgettable day trip by car or tour bus from Cordova, but if you have a couple of days, you can do much more. The backwaters, sloughs, and ponds beg to be explored by canoe. Bird-watchers will especially enjoy paddling here and visiting the boardwalks and blinds set up by the Forest Service. You can raft the rivers. There are excellent hiking trails and mountain-biking routes branching from the road, and Forest Service cabins to stay in.

The delta seems to go on forever, a vast patchwork of marsh, pond, small hills of trees, and the huge, implacable gray river itself. The glacial silt it carries away—some two million tons a day—has built this 700,000-acre wetland. A well-maintained gravel road leads across it, all in Chugach National Forest, and the rangers have done a good job of providing ways and places to enjoy and learn about the area. The road itself is the old bed of the Copper River and Northwestern Railroad. It leads 48 miles to the **Million Dollar Bridge.** Built by

Michael Heney, a magician of a 19th-century railroad builder who also constructed the White Pass and Yukon Route in Skagway, the 200-mile Copper River line was an engineering triumph that brought the mind-boggling wealth of the Kennecott Copper Corporation to ships in Cordova (read more about the mine in section 8 in chapter 9). The bridge over the Copper River was built in a race against time between two surging glaciers in 30-foot-deep, fast-flowing glacial water, in winter. It stood for 56 years, until the 1964 earthquake knocked down one end of one of the spans, driving it into the riverbed. Now your highway dollars are at work repairing that span, although there is nowhere to drive on the other side, only an unmaintained road that soon peters out into a rough trail.

GETTING THERE

BY CAR   Driving gives you the most freedom. The road is gravel, but it's wide and level. Beyond the Million Dollar Bridge, however, it's a rough four-wheel-drive track at best, and if you get stuck you'll be there for a long time. Check at the Forest Service Cordova Ranger Station for the latest news about the road and pick up their road guide.

BY BIKE   Mountain biking the highway is the adventurous way to travel, camping or staying in a Forest Service cabin on the way. The drawbacks are the distances, the delta's strong winds, and a lot of road dust. Of course, you don't have to ride all the way to see lots of birds and wildlife, and there are good mountain biking routes on the delta away from the road. The 3-mile **Saddlebag Glacier Trail,** at mile 25 of the Copper River Highway, leads to a stunning vista of a glacial lake surrounded by rocky peaks. Bikes are for rent from Cordova Coastal Outfitters (see "Out on Prince William Sound," below) for $15 a day.

ALONG THE ROAD

Keep your eyes scanning the wetlands and mountains around you as you drive out the road. The **wildlife** you may see along the way includes black and brown bears, wolf, coyote, moose, and mountain goats. The entire world population of dusky Canada geese nests on the delta, and you're likely to see eagles and trumpeter swans without really looking. The ranger station provides a wildlife-viewing guide and several places to stop along the way designed for bird-watching. The first is a platform with interpretive signs as you leave town, an introduction to the delta; this stretch of the road is fine for bird-watching.

Don't skip the **Alaganik Slough Boardwalk.** Take the 3¼-mile spur road to the right 17 miles out the Copper River Highway; it's marked. The sky here is big and certain while the land is ambivalent—it doesn't know if it wants to be waving grass of green and gold or shallow, shimmering ponds and tendrils of water. The road leads to the start of the 1,000-foot boardwalk. One part leads to a large blind where you can watch the ponds and brush for birds. The other takes you above a large pond that reflects the sun and the colors of the marsh. We were speechless when we stood there one evening at sunset, even in the complete absence of birds. Often in the summer you can see breeding trumpeter swans, ducks, and grebes, and in the spring and fall migrating waterfowl and shorebirds make appearances. Just before the Alaganik boardwalk, the 1-mile Fisherman's Trail is a meandering boardwalk route among streams and ponds.

The highway ends with the area's best attraction, the advancing **Childs Glacier.** This is the most amazing glacier I've ever seen and no one seems to know about it outside Cordova. The advancing wall of ice, 300 feet tall, comes right down to the quarter-mile-wide river, battling the flowing water for control of the land here. The glacier tries to divert the river while the river tries to cut the glacier like a knife, eroding the base and bringing down huge ice chunks. As you sit on the opposite bank, the glacier on the opposite side is too large to see—it completely fills your field of vision, creating an eerie and hypnotic sense of scale. On a warm summer day, you can feel the glacier's thunder as the ice shifts, and see pieces fall off. A chunk the size of a car barely registers, but when an office building–size hunk falls, there's a roar and gray breakers radiate out across the river. Falling glacier pieces have made waves large enough to uproot trees here, not to mention hurl a few fish around—at the Forest Service viewing and picnic area across the river, salmon have been found high up in the trees and boulders in odd places. Several years ago, such a wave injured some visitors, and now the Forest Service warns that anyone who can't run fast should stay in the observation tower. A bit farther from shore there's a campground with pit toilets. A path leads less than a mile to the **Million Dollar Bridge** or drive by on your way out.

ACTIVITIES

CANOEING The delta's canoe routes are little used, leading to remote places where birds and aquatic animals rule. You can launch on Alaganik Slough at a picnic area at mile 22 on the Copper River Highway, paddling placid waters into stunningly beautiful marsh lands. Taking the "Wrong Way" route that starts a couple of miles up the road, you can float several miles of challenging water down to McKinley Lake, stay at the Forest Service cabin, then float downstream again to the slough launch, back at the road. It's ideal overnight, or you could do it in a day, or, as we did, spend an extra day and night at the cabin. The couple who run **Cordova Coastal Outfitters** (see below, under "Out on Prince William Sound") rents canoes for $35 a day and drops them off, and will help you decide what route to take. You can ride out on one of their bicycles and pick up the canoe already at the launch site. They rent camping gear, too. Make sure to get their advice on current conditions before setting out on the water.

FISHING The delta's lakes and streams harbor all five species of Pacific salmon, as well as Dolly Varden char and rainbow and cutthroat trout. The Cordova Ranger Station can offer guidance, or contact the Cordova office of the **Alaska Department of Fish and Game** (© 907/424-3213; www.alaska.gov/adfg, click "Sport Fishing" then the southcentral region). See "Fishing" in chapter 2 for general guidance.

HIKING The Forest Service maintains several trails on the delta. The **Alaganik Slough Boardwalk** and **Saddlebag Glacier Trail** are mentioned on p. 313.

The **Haystack Trail,** starting on the right just past the 19-mile marker on the highway, climbs through mossy rainforest from the delta's floor onto an odd little hill. The glaciers that once covered the delta spared this bedrock outcropping. The trail is steep in places but only .75 mile in length, and it leads to an overlook.

The **McKinley Lake Trail,** at mile 21.6 on the highway, leads 2.5 miles through rainforest vegetation to a lake bearing trout (although we got no bites), and a little further to the overgrown ruins of a gold mine. You can also get there by canoe (see below). There are two Forest Service cabins on the trail, the small McKinley Trail Cabin near the highway and the McKinley Lake Cabin, beautifully situated among big trees above the lake. Each costs $35 a night and can be reserved through the national system described in section 3 of this chapter, on the Chugach National Forest.

You can also join a guided nature hike of a few hours, or all day, with Alaska River Rafting (see "Rafting," directly below).

RAFTING   The immense quantity of water draining the Wrangell–St. Elias Mountains through the Copper River Delta, and the Copper River Highway that provides river access, make this a perfect venue for rafting. **Alaska River Rafting** (© 800/776-1864 or 907/424-7238) is well regarded by locals. Their diverse territory means they can offer quite a range of trips, from easy floating to white water, or even rafting right in front of the Childs Glacier. Trips range in duration from half- to multiday. A 3½-hour trip is $65 adults, $45 ages 6 to 12; all day, with flightseeing, $250. They guide nature hikes, too.

OUT ON PRINCE WILLIAM SOUND

The waters of Prince William Sound around Cordova, although lacking the tidewater glaciers found in the western Sound, are protected and rich in marine life. Sea otters, congregating in rafts of many dozens or even hundreds, don't receive a second glance from locals,. Sea lions can be found predictably, too, and orcas and humpback whales are not out of the ordinary. Bird-watchers can expect harlequin ducks and many other marine birds.

Cordova Coastal Outfitters is a good place to start for any outdoor activities (© 800/357-5145 or 907/424-7424; www.cdvcoastal.com). Andy Craig and Seawan Gehlbach know the equipment, the skills, and the area, and they convey that knowledge with casual enthusiasm. Their booth is on the dock below the Alaska Commercial grocery store, on the south side of the boat harbor. They guide sea kayaking and rent kayaks. If your group isn't up to kayaking, go with them on a guided boat tour to see the scenery and wildlife (prices and length of tour are flexible), or rent a motorboat to operate yourself—you won't believe the sense of freedom you feel clearing the harbor breakwater to explore Orca Inlet and the bays of Hawkins Island, on the far side. Boats rent for $115 to $135 a day, fishing gear extra. The **guided sea-kayaking trip** for beginners lasts 4 hours and costs $75, concentrating on wildlife sightings. A 4-hour trip for the same price paddles on Eyak Lake to see brown bears and great blue herons. Single kayaks rent for $35 a day, doubles $50.

Several vessels are available for fishing charters or day trips to see whales and other wildlife. The chamber of commerce (p. 310) has links to other charter operators on its website, or call them for a referral.

WHERE TO STAY

The Northern Nights Inn ⭐ *(Value)*   These large rooms, some with views and all loaded with amenities, are an almost unreal value. All but one has a full kitchen, and breakfast supplies are provided. They're upstairs in Becky Chapek and Bill Myers's historic 1906 house, a couple of blocks above the main street. The family is charming and will make you feel like a local. Each room has been lovingly renovated, with antiques and quilts. Two rooms are entire apartments.

500 3rd St. (P.O. Box 1564), Cordova, AK 99547. © 907/424-5356. Fax 907/424-3291. 5 units. $60–$95 double. Extra adult $10. Children stay free in parents' room. AE, DISC, MC, V. **Amenities:** Free bike loan; car rental; babysitting; free laundry machines; fish freezing. *In room:* TV/VCR, fridge, coffeemaker, hair dryer, iron, microwave.

Orca Adventure Lodge ⭐   A picturesque old cannery north of town was renovated into comfortable guest rooms with private bathrooms (no phones or TVs, however) while retaining the exterior that made it attractive in the first place. They've got a good chef, too, who produces a lot of seafood. But it's the location and the things you can do here that make the place: on a gravel beach with a dock where sea kayaks, fishing boats, and float planes pick up guests, and where thousands of pink salmon spawn in a small creek. In the late winter helicopters land on the grounds to carry guests to ski in the vast and trackless Chugach Mountains. Guests can use the place as a hotel, paying the regular nightly rates listed below, or come with a package, which includes all meals and outdoor equipment, such as kayaks, bikes, and fishing poles (guiding is extra), for $135 per person per day.

2500 Orca Rd. (P.O. Box 2105) Cordova, AK 99574. ✆ **866/424-ORCA** or 907-424-7249. www.orca adventurelodge.com. 34 units. Summer $125 double, $150 suite; winter $95 double, $110 suite. **Amenities:** Restaurant.

Prince William Motel This is a clean, comfortable motel. The lower rooms look out onto an air shaft, but that may be an advantage if you're trying to get to sleep when it's still light out. Seven recently remodeled rooms have kitchenettes, with a $20 premium. It's not a good choice if you have trouble with stairs. For anglers, the motel provides barbecues and freezer space.

2nd St. and Council (P.O. Box 908), Cordova, AK 99574. ✆ **907/424-3201.** Fax 907/424-2260. www.ak-biz. com/princewilliammotel. 16 units. Summer $100–$120 double. Extra adult $10. Children 11 and under stay free in parent's room. AE, MC, V. **Amenities:** Coin-op laundry; fish freezing; barbecue. *In room:* TV, fridge, coffeemaker, microwave.

WHERE TO DINE

Some of Cordova's best lunches come from **Baja Taco** (✆ **907/424-5599**), with a bus and a building at the boat harbor. The proprietor, who lives in Baja in the winter, specializes in salmon tacos and operates here May through September.

Ambrosia ITALIAN   This is a comfortable family restaurant with an extensive menu, including pizza. It's the kind of place that stays in business in a small town: The food is reliable and the portions large, but nothing too challenging or unusual. They serve beer and wine.

410 First St. ✆ **907/424-7175.** Main courses $9.75–$21. AE, MC, V. Summer daily 4-10pm.

Killer Whale Café CAFE   This is a good breakfast or lunch stop. It's welcoming to kids—they even have a separate play area. The cafe co-exists within a bookstore, **Orca Book and Sound,** but is not associated with it; you walk through the shelves to order at a counter, then carry your meal to lofts up above. (I have to mention the bookstore owner, however, a local institution: Kelly Weaverling was an oil spill hero and the only member of the Green Party to hold elected office in the United States when he was Cordova's mayor a few years ago.) The cafe serves a full breakfast menu in the morning, soups, sandwiches, and daily specials for lunch, fresh baked goods all day, and low-carb items. They also make smoothies and espresso.

In Orca Book and Sound, 507 First St. ✆ **907/424-7733.** All items $3.50–$9.75. No credit cards. Mon–Fri 7am–3pm; Sat 8am–2pm.

8

The Denali National Park Region

Denali (Den-*al*-ee) stands alone among the national parks: It gives regular people easy access to real wilderness, with sweeping tundra vistas, abundant wildlife, and North America's tallest mountain. Other wilderness areas in Alaska may have equally inspiring scenery and even more animals, but Denali is unique because of its accessibility to visitors—and because that accessibility hasn't spoiled the natural experience, as it has at so many other parks.

It's a sad truth that even the largest national parks in the Lower 48 are too small to comprise complete ecosystems. The dream of leaving nature undisturbed is essentially lost in those places, and only through human intervention do the natural systems within the parks stay as close to their primeval state as they do (this is demonstrated by the efforts of Yellowstone rangers to drive bison back within park boundaries so they won't come to harm outside). Millions of cars driving through the parks further interfere with nature. At Rocky Mountain National Park, there's a crossing guard for bighorn sheep. Yosemite Valley and Grand Canyon Village can be choked with cars in summer, yet attempts to get rid of the cars have so far been thwarted.

On the other end of the spectrum, Alaska has many parks with immense, intact ecosystems that have remained unchanged, still existing as they did before the first white contact. More than two-thirds of America's national park acreage is in Alaska, taking in inconceivably huge swaths of land without roads, buildings, or landing strips. They're natural, all right, but almost no one goes there. Some of these parks receive a few hundred visitors a year—only the indigenous people of the surrounding villages and the hardiest and wealthiest outdoors people. Just chartering a plane to get to some of these places can cost as much as most people spend on their entire vacations. With so many people on the earth, wilderness survives only when it's rationed somehow. In most of Alaska, the rationing system is simply the expense and difficulty of getting to the wilds.

At Denali, on the other hand, you can see the heart of the park for little more than it would cost you to visit Yellowstone. And when you get there, it's a pristine natural environment where truly wild animals live in a nearly complete ecosystem pretty much without human interference. A single National Park Service decision makes this possible: The only road through the park is closed to the public. This means that to get into the park, you must ride a bus over a dusty gravel road hour after hour, but it also means that the animals are still there to watch and their behavior remains essentially normal. From the window of the bus, you're likely to see grizzly bears doing what they would be doing even if you weren't there. It may be the only $30 safari in the world.

What's even more unique is that you can get off the bus pretty much whenever you want to, walk across the tundra, out of sight of the road, and be alone in this primeval wilderness.

> ⸧ **Tips** **Denali Changes**
>
> Massive changes to the main Denali National Park visitor area underway for several years should be nearing completion for the 2005 season, but other changes farther inside the park are just getting started. Here are the major changes not finished in time to cover with great certainty in this edition.
>
> - The Eielson Visitor Center, 66 miles within the park, was scheduled to be demolished and rebuilt in a new version four times larger than the original—but at press time it was unclear if the funding was in place for the overhaul. If the project procedes, shuttle buses that formerly turned around at Eielson will probably turn around a few miles short of there, at Stony Overlook. Pricing details were not yet available for that shorter ride at press time.
> - The new Murie Science and Learning Center is due to open by the time this edition is published. It will add an educational resource in the easily accessible, front-country area.
> - The Visitor Center Campus is scheduled for completion during the 2005 season. The campus as a whole will have programs, exhibits, a theater, food courts, a bookstore, parking, and so on.
> - The existing Visitor Access Center will become a transit center, just for boarding buses and getting tickets and permits for the buses, campgrounds, and backcountry.
> - If you've been to Denali before, you will be pleased to see the improvements along the highway in the commercial Glitter Gulch area. New lighting, street lights, and pathways make it more pleasing to the eye and, more important, much safer for pedestrians. A pedestrian bridge over the Nenana River is due to be completed by 2005.

Unfortunately, many Denali visitors never take the opportunity, which normally would cost a lot of money or require a lot of muscle and outdoor skill. Being alone under God's big sky makes many people nervous. Most people have never been entirely away from other people, much less apart from anything people have made. But that's the essence of Alaska—learning, deep down, how big creation is and how small you are, one more mammal on the tundra under the broad sky. At Denali, you can experience that wonder, and then, when you're ready to return to civilization, you can just walk to the road and catch the next bus—they come every half hour.

The Denali experience spreads beyond the park. After all, the park boundary is an artificial line—the

wildlife and the scenery of the Alaska Range don't observe its significance. Several outstanding fly-in wilderness lodges bracket the park in country just as beautiful, where you can explore open country on foot, horseback, or dog sled. To the east, the **Denali Highway** runs through the same extraordinary terrain, with opportunities for hiking over the tundra and canoeing on the lakes managed by the Bureau of Land Management. To the south, **Denali State Park** and the town of **Talkeetna** provide another vantage on Mount McKinley, with the advantage of salmon fishing in the rivers. The construction of comfortable new lodges and a variety of good outdoor guides have helped make Talkeetna a popular alternative gateway to Denali. Even though it's 150 miles from the park entrance by car, Talkeetna is physically closer to the mountain than is the park headquarters.

Visitors often skip the area's other attractions, however, and focus on **Mount McKinley,** which, at 20,320 feet, is the tallest mountain in North America. It is an impressive peak, but you don't need to go to the park to see it—in fact, most people who do go *don't* see it. Summer weather patterns usually sock in the mountain by mid-afternoon, at least as seen from the ground in the park.

Unfortunately, Denali has become a thing people feel they must do, and seeing Mount McKinley is a thing they must do when they visit Denali. Many package tours rush through the park so quickly it becomes a blur outside a window rather than an experience. If they miss the mountain, passengers may wonder why they traveled so far to stay at the ticky-tacky roadside development at the park's entrance and then ride on a bus over a bumpy road. A friend swears she overheard a tourist ask, as she boarded the train leaving Denali, "Why did they put the park way out here in the boondocks?"

The answer is there for you to find, at the bottom of the steps of the shuttle bus door.

1 Planning a Visit to the Park

ORIENTATION

Denali National Park and Preserve is rock and ice-robed in tundra and stands of stunted black spruce, a huge slice of the Alaska Range that stands like a pivot in the center of Alaska. It encompasses 6 million acres, a roughly triangular polygon about 20% larger than Massachusetts. The only park entrance is 237 miles north of Anchorage and 120 miles south of Fairbanks on the paved George Parks Highway or the Alaska Railroad. Although **Mount McKinley** is visible from as far away as Anchorage, you can't see it at all from the park entrance (where you will find the railroad depot and all services accessible by private vehicle), because it's on the far side of the park. A mile north of the park entrance on the Parks Highway, along a cliff-sided canyon of the Nenana River, is **Glitter Gulch,** the local term for the seasonal roadside strip that's home to hotels and restaurants (boosters call it the **Nenana Canyon Area**). Other services are at **Carlo Creek,** 13 miles south on the Parks Highway; at another roadside development 7 miles south of the park entrance; and in the year-round town of **Healy,** 12 miles north of the park entrance. From the park entrance, a road accessible only by shuttle bus leads west 89 miles through the park, past a series of campgrounds and a visitor center, and ends at the **Kantishna district,** a patch of park-surrounded private land with wilderness lodges.

WHEN TO GO & HOW FAR AHEAD TO PLAN

Crowding is relative. Once you're out in the park, Denali is never crowded. The bottleneck created by the shuttle and tour bus system, which prevents vehicles from entering the heart of the park, protects it from overuse. What makes the July to mid-August busy season difficult is getting through that bottleneck from the crowded park entrance into the wilderness. At that time, travelers who just show up at the visitor center without any reservations might have to spend a day or two outside the park before they can get a desirable shuttle bus seat, a campground site, or a backcountry permit.

The flow of visitors varies greatly from year to year. After dropping for four years, it leaped recently. Some years, you needed to make **reservations** by March for a July visit; other years, a few weeks of advance planning has been enough. I can't predict what it will be like in 2005, so to be on the safe side, get your shuttle tickets and campsites as soon as you know the dates of your visit. Lodgings also get tight in July, but are not as critical to the success of your visit. Reserve as far ahead as you can, but don't worry about getting stuck in a dive if you don't get your first choice of rooms or cabins, as there are few really bad places near the park.

Summer residents come to the park beginning in early May, when snow remains; they migrate south again in mid- to late September, when winter is closing in. In the off season, fewer than 200 residents stay in the area, and sled-dog-driving rangers patrol the backcountry. The shuttle bus system doesn't begin operation until Memorial Day, so May visits are inadvisable. The visitor season gets into high gear in mid-June and starts to wind down in mid-August. There are several weeks of relative quiet, reduced prices, and easy reservations at the end of the season, a wonderful time to go to Denali. The weather gets nippy at night, and there can be surprise snowfalls, but rain is less likely, and the trees and tundra turn wonderful colors. By early September, visitors are so few that the park no longer takes telephone reservations. By mid-September, private cars can drive on the park road for a few days—the park service holds a lottery in July to determine who will get that treat.

Another way to avoid the crowds is to book a stay in a **wilderness lodge.** Lodges in Kantishna, listed in section 11 of this chapter, have the right to carry clients to their businesses over the park road in buses and vans, avoiding the bottleneck. Also in section 11 are reviews of remote lodges outside the park's boundaries that you can reach by air.

SAMPLE ITINERARIES

The more you're willing to rough it, the closer you can get to the real Denali. There are no hotels inside the park.

THE HOTEL-STAY ITINERARY

Drive to the park or arrive by train and choose accommodations near the park—shuttles and courtesy vans can get you around. Attend a ranger talk, the *Cabin Nite* dinner-theater show, or go on a short **nature walk** around the park hotel in the evening. Get to bed early, and the next morning take a shuttle bus before 7am into the park to see the terrain and animals, and possibly to get a view of the mountain. By late morning you'll be at Stony Overlook, with a commanding view of McKinley (in good weather). Now ride partway back toward the entrance before getting off the bus at a place of your choosing for a walk and to eat the bag lunch you've brought along with you (pack out all trash, of course), or take one of the **park service guided walks.** After enjoying the wilderness for a few hours, head back on the bus, finishing a long day back at the hotel. Next day try a rafting ride, a flightseeing trip, or another activity near the park entrance before driving onward or reboarding the train.

THE FAMILY CAMPING ITINERARY

Arrive at the park entrance by car with your camping gear and food for a couple of nights. (You can rent the camping gear and car in Anchorage or Fairbanks.) Camp that evening at the **Riley Creek Campground** near the visitor center and enjoy the evening ranger program or a nature walk, or go straight to a campsite farther within the park (either way, you'll need to reserve well ahead).

Denali National Park

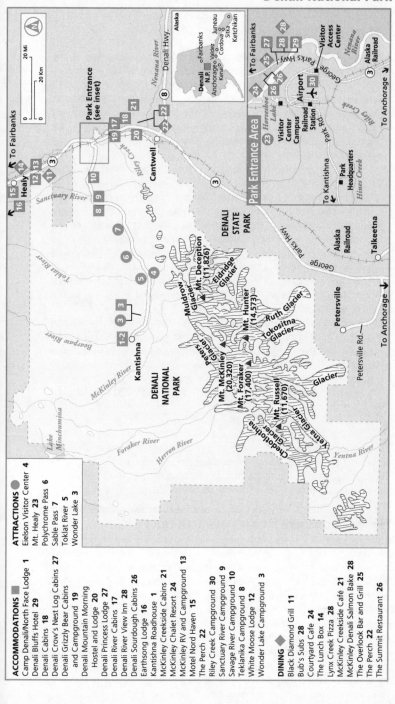

The Denali Highway: The Drivable Denali

From Cantwell, 27 miles south of the Denali National Park entrance, the Denali Highway leads 133 miles east to another tiny village, Paxson, on the Richardson Highway. The little-known road is a lesson in how labels influence people. It runs due east from the Denali National Park border, a natural extension of the park over the Alaska Range, with scenery that's equal to and in some ways more impressive than the park's. Yet without the national park name, the terrain along the Denali Highway is comparatively little used.

The Bureau of Land Management controls the land along the Denali Highway, and it's pretty much open for any recreational activity. The **Tangle Lakes** start a 3-day, 35-mile float trip (for experienced paddlers) to the Richardson Highway and host fine lake canoeing, where you can see an extraordinary variety of waterfowl, including trumpeter swans, sandhill cranes, and loons. Much of the highway passes through high, alpine terrain, with views that extend infinitely and good chances of seeing caribou, moose, and black and grizzly bear. At **Maclaren Pass,** at 4,086 feet, you stand in high Alaska Range terrain of tundra and rock, with views of Maclaren Glacier. The land invites you to walk at least a little way out across it.

Simply driving the road is an experience. If you're traveling to Denali National Park from Anchorage or Fairbanks, consider making a return trip via the Denali Highway and Richardson Highway. But check out road conditions first. The road is gravel and state budget cuts sometimes leave it in poor condition. Check with the Alaska Department of Transportation's **road condition hotline** (© 511; http://511.alaska.gov).

The next day, catch a shuttle bus or camper bus to get deeper into the park for sightseeing and **hiking.** If you have another day after that within the park, you can do more hikes and have the cushion of a weather day. Add a rafting excursion at the park entrance before driving on, if you like, and possibly a night at a hotel to get washed up.

THE BACKCOUNTRY CAMPING ITINERARY

Arrive by train, bus, or car with your backpack, camping gear, and food for at least several days' hiking. Go immediately to the visitor center to orient yourself to the backcountry permit process, buy the information you need for your trek (see section 4 of this chapter), and choose the unit area that looks most promising. **Backcountry permits** cannot be reserved in advance; you can only apply for them in person two days in advance, and they go fast. If you're lucky, permits will be left for the day after you arrive; more likely, you'll need to camp for a night nearby and arrive at the visitor center by the 7am opening (in high season) to get your permit for the following day. Now you've got another day to wait; if you've reserved a shuttle-bus seat, you can get a preview of the park and see some wildlife or, outside the park, go on a rafting trip. The next morning you can start your backcountry hike, taking the camper bus to your unit, then traveling for up to 2 weeks in a huge area of wilderness reserved almost exclusively for your use.

When the road is good, you can cover its length in less than 4 hours. (Agencies that rent cars and RVs for these gravel highways are listed under "Equipped for the Backroads" on p. 369, for Fairbanks; and "Car Wheels on Gravel Roads" on p. 198, for Anchorage. Most other companies don't allow their vehicles on the Denali.) Small roadhouses are found along the way. **Biking** the road is one of the best ways to see it. Trails and remote roads from the highway offer some exceptional mountain biking and hiking routes, especially in the Tangle Lakes National Register Archaeological District. There are **Bureau of Land Management campgrounds** along the highway at Brushkana Creek and Tangle Lakes, and you can camp anywhere you want outside a campground.

Be sure to get the BLM's *Denali Highway Points of Interest* road guide and *Trail Map and Guide to the Tangle Lakes National Register District.* They're available at the Alaska Public Lands Information Centers in Fairbanks, Anchorage, or Tok, or directly from the **Bureau of Land Management.** Their Glennallen Field Office, P.O. Box 147, Glennallen, AK 99588 (© **907/822-3217;** www.glennallen.ak.blm.gov; open Mon–Fri 8am–4:30pm), manages the area, and rangers there can give you guidance on where to go.

CampAlaska Tours (© **800/376-9438** or 907/376-9438; www.camp alaska.com) covers this ground, too, with group camping excursions that use a van to get from destination to destination, camping each night along the way.

THE WILDERNESS LODGE ITINERARY

For those who can afford it, this may be the best way to see Denali. The lodge will fly you in—or, if it's in Kantishna, drive you through the park—and you'll immediately be away from the crowds in remote territory. The lodges all have activities and guides to get you out into the wilderness. If you're not staying in Kantishna, you may want to schedule a day to ride the shuttle bus into the park to see the mountain and wildlife anyway, with an evening in a hotel near the park or in Healy.

THE TALKEETNA OPTION

Drive only as far as Talkeetna, about 110 miles north of Anchorage, and board a flightseeing plane from there to the park, perhaps landing on a glacier on Mount McKinley. You'll stand a better chance of seeing the mountain than anyone else, since the weather tends to be better on the south side and you can fly above most clouds. You'll also save yourself hours of driving to the park and the bus ride into the park, and you'll have the pleasure of staying in a town with some character, unlike the park entrance area. If you want the on-the-ground wildlife-viewing opportunities that can be had only in the park, you can fly from Talkeetna for the day, for a price. (See section 10 of this chapter for more information.)

2 Park Essentials

VISITOR INFORMATION

Getting the information you need to plan your visit is especially important at Denali because of the need for advance reservations.

The most important resource for setting up a trip is the concessionaire: **Denali Park Resorts,** 241 W. Ship Creek Ave., Anchorage, AK 99501 (© **800/ 622-7275** or 907/272-7275; fax 907/264-4684; at Denali, from May 15 through the visitor season, the number is © 907/683-8200; www.denalipark resorts.com; for reservations www.reservedenali.com). The concession is operated by a joint venture of ARAMARK and the Doyon Native corporation; for the purposes of visitors, any of those names refer to the same outfit. They handle the reservations system for the campgrounds and shuttle buses, as well as two hotels, bus tours, a rafting operation, and a dinner theater that you can reserve.

The easiest place to make in-person contact with the concessionaire or the park service itself is the **Denali National Park Visitor Center,** also known as the Visitor Access Center, on Denali Park Road, half a mile from the park entrance (P.O. Box 9), Denali National Park, AK 99755 (© **907/683-2294;** www.nps.gov/dena). The visitor center is open from June to mid-September daily from 7am to 8pm, May 8am to 5pm, and late September 10am to 4pm. It's closed October through April. Here you will find the Denali Park Resorts reservation and ticketing desks and the park backcountry desk. You can even buy an espresso to drink in line. Since there's no park entrance station, this center is also the stop for the park map, a copy of the *Alpenglow* park newspaper, and other handouts. A small bookstore offers a limited selection on the area, and films and programs take place in an auditorium. *Note:* The plan is that some of these services will move to the new visitor center campus up the road during the 2005 season; see "Denali Changes," p. 318.)

Besides the centers at the park, you can get park information on the way there at the interagency **Alaska Public Lands Information Centers;** they are in Anchorage, Fairbanks, and Tok, listed in chapters 6 and 9. The park website (www.nps.gov/dena) is handy too. The park's nonprofit publishing arm is the **Alaska Natural History Association,** Denali Branch, P.O. Box 230, Denali National Park, AK 99755 (© **907/683-1272** summer, 907/683-1258 off season; www.alaskanha.org). They operate the shops in the park visitor centers, and you can use their website to order books and maps before coming.

THE RESERVATIONS SYSTEM

Here's the system for reserving shuttle-bus tickets and sites at the developed campgrounds. This section may look long, but paying attention to the details of the reservations system greatly improves your chances of a good visit to the park. (The backcountry permit system is covered in section 4 of this chapter.)

FOR ADVANCE RESERVATIONS

Sixty-five percent of shuttle-bus seats and all campground sites (except Sanctuary) are offered for booking by Internet, telephone, fax, or mail; the balance is held back for walk-ins up to 2 days before the trip. Use the Denali Park Resorts information above under "Visitor Information."

Reservations by mail or fax open for the whole summer on December 1 of the preceding year. Reservations by Internet or phone open in mid-February. After that date, lines are answered daily from 7am to 5pm Alaska time (remember, that's 4 hr. earlier than Eastern Standard Time). By faxing, you can get in before the phone lines open. Reservation forms to fax or mail are available on the park's website (www.nps.gov/dena, click "Reservations," on the left side of the page). You will need to include the dates, times of the bus or names of campgrounds you want, plus alternate dates; the names and ages of the people in your party; and the number of your Visa, MasterCard, American Express, or Discover Card, with expiration date and signature. They will add entrance and reservation fees (see "Fees," below) and figure the total. You can also pay by check if you're reserving by mail. *Note:* Don't use the mail unless you write several months ahead, as you could miss getting a reservation. Mail to Alaska takes about 5 days from the U.S. East Coast.

A **confirmation** should be sent out by mail or fax within 2 days of receipt. Take the confirmation to the "will call" desk at the visitor center when you arrive to exchange it for a camping permit and bus ticket. If you'll be arriving after the center closes at 8pm, you must call © **907/683-1266** in advance to avoid losing your site or shuttle seat.

FOR WALK-INS

Phone, mail, and fax orders are not accepted the day before the visit starts, but walk-in reservations begin 2 days out, offering the remaining 35% of the shuttle-bus seats and any leftover car-camping sites, and all sites at Sanctuary Campground. If it's a busy time of year, desirable shuttle reservations are snapped up early in the day. That means you may not get a good reservation for the day of your arrival or even the day after, only the next day after that. That's why it's so critical to reserve in advance.

On the other hand, don't despair if you arrive without reservations, as the flow of visitors rises and falls unpredictably. It's perfectly possible that you'll walk into the visitor center and get a shuttle seat on the same day.

FEES

Park entrance fees were increased for 2005 to $20 per family (up to eight) or $10 per person, good for 7 days. There is no entrance station to collect the fee, but it is automatically added to your bill when you make shuttle or campground reservations. If you have a National Parks Pass or a Golden Age or Golden Access pass, mention it when you call to get your discount.

Campground fees are $16 to $18 per night for car or RV camping, $12 for walk-in tent camping at Riley Creek Campground, and $9 in Sanctuary Campground. A reservation fee of $4 is charged for the first night of stays in campgrounds other than Riley Creek and Savage River. (See "Where to Stay" later in the chapter for more particulars.)

Another $4 fee is charged for canceling or changing a campsite or bus ticket, except for free children's tickets. You can cancel until 6pm for campground reservations, or 2 hours before departure for bus tickets.

Bus fees are listed in the chart "Denali Park Road Bus Facts," in section 3 of this chapter.

GETTING THERE
BY TRAIN

The **Alaska Railroad** (© **800/544-0552** or 907/265-2494; www.alaskarailroad. com) pioneered tourism to the park before the George Parks Highway was built in 1972. In summer, trains leave both Anchorage and Fairbanks daily at 8:15am, arriving at the park from Anchorage at 3:45pm and from Fairbanks at noon, crossing and going on to the opposite city for arrival at 8:15pm in each. The fare from Anchorage to Denali is $125 one-way for adults, half price for children.

Tips Train Choices

Alaska Railroad executives know that their fares are high for a simple ride to Denali. As one told me, "We're selling entertainment," and that's how you should judge your choices. So, to review the entertainment: All the cars are luxurious, and some are grand and highly memorable; the rail line follows a historic, unspoiled route through beautiful countryside; there's a good chance of seeing moose and caribou; the commentary by well-trained Alaska high school students is fresh and engaging; and the food is good—you can dine in a beautiful bistro car or in a truly extraordinary white-tablecloth dining car. There are disadvantages, too. The train is very expensive. You can rent a small car for a week for the same price as one round-trip on the train. It's slow, adding 3 hours to a trip from Anchorage to the park, and when it's late, it can be very late. And, once you arrive, you have to rely on shuttles and courtesy vans to get around outside the park.

After you decide to ride the train, you have to choose which part of the train. One set of Alaska Railroad locomotives pulls the Alaska Railroad cars and three other sets of cars with full domes owned by cruise lines, two of which have seats for independent travelers (although 90% or more are filled with their older cruise-ship customers). **Princess Cruises and Tours** (© 800/426-0500; www.princesslodges.com/rail. htm) has tall all-dome cars with table seating upstairs and dining rooms downstairs; there's plenty of head room and you can see a long way. Their special advantage is large balconies at the ends of the cars where you can ride outdoors. **Grayline of Alaska Package Tours** (a part

---

The full train runs only from mid-May to mid-September, with somewhat lower fares in the first and last few weeks of the season. During the winter, the Alaska Railroad runs a single passenger car from Anchorage to Fairbanks and back once a week—a truly spectacular, truly Alaskan experience.

BY CAR

Renting a car and driving from Anchorage or Fairbanks is far cheaper and far faster than taking the train. The drive is about 4½ hours from Anchorage and 2½ hours from Fairbanks, on a good two-lane highway. Many of the views along the **Parks Highway** are equal to the views on the train, but large stretches, especially in the Matanuska and Susitna valleys, near Anchorage, have been spoiled by ugly roadside development (which you don't see from the train). A long but spectacular detour around the mess leads through **Hatcher Pass** on a mountainous gravel road open only in the summer. See "Through Hatcher Pass" in section 10 of chapter 6. Farther north from Anchorage, the Parks Highway passes through Denali State Park. If the weather's clear, you can see Mount McKinley from the pull-outs there. The state park also contains several campgrounds, hiking trails, a lake with canoe rental, and a veterans' memorial.

From Fairbanks, the drive is pleasant but rarely spectacular. Allow an hour to stop in the quaint, riverside town of Nenana, where you can see an old railroad depot museum (p. 380).

of Holland America) ((C) **800/544-2206** or 907/277-5581; www.grayline alaska.com) has some brand new cars that are even better than Princess's. They're huge and comfortable, with all seats facing forward upstairs—an advantage over table seating—and dining rooms below that are large enough so only two seatings are needed for each meal. (All meals are served at assigned seatings in the cruise line cars.) Small outdoor and lounge areas are at the rear of each pair of cars for passengers to stretch out, and there are elevators and accessible restrooms. The Alaska Railroad cars are more traditional, with all seats facing forward, and you have more freedom to get up and wander around and choose between the two dining options—not just march from one assigned seat to another. However, there is a 20-minute limit to sitting in the dome seats. Passenger seats are assigned on all three offerings. You can't walk from one company's cars to another, but you can walk between cars in your own train section. Fares on the cruise-line operations run even higher than the railroad's fares, but they're mainly sold (and much more advantageously priced) as part of lodging packages with the companies' Denali hotels.

Personally, I would choose the Alaska Railroad experience because I love trains, and their cars feel more authentic and less controlled than the cruise-line offerings. All provide superb service, however, as a sort of Orient Express of the north that's as much about the ride as the destination.

BY BUS

Several van and bus services inexpensively connect Anchorage and Fairbanks to Denali. Most will carry bikes and other gear for an additional fee.

Alaska Trails ((C) **888/600-6001**; www.alaskashuttle.com) offers twice daily service from Anchorage, once a day from Fairbanks, with stops at any other point on the way. In Anchorage, it leaves from the downtown Anchorage Youth Hostel, and in Fairbanks, from Billie's Backpackers Hostel. The one-way fare is $64 from Anchorage, $44 from Fairbanks.

The Park Connection Motorcoach Service ((C) **800/266-8625** or 907/245-0200; www.alaskacoach.com) runs big, comfortable coaches to Seward and Anchorage, with two buses daily in each direction. The fare is $69 to Anchorage, $118 to Seward, and children ride for half price.

BY AIR

Talkeetna Aero Services ((C) **800/660-2688** or 907/733-2899, www.talkeetna aero.com) offers the only scheduled air service to Denali from Talkeetna, their base, or from Anchorage, in the summer only. The flights are sold as one-day packages, including flightseeing on the way, a bus tour at the park, a box lunch and ground transfers. It's the only way to "do" Denali in a day. The package from Anchorage is $455, from Talkeetna $260.

Tips **Driving Times**

It isn't as far from Anchorage to Denali or Fairbanks as you might guess from looking at the train schedule, it's just that the train averages less than 40 miles per hour. The speed limit on the two-lane Parks Highway is 65 miles per hour, and traffic often goes faster. It is Alaska's fastest extended highway. A car gets from Anchorage to Fairbanks in less than 7 hours and from Anchorage to Denali in less than 5 (as opposed to 12 and 7½ hr. by rail, respectively). A road mileage chart is shown with the map on p. 6.

GETTING AROUND

If you take the train or bus, you'll find that most accommodations have arrangements to get you around, although this becomes less convenient as you get farther from the park entrance. Ask how courtesy transportation works when you book your room. There are cabs available, too, but they have been a poor option because of sky-high rates. If you must rely on cabs, get a firm quote when you call. Companies include **Caribou Cab** (© **907/683-1377**) and **Ask Denali Transportation & Tours** (© **877/683-4465** or 907/683-4765). You can also take the train to Denali, rent a car there, and drop it in Fairbanks or Anchorage. **Teresa's Alaskan Car Rentals** (© **907/683-1377;** www.denalicarrental.com) is in Healy, and **Drive Denali** (© **907/683-3327;** www.drivedenali.com) is near the park entrance.

If you drive to the park, you'll still need to take the shuttle bus, described below, to get into its heart, except under certain circumstances. You can drive past mile 14 on the park road only if you have a 3-day camping permit at Teklanika Campground, 29 miles in; then your vehicle must remain parked at the campground for the entire 3 days. The rules loosen at the end of the season, when winners of a drawing can drive the road for a few days in late September (check with the park service for lottery details). After the permit driving is over, the road is open to anyone as far as mile 30 until the snow flies; then it's maintained only as far as the headquarters, 3 miles from the entrance.

Bicycles have free access to the park road. For that option, see section 5 of this chapter.

FAST FACTS: **Denali National Park**

Banks A couple of ATMs are in the Glitter Gulch (Nenana Canyon) area, including one at the Lynx Creek Store and Deli. A couple more are at gas stations in Healy, 12 miles north of the park. Do your banking before leaving Anchorage or Fairbanks.

Emergencies © **911** will work inside the park, but be sure to tell the operator you are within Denali National Park.

Gear Rental **Denali Mountain Morning Hostel and Lodge** (© **907/683-7503**), listed in full on p. 345, rents camping gear; a complete kit is $40 for the first day, $10 each additional day. Bikes are for rent at **Denali Outdoor Center** (© **888/303-1925** or 907/683-1925; www.denalioutdoorcenter.com);

see p. ###. Binoculars are for rent at **Riley Creek Mercantile** and at **Lynx Creek Store** (see "Stores," below).

Hospital A **health clinic** (℃ **907/683-2211**) is located in Healy, 12 miles north of the park entrance; it's open 24 hours a day for emergencies, or normal office hours for non-emergencies.

Police The **Alaska State Troopers** (℃ **907/683-2232** or 907/768-2202) has a post in Healy, 12 miles north of the park, and in Cantwell, 28 miles south.

Post Office The post office is just within the park entrance, right before the Riley Creek Campground.

Stores You should do major shopping before leaving Anchorage or Fairbanks, but there are two handy little stores at Denali. **Riley Creek Mercantile** (℃ **907/683-9246**) is at the Riley Creek Campground, near the park entrance. It's open daily from 5am to 10pm in the summer. It's an invaluable stop. Besides convenience groceries, they have firewood, some basic camping supplies, RV supplies, made-to-order sandwiches, postal services, Internet access, fax and copy service, binocular rentals, showers, and laundry. A convenience store and gas station, the **Lynx Creek Store and Deli** (℃ **907/683-2548**), is on the Parks Highway in the Glitter Gulch (Nenana Canyon) area, just north of the park entrance. They have an activity desk for concessionaire services such as rafting and the Cabin Nite show.

Taxes The local bed tax is 7%. There is no sales tax.

3 Denali by Shuttle Bus

Your visit to Denali will likely revolve around a ride on the shuttle bus into the park to see the wildlife and to stop for a walk in the wilderness. Some planning will make it a more successful trip.

CHOOSING YOUR DESTINATION

You can buy shuttle tickets to the Toklat (*toe*-klat) River, 53 miles into the park; to Stoney Overlook (the stop taking the place of the Eielson Visitor Center while it is rebuilt) at around 61 miles; Wonder Lake at 85 miles; or Kantishna, at 89 miles (fares are listed in the "Denali Park Road Bus Facts" chart that accompanies this section). On any day trip, you have to go both ways, so you're in for a long drive. If you don't get off the bus along the way, the round-trip takes 6½ hours to Toklat, nearly 8 hours to Stony Overlook (or Eielson Visitor Center, when it is in operation), 11 hours to Wonder Lake, and 12 hours to Kantishna.

In choosing your destination, you need to balance your stamina, your desire to save time for a day hike, and your desire to see wildlife. There are no firm rules about where wildlife shows up, but my own observations are that in the early morning, you can often see moose on the first part of the road; in mid-summer, brown (grizzly) bears seem to appear most in the higher country, beyond Toklat, which also is the best area for caribou; in the fall berry season, the grizzlies show up all along the drive.

The best views of Mount McKinley show up around Stony Overlook, at about mile 61, beyond Toklat. The mountain is most likely to be visible in the morning, as clouds often pile up during the day. Going beyond Stony to

---

Tips Bus Concerns & Complaints

The Denali concessionaire uses only school bus–type vehicles over the park road. We've received complaints from readers who allegedly were stuck on these buses while other visitors toured the park in luxury motor coaches, but this just isn't so: Only these tough, lightweight buses are allowed on the narrow, gravel park road. I've also heard from visitors complaining of white knuckles on the ride. It's true the buses act a bit like mountain goats on the heights of Polychrome Pass and near Eielson Visitor Center. The road climbs without guardrails, and if you're afraid of heights, it might not be to your liking.

Wonder Lake provides more amazing views, including the land-covered Muldrow Glacier and many classic images of Mount McKinley. There's really no reason to go as far as Kantishna unless you are headed to a lodge there (see "Wilderness Lodges" in section 11 of this chapter). In general, I think Stony Overlook (or Eielson Visitor Center, when open) is the best destination for most people, offering them the chance to see the mountain and some wildlife while leaving them time to get out and walk (I've included ideas on where to hike later).

You won't be able to time your trip for good weather, as you need to book ahead. But don't despair if it rains—the sun may be out at the other end of the park. The best weather for wildlife sightings is cool, overcast skies without rain. One trick of the system that allows visitors to wait for sun is to stay at Teklanika Campground. If you drive to a campsite there, agreeing to stay for 3 days, you're eligible to buy a special shuttle ticket for $23 that is good for rides deeper into the park the entire time you're staying at the campground. Wherever you stay, you can buy a three-trip pass for the price of two.

Denali can be a challenge for families. Young children will go nuts on an 8-hour bus ride, and often can't pick out the wildlife—this isn't a zoo, and most animals blend in with their surroundings. Older children also have a hard time keeping their patience on these trips, as do many adults. The only solution is to get off the bus and turn your trip into a romp in the heather. When you've had a chance to revive, catch the next bus. Besides, just because you buy a ticket to Wonder Lake doesn't mean that you have to go that far. Keep in mind, too, that if your child normally needs a car seat, you must bring it along on the bus, or arrange to borrow one when you reserve your seats.

The park has other alternatives to the Shuttle Bus with commentary and other amenities. Denali Park Resorts operates two narrated bus tours, booked mostly as part of package tours. The **Denali Natural History Tour** provides just a taste of the park, going 17 miles down the park road. The **Tundra Wilderness Tour** goes to Toklat when the mountain is hidden by clouds, and 8 miles farther, across Highway Pass to Stony Hill, when it is visible. New in 2004, buses carried video monitors connected via close circuit to a telephoto lens so passengers could see far-off wildlife without binoculars. Food is provided, but you can't get off the bus along the way. Also new in 2004, the Denali Institute and Murie Science and Learning Center (© **866/683-1269** or 907/683-1269; www.denali institute.org) began offering a tour called **Wolves of Denali: A Guided Learning Excursion.** The 5-hour tour takes groups of just 12 to the Igloo Creek area to look for wolf tracks, experiment with radio tracking, and maybe see the wolves that frequent the area.

Two other narrated tours are offered by privately-owned lodges in the Kantishna area, at the far end of the park road. **Kantishna Wilderness Trails** (© **800/230-7275** or 907/683-1475; www.seedenali.com) and **Denali Backcountry Tours** (© **888/560-2489** or 907/683-2643) each cover 190 miles in around 13 hours, with a stop halfway through, at the far end, for a meal and gold panning (with either), or a sled dog demonstration (with Kantishna) or a hike (with Denali Backcountry). Either way, it's a marathon and you can't get off the bus along the way, but there is no other choice for a one-day, narrated tour that covers the whole road. The cost is $115 for adults; on the Denali Backcountry version children can go for $55, but no kid I know can stay sane on a 13-hour bus ride.

GETTING READY

Reserve your shuttle ticket for as early as you can stand to get up in the morning. This strategy will give you more time for day hikes and enhance your chances of seeing the mountain and wildlife. Many animals are more active in the morning, especially on hot days. During peak season, the first bus leaves the visitor center at 5:15am and then one leaves roughly every 15 to 30 minutes in the morning. A few buses leave in the afternoon, mostly to pick up stragglers on the way back, returning late under the midnight sun.

By taking an early bus, you have more time to get off along the way for a hike, walking back to the road and getting the next bus that comes along with a spare seat. Time it right, and you could have more than 8 hours for hiking plus a tour of most of the park road before returning on a late bus. (To be on the safe side, don't push it to the very last bus.) The sun won't set until after 11pm May through July and it will be light all night. If you need to get back to the park entrance at a certain time, leave yourself plenty of time, because after getting off your westbound bus, you can't reserve seats going back the other way, and you may have to wait an hour for a bus with room to take you.

Before you leave for the visitor center to get on your shuttle bus, you'll need a packed lunch and plenty of water. You should wear sturdy walking shoes and layers of warm and lighter clothing with rain gear packed; you should have binoculars or a spotting scope at the ready; and you should have insect repellent. You may also want a copy of Kim Heacox's worthwhile booklet *Denali Road Guide,* available for $6 at the visitor center bookstore and published by the Alaska Natural History Association (listed in section 2 under "Visitor Information"). It provides a milepost commentary you can follow as you ride. ANHA also publishes guides to Denali birds, mammals, geology, and trails. If you'll be doing any extensive day hiking, you may also want to bring a detailed topographic map printed on waterproof plastic (published by Trails Illustrated and sold for $9.95 from the visitor center or by ordering from ANHA) as well as a compass; if you're just going to walk a short distance off the road, you won't need such preparations.

ON YOUR WAY

There are no reserved seats on the bus, but if you arrive early you can find a place on the left side, which has the best views on the way out. Bus riders often see grizzly bears, caribou, Dall sheep, and moose, and occasionally wolves, but, as one driver said, the animals aren't union workers, and it's possible that you won't see any at all. Of course, you have to stay on the bus when animals are present.

The shuttle-bus drivers generally offer commentary about the sights on the road, but they aren't required to do so. Some do a great job and some don't say much. The tour bus drivers do a running commentary.

> **Tips** **Shuttle-Bus Etiquette**
>
> It's common courtesy on the shuttle bus to yell out when you see wildlife so others can see it, too. The driver will stop and everyone will rush to your side of the bus. After you've had a look give someone else a chance to look out your window or get a picture. Try to be quiet and don't stick yourself, your camera, or anything else out of the bus. You will scare away the animals or, worse, help habituate them to humans.

A ROAD LOG

Here are some of the highlights along the road (check the visitor center or the park service information handouts to confirm times of the guided walks):

MILE 9   In clear weather, this is the closest spot to the park entrance with a view of Mount McKinley. This section also is a likely place to see moose, especially in the fall rutting season.

MILE 14   At the end of the paved road at the Savage River Bridge, this is generally as far as private vehicles can go. A park service checkpoint stops anyone who doesn't have a proper permit. From the parking lot by the bridge, a simple climb over dry tundra leads to Primrose Ridge, also known as Mount Wright.

MILE 17   The portable toilets here are as far as the Natural History Tour bus goes.

MILE 29   An hour and 10 minutes into the drive, a large rest stop overlooks the Teklanika River, with flush toilets, the last plumbing on the road (until completion of the Eielson Visitor Center rehab). The Teklanika, like many other rivers on Alaska's glacier-carved terrain, is a braided river—a stream wandering in a massive gravel streambed that's much too big for it. The braided riverbeds, sometimes miles wide, were created by water from fast-melting glaciers at the end of the last ice age. Each is kept free of vegetation by its river, which constantly changes course as it spreads the debris of rock and dust from the glaciers. Flat plains in glacial terrain usually are laid down by this mechanism.

MILE 34   Craggy Igloo Mountain is a likely place to see Dall sheep. Without binoculars, they'll just look like white dots. Manageable climbs on Igloo, Cathedral, and Sable mountains take off along the road in the section from Igloo Creek to Sable Pass.

MILE 38–43   Sable Pass, a critical habitat area for bears, is closed to people. A half-eaten sign helps explain why. Bears show up here mostly in the fall. This is the start of the road's broad alpine vistas.

MILE 46   Here you'll find the top of 5-mile-wide Polychrome Pass, the most scenic point on the ride, and a toilet break, 2 hours and 25 minutes into the trip. Caribou look like specks when they pass in the great valley below you, known as the Plain of Murie after Adolph Murie, a biologist who pioneered study here and helped develop the park service's scientific ethic (the name does not always appear on maps, however). Note how the mountains of colored rock on either side of the plain match up—they once were connected before glacial ice carved this valley. Huge rocks on its floor are glacial erratics, plucked from the bedrock by moving ice and left behind when the ice melted.

Denali Park Road Bus Facts

Bus	Purpose	Route	Frequency	Fare
DPR courtesy shuttle	Links Denali Park Resorts hotels to park entrance	Hotels 1 mile north and 7 miles south	Continuous loop	Free, even if not staying at a DPR hotel
Riley Creek Loop	Links facilities within park entrance area	Visitor center, Riley Creek Campground, rail depot	Continuous loop	Free
Savage River Shuttle	Public transport to hiking near the Savage River, which can also be reached by car	From visitor center to Savage River Day use area, about 14 miles into the park	Peak season every hour from 9am–9pm	Free
Camper shuttle (Green Bus)	Access to campgrounds beyond the park entrance	From the visitor center to Wonder Lake Campground, 85 miles into the park	Several times a day	$23 adults, half price ages 15–17, free 14 and younger
Shuttle Bus (or just "the shuttle") (Green bus)	General access to the park and wildlife viewing; limited commentary, depending on the driver; no food service	From the visitor center as far as Kantishna, 89 miles away through the park	Every 30 minutes to Toklat River, every hour to Wonder Lake, once daily to Kantishna	$18 to Toklat, $23 to Eielson (Stony), $32 to Wonder Lake, $35 to Kantishna; half price ages 15–17, free 14 and younger
Tundra Wilderness Tour (Tan bus)	6- to 8-hour guided bus tour with lunch provided; passengers may not get off en route	From the visitor center to the Toklat River or Highway Pass, 53 to 61 miles into the park	Twice daily	$77 adults, $41 ages 14 and younger (includes park entrance fee)
Natural History Tour (Tan bus)	3- to 5-hour guided bus tour at the edge of the park	From the visitor center 17 miles into the park	Three times daily	$42 adults, $23 ages 14 and younger (includes park entrance fee)
Wolves of Denali	5-hour educational tour about wolf biology (p. 330)	From the visitor center 32 miles into the park	Once a day	$75 adults, $55 ages 15 and younger

MILE 53   The Toklat River, another braided river, is a flat plain of gravel with easy walking. The glaciers that feed the river are 10 miles upstream; the river bottom is habitat for bears, caribou, and wolves, and a good place for picnics.

MILE 58   Highway Pass is the highest point on the road. In good weather, dramatic views of Mount McKinley start here. The alpine tundra from here to the Eielson Visitor Center is inviting for walking, but beware: Tundra is soft underfoot and can conceal holes and declivities that can twist an ankle.

MILE 61   Stony Overlook, the road point on the mountainous highway point between Stony Dome and Stony Hill, is the turn-around point for most buses while the Eielson Visitor Center is being reconstructed.

MILE 64   Thorofare Pass, where the road becomes narrow and winding, is a good area to look for bears and caribou. Bus drivers know best where the animals are on any particular day, since they talk to fellow drivers.

MILE 66   This is the site of the **Eielson Visitor Center,** scheduled for closure and reconstruction during 2005 and 2006. It is a fine vantage point for seeing McKinley, the summit of which is just 33 miles away. Seismic measurements here show frequent small earthquakes accompanying McKinley's prodigious growth—about an inch every 3 years. This region is a jumble of rocks pushed together by the expanding Pacific tectonic plate; the mountain, and the whole Alaska Range, are folding upward in that great collision.

MILE 68.5   The incredibly rugged terrain to the north is the earth and vegetation covering Muldrow Glacier. The ice extends to McKinley's peak and was an early and arduous route for climbers; these days, they fly to a base camp at 7,200-feet elevation on the Kahiltna Glacier, on the south side. McKinley's glaciers, falling 15,000 vertical feet and extending up to 45 miles in length, are among the world's greatest. The Ruth Glacier has carved the Great Gorge on the south side, which is almost 6,000 feet deep above the ice and another 4,000 below—almost twice the depth of the Grand Canyon. The park road comes within a mile of the Muldrow's face, then continues through wet, rolling terrain past beaver ponds, and finally descends into a small spruce patch near mile 82.

MILE 86   Wonder Lake campground is the closest road point to Mount McKinley, 27 miles away. Some buses continue another half hour to Kantishna. The fact that McKinley looks so massive from this considerable distance, dominating the sky, is testament to its stupendous size. You'll likely never see a larger object on this planet. From its base (your elevation here is only 2,000 ft.) to its top is an elevation gain greater than that of any other mountain on earth. Other mountains are taller overall, but they stand on higher ground.

4 Denali on Foot: Day Hiking & Backpacking

DAY HIKING IN THE BACKCOUNTRY

One of the unique aspects of Denali is the lack of developed trails—you really can take off in any direction. I've covered some of the best hiking areas above, in "A Road Log," including Primrose Ridge, Teklanika River, Igloo and Sable mountains, and the Toklat River. The park service long resisted building any trails, but finally gave in and recognized some trails visitors had created, including those at the Eielson Visitor Center (currently a construction site) and the 2-mile path that leads from the Wonder Lake Campground to the McKinley River Bar, which extends far to the east and west. You can drive or take a free shuttle to the Savage River Day Use Area, at mile 15, which has a 1-mile loop

---

> **Tips** **Ranger Programs in the Park**
>
> Check the park newspaper, *The Alpenglow,* for ranger talks and slide
> shows that happen as often as several times a day in the front-country
> area (near the entrance) and at the Riley Creek, Savage River, and
> Teklanika campgrounds.

---

trail and longer, informal routes for great alpine tundra hiking. No permit is
needed for day hiking.

The broad, hard gravel flats of the **braided riverbeds,** such as the McKinley,
Toklat, Teklanika, and Savage, are among the best routes for hiking in the park.
Stony Creek, leading up a gorge to the north from the road at mile 60, is an
excellent walk into the mountains. You can also hike on the tundra, of which
there are two varieties: The **wet tundra** lies on top of permanently frozen
ground called permafrost; it's mushy at best, like hiking on foam rubber laid
over bowling balls. At worst, it's swamp. **Dry tundra** clothes the mountainsides,
and generally makes for firmer footing and easier walking. The brush and
stunted forest of the region are virtually impenetrable.

The major risks of hiking here relate to the weather and rivers. It can get cold
and wet in midsummer, and if you're not prepared with warm, waterproof clothing, you could suffer the spiraling chill of hypothermia. The rivers are dangerous because of their fast flow and icy cold water. Experienced backcountry
trekkers plan their routes to avoid crossing sizable rivers. See the notes on river
crossings, hypothermia, and getting lost in the "Outdoors Health & Safety" section of chapter 2. Bears, which people worry most about, have never killed a
Denali visitor. Tips on avoiding them are in chapter 2, and are widely distributed at the park.

For a first foray beyond the trails, consider joining one of the park service
guided hikes. As many as two daily **Discovery Hikes** take off from the park
road. One follows a route well inside the park toward the Eielson Visitor Center and the other goes nearer to the entrance end of the park. A ranger takes only
15 hikers, leading them into wilderness while teaching them about the nature of
the places they visit. Plan a 5- to 11-hour day, including the shuttle ride; actual
hiking time is about 4 hours. The hikes generally are not too strenuous for families with school-age children, although it is wise to inquire how steep it will be
if you have any doubts. They cost no more than the price of your shuttle ticket.
You need to wear hiking shoes or boots and bring food, water, and rain gear.
Reserve a place in advance, as hikes fill up in July and you'll need to know when
and where to catch the special bus. Rangers lead other walks, too, although the
line-up can change each year. There often is a walk on the short Savage River
Loop, 15 miles into the park, and another along the Toklat River, at mile 53.
Check with the visitor center for the current offerings and crucial details about
which bus to take.

DAY HIKING IN THE PARK ENTRANCE AREA

There are several trails at the park entrance, weaving through the boreal forest
around small lakes. Only one strenuous trail leads from the entrance area, but
it is a gem. The steep and spectacular hike to the **Mount Healy overlook** is a
5-mile round-trip. The trail breaks through the tree line to slopes of tundra and
rock outcroppings, where you can see just how small is the pocket of human
infestation at the park entrance area: The Alaska Range and its foothills extend

far into the distance. If you continue on an all-day hike right to the top of Mount Healy, you can see all the way to McKinley on a clear day. Several new trails have just been completed or are planned with the current construction program. A new bike trail connects the entrance area, near the Riley Creek Mercantile, to Glitter Gulch, allowing pedestrians to get back and forth without walking on the road. The trail is free of barriers to people with disabilities. Three new interpretive trails are planned for completion in time for the 2005 season. The *Alpenglow* park newspaper contains a brief guide for the trails and may be the best source of up-to-date information on the new trails.

BACKPACKING

Imagine backpacking over your own area of wilderness, without trails, limits, or the chance of seeing other people. There's no need to retrace your route to get back: Anywhere you meet the 89-mile Denali Park Road you can catch a bus back to the world of people. Any experienced backpacker should consider a backcountry trek at Denali.

Yes, it can be challenging. Hiking on the tundra, broken-rock mountainsides, and braided rivers is tiring, and it's easy to fall or turn an ankle. You must be prepared for river crossings and cold weather, know how to find your way with a map and compass, and know how to avoid attracting bears. But if you've done a backpacking trip in a less challenging area, you surely can manage it here, so long as you prepare and don't underestimate the additional time you'll need in trail-less terrain. Nor do you need to trek far—you can camp just a few miles off the road and still be in a place that looks like no one has ever been there before.

You must be flexible about where you're going and be prepared for any kind of terrain, because you can't choose the **backcountry unit** you will explore until you arrive at the backcountry desk at the visitor center and find out what's available. This information, and a map of the units, is posted on a board behind the desk. Groups of four or more may have a hard time finding a place to hike, but there's almost always *somewhere* to go. You can reserve permits only 2 days in advance, and you're unlikely to get one for the day you arrive, but you can reserve permits for continuation of your trip for up to 14 days at the same time. The first night of a trip is the hard one to get—for one thing, you can reserve only units that are contiguous to the park road for the first night—but after that, each night gets progressively easier. A couple of rangers are there to help you through the process.

Buy the ***Denali National Park and Preserve* topographical map,** published by Trails Illustrated, available for $9.95 from the Alaska Natural History Association, listed earlier under "Visitor Information." Printed on plastic, the map includes the boundaries of the 43 backcountry units and much other valuable information. Also, you'll want a copy of ***Backcountry Companion,*** by Jon Nierenberg, which describes conditions and routes in each area and is published and sold by ANHA for $8.95. You'll find it at the visitor center, or you can glance at a well-thumbed copy kept at the backcountry desk.

The alpine units from the Toklat River to Eielson Visitor Center are the most popular. That's where you get broad views and can walk across heathery dry tundra in any direction. But to travel far, even there, you may have to climb over rugged, rocky terrain, and the tundra can be deceptively difficult to walk on—it's soft and hides ankle-turning holes. The wooded units are the least popular, since bushwhacking through overgrown land is anything but fun. The best routes for making time here (and anywhere in the Alaska Bush) are along the braided river valleys and streambeds. Be ready to walk in water. You'll have to take the **camper bus** to get to your backcountry unit, at a cost of $23 for each adult.

Before venturing into the backcountry, everyone is required to watch an **orientation film** called *Hiking the Denali Wilderness*. Among its goals is to teach you how not to attract bears, but some people find that intimidating. Don't worry, just follow the instructions and you will be OK. The park service provides bear-resistant food containers in which you are required to carry all your food. Guns are not permitted in the park; carrying a pepper spray such as Counter Assault for self-defense from bears is allowed. Bear safety is covered in chapter 2 under "Outdoors Health & Safety."

Before you decide to go backpacking at Denali, however, you may want to broaden your thinking—if you're up to a cross-country hike without a trail, there are tens of millions of acres in Alaska available for backpacking that don't require a permit. Check with the Alaska Public Lands Information Center in Anchorage or Fairbanks for ideas about road-accessible dry tundra and other suitable areas on the Denali Highway (see earlier), and on the Dalton Highways and in Wrangell–St. Elias National Park (in chapter 9). I've listed some great trail hikes in chapter 7, under Chugach National Forest, and in chapter 9, in the sections on Chena Hot Springs Road and the Steese Highway.

5 Activities Within the Park

MOUNTAIN BIKING

A bicycle provides special freedom in the park. Bicyclists can ride past the checkpoint where cars have to turn back, at mile 14 on the park road. Park campgrounds have bike stands, and, with a reservation or if there is space available, you can take a bike on the shuttle or camper bus, so you can get a lift when you need one, or ride one way. (Groups larger than two may need to split up to fit on camper buses.) The longest stretch on the park road between campgrounds is 52 miles. On the downside, the buses kick up a lot of dust, and bikes are not permitted off-road. Pick up a copy of the bicycle rules from the backcountry desk before you start. **Denali Outdoor Center** (© 888/303-1925 or 907/683-1925; www.denalioutdoorcenter.com), located just north of the overlook in the Glitter Gulch area, rents front-suspension bikes for $40 for 24 hours, $25 for 6 hours, with discounts for longer rentals.

SLED DOG DEMONSTRATIONS

In the winter, rangers patrol the park by dog sled, as they have for decades. In the summer, to keep the dogs active and amuse the tourists, they run a sled on wheels around the kennel, and a ranger gives a talk, normally at 10am, 2pm, and 4pm. Although it's no substitute for seeing dogs run on snow, you can get a sense of their speed and enthusiasm from the show. It was the highlight of my older son's trip to Denali when he was 3 years old. There's no parking at the kennels, near the headquarters at mile 3.4 on the park road, so take a free bus that leaves the visitor center 40 minutes before each show. Times are listed in the *Alpenglow* park newspaper.

FISHING

Fishing is poor at Denali. There are grayling in some rivers, but the water is too cold and silty for most fish. Those who don't care if they catch anything, however, do enjoy fishing in this wonderful scenery. You don't need a fishing license within park boundaries, but you do have to throw back everything you catch. Bring your own gear.

First to the Top

It's the biggest. That's why climbers risk their lives on Mount McKinley. You can see the mountain from Anchorage, more than 100 miles away. On a flight across Alaska, McKinley stands out grandly over waves of other mountains. It's more than a mile taller than the tallest peak in the other 49 states. It's a great white triangle, always covered in snow, tall but also massive and strong.

The first group to try to climb Mount McKinley came in 1903, led by Judge James Wickersham, who also helped explore Washington's Olympic Peninsula before it became a national park. His group made it less than halfway up, but on the trip they found gold in the Kantishna Hills, setting off a small gold rush that led to the first permanent human settlement in the park area. Wickersham later became the Alaska Territory's nonvoting delegate to Congress and introduced the bill that created the national park, but the government was never able to get back land in the Kantishna area from the gold miners. Today, that land is the site of luxurious wilderness lodges, right in the middle of the park.

On September 27, 1906, renowned world explorer Dr. Frederick Cook announced to the world by telegraph that he had reached the summit of Mount McKinley after a lightning-fast climb, covering more than 85 miles and 19,000 vertical feet in 13 days with one other man, a blacksmith, at his side. On his return to New York, Cook was lionized as a conquering explorer and published a popular book of his summit diary and photographs.

In 1909, Cook again made history, announcing that he had beat Robert Peary to the North Pole. Both returned to civilization from their competing treks at about the same time. Again, Cook was the toast of the town. His story began to fall apart, however, when his Eskimo companions mentioned that he'd never been out of sight of land. After being paid by Peary to come forward, Cook's McKinley companion also recanted. A year later, Cook's famous summit photograph was re-created—on a peak 19 miles away and 15,000 feet lower than the real summit.

In 1910, disgusted with Cook, four prospectors from Fairbanks took a more Alaskan approach to the task. Without fanfare or special supplies—they carried doughnuts and hot chocolate on their incredible final ascent—they marched up the mountain carrying a large wooden

CLIMBING MOUNT MCKINLEY

Because of its altitude and weather, Mount McKinley is among the world's most challenging climbs. Summer temperatures at the high camp average 20° to 40°F below zero (–28° to –40°C). If you're looking here for advice, you're certainly not up to an unguided climb. A guided climb is a challenging and expensive endeavor requiring months of conditioning and most of a month on the mountain. Get names of guides from the park service's **Talkeetna Ranger Station,** P.O. Box 588, Talkeetna, AK 99676 (© **907/733-2231**). The climbing season lasts from late April or early May until the snow gets too soft, in late June or flagpole they could plant on top to prove they'd made it. But on arriving at the summit, they realized that they'd climbed the slightly shorter north peak. Weather closed in, so they set up the pole there and descended without attempting the south peak. Then, when they got back to Fairbanks, no one could see the pole, and they were accused of trying to pull off another hoax.

In 1913, Episcopal archdeacon Hudson Stuck organized the first successful climb to reach the *real* summit—and reported he saw the pole on the other peak. Harry Karstens led the climb (he would become the park's first superintendent in 1917), and the first person to stand at the summit was an Alaska Native, Walter Harper.

Although McKinley remains one of the world's most difficult climbs, about 10,000 people have made it to the top since Hudson Stuck's party. Since 1980 the number of climbers has boomed. Garbage and human waste disposal are a major problem. One recent June day, 115 climbers made it to the summit. In 1970, only 124 made the attempt all year; now more than 1,200 try to climb the peak each year, with about half making it to the summit. The cold, fast-changing weather is what usually stops people. From late April into early July, climbers fly from the town of Talkeetna to a base camp at 7,200 feet elevation on the Kahiltna Glacier. From there, it takes an average of about 18 days to get to the top, through temperatures as cold as –40°F (–40°C).

Climbers lose fingers, toes, and other parts to frostbite, or suffer other, more severe injuries. More than 90 climbers have died on the mountain, not counting plane crashes. During the season, the park service stations rescue rangers and an emergency medical clinic at the 14,200-foot level of the mountain, and keeps a high-altitude helicopter ready to go after climbers in trouble. In 2002, under pressure from Congress, the park service started charging climbers a $150-a-head fee, defraying a portion of the rescue costs. The park and the military spend about half a million dollars a year rescuing climbers, and sometimes much more. The cost in lives is high, as well. Volunteer rangers and rescuers die as well as climbers. Plane crashes, falls, cold and altitude all take a toll. Monuments to those who never returned are in the cemetery near the airstrip in Talkeetna.

early July. Climbers fly from Talkeetna to a 7,200-foot base camp on Kahiltna Glacier. About 1,200 climbers attempt the mountain annually in about 300 parties; about half typically make it to the top each year, and usually a few die trying.

6 Attractions & Activities Outside the Park

FLIGHTSEEING

Getting a good, close look at Mount McKinley itself is best accomplished by air. Frequently you can see McKinley from above the clouds even when you can't see it from the ground. Best of all, some Talkeetna operators that fly mountaineers also land visitors on the mountain, a unique and unforgettable experience (see section 10 of this chapter). Regardless of how close you approach the mountain, a flight shows how incredibly rugged the Alaska Range is.

Small planes and helicopters fly from the park airstrip, from private heliports and airstrips along the Parks Highway, and from the Healy airstrip. **Denali Air** (© **907/683-2261;** www.denaliair.com) has an office in the Nenana Canyon area, and operates flights at mile 229.5 of the Parks Highway. An hour-long flight going within a mile of the mountain costs $240 for adults, $120 for children ages 2 to 12. **Era Helicopters** (© **800/843-1947** or 907/683-2574; www. flightseeingtours.com), with bases in Denali and Talkeetna, has 50-minute flights for $259, including van pickup from hotels in the area. Their heli-hikes land for a 4-hour walk on a mountain ridgeline, the difficulty tailored to the customers' ability. They also offer a 75-minute glacier-landing flight. Either tour costs $359 per person.

RAFTING

Rafting on the Nenana River, bordering the park along the Parks Highway, is fun and popular. Several commercial guides float two stretches of the river: an upper portion, where the water is smoother and the guides explain passing scenery; and the lower portion, where the river roars through the rock-walled Nenana Canyon, and rafts take on huge splashes of silty, glacial water through Class III and IV rapids. Guides take children as young as 5 on the slow trip (although I wouldn't let my kid go at that age); the youngest accepted for the fast portion is age 12. White-water rafting carries risks you shouldn't discount just because a lot of people do it, as a fatal accident on the supposedly easy tour confirmed in 1999. Each session takes 2 to 2½ hours, including safety briefings, suiting up, and riding to and from the put-in and take-out points. Prices vary from $65 to $90 for adults, with discounted rates for children (from $10 less to half off).

Denali Outdoor Center (© **888/303-1925** or 907/683-1925; www.denali outdoorcenter.com) is a professional operation, offering rafting trips and instruction in river techniques. Although several other firms compete and you can shop around, DOC's strong safety ethic would be the decisive factor in my choice. Moreover, they provide specialized dry suits that keep passengers comfortable, not just Mustang flotation suits that allow you to get drenched. DOC also offers self-paddled inflatable kayaks, popular with those who want to take an active hand in their float. In any event, plan a shower afterward—the silt in the river water will stick to your skin and hair.

HORSEBACK RIDING

There is no riding in the park itself, but various companies offer rides in similar terrain outside the Park's boundaries. One- to two-hour rides cost from $65 to $95. Among the operators are **Denali Saddle Safaris** (© **907/683-1200;** www. denalisaddlesafaris.com), which also offers pack trips and extended journeys; and **Tumbling B Ranch** (© **907/683-6000;** www.tumblingbranch.com).

7 Where to Stay
PARK SERVICE CAMPGROUNDS

I've explained how to make camping reservations in section 2 of this chapter, under "The Reservations System." Note that reservation fees may be added to camping fees.

Only Riley Creek Campground is open after September (water is off in winter). The rest reopen when the snow is gone in May, except Wonder Lake, which opens in June.

I have noted where RVs are permitted in the description of each campground. There are no RV hook-ups at any campground in the park.

CAR-ACCESSIBLE CAMPGROUNDS

In addition to these, see **Teklanika River campground** under "Bus-Accessible Campgrounds," below; you can drive to it as long as your stay is at least 3 nights.

Riley Creek   This large campground right across the road from the visitor center is best for those who want to be in the middle of things. It's near the Riley Creek Mercantile, with its showers, laundry, Internet access, and a sewage dump station. The free front-country shuttle connects the campground with other facilities. Reservations are relatively easy to get. Sites are wooded with small birch and spruce, and they're adequately separated, but this isn't exactly wilderness camping. Twenty-seven walk-in sites are only for tent-users without vehicles.

Near the visitor center. 146 sites; RVs or tents. $18 vehicle sites, $12 walk-in sites. Campfires allowed; flush toilets.

Savage River   On the taiga—the thin spruce forest and tundra—this is a wonderful campground with unforgettable views. Campers can wander from their sites on some of the park's best hikes. This is the only campground you can readily drive to that's away from the activity at the park entrance. There is no telephone.

On Denali Park Rd., 13 miles from entrance. 33 sites; RVs and cars or tents. $18 per site. Campfires allowed; flush toilets.

BUS-ACCESSIBLE CAMPGROUNDS

To use these campgrounds, you'll need a camper ticket on the shuttle bus, which costs $23 for adults, half price ages 15 to 17, free ages 14 and under. There are no businesses and no phones beyond the park entrance area; you must bring in everything you need. Wildlife management concerns sometimes close these campgrounds unexpectedly.

Sanctuary River   This small, primitive campground offers a backcountry experience away from cars. You can't reserve sites in advance; permits are available only in person at the visitor center when you arrive.

On Denali Park Rd., 23 miles. 7 sites; tents only. $9 per site. No campfires; stoves permitted; chemical toilets.

Teklanika River   This is the only car campground beyond the checkpoint on the Park Road. To hold down traffic, the park service requires campers to keep their vehicles in place for 3 days. In the past couple of years, tents have not been

---

Tips Keeping Clean at Denali

The only showers within the park are at **Riley Creek Mercantile,** the store near the Riley Creek Campground, which also has laundry machines and other services. You pay by the shower, so there's no coin-operated timer to feed. You can also wash your clothes and shower at **McKinley RV and Campground** in Healy, covered below under "Commercial Campgrounds." The larger park campgrounds have the typical cold-water bathrooms found in the national parks, while others have vault toilets.

allowed here because wolves in the area were showing too much interest; at this writing, that policy still stands. Sites are among the small trees of the boreal forest. The big advantage of staying here is that you begin the morning much closer to the heart of the park, cutting the time you have to spend on the bus. You can buy one bus ticket for the regular price and use it for your entire 3-day stay. That makes Teklanika a good base to really explore different areas of the park in varying kinds of weather.

On Denali Park Rd., 29 miles from entrance; access by camper bus, or drive in with a minimum 3-night stay. 53 sites; RVs only, no tents. $16 per site. Campfires allowed; flush toilets.

Wonder Lake ★★★   It takes almost 6 hours to get here on the bus, but this campground by placid Wonder Lake, at the foot of Mount McKinley, puts you in the most beautiful and coveted area of the park. Set among a patch of spruce trees on the mountain side of the lake, the sites can be tough to get. On the other hand, the mosquitoes can be horrendous.

On Denali Park Rd., 85 miles from entrance. $16 per site. 28 sites; tents only. No campfires, stove only; flush toilets.

COMMERCIAL CAMPGROUNDS

There are several commercial campgrounds in the general vicinity of the park entrance, although none in walking distance.

Denali Grizzly Bear Cabins and Campground (© **907/683-2696;** www.alaskaone.com/dengrzly) is about 7 miles south of the park entrance at mile 231.1 of the Parks Highway. Some sites sit on an exposed hillside while others are among small trees. Small cabins and tent cabins dot the property as well; they range from $49 without a bathroom to $173 for a unit with a kitchen and full bathroom. There is a coin-operated shower. Tent sites are $19 for up to four people, with electrical and water hookups $6 more.

A campground with birch trees and attractive sites is 10 miles north of the park, in Healy. **McKinley RV and Campground,** at mile 248.5 on the Parks Highway (© **800/478-2562** or 907/683-2379; www.mtaonline.net/~rvcampak), has a deli and espresso bar, a gas station, token-operated laundry, and hot showers. Basic tent sites are $16, full hookups $27.

HOTELS

Patterns of land ownership and the uncontrolled development around Denali have led to a hodgepodge of roadside hotels, cabins, lodges, campgrounds, and restaurants in pockets arrayed along more than 20 miles of the Parks Highway. There are rooms of good quality in each of the pockets, but the going rates vary widely.

The most expensive rooms, and the first booked, are in the immediate vicinity of the park entrance. Next are the hotels south of the park. Both these areas are entirely seasonal. The best deals are in **Healy,** 12 miles north of the park, where you can find a room for $50 less than a comparable room near the park entrance. You can find a few links to B&B websites through the **Healy Chamber of Commerce** (www.denalichamber.com, click "Directory"). If you don't have a car Healy is not convenient; in that case, stay nearer the park entrance.

The other choices are **Talkeetna,** the back door to the park (described in section 10 of this chapter); or a wilderness lodge in the **Kantishna** area or outside the park (see section 11 of this chapter).

Despite their high prices, rooms can be hard to find at the peak of the season, and it's wise to book ahead.

NEAR THE PARK

This area, known formally as Nenana Canyon or more commonly as "Glitter Gulch," extends about a mile north of the park entrance on the Parks Highway. Two huge, luxurious hotels dominate the area. Owned by the Princess and Holland American cruise lines, each has superb rooms and public areas that were rebuilt in grand style between 2002 and 2004. Objectively the best lodgings in the area, I give them brief mention mainly because they serve package-tour passengers nearly to the exclusion of other guests. These two hotels are: the **Denali Princess Lodge,** Mile 238.5, Parks Hwy. (© **800/426-0500** reservations, 907/683-2282 local; fax 907/683-2808; www.princesslodges.com), and the **McKinley Chalet Resort,** Mile 239.1, Parks Hwy. (book through Denali Park Resorts, under "Visitor Information," earlier). Rack rates are high at each of these places, but you can stay for much less if you arrive on one of the days when the flow of cruise ship passengers is down, or early or late in the season, or if you book one of their packages. Good deals are to be had there as packages with the Alaska Railroad, or out of peak season.

Since most readers of this book are independent travelers, I've concentrated on smaller lodgings that cater to individual bookings. In addition to those described in full below, you'll find good standard rooms at **Denali River View Inn,** Mile 238.4, Parks Hwy. (© **866/683-2663** or 907/683-2663; www.denali riverviewinn.com), for $144 double; and at **Denali Sourdough Cabins,** Mile 238.5, Parks Hwy. (© **800/544-0970** or 907/683-2773; www.denalisourdough cabins.com), which has comfortable little cabins with private bathrooms in the woods below the highway for $145 at peak season.

All of the hotels in this area are open only during the tourist season, roughly from May 15 to September 15.

Denali Bluffs Hotel ★★   A series of 12 buildings on a steep mountainside looks down on the Nenana Canyon area from above the highway. The light, tastefully decorated rooms have two double beds and good amenities, and those on the upper floor have vaulted ceilings and balconies with great views. The courtesy van will take you anywhere in the area. The same owners have the **Grande Denali Lodge,** which perches impossibly high above the Nenana Canyon and charges a bit more for the view. Use caution and observe the mirrors at the switchbacks on the gravel road up from the highway. Contact information is for Denali Bluffs, but the toll free number and website are good for either.

Mile 238.4, Parks Hwy. (P.O. Box 72460, Fairbanks, AK 99707). © **866/683-8500** or 907/683-8500. Fax 907/ 683-8599. www.denalialaska.com. 112 units. High season $206 double; low season $133 double. Extra person $20. AE, DISC, MC, V. **Amenities:** 2 restaurants; tour desk; courtesy van; coin-op laundry. *In room:* Satellite TV, fridge, coffeemaker.

Denali Crow's Nest Log Cabins ★   Perched in five tiers on the side of Sugarloaf Mountain above the Nenana Canyon area, looking down on Horseshoe Lake and the other, larger hotels, the regularly updated cabins are roomy and comfortable, especially those on the 100 and 200 level. A log cabin and the warmth of the Crofoot family create a truer Alaskan feeling than the modern, standard rooms that have filled the canyon, and the rates are quite reasonable for the area (believe it or not). You spend a lot of time climbing stairs, however; and the rooms have shower enclosures, not tubs. All rooms are nonsmoking. The restaurant, **The Overlook,** is recommended separately under "Where to Dine," later in this chapter.

Mile 238.5, Parks Hwy. (P.O. Box 70), Denali National Park, AK 99755. © **888/917-8130** or 907/683-2723. Fax 907/683-2323. www.denalicrowsnest.com. 39 cabins. High season $149 cabin for 2; low season $99 cabin for 2. Extra person $10. MC, V. **Amenities:** Restaurant; bar; outdoor hot tub; tour desk; courtesy van.

IN HEALY

Healy is 10 miles north of the park entrance, but a world away. It's a year-round community with an economy based partly on a coal mine. It sits in a large, windy valley with a few patches of stunted trees and big, open spaces of tundra. There are many hotels and B&Bs with rooms that cost from $20 to $90 less than those near the park. Also, unlike hotels at the park entrance, most Healy businesses are open year-round. They say the water tastes better, too. On the downside, you need a car to stay in Healy.

Besides the lodgings listed below, **Dome Home Bed & Breakfast** (© **800/683-1239** or 907/683-1239; www.denalidomehome.com) is a great place, a huge house in a geodesic dome. The seven rooms are $115 double in summer and have many amenities.

Earthsong Lodge ★★ Value   This place is well off the beaten path, but it's worth the trip to stay in an authentically Alaskan dwelling and meet interesting people, year-round residents Jon and Karin Nierenberg. Guests gather in the main lodge building, with its library, living room, and piano. There's a coffee house, Henry's, serving breakfast and dinner and packing sack lunches. The lodge and individual cabins are all solid log construction. The cabins, with one or two bedrooms, have quilts on the beds and other cozy features, as well as private bathrooms (these are operational only in the summer; in the off season, guests use a shower house). Outside is the windy open tundra with sweeping views of the Alaska Range and Mount McKinley. In the evening, Jon puts on slide shows of his Alaska life and adventures. In the winter they offer dog sledding, and in the summer rides in a dog cart and kennel tours. The lodge is 17 miles north of Denali National Park, 4 miles down the scenic Stampede Road.

Stampede Trail, off the Parks Hwy. at mile 251 (P.O. Box 89), Healy, AK 99743. © **907/683-2863**. Fax 907/683-2868. www.earthsonglodge.com. 10 cabins. Summer $115–$135 double; winter $75–$85 double. $10 each additional person over age 12. DISC, MC, V. **Amenities:** Restaurant (coffeehouse). *In room:* Coffeemaker, hair dryer.

Motel Nord Haven ★★   This fresh little gray hotel with a red roof has large, immaculate rooms, each with one or two queen-size beds. They're equal to the best standard rooms in the Denali Park area and a lot less expensive. Bill and Patsy Nordmark offer free continental breakfast in the summer, and newspapers, coffee, tea, hot chocolate, extra phone lines for the Internet, and a sitting room with a collection of Alaska books. The rooms, decorated with Alaska art and oak trim, all have interior entrances and have been smoke-free since their construction. Up to four people can stay in the rooms with two beds for the price of a double. There are three kitchenette units. The Nordmarks pack sack lunches for $8.

Mile 249.5, Parks Hwy. (P.O. Box 458), Healy, AK 99743. © **800/683-4501** or 907/683-4500. Fax 907/683-4503. www.motelnordhaven.com. 28 units. Summer $124–$150; spring/fall $89–$99; winter $75–$80. AE, MC, V. *In room:* TV, dataport.

White Moose Lodge Value   This old, low-slung building among stunted black spruce contains an unlikely find—comfortable, cheerfully decorated rooms with flower boxes, and a small greenhouse. All have two double beds and private bathrooms. The breakfast served in the small lobby consists of coffee, tea, orange juice, and pastries.

Mile 248, Parks Hwy. (P.O. Box 68), Healy, AK 99743. © 800/481-1232 or 907/683-1231. Fax 907/683-1232. www.whitemooselodge.com. 12 units. High season $90 double; low season $70 double. Extra adult $10, extra child $5. Rates include continental breakfast. AE, DC, DISC, MC, V. Closed Oct to mid-May. In room: TV.

SOUTH OF THE PARK

Lodgings south of the park are in widely separated pockets of private land concentrated 7 and 14 miles south of the park. (Anything south of that is covered with Talkeetna, in section 10 of this chapter.) I've listed just a few in detail below, but you may also want to try these others that may be just as good: **McKinley Creekside Cabins,** 13 miles south at mile 224, Parks Hwy. (© 888/ 5DENALI or 907/683-2277; www.mckinleycabins.com), which offers comfortable, carpeted cabins, all with small private bathrooms, for reasonable prices starting at $79 double, or $169 for a family suite with a kitchenette; or, five miles closer to the park, **Denali Cabins,** Mile 229, Parks Hwy. (© 888/560-2489 or 907/644-9980; www.denali-cabins.com).

Denali Mountain Morning Hostel and Lodge ★ Value This extraordinary hostel is operated by energetic outdoors people who offer a cozy place to stay in an octagonal log building as well as support for forays into the park. Their well-stocked store and equipment rental operation offer everything needed for a backpacking trip, and their free shuttle runs to the park entrance four times a day. Accommodations include hostel bunks, private rooms, or separate private cabins, all advantageously priced. All guests use the shared bathhouse and have access to a fully equipped kitchen and Internet access, which carries an additional fee. They are located near McKinley Creekside Cafe and the Perch.

Mile 224.5, Parks Hwy. (P.O. Box 208), Denali National Park, AK 99755. © 907/683-7503. Fax 907/683-7504. www.hostelalaska.com. 3 private rooms, 3 private cabins. Bunk $25 adult, $19 children 12 and under. Private room $65 double; cabin $75 double; $10 each additional adult, $5 ages 5–12, free under 5. 2-night minimum in private rooms and cabins. DISC, MC, V.

Denali River Cabins ★★ These cedar cabins arrayed on a maze of boardwalks above the Nenana River are fresh and well appointed. Unlike some accommodations outside Denali, they have an outdoorsy, national park feel, lent in part by the riverside location. They have shower stalls, not tubs, and lack closets. They do have phones. The cabins on the river, with decks over the water, are $30 more. The sauna has a picture window on the river. Ride the free Denali Park Resorts shuttle to the park entrance and rail depot. Don't confuse this place with Denali Cabins.

Mile 231.1, Parks Hwy. (P.O. Box 210), Denali National Park, AK 99755. (Winter mailing address: 1 Doyon Place, Ste. 200, Fairbanks, AK 99701.) © 800/230-7275 or 907/683-8000. Fax 907/683-8095. (Winter © 907/459-2121; fax 907/459-2160.) www.seedenali.com. 54 cabins. High season $139–$169 cabin for 2; low season $99–$119 cabin for 2. Extra adult $10, free for children under 11. AE, DISC, MC, V. **Amenities:** Restaurant; bar; sauna; tour desk; coin-op laundry. In room: TV.

The Perch ★ Value In the trees along rushing Carlo Creek, 13 miles south of the park entrance, cabins range from large, modern units with private bathrooms to adorable if spartan A-frames with lofts that share a bathhouse. Two cabins have kitchens. There's a sense of privacy and of being out in the woods along the wooden and gravel walkways. The Perch is an exceptional value, open year-round. You will need a car to stay here. The **restaurant and bar,** set atop a steep hill, are described below under "Where to Dine"; down on the highway level, their Panorama Pizza Pub is a local gathering place.

Mile 224, Parks Hwy. (P.O. Box 53), Denali National Park, AK 99755. © 888/322-2523 or ©/fax 907/683-2523. www.denaliperchresort.com. 22 cabins, 14 with private bathroom. $75–$95 cabin for 2. Extra adult $16. Rates include breakfast. AE, DISC, MC, V. **Amenities:** 2 restaurants; bar; tour desk.

WILDERNESS LODGES

For those who can afford it, a lodge allows you to experience real wilderness in complete comfort. For understandable reasons, lodges with any view of Mount McKinley or proximity to the park call themselves Denali lodges. Some are actually within the park's boundaries in the old gold-mining inholding of the Kantishna District, while others are reached only by air and lie well outside the park. In either case, a wilderness lodge experience revolves around the lodge and its immediate surroundings, not the park activities described above, so I've grouped them in section 11.

8 Where to Dine

Since Denali is entirely seasonal, it lacks the range of inexpensive family restaurants that develop in year-round communities. While you may find reasonably priced food in Healy, to the north, or Carlo Creek, to the south (see below), near the park most meals are overpriced by 25% to 50% due to the short season and captive audience.

NEAR THE PARK ENTRANCE

You'll have no trouble finding an espresso at Denali. The large hotels in the canyon each have fine dining and casual restaurants; I've described the best in detail below. There are plenty of spots to get a low-key or take-out meal. The **Courtyard Cafe** at the McKinley Chalet Resort serves a buffet and has a children's menu. You can't miss the tacky highway frontage of the **McKinley Denali Salmon Bake** in Glitter Gulch. Although casual to the point of indifference, it can be a fun place to eat in a picnic setting, and the food is adequate and relatively inexpensive. **Lynx Creek Pizza** is something of a tradition but terribly inconsistent from year to year. For take-out sandwiches and a great Greek salad, it's hard to beat **Bub's Subs,** on the highway (© **907/683-7827**); call ahead to avoid waiting. It's next to Denali Outdoor Center. They have no seating.

Nenana View Bar & Grill ⭐ PIZZA/STEAK/SANDWICHES   This attractive restaurant in the McKinley Chalet Resort has an open kitchen to watch the cooking and outdoor seating overlooking the river. They serve some of the best pizza in the area and great fire-grilled steaks.

Mile 238.9 Parks Highway, in McKinley Chalet Resort. © **907/683-8200.** All items $12–$27. AE, DISC, DC, MC, V. May–Sept daily 11am–4:30pm and 5–10:30pm. Closed off season.

The Overlook Bar and Grill ⭐ BURGERS/STEAK/SEAFOOD   This fun, noisy place has the feel of a classic bar and grill, with a vaulted ceiling of rough-cut lumber and a spectacular view of the Nenana Canyon. There are two dining rooms, one with the bar, and another, behind a glass partition, which is quieter and has tablecloths. A huge variety of craft beers is available, with several on tap. At times I've gotten superb fare here and at other times it has been merely acceptable. Call © 907/683-2723 for courtesy transportation from all area hotels.

Mile 238.5, Parks Hwy., up the hill above the Denali Canyon area. © **907/683-2641.** Lunch main courses $9–$15; dinner main courses $16–$30. MC, V. Daily 11am–11pm, bar till midnight. Closed mid-Sept to mid-May.

The Summit Restaurant ⭐⭐ STEAK/SEAFOOD   This is a terrific place for a special night of dining out right near the park. First, there's the dining room, perched on the edge of the Nenana Canyon, where you can watch rafters float by during your meal. Then there's the food and service, which are up to Princess Tours' excellent standards—steak and salmon, the usual choices for Alaska tourists—prepared expertly. For something a bit more casual the Basecamp Bistro is in the same building.

In the Denali Princess Lodge, Mile 238.5, Parks Hwy. ✆ **907/683-8812**. Reservations recommended. Dinner main courses $17–$37. AE, DC, DISC, MC, V. Summer daily 5–10:30am, 11am–2pm and 5–10pm.

IN HEALY

These places are 12 miles north of the park, so you will need a car.

Black Diamond Grill ★★ STEAK/SEAFOOD/ITALIAN   A unique nine-hole golf course lies amid the mountains and rolling taiga north of the park. The associated restaurant brings a new class of food to the area with a menu mostly influenced by Northern Italian cookery. For lunch, sandwich choices include a pesto chicken hoagie for $7.50, and for dinner there is halibut in parchment with fresh rosemary and garlic for $20. Although not as perfect as at the best restaurants in Anchorage, the cuisine is really something for the Denali area. The dining room is light and cheery, with pine furniture and flowers on the table. Children will enjoy the mini-golf course or wagon rides.

Mile 247, Parks Hwy. (take the hwy. north 10 miles, then turn left at Otto Lake Rd.). ✆ **907/683-4653**. www. blackdiamondgolf.com. Lunch $7.50–$9, dinner main courses $14–$24. AE, DISC, MC, V. Daily 7am–11pm. Closed off season.

The Lunch Box *Value* TAKEOUT   This trailer produces good, inexpensive food in Asian, Italian, Mexican, and deli styles, with low carb choices, to take on a picnic or eat back at the room. The teriyaki rice bowl is delicious. They're also famous for the ribs produced on Saturdays only. A hearty box lunch is about $8, and they'll bring it to your hotel the night before so you can catch an early park bus.

Healy Spur Rd. (just off the Parks Hwy. across the street from the Mountain View Store). ✆ **907/683-6833**. Lunch $3–$8. MC, V. June–Aug Mon–Fri 11am–2pm and 4–7pm; Sat 11am–2pm. Closed Sun, holidays, and off season.

SOUTH OF THE PARK

McKinley Creekside Cafe ★ *Kids* STEAK/SEAFOOD/SANDWICHES   This cozy and friendly spot in the Carlo Creek area, south of the park, is a favorite of the locals. You can dine on steak or baked salmon with brown sugar, apples, and toasted almonds for around $20, or order a main-course salad or burger for around $8. The food is consistently good, including breakfast, and craft brews and wine are served. There is a playground outside and a kid's menu. They also pack substantial sack lunches for the shuttle-bus ride.

Mile 224, Parks Hwy. ✆ **907/683-2277**. www.mckinleycabins.com. Lunch $6–$10, dinner $8–$21. DISC, MC, V. Summer daily 6am–10pm.

The Perch/Panorama Pizza Pub ★ STEAK/SEAFOOD/PIZZA/DELI   An odd, knoblike hill gives the Perch its name (the attractive cabins described above sit below the restaurant). It's a friendly, family-run place serving a straightforward steak and Alaskan seafood menu—they don't try anything fancy, just good ingredients done right. The home-baked bread is noteworthy. The dining room is light, with well-spaced tables and big picture windows on three sides. Down on the highway level, the Panorama Pizza Pub is a hot spot for pizza, and also includes a bakery/deli that packs lunches in cloth tote bags for the park bus. You can often hear local musicians playing there in the evening.

Mile 224, Parks Hwy., 13 miles south of the park. ℂ 888/322-2523 or 907/683-2523. www.denaliperch resort.com. Perch dinner main courses $14–$40; Panorama Pizza Pub pizza $12–$30. AE, DISC, MC, V. Summer daily 6am–11pm. Winter hours vary.

9 Denali Nightlife

The main evening event is the concessionaire's **Cabin Nite Dinner Theater,** at the McKinley Chalet Resort (ℂ **800/276-7234** or 907/683-8200), a professionally produced musical revue about a gold rush–era woman who ran a roadhouse in Kantishna. You can buy the $49 tickets (half price ages 2–12) virtually anywhere in the area. The actors, singing throughout the evening, stay in character to serve big platters of food to diners sitting at long tables, doing a good job of building a rowdy, happy atmosphere for adults and kids.

Princess Cruises and Tours puts on its own evening show, **The Music of Denali,** at the Denali Princess Lodge. The performance lasts an hour; with dinner, it lasts 2 hours. Tickets are for sale at the hotel's tour desk (ℂ **800/426-0500** or 907/683-2282) for $45 (half price ages 6–12).

10 Talkeetna: Back Door to Denali

Talkeetna, a historic and funky little town with a sense of humor but not much happening, slept soundly from its decline around World War I until about a decade ago. Now there are paved streets (both of them), a fancy National Park Service building, a new railroad depot, and two large luxury lodges. It seems that while Talkeetna slumbered in a time capsule, an explosion of visitors was happening at Denali National Park. Now, not entirely voluntarily, Talkeetna finds itself enveloped in that boom.

As a threshold to the park, Talkeetna has significant pros and cons that you should take into account. On the positive side, it's closer to Anchorage; the development is much more interesting and authentic than that at the park entrance; there's lots to do outdoors; and great views of the mountain are less frequently obscured by clouds. On the negative side, a big minus: You can't get into the park from here without a long drive or a flight. That means you miss the dramatic scenery, easy backcountry access, and unique wildlife viewing on the park road.

The town dates from the gold rush, and has many charming log and clapboard buildings. With 15 sites of historic note, the entire downtown area has been listed on the National Register of Historic Places. You can spend several hours looking at two small museums and meeting people in the 2-block main street, then go out on the Talkeetna or Susitna rivers for rafting, a jet-boat ride, or fishing, or take a flightseeing trip to the national park.

ESSENTIALS

GETTING THERE Talkeetna lies on a 13-mile spur road that branches from the Parks Highway 99 miles north of Anchorage and 138 miles south of the park entrance.

The **Alaska Railroad** (ℂ **800/544-0552** or 907/265-2494; www.alaskarail road.com) serves Talkeetna daily on its runs to Denali National Park during the summer, and weekly in the winter. (See section 2 of this chapter for additional details.) The summer fare from Anchorage to Talkeetna is $78 one-way for adults, half price for children.

The **Talkeetna Shuttle Service** (ℂ **907/733-1725** office or 907/373-8548; www.denalicentral.com) runs to and from Anchorage for $55 one-way, $100 round-trip. **Alaska Trails** (© **888/600-6001;** www.AlaskaShuttle.com), listed earlier in section 2, serves Talkeetna from Anchorage or Fairbanks.

It's possible to stay in Talkeetna and do the Denali National Park shuttle bus ride and other park activities by flying there for the day. **Talkeetna Aero Services** (© **800/660-2688** or 907/733-2899; www.talkeetna-aero.com) offers daily round trips for this purpose during the summer. They charge $260 as a package with ground transfers, a bus tour, and a box lunch.

VISITOR INFORMATION   Built to serve people aiming to climb Mount McKinley, the **Denali National Park Talkeetna Ranger Station,** downtown Talkeetna (P.O. Box 588), Talkeetna, AK 99676 (© **907/733-2231;** www. nps.gov/dena), makes a fascinating stop for anyone curious about mountaineering. Inside the handsome structure a large sitting room contains a river-rock fireplace, climbing books, and pictures of the mountain—it's like an old-fashioned explorers' club. Fascinating records open for inspection cover the history of McKinley climbs. Rangers are on hand to answer questions, too. It's open May through August daily from 8am to 6pm; off season, Monday through Friday from 8am to 4:30pm.

The **Talkeetna/Denali Visitor Center,** located in a tiny cabin at the intersection of the Parks Highway and Talkeetna Spur Road and on Main Street next to Nagley's General Store (P.O. Box 688), Talkeetna, AK 99676 (© **800/660-2688** or 907/733-2688; www.alaskan.com/talkeetnadenali), is a commercial center belonging to a local flight service and providing brochures, information, and advice while earning commissions from bookings. It's the handiest commercial information stop in the region. The center is open daily from 8am to 8pm in summer, and they respond to inquiries year-round with free trip-planning help.

Like several small towns around Alaska, Talkeetna has a neat little online newspaper (there's also a printed version) that lets anyone eavesdrop on the community as well as gather information for a visit; it's the *Talkeetna Times Newspaper,* www.talkeetnanews.com. The tourist information version is the *Talkeetna Good Times.*

FAST FACTS: Talkeetna

Bank There is none, but ATMs are on Main Street at Nagley's General Store and at the coin-operated Three Rivers laundry.

Hospital Go to **Sunshine Community Health Center,** mile 4.4 on the Talkeetna Spur Road (© **907/733-2273**).

Internet Access At **Talkeetna Natural Foods,** with coffee, broadband, and a small fee; or for free at the **Talkeetna Public Library,** at mile 13 of the Spur Road, just across the tracks.

Police For non-emergencies, call the **Alaska State Troopers** at © **907/ 733-2256.** The station is at mile 1 of the Talkeetna Spur Road, near the highway.

Post Office In the town center, near the intersection of Talkeetna Spur Road and Main Street.

Taxes There is no sales tax. Bed tax in the area is 5%.

SPECIAL EVENTS **The Talkeetna Moose Dropping Festival,** held over the second weekend in July, is the big event of the year; it's a community fair finishing its third decade as a fundraiser for the Talkeetna Historical Society (© **907/733-2487**). The named event doesn't involve dropping moose, as an aggrieved animal-lover once complained, but dropping moose droppings. Another event, the **Mountain Mother Contest,** open only to mothers, is a race of Bush skills, including crossing a stream, splitting wood, and diapering a baby.

EXPLORING THE TOWN

Talkeetna is famous for its laid-back atmosphere and outdoors, not for "attractions," but there are several places to stop in to get the sense of the place. One is the ranger station mentioned above under "Visitor Information." If you come in May or June, you're sure to meet many international mountain climbers; you'll have no difficulty picking them out. The **Fairview Inn** is a historic bar with the rough edges still in place. Along Main Street are shops where artists and craftspeople often can be found at work.

The **Talkeetna Historical Society Museum,** in four buildings on the Village Airstrip a half block south of Main Street (© **907/733-2487;** www.talkeetna history.org), is well worth a stop. The first building contains artifacts and displays on local mining history, including engaging photographs and biographies of individual characters. The second is an attempt to re-create the old railroad depot. The third holds climbing displays and a huge scale model of Mount McKinley and the nearby mountains (don't miss it if you plan to fly over the mountain). The fourth is a 1916 trapper's cabin. The museum also is a handy information stop. It's open daily in summer from 10am to 6pm; closed in winter. Admission is $3, free for children 12 and under.

I've found the most affecting site in town to be the **mountain climbers' memorial** at the town cemetery, near the airstrip on the east side of the railroad tracks. Besides a granite memorial of plaques for lost mountaineers, there is a small garden of monuments to many individual climbers, some in Japanese. The bodies of 34 climbers who died on the mountain have never been recovered.

GETTING OUTSIDE
FLIGHTSEEING

The only way you'll get into the park from Talkeetna is by flying with one of the glacier pilots who support McKinley climbs, which typically begin with a flight from here to the 7,200-foot level of the Kahiltna Glacier. There is no more dramatic or memorable experience available to the typical tourist in Alaska. These immense mountains grow ever larger as you fly toward them until, like a tiny insect, you fly among their miles-tall folds, watching the climbers toiling on the ice below you. I was simply speechless.

Several operators with long experience offer the flights. The least expensive excursions cost around $140 (if the plane is full) and approach McKinley's south face. Rates often depend on how many are going, so you can save by putting together a group of four or five, or if the operator can add you to a group. Another way to save money is to call ahead, if only the day before, and ask for a reservation at a guaranteed price, which an operator will often do at the high season if they know you are coming. If at all possible—and if the weather is good—buy an extended tour that circles the mountain and flies over its glaciers, for $180 to $205 with a full plane. Best of all, in early summer and in the fall you can arrange a landing on the mountain itself, just as the climbers do (the snow is usually too soft starting in mid-July, but sometimes planes can land on the glaciers all summer). The Don Sheldon Amphitheater on the Ruth Glacier is a stunning spot high on McKinley; only after you stand there do you realize the incredible scale of what you have seen from above. These landings are usually treated as add-ons to the tours mentioned above, for an additional price of around $60 per person.

A number of air taxi companies offer these flights, all operating out of the Talkeetna airport, including these two: **Talkeetna Air Taxi** (© **800/533-2219** or 907/733-2218; www.talkeetnaair.com), and **Talkeetna Aero Services** (© **800/660-2688** or 907/733-2899, www.talkeetna-aero.com).

FISHING & JET BOAT TOURS

Talkeetna is at the confluence of the big Talkeetna and Big Susitna rivers. **Mahay's Riverboat Service** (© **800/736-2210** or 907/733-2223; www.mahays riverboat.com) is a large guide service, with 2-hour tours on a unique 51-foot jet boat for $50 per person, operating several times a day from a dock near the public boat launch on the Talkeetna River. Owner Steve Mahay is legendary, the only person ever to shoot Devil's Canyon in a jet boat. He offers fishing charters as well.

RAFTING

Talkeetna River Guides, on Main Street (© **800/353-2677** or 907/733-2677; www.talkeetnariverguides.com), offers a 2-hour wildlife river-rafting tour, without white water, over 9 miles of the Talkeetna three times a day for $54 adults, $22 children under 12. They also offer guided fishing and longer rafting outings and overnights by air, including the wild and hazardous class IV whitewater of the Talkeetna Canyon.

WHERE TO STAY & DINE

There are good restaurants at each of the lodgings listed here. One other place stands out, **Café Michele,** in a quaint little house at the corner of Talkeetna Spur Road and Second Street (© **907/733-5300**). It's a classy little bistro, serving sandwiches on homemade focaccia bread for lunch, and dinner entrees under $25.

It's easy to find a burger or sandwich on the Main Street, and a large campground is at the boat launch (cross the railroad tracks to the airport, then turn left).

Mt. McKinley Princess Lodge ★★   The Princess Cruise Line built the main lodge building to take advantage of a striking view of the mountain, only 42 miles away as the crow flies. The property isn't really near anything—100 miles south of the park entrance and about 45 road miles from Talkeetna—but, like a resort, they offer everything you need on-site and a full set of activities, including a short network of trails. The design and decoration are an inspired modernization of the classic national park style. There are several dining choices, including a steak and seafood place, a cafe, and a pizzeria.

Mile 133.1, Parks Hwy., Denali State Park, AK 99683 © 800/426-0500 or 907/733-2900. Fax 907/733-2922. www.princesslodges.com. 238 units. Summer $179 double; $289 suite. Spring and fall $139 double; $199 suite. AE, DISC, DC, MC, V. Closed mid-Sept to mid-May. **Amenities:** 2 restaurants; bar; exercise room; tour desk; coin-op laundry. *In room:* TV, hair dryer.

Swiss-Alaska Inn *Finds*   This is the essence of Talkeetna: a family business in the same hands for decades where guests are made to feel like old friends among the real old friends often found sipping coffee with the proprietor in the small restaurant. They serve good, familiar American meals, plus a few German dishes.

Rooms are decorated in light colors and, although small, are clean, comfortable, and reasonably priced.

F St., near the boat launch (P.O. Box 565), Talkeetna, AK 99676. ℂ **907/733-2424.** Fax 907/733-2425. www. swissalaska.com. 20 units. $110 double. Extra person $10. AE, DISC, MC, V. **Amenities:** Restaurant; bar; courtesy car (to railroad station). *In room:* TV/VCR, hair dryer.

Talkeetna Alaskan Lodge ★★   The Cook Inlet Region Native corporation spared no expense building this magnificent hotel of big timbers and river rock, but it's not a gaudy showplace. Rooms and hallways are hung with Native art and trimmed with understated geometric designs fashioned from regionally harvested birch. Because the hotel is located atop a high bluff, every common room and many guest rooms orient to a broad-canvas masterpiece of the Alaska Range. Although just 2 miles from the town, the hotel feels like it's out in the wilderness. Rooms in the main building are preferable as they're somewhat larger and have either one king- or two queen-size beds. Hallways connect to several sumptuous lobbies with reading areas.

Mile 12.5, Talkeetna Spur Rd. (P.O. Box 93330, Anchorage, AK 99509-3330). ℂ **888/959-9590** or 907/265-4501 reservations; 907/733-9500 at lodge. Fax 907/263-5559. www.talkeetnalodge.com. 200 units. Summer $229 double; off season $149 double. Extra person $12. AE, DISC, MC, V. Closed Oct–Apr. **Amenities:** 2 restaurants (international, cafe); bar; tour desk; courtesy van. *In room:* TV, dataport, coffeemaker, hair dryer.

11 Denali Wilderness Lodges

Staying in a wilderness lodge is expensive and requires a significant commitment of time. It doesn't make sense to spend less than 3 days, and some lodges require longer minimum stays. You need some time to slow down and feel the pace of the Bush. Here I've listed the best lodges in the Denali region; see chapter 7 for lodges on Kachemak Bay, near Homer.

KANTISHNA DISTRICT

The Kantishna district is an inholding of private land within Denali National Park where gold miners staked claims before the park was created. The lodge operators who later obtained this land gained something more valuable than gold: the opportunity to bring visitors to the far end of the park from the entrance, as near as a vehicle can get to Mount McKinley. Hosts drive visitors to Kantishna in private buses or vans over the 89-mile park road. These lodges are open only in summer. Besides those listed here, another excellent choice is **Denali Backcountry Lodge** (ℂ **800/841-0692** or 907/644-9980 ext. 204; www.denalilodge.com). All of these lodges are open only in summer.

Camp Denali/North Face Lodge ★★★   At this pioneering eco-tourism establishment, you can wake to the white monolith of Mount McKinley filling your window. The naturalist guides here have the right to use the park road free of the shuttle system for hikes, biking, lake canoeing, bird-watching, photography sessions, and other outdoor learning activities, all included in the substantial price. During some sessions, nationally respected academics and other experts lead the program. All arrivals and departures are on fixed session dates of 3, 4, or 7 days and start with a picnic supper on the park road on the way out to the lodges. Each of the Camp Denali cabins has its own outhouse, and all share a central bathhouse and wonderful lodge common rooms—it has the best views, and would be my first choice for anyone who can get by without his or her own flush toilet. North Face Lodge has smallish traditional rooms with private bathrooms. Each lodge has its own dining room for family-style meals. A conservation ethic pervades the operation, from the homegrown vegetables to the proprietors' efforts to preserve the natural values of private land in the park.

Kantishna District (P.O. Box 67), Denali National Park, AK 99755. ℂ **907/683-2290.** Fax 907/683-1568. www.campdenali.com. 17 cabins, none with private bathroom (Camp Denali); 15 units with bathroom (North Face Lodge). $400 per person per night, double occupancy. Rates include all meals and guided activities. Minimum stay 3 nights. No credit cards. No smoking in buildings or vehicles.

Kantishna Roadhouse ★★   This well-kept property of many buildings along Moose Creek in the old Kantishna Mining District trades on both the mining history and outdoor opportunities of the area. Some rooms are large and luxurious, while others are in smaller single cabins with lofts. The log central lodge has an attractive lobby with people coming and going—it's got more of a hotel feel and might be more attractive to an older, less active set or to families than the other lodges in the Kantishna District. It's also somewhat less expensive, has a bar, and accommodates 2-night stays. Guided hikes, wagon rides, biking, gold panning, a daily sled dog demonstration, and the bus ride from the park entrance are included in the rate.

Kantishna District, Denali National Park (Mailing address: P.O. Box 81670, Fairbanks, AK 99708). ℂ **800/942-7420** or 907/683-1475. Fax 907/683-1449. (Winter: ℂ 907/459-2120; fax 907/459-2160.) www.see denali.com. 27 units. $335 per person per night, double occupancy; $250 ages 3–11. Rates include all meals and guided activities. 2-night minimum. AE, DISC, MC, V. **Amenities:** Restaurant; bar; sauna; mountain bikes.

Skyline Lodge ★ *Value*   This new lodge run by pilot Greg Lahaie, owner of Kantishna Air Taxi, offers a unique alternative in Denali's backcountry: a place you don't have to be a millionaire to afford. With room for only eight guests and a self-serve philosophy, it's far simpler and more casual than the full service lodges in Kantishna, and costs less than a fourth as much. Also, there's no minimum stay, and you can fly there economically with Greg. It costs $25 a day to join the family-style lunch and dinner (breakfast is already included in the price). Rooms are in cabins, each with a double or queen-size bed and a loft. Large windows overlook Moose Creek. The kitchen, TV, and other amenities are in the central lodge building. The most important amenity, however, is that you are in the heart of Denali's backcountry. No smoking.

Kantishna District (P.O. Box 46), Denali Park, AK 99755. ℂ **907/683-1223.** Fax: 907/683-1223. www.katair.com. 3 units, none with private bathroom. $155 double, $40 each additional person age 2 and over. DISC, MC, V. Rates include continental breakfast. **Amenities:** Sauna; courtesy van; free mountain bikes.

FLY-IN LODGES

These lodges are outside the park proper, but share the same kind of terrain and some of the same views. Each offers its own version of the real wilderness lodge experience, far from roads and accessible only by small aircraft in places where wildlife far outnumbers people.

Caribou Lodge ★★   There's a lot to love about this place: the location above tree line, on its own alpine lake, miles from any other structure; the unlimited dry tundra hiking and views along the rounded ridge tops; the wildlife and the quiet. But what I love best, and what I suspect will matter most to visitors, is that it's real. This is home to Mike and Pam Nickols, the couple who personally host just three parties at a time, and for a decade they've lived out here in true Bush style, year-round, far off the grid. They guide hiking, canoeing on the lake, and watching the wildlife; in the winter, they teach guests to drive a dog team over endlessly rolling hills of snow. Mainly, a visit is a chance to experience another way of life, one that exists in few places. The accommodations are simple but comfortable, each cabin with its own outhouse and a shared shower facility. Access is by small aircraft only, on skis in winter or floats in summer; in spring and fall, when the ice on the lake is soft, it's just about impossible to get there. For rough figuring, a plane from Talkeetna costs $135 to $180 per person, but inquire to get a more exact cost.

20 miles east of Talkeetna (P.O. Box 706), Talkeetna, AK 99676. ©/fax **907/733-2163**. www.cariboulodge alaska.com. 3 cabins. $265 per person per day. Rates include all meals and guiding and are based on double occupancy, 2-day minimum. No credit cards. **Amenities:** Restaurant (family style, included in rate); guided activities included in rate; sauna.

Denali West Lodge ★★★   The log buildings look down through birch trees onto the shore of huge Lake Minchumina, far out in the Bush west of Denali National Park. The place balances authenticity and comfort so that you can sit at the bar and munch on great food while feeling like an adventurer. The real log cabins are cozy with quilts and barrel stoves that the staff lights when they bring your coffee in the morning; each has its own outhouse and there are shared showers. But what's truly unique are the activities, included in the price and led by guides who are assigned one to each party (the lodge has a 10-guest maximum in summer, six in winter). In summer, there's canoeing, hiking, and lake fishing. In the winter, go on dog mushing expeditions unlike any other in Alaska: Guests are met at the landing strip across the lake and drive their own teams to the lodge. The 9-day stay takes off on an expedition to McKinley, with participants sleeping in heated tents at night and mushing during the day; few people will ever live such an adventure in such comfort and safety. Obviously, a stay costs more than most people can afford; you should also figure in the cost of chartering a plane to get there, which is around $525 from the Denali Park entrance.

P.O. Box 40AC Lake Minchumina, AK 99757. © **888/607-5566** or 907/674-3112. Fax 907/674-3112. www. denaliwest.com. 5 cabins. Summer $1,470 3-night stay, $1,960 4 nights, per person. Winter $3,450 6 days mushing at lodge, $6,550 9 day-mushing expedition. Half price for children 12 and under. AE, DISC, MC, V. Rates include all meals and guiding, 3-night minimum. **Amenities:** Restaurant (family style, included in rate); guiding; sauna.

9

The Alaskan Interior

A warm summer evening in a campground; a slight breeze rustling the leaves of ghostly paper birches, barely keeping the mosquitoes at bay; the sounds of children playing; a perpetual sunset rolling slowly along the northern horizon—this is Interior Alaska. You know it's time to gather up the kids, separate them according to who belongs to whom, and put them to bed; it's 11 o'clock, for heaven's sake. But it's too difficult to feel that matters, or to alter the pace of a sun-baked day that never ends, meandering on like the broad, silty rivers and empty two-lane highways. Down by the boat landing, some college kids are getting ready to start on a float in the morning. An old, white-bearded prospector wanders out of the bar and, offering his flask to the strangers, tries out a joke while swatting the bugs. "There's not a single mosquito in Alaska," he declares. Waits for the loud, jocular objections. Then adds, "They're all married with big, big families." Easy laughter; then they talk about outboard motors, road work, why so many rabbits live along a certain stretch of highway. Eventually, you have to go to bed and leave the world to its pointless turning as the sun rotates back around to the east. You know it'll all be there tomorrow, just the same—the same slow-flowing rivers, the same long highways, the same vast space that can never be filled.

Interior Alaska is so large—it basically includes everything that's not on the coasts or in the Arctic—you can spend a week of hard driving and not explore it all. Or you can spend all summer floating the rivers and still have years of floating left to do before you see all the riverbanks. It's something like what the great mass of America's Midwest once must have been, perhaps a century and a half ago, when the great flatlands had been explored but not completely civilized and Huckleberry Finn could float downriver into a wilderness of adventures. As it happens, I have a friend who grew up on a homestead in the Interior and ran away from home at age 15 in that exact same fashion, floating hundreds of miles on a handmade raft, past the little river villages, cargo barges, and fishermen. During an Interior summer, nature combines its immensity with a rare sense of gentleness, patiently awaiting the next thunderstorm.

Winter is another matter. Without the regulating influence of the ocean—the same reason summers are hot—winter temperatures can often drop to –30°F or –40°F (–34°C or –40°C), and during exceptional cold snaps, even lower. Now the earth is wobbling over in the other direction, away from the sun. The long, black nights sometimes make Fairbanks, the region's dominant city, feel more like an outpost on a barren planet, far off in outer space. That's when the northern lights come, spewing swirls of color across the entire dome of the sky and crackling with electricity. Neighbors get on the phone to wake each other and, rising from bed to put on their warmest parkas and insulated boots, stand in the street, gazing straight up. Visitors lucky enough to come at such times may be watching from a steaming hot-spring tub. During the short days, they can bundle up and watch sled-dog racing or race across the wilderness themselves on snowmobiles.

Fairbanks stands second in Alaska in population, with over 80,000 in the greater area, but the Interior otherwise is without any settlements large enough to be called cities. Instead, it's defined by roads, both paved and gravel, which are strands of civilization through sparsely settled, often swampy land.

Before the roads, development occurred only on the rivers, which still serve as thoroughfares for the Athabascan villages of the region. In the summer, villagers travel by boat. In the winter, the frozen rivers become highways for snowmobiles and sled-dog teams. White homesteaders and gold miners live back in the woods, too. Gold rush history is written on the land in piles of old gravel tailings and abandoned equipment, as well as in the prettier tourist attractions and historic sites. Gold mining goes on today, in small one-man operations and huge industrial works employing hundreds.

1 Exploring the Interior

More than anywhere else in Alaska, the Interior is the place where having your own car provides you with the freedom to find the out-of-the-way places that give the region its character. Trains and buses run between Fairbanks and Anchorage, but that approach will show you only the larger, tourist-oriented destinations.

If you have the time and money, you may enjoy driving one of the remote gravel highways, or just poking along on the paved highways between the larger towns, ready to stop and investigate the roadhouses and meet the people who live out in the middle of nowhere. You'll find them mostly friendly and often downright odd—*colorful,* to use the polite term. As I drove an abandoned highway a few years ago, I saw a hand-lettered sign advertising coffee. It wasn't your typical espresso stand, just a log cabin dozens of miles from the next nearest building. A squinting high plains drifter stepped out of the cabin, wearing a cowboy hat on his head and a huge revolver on his hip, and asked, "Yeah?" The coffee came from a percolator warming on the woodstove, and the proprietor and I struck up a good conversation in his dark little dwelling. He was living the life of the old-time frontier. Another favorite roadside sign, sighted on the Alaska Highway, in spray paint on plywood: SALE—EEL SKINS—ANVILS—BAIT. I've always wished I'd stopped in to window-shop and meet the person who came up with that business plan.

Of course, not every mile of back road is scenic, nor are all the stops interesting. Driving a car through Alaska takes a long time, including many hours spent in dull, brushy forest, and calls for a high tolerance for greasy hamburgers. Paved highway sections can develop frost heaves in this often-frozen land—backbreaking dips and humps caused by the freeze and thaw of the road base and ground underneath. The gravel roads generate clouds of dust and quickly fatigue drivers, and windshields and headlights often succumb to their flying rocks. For information on renting a vehicle in Fairbanks to drive on gravel roads, see "Equipped for the Backroads," on p. 369; for Anchorage, see "Car Wheels on Gravel Roads," on p. 198.

Finds   Rollin' on the River

Floating any of the thousands of miles of the Interior's rivers opens great swaths of wilderness. Beginners will want to take a guided trip before venturing out on their own. (See the lists of operators in chapter 2.) To plan your own trip, get Karen Jettmar's *The Alaska River Guide* (Alaska Northwest Books, $17), which includes details for floats on more than 100 river trips across the state. Also, check with the **Alaska Public Lands Information Center** in Fairbanks (p. 362), Tok (p. 390), or Anchorage (p. 198) for guidance on setting up your trip. Among the most accessible and historic rivers in the region are the Chena, Chatanika, and Yukon (see the sections on Fairbanks and Chena Hot Springs Rd. and the boxes on the Steese Hwy. and Dawson City in this chapter).

2 Fairbanks: Alaska Heartland

If the story of the founding of Fairbanks had happened anywhere else, it wouldn't be told so proudly, for the city's father was a swindler and its undignified birth contained an element of chance not usually admitted in polite society. As the popular story goes (and the historians' version is fairly close), it seems that in 1901, E. T. Barnette decided to get rich by starting a gold-mining boomtown like the others that had sprouted from Dawson City to Nome as the stampeders of 1898 sloshed back and forth across the territory from one gold find to the next. He booked passage on a riverboat going up the Tanana with his supplies to build the town, having made an understanding with the captain that, should the vessel get stuck, he would lighten the load by getting off with the materials on the nearest bank. Unfortunately, the captain got lost. Thinking he was heading up a slough on the Tanana, he got sidetracked into the relatively small Chena River. That was where the boat got stuck and where Barnette got left, and that was where he founded Fairbanks.

Fortunately for Barnette, an Italian prospector named Felix Pedro had been looking for gold in the hills around the new trading post and made a strike on the Tanana. On that news, Barnette dispatched his Chinese cook off to Dawson City to spread the word. The cook's story showed up in a newspaper that winter, and a stampede of hundreds of miners ensued, heading toward Fairbanks in weather as cold as −50°F (−46°C). Barnette's town was a success, but the cook nearly got lynched when the stampeders found out how far he'd exaggerated the truth. Much more gold was found later, however, and half the population of Dawson City came downriver to Fairbanks. Barnette had made it big.

The town's future was ensured thanks to a political deal. Barnette did a favor for the territory's judge, James Wickersham, by naming the settlement for Wickersham's ally in Congress, Sen. Charles Fairbanks of Indiana, who later became vice president. Wickersham then moved the federal courthouse to Fairbanks from Eagle—he loaded his records on his dog sled and mushed here, establishing the camp as the region's hub. Wickersham's story is interesting, too. He was a notable explorer, Alaska's first real statesman as a nonvoting delegate to Congress, and father of the Alaska Railroad. Houses he lived in are preserved at Pioneer Park (formerly known as Alaskaland) in Fairbanks and in Juneau just up the hill from the capitol building. Barnette didn't do as well in history's eyes: He was run out of the town he founded for bank fraud.

Alaska's Highways a la Carte

You won't need a detailed highway map of Alaska, because Alaska doesn't have detailed highways. A single triangle of paved two-lane highways connects Tok, Fairbanks, and Anchorage. From this triangle, a few routes reach to discrete destinations, and gravel roads penetrate the periphery of the Bush. Beyond a few miles of freeway around Fairbanks and Anchorage, highways all are narrow strips of asphalt or gravel through the wilderness. A centralized report on road conditions, construction and weather is operated by the Alaska Department of Transportation (© 511; http://511.alaska.gov).

MAIN HIGHWAYS

Alaska Highway (Rte. 2 from the border to Delta Junction)   Running nearly 1,400 miles from Dawson Creek, British Columbia, to Delta Junction, Alaska, a couple of hours east of Fairbanks on the Richardson Highway, this World War II road today is paved and generally easy driving. Two tiny towns lie on the Alaska portion of the road, Delta Junction and Tok. The prettiest part is on the Canadian side, in the Kluane Lake area. See section 5, later in this chapter.

Glenn Highway (Rte. 1 from Anchorage to Tok)   From the Alaska Highway, this is how you get to Southcentral Alaska, including Anchorage, 330 miles southwest of Tok. The northern section, from Tok to Glennallen (sometimes called the "Tok Cut-Off"), borders Wrangell–St. Elias National Park, with broad tundra and taiga broken by high, craggy peaks. Glennallen to Anchorage is even more spectacular, as the road passes through high alpine terrain and then close by the Matanuska Glacier, where it winds through a deep canyon valley carved by the glacier's river. See section 6, later in this chapter.

Parks Highway (Rte. 3)   The George Parks Highway goes straight from Anchorage to Fairbanks, 358 miles north, providing access on the way to Denali National Park. There are some vistas of Mount McKinley from south of the park, but the Parks Highway is mostly just a transportation route, less scenic than the Richardson or Glenn highways. From the northern (Fairbanks) end, the highway passes Nenana (p. 380), then Denali and Talkeetna (chapter 8), and finally the towns of the Matanuska and Susitna valleys (chapter 6).

Richardson Highway (Rte. 4 from Valdez to Delta Junction, Rte. 2 from Delta Junction to Fairbanks)   The state's first highway, leading 364 miles from tidewater in Valdez to Fairbanks, lost much of its traffic to the Parks Highway, which saves more than 90 miles between Anchorage and Fairbanks, and to the Glenn Highway, which saves about 120 miles from Glennallen to Tok. But it's still the most beautiful paved drive in the Interior. From the south, the road begins with a magnificent climb through Keystone Canyon and steep Thompson Pass, just out of Valdez (see chapter 7), then passes the huge, distant peaks of southern Wrangell–St. Elias National Park. North of Glennallen, the road climbs into the Alaska Range, snaking along the shores of long alpine lakes. The road descends again to the forested area around Delta Junction and meets the Alaska Highway before arriving in Fairbanks. See section 7, later in this chapter.

Seward Highway (Rte. 1 from Anchorage to Tern Lake, Rte. 9 from Tern Lake to Seward)   The highway leaves Anchorage on the 127-mile drive to Seward following the rocky edge of mountain peaks above a surging ocean fjord. Abundant wildlife and unfolding views often slow cars. Later, the road climbs through high mountain passes above the tree line, tracing sparkling alpine lakes. Alaska's best trail hikes are here. The section from Anchorage 50 miles south to Portage Glacier is covered in chapter 6; the remainder, to Seward, in chapter 7.

Sterling Highway (Rte. 1 from Tern Lake to Homer)   Leading 142 miles from the Seward Highway to the tip of the Kenai Peninsula, the highway has some scenic ocean views on its southern section, but is mostly a way to get to the Kenai River, the Kenai National Wildlife Refuge, Kachemak Bay, and the towns of Cooper Landing, Soldotna, Kenai, and Homer.

RURAL ROADS

These mostly gravel roads are all in the Interior region covered by this chapter.

Chena Hot Springs Road   A relatively civilized road into the outdoors, this paved 57-mile highway east of Fairbanks meets hiking and river routes on the way to Chena Hot Springs.

Dalton Highway (Rte. 11)   Built to haul equipment to the Prudhoe Bay oil fields, about 500 miles north of Fairbanks, the supremely scenic Dalton reaches the heart of the wilderness, crossing the Brooks Range and the North Slope.

Denali Highway (Rte. 8)   This 133-mile gravel road connects the midpoints of the Parks and Richardson highways, passing stunning alpine vistas high in the Alaska Range that rival those within Denali National Park. Along the way are a rich network of trails and mountain lakes and a good chance to see caribou, bear, moose, and waterfowl. See chapter 8.

Edgerton Highway & McCarthy Road (Rte. 10)   Running east from the Richardson Highway south of Glennallen, the Edgerton leads to the tiny town of Chitina, where the McCarthy Road, a one-lane track, penetrates Wrangell–St. Elias National Park to the historic sites at McCarthy and Kennecott. The journey of 93 miles takes half a day.

Steese Highway (Rte. 6)   This gravel road climbs the rounded tundra mountains 162 miles east of Fairbanks to the Native village of Circle, on the Yukon River. It's a rare road deep into Bush Alaska.

Taylor Highway (Rte. 5)   At times rough, narrow, and a little scary, this dirt road leads 161 miles from a junction on the Alaska Highway east of Tok to the fascinating Yukon River village of Eagle, an island in time.

Top of the World Highway (Yukon Rte. 9)   Connecting to the Taylor Highway and crossing the Canadian border to Dawson City, a distance of 79 miles, the road rides mountaintop to mountaintop, above the tree line nearly the entire way.

Fairbanks is Alaska's second-largest city now, with a population of about 30,000 in the city limits and 82,000 in the greater metropolitan area, but it has never learned to put on airs. It sprawls, broad and flat, along big highways and the Chena. It's a friendly, easygoing town, but one where people still take gold and their independence seriously. They're still prospecting and mining around here, fighting off environmental regulation and maintaining a traditional Alaskan attitude that "it's us against the world." Fairbanks is the birthplace of strange political movements, including the secessionist Alaskan Independence Party. It's an adamant, loopy, affable place; it doesn't seem to mind being a little bizarre or residing far from the center of things. And that makes it an intensely Alaskan city, for those are the qualities Alaskans most cherish in their myth of themselves.

Fairbanks can strike a visitor a couple of ways, depending on what you expect and what you like. Fairbanks can come across as a provincial outpost, a touristy cross between Kansas and Siberia. Driving one of the franchise-choked commercial strips, you can wonder why you went out of your way to come here. Or you can relax and take Fairbanks on its own terms, as a fun, unpretentious town that never lost its sense of being on the frontier.

My children love it here. There's plenty for families to do in Fairbanks, much of it at least a little corny and requiring drives to widespread sites at the university, on the Chena River, in the gold mining area north of town, and at Pioneer Park. (You *must* have wheels in Fairbanks.) There are good opportunities for hiking and mountain biking, and great opportunities for canoeing and slow river-float trips.

ESSENTIALS

GETTING THERE   By Car or RV   Fairbanks is a transportation hub. The Richardson Highway heads east 98 miles to Delta Junction, the end point of the Alaska Highway, then south to Glennallen and Valdez. The Parks Highway heads due south from Fairbanks to Denali National Park, 120 miles away, and Anchorage, 358 miles south.

By Bus   Alaska Trails (© 888/600-6001; www.AlaskaShuttle.com) offers daily service in summer (less frequently in winter) to and from Denali National Park and Anchorage (one-way fares are $46 and $86, respectively). In Fairbanks, the bus stops at Billie's Backpackers Hostel (p. 377). The shuttle also runs to Dawson City and, when it has at least four passengers, to Valdez. They pick up and drop off along the way on each route.

By Train   The **Alaska Railroad** (© 800/544-0552; www.alaskarailroad.com) links Fairbanks with Denali National Park and Anchorage, with tour commentary provided along the way. High-season, the one-way Denali fare is $50, Anchorage $175 (around twice the cost of flying between the cities).

By Air   Alaska Airlines (© 800/252-7522; www.alaskaair.com) connects Fairbanks to Anchorage. A good round-trip fare is under $200. The airport is a hub for various small carriers to Alaska's Interior and Arctic communities.

A cab downtown from the airport is $16 to $18 with **Yellow Cab** (© 907/455-5555).

VISITOR INFORMATION   The **Fairbanks Log Cabin Visitor Information Center** is in a large log building with a sod roof at 550 1st Ave., on the Chena River at the center of town, at Cushman Street, Fairbanks, AK 99701 (© 800/327-5774 or 907/456-5774; fax 907/452-2867; www.explorefairbanks.com). Besides answering questions, the staff and volunteers provide useful maps and can

Greater Fairbanks

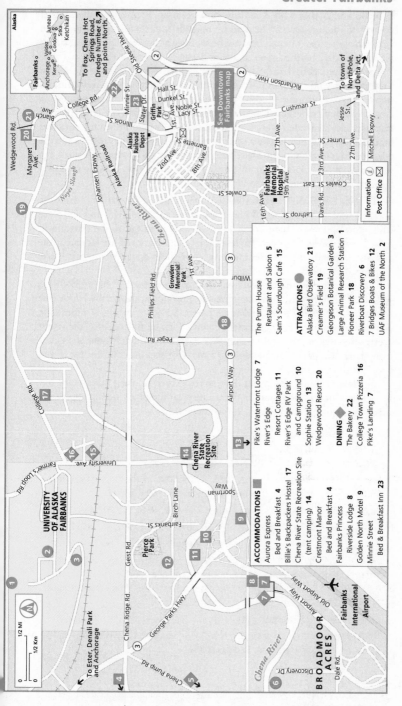

To Fox, Chena Hot Springs Road, Dredge Number 8, and points North.

To town of NorthPole, and Delta Jct.

To Ester, Denali Park and Anchorage

Alaska

Anchorage · Valdez · Juneau
Kenai · Cordova · Sitka
Fairbanks · Ketchikan

College Rd.
Wedgewood Rd.
Blanch Ave.
Margaret Ave.
Old Steese Hwy.
Hall St.
Dunkel St.
Noble St.
Lacy St.
1st. Ave.
Slater Dr.
Minnie St.
Illinois St.
Griffin Park
Alaska Railroad Depot
Barnette St.
2nd Ave.
8th Ave.
See Downtown Fairbanks map
Cushman St.
Richardson Hwy.
Johansen Expwy.
Alaska Railroad
Noyes Slough
Chena River
Growden Memorial Park
Phillips Field Rd.
Peger Rd.
1st Ave.
Wilbur
Airport Way
Fairbanks Memorial Hospital
16th Ave.
17th Ave.
19th Ave.
Cowles St.
Lathrop St.
Davis Rd.
23rd Ave.
27th Ave.
Turner St.
Jesse St.
Mitchell Expwy.
College Rd.
Farmer's Loop Rd.
University Ave.
UNIVERSITY OF ALASKA FAIRBANKS
Pierce Park
Geist Rd.
Birch Lane
Fairbanks St.
Sportman Way
Chena Ridge Rd.
George Parks Hwy.
Chena Pump Rd.
BROADMOOR ACRES
Dale Rd.
Discovery Dr.
Chena River
Fairbanks International Airport
Airport Way
Old Airport Way
Chena River State Recreation Site

0 1/2 Mi
0 1/2 Km

ACCOMMODATIONS

Aurora Express
Bed and Breakfast **4**
Billie's Backpackers Hostel **17**
Chena River State Recreation Site
(tent camping) **14**
Crestmont Manor
Bed and Breakfast **4**
Fairbanks Princess
Riverside Lodge **8**
Golden North Motel **9**
Minnie Street
Bed & Breakfast Inn **23**
Pike's Waterfront Lodge **7**
River's Edge
Resort Cottages **11**
River's Edge RV Park
and Campground **10**
Sophie Station **13**
Wedgewood Resort **20**

DINING

The Bakery **22**
College Town Pizzeria **16**
Pike's Landing **7**
The Pump House
Restaurant and Saloon **5**
Sam's Sourdough Cafe **15**

ATTRACTIONS

Alaska Bird Observatory **21**
Creamer's Field **19**
Georgeson Botanical Garden **3**
Large Animal Research Station **1**
Pioneer Park **18**
Riverboat Discovery **6**
7 Bridges Boats & Bikes **12**
UAF Museum of the North **2**

361

help you find a room with their daily vacancy listing. Several computers are set up for free Internet access. The center is open daily in summer and Monday to Friday in winter; exact hours could not be specified at this writing. They also have information desks at the airport and train depot.

The **Alaska Public Lands Information Center,** down the stairs at 3rd and Cushman streets (© **907/456-0527;** www.nps.gov/aplic), is an indispensable stop for anyone planning to spend time in the outdoors, and an interesting one even if you're not. The staff is remarkably knowledgeable and can tell you about trips and activities based on first-hand experience. Besides providing maps and other details, the center houses a small museum about the state's regions and the gear needed to explore them. Daily free films and naturalist programs show in a small auditorium. Open in summer daily from 9am to 6pm, in winter Tuesday through Saturday from 10am to 6pm.

GETTING AROUND   Fairbanks is designed around the car, and that's the practical way to get around. Without one, sticking downtown, you will leave with a low opinion of the place. The city is too spread out to use taxis much. **Avis, Hertz, Dollar, Budget, Payless, Alamo** and **National** are located at the airport. **National** rents vehicles for gravel roads at its downtown location (see, "Equipped for the Back Roads," p. 369).

The Fairbanks North Star Borough's **MACS bus system** (© **907/459-1011;** www.co.fairbanks.ak.us) links the university, downtown, the nearby North Pole community, shopping areas, and some hotels. Service is every 30 minutes, at best, worse Saturday, and nonexistent Sunday. Pick up timetables at the visitor center. All buses connect at the transit park downtown, at 5th Avenue and Cushman Street. The fare is $1.50 adults, 75 cents for seniors, children, teens, and people with disabilities, free under age 5.

Fairbanks's car-oriented layout does not lend itself to using bikes as the primary means of transportation, but there are great mountain biking opportunities (see "Getting Outside," later in this chapter).

FAST FACTS: **Fairbanks**

Banks Fairbanks has numerous banks with **ATMs** in the downtown area and along the commercial strips. **Key Bank** is at 100 Cushman.

Business Services **Kinko's Copy Center** is at 418 3rd St. (© **907/456-7348**).

Hospital **Fairbanks Memorial** is at 1650 Cowles St. (© **907/452-8181**).

Internet Access Free at the **Log Cabin Visitor Center** on Cushman Street at the river downtown (see above).

Police For nonemergency police business, call the **Alaska State Troopers** (© **907/451-5100**) or, within city limits, the **Fairbanks Police Department** (© **907/459-6500**).

Post Office At 315 Barnette St.

Taxes Fairbanks has no sales tax. North Pole charges 3% with a cap of $6 in tax on any one purchase. Bed tax is 8%.

SPECIAL EVENTS   A recording of current local happenings can be reached at © **907/456-INFO,** maintained by the Fairbanks Convention and Visitors Bureau, which also posts an event calendar at **www.explorefairbanks.com.**

The **Yukon Quest International Sled Dog Race** (℃ 907/452-7954; www. yukonquest.com) starts February 13, 2005, in Whitehorse and ends more than a week later in Fairbanks (in even-numbered years, the direction is reversed). Mushers say this rugged 1,000-mile race is even tougher than the Iditarod.

The **Nenana Ice Classic** (℃ 907/832-5446; www.nenanaakiceclassic.com) is a sweepstakes held annually since 1917 based on who can guess closest to the exact minute when the ice will go out on the Tanana River. The classic starts with Tripod Days, the first weekend in March, when they set up the so-called four-legged tripod; when it moves 100 feet it trips a clock, determining the winner. The Tripod Days celebration includes dance performances, dog mushing, and other activities.

Later in March, the **World Ice Art Championships** (℃ 907/451-8250; www.icealaska.com) brings carvers from all over the world to sculpt immense, clear chunks cut from a Fairbanks pond. Ice sculptures stand in an Ice Park at the corner of Peger and Phillips Field roads. In 2005 carving will be March 2 to 4 and 7 to 12 with the best viewing from March 13 to 27. Among ice carvers, Fairbanks' ice is famous for its clarity and the great size of the chunks. Some spectacular ice sculptures stand as tall as two-story buildings. Check the website for pictures of past winners.

The **North American Sled Dog Championships** (℃ 907/457-MUSH; www. sleddog.org) are the oldest running, taking place over 2 weekends in mid-March. Sprint mushers from all over the world compete with teams of as many as 24 dogs, streaking away from the starting line on 2nd Avenue or the Chena River.

Lots of events happen around the **summer solstice,** usually June 21. The **Midnight Sun Run** (℃ 907/452-6046; www.midnightsunrun.org) is a 10K race and walk with winners chosen both for their times and their funny costumes. It begins at 10pm on the university campus and ends at Pioneer Park. The **Midnight Sun Baseball Game,** hosted by the semipro Fairbanks Goldpanners (℃ 907/451-0095; www.goldpanners.com), begins at 10:30pm; the game is played with no artificial lights.

Also in June, the free **Fairbanks Summer Folk Fest** (℃ 907/488-0556; www.alaskafolkmusic.org) fills a Pioneer Park lawn with music, food, and art booths; live music starts at noon and lasts late into the night.

The **Fairbanks Summer Arts Festival,** held on the University of Alaska Fairbanks campus (℃ 907/474-8869; www.fsaf.org), brings artists of international reputation for performances and classes for all levels in music, dance, theater, opera, creative writing, and visual arts and other subject areas over the last 2 weeks in July (July 17–31, 2005).

The **Tanana Valley State Fair** (℃ 907/452-3750; www.tananavalleyfair.org), in early August, shows off the area's agricultural production, arts and crafts, businesses, and entertainment, and includes rides and competitive exhibits.

The last week of August, Friends of Creamer's Field (℃ 907/459-7307) hosts an annual **Sandhill Crane Festival,** with nature walks, lectures, and other activities, mostly at Creamer's Field (see "Special Places," later in this chapter).

The **BP Top of the World Classic,** Nov 17–20, 2005, brings NCAA Division I basketball teams to the University of Alaska–Fairbanks for a weekend tournament (℃ 907/474-6830; www.towc.org).

EXPLORING THE TOWN
STROLLING AROUND DOWNTOWN

If you want to explore downtown for an hour or two, pick up the walking tour booklet available for a nominal fee at the log cabin visitor center at 1st and

Cushman. It points out what's interesting (and more) about places you otherwise wouldn't look at twice. Among the highlights is the **Golden Heart Park,** a waterfront plaza next to the center, with a fountain and a bronze of a Native family, where community events often occur. A graceful footbridge spans the river, and on the other side is the town's most interesting building, the Roman Catholic **Church of the Immaculate Conception.** The white clapboard structure, built in 1904, has ornate gold rush decoration inside, rare for its authenticity, including a pressed-tin ceiling and stained-glass windows—an appealing if incongruous mix of gold rush and sacred decor.

At 1st Avenue near Kellum Street, east from the visitor center, **St. Matthew's Episcopal Church** is a cute old log church with a working rope-pull bell. It was founded by missionary and dog-sled explorer Hudson Stuck in 1904, who organized the first successful climb of Mount McKinley. The original church burned; the present structure dates from 1948.

At 500 2nd Avenue, the **Fairbanks Ice Museum** ⚑ (© **907/451-8222;** www.icemuseum.com) aims to show summer visitors what winter is like, with seven large ice displays and a freezer you can enter to feel –20°F (–28°C). A big-screen, high-tech slide show plays hourly, explaining the annual World Ice Art Championships (see "Special Events," above), and the freezers contain impressive ice tableaux. Admission is $10 for adults, $6 ages 6 to 12, except noon lunch shows, which include food and cost $15 for everyone. It's open from 10am to 8pm daily from mid-May to mid-September.

The Fairbanks Community Museum ⚑, in the old city hall at 410 Cushman St. (© **907/451-8985**) is well worth a stop for the charming historical

---

Moments   Seeing the Aurora Borealis

One fall evening I left the house of friends in Fairbanks to the sight of a swirling green glow that filled the dark sky. I knocked on the door and brought them out to see, only to have my friends laugh in my face. They informed me, with mock contempt for my Anchorage home, that in Fairbanks they don't even bother to bend their necks back for northern lights as dim as these. It's true—a bright aurora borealis is routine in Fairbanks. Some of the world's top experts on the phenomenon work here, at the University of Alaska's Geophysical Institute (their aurora predictions, in season, and extensive background on the aurora are posted at **www.gi.alaska.edu**). Hours-long displays can be incredibly spectacular and even moving.

Unfortunately, few visitors see these wild strands of bright colors whipping across the sky, because when most visitors come, the sky is never dark. Alaskans rarely see the stars from late May to early August, and to see the aurora well you need an especially dark night sky. To improve your chances, plan your trip in the fall or winter. An early September trip offers brilliant fall foliage, dark night skies, and the remnants of summer weather. In midwinter, the sky is dark all night and most of the day. Many hotels near Fairbanks cater to travelers coming to see the aurora in winter, as well as visitors who come for such winter sports as dog mushing and snowmobiling; the best for that kind of trip is Chena Hot Springs Resort, covered in the next section.

exhibits and the sense of local pride it contains. A series of cramped galleries in the former city offices offer up old photographs, maps, newspapers and other bric-a-brac, as well as skillfully created explanatory exhibits, mostly focusing on the area's gold mining history and development. You could spend quite some time wandering this maze of small discoveries. The Yukon Quest International Sled Dog Race (see "Special Events," above) shares these quarters, teaching about mushing with displays of equipment and supporting the race with souvenirs sold in the tiny gift shop. The museum is open summer Monday through Saturday from 10am to 6pm, winter the same hours Tuesday through Saturday.

PIONEER PARK ★★

Built for the Alaska purchase centennial in 1967, **Pioneer Park** (formerly **Alaskaland**) is the boiled-down essence of Fairbanks on grounds at the intersection of Airport Way and Peger Road (✆ **907/459-1087;** www.co.fairbanks. ak.us, click "Pioneer Park"). It's called a theme park, but don't expect Disneyland or anything like it. Instead, Pioneer Park is a city park with a theme. It's relaxing and low-key, entrancing for young children and interesting for adults if you can give in to the charm of the place. Admission to the park is free and the tours and activities are generally inexpensive. The park is open year-round, but the attractions operate only Memorial Day weekend to Labor Day, daily from 11am to 9pm. Pick up a map and schedule when you arrive; here I've listed the highlights, but there is more to see. Depending on the pace you like to keep and the age level of your group, you can spend anything from a couple of hours to most of a day here.

The **SS Nenana** ★★ (✆ **907/456-8848**) is the park's centerpiece. Commissioned by the federally owned Alaska Railroad in 1933, the large sternwheeler plied the Yukon and Tanana rivers until 1952. In 1967 the *Nenana* came to what was then Alaskaland but was unmaintained and had nearly collapsed from rot when it was saved by a community restoration effort, completed in 1992. There are two decks of sumptuous mahogany, brass, and white-painted promenades to see, plus the wheelhouse, well-preserved engine room, and the like. Self-guided entry to the entire boat is $3 (free for ages 5 and younger), or for $2 you can see the ground-floor cargo deck with its engaging set of dioramas showing all the riverside towns and villages where the boat called, modeled as they looked in its heyday.

Much of Fairbanks's history has been moved to Pioneer Park. A village of log cabins contains shops and restaurants, each marked with its original location and place in town history. **Judge Wickersham's house,** built around 1904, is kept as a museum, decorated appropriately according to the period of the town's founding. The house is less than grand—it may remind you of your grandmother's—but it's worth a stop to strike up a conversation with the historical society volunteers who keep it open. **Pres. Warren Harding's railcar,** from which he stepped to drive the golden spike on the Alaska Railroad, sits near the park entrance. The **Pioneer Air Museum** (✆ **907/451-0037**) is housed in a geodesic dome toward the back of the park. Besides the aircraft there are displays and artifacts of the crashes of Alaska's aviation pioneers. Admission is $2 adults, free 12 and under with parent. Other attractions include a gold rush museum, an illustrated gold rush show, kayak and bike rentals, a dance hall, and an art gallery.

If you have children, you certainly won't escape Pioneer Park without a ride on the **Crooked Creek and Whiskey Island Railroad** that circles the park twice, with a tour guide pointing out the sights; rides cost $2 for adults, $1 for children and seniors. Kids also will enjoy the large **playground,** with equipment for toddlers and older children, where lots of local families come to play, and the 36-hole miniature golf course. The only carnival ride is a nice old **merry-go-round,** which costs $1.

Tour groups generally come to Pioneer Park in the evening from mid-May to mid-September for the **Alaska Salmon Bake,** at the mining valley area, and the **Golden Heart Revue,** at the Palace Theatre (© **800/354-7274** or 907/452-7274; www.akvisit.com for both). Cost for prime rib and fish (halibut, cod, or salmon) is $24. Beer and wine are available. The seating area is pleasant, with indoor or outdoor dining. The revue, nightly at 8:15pm from mid-May to mid-September, covers the amusing story of the founding of Fairbanks with comedy and song in a nightclub setting; admission is $15 for adults.

UNIVERSITY OF ALASKA FAIRBANKS

The state university's main campus contains several interesting attractions and makes a point of serving tourists. The campus is on the west side of town; the main entrance is at the intersection of University Avenue and College Road. A widely distributed brochure lists tours, hours, and fees. A free 2-hour **walking tour,** led by students, meets at the museum Monday through Friday at 10am, June through August except July 1 and 2. Call ahead (© **907/474-7581**) to confirm the time and any weather cancellations. A shuttle bus is provided in case of rain. More campus attractions are listed below; for a complete list, go to www.uaf.edu/univrel/tour and click "Activities and Tours." The university's ski trails are covered later in this chapter under "Winter Activities."

UAF Museum of the North ✪✪✪   This rich, interdisciplinary on-campus museum, long one of Alaska's best, will open a spectacular new expansion in 2005 that promises to make a stir well beyond the state. First, the old part of the museum: Alaska's best natural history collection and its most scholarly, with information presented at advanced as well as elementary levels. Some of the objects have a real wow factor, such as Blue Babe, the mummified steppe bison; a 5,400-pound copper nugget; and the state's largest collection of gold. There is an audio tour guide, or in the summer you can join free 20-minute talks offered through the day on the university's specialties. All this will remain, and it already provided enough to keep your interest for much of a day. Now the new part: a swooping combination of grand, graceful shapes, designed by Joan Soranno, a disciple of Frank Gehry, it is reminiscent of moving icebergs, or perhaps of the Northern Lights. Inside, the towering new gallery will be devoted to art. The museum director, herself an art historian, has planned something new and innovative here, with thematic presentation of western art alongside Native and archeological objects, interactive exhibits, sound, crafts, and much more. Completion of the $33 million project will happen at some time during the season, but the exact date is not yet known.

907 Yukon Dr. (P.O. Box 756960), Fairbanks, AK 99775-6960. © **907/474-7505.** www.uaf.edu/museum. Admission $5 adults, $4.50 ages 60 and older, $3 ages 7–17, free ages 6 and under. Summer daily 9am–7pm; winter Mon–Fri 9am–5pm, Sat–Sun noon–5pm.

Georgeson Botanical Garden ✪   I really enjoy the mix of science and contemplation I find at this relaxed working garden. Plots are laid out to compare seeds and cultivation techniques, usually well posted with explanatory information on the experiment; but at the same time the flowers and vegetables are spectacular, and there are peaceful memorials and places to picnic. You don't need a tour to enjoy the garden. Nearby, the barn of the university's experimental farm is open for visitors to wander through and view the reindeer.

W. Tanana Dr., Fairbanks, AK 99775. (C) **907/474-1744.** www.uaf.edu/salrm/gbg. Admission $1. Open day-light hours; store open May 15–Labor Day daily 8am–8pm; free guided tours Fri at 2pm.

Large Animal Research Station ✦   The university studies captive musk ox, reindeer, and caribou here, on a property often called the musk ox farm. Hour-long tours are given daily in the high season, with naturalists bringing animals into an amphitheater for close-up viewing. At any time, on a walk along the fence from the parking lot on Yankovich Road, you can see the animals behaving naturally in the large pastures. Best times are the cool morning or evening hours, and binoculars help.

Yankovich Rd., Fairbanks, AK 99775. (C) **907/474-7207.** www.uaf.edu/lars. Tour $10 adults, $9 seniors, $6 students, free ages 6 and under. Tours Memorial Day–Labor Day daily 1:30 and 3:30pm; Tues–Sat 6:30pm. Drive north from campus, turn left on Ballaine Rd., left again on Yankovich.

COMMERCIAL TOURIST ATTRACTIONS AROUND FAIRBANKS

Three major for-profit attractions around Fairbanks pack in visitors by the hundreds of thousands, most of them on group tours. These places are educational and fun, as I've described below, but I think they all charge excessive prices. Whether they're worth your money depends on how much you've got and your level of interest; however, I doubt most independent budget travelers would feel they got their money's worth.

The Riverboat *Discovery* ✦✦   The *Discovery* belongs to the pioneering Binkley family, which has been in the riverboat business since the Klondike gold rush and have run this attraction since 1950. The *Discovery* is a real sternwheeler, a 156-foot steel vessel carrying 700 passengers on as many as three trips a day. There's nothing intimate or spontaneous about the 3½-hour ride, which mostly carries package-tour passengers off fleets of buses, but the Binkleys still provide a diverting outing that doesn't feel cheap or phony. After loading at a landing with shops off Dale Road, near the airport, the boat cruises down the Chena and up the Tanana past demonstrations on shore—among others, a bush plane taking off and landing, fish cutting at a Native fish camp, and a musher's dog yard (in recent years, it was four-time Iditarod champion Susan Butcher's yard, and she'd often show off the dogs herself). Finally, the vessel pulls up at the bank for an hour-long tour of a mock Athabascan village.

1975 Discovery Dr., Fairbanks, AK 99709. (C) **866/479-6673** or 907/479-6673. www.riverboatdiscovery.com. Tours $45 adults, $30 ages 3–12, free ages 2 and under. Sailings mid-May to mid-Sept daily at 8:45am and 2pm.

The El Dorado Gold Mine ✦   A train such as you would find at an amusement park carries visitors though an impressively staged educational tour, including a trip through a tunnel in the permafrost. This is like a land version of the riverboat tour that's operated by the same family, the Binkleys. But the gold miners who act as hosts are the real attraction here. Visitors gather around a sluice to hear the amusing and authentic Dexter and Lynette (aka Yukon Yonda) Clark and watch a swoosh of water and gold-bearing gravel rush by. You pan the resulting pay dirt, and everyone goes home with enough gold dust to fill a plastic locket—typically $5 to $35 worth. Drive out to the mine after making reservations, or take a free shuttle.

Off the Elliott Hwy., 9 miles north of town. (C) **866/479-6673** or 907/479-6673. www.eldoradogoldmine.com. Tours $30 adults, $20 ages 3–12, free ages 2 and under. Tours daily; call for times.

Gold Dredge Number 8 ✦   Authenticity makes this is the area's best historic gold-mining site. The centerpiece is a 1928 gold dredge, similar to machines in Dawson City and Nome, standing five decks tall on a barge in a pond it created. When it operated, huge scoops would dig from one end, the mechanism inside would digest the gold from the gravel, and then it would dump the spoils out the back—in this way, the pond and the dredge it supports crept 3½ miles across the frozen ground north of Fairbanks. Many sterile areas you see in this area were created by these earth-eaters, for nothing grows on their tailings for decades after. The tour company that bought the historic site added to the dredge with museums housed in relocated gold camp buildings, showing the harsh, colorless life lived by the miners. A 90-minute tour starts with a film, then a half hour on the dredge, and finally a chance to pan for gold yourself, with success assured. It's a fascinating machine, but, as noted above, the price is high for what is essentially a single-subject museum.

1755 Old Steese Hwy., Fairbanks, AK 99712. ℂ 907/457-6058. www.golddredgeno8.com. Admission $19 tour only, $23 with gold panning, $33 with cafeteria lunch. Mid-May through mid-Sept tours start hourly 9:30am–3:30pm. To get there, go north on the Steese Expressway from town, turn left on Goldstream Rd., turn left again on the Old Steese Hwy.

GETTING OUTSIDE
In this section, I've described the outdoor opportunities local to Fairbanks, but some other choices are barely farther afield: Check out section 3 of this chapter, on Chena Hot Springs Road, and the feature later, "The Steese Highway: Drive into the Wild."

The **Alaska Public Lands Information Center,** 250 Cushman St. (at 3rd Ave.), (ℂ **907/456-0527;** www.nps.gov/aplic), is a great resource. The staff will advise you on outings, outfitters, and where to find rental equipment.

GEARING UP
You can rent most of what you need for outdoor explorations around Fairbanks and along the region's extraordinary rural highways from a set of local businesses that have grown up around the needs of adventurers.

Some of the outdoor opportunities described below require a drive on unpaved roads, including anything on the Steese Highway. Two businesses that rent vehicles you can take on these roads are listed in the feature "Equipped for the Backroads," on p. 369. One of those, GoNorth Alaska Adventure Travel Center, also rents canoes, bikes, and camping gear and offers a shuttle for canoeists and hikers.

Alaska Outdoor Rentals & Guides, owned by the knowledgeable Larry Katkin, has its main location on the river bank at Pioneer Park (ℂ **907/457-BIKE;** www.akbike.com). The company rents canoes and bikes and offers pickup or drop off for canoeists in town or far afield—even for trips on the great Yukon River. For an easy in-town paddle, say from the park to Pike's Landing, you would pay $29 for the canoe and $15 for the pick up. If you want to go beyond the road system, Larry also carries foldable canoes and kayaks that will fit in a Bush plane. He also offers canoeing lessons. This is a good place to start a mountain biking outing, too. They have a large fleet of quality bikes at five locations: Pioneer Park, the Fairbanks Hotel (downtown), River's Edge Resort (p. 372), Chena Hot Springs Resort (p. 384), and at Dalton Highway's Coldfoot Camp (p. 387). Bikes rent for $27 for an 8-hour day in summer.

You can also rent from the long-established **7 Bridges Boats and Bikes,** at 7 Gables Inn, 4312 Birch Lane (ℂ **907/479-0751;** www.7gablesinn.com/7bbb) for $35 per day or $100 per week, and they will drop you off at the river and pick you up at your destination for $1.50 per mile out of town, with a $15 minimum. Guests at the inn get free rentals (same phone, Web: www.7gablesinn.com). Street and mountain bikes go for $20 a day.

For ski rentals, see the appropriate sections below.

Tips Equipped for the Backroads

Exploring Alaska's gravel highways—camping and fishing along the way, perhaps launching a canoe in a remote lake—has been tough for visitors to arrange because of the policies of most rental car agencies, which don't allow clients to drive off pavement. An exception is the **Alamo/National** franchise in Fairbanks, with locations at the airport and downtown at 4960 Dale Rd. (© **800/227-7368** or 907/451-7368). They rent SUVs and will allow some vehicles to go on gravel roads such as the Dalton, Steese, and Denali highways. **GoNorth Alaska Adventure Travel Center,** at 3500 Davis Rd. (© **866/236-7272** or 907/479-7272; www.gonorthalaska.com) goes a step further, renting campers on four-wheel-drive pickup trucks, perfect for exploring gravel roads. The firm also runs a nice tent-camp hostel, arranges self-guided outdoor trips, rents canoes, bikes, and camping gear, and drives a shuttle for canoeists and hikers. With required insurance and unlimited mileage, a pickup camper is about $160 a day.

SPECIAL PLACES

CREAMER'S FIELD   At 1300 College Rd., right in Fairbanks, this migratory waterfowl refuge is an 1,800-acre former dairy farm that was saved from development in 1966 by a community fund drive. The pastures are a prime stopover point for Canada geese, pintails, and golden plovers in the spring and fall. I saw many swans there last spring. Sandhill cranes, shovelers, and mallards show up all summer. The **Friends of Creamer's Field** (© **907/459-7307;** www.creamers field.org) operates a small visitor center in the old farmhouse with displays on birds, wildlife, and history, open June through August daily from 10am to 5pm. They offer guided nature walks in summer Saturday and Wednesday at 9am and Tuesday and Thursday at 7pm. You don't need a guide, however: during migrations, use the blinds around the edge of the field; other times, explore the 3 miles of trails through forest, field, and wetland. I especially enjoy the boreal forest nature walk, interpreted by an excellent booklet you can pick up at the visitor center or from a kiosk at the trailhead when the visitor center is closed.

The **Alaska Bird Observatory** (© **907/451-7159;** www.alaskabird.org) conducts research and educational programs on the Creamer's Field refuge, including bird walks and daily bird banding that visitors can observe. It is the farthest north facility of its kind in North America. Their office is just west of the refuge on the grounds of the Wedgewood Resort (see below).

CHENA LAKES RECREATION AREA   This is a wonderful and unique place for a family camping trip. A birch-rimmed lake created for a flood-control project has been developed by the local government to provide lots of recreational possibilities: flat walking and bike trails; a swimming beach; fishing; a place to rent canoes and paddleboats; a self-guided 2½-mile nature trail; a playground; big lawns; and the terrific campground, with 80 camping sites, from pull-throughs for RVs to tent sites on a little island you can reach only by boat. In the winter, it's a popular area for cross-country skiing, ice fishing, and dog mushing. Camping costs $10; day use is $4. Drive 17 miles east of Fairbanks on the Richardson Highway and turn left on Laurance Road as you leave North Pole. For information, contact Fairbanks North Star Borough Chena Lakes Recreation Area (© **907/488-1655**). Follow the same directions (drive along the dam past the recreation area) to the **Moose Creek Dam Salmon Watch,** a picnic and viewing area built by the U.S. Army Corps of Engineers atop the flood control project, to watch spawning salmon in crystal-clear water from late June to the end of July. Use of the salmon watch is free, so tell the recreation area gatehouse you are going there.

SUMMER ACTIVITIES

CANOEING   The rivers in and around Fairbanks are best seen by floating slowly along in a canoe. Paddling is more popular than hiking around here. See "Gearing Up," on p. 368, for companies that rent equipment and offer shuttle services.

The Chena River is slow and meandering as it flows through Fairbanks, and you have your pick of restaurants on the bank. Farther upriver, the canoeing passes wilder shores, and near the headwaters becomes more challenging (covered in the "Chena Hot Springs Road" section, later). For beginners, try the wilderness section from the Chena Lakes Recreation Area downstream (described above). It's 12 to 16 hours from there all the way into town, or you can take out at one of the roads crossing the river along the way. The **U.S. Army Corp of Engineers** (© 907/488-2748) produces a float map with put-in and take-out points and float times, available at the Alaska Public Lands Information Center (see "Visitor Information," earlier).

For something a bit more challenging but still manageable, the clear, Class I water of the Chatanika River is perfect for day trips or relaxed expeditions of a week or more, if you know how to handle river hazards such as sweepers and snags that show up on any Alaska stream. Alaska State Parks produces a brochure covering the float from the Upper Chatanika River Campground, at mile 39 of the Steese Highway, to another campground on the Elliot Highway. Low water and logjams requiring portages can slow down the trip so that it takes a long day; in better conditions, expert canoeists can do it in a few hours.

The Steese Highway also meets two National Wild and Scenic Rivers: Beaver Creek, for trips of a week or more over easy Class I water, and Birch Creek, for more expert paddlers. Get *The Alaska River Guide*, mentioned on p. 357, for detailed guidance, and check with the Alaska Public Lands Information Center in Fairbanks. Also see "The Steese Highway: Drive into the Wild," p. 383.

BIKING & HIKING   Traffic goes fast in Fairbanks and the separated bike trails are few, but strong cyclists can get by. Mountain biking is good on many dirt roads and byways within and beyond Fairbanks and on the ski trails at Birch Hill Recreation Area and the University of Alaska Fairbanks (see "Winter Activities," below). The ski trails are also good for easy summer hikes, or go farther afield for more ambitious trail hikes off Chena Hot Springs Road (in the next section of this chapter) or the Steese Highway (p. 383). Inquire about all the options or other ideas at the Alaska Public Lands Information Center (p. 362).

FISHING   Salmon season here is brief and the fish, this far inland, have turned spawning colors and have softer, less palatable flesh compared to coastal salmon. Most fishing is in the streams for Arctic grayling, Northern pike, and burbot, and in stocked lakes for rainbow trout, Arctic char, and silver salmon. You can fish right in the Chena as it flows through town, although getting out of town and hiking away from a road yields better results. Fly-in fishing will further increase your chances and add sheefish and Dolly Varden char to your list, but the expense of around $300 a day is easier to justify from Anchorage, where you can target salmon as well as freshwater fish. The Alaska Public Lands Information Center (p. 362) offers guidance, or contact the **Alaska Department of**

Fish and Game, at Creamer's Field, 1300 College Rd., Fairbanks, AK 99701 (© **907/459-7207;** sport fish information recording 907/459-7385; www.alaska. gov/adfg, click on "Sport Fishing," then "Region 3," then "Lower Tanana Drainage").

WINTER ACTIVITIES

Fairbanks has real Jack London winters. The visitor bureau guarantees it. For the growing number of visitors who want to experience real cold, see the aurora borealis, and ride a dog sled, Fairbanks is the place. Chena Hot Springs Resort (p. 384) and A Taste of Alaska Lodge (p. 374) are the best destinations for winter immersion, but you can also have a good time in town, especially in March, when the days lighten up, the temperatures are moderate, and the town gets busy with dog mushing and the ice carving contest (see "Special Events," earlier).

DOG MUSHING   The long winters and vast wild lands make the Fairbanks area a center of dog sledding, both for racers and recreationists, and there are plenty of people willing to take you for a lift, which is really an experience not to be missed. I've heard good things about **Sun Dog Express Dog Sled Tours** (© **907/479-6983;** www.mosquitonet.com/~sleddog), which charges $25 for a quick spin, up to $250 to learn to drive a team in a half day. They also have summer cart tours.

Two local accommodations include mushing in their offerings, A Taste of Alaska Lodge and Chena Hot Springs Resort. The Denali West Lodge, covered in chapter 8, offers real mushing expeditions.

CROSS COUNTRY SKIING   The **Birch Hill Recreation Area,** off the Steese Expressway just north of town, has about 25km of good cross-country ski trails, most groomed for classical or skate skiing, and a warm-up building in which to change clothes. Several loops of a few kilometers each offer advanced skiing on the steep southern side of the hill; loops of up to 10km provide more level terrain to the north. There is a lighted loop, too. The **University of Alaska Fairbanks** offers a network of roughly the same length, two-thirds of it groomed for skate technique. Although I prefer Birch Hill, with its mix of ability levels, the University trails pass through lovely lands and have the advantage of a nearby source of rental equipment: the **Outdoor Adventures Program** at the Wood Student Center (© **907/474-6027;** www.uaf.edu/outdoor). You can rent skis, poles, and boots for a mere $8 a day. One trailhead is at the west end of campus, near the satellite dishes at the top of Tanana Loop. Another is off Farmers Loop Road at Ballaine Lake.

DOWNHILL SKIING   Fairbanks has several community-sized downhill skiing areas, including the relatively large **Moose Mountain Ski Resort** (© **907/479-4732;** www.shredthemoose.com), with 1,250 vertical feet of skiing. Instead of freezing on a lift, you ride back up the hill and socialize in heated buses.

SHOPPING

Fairbanks has a few good shops downtown. **New Horizons Gallery,** at 519 1st Ave. (© **907/456-2063**), occupies a large space with a combination of large oils by Alaska's best serious artists, inexpensive prints, and gifts, and is open every day. The **Arctic Travelers Gift Shop,** at 201 Cushman St. (© **907/456-7080**), specializes in Native art and crafts, carrying both valuable art and affordable but authentically Alaskan gifts. The staff is knowledgeable about what they sell. Right next door, at 215 Cushman, **If Only . . .** (© **907/457-6659**) is a charming gift and stationary shop with items to hold locals' as well as visitors' interest—not just tourist stuff.

Near the airport, at 4630 Old Airport Rd., the **Great Alaskan Bowl Company** (© **907/474-9663;** www.woodbowl.com) makes and sells bowls of native birch—salad bowls, of course, but also bowls for many other purposes. Some of these bowls are simply amazing. They can carve up to eight nested bowls from one piece of wood and even laser-engrave a photo inside one. Through a glass wall looking into the shop, you can see workers cutting the bowls from raw logs. It's hard to depart without buying a bowl.

WHERE TO STAY

Going the bed-and-breakfast route is a good choice in Fairbanks. At the B&Bs I've listed below, you can save money over a hotel and get a private room just as good while staying in a unique place with interesting people. The **Fairbanks Association of Bed and Breakfasts** lists about 20 more on its website at **www.ptialaska.net/~fabb**. You also can get B&B information at the Fairbanks Log Cabin Visitor Information Center (p. 360).

EXPENSIVE

There are many more hotels in the expensive category than there is any need to describe here, so I have followed my usual practice of including one for each taste. **Pike's Waterfront Lodge** (© **877/774-2400** or 907/456-4500; www.pikes lodge.com) is also quite good, and has several memorable features: an extraordinary wildlife art collection, a greenhouse, and an ice cream parlor with an airplane sticking out of it. The rooms, however, are comparable to the Fairbanks Princess Riverside Lodge, which is next door and has a more pleasant setting.

Fairbanks Princess Riverside Lodge ★★ This enormous cruise-line-operated hotel extends in three long wings of gray clapboards on the banks of the Chena. Rooms and common areas maintain an opulent style of lavish colors and prints, a pleasing mish-mash of faux-rustic Alaskan touches and gold rush excess. Rooms are not large but are well turned out and many have river views (commanding a $10 premium). Business travelers will like the airport location, crisp, efficient service, and wireless Internet in some of the building, including all public spaces. Food is from a bar and grill, or, in the summer, a riverfront cafe with outdoor dining.

4477 Pikes Landing Rd., Fairbanks, AK 99709. © **800/426-0500** or 907/455-4477. Fax 907/455-4476. www. princessalaskalodges.com. 325 units. High season $199 double, $289–$499 suites; low season $109 double, $199–$349 suites. Extra person $10. AE, DC, DISC, MC, V. **Amenities:** Restaurant; cafe; bar; exercise room; steam room; tour desk; courtesy van; business center; laundry service; coin op laundry. *In room:* A/C, TV, dataport, hair dryer, iron.

River's Edge Resort Cottages ★★ *Kids* An afternoon on a sunny riverbank exemplifies the best of Interior Alaska; this place is built around that knowledge. Trim little cottages stand in a grassy compound along the gentle Chena River, where guests can fish for grayling. Inside, each light, airy cottage is an excellent standard hotel room, with high ceilings and two queen beds. Outside, they're like a little village, where guests can sit on the patio, watch the river go by, and socialize. The owners got the idea for the place from their RV park next door, when they noticed how their guests enjoyed visiting together in the open with their own private units to retreat to. It's perfect for families, as the outdoor areas are safe for playing and noise inside won't bother the neighbors. A large, summer-only restaurant sits at river's edge, with dining on a deck or inside at round,

Downtown Fairbanks

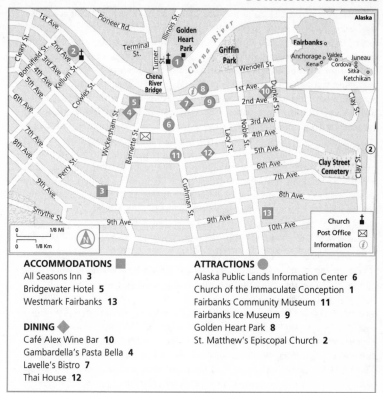

ACCOMMODATIONS ■
All Seasons Inn **3**
Bridgewater Hotel **5**
Westmark Fairbanks **13**

DINING ◆
Café Alex Wine Bar **10**
Gambardella's Pasta Bella **4**
Lavelle's Bistro **7**
Thai House **12**

ATTRACTIONS ●
Alaska Public Lands Information Center **6**
Church of the Immaculate Conception **1**
Fairbanks Community Museum **11**
Fairbanks Ice Museum **9**
Golden Heart Park **8**
St. Matthew's Episcopal Church **2**

oak tables. Dinner entrees—steak, seafood, and down-home cooking—range up to $30; a burger is $8.

4200 Boat St., Fairbanks, AK 99709. ✆ **800/770-3343** or 907/474-0286. Fax 907/474-3665. www.rivers edge.net. 86 cottages, 8 suites. High season $173 double; low season $89 double. Extra person over age 11 $10. AE, DISC, MC, V. Take Sportsman Way off Airport Way to Boat St. **Amenities:** Restaurant; bar; tour desk; courtesy van; laundry service. *In room:* TV, dataport, coffeemaker, hair dryer.

Sophie Station ★ This all-suite hotel, near the University and airport, is well equipped for business travelers or longer stays, with fully equipped kitchens, sitting rooms, and separate bedrooms in every suite. The decoration in the rooms is muted and even dated, but everything is very clean, well maintained, and comfortable. Bathrooms and closets are quite large. The newly remodeled lobby contains a free Internet work station. I was startled by the quality of the food and service in the hotel restaurant, called **Zack's,** which looks like it would produce typical, unmemorable hotel cafe dining. Each dish I selected was perfectly seasoned and done to a turn, servers were attentive without being annoying, and the meals came quickly. The cuisine includes Alaska seafood and familiar American dishes. Prices are reasonable—dinner main courses top out at $23—and they're open year round.

1717 University Ave., Fairbanks, AK 99709. ✆ **800/528-4916** reservations or 907/479-3650. Fax 907/479-7951. www.fountainheadhotels.com. 148 units. High season $149–$180 double; low season $89–$120. Extra person $10 in high and low seasons. AE, DC, DISC, MC, V. **Amenities:** Restaurant; courtesy van; coin-op laundry. *In room:* A/C, TV, kitchen, hair dryer, iron.

A Taste of Alaska Lodge 🌟 Situated atop a grassy slope on 280 acres, facing Mount McKinley, the hand-crafted log main building feels like a wilderness lodge but is less than half an hour from Fairbanks. The family that originally homesteaded this property still lives here and runs the lodge, with the third generation now training to take over. Each family member I've met is an Alaskan original. A musher offers rides with an on-site dog team in winter (although they were between mushers at this writing), when visitors come for exceptional aurora viewing. In summer visitors can enjoy the hot tub and peer at goldfish in a manmade pond set amid a large field of hay. Rooms are decorated with handmade quilts, brass beds, and other reproductions, and an incredible array of knickknacks and collectibles (some will love all this, some may find it a little corny). Each room has a door straight onto the grounds, where moose often wander. The cabins are large and especially luxurious. They are reasonably priced, while the standard rooms are too dear. Breakfast is served at 8am on the dot, and guests have to remove their shoes at the door. Smoking is not allowed.

551 Eberhardt Rd., Fairbanks, AK 99712. ⓒ 907/488-7855. Fax 907/488-3772. www.atasteofalaska.com. 8 units, 2 cabins. $175 double; cabin $175–$200. Extra person $25. Rates include full breakfast. AE, MC, V. Turn right 5½ miles out Chena Hot Springs Rd. **Amenities:** Hot tub. In room: TV, wireless Internet with $10 fee.

Wedgewood Resort 🌟🌟 Off College Road near the Creamer's Field Refuge, this well-kept hotel sprawls across a grassy, 23-acre complex in eight large buildings. Seven of them are converted three-story apartment buildings, regularly refitted, without elevators but with large living rooms, separate dining areas, fully equipped kitchens, air conditioners, two TVs, balconies, and phones with voice mail in both the living room and bedroom. The main difference from home is that someone else cleans up after you. Another 157 units are large standard hotel rooms, all on the ground floor and with indoor connection to the lobby; however, those are closed in winter. A scheduled courtesy van runs to the airport and train depot and various tourist sites in the summer. A footbridge connects the hotel to Creamer's Field and the Alaska Bird Observatory has opened its research and educational center on the grounds (p. 369).

212 Wedgewood Dr., Fairbanks, AK 99701. ⓒ 800/528-4916 reservations or 907/452-1442. Fax 907/452-8184. www.fountainheadhotels.com. 157 units, 294 apts. High season $185 double, $135–$195 apt for 2; low season $75–$120 apt, regular double rooms not offered. Extra person in apt $10. AE, DC, DISC, MC, V. **Amenities:** 2 restaurants (summer only); bar; tour desk; courtesy van; coin-op laundry; dry cleaning. In room: A/C, TV, dataport, coffeemaker, hair dryer, iron.

Westmark Fairbanks Hotel & Conference Center 🌟🌟🌟 This Fairbanks landmark, the town's grand meeting place, declined until two years ago, when the owner, Holland America Lines, demolished most of it and built a showplace

---

⌐Tips Going with the Flow

Many of the large, top quality hotels in Fairbanks, including the Princess, Westmark, and Pike's Landing, cater to enormous escorted tours, which flow through town on a rhythm set by the arrival of cruise ships hundreds of miles away. As a result, certain nights are booked up every week many months in advance, while others are wide open. Fortunately, this flow alternates on different nights for different companies, so when one hotel is full another is empty. If you find your first choice is booked, just call one of the others. If they have rooms, ask for a discount, as they may have a lot of empty rooms.

and the city's tallest tower (not exactly a skyscraper, but you don't need to be very high for good views in Fairbanks). The decor leaped 30 years forward and now the hotel is the city's most stylish, with a post-mod pastiche that includes fabrics and lamps from the Jetsons along with colonial woodwork, big, manly furniture, and lots of color. I liked it. The rooms are packed with all the latest amenities, including WiFi throughout the new section. They built little shelves for the coffeemakers so they're not down with your toothpaste. Downstairs, the hotel has a cafe with a dining room that's a work of art and a comfortable steak house (neither were open yet for my tour), as well as a large fitness center, large guest laundry, and a sort of communication center, with an ATM, newspapers, Internet kiosks, phones, and so on. The company has made a good choice in eschewing the phony Alaskan motif you get so sick of if you spend much time touring here. Instead, they made a cool hotel, a fun place to stay. Prices are quite reasonable for this class.

813 Noble St., Fairbanks, AK 99701. ⓒ **800/544-0970** reservations, or 907/456-7722. Fax 907/451-7478. www. westmarkhotels.com. 400 units. Summer $179 double, $209–$500 suite; winter $129 double, $159–$500 suite. Extra person over age 12 $15. AE, DC, DISC, MC, V. **Amenities:** 2 restaurants; bar; fitness center; tour desk (seasonal); courtesy van; coin-op laundry; laundry service. *In room:* A/C, TV, dataport, coffeemaker, hair dryer, iron.

MODERATE

All Seasons Inn ★★ This charming and comfortable country inn on a pleasant residential street a couple of blocks from the downtown core is the creation of Mary Richards, a longtime transplant from the southern United States who retains, along with a slight accent, the gentle hospitality and refined style she brought with her. Each cozy room has its own inspired decorative details in bold colors, and the housekeeping has always been perfect on our many visits. For socializing with Mary or other guests a series of large, elegant common rooms connect downstairs, where you'll find a bar with hot drinks and a sun porch with books and games. Complimentary newspapers come with the full breakfast and wireless Internet reaches all the rooms. Shoes are removed at the front door in winter. Smoking is not allowed.

763 Seventh Ave., Fairbanks, AK 99701. ⓒ **888/451-6649** or 907/451-6649. Fax 907/474-8448. www.all seasonsinn.com. 8 units. High season $135–$160 double; low season $75–$90 double. Extra person $25. Rates include full breakfast. DC, DISC, MC, V. No smoking. **Amenities:** Coin-op laundry. *In room:* TV, dataport, hair dryer, iron.

Aurora Express Bed and Breakfast ★★ *Finds* Susan Wilson's late grandmother appeared to her in a dream and told her there would be a train on a bank below her house, on the family's 15 acres high in the hills south of Fairbanks. So Wilson went out and got a train—a still-growing collection that includes a pair of 1956 Pullman sleepers, a dining car, a locomotive, a caboose, and a World War II hospital car—and her husband, Mike, brought it all up the mountain to install below the house, right in the spot indicated. Some cars are close to their original form, and Susan says older guests sometimes weep over the memories they bring back. Others were elaborately remodeled into small rooms on themes related to Fairbanks history. A full breakfast is served in the dining car, which also houses the common area, TV, and phone. One 85-foot-long car is meant for families, with railroad-theme decor, puzzles, and toy trains. Then there's the incredible caboose, dedicated to Grandma. They're located 6½ miles out of town, so you will need your own car if you stay here. Smoking is prohibited.

1540 Chena Ridge Rd. (P.O. Box 80128), Fairbanks, AK 99708. ⓒ **800/221-0073** or 907/474-0949. Fax 907/ 474-8173. www.aurora-express.com. 7 units. $115–$150 double. Extra person $15–$25. Rates include full breakfast. MC, V. Closed mid-Sept to mid-May.

Bridgewater Hotel ⭐ Value   This older building in a prime downtown location near the river contains comfortable, immaculate rooms that sacrifice little of substance to places charging as much as $50 a night more. Decoration in pastels creates a feminine, boutique tone in common areas. Rooms are bright and airy and those on the corners have exceptional views. All have shower stalls only, not tubs. A cafe serves breakfast and one of Fairbanks' best restaurants, Gambardella's, is just steps away and allows guests to charge meals to the rooms. A great choice for summertime travelers who like staying in a traditional downtown hotel but don't need luxury hotel trappings.

723 1st Ave., Fairbanks, AK 99701. © 800/528-4916 or 907/452-6661. Fax 907/452-6126. www.fountain headhotels.com. 94 units. $115–$140 double. Extra person $10. AE, DC, DISC, MC, V. Closed mid-Sept to mid-May. **Amenities:** Tour desk; courtesy van; laundry service. In room: A/C, TV, dataport, coffeemaker, hair dryer.

Minnie Street Bed & Breakfast Inn ⭐⭐   Just across the river from the downtown center, near the rail depot, two buildings around a garden courtyard contain clean, large, brightly decorated rooms with many amenities, custom-designed carpeting, handmade quilts, and stylish furniture. The inn, both homey and perfect, reflects the personality of its serene but exacting owner, Marnie Hazelaar. A full breakfast is served in a dining room with a high vaulted ceiling. Huge one- and two-bedroom suites have kitchens, one guest room has a Jacuzzi, and the common area has a guest Internet-connected computer.

345 Minnie St., Fairbanks, AK 99701. © 888/456-1849 or 907/456-1802. Fax 907/451-1751. www.minniestreet bandb.com. 10 units, 6 with private bathroom. High season $110–$145 double, $150–$195 suite; low season $65–$75 double, $125 suite. Extra person $25. Rates include full breakfast. AE, DISC, MC, V. **Amenities:** Business center; massage; coin-op laundry. In room: TV, hair dryer, CD player.

INEXPENSIVE

Besides the other inexpensive places listed below, **Cloudberry Lookout Bed and Breakfast,** off Goldhill Rd. at 351 Cloudberry Lane, Fairbanks, AK 99709 (© **907/479-7334;** fax 907/479-7134; www.mosquitonet.com/~cloudberry), is an exceptional place, a handcrafted house with a spiral staircase leading up to a 60-foot tower in the woods west of town and an eco-couple as hosts.

Crestmont Manor Bed and Breakfast ⭐   Phil and Connie Horton built this masterpiece of pale custom woodwork to be their home and inn (Phil is a builder), and filled it with handmade quilts (Connie is a quilter), splashes of bright colors, warm decorative themes, and huge impressionistic oil paintings (their son is an artist). The feel is crisp and airy, but the house is traditional, furnished with antiques and reproductions, like an old fashioned home but more perfect. It sits on the side of Chena Ridge, overlooking the west side of town, near the university and some good restaurants. One small room with two twin beds and a separated bathroom rents for $85 in summer; the rest are typically sized with attached bathrooms with shower stalls. The full breakfast is served 7:30 to 8:30am.

510 Crestmont Dr., Fairbanks, AK 99709. © **907/456-3831.** Fax 907/456-3841. www.mosquitonet.com/~crestmnt. 5 units. High season $85–$110 unit; low season $55–$75 unit. Rates include full breakfast. AE, DISC, MC, V. In room: TV.

Golden North Motel Value   The Baer family, owners since 1971, are constantly improving the rooms in this two-story motel, making it the best bargain in town for those seeking a basic budget room. They make their money on return business from Alaskans who know this secret. The Baers are always replacing something, and where carpets and furniture are worn they're still quite clean. You have a choice of small rooms and units that combine two of the smaller rooms; although strictly functional, they're very reasonably priced and have extras such as voice mail, coffeemakers, and VCRs or DVD players in the room or free to borrow. The building, on a side street near the airport, is a nondescript brown rectangle brightened by flower boxes on the outdoor walkways. Family members greet guests warmly with free pastries and coffee in the small lobby, which adjoins a room with a computer for Internet access and business machines free for guest use.

4888 Old Airport Rd., Fairbanks, AK 99709. (C) 800/447-1910 or 907/479-6201. Fax 907/479-5766. www.goldennorthmotel.com. 62 units. Summer $74–$99 double, $10 each additional person over age 12; winter $55–$63 double. Rates include continental breakfast. AE, DC, DISC, MC, V. **Amenities:** Courtesy van, business center. *In room:* TV, coffeemaker.

A HOSTEL & CAMPING

There are several hostels in Fairbanks. Among the best is the homey **Billie's Backpackers Hostel,** near the university, at 2895 Mack Blvd. ((C) **907/479-2034;** www.Alaskahostel.com). It's a charming place with a charming owner—a real home, but quirky and fun. Billie assigns bunks as people arrive, and you could luck into a private room for the same $22 a night she charges everyone. The price includes all linens, coffee and tea, the Internet, and much else. The Alaska Trails shuttle, which her son owns, stops out front (see "Getting There," p. 360). To find the hostel, turn south off College Road on Westwood Way and look for the first house on the left.

Tent camping is a good way to go in Fairbanks, with its mild summers and ample public lands, but stock up on the mosquito repellent. Right in town, the **Chena River State Recreation Site** (not to be confused with the recreation "area" of the same name described in the next section of this chapter), is located where University Avenue crosses the river. Sites are surrounded by birch, some are near the river, and there are flush toilets. Arrive early to camp close to the river instead of at one of the noisier sites nearer the road. The self-service fee for one of the 56 drive-in sites is $15, for five tent-only sites $10. Getting a bit out of town, there are superb public campgrounds at Chena Lakes Recreation Area (see "Special Places," earlier in this chapter) and along Chena Hot Springs Road (covered in section 3 of this chapter).

Fairbanks has plenty of RV parks, some with full service and then some. Pick up a list at the visitor center. Among the best is **River's Edge RV Park and Campground,** at a wooded riverside bend of the Chena at 4140 Boat St., off Airport Way and Sportsman Way ((C) **800/770-3343** or 907/474-0286; www.riversedge.net), with lots of services, including free shuttles and organized tours. Full hookups are $27 and tent camping $16. The same people operate the cottage resort and restaurant next door.

WHERE TO DINE
DOWNTOWN

Gambardella's Pasta Bella ★★ ITALIAN   This warm, charming restaurant is right in the center of things. The chicken rustico (which sits on polenta) is tasty, they serve seafood in interesting ways, and the lasagna, made with sausage, thin noodles, and a rich, dusky tomato sauce will improve your opinion of this abused dish. Dining rooms are narrow and segmented, so you always seem to be sitting with just a few other people, with elaborate decoration that adds to a pleasingly busy feeling. Unlike the synthetic ambience of some of Fairbanks's other fine dining places, Gambardella's feels real, a place where a family shares its cuisine. Perfect, no—but pleasant and satisfying. On a sunny day, eat on the patio among the hanging flowers. They serve beer and wine.

706 2nd Ave. ℭ 907/457-4992. www.nvo.com/gambardellas. Lunch $6–$10; dinner main courses $9.50–$20. 15% gratuity added for parties of 5 or more, or for split checks. AE, MC, V. Mon–Sat 11am–10pm; Sun 4:30–10pm; closing an hr. earlier off season.

Lavelle's Bistro ★★★ ECLECTIC   In a big room of chrome, stone, and glass right downtown (at the base of the Marriott SpringHill Suites), Lavelle's has a grown-up, cosmopolitan feel that is quite welcome when you weary of the Alaskan rustic or gold rush themes of many of the area's restaurants. It's also got the advantage of consistently superb food, ambitious in conception and fine in execution, and expert service. The cuisine is difficult to categorize, as southwest and Italian influences might be brought to a single dish, and Northwest, Asian, and French influences turn up variously. Main courses are mostly over $20, but you can dine economically on the ample appetizers and salads, or choose a vegetarian lasagna that for only $15 comes with soup or a salad and side dishes. The wine list is impressive and the 3,000-bottle cellar is behind glass in the middle of the dining room; the owners are on a mission to educate Fairbanks about wine, as they've already done with food by creating one of Alaska's best restaurants.

575 1st Ave. ℭ 907/450-0555. www.lavellesbistro.com. Reservations recommended. Main courses $15–$30. AE, DC, DISC, MC, V. Mon–Sat 4:30–10pm, Sun 4:30–9pm.

Thai House ★★ THAI   In a small, brightly lit storefront in the downtown area, this is a simple, family-run restaurant with authentic Thai cuisine. Every time we've dined here the food came quickly and was deftly seasoned and cooked to a turn. You can rely on the servers, beautifully attired in national costumes, to help you order; just believe that when they say "hot" they really mean it. The first time I ate here, I rechecked the bill because it seemed too small. Such gems may be common in cities with large ethnic communities, but in Fairbanks, this place stands out.

526 5th Ave. ℭ 907/452-6123. Lunch items $6.75–$8; dinner main courses $9–$12. MC, V. Mon–Sat 11am–4pm and 5–10pm.

WITHIN DRIVING DISTANCE

Besides the restaurants listed here, there's the salmon bake at Pioneer Park, described earlier, and the buffet at Ester Gold Camp, below. Also, consider the excellent restaurant at Sophie Station Hotel (p. 373).

Also, in town, near the University at 3702 Cameron St. off University Ave., **Sam's Sourdough Cafe** (ℭ 907/479-0523) is a masterpiece in the art of the greasy spoon, with quick, friendly service, good burgers, great milkshakes, and breakfast all day. They're open from 6am to 10pm.

Some of the best pizza in town comes from **College Town Pizzeria,** near the intersection of College and University roads (ℭ 907/457-2200), an east coast, order-at-the-counter, family place. The crust is wonderful—crisp yet chewy— and they prepare it either in the American style or as Italian gourmet pizza with pesto, spinach, and the like and without tomato sauce. A large combo is $20. They don't deliver and are closed Sunday.

The Bakery *Finds* DINER   There are an infinite number of old-fashioned coffee shops in and around Fairbanks—the kind of place where a truck driver or gold miner can find a hearty, down-home meal, a motherly waitress, and a bottomless cup of coffee. This is one of the better versions. The sourdough pancakes are good, the menu is long and inexpensive, portions are huge (sometimes they require two plates), the service is fast and friendly. You can get breakfast all day (of course). They have no liquor license.

69 College Rd. © **907/456-8600.** Lunch items $5.50–$9; dinner main courses $8–$16. MC, V. Mon–Sat 6am–9pm; Sun 7am–4pm.

Pike's Landing ⭐ STEAK/SEAFOOD   The dining room of the fine dining section overlooks the Chena River near the airport from a series of tiered levels, each with tables well separated and covered with linens. The menu includes a nice range of simple to more ambitious selections; highlights I have found included the appetizer of spicy crab-stuffed mushrooms with a thick, chowder-like sauce and a lunch of a deftly seasoned seafood burrito. Main courses for dinner come with a choice of three salads, including a flavorful Caesar. Portions are quite large. Sunday brunch is big and delicious. Service, in my experience, is not always perfect, however, and the entire restaurant is a bit dated. For an inexpensive meal, the bar serves basic food on the deck over the river from 2:30 to 10pm. It's a pleasant choice on a sunny day, less so in cool or rainy weather, when it remains in operation behind plastic.

4438 Airport Way. © **907/479-6500.** Lunch items $7.50–$11; dinner main courses $22–$33. AE, DC, DISC, MC, V. Mon–Sat 11am–2pm and 5–9pm; Sun 10am–2pm and 5–9pm.

The Pump House Restaurant and Saloon ⭐⭐ STEAK/SEAFOOD   The historic, rambling, corrugated tin building on the National Register is elaborately decorated and landscaped with authentic gold rush relics. Sitting on the deck over the Chena, you can watch the riverboat paddle by or a group in canoes stop for appetizers and drinks from the full bar. For dinner, the cuisine is a cut above the area's typical steaks and seafood and includes game you may not have tried, including caribou and musk ox. Dishes such as the smoked salmon salad and the fish chowder—hearty, creamy, and flavorful—make the most of the regional ingredients without trying to get too fancy. The food is award-winning, and I have usually been happy, but I think the sauces can be too heavy. Portions are ample—save room for one of the exceptional desserts. They serve a big Sunday brunch, too.

Mile 1.3, Chena Pump Rd. © **907/479-8452.** www.pumphouse.com. Main courses $16–$30. AE, DISC, MC, V. Summer Mon–Sat 11:30am–2pm and 5–10pm, Sun 10am–2pm and 5–10pm; winter Mon–Sat 5–9pm, Sun 10am–2pm and 5–9pm.

The Turtle Club ⭐ *Finds* BEEF/SEAFOOD   Locals pack into this squat, windowless building, with its vinyl tablecloths and stackable metal chairs, for a menu with just a few famous selections: prime rib, lobster, king crab, prawns and, Tuesday through Thursday, barbecue ribs. These are simple, burly meals with roadhouse-style service; the menu is printed on the placemat and vegetables are an afterthought from an indifferent salad bar. But when the beef comes, you know it—the middle-sized prime rib cut is over an inch thick and covers a large plate, an insanely large portion—and the meat is tender and cooked right. The atmosphere is noisy and super-casual; people laugh loud and don't worry about putting their elbows on the table or spilling a little beer. You won't run into many other tourists here, north of the city in Fox, but you do need reservations, and even with them you often wait half an hour in the smoky bar or a narrow corridor. If this doesn't sound like fun, don't go; but if you get it, the place is energizing.

Mile 10 Old Steese Hwy., Fox. © **907/457-3883.** Reservations recommended. Main courses $19–$29. AE, DISC, MC, V. Mon–Sat 6–10pm, Sun 5–9pm.

FAIRBANKS NIGHTLIFE

Fairbanks has a lot of tourist-oriented evening activities, as well as entertainment also attended by locals. Call the 24-hour event recording of what's playing currently (© **907/456-INFO**) or get a copy of the *Fairbanks Daily News-Miner.* A

Finds Nenana: Tom Sawyer's Alaska

If you are driving south from Fairbanks toward Denali National Park or Anchorage, plan a short stop in the town of Nenana, about 60 miles along your way. It's a town out of a Mark Twain novel, a sleepy, dusty riverside barge stop left over from the past. Here Pres. Warren Harding drove the golden spike on the Alaska Railroad in 1923; it is still on display outside the memory-stirring old depot museum, although the train hasn't stopped regularly in 20 years. On the waterfront, riverboats are still loaded with cargo for villages up and down the Tanana River. That's also where you can see the cultural center, with its own little museum and Native craft shop. The oldest building in town is the picturesque 1905 log cabin church on Front Street. Stop in at the visitor center on the Parks Highway to learn more and to see the big book of guesses from the Nenana Ice Classic (www.nenanaakiceclassic.com). The contest is a drawing to guess the exact minute the ice on the Tanana will go out, with a jackpot over $300,000. Thanks to the game, this is one of the most carefully kept climate measurements in the north; scientists are using it to demonstrate long-term warming of the weather. See "Special Events," earlier, to learn about ice classic festivities.

---

large multiplex **movie theater** is located on Airport Way. The evening show at the **Palace Theatre** is discussed earlier under "Pioneer Park."

The **Ester Gold Camp** (© 800/354-7274 or 907/452-7274; www.akvisit.com) is an 11-building historic site, an old mining town that's been turned into an evening tourist attraction. The main event is a gold rush theme show at the Mala-mute Saloon, with singing and Robert Service poetry, nightly at 9pm; admission is $15, half price age 12 and under. A "photosymphony" slide show about the aurora takes place a couple of times a night in the summer and costs $8. There's also a restaurant that serves a buffet 5 to 9pm with mess-hall seating; it costs $22, or $33 if you have crab. Kids' prices $12 and $19, respectively. The gift shop is open in the evening, and there are simple, inexpensive rooms in the old gold mine bunkhouse and a campground.

Here are a couple of places to go out in the evening without having to hear about the gold rush (in other words, places real locals go). Downtown, **Café Alex Wine Bar,** at 310 1st Ave. (© 907/452-2539), a trendy and popular place with a pianist to sip wine and nosh on shared plates from an all-appetizer menu of truly delicious food.

Or, three miles south of town on the Parks Highway, **The Blue Loon** (© 907/457-5666; www.theblueloon.com) has live music—both local and famous imported acts—lots of beers on tap, good burgers, and a volleyball court outside. They even show movies and call themselves the "cultural epicenter of Fairbanks."

3 Chena Hot Springs Road

The 57-mile paved road east from Fairbanks is an avenue to an enjoyable day trip or a destination for up to a week's outdoor activities and hot-spring swimming. Of all the roads radiating from Fairbanks, this short highway will be most rewarding to outdoors people, and there is a funky and relaxing resort at the end.

The road travels through the Chena River State Recreation Area, with spectacular hikes and float trips and well-maintained riverside campgrounds, and leads to the Chena Hot Springs, where there's a year-round resort perfect for soaking in hot mineral springs and for use as a base for summer or winter wilderness day trips. The resort is open to people who want to rent one of the comfortable rooms or to campers and day-trippers, and it's even more popular in the winter than in the summer (it's slowest Apr–May).

The paved road leads through a forest of birch, spruce, and cottonwood, first passing an area of scattered roadside development and then following the Chena River through the state recreation area. On a sunny summer weekend, the people of Fairbanks migrate to the riverside and the hiking trails; on a sunny winter weekend, they take to the hills on snowmobiles, cross-country skis, or dog sleds. It's a pleasant drive at any time, around 1¼ hours each way from Fairbanks, but not particularly scenic.

A pair of prospectors, the Swan brothers, discovered the hot springs in 1905, having heard that a U.S. Geological Survey crew had seen steam in a valley on the upper Chena. Thomas Swan suffered from rheumatism; incredibly, he and his brother poled up the Chena River from Fairbanks, found the hot springs, built a cabin and rock-floored pool, and spent the summer soaking. He was cured! More visitors followed, drawn by stories that whole groups of cripples were able to dance all night after soaking in the pools—by 1915 a resort was in operation, drawing worn-out miners and gold rush stampeders and many others as well. The resort has been in constant use ever since.

ESSENTIALS
GETTING THERE   The Chena Hot Springs Road meets the Steese Expressway about 10 miles north of downtown Fairbanks. (Details on renting a car in Fairbanks can be found at the beginning of section 2 of this chapter.) The resort offers rides from anywhere in Fairbanks for $80 round-trip for one or two people, $40 for each additional person.

VISITOR INFORMATION   For outdoors information, check the Fairbanks **Alaska Public Lands Information Center,** 250 Cushman St. (at 3rd Ave.), (© **907/456-0527;** www.nps.gov/aplic).

The **Alaska Division of Parks,** at 3700 Airport Way, Fairbanks, AK 99709 (© **907/451-2695;** www.alaskastateparks.org, click on "Individual Parks"), manages the recreation area and produces trail, river, and road guides, which are also available at trail-head kiosks, from the public lands center, on the website, or in the area's *Trailmaker* newspaper, which you can also order from the Web. You can also contact the parks office with questions about the public cabins in the area (see "State Parks Cabin Reservations," in section 1 of chapter 7, for how to reserve).

THE CHENA RIVER STATE RECREATION AREA
The recreation area takes in 254,000 acres along the river valley and over the rolling mountains of heather around it. Some of Interior Alaska's best hiking and floating are found here. As everywhere in the Interior, the mosquitoes are brutal.

ACTIVITIES
HIKING & BACKPACKING   The best trail hikes in the Fairbanks area are in the Chena Hot Springs State Recreation Area. Backcountry camping requires no permit, and many of the trails go above the tree line, so it's a good area for backpackers to get into the wilderness.

The **Angel Rocks Trail** is a sometimes steep 3.5-mile loop to a large granite outcropping, an impressive destination with good views of the valley below. The trail mostly stays below the tree line; the blackened areas you see are from a 22,000-acre fire in 2002. The trailhead is well marked, at mile 48.9 of the road.

The 15-mile loop of the **Granite Tors Trail,** starting at mile 39 of the road, is a challenging day hike, rising through forest to rolling alpine terrain, but the towering tors more than reward the effort. Like surrealist experiments in perspective, these monolithic granite sentinels stand at random spots on the broad Plain of Monuments, at first confounding the eye's attempts to gauge their distance and size. Like the Angel Rocks, they were created when upwelling rock solidified in cracks in the surrounding earth, which then eroded away. Water is scarce, so bring along plenty. This is an excellent overnight hike, with the driest ground for camping right around the tors. There is also a public shelter halfway along the trail.

For a longer backpacking trip, the **Chena Dome Trail** makes a 30-mile loop, beginning at mile 50.5 and ending at mile 49. The 3 miles nearest the road at either end pass through forest, but the remaining 23 miles are above the tree line, marked with cairns and with expansive views. The trail summits 4,421-foot Chena Dome after the 10-mile mark. The trail can be quite wet and muddy in parts and steep and rocky elsewhere and you must bring water with you. A public shelter is on the trail.

RIVER FLOATING The Chena is a lovely river, growing from a clear, frothy creek near the end of the road to a lazy, brown Class I river as it flows off toward Fairbanks, several days downstream. Where you choose to start depends on your expertise. Easier water is downstream from Rosehip Campground (mile 27), with the slowest of all nearer Fairbanks, but the upper portion is more popular if you are up for something a bit more challenging. The road crosses the river several times, and the state park system has developed other access points, so it's possible to plan a float that exactly matches your time and abilities. Choose your route with the help of the river guide produced by the Alaska Division of Parks (see "Visitor Information," above).

Canoe Alaska (© **907/883-2628;** www.canoealaska.net) specializes in white-water canoe instruction for beginners and intermediate paddlers and leads guided canoe and raft outings and expeditions; a guided trip is around $100 a day. They also rent canoes and offer shuttle service. Other agencies offering such services are covered in the Fairbanks section, earlier in this chapter (two are under "Canoeing" and one in the feature "Equipped for the Backroads").

FISHING Several of the ponds in the recreation area are stocked with rainbow trout, which you can keep subject to harvest limits. Signs along the road mark access points to the ponds and river. You can catch and release Arctic grayling in the Chena, but check current regulations and bait restrictions. Contact the **Alaska Department of Fish and Game,** 1300 College Rd., Fairbanks, AK 99701 (© **907/459-7207;** www.alaska.gov/adfg, click on "Sport Fishing," then on the Interior region on the map, then "Lower Tanana Drainage").

CAMPING & CABINS

Three beautiful campgrounds with water and pit toilets lie along the road by the Chena River, managed by the Alaska Division of Parks (see "Visitor Information," above). Although they can't be reserved ahead, the campgrounds are unlikely to be full. The **Rosehip Campground,** at mile 27, has 37 sites, well separated by spruce and birch, with six suitable for RVs. Some sites are right on the river, and some are set up for more private tent camping, in the woods. The **Granite Tors Campground** is across from the trail head at mile 39; it has 24

The Steese Highway: Drive into the Wild

Driving the Steese Highway north from Fairbanks is like following a river upstream as it diminishes into its headwaters. First it's a 4-lane freeway, then a two lane highway, then the pavement gives out, then the gravel gives out. The road climbs over round tundra mountains, leaves behind the last tiny town, then drifts through uninhabited woods before ending on the banks of the Yukon River at a tiny Athabaskan village, Circle (named for the Arctic Circle, which it isn't on). It's a rough 162-mile drive to nowhere. But if nowhere is where you want to go, the Steese Highway may be the right adventure for you. Just don't forget the mosquito repellent.

Most of the land along the Steese is controlled by the federal **Bureau of Land Management** (BLM), 1150 University Ave., Fairbanks, AK 99709 (© **800/437-7021** or 907/474-2200; http://aurora.ak.blm.gov). Small- and large-scale gold mining takes place in the area, but most of the land is managed for recreation, with several campgrounds, some popular river floats, and a couple of beautiful hikes. The BLM website above contains detailed information: click on "Site Map" and the links for the Steese area and the White Mountains National Recreation Area. In addition, State Parks manages the **Upper Chatanika River Campground,** at mile 39, with 25 sites, pit toilets, a hand pump for water, and a $10 fee. This is the starting point for the most popular river float on the highway (covered, with others, in the Fairbanks section under "Canoeing," p. 370).

Without driving to the bitter end at Circle (where the only attraction is the Yukon River itself), you can make a goal of **Eagle Summit,** at mile 107, the highest place on the highway (3,624 ft.), and a good place to be on June 21 each year, the summer solstice. Although it's still a degree of latitude below the Arctic Circle, the sun never sets here on the longest day because of the elevation and atmospheric refraction. People come out from Fairbanks and make a celebration of it. The midnight sun is visible for about 3 days before and after the solstice, too, assuming the sky is clear. The BLM has installed a toilet and a viewing deck on a 750-foot loop trail at the trailhead to the 27-mile **Pinnell Mountain National Recreation Trail.** This is a challenging 3-day hike over amazing terrain of rounded, windblown, tundra-clothed mountaintops. To hike it downhill, start at Eagle Summit and end at Twelvemile Summit, mile 86. Two emergency shelters along the trail provide protection from the ferocious weather that can sweep the mountains. Get the free BLM trail brochure before going.

The next sensible destination is the tiny town of Central, 128 miles along the highway. It's a real, old-fashioned gold mining community where the current price of gold is posted in the bar and you can use your gold dust to pay for your drinks. There are a couple of simple diners, lodgings, and a campground, and the **Circle District Historical Museum** (© **907/520-1893**), which concentrates on the gold mining that has sustained the area since 1893. Admission $1 adults, 50 cents 12 and under, and it is open during summer daily noon to 5pm.

sites, seven suitable for RVs. Some sites have river frontage, and, as at Rosehip, float trips start there. The **Red Squirrel Campground,** at mile 42.8, has 12 sites and a pleasant picnic area on the grassy edge of a small, placid pond, where swimming is permitted. Camping is $10 a night at each of these campgrounds.

There are several public-use cabins in the recreation area, two of them easily accessible to summer visitors and not hard to book a month or two ahead. (See "State Parks Cabin Reservations" in section 1 of chapter 7 for how to get one.) These are primitive cabins; you must bring your own sleeping bags, lights, and cooking gear. The **North Fork Cabin** is at mile 47.7 of the road, and the **Chena River Cabin** faces the river at mile 32.2. You can get to either by car or canoe, and each costs $40 a night. Other public cabins in the area primarily serve winter users and are difficult to reach when the ground thaws.

THE HOT SPRINGS

Chena Hot Springs Resort ★★ Several years ago, Bernie Karl, a Fairbanks recycling entrepreneur, bought the hot springs, the 440-acre valley they lie in, and the old resort there, which had perennially struggled to stay out of the red. As I walked around the grounds with him he waved his hand here and there while outlining his audacious plans. I admit I nodded patronizingly. Each time I've gone back, however, more of his dream has been realized: an outdoor, boulder-rimmed swimming pond of hot mineral water, without chlorine or treatment; a building of large, modern bedrooms and a recreational center; and, incredibly, a large arched structure made of ice. Bernie built the ice hotel and filled it with expertly carved ice sculptures and got international publicity—then the building inspectors shut it down, citing, of all things, the lack of fire extinguishers. (Their real concern was the complete lack of engineering.) Bernie hired an engineer, got the disagreement worked out, and operated the ice hotel for a winter. Folks paid $15 each ($7.50 ages 6–12) just to walk through it, and overnight guests plunked down $575 for a double to sleep on a block of ice. Whatever Bernie says he will do next, I will believe him.

Unfortunately, Bernie is not as good at maintaining as he is at dreaming and building. Even some of the new facilities had fallen into a sad state on my last visit, and some of the older buildings were below the standards most travelers would find acceptable. That said, I recommend a visit, if you can overlook such issues or if you rent the best rooms in the place, which are still quite good. Or camp out. Our family has enjoyed wonderful days here swimming and exploring. Soak in the pools, hike through the woods, and enjoy the sound of the wind in the trees.

The hot springs supply an indoor pool, a series of indoor and outdoor hot tubs and spas, and the outdoor hot pond (100°–104°F/38°–40°C). Kids are limited to the indoor swimming pool, which is kept cool enough to swim, allowing adults to escape the noise outside. The locker rooms are tiny, so guests will want to change in their rooms. The swimming facility is open daily from 9am to midnight. Swim passes come with your room if you're staying at the resort; for campers or day-trippers, a day pass is $10 adults, $7 ages 6 to 17, free children 5 and under; a 10-punch pass is $60 for all ages.

Winter is the high season, when the aurora viewing is exceptional, away from city lights, and you can enjoy Nordic skiing groomed for classical or skating techniques, Sno-Cat and snow-machine tours, ice skating, sled-dog rides, winter biking, and more. An aurora viewing station, with a warm-up lodge, is established on a hilltop, where guests can flop back in the snow under a dizzying dome of stars and colors. In the summer, you can go horseback riding, rafting, canoeing, hiking, gold panning, flightseeing, or mountain biking. All activities are guided and carry extra fees.

The accommodations range from the crude, original cabins built by the prospectors who discovered the area to the large new hotel rooms with televisions, phones, and coffeemakers. The newest rooms, in the Moose building, are large and nicely done up, but noise can be a problem at night as guests come and go to look at the aurora. The larger cabins—not the prospectors' originals—are crude but adequate for a family or group looking for inexpensive lodgings and not particular about indoor plumbing. The intermediate rooms tend to be worn out. Even when they were new they were blah and cheaply made. The main lodge building contains the restaurant and bar. The menu and staff change fairly frequently and a new set-up was not ready to be reviewed at this writing. Over all, this is a good place to have fun in the real Alaska, but be ready for some rough spots.

Mile 56.5, Chena Hot Springs Rd. (P.O. Box 58740), Fairbanks, AK 99711. ✆ 800/478-4681 or 907/451-8104. Fax 907/451-5181. www.chenahotsprings.com. 80 units, 11 cabins. $105–$200 double. Extra person $20. AE, DC, DISC, MC, V. **Amenities:** Restaurant; bar; indoor and outdoor pools; hot tubs and Jacuzzis; guided activities; tour desk; massage; coin-op laundry. *In room* (excluding cabins): TV.

4 The Dalton Highway

The original purpose was utilitarian: to haul equipment north from Fairbanks for the trans-Alaska oil pipeline, which runs from Prudhoe Bay, on the Arctic Ocean, to Valdez, on the Pacific. But the experience of the Dalton Highway for a traveler is so far beyond the ordinary as to require a whole new frame of reference to take it all in. The road is so very long, so remote and free of traffic, and the scenery is so mind-boggling in its grandeur and repetition, that after a time it feels like you're living in a dream. At some point you have to swallow and say to yourself, "I guess I didn't know that much about the world after all."

Part of the wonder comes in the difficulty of the drive. There are extreme sports—throwing yourself off the side of a mountain and so forth—and this is an extreme road trip, one that dives into deep wilderness as far from help as most people ever get. In 500 miles there are only two service stations. Driving the Dalton is not to be taken lightly or done on a whim. You need to prepare and you need to know you want to do it, because you will be rumbling over gravel for many, many hours, breathing dust, and beating the crud out of your car.

The drive starts in Fairbanks (officially, you drive parts of the Steese Highway and Elliot Highway before the real Dalton Highway begins), crossing the rounded hills and low forest of that region before crossing the Yukon River on a high, wood-decked bridge. Over the miles that follow trees grow sparser and the road crosses some spectacular alpine plateaus until, entering the Brooks Range, Arctic vegetation and the mountains' rocky ferocity take over. Beyond towering Atigun Pass, the Arctic Slope extends 170 miles, first through sensuous tundra foothills, then over the broad, lake-dotted flatlands that extend to the Arctic Ocean. Arrival at the oil facilities can be a let down, especially if you haven't made arrangements for the tour that is the only way through to the shore. More on that below.

Wildlife shows up all along the road: moose, caribou, and grizzly bears, and sport fish and songbirds. Animals far outnumber people. A highway business is next to the Yukon, and at Coldfoot there is a truck stop, and Wiseman is 15 miles up the road from Coldfoot, where the 2000 census counted 21 people. And that's it for another 240 miles of gravel to Prudhoe Bay. There are no

ATMs, no grocery stores, no cell phone coverage, no medical facilities—civilization just isn't there. Drive carefully.

DALTON HIGHWAY ESSENTIALS

PRACTICAL TIPS You can drive the highway yourself, staying in the few motels along the way or in a tent or motor home. From Fairbanks take the Steese Highway north to the Elliot Highway. The total road distance from Fairbanks to the Arctic Ocean is 497 miles. Road conditions are notorious on the gravel-and-dirt Dalton, but now much of it is kept in good condition with pavement working its way steadily north. Speeds of 50 miles per hour are possible on some parts of the road, while doing 35 will keep you in one piece on rougher spots. The drive takes 12 hours each way, without stops. It's dusty, shoulders are soft, and flat tires are common. In the Fairbanks section I have listed a business that rents SUVs for the highway and another that rents campers on four-wheel-drive pickups (See "Equipped for the Backroads," on p. 369). Generally, other rental companies don't allow their vehicles on the Dalton.

Preparing for the drive is essential. Pick up the road guide produced by the BLM and get first-hand, personal advice (see "Visitor Information," below). Check road conditions, construction, and weather with the Alaska Department of Transportation (✆ **511;** http://511.alaska.gov). Bring at least one full-sized spare tire and extra gasoline in jugs. Most vehicles can make it from one gas station to the next, but what if the station is closed or you have to turn around short of a refill? Insect repellent is an absolute necessity. (See further suggestions to prepare for rural highways in "Driving Safety," p. 33). Drive with your headlights on at all times. Truck traffic is dominant. Slow down or even stop to allow trucks to pass you either way, and be careful on bridges, as some are narrow. Also, pull off for views or pictures—don't just stop in the middle of the road, as some people do.

For those who want to let someone else do the driving, a bus package is listed in section 9 of chapter 10, on Prudhoe Bay.

VISITOR INFORMATION Getting up-to-date advice is critical before heading off on the Dalton Highway, and the best place to do that is the Fairbanks **Alaska Public Lands Information Center,** at 250 Cushman St. (at 3rd Ave.), Fairbanks, AK 99701 (✆ **907/456-0527;** www.nps.gov/aplic). Staffers there drive the road annually to stay on top of current conditions.

Much of the road runs through land managed by the **Bureau of Land Management,** 1150 University Ave., Fairbanks, AK 99709 (✆ **907/474-2200;** http://aurora.ak.blm.gov/arctic). They publish information on driving, recreation, and natural history on their Web page and in the very handy free guide *The Dalton Highway,* a 24-page booklet available at the public lands information center or from any of the BLM information centers.

Two information stops are along the highway, both open summer only. A **contact station** at the Yukon River crossing is staffed by BLM volunteers and open daily in summer from 9am to 6pm. It has no phone. The brand new **Arctic Interagency Visitor Center** is at mile 175 on the west side of the highway in Coldfoot (✆ **907/678-5209**), open from 10am to 10pm daily. The center has exhibits about the North, a theater for nightly educational programs, a trip-planning room, a bookstore, and knowledgeable staff. Even if you don't have any questions, it's hard to imagine not stopping at this one real tourist attraction in your many hours of driving.

ON THE ROAD

The bridge over the Yukon River at mile 56 is the only crossing in Alaska, and many people drive the Dalton just to get to the **Arctic Circle** at mile 115, where you'll find a sign for pictures as well as a crude camping area. Many, many places along the highway have incredible views; among the most famous are Finger Mountain at mile 98; Gobbler's Knob at mile 132, which offers the first view of the Brooks Range; and 4,739-foot Atigun Pass at mile 245, where the road crosses the Brooks Range, winding through impossibly rugged country. The pass is the highest point on the Alaska road system, and you may find summer snow. All along the highway are opportunities to see birds and animals, including rabbits, foxes, wolves, moose, Dall sheep, bears, and caribou. Sit still if you want to see the skittish caribou, as they may wander closer to an unmoving vehicle.

The road parallels the 4-foot-wide **trans-Alaska pipeline.** The line, completed in 1977, serves America's largest and second-largest oil fields, Prudhoe Bay and Kuparuk, carrying the hot crude 900 miles from the Arctic Ocean to docks in Valdez, where tankers pick it up for shipment primarily to the West Coast. The public road ends before reaching the Prudhoe Bay complex and the Arctic Ocean. The only way through the gate is with a tour operator, and you must make arrangements at least 24 hours ahead to clear security. Call the **Arctic Caribou Inn** (© **877/658-2368** or 907/659-2368; www.arcticcaribouinn. com). See section 9 of chapter 10, on Prudhoe Bay, for more details.

HIGHWAY SERVICES: FOOD, FUEL & LODGINGS

Among the three places offering services along the 414 miles of the Dalton, you won't find anything luxurious, or even approaching budget chains.

Yukon River Camp, with a motel, a restaurant, a gift shop, fuel, and tire repair, is at Mile 56, just past the Yukon River Bridge (© **907/474-3557**). The motel is a former pipeline construction camp.

The **Coldfoot Camp** truck stop at Mile 175 (© **866/474-3400** or 907/ 474-3500; www.coldfootcamp.com) is the one big stopping place along the road. After the endless wilderness miles on the road, no one could stand to pass it by. The camp includes several buildings on a large gravel pad. Most important are the gas pumps and the 24-hour restaurant where you pay for the fuel—a typical but friendly highway diner. Across the lot, the hotel, known as the Slate Creek Inn, is built of left-over construction camp modular units. The small rooms with low ceilings are perfectly comfortable, with private bathrooms, but far from grand. The camp also offers minor vehicle repairs, towing, RV hookup, laundry, a post office, a gift shop, and a saloon. They guide rafting on the Middle Fork of the Koyukuk River, offer mountain bike rentals, and shuttles for hiking and guided hiking. An air taxi, **Coyote Air** (© **800/252-0603** or 907/678-5995; www.flycoyote.com), can show you this amazing country from the air. There are other activities farther afield offered by **Northern Alaska Tour Company** (© **907/474-8600;** www.northernalaska.com). Don't miss the new interagency visitor center, described above. The pleasant BLM Marion Creek Campground is 5 miles north of Coldfoot.

After Coldfoot, the next service area is **Deadhorse,** at the end of the road another 240 miles north, with rooms, fuel, restaurants, a post office, vehicle maintenance, a general store, and an airport. See the Prudhoe Bay section in chapter 10.

GETTING OUT OF THE CAR
ACTIVITIES

FISHING   The streams and lakes of the Arctic are cold, poor in nutrients, and frozen much of the year; fishing is not a good reason to drive the Dalton. However, if you are taking the adventure anyway, there are fish in streams from July to mid-September and in lakes that don't freeze to the bottom. Many of the streams have Arctic grayling, but you'll want to hike farther than a quarter mile from the road to increase your chances. A good bet is the **Jim River area** between miles 140 and 144, where the river follows the road and fishing pressure is more spread out. Most North Slope rivers have good Dolly Varden fishing in late August and early September. Many of the lakes along the road have grayling, and the deeper ones north of the Brooks Range have lake trout. Check current regulations. Contact the **Alaska Department of Fish and Game,** 1300 College Rd., Fairbanks, AK 99701 (© **907/459-7207**); they produce a booklet called *Sportfishing Along the Dalton Highway.*

HIKING   The road has no established hiking trails, but most of the area is open to self-reliant hikers who know how to pick their own route. Hiking brushy or marshy Interior country isn't fun, but the dry tundra of the ridgetops and mountains creates a wonderful sense of freedom. The country opens up north of the Chandalar Shelf at mile 237. The best hiking area is the zone of dry tundra in the foothills north of the Brooks Range. But even at upper elevations you still run into tussocks, wet ground, and stream crossings. Topographical maps and advice on hiking the Brooks Range are available at the sources listed under "Visitor Information," above. Remember, this is remote wilderness; do your research, be prepared, and tell someone where you're going and when you'll be back.

CAMPING

The Bureau of Land Management has a few campgrounds along the road, but there seems little reason to wait to reach them, as there are any number of places to pull off the road on a spot of gravel and spend the night, often in places of stunning beauty. The only requirements are for safety and the environment: get far enough off the road to avoid the fast-moving truck spewing gravel as far as 30 feet; read up on bear avoidance on p. 30; and don't leave toilet paper or anything else behind. I have listed the BLM's developed areas along the road, which include campgrounds and spots where you can park for a while and obtain water. Unless the description mentions a formal campground, these are just pullouts where you can park and camp or sleep in your car (add 83 miles to the mileposts to get the distance from Fairbanks):

- **Mile 60:** Artesian well, outhouses, and dump station.
- **Mile 98** (Finger Mountain): Nice views, outhouse, and wheelchair-accessible trail with interpretive signs.
- **Mile 115** (Arctic Circle): Outhouses, picnic tables, and an interpretive display; camp only in the undeveloped campground up the hill, which does not have water.
- **Mile 150** (Grayling Lake): Pull-out with outhouse.
- **Mile 175** (Coldfoot): A private campground with hookups is part of the truck stop described above.
- **Mile 180** (Marion Creek): A developed BLM campground with 27 campsites, 11 of them for large RVs (no hookups). The campground has a well and outhouses; the fee is $8.

- **Mile 235** (Arctic tree line): Outhouse; not an attractive camping site due to truck traffic on a steep grade.
- **Mile 275** (Galbraith Lake): Undeveloped campground with outhouses but without water about 4 miles off-road; follow the access road to the state-operated landing strip, then continue 2.5 miles on an unimproved road.
- **Mile 355** (on the North Slope): wayside with an outhouse.

5 The Alaska Highway

Detailed coverage of the entire 2,400-mile drive to Alaska is beyond our scope, but chapter 2's "Getting There" section provides the planning basics. Here I've covered the Alaska portion of the road, the 200 miles of the Alaska Highway that run from the border with Canada to the terminus in Delta Junction. This is mostly boring driving, miles of stunted black spruce and brush, either living or burned out. It's a relief when you hit the first major town, **Tok** (rhymes with Coke), 100 miles along. But don't get your hopes up. This is the only place where I've ever walked into a visitor center and asked what there is to do in town, only to have the host hold up her fingers in the shape of a goose egg and say, "Nothing." Another 100 miles (I hope you brought plenty of cassette tapes, because no radio station reaches out here) and you've made it to **Delta Junction.** There's a little more to do here, but it's still not a destination. Another 100 miles and you're in Fairbanks.

The main sources of information for the drive are based in Tok, the first town you hit after you cross the border. It acts as a threshold for the entire state. To plan the journey ahead, contact them, and see "Exploring the Interior," at the beginning of this chapter. If you're headed to Anchorage or other points south, see the sections on the Glenn and Richardson highways later in this chapter; those roads branch from the Alaska Highway at Tok and Delta, respectively.

I've arranged this section in order from the border with Canada heading west.

CROSSING THE BORDER

Remember to set your watch back an hour when crossing the border in Alaska—it's an hour later in Yukon Territory. Also, if you make significant purchases or rent rooms in Canada, you may be able to get a refund on the 7% goods and services tax (GST). Ask at the border station.

CUSTOMS   Crossing the U.S./Canadian border requires a little preparation even for U.S. citizens to make sure you have the necessary identification. U.S. and Canadian citizens don't need passports or visas going either way, but should carry **proof of citizenship** and **proof of residence.** (Citizens of other countries probably need passports, and those from some countries may need visas; see chapter 3.) Canadian authorities now require American citizens to produce a piece of photo identification such as a driver's license combined with either a birth certificate or a passport. **Children** with their parents may need a birth certificate; children or youths under 18 unaccompanied by parents may need a letter from a parent or guardian; and children with a single parent should carry a letter from the other parent. There are no duties on products made in the United States or Canada. For duties on items that you buy that originated in other countries or on alcohol or smoking supplies see chapter 3. Products you buy in Alaska made of **ivory, fur, or other wildlife** will probably require special permits to be taken out of the United States, and it's easiest to have the store where you bought the item take care of it (see chapter 3 for details). U.S. authorities no longer let non-citizens into the country with firearms except for permanent resident aliens or foreigners holding both a special permit from the Bureau of Alcohol Tobacco and Firearms and a non-resident hunting license (see chapter 3). Going into Canada, **firearms** other than hunting rifles or shotguns generally are not allowed, and you need to fill out a form and pay a $50 fee for guns that are allowed; contact the Canadian Firearms Center (© **800/731-4000;** www.cfc.gc.ca) before you go to avoid problems. Entering the U.S., **dogs** more than 3 months old require a rabies certificate signed by a licensed veterinarian. **Beef** from Canada and **poultry** from British Columbia are not allowed to enter into the U.S., even as ingredients in pet food, nor are **citrus fruits** (except fruit clearly identified as being of U.S. origin). If in doubt about any of these issues call before you go, as the border is a long way from anywhere: **Canadian Customs** in Whitehorse (© **867/667-3943**) or **U.S. Customs** in Anchorage (© **907/271-2675**).

FROM THE BORDER TO TOK

The first 60 miles after entering the United States the road borders the Tetlin National Wildlife Refuge. These broad wetlands and low forests are a migratory stop-over in May for thousands of songbirds, birds of prey, and swans and other waterfowl, and are the summer home of lesser sandhill cranes, among 143 other species. Caribou show up along the road, especially in the early spring and fall. A **Fish and Wildlife Service Visitor Center,** 8 miles past the border, at mile 1,229 (© **907/774-2245** or 907/883-5312 headquarters; http://tetlin.fws.gov), is open May 15 to September 15 daily from 8am to 5pm. There are exhibits and the observation deck has a great view. The refuge also has two small lakeside campgrounds over the next 27 miles: Deadman, at Mile 1,249, with 16 sites (OK for RVs); and Lakeview, at mile 1,256, with eight (no RVs allowed). Rangers give evening campground programs in the summer. The campgrounds do not have water.

TOK

Born as a construction station on the highway, Tokyo Camp's name was shortened to Tok after Pearl Harbor. Since then, Tok's role in the world hasn't expanded much beyond being a stop on the road. With its location at the intersection of the Alaska Highway and the Glenn Highway to Anchorage and Prince William Sound (see the next section), the town has built an economy of gas stations, gift stores, cafes, and hotels to serve highway travelers.

ESSENTIALS

GETTING THERE You're surely passing through Tok with your own set of wheels. If you get stuck for some reason, one bus service or another can get you on your way. Inquire at the visitor center. **Alaska Trails** (© **888/600-6001;** www.AlaskaShuttle.com) runs through Tok between Fairbanks and Dawson City.

VISITOR INFORMATION Public land agencies jointly operate an informative visitor center to introduce highway travelers to Alaska's outdoors. The **Alaska Public Lands Information Center,** P.O. Box 359, Tok, AK 99780 (© **907/883-5667;** www.nps.gov/aplic), is on the right (north) side of the road coming from the direction of Canada on the Alaska Highway. It is open daily from 8am to 7pm in summer and from 8am to 4:30pm in winter. Besides answering questions, rangers offer talks and nature walks in the summer, and you can make ferry reservations on the Alaska Marine Highway System.

Dawson City & Eagle: Detour into History

Instead of taking the Alaska Highway directly from Whitehorse, Yukon, to Tok, consider driving north on the Klondike Highway (Yukon Hwy. 2) to Dawson City, then west and south over the Top of the World Highway and partially unpaved Taylor Highway to rejoin the Alaska Highway just east of Tok. This represents 502 miles of driving, about 127 miles more than if you just stay on the Alaska Highway, and includes 43 miles of sometimes rough dirt road, but it's worth doing at least one way to see historic Dawson City and the fabulous mountain scenery of the Top of the World Highway. Dawson was the destination of the 1898 Klondike Gold Rush; the bed of the Klondike River near here contained thick veins of gold. The town maintains the look of those days, when it was the second largest city on the west coast, after San Francisco. Many buildings, a gold dredge, and a river boat were restored as part of the Klondike National Historic Sites, managed by **Parks Canada.** Besides the buildings and their setting, there are museums, a working non-profit casino, a vaudeville show, a center of indigenous culture, and other attractions, easily enough for two days of sightseeing. The **Klondike Visitor Association** (P.O. Box 389, Dawson City, YT, Canada Y0B 1G0; ℂ **867/993-5575**; fax 867/993-6415; www. DawsonCity.ca), offers information on local businesses, accommodations, and community events. For information on the historic sites, contact Parks Canada at P.O. Box 390, Dawson City, YT, Canada Y0B 1G0 (ℂ **867/993-7200**; www.parkscanada.gc.ca, click on "National Historic Sites," then "Yukon"). For information on the **Han Nation people** here and their cultural center, call ℂ **867/993-5385**, (www.trondek.com).

After passing into the United States on the Top of the World Highway (note, this border crossing is open only during the day, and only during the summer), a further detour leads north on the Taylor Highway to the forgotten town of Eagle on the bank of the Yukon River (going south on the Taylor leads you back to the Alaska Hwy.). The trip to Eagle adds 66 miles each way on a winding, narrow dirt road; allow 2 hours each way. But, if you have the time, the destination more than rewards the effort. Eagle is lost in time, a treasure of a gold rush river town with many original buildings full of original artifacts from a century ago. It's entirely authentic and non-commercial, with few businesses other than the store, cafe, motel, and a B&B. The **Eagle Historical Society and Museums** (ℂ **907/547-2325**; www.eagleak.org) shows off the buildings and several museums of materials left behind in this eddy in the stream of history. Their 3-hour walking tour starts once a day at 9am daily Memorial Day to Labor Day and costs $5.

To plan a float trip on the Yukon River from Eagle, or for other outdoor information, contact the Eagle Field Office of the **Yukon–Charley Rivers National Preserve,** P.O. Box 167, Eagle, AK 99738 (ℂ **907/547-2233**; www.nps.gov/yuch). The office lies on the far side of the airstrip from the main part of town.

A few doors down at the intersection of the Alaska Highway and Tok Cut-Off (also known as the Glenn Highway), the town's **Main Street Visitor Center** is operated by the Tok Chamber of Commerce, P.O. Box 389, Tok, AK 99780 (℡ **907/883-5775;** www.TokAlaskaInfo.com). The center provides information on Tok and anywhere else you may be bound on the highway. They're open from May 1 to September 15 daily from 8am to 7pm.

FAST FACTS: Tok

Bank **Denali State Bank** is in the Three Bears Store and has an ATM; another ATM is at the Texaco station across the road from Fast Eddy's restaurant.

Hospital **Tok Clinic** is on the Tok Cut-Off across from the fire station (℡ **907/883-5855**).

Police Contact the **Alaska State Troopers** (℡ **907/883-5111**), near the intersection of the Alaska Highway and Glenn Highway.

Post Office At the highway junction next to the Westmark Hotel.

Taxes There are none in the region.

WHERE TO STAY

The motels are numerous and competitive in Tok. There also are many B&Bs. Check at the visitor center.

The **Tok International Youth Hostel** (℡ **907/883-3745;** stout@aptalaska. net) occupies a MASH tent a mile off Mile 1322.5 Alaska Highway, 8 miles west of town, on Pringle Drive. Guests use an outhouse and need mosquito repellent. The hostel offers a shower and cooking facilities. Beds are $10 apiece; reservations are not necessary. It's closed from September 15 to May 15.

Be sure to get the 25¢ state highway and campground map from the public lands center (see above), which includes all the public campgrounds in Alaska. Three attractive state park campgrounds lie near Tok on the three highway links that radiate from the town. Each has a $10 self-service fee.

There are lots of competitive RV parks in Tok, too. One that has wooded sites suitable for tent camping as well is the **Sourdough Campground,** 1½ miles south of town on the Glenn Highway (℡ **800/789-5543** Alaska and Yukon only, or 907/883-5543; www.sourdoughcampground.com). They charge $26 for full hookups, $16 dry, and serve pancake breakfasts.

Snowshoe Motel & Fine Arts and Gifts *(Value*   The 10 newer nonsmoking rooms near the front are a real bargain. Each is divided into two sections by the bathroom, providing two separate bedrooms—great for families. They have phones. Outside walkways are decorated with flowers. The gift shop carries some authentic Native art as well as highway kitsch.

Across the hwy. from the information center (P.O. Box 559), Tok, AK 99789. ℡ 800/478-4511 in Alaska, Yukon, and part of B.C.; or 907/883-4511. Fax 907/883-4512. snowshoe@aptalaska.net. 24 units. High season $72 double; low season $57 double. Rates include continental breakfast in summer. Extra person $5. MC, V. *In room:* TV.

Westmark Tok   The central hotel in town is closed in the winter, as its clientele is primarily the package tour bus trade. It's made up of several buildings connected by boardwalks. The older rooms are narrow, without enough room at the foot of the bed for the TV, but they're comfortable and up-to-date. The new section has larger rooms for the same price. There's a "factory outlet" gift store in the lobby that sells remainders from Westmark's other shops for lower prices. A greenhouse grows huge vegetables. The restaurant serves three meals a day, with dinners in the $14-to-$20 range.

Intersection of Alaska and Glenn highways (P.O. Box 130), Tok, AK 99780-0130. © **800/544-0970** (reservations) or 907/883-5174. Fax 907/883-5178. www.westmarkhotels.com. 93 units. $129 double. AE, DC, DISC, MC, V. Closed mid-Sept to mid-May. **Amenities:** Restaurant; bar. *In room:* TV, coffeemaker, hair dryer, iron.

Young's Motel   Good standard motel rooms occupy three one-story structures on the parking lot behind Fast Eddy's restaurant (described below), where you check in. Eighteen newer, smoke-free rooms are the pick of the litter, but all are acceptable.

Behind Fast Eddy's Restaurant on the Alaska Hwy. (P.O. Box 482), Tok, AK 99780. © **907/883-4411**. Fax 907/ 883-5023. edyoung@aptalaska.net. 43 units. High season $79 double; low season $67 double. Extra person $5. AE, DISC, MC, V. **Amenities:** Restaurant (described below); bar. *In room:* TV, dataport.

WHERE TO DINE

A reliable restaurant of many years tenure, **Fast Eddy's** (© **907/883-4411**), is on the right as you enter town from the east. Begun as a typical roadside cafe, it has developed into a place where a wine list and fine-dining entrees don't seem out of place. Yet the proprietor knows that most highway travelers just want a simple, relaxing meal, and the varied menu offers anything they might have in mind. I relish the salad bar and light dishes that offer a break from the usually carnivorous greasy-spoon choices found elsewhere along the highway. The dining room is decorated in maroon, dark wood, and brass. They're open in summer from 6am to 11pm, in winter from 6am to 10pm.

DELTA JUNCTION

This intersection with the Richardson Highway, which runs from Valdez to Fairbanks (see section 7, below), is the official end of the Alaska Highway. It's an earnest little roadside town set in a broad plain between the Delta and Tanana rivers. People make their livings from farming and tourism, by working at a trans-Alaska pipeline pump station south of town, and from construction at Fort Greely, a defunct Army base recently reborn as the "test bed" for President Bush's missile defense system. For visitors, there are two historic roadhouse museums, several good campgrounds, and an unpredictable chance to spy a herd of bison—but not enough to hold most for more than a few hours.

ESSENTIALS

VISITOR INFORMATION   A helpful **visitor center** run by the Delta Chamber of Commerce, P.O. Box 987, Delta Junction, AK 99737 (© **877/895-5068** or 907/895-5068, 907/895-5069 summer only; www.deltachamber.org), stands at the intersection of the Alaska and Richardson highways, in the middle of town; it's open from mid-May to mid-September.

FAST FACTS: **Delta Junction**

Bank **Wells Fargo,** with an ATM, is next door to the IGA Food Cache on the Richardson Highway at the center of town.

Hospital The **Family Medical Center** is at Mile 267.2 Richardson Highway, 2 miles north of the visitor center (© **907/895-4879** or 907/895-5100).

Police The **Alaska State Troopers'** emergency number is ℂ **907/895-4800.**
For nonemergencies, call ℂ **907/895-4344.**

Post Office On the Richardson, 2 blocks north of the visitor center.

Taxes None of any kind.

EXPLORING THE AREA

Before construction of the first road to Fairbanks in 1917 (today's Richardson
Hwy.), travelers to the Interior followed a trail on basically the same route by
horse in summer and dog sled in winter, stopping at roadhouses that provided
food and shelter a day apart on the 2-week trip. Two well-preserved examples of
the roadhouse system survive near Delta Junction.

In 1996, the Army saved the 1905 **Sullivan Roadhouse** (ℂ **907/895-4415**),
which had stood abandoned since 1922 on what became an Army bombing
range. Today the log building stands near the town visitor center and is open in
summer Monday through Friday 9am to 5pm. Many of the Sullivan's original
belongings have been set back in their original places, giving a strong feel for
frontier life, but the heart of the restoration is the authentic hospitality of the
local volunteers who show off the place with great pride.

The next stop on the trail beyond Sullivan's Roadhouse was 16 miles toward Fairbanks. **Rika's Roadhouse and Landing,** 10 miles northwest of Delta at Mile 275
on the Richardson Highway (ℂ **907/895-4201;** www.rikas.com), still makes a
pleasant stop on your drive. This roadhouse lasted later than the Sullivans' because
drivers had to board a ferry here to cross the Tanana River until the 1940s, and the
shore was the end of the line for Tanana sternwheelers. The 1906 log building, on
the National Register of Historic Places, has been altered too much by its gift shop
to feel authentic, but the grassy 10-acre compound completes a vivid scene of
Alaska pioneer life with surviving outbuildings, including telegraph cabins, a
museum, a barn, a gorgeous vegetable garden, and livestock pens. A concessionaire
manages the site for the Big Delta State Historical Park, with a restaurant serving
soups, salads, and sandwiches daily from 9am to 5pm; the grounds and museum
are open from 8am to 8pm from May 15 to September 15. An impressive suspen-
sion bridge carries the trans-Alaska pipeline over the Tanana River, and boaters use
the shoreline, at the confluence of the Tanana and Delta rivers.

WHERE TO STAY

The cute, funny, and hospitable **Kelly's Alaska Country Inn,** at the intersection
of Richardson and Alaska highways (ℂ **907/895-4667;** www.kellysalaskacountry
inn.com), has rooms for $99 (double) right in the middle of town. The 20 rooms
have TVs, telephones, microwave ovens, refrigerators, and coffee machines; most
are small and ordinary, but a funky few are in an old Quonset hut and have arched
wood ceilings. This is a family-run business going way, way back.

You'll find basic rooms with refrigerators and satellite TV for $75 (double)
at **Alaska 7 Motel,** 3548 Richardson Hwy. (ℂ **907/895-4848;** www.alaska7
motel.com).

Check at the visitor center for a referral to one of the many B&Bs.

CAMPING

Alaska State Parks maintains five campgrounds on the rivers and lakes in and
around Delta Junction and a couple of public cabins. Right on the highway near
town, the **Delta State Recreation Area campground** lies among large spruce

and birch trees, the sites well separated, some with walk-in privacy. It is among the most attractive campgrounds on the highway. The **Quartz Lake State Recreation Area,** 11 miles northwest of town on the Richardson Highway and down a 3-mile turnoff, has an 80-site campground on the shallow fishing lake. The camping fee at each is $10. For information, contact the **Department of Natural Resources Public Information Center,** 3700 Airport Way, Fairbanks, AK 99709 (© **907/451-2705;** www.alaskastateparks.org, click on "Individual Parks").

To park an RV, or if you're tent camping and need a shower, **Smith's Green Acres RV Park and Campground,** 1½ miles north on the Richardson Highway from the visitor center (© **800/895-4369** or 907/895-4369), has grassy RV sites and tent sites among the trees. The place also has cabins, a small playground, and laundry facilities. Full hook-up sites are $24, tent sites $12.

WHERE TO DINE

Buffalo Center Diner DINER   The locals eat here, for good reason. The dining room is light and clean, decorated with wood and plants, and the menu covers everything you would hope for in a simple family restaurant—plus a seasonal list of buffalo dinners in honor of the Delta herd. Each time I've stopped the food has been good and the atmosphere relaxing. Service has always been friendly and quick and the waitress called me Hon.

1680 Richardson Hwy. © **907/895-5089.** Lunch $4.75–$12; dinner $8–$27. MC, V. Summer daily 6am–9pm; winter daily 6am–8pm.

6 The Glenn Highway

The Glenn Highway, Alaska Route 1, leads from the Alaska Highway at Tok to Anchorage (the section from Tok to Glennallen is also called the Tok Cut-Off). It connects the most populous part of the state to the outside world, a 328-mile strip of blacktop that grows from two lanes in Tok to six or more in urban downtown Anchorage. In this section, I cover the stretch from Glennallen to Palmer. From Tok to Glennallen, the road passes through wilderness. The portion from Palmer to downtown Anchorage is all part of the greater city and encompassed in chapter 6.

GLENNALLEN

It may look like just a wide place in the road, but this little town is the commercial hub for the Copper River Country, a great, thinly settled region.

Other than Wrangell–St. Elias National Park, most of the public land in the Copper River Country is managed by the **Bureau of Land Management Glennallen Field Office,** with a log cabin office in town on the north side of the Glenn Highway, P.O. Box 147, Glennallen, AK 99588 (© **907/822-3217;** www.glennallen.ak.blm.gov), open Monday through Friday from 8am to 4:30pm. Information also is available from the public land information centers in Anchorage, Fairbanks, and Tok. This huge area, about as large as a midsize eastern U.S. state, is more accessible than the park, an advantage for outdoor recreation, but it's still a rough, remote land with few high-quality visitor facilities. There are several large alpine lakes, two National Wild Rivers, many hiking trails, and five campgrounds (including the State Parks campground just north of Glennallen), all reached on the Richardson, Glenn, and Denali highways. Guides are available for **rafting** and **fishing** in the rivers. Check at the visitor center or BLM office for a list of operators.

For commercial information, the volunteer-run **Copper River Visitor Center** is in a gray building at the intersection of the highways (P.O. Box 469, Glennallen, AK 99588; ℂ **907/822-5555;** www.traveltoalaska.com). The center operates from May 15 to September 15; June through August it is open daily 8am to 7pm; at the beginning and end of the season the hours are 9am to 6pm. Glennallen has a bank with an ATM, a post office, a medical center, and government offices, all centered along a strip of the Glenn Highway around Mile 187.

Good standard accommodations are at the **New Caribou Hotel,** in town at Mile 187 of the Glenn Highway (ℂ **800/478-3302** or 907/822-3302; www.caribouhotel.com). The rooms, although not large, have the amenities of a roadside chain, but the hotel as a whole has the character of its place. It's a good stop on a long drive. A double is $139 in the summer. They book up in the summer, so reservations are important. *Note:* the annex building, a former construction camp, is much less desirable. Their **Caribou Restaurant** is inexpensive but quite fancy inside, with lots of brass and booths. Choices include burgers, steak, meatloaf, pork chops, and salmon.

THE MATANUSKA GLACIER AREA

From Glennallen, the highway traverses a broad tundra area where there's a good chance of seeing caribou and other wildlife from a distance. Next, the road then climbs between two mountain ranges—the coastal Chugach Mountains that hold the glaciers around Prince William Sound, and the craggy old Talkeetna Mountains to the north. The road winds through steep, rocky terrain with wonderful, scary views, including a good look at the Matanuska Glacier. In the fall, when the tundra and the birches, aspens, and cottonwoods turn yellow and red, this drive is dizzying in its beauty.

The Matanuska Glacier State Recreation Area overlooks the glacier and has a 1-mile interpretive nature trail and a good, 12-site campground (sites are $15). To get closer to the glacier, you have to take a rough side road and pay a $10 per person fee to the people who own the land in front of it. Turn at mile 102. The side road is three miles, followed by a 15 minute walk to the glacier's face.

There are several other good trails and camping areas along the road, too.

Two exceptionally good remote lodges lie along the highway near the glacier, about 70 miles from Glennallen or 115 miles from Anchorage. In this remote area there is no TV and phones are in common rooms.

Majestic Valley Wilderness Lodge ★ *Finds*   This friendly lodge offers basic rooms with private bathrooms and serves excellent family-style meals to guests and others who reserve in advance. Dining is in an extraordinary log lodge building with a towering ceiling and wonderful mountain views—a quintessentially Alaskan space that is understandably popular for weddings and the like. While most of the rooms are small and basic, they're set in a gorgeous, quiet spot out of sight of the highway. A 20km network of superb cross-country skiing trails is groomed with top quality equipment for diagonal or skate skiing—we enjoy going there for spring skiing weekends on the spectacular terrain. In the summer, the hiking here, mostly above treeline, is exceptional. The lodge offers guides for hikes, skiing, and snowmobiling.

Mile 114.9, Glenn Hwy., HC03, Box 8514, Palmer, AK 99645. ℂ 907/746-2930. Fax 907/746-2931. www.majesticvalleylodge.com. 10 units, 2 cabins. $100 double; $119 cabin double. Extra adult $10; extra child ages 4–12 $5. MC, V. **Amenities:** Restaurant; free-standing wood-fired sauna; activity desk.

Sheep Mountain Lodge ★   On a mountainside above the road, a well-loved couple, Zack and Anjanette Steer, preside at this historic log lodge. Zack is a top competitive dog musher, so the operation is mostly oriented to the summer. Guests hike and mountain bike over spectacular trails on the tundra mountains. Cabins are large and stylishly decorated, with high ceilings and walls of rough wood to remind you of the rural location. The sitting porches have wonderful views down the mountainside. They rent a sleeping-bag bunkhouse, too, and have a guest sauna and indoor hot tub. The little cafe serves simple, healthy food in the summer. Service is very friendly.

Mile 113.5, Glenn Hwy., HC 03, Box 8490, Palmer, AK 99645. © **877/645-5121** or 907/745-5121. Fax 907/745-5120. www.sheepmountain.com. 10 cabins. Summer $135 double, extra person $15; winter $115 double, extra person $10. Bunkhouse $60 for 4, extra person $5. DISC, MC, V. Closed one month each in spring and fall (call ahead). **Amenities:** Restaurant; Jacuzzi; sauna.

CHICKALOON & SUTTON

More country-style development crops up along the road as you approach urban Alaska. Chickaloon is the base of Nova Raft and Adventure Tours, the river riding company listed in the Anchorage chapter; if you're already passing through here, you may want to arrange a float. Sutton is a little town left behind by a coal mine that once operated in these mountains. The charming little historic park there is worthy of a stop to stretch your legs.

7 The Richardson Highway & Copper Center

The 364-mile drive from Fairbanks to Valdez unfolds as a grand cross-section of Alaska. It begins in the broad Interior valleys at the north, rises to the tundra and lakes of the Alaska Range, descends back down to the Copper River Country, and finally climbs over the steep coastal mountains into the Prince William Sound fjord where Valdez resides. This was the first route into Alaska, but today it is little traveled and mostly free of development, an opportunity to see real wilderness by car on paved road.

Delta Junction is covered in section 5, on the Alaska Highway. The intersection with the Denali Highway (see chapter 8) comes 81 miles south of there. This section has the most extraordinary scenery—broad vistas, the Delta River, amazing alpine lakes including long Summit Lake, and many views of the trans-Alaska pipeline. Don't plan on stops or services, although there are a few widely scattered campgrounds and seasonal businesses. The spot on the map known as Paxson, the intersection with the Denali Highway, has one main business, the Paxson Inn. You can fill your tanks there 24 hours a day or buy a snack, but I wouldn't recommend the restaurant or the rooms.

South from Paxson the views remain lovely, with more lakes, increasingly surrounded by trees, as latitude and elevation decrease going into the Copper River Valley. After 15 miles you reach the only noteworthy business on this 70-mile section of road from Paxson to Glennallen: the **Meiers Lake Roadhouse and Atwater Chateau Motel,** at Mile 170 (© **907/822-3151**). Way out here, where they have to make their own electricity, a rugged and cheerful little family has built a fine motel of 16 cozy, immaculate rooms with satellite TVs and private bathrooms. They charge $100 a night regardless of the number of people in the room and have a restaurant, bar, and hardware store.

The next town on the Richardson is Glennallen, which is covered above, in section 6. Fourteen miles south of Glennallen, **Copper Center** is a tiny Athabascan community on the old Richardson Highway. There is one country-road attraction, a big model train diorama of the Copper River and Northwestern Railroad and Kennecott Mine (see the next section), showing McCarthy, Chitina, and the Motherlode Mine. Ron Simpson built the set-up in his bar,

The Copper Rail Depot (© 907/822-3522; www.crnwrailway.com). It's on the loop road off the Old Richardson Highway, near the Copper Center Lodge.

That historic roadhouse, the **Copper Center Lodge** (© 907/822-3245) has long been worthy of a stop for dinner or even overnight. The history of the lodge dates from the bizarre gold rush origins of Copper Center and Valdez, when about 4,000 stampeders to the Klondike tried a virtually impossible all-American route from Valdez over the glaciers of the Wrangell–St. Elias region. Few made it, and hundreds who died are buried in Copper Center. The original lodge was built of the stuff they left behind. The existing building dates from 1932. A double room is $109 and they're open year round.

Copper River Princess Wilderness Lodge ★★   Completed in 2002, this first-class lodge built by the Princess Cruise Line brings a whole different world to a formerly rough and isolated corner of the planet. Where once a room with its own phone or toilet was a rarity, now you can get one with a dataport and hair dryer and with a fine restaurant down the hall. Princess has tried to capture the trim, red-and-white look of the historic Kennecott mining district. Inside, common areas are spacious and warm, with a big slate fireplace in the lobby. Rooms are in earth tones, with faux rustic furniture and art reflecting mining history, and have king- and queen-size beds. The restaurant serves three meals a day, including sophisticated cuisine for dinner; those meals are not just in another league, but a completely different game than anything else found on the highway. Main courses are $16 to $29.

Mile 102 Richardson Hwy. (P.O. Box 422), Copper Center, AK 99573. © **800/426-0500** or 907/822-4000. Fax 907/822-4044. www.princesslodges.com. 85 units. High season $179 double; low season $139 double. AE, DISC, MC, V. **Amenities:** Restaurant; tour desk; courtesy van to Gulkana airport. *In room:* TV, dataport, hair dryer.

8 Wrangell–St. Elias National Park & Kennecott

Looking at a relief map of Alaska, you'd think the portion drained by the Copper River was so overweighted with mountains that it might topple the whole state into the Pacific. The Alaska Range, in the center of the state, has the tallest mountain, but this Gulf of Alaska region, straddling the Alaska-Yukon border, has more mass—the second- and fourth-tallest mountains in North America (Logan and St. Elias), plus nine of the tallest 16 peaks in the United States. Four mountain ranges intersect, creating a mad jumble of terrain covering tens of millions of acres, a trackless chaos of unnamed, unconquered peaks. The Copper River and its raging tributaries slice through it all, swallowing the gray melt of innumerable glaciers that flow from the largest ice field in North America. Everything here is the largest, most rugged, most remote; words quickly fall short of the measure. But where words fail, commerce gives a little help: These mountains are so numerous and remote that one guide service makes a business of taking visitors to mountains and valleys that no one has ever explored before.

Ironically for such a wild land, the area's main attraction for visitors is its history. The richest copper deposit in the world was found here in 1900 by a group of prospectors who mistook a green mountaintop for a patch of green grass where they could feed their horses. It was a mountain of almost pure copper, with metallic nuggets the size of desks (one is at the UAF Museum of the North in Fairbanks). The deposit produced trainloads of 70% pure copper. The first ore was so rich it required no processing before shipping, then came lots more copper that did need minimal processing. Much more lower-grade ore still lies underground. The Alaska Syndicate, an investment group that included J. P. Morgan and Daniel Guggenheim, built the Kennecott Copper Corporation from this wealth (its name was a misspelling of the Kennicott River and Glacier, where the copper was found). To get the copper out, they paid for an incredible 196-mile rail line up from Cordova (see section 12 in chapter 7), and created a self-contained company town deep in the wilderness, called **Kennecott.** When the high-grade ore was gone, in 1938, they pulled the plug, leaving a ghost town of extraordinary beauty that still contains machinery and even documents they left behind.

Wrangell–St. Elias National Park and Preserve now owns Kennecott and more than 13 million acres across this region of Alaska. It's the largest national park in the United States by a long shot, six times the size of Yellowstone and about 25% larger than the entire country of Switzerland. The protected land continues across the border in Canada, in **Kluane National Park,** which is similarly massive. Most of that land is impossibly remote, but Wrangell–St. Elias has two rough gravel roads that allow access to see the mountains from a car. The main route is the abandoned roadbed of the Copper River and Northwestern Railroad leading to Kennecott and the historic sites there. It's an arduous but rewarding journey by car, requiring at least 2 days to do it right. Air taxis, river guides, and remote lodges offer other ways into the park's untouched wilderness, mostly starting from **McCarthy,** a historic village near Kennecott. There are a few trails near Kennecott, but only for day hikes. This is a country where experienced outdoors people can get away from any trace of humans for weeks on end.

THE KENNECOTT & MCCARTHY AREA

This historic copper area is the only part of the park most visitors see, as it's the most accessible and has the most services, interesting sites, and paths to explore. It's still not easy to get to, however—that's why it's still so appealing—and there's little point in going without adequate time. You can hit the highlights at Kennecott and McCarthy in 1 full day, but just getting there takes time. My family and I spent 3 nights on our last visit and could have stayed longer.

The main event is the ghost town at **Kennecott,** whose red buildings gaze from a mountainside across the Kennicott Glacier in the valley below. Now owned by the park service, the buildings made up an isolated company town until 1938, when it abruptly shut down. Tourists coming here as late as the 1960s saw it as if frozen in time, with breakfast dishes still on the tables from the day the last train left. Most of that was looted and destroyed in the 1970s, but when I toured the company store a few years ago, old documents still remained, and the powerhouse and 14-story mill buildings still had their heavy iron and wood equipment. Besides the buildings, there are excellent hiking trails, including one that traverses the glacier. The town now has only a few year-round residents, but in summer is busy with a lodge, a couple of bed-and-breakfasts, guide services, and park rangers.

Five miles down the road, Kennecott's twin town of **McCarthy** served the miners as a place to drink, gamble, and hire prostitutes on their rare days off—the company didn't allow any frivolity in Kennecott or in the bunkhouses high up on the mountain. McCarthy retains the relaxed atmosphere of its past, with businesses and residents living in false-front buildings not much changed from Wild West days. More of a year-round community, McCarthy has a restaurant, lodging, flight services, and other businesses.

Yet even this most populous part of the park is isolated and sparsely inhabited, with few services. Only 42 people live in the greater area year-round. You will find no banking services, general stores, gas stations, clinics, police, or anything else you're used to relying on. Phones came to McCarthy and Kennecott only in the late 1990s and still are few. Bring what you need.

ESSENTIALS

GETTING THERE   By Car   The paved **Edgerton Highway** starts 17 miles south of Copper Center on the Richardson Highway, then runs east for 33 miles to the tiny, dried-up former railroad town of **Chitina** (*chit*-na), the last reliable stop for groceries, gas, and other necessities until you return here. Do fill your tank; prudence also demands a full-sized spare tire. Heading east, into the park, the **McCarthy Road** continues along the roadbed of the Copper River and Northwestern Railway. This is 60 miles of narrow dirt road, muddy in wet weather and clouded with dust when it's dry. Each year it has been improved a little, and two-wheel-drive cars can normally make it. The drive is a fun adventure, passing through tunnels of alders and crossing rivers on some of the original wooden railroad trestles; one wood-decked bridge spans a canyon more than 200 feet deep. There are virtually no services, very few buildings, and little traffic on the 3-hour drive.

The road ends at a parking lot and collection of temporary businesses on the banks of the Kennicott River. You can drive no further. A fee applies to park at the riverside lot, but you can park free for the day ($5 overnight) a little way off at Glacier View Campground (see below). Next, you walk across a footbridge or two. Late in the summer the Kennicott Glacier releases a flood from a glacier-dammed lake, but at other times the second channel is a dry wash and the second bridge isn't needed. Handcarts are available to move your luggage across, and on the other side you can catch a van. The place where you are staying will send one, or you ride the **van** operated by **Wrangell Mountain Air** (© **907/554-4411**), $2 to McCarthy or $5 per person, one-way, to Kennecott. A public telephone is near the bridge; use it to call the van or your lodgings.

By Bus   The **Backcountry Connection** (© **866/582-5292** in Alaska only, or 907/822-5292; www.alaska-backcountry-tours.com) runs vans from Glennallen and Chitina to the footbridge daily in summer, many of them with park rangers on board offering commentary. The van leaves Glennallen at 7am and Chitina at 8:30am, arriving at the bridge at 11:30am. The trip departs from the bridge at 4pm, getting back to Chitina at 7pm and Glennallen at 8:30pm. The fare is $79 round-trip from Chitina, $89 from Glennallen and Copper Center. The shuttle operators also offer narrated tours around Glennallen, Chitina, and Copper Center.

By Air   The simplest way to Kennecott and McCarthy is to fly there on one of the air taxis, then get around on one of the vans that shuttles back and forth over 5 miles of dirt road. **Wrangell Mountain Air** (© **800/478-1160** or 907/554-4411; www.wrangellmountainair.com) offers twice-daily service from Chitina to McCarthy for $150 round-trip. Another reputable service operating on an on-demand basis is **McCarthy Air** (© **888/989-9891** or 907/554-4440; www.McCarthyAir.com). You can charter from anywhere. A one-way charter with a three- to seven-passenger plane from Anchorage is $1,000 to $1,150, from Valdez $550 to $600. Both operators also offer charters to remote park valleys and glaciers for backcountry trips, covered later under "Getting Outside: Hiking & Backpacking." Use the same flight services for a sightseeing outing over the national park.

Wednesday or Friday, it's possible to fly in a small prop plane carrying the mail from Anchorage to Gulkana and then from Gulkana to McCarthy for a total of about $260 one-way. **Security Aviation** (✆ **800/478-7880** in Alaska only, or 907/248-2677; www.securityaviation.biz) flies Anchorage to Gulkana, and **Ellis Air Taxi** (✆ **800/478-3368** in Alaska only or 907/822-3368; www.ellisair.com) flies from Gulkana to McCarthy. Call Ellis for booking clear through.

VISITOR INFORMATION   The main park visitor center is on the Richardson Highway near Copper Center (✆ **907/822-5234;** www.nps.gov/wrst). Stop in to buy maps and publications, watch a movie, or to get advice from a ranger on outdoor treks. Hours are Memorial Day to Labor Day, daily from 8am to 6pm; in winter, Monday through Friday from 8am to 4:30pm. You can write for information to P.O. Box 439, Copper Center, AK 99573. The park service is restoring buildings and developing visitor services in Kennecott itself. A former train depot has become a visitor center, a good place to stop with questions for rangers, plan a backcountry trip, or to join one of the daily guided activities.

The **Kennicott-McCarthy Chamber of Commerce,** P.O. Box MXY, McCarthy, AK 99588, lacks a phone or office, but you can find lots of information about the area on the Web at **www.mccarthy-kennicott.com,** including the charming bimonthly newspaper, a link to the chamber, and an online visitor guide.

EXPLORING THE TOWNS

CHITINA   Chitina lost its reason to exist in 1938, when the last train ran on the Copper River line, but it lives on with 123 residents supporting themselves largely with salmon from the river, produce from their gardens, berries from the forests, and the few tourists who stop. There's a general store and a couple of gas stations (the last gas for many a mile), a wayside interpretive area at the site of the old depot, a pond where you can often see trumpeter swans, and, down by the river, lazily rotating fish wheels plucking fish from the river. The Copper River is too turbid for angling, but clear water tributaries and stocked lakes in the area have fish. You can also explore south on the old Copper River rail line and even through the tunnels; check with a local or the park headquarters for advice and current conditions before trying it, as landslides sometimes block the way.

MCCARTHY   McCarthy feels authentic as soon as you walk down the dirt main street between the false fronts. There are flight service offices to arrange a trip out, a lodge, and hotel. Then, a street beyond, unbroken wilderness for hundreds and perhaps thousands of miles. On a summer evening young backpackers and locals stand in the road—there is no traffic, since there are almost no vehicles—meeting and talking, laughing loudly, walking around dogs having their own party. Visitors quickly mix in, as everyone seems eager to talk about the town and its history and their own peculiar wilderness lives. The people here know it's unique, and everyone hopes it doesn't change much.

KENNECOTT   This has got to be one of the world's greatest ghost towns, with some 40 buildings, mostly in good enough condition to be reused today—indeed, until the current park service restoration project began, the community still played basketball in one structure. Some historic buildings have become lodgings, and the park service is using others. Locals still pick rhubarb and chives from the company garden. History has the same kind of immediacy here that you get from holding an old diary in your hand, quite different from the sanitized history-through-glass that you're used to at more accessible sites.

The park service bought most of the buildings a few years ago. When we walked through, on the eve of the takeover, items remained out on the ground or on store shelves that would be in museums in many places. If Kennecott were an ordinary industrial site, that would be interesting enough, but this place was something well out of the ordinary: an outpost beyond the edge of the world where men built a self-contained city almost a century ago. The hardship of the miners' lives and the ease of the managerial families' lives also present a fascinating contrast.

You can take in some of the story by wandering around with a walking tour booklet available from the Park Service and reading signs, but it would be a mistake to miss going inside the buildings, and to do that you need to join a **guided tour** with **St. Elias Alpine Guides** (② **888/933-5427** or 907/544-4445 in season; full listing below under "Hiking & Backpacking"). They have an office in the old Chinese laundry right in the ghost town. Tours, which happen twice a day, last much of the morning or afternoon and go into real depth on the geology and history, climbing to the perilous 14th floor of the mill building. They operate mid-May to mid-September and charge $25 per person. The guides will arrange a custom tour, too.

GETTING OUTSIDE

HIKING & BACKPACKING   There are a few trails radiating from Kennecott, for which crude maps are available from the rangers and others around town; or buy the **Trails Illustrated** topographic map, printed on plastic, for sale from some local businesses, or order ahead (see "Fast Facts: Alaska" in chapter 2). An impressive walk continues through the ghost town up the valley, paralleling the Kennicott Glacier and then its tributary, the Root Glacier. You can either climb along the Root's edge to a towering ice fall, or traverse the glacial ice on a trail branch. It's wise to join a group if you want to walk on the glacier itself, as that can be dangerous. St. Elias Alpine Guides, listed below, accepts walk-ins for daily glacier day hikes and other hikes and tours. A half day on the glacier goes for $50 a person, while all-day hikes are $95 and ice-climbing lessons $100. Another fascinating hike you can do on your own leads straight up the mountain behind the Kennecott buildings to the old Bonanza Mine and bunkhouses, 3,000 feet higher on the alpine tundra.

Beyond the trails, the park is endless miles of trackless wilderness—one of earth's last few places that really deserves that name. Fit hikers without the backcountry experience to mount their own expedition should join one of the guides who work in the area. **St. Elias Alpine Guides** (② **888/933-5427** or 907/554-4445 June–Sept; 907/345-9048 Oct–May; www.steliasguides.com) offers day hikes, rafting, backpacking trips, and alpine ascents, but specializes in guiding extended trips to unexplored territory. Bob Jacobs, president of the company, stopped guiding on Mount McKinley years ago because of the crowds. He claims never to have seen another party in more than 25 years of guiding expeditions in Wrangell–St. Elias, and has led more than 45 parties of customers up previously unclimbed peaks. You can't get farther from civilization. A 2-week trek and climb, including 4 days of mountaineering instruction, is a big commitment and costs $3,000 and up, but then, first ascents are a finite resource. The St. Elias catalog will make anyone who loves backpacking drool. Trips begin at $775 for a 4-day Donoho Peak trek. They are all-inclusive, but not without hardship and risk—nothing can take away from the severity of this wild country.

Hiking on your own in a wilderness largely without trails is a whole new kind of experience for experienced backpackers and outdoors people who are used to more crowded parts of the planet. You feel like an explorer rather than a follower. At times, there's a fairy-tale sense of the world unfolding around you, as fresh as creation. If you're not prepared to select your own route—a task only for those already experienced in trackless, backcountry traveling—there are various established ways through the park you can follow with a topographic map. You can get a trip synopsis from the visitor center or ranger station, or download from their website (www.nps.gov/wrst). Rangers can help you choose a route to suit your party, although none are easy.

Some routes start from the roads, but a better way to go is to charter a flight into a remote valley from one of the two **air services** in McCarthy, Wrangell Mountain Air or McCarthy Air (p. 400). The planes land on gravel strips, river bars, glaciers, alpine tundra, or any other flat place the pilots know about. These companies make a business of flying out backpackers, and so have established rates for different landing sites and can help you determine a route that's right for you, as well as provide a list of supplies. Wrangell Mountain Air rents bear-proof containers and two-way radios, and McCarthy Air and the Park Service lend the containers. You can charter a flight for $70 to $300 per person, with at least two passengers. Or fly in to a lake or river for fishing and exploring from a base camp, reducing the worry about how much you pack.

Note: I wouldn't want to scare off anyone who would really be able to manage one of these trips, but people do get into trouble in the Alaska wilderness every year, and some of them don't come back. Before you head out into the backcountry, you must know how to take care of yourself where help is unavailable; this includes handling river crossings, bear avoidance, preventing hypothermia, basic first aid, and other issues. Unless you have plenty of backpacking experience in less remote areas, I don't recommend starting here.

MOUNTAIN BIKING   Anywhere else, the 60-mile road that leads to this area would be considered a mountain-biking trail. You also can make good use of bikes between McCarthy, Kennecott, and the footbridge. An old **wagon road** parallels the main road that connects the two towns, 4½ miles each way; the road itself is a one-lane dirt track. Advanced cyclists can also ride the trails around Kennecott described above under "Hiking & Backpacking."

RAFTING   Many great, wild rivers drain these huge mountains, which are still being carved by enormous glaciers. The **Kennicott River,** starting at the glacier of the same name, boils with Class III rapids for some 40 minutes starting right from the footbridge at the end of the McCarthy Road. As the area lacks roads, however, most trips must include a plane ride at least one-way, and that makes white-water rafting day trips here more expensive than outings near Anchorage or Valdez. At Wrangell–St. Elias, floats punch deep into the backcountry. The Kennicott River meets the Nizina, passing through a deep, dramatic canyon; then the Nizina River flows into the Chitina River, which meets the Copper River near the town of Chitina, 60 miles from the starting point. The Copper River flows to the ocean. A float from the footbridge through the Nizina Canyon takes all day, with lunch and bush plane flightseeing back, which could include a glacier fly-over. St. Elias Alpine Guides (see "Hiking & Backpacking," above) charges $235. Other trips continue for 3 or 4 days to Chitina, for $575 to $850 per person; or for 10 to 13 days, 180 miles all the way to the Copper River Delta and the sea (see "Cordova: Hidden Treasure" in chapter 7), for $2,500 to $2,900 per person. This is Alaska on its largest and most grandiose scale, accessible only from the banks of these great rivers.

WHERE TO STAY & DINE

The closest standard hotel room is in Copper Center (in the previous section). In the Kennecott-McCarthy area itself there are several attractive places to stay, all thick with the history the towns represent, but unlike ordinary American lodgings. Dining is mainly at the lodges. If you're not staying there, it is a good idea to check ahead to make sure they will be ready for you for a meal.

CAMPING & HOSTELLING There is no campground on the Kennecott-McCarthy side of the Kennicott River footbridge. The park service allows camping anywhere in the park without a permit, but there are few handy spots on public land (remember, much of the land along the roads is private).

A couple of primitive private campgrounds and a hostel are at the end of the McCarthy Road. **Glacier View Campground** (© **907/554-4490,** 907/345-7121 off season; www.glacierviewcampground.com) charges $12 a night for camping and has a cabin for rent. The owners also rent mountain bikes and offer showers and free day parking. Their cafe serves barbecue for lunch and dinner.

Besides the backpacker's hotel mentioned in the review of the McCarthy Lodge (see below), **Kennicott River Lodge and Hostel** (© **907/554-4441** summer, 907/447-4252 winter; www.kennicottriverlodge.com), located at the end of the road 400 feet from the footbridge, offers bunks for $28 per person. Sheets and pillows are included; other bedding is extra. The lodge also rents cabins for $100 double plus $25 for each additional person. They have a common kitchen, lounge, sauna, and showers.

There are three campgrounds on the way to the footbridge. The most attractive is the state parks' **Liberty Falls Campground,** at mile 23 on the Edgerton Highway, which is set among big trees at the foot of a crashing waterfall. Many of the sites are walk-ins, with wooden tent platforms and lots of privacy. The self-service camping fee is $10 per vehicle; the day use fee is $1. There are pit toilets and no running water.

Kennicott Glacier Lodge ★★ This is the largest and most comfortable accommodation in the Kennecott-McCarthy area, taking the edges off the isolation. The lodge accurately re-creates an old Kennecott building, with the same red-and-white color scheme, and stands among the historic structures of the ghost town. You can't get any closer to what you want to see. Guests can sip drinks on a long front porch overlooking the glacier, or relax on a lawn with the same view. The rooms are not large, and most have bathrooms down the hall, but all were quite clean each time we visited. An annex with ten new rooms, with two queen-sized beds and private bathrooms, was added in 2004, bringing an even more mainstream experience to this Bush outpost.

Filling dinners are served family style, at long tables, with a fixed menu for a fixed price (a turkey dinner was $26, for example). Breakfast and lunch are a la carte. There's nowhere else to eat right in Kennecott, so plan to spend about $50 per person on food, or book the package that includes meals for $265 per person for two. If staying in the new annex, the package rate is $315 per night. A brief tour of the ghost town is included.

P.O. Box 103940, Anchorage, AK 99510. © **800/582-5128** or 907/258-2350; in season only, 907/554-4477. Fax 907/248-7975. www.KennicottLodge.com. 35 units, 10 with private bathroom. $179 double shared bathroom, $229 private bathroom. AE, DISC, MC, V. Closed mid-Sept to mid-May. **Amenities:** Restaurant; tour desk; courtesy van.

McCarthy Lodge ★ The lodge is the center of the relaxed village of McCarthy, 5 miles from the historically more buttoned-up Kennecott, and is open year round. Although you are not among the mining ruins when you stay here, you are in a real community where you can meet year-round residents and the many interesting characters who spend the summer here. The lodge was taken over by energetic owners who have created rooms full of historic charm, with antiques, quilts, and memorabilia—a living museum, as they call it. Even the soap is authentic, made by hand. The bedrooms—which are small, as always in a historic building—are in a false-front structure that you might see in an old Western movie. They have shared bathrooms. The lodge, across the street, is an authentic Bush roadhouse, an unmistakably backwoods log building. It serves a three-course dinner nightly in summer with seatings from 6 to 10pm for $28, or you can eat in the saloon until 11pm for $6 to $10. The same owners operate **Lancaster's Backpacker's Hotel,** with double rooms for $65.

P.O. Box MXY, McCarthy, AK 99588. ⓒ **907/554-4402.** Fax 907/554-4404. www.mccarthylodge.com. 20 units, none with private bathroom. $159 double year round. MC, V. Rate includes full breakfast. **Amenities:** Restaurant; bar; courtesy van.

10

The Bush

The Bush is most of Alaska. On a map of the state, the portion with roads and cities is a smallish corner. Yet most visitors—and, indeed, most Alaskans—never make it beyond that relatively populated corner. Several years ago a lifelong Anchorage resident was elected to the legislature and appointed chair of its rural issues committee, only to admit he had never been to the Bush. It's common for children to grow to adulthood in Anchorage, Fairbanks, or Southeast Alaska without traveling to the Arctic, the Aleutians, or the vast wetlands of western Alaska. It happens for the same reason most tourists don't go to Bush Alaska—getting there is expensive, and there's not much in the way of human activity once you arrive. Bush Alaska is one of the planet's last barely inhabited areas. But that's a reason to go, not a reason to stay away. You can meet indigenous people who still interact with the environment in their traditional way and see virgin places that remain to be explored by self-reliant outdoors people.

Although there are few people in the Bush, the hospitality of those you do meet is special and warming. In Bush Alaska, where the population is overwhelmingly Alaska Native, it's not uncommon to be befriended by total strangers simply because you've taken the trouble to come to their community and are, therefore, an honored guest. Even in the larger towns, people smile as you pass in the street. If you have a questioning look on your face, they'll stop to help. Living in a small place where people know each other and have to work together against the elements makes for a tight, friendly community.

Alaska's Native culture is based more on cooperative than competitive impulses. Respect and consensus carry greater weight than in individualistic white society. Cooperation requires slowing down, listening, not taking the lead. People from our fast-paced culture can leave a village after a visit wondering why no one spoke to them, not realizing that they never shut up long enough to give anyone a chance. The cultural differences here are real, unlike the shadows of past differences we celebrate in most regions of the homogenous United States. Long pauses in conversation are normal, looking down while addressing a person demonstrates respect, punctuality is highly relative, child care is a community function, and when gifts are offered, people really mean it—turning down even a cup of coffee is gauche. (For more on the culture of Alaska's Native peoples, see the appendix.)

The Native people of the Bush also have terrible problems trying to live in two worlds. There's too much alcohol and too many drugs in the Bush, too much TV, but not enough of an economic base to provide safe drinking water or plumbing in many villages. Even in some of the relatively prosperous village hubs described in this chapter, visitors will glimpse a kind of rural poverty they may not have seen before—where prices are extremely high and steady jobs scarce and difficult to hold while pursuing traditional hunting and food gathering. But if you ask why Natives stay, you're missing something. In a world where so few indigenous cultures survive, people here are working to retain traditions that give their lives meaning—a sense of place and a depth of belonging that most of us can only envy. It's a work in progress, this combination of tradition and modernity, but there's no question they're slowly succeeding. They control their own land, they're building an economic base, and Native ways are being passed on to younger generations.

The Natives' physical environment is extreme in every respect—the weather, the land, even the geography. There's a special feeling to walking along or upon the Arctic Ocean, the virtual edge of the earth. The quantity and accessibility of wildlife are extreme, too, as are the solitude and the uniqueness of what you can do. Unfortunately, the prices also are extreme. Getting to a Bush hub from Anchorage costs more than getting to Anchorage from Seattle; it can be cheaper to get to Europe from Anchorage than to the

Aleutians. And once you're at the hub, you're not done. Getting into the outdoors can cost as much again. Many travelers can't afford a Bush sojourn, instead satisfying their curiosity about the state's unpopulated areas on Alaska's rural highways. Most who can afford the trip usually make the most of their time and money with brief prearranged tours or trips directly to wilderness lodges. Only a few explorers head for the Bush unguided, although there are some good places to go that way—Nome, Barrow, Kodiak, and Unalaska among them.

Covering the Bush is also a challenge for the writer of a book like this one. There are more than 200 Alaska villages; many lodges, camps, and guides; and a vast, undefined territory to describe. All that information would fill a larger book than this one. I've chosen to provide sections on those few Bush hubs that are most accessible and popular with visitors, those that have modern facilities and can be used as gateways to more of the state for visitors who want to venture beyond the fringe of civilization.

1 Exploring the Bush

Alaska's Bush is better defined by what it's like than by where it is. The most common and convenient conception says the Bush is everything beyond the road system. On a map, everything north and west of Fairbanks obviously meets that definition, but many Bush villages lie elsewhere in the Interior, in Southcentral, and in Southeast Alaska. In fact, there are some Bush villages you can drive to. No simple definition works. You know a Bush community by how it feels. It's a place where the wilderness is closer than civilization,

Map Pointer
To locate these towns and regions, refer to the "Alaska" map on p. 6.

where people still live off the land and age-old traditions survive, and where you have to make a particular effort to get in or out.

THE REGIONS
THE ARCTIC The Arctic Circle is the official boundary of the Arctic. The line, at 66° 33' north latitude, is the southern limit of true midnight sun—south of it, at sea level, the sun rises and sets, at least a little, every day of the year. But in Alaska, people think of the Arctic as beginning at the **Brooks Range,** which is a

bit north of the circle, including **Barrow** and **Prudhoe Bay.** The northwest Alaska region, which includes **Kotzebue** and, slightly south of the Arctic Circle, **Nome,** also is Arctic in climate, culture, and topography. The biggest geographic feature in Alaska's Arctic is the broad **North Slope,** the plain of tundra that stretches from the northern side of the Brooks Range to the Arctic Ocean. It's a swampy desert, with little rain or snowfall, frozen solid all but a few months a year.

WESTERN ALASKA This is the land of the massive, wet **Yukon-Kuskokwim Delta** and the fish-rich waters of Bristol Bay. The Y-K Delta, as it's known, was never really exploited by white explorers, and the Yup'ik people who live there have maintained some of the most culturally traditional villages. In some, Yup'ik is still the dominant language. **Bethel** is the main hub city of the delta but holds little attraction for visitors. **Bristol Bay** is known for massive salmon runs, and avid anglers may be interested in its wilderness lodges, using **Dillingham** as a hub.

SOUTHWEST ALASKA Stretching from the Aleutians—really a region of their own—to the Alaska Peninsula, Kodiak Island, and the southern part of the mountainous west side of Cook Inlet, this is a maritime region, like Southeast, but far more remote. The hub of the wet, windy **Aleutians** is **Unalaska** and its port of **Dutch Harbor. Katmai National Park** and the adjoining wild lands are the main attraction of the Alaska Peninsula, although there also are fishing lodges on the salmon-rich rivers and on the lakes to the north, including areas in **Lake Clark National Park** and **Iliamna Lake.** The lakes and west side of **Cook Inlet** are accessed primarily by Kenai, Homer, and Anchorage flight services for fishermen and hunters. **Kodiak** is hardly a Bush community, but it fits better in this chapter than anywhere else, and the town is a hub for villages and bear viewing on Kodiak Island.

GETTING AROUND

With a few exceptions for strongly motivated travelers, who can take the ferry to Kodiak and Unalaska or drive to Prudhoe Bay, getting to each town in this chapter will require flying. **Alaska Airlines** (© 800/252-7522; www.alaskaair.com) offers the only jet service to Bush hubs.

Other, smaller operators serve these towns with prop aircraft. Throughout the chapter, I've listed the plane fare to various communities from Anchorage, based on flying coach and getting a significant discount for advance purchase, weekend stay over, and some restrictions. Full Y-class fares cost more. With the way airfares fluctuate, it would be unwise to use these numbers as anything more than rough guides. To get the current best fare, use a travel agent or the Internet.

Kodiak, which barely fits in a chapter on the Bush, is the most accessible of the communities in this chapter, but it still requires either a 10-hour ferry ride from Homer or a $250 round-trip plane ticket from Anchorage. This charming, historic town is similar to towns in Southeast Alaska or Prince William Sound, but it is also a hub for Native villages on the island and remote wilderness. **Unalaska/Dutch Harbor,** in the Aleutian Islands, is an interesting place to go way off the beaten path while staying in complete comfort. From Anchorage a visit requires a 3-hour flight on a turbo prop aircraft, and fares of $850 are typical. **Kotzebue** and **Barrow** are the most purely Native of the communities in the chapter. **Nome** has the advantages of Arctic surroundings easily accessible on gravel roads, but is more of a gold rush town than a Native village. **Prudhoe Bay,** at the end of the Dalton Highway, is an industrial complex without a real town associated with it. Fares from Anchorage range from $400 to $700 for these communities. Buying an **Alaska Airlines package tour** saves money to Nome, Kotzebue, or Barrow, and gives you something to do when you arrive.

2 Kodiak: Wild Island

The habitat that makes Kodiak Island a perfect place for bears also makes it perfect for people. Runs of salmon clog unpopulated bays and innumerable, unfished rivers; the rounded green mountains seem to beg for someone to cross them; the gravel beaches and protected rocky inlets are free of people, but full of promise. But, in this respect, bears are smarter than people. Brown bears own the island, growing to prodigious size and abundant numbers, but Kodiak is as yet undiscovered by human visitors. That's part of the wonder of the place. I'll never forget flying over the luxuriant verdure of Kodiak's mountains and the narrow string of glassy Raspberry Strait on a rare sunny day, seeing no sign of human presence in the most beautiful landscape I had ever beheld.

The narrow streets of the town of Kodiak are a discovery, too. Twisting over the hills in little discernible order, they were the original stomping grounds of **Lord Alexander Baranof,** the first Russian ruler of Alaska, who arrived here in 1790. Kodiak has the oldest Russian building in North America. It was nearly lost in the 1964 Good Friday earthquake, which destroyed most of the town, explaining the general lack of old buildings. The quake brought a 30-foot wave that washed to the building's doorstep. A marker near the police station on Mill Bay Road shows the wave's incredible high-water point. Before the Russians, the **Koniag** people lived off the incomparable riches of the island. They're still here, recovering their past in a fascinating little research museum.

The town looks to the sea. Along with the Coast Guard base, fishing makes Kodiak prosperous, creating a friendly, energetic, unpolished community. Kodiak is separate from the rest of Alaska, living its own commercial fishing life without often thinking of what's going on in Anchorage or anywhere else. It's off the beaten path because it doesn't really need anything the path provides.

For the visitor, Kodiak is an undiscovered gem. A few days just scratch the surface of the charming, vibrant town and the easily accessible wild places around it, yet, even in midsummer, you will see few if any other tourists.

There are six **Native villages** on the island. A flight to one of them and back on a clear day is a wonderful, low-cost way to see remote areas of the island and to get a taste of how Alaska Natives live. It's also popular to fly out to see the famous bears on a day trip, or stay at one of several **wilderness lodges** for wildlife-watching, fishing, sea kayaking, and hunting, or even participating in a Native-led archaeological dig.

ESSENTIALS

GETTING THERE   It's a 1-hour flight from Anchorage to Kodiak on **Alaska Airlines** (© 800/252-7522; www.alaskaair.com). **ERA Aviation** (© 800/866-8394; www.FlyEra.com) also serves the route with prop aircraft, which may save money. A round-trip ticket from Anchorage costs around $250, but you can often get a better deal. A cab, from **A&B Taxi** (© 907/486-4343), runs about $15 from the airport.

The ferry *Tustumena,* of the **Alaska Marine Highway System** (© 800/642-0066 or 907/486-3800; TDD 800/764-3779; www.FerryAlaska.com), serves Kodiak from Homer and Seward. If you have the time for the 10-hour run from Homer—the closest port with a road—this boat ride is truly memorable. The vessel leaves land behind and threads through the strange and exposed Barren Islands. The ocean can be quite rough, and when it is, lots of passengers get seasick; take Dramamine *before* boarding. A cabin is a good idea for an overnight run. The U.S. Fish and Wildlife Service staffs the trips with a naturalist. The adult passenger fare from Homer is $63, children half price.

VISITOR INFORMATION The **Kodiak Island Convention and Visitors Bureau,** 100 Marine Way, Ste. 200, Kodiak, AK 99615 (© **907/486-4782;** fax 907/486-6545; www.kodiak.org), occupies a small building on the ferry dock. Hours vary according to the ferry schedule, but essentially follow this pattern: summer Monday from 8am to 8:30pm, Tuesday through Friday 8am to 5pm, Saturday from 10am to 4pm, Sunday from 1 to 8:30pm; winter Monday through Friday from 8am to 5pm, closed for lunch.

The **Kodiak National Wildlife Refuge Visitor Center,** 1390 Buskin River Road, Kodiak, AK 99615 (© **888/408-3514** or 907/487-2600; http://alaska. fws.gov/nwr/kodiak), is headquarters for a refuge that covers most of the island and is home of the famous Kodiak brown bear. There are remote public-use cabins all over the refuge, reachable by chartered plane. Permits are $30 a night, available though a quarterly drawing of names (Jan. 2 for April–June, April 1 for July–Sept). The center has exhibits and is a good place to stop for outdoors information. They're open from mid-June to August daily from 8am to 4:30pm; the balance of the year Monday through Friday only.

ORIENTATION The Kodiak Archipelago contains Kodiak, Shuyak, and Afognak islands, and many other, smaller islands. Kodiak is the nation's second-largest island (after Hawaii's Big Island). The city of Kodiak is on a narrow point on the northeast side of Kodiak Island, surrounded by tiny islands. There are six Native villages on other parts of the island. The airport and Coast Guard base are several miles southwest of town on **Rezanof Drive,** which runs through town and comes out on the other side. The center of Kodiak is a hopeless tangle of steep, narrow streets—you need the excellent map given away by the visitor center, but it's all walkable. The ferry dock is on **Marine Way,** and most of the in-town sights are right nearby. Several gravel roads, totaling 100 miles, make wonderful exploring from Kodiak to deserted shorelines, gorgeous views, pastures, recreation areas, and salmon streams. The visitors guide contains a mile-by-mile guide to each drive.

GETTING AROUND Several companies rent cars, including **Budget** (© **800/527-0700** national or 907/487-2220 local; www.budget.com), which has offices at the airport and downtown.

If it's not raining, a bike is a great way to get around Kodiak, and strong riders will enjoy touring the roads out of town. Bikes are for rent at **Fifty-Eight Degrees North,** a full-service bike shop at 1231 Mill Bay Rd. (© **907/486-6249**). Front-suspension mountain bikes rent for $30 for 24 hours.

FAST FACTS: Kodiak

Banks Several banks downtown have ATMs, including **Key Bank** and **Wells Fargo** on the mall at the waterfront.

Hospital **Providence Kodiak Island Medical Center** is at 1915 E. Rezanof Dr. (© **907/486-3281**).

Internet Access **The Treasury** gift and bookstore, on the mall at 104 Center St., Ste. 104 (© **907/486-0373**); or the **A. Holmes Johnson Public Library,** 319 Lower Mill Bay Rd. (© **907/486-8686**).

Police Contact the **Kodiak Police Department** at © **907/486-8000.**

Post Office 419 Lower Mill Bay Rd., at Hemlock Street.

Taxes Sales tax is 6% within city limits and the room tax is 5% everywhere on the island. So rooms are taxed 11% in Kodiak city, 5% elsewhere.

SPECIAL EVENTS **Russian Orthodox Christmas,** January 7, includes the evening **Starring Ceremony.** A choir follows a parishioner carrying a star to sing at the homes of church members.

The **Pillar Mountain Golf Classic** (© **907/486-2931,** organizer's home phone) is played on a one-hole par-70 course that climbs 1,400 feet from tee to flag; dogs, chain saws, two-way radios, and tracking devices are prohibited, and cursing the officials carries a $25 fine. Handsaws and hatchets are allowed. March 26–27, 2005.

The 5-day **Kodiak Crab Festival** (© **907/486-5557;** www.kodiak.org/crabfest. html), on Memorial Day weekend, is a big event, including many a carnival, fun community events, the solemn blessing of the fleet, and memorial service for lost fishermen and mariners.

On Labor Day weekend, the **Kodiak State Fair and Rodeo** (© **907/ 486-6380**) has all kinds of small-town contests and family entertainment. The **Harbor Stars Fleet Parade** (© **907/486-8080**), in mid-December, includes many brightly decorated vessels to celebrate Christmas.

The visitor bureau maintains a community calendar online at **www. kodiak.org/calendar.html**.

EXPLORING THE TOWN

The highlights downtown include the **Fishermen's Memorial,** near the harbormaster's office at the head of the St. Paul Harbor, where a staggeringly long list of Kodiak fishermen who have lost their lives at sea is posted on plaques. The warship set in concrete on Mission Way is the *Kodiak Star,* the last World War II Liberty Ship built. It came here as a fish processor after the 1964 earthquake destroyed the canneries and is still in use. At Kashevarof and Mission streets, the **Holy Resurrection Russian Orthodox Church** was founded in 1794, although the present building dates only to 1945, when the original church burned. Along Shelikof Avenue, overlooking St. Paul Harbor, the **Kodiak Maritime Museum** has mounted eight attractive and interesting signs explaining the parts of a boat, North Pacific crabbing and geography, and other nautical topics.

The **Kodiak Alutiiq Dancers** give half-hour performances June to mid-September at 2:30pm daily at the Shoonaq' Tribal Council, at 312 W. Marine Way (© **907/486-4449**). Admission is $15 adults, $7.50 children.

Alutiiq Museum ⭐ This exceptional museum, funded and governed by Natives, seeks to document and restore the Koniag Alutiiq people's culture, which the Russians virtually wiped out in the 18th century. Besides teaching about Alutiiq culture in a single gallery, the museum manages its own archaeological digs (see "Getting Outside," below) and repatriates Native remains and artifacts, which researchers removed by the thousands in the 1930s. The archaeological repository now includes 100,000 objects.

215 Mission Rd. ⓒ **907/486-7004.** www.alutiiqmuseum.com. Admission $3 adults, free for kids under age 12. Summer Mon–Fri 9am–5pm, Sat 10am–5pm; winter Tues–Fri 9am–5pm, Sat 10:30am–4:30pm.

The Baranov Museum ★ The museum occupies the oldest Russian building of only a few left standing in North America; it was built in 1808 by Alexander Baranof as a magazine and strong house for valuable sea otter pelts. It stands in a grassy park overlooking the water across from the ferry dock. Inside is a little museum rich with Russian and early Native artifacts. The guides know a lot of history and show 45 educational albums on various topics. The gift store is exceptional, selling antique Russian items and authentic Native crafts.

101 Marine Way. ⓒ **907/486-5920.** www.baranov.us. Admission $3; free for children 12 and under. Summer Mon–Sat 10am–4pm, Sun noon–4pm; winter Tues–Sat 10am–3pm. Closed Feb.

GETTING OUTSIDE
TWO RECREATION AREAS
A couple of miles north of town on Rezanof Drive, the **Fort Abercrombie State Historical Park** encompasses World War II ruins set on coastal cliffs amid huge trees. Paths lead to the beaches and good tide-pool walking, a swimming lake, and lots of other discoveries. The gun emplacements, bunkers, and other concrete buildings defended against the Japanese, who had seized islands in the outer Aleutians and were expected to come this way. A group of local World War II buffs have built a museum of artifacts left over from the Alaska fighting. It occupies the ammunition bunker at the historical park. Hours change annually, but will be posted at www.kadiak.org, or the volunteers will open it any time by appointment (ⓒ **907/486-7015**). The website is extensive. A wonderful 13-site campground sits atop the cliffs among the trees and ruins. Camping is $10. The **Alaska Division of State Parks,** Kodiak District Office, 1400 Abercrombie Dr., Kodiak, AK 99615 (ⓒ **907/486-6339;** fax 907/486-3320; www.alaskastateparks. org, click on "Individual Parks," then "Kodiak Islands"), maintains an office here where you can pick up a walking-tour brochure or, during the summer, join the Saturday-night interpretive program or a guided tide-pool walk, scheduled to coincide with low tides. Or investigate the tide pools on your own, picking up an identification guide at the park's natural history bookstore.

The **Buskin River State Recreation Site,** 4 miles south of town off Rezanof Drive near the Fish and Wildlife Service visitor center, has 15 campsites, a hiking trail, and access to fishing. Camping is $10.

OUTDOOR ACTIVITIES
ARCHAEOLOGY Dig Afognak, 215 Mission Rd., Suite 212 (ⓒ **800/ 770-6014** or 907/486-6014; www.afognak.org/dig.php), operated by the Afognak Native Corporation, offers visitors a chance to help in scientific excavations of Koniag sites on Afognak Island, an effort by the Native group to reassemble their cultural heritage. Visitors are instructed in the natural history of the beautiful area as well as archaeology, but they're also expected to work, doing digging and other tasks in a remote lab. Each weeklong session has a different educational emphasis, with scientists or elders on hand to enrich the learning. Accommodations are in heated tents, and you have to bring your own sleeping bag. Dinner often is seafood caught in nets at the beach. A 7-day session is $1,650, including transportation from Kodiak.

BROWN BEAR VIEWING To see Kodiak's famous bears you need to get out on a plane or boat. The easiest way is a Kodiak-based floatplane; expect to pay at least $400 per person, with a two- or three-person minimum for a half-day trip (larger groups can get discounts). Landing on the water, you can occasionally watch from the dry platform of the plane's floats, but it's usually necessary to put on rubber boots (provided) and walk up to half an hour to get to where bears congregate. Binoculars and telephoto camera lenses are essential, as no responsible guide would crowd Kodiak brown bears so closely that such lenses become unnecessary (although the bears could choose to approach within 50 yards of you). Bears congregate only when salmon are running, so the timing of your visit is critical. From early July to mid-August you have a good chance of seeing bears fishing in streams on Kodiak, sometimes in numbers. In June, Kodiak air services fly to the east coast of the Alaska Peninsula to watch bears digging clams from the tidal flats and eating grass and greens on the coastal meadows. That's interesting to see and the flight is spectacular, but the viewing may be from a greater distance and the bears will more likely be on their own. Generally, the flight services charge their standard bear viewing seat rate regardless of how far they have to fly to find bears; if you charter, it may cost much more, but you will have freedom to determine where the plane goes for added sightseeing. If bears are your primary interest, however, additional money might be better spent on a longer outing rather than a charter: the flight services can leave you at a lodge for a full day of viewing or an overnight, away from the daytrippers. For more advice, and particulars on where the bear viewing is hot, contact the Kodiak National Wildlife Refuge (see "Visitor Information," above). If bear viewing is the whole reason you're going to Kodiak, consider saving money and using Homer as your base (see chapter 7), or spending more money to go to Katmai National Park to see bears really close (see section 3 of this chapter).

Several small flight services offer bear viewing, including **Sea Hawk Air** (© **800/770-4295** or 907/486-8282; www.seahawkair.com). See "Sea Kayaking," below, for another option.

FISHING The 70 miles of road leading from Kodiak reach eight good-sized rivers with good fishing for salmon and Dolly Varden char. At times you can drive to places with fishing pressure as light as some fly-in locations on the mainland. Going beyond the road network puts you on some of the best and least used fishing opportunities in Alaska. The visitor center provides a list of where to fish and the names and addresses of guides for remote fishing. You can also seek advice and regulations from the **Alaska Department of Fish and Game,** 211 Mission Rd., Kodiak, AK 99615 (© **907/486-1880;** www.alaska.gov/adfg; click on "Sport Fishing," then on the Southcentral region, then on "Kodiak"). To fish the remote areas, you'll need to charter a plane, going for a day or staying at a remote public-use cabin or wilderness lodge.

About 50 boats are available in the boat harbors for ocean fishing. An advantage of coming to Kodiak is that it puts you near rich halibut grounds—you don't have to take a long boat ride for excellent fishing. Trolling for silvers is good in August. Check with the visitor center for a referral.

HIKING & BIRD-WATCHING There are some good day hikes in Kodiak, some starting from downtown. You can get a guide and a schedule of guided hikes from the visitor center.

SEA KAYAKING The Kodiak Archipelago, with its many folded, rocky shorelines and abundant marine life, is a perfect place for sea kayaking. Kayaks were invented here and on the Aleutian Islands to the west. Several operators offer kayaking services and tours around Kodiak and on the shore of Katmai National Park. **Mythos Expeditions** (© **907/486-5536**) takes kayakers along the Katmai coast for multiday bear-viewing trips; guests paddle by day and sleep and eat aboard a converted commercial fishing boat. They also go to **Shuyak Island State Park,** 54 miles north of Kodiak and rent kayaks for use there. The park is a honeycomb of islands and narrow passages in virgin Sitka spruce coastal forest.

The Division of State Parks (see address under "Two Recreation Areas," above) distributes a free kayaking guide with route descriptions and maintains four public-use cabins, which rent for $65 a night. These cabins can be quite hard to get in August. See "State Parks Cabin Reservations," in section 1 of chapter 7, and read up on the special rules for Shuyak Island on www.alaska stateparks.org.

For a simple beginner's kayaking day trip near town, check with the visitor center. It is a lovely spot for a short paddle, through the boat harbors and to the islands around the town.

WHERE TO STAY

I've listed places in town and nearby on the roads, but Kodiak also has some of Alaska's best wilderness lodges in remote areas and near Native villages around the island. You can get a list from the visitor center, and their website contains links to most of them.

Best Western Kodiak Inn ⭐   This is the best hotel in downtown Kodiak, with attractive, up-to-date rooms perched on the hill overlooking the boat harbor, right in the center of things. Rooms in the wooden building vary in size and view, but all are acceptable standard rooms with good amenities, including wireless Internet.

The **Chart Room** restaurant, specializing in seafood and with a great view of the water, is a good choice for a nice dinner out, with entrees in the $15 to $25 range.

236 W. Rezanof Dr., Kodiak, AK 99615. 📞 **888/563-4254** or 907/486-5712. Fax 907/486-3430. www.kodiak inn.com. 81 units. High season $149 double; low season $99 double. Extra person over age 12 $15. AE, DC, DISC, MC, V. **Amenities:** Restaurant; bar; outdoor Jacuzzi; tour desk; courtesy van. *In room:* TV, wireless Internet, fridge, coffeemaker, hair dryer, iron, microwave.

Buskin River Inn ⭐   This quiet hotel with standard rooms is near the airport rather than the downtown sights; you will need a rental car if you stay here. Rooms on one side look out on the river, the other side on the parking lot. It's near the wildlife refuge visitor center, a hiking trail, and the nine-hole golf course at the Coast Guard base. The **Eagle's Nest Restaurant** has a complete beef and seafood menu and a pleasant setting.

1395 Airport Way, Kodiak, AK 99615. 📞 **800/544-2202** or 907/487-2700. Fax 907/487-4447. www.kodiak adventure.com. 50 units. High season $145 per unit; low season $125. No charge for additional person, $15 charge for roll-away bed. AE, DC, DISC, MC, V. **Amenities:** Restaurant; tour desk; courtesy van; coin-op laundry; free Internet access in business office. *In room:* TV, fridge, coffeemaker, hair dryer.

Kodiak Bed and Breakfast   Hospitable, active Mary Monroe runs this comfortable, homey place with a friendly retriever, Kody. There is a porch overlooking the harbor where you can eat breakfast on sunny mornings (fish is often on the morning menu). The location is convenient, right downtown, and the entry for the bedrooms and shared sitting room downstairs doesn't require you to walk through Monroe's own living quarters. A telephone and TV are shared in the sitting room and a freezer is available for guests' fish.

308 Cope St., Kodiak, AK 99615. 📞 **907/486-5367.** Fax 907/486-6567. 2 units, both with shared bathroom. $105 double. Rate includes breakfast. No credit cards.

Wintels Bed and Breakfast   A long walk from downtown (you'll need a car if you stay here), this house stands with the ocean on one side and a lake on the other, so all rooms have water views. The owners, a family of longtime residents, can tell you a lot about Alaska and show off their mounted sea ducks and furs. The rooms are attractive and the breakfasts large; they will also freeze your fish.

1723 Mission Rd. (P.O. Box 2812), Kodiak, AK 99615. ©/fax 907/486-6935. www.wintels.com. 3 units, 1 with private bathroom. $90–$110 double. Extra person $35. Rates include full breakfast. No credit cards. **Amenities:** Jacuzzi; sauna; laundry service. *In room:* Hair dryer.

WHERE TO DINE

Besides the hotel restaurants listed above at the Best Western Kodiak Inn and Buskin River Inn, Kodiak has a typical selection of family restaurants. But one place to eat is unique, and could be a highlight of your trip. Mary and Marion Owen serve dinner for six on their 42-foot yacht the *Sea Breeze.* The meals from **Galley Gourmet** (© 800/253-6331 or 907/486-5079; www.kodiak-alaska-dinner-cruises.com) are usually elaborate seafood creations. The evening starts at 6pm with a 45-minute harbor cruise, then dinner at anchor; you're back at the dock at 9:30pm. The price is $100 per person. They'll also do a 2-hour harbor cruise without food service for $50 per person.

Downtown, **El Chicano,** at 103 Center St. (© **907/486-6116**), is a Mexican place with friendly service and reasonable prices.

Eugene's Restaurant, upstairs at 202 E. Rezanof Dr. (© **907/486-2625**), is the same kind of place, but with Chinese and American food—big portions, a pleasant family running things, and a comfortable dining room. We enjoyed the curried chicken and kung pao shrimp.

Harborside Coffee and Goods, at 210 B, Shelikof St. (© **907/486-5862**), on the south side of the boat harbor, is a comfortable coffeehouse with soup, bagels, and fresh pastries, popular with young people.

Henry's Great Alaskan Restaurant, at 512 Marine Way (© **907/486-8844**), on the waterfront mall, is a bar and grill where you will meet many commercial fishermen and other locals.

3 Katmai National Park

Most of the land of the Alaska Peninsula, pointing out to the Aleutian Archipelago, is in one federally protected status or another, centering on Katmai National Park. The park, pronounced "*cat*-my," lies just west of Kodiak Island, across the storm-infested Shelikof Strait. Bear and salmon are the main attractions. **Brooks Camp,** with a campground and lodge within Katmai, is probably the most comfortable place for foolproof bear viewing in Alaska. Here, in July and September only, you can sit back on a deck and watch 900-pound brown bears walk by, going about their business of devouring the spawning salmon that contribute to their awesome size. (A brown bear is the genetic twin of the grizzly, but generally larger due to its coastal diet of salmon.) Staying the night will require you to reserve a place in the 16-space campground the previous winter or stay in the pricey lodge, where rooms can book up over a year ahead for the bear season. You can go for a day trip with less planning if you can stand to pay around $500 round-trip airfare from Anchorage for 2 or 3 hours at the camp (this information is covered in "Getting There," below).

Katmai was set aside in 1918 for entirely different reasons. The area exploded into world consciousness in 1912 with the most destructive volcanic eruption to shake the earth in 3,400 years. When Katmai's Novarupta blew, it released ten times more energy than Mount St. Helen's eruption of 1980 and displaced twice as much matter as 1883's Krakatoa. In Kodiak, the sky was black for 3 days and 2 feet of ash crushed houses and choked rivers. People could clearly hear the blast in Juneau; acid rain melted fabric in Vancouver, British Columbia; and the skies darkened over most of the Northern Hemisphere. At the blast site all life within a 40-square-mile area was wiped out and buried as deep as 700 feet. But so remote was the area, then still unnamed, that not a single human being was killed. The **Valley of Ten Thousand Smokes,** the vast wasteland created by the blast, belched steam for decades after. Today Novarupta is dormant and the steam is gone, but the area is still a barren moonscape, making a fascinating day tour or hiking trip.

ESSENTIALS

GETTING THERE   Most people fly to Katmai from Anchorage by way of the village of **King Salmon,** which lies just west of the park. **Alaska Airlines** (© **800/252-7522;** www.alaskaair.com) flies to King Salmon twice a day in the summer, charging around $400 round-trip. For more flight options, you can use their prop partner, **PenAir** (© **800/448-4226;** www.penair.com).

Air taxis carry visitors the last leg from King Salmon to **Brooks Camp** for a fare of around $160, round-trip. **Katmai Air,** operated by park concessionaire Katmailand (© **800/544-0551** or 907/243-5448; www.katmaiair.com), does these flights, and offers round-trip airfare packages from Anchorage that can save a little money (total around $500) and add simplicity to your planning.

As an alternative to Brooks Camp, more and more visitors are exploring the supremely rugged wilderness on the east side of the park from the beaches along **Shelikof Strait.** Air-taxi operators make drop-offs and do bear-viewing day trips from Homer or Kodiak (see section 2 of this chapter, earlier, on Kodiak, or see the Homer section in chapter 7), and boats out of Kodiak go across for extended cruising and kayak expeditions. In this park, with more than 2,000 brown bears resident (the world's largest protected population), it's easy for pilots to find them digging clams on the tidal marshes, then land on floats for a good, close look.

RESERVATIONS & FEES   No entry fee or permit applies for day trips to Katmai, but once you're there you have to sign up for an hour on the bear-viewing platforms (see below). Camping costs $8 per person per night. There are only 20 sites, and they are in very high demand during the bear season in July. The crowds are smaller in September, but the bears are not quite as numerous. All sites become available for the entire summer on January 15. To reserve, call or log on to the **park service national reservation system** (© **800/365-2267** or 301/722-1257; http://reservations.nps.gov). If you're using the phone system, enter **KAT#** at the prompt.

VISITOR INFORMATION   Besides the **Katmai National Park Headquarters,** 1 King Salmon Mall (P.O. Box 7), King Salmon, AK 99613 (© **907/246-3305;** www.nps.gov/katm), there's also a **visitor center** next door to the airport in King Salmon (© **907/246-4250**), staffed jointly by the National Park Service, U.S. Fish and Wildlife Service, and local governments. It is open 8am to 5pm daily in the high season, Monday through Friday in winter. At Brooks Camp the park service has a center where all visitors are required to attend a 20-minute orientation called "The Brooks Camp School of Bear Etiquette," designed to train visitors (not bears) and keep them out of trouble. In Anchorage, you can get information at the **Alaska Public Lands Information Center,**

at 4th Avenue and F Street (© **907/271-2737;** see the complete listing under "Visitor Information" in section 1 of chapter 6).

GETTING AROUND   Once you've made it to Brooks Camp, a **bus** carries visitors to the Valley of Ten Thousand Smokes, 23 miles by gravel road from the camp. The park concessionaire, **Katmailand,** charges $88 per person, round-trip, for the all-day excursion, plus $8 more for lunch. One-way transfers for hikers are $51.

FAST FACTS: Katmai

Bank **Wells Fargo,** with an ATM, is in the King Salmon Mall on the Peninsula Highway in King Salmon.

Hospital The **Camai Clinic,** in Naknek (© **907/246-6155),** is open during normal business hours; calls to the number go to emergency dispatchers after hours.

Police In **King Salmon,** call © **907/246-4222;** elsewhere, call **Alaska State Troopers** at © **907/246-3346** or 907/246-3464. There are no phones or cellular service out in the park.

EXPLORING THE TOWN

Katmai's famous bear viewing occurs at **Brooks Camp** when the bears congregate near the Brooks River to catch salmon during July and September, and maybe the last week of June or the first week of August. This is when you're assured of seeing bears from the elevated platforms near the Brooks River falls, half a mile from Brooks Camp, even on a day trip. Forty to sixty bears feed here. Rangers escort visitors to the platforms to keep them separate from the bears, but you do get quite close to them. The park service recommends that people with mobility problems avoid this trail when bears are present, which pretty much means you shouldn't go to Brooks Camp if you have trouble getting around. Due to the popularity of the experience, there is a 1-hour limit on the falls platform during the peak season. After your turn is up, you can sign up on a waiting list to get another chance. Outside of the short salmon runs, there are better places to see bears, so don't spend the money to come here. Bears feed all summer on clams on Katmai's east shore. See "Getting There," above.

The Brooks Camp area has a small park service campground, visitor center, and lodge, located where the Brooks River flows into Naknek Lake. When the area was first developed for fishing in the 1950s the camp was built in the middle of a major bear corridor, where it never would be allowed today, creating a unique opportunity to stay right in some the most concentrated bear habitat on the globe. The most comfortable way is at the **Brooks Lodge,** operated by Katmailand (© **800/544-0551** or 907/243-5448; www.katmainationalpark.com). The lodge has 16 units, with private bathrooms with shower stalls. To save money, book the lodge rooms as packages with air travel. The least expensive, 1-night visit is $754 per person, double occupancy, meals not included; 3 nights is $1,306. A double room without airfare is $560. Peak dates (when the bears are around) book up 12 months out or earlier; for your choice, call as soon as the reservation system opens 18 months ahead, January of the year before the visit. Three buffet-style meals are served daily for guests and visitors who aren't staying in the lodge. Breakfast is $12, lunch $18, and dinner $26. For food, they take MasterCard and Visa at the lodge. Also at Brooks Camp, there's a small store, the park service visitor center, and the 16-site campground. See "Reservations & Fees," above, for info on campground reservations, which should be made 6 months in advance. The rangers require special precautions to keep bears away from campers.

The rivers and lakes of Katmai lure human anglers as well as ursine ones. Katmailand operates two lodges within the park other than Brooks Lodge for remote fishing, the **Kulik** and **Grosvenor lodges.** Check their website at www. katmailand.com for fishing details.

The park service also has a list of dozens of fishing, hiking, and air guides. There is no central clearinghouse for remote fishing, but you can find and book a good place through an agency such as **Sport Fishing Alaska,** 9310 Shorecrest Dr., Anchorage, AK 99502 (© **888/552-8674** or 907/344-8674; www.Alaska TripPlanners.com), listed in full under "Planning an Outdoor Vacation" in chapter 2.

Backcountry hiking in Katmai means crossing a wilderness without trails, and only experienced backpackers should plan extended trips. The park service asks hikers to obtain a voluntary permit for backcountry travel, thereby clueing them in to your plans in case you need to be rescued. Anyone can walk for the day without such precautions in the desolate **Valley of Ten Thousand Smokes.** This 40-square-mile plain remains a moonscape 90 years after the titanic volcanic blast that buried it, little changed except that the famous plumes of smoke are gone and rivers have sliced through the debris in places to create narrow, white-walled canyons. Although it looks like a desert and is subject to dust storms, rain is common and temperatures rarely go higher than 65°F (18°C). Katmailand operates a tour bus from Brooks Camp, mentioned above under "Getting Around." The visitors on those tours usually stay on a short trail on the valley's rim. Longer hikes into the valley bring you into contact with more of the bizarre landforms created by the eruption.

4 Unalaska/Dutch Harbor: Aleutian Boomtown

After a lifetime of hearing how desolate the Aleutians (uh-*loo*-shens) were, I felt like I was leaving the edge of the earth the first time I traveled to Unalaska (oon-ah-*las*-ka). Shortly after I arrived, a storm started slinging huge raindrops horizontally through the air so hard that they stung as they splattered on my face. People went on about their business as if nothing special was happening— stormy weather constantly batters these rocks that pop up from the empty North Pacific. My expectations seemed justified.

But the next day, the storm cleared like a curtain opening on a rich operatic scene—simultaneously opening the curtain of my dark expectations. Unalaska may lack trees, but it's not a barren rock. The island is covered with heather and wildflowers. Rounded mountains that invite wandering exploration rise from the ocean like the backs of huge beasts. For sightseeing, it has barely a day's attractions, but for outdoor exploring, bird-watching, and halibut fishing, few places come close.

With the protected port of Dutch Harbor so far out in a ferocious ocean habitat rich in crab and bottom fish, Unalaska has grown in 3 decades from a tiny, forgotten Native village to the nation's largest fishing port. The pattern of growth followed the form of the early gold rushes. There was a wild, lawless time in the 1970s when crab fishermen got rich quick and partied like Old West cowboys. Then the overfished crab stocks crashed, only to be replaced, starting in the mid-1980s, by an even bigger boom, when waters within 200 miles of the U.S. shore were rid of foreign vessels and American bottom fishing took off. Big factory ships began unloading here and huge fish plants were built on flat ground chipped from the rock. Today that expansion has reached a steady state and women and families have come to town—another part of the gold rush pattern. But domestication isn't done yet. Most of the population lives in bunkhouses and flies back to Seattle, Mexico, and the Philippines when the processing plants close for the season. Unalaska may be the best current example of the American cultural phenomenon of the frontier boomtown.

Ironically, Unalaska is Alaska's oldest town as well as its newest city. The value of a good port out in the middle of the ocean was recognized from the beginning by the Aleuts. In 1759, the Russians began trading here, and fought a war with the Aleuts from 1763 to 1766, the outcome of which was slavery for the Aleut hunters and the massacre of their people. The Russians built a permanent settlement here in 1792, their first in Alaska. Unalaska also was a key refueling stop for steamers carrying gold rush stampeders to Nome a century ago, which brought an epidemic that killed a third of the indigenous population. In 1940, Dutch Harbor—the seaport on Amaknak Island associated with the town and island of Unalaska—was taken over by the U.S. Navy to defend against Japanese attack. That attack came: In June 1942, Japanese planes bombed Unalaska, killing 43. The Aleut people were removed from the islands for the duration of the war and interned in inadequate housing in Southeast Alaska, where many died of disease. The military pulled out in 1947, but the remains of their defenses are interesting to explore, part of a unique unit of the national park system. Thanks to a 1971 act of Congress settling Native claims, the Aleut-owned Ounalashka Corporation owns much of the land around town. But the National Park Service protects and interprets the World War II historic sites on Native-owned land.

ESSENTIALS

GETTING THERE   **Alaska Airlines** (© 800/252-7522; www.alaskaair.com) stopped serving Dutch Harbor (the Unalaska port and airport) recently because the bad weather and short runway made the schedule too unreliable. Instead, they book flights on **PenAir** (© 800/448-4226; www.penair.com), which operates 30-passenger turbo prop aircraft (of course, you can also book directly with PenAir). When a squall is hitting Dutch, these smaller planes can land on a different island and wait for it to clear. The flight takes 3 hours and a ticket is $850 or more round-trip.

The **Alaska Marine Highway System** ferry *Tustumena* (© 800/642-0066; www.FerryAlaska.com) runs once a month from Homer, leaving Tuesday and arriving in Unalaska on Saturday after stopping in Kodiak and the villages along the way. The passenger fare is $295, and a two-berth cabin with facilities is $273 more. I'm told this open sea adventure is a great way to see beautiful country and encounter the people of the villages along the way. Of course, unless you want to spend half a day in Unalaska and then make the long return trip, you'll need to fly back.

VISITOR INFORMATION   The **Unalaska/Port of Dutch Harbor Convention and Visitors Bureau,** P.O. Box 545, Unalaska, AK 99685 (© 877/581-2612 or 907/581-2612; www.unalaska.info), is at 5th Street and Broadway, in the old part of town.

A visitor center for the **Aleutian WW II National Historic Area** (© 907/ 581-1276; www.nps.gov/aleu) occupies a war-era building at the airport. The historic area encompasses World War II ruins on the island that, like the center, stand on Native-owned lands. The National Park Service helped fund the improvements and interpret the history. A $4 entry fee at the visitor center also covers the permit to hike to the ruins (see "Exploring the Town," below). The website is interesting, too (click on "In Depth").

GETTING AROUND   The main historic part of the town is a tiny street grid on a narrow peninsula facing Iliuliuk Bay. The **Bridge to the Other Side** (that's the official name) leads to Amaknak Island, the site of the airport, the Grand Aleutian Hotel, and the fishing industrial area of Dutch Harbor. Traveling down the road in the other direction leads a little way up into the mountains, a starting point for walks. Van taxis are the main way of getting around town for the hordes of fishermen. One company is **Blue Checker Taxi** (© 907/581-2186).

FAST FACTS: **Unalaska/Dutch Harbor**

Bank   **Key Bank** is attached to the Alaska Commercial Store and has an ATM.

Hospital   **Iliuliuk Family and Health Services** (© 907/581-1202) offers clinic services.

Internet Access   Free at the **public library** (© 907/581-5060).

Police   **Unalaska** Department of Public Safety (© 907/581-1233) is just above the bridge on the Unalaska side.

Taxes   Sales tax is 3%; the total tax on rooms is 8%.

EXPLORING THE TOWN

Unalaska's most significant historic site is the **Holy Ascension Cathedral.** Completed in 1896 on the site of churches that had stood since 1808, the white church with green onion-shaped domes contains 697 icons, artifacts, and artworks—a significant collection that has been continuously in use by the Aleut congregation. The congregation was founded by Father Ivan Veniaminov, who translated the Gospel into Aleut and has been canonized as St. Innocent. A $1.3-million restoration saved the church from collapse in 1996. It is a dignified, geometric counterpoint to the soft edge of sparkling Iliuliuk Bay.

The professionally curated **Museum of the Aleutians,** next door to the Ounalashka Corporation on Margaret Bay in Dutch Harbor (© 907/581-5150; www.aleutians.org), contains some of the region's best artifacts, including some from North America's oldest coastal sites on Umnak and Unalaska islands. Exhibits also cover the town's history, with World War II artifacts and other items left behind by the successive waves of occupiers. Every summer the museum mounts archaeological digs on the island, inviting visitors to join in the work, earn college credit while digging, work to clean the artifacts in the museum, and hear evening lectures. Admission is $4. It's open summer Monday through Saturday from 11am to 4pm, Sunday from noon to 5pm; in winter Tuesday through Saturday from 11am to 4pm.

There are remains of **World War II military structures** around town, including some that are still in use, such as the submarine dry dock that today fixes fishing boats. Trails lead over the island to other sites included in the Aleutian

World War II National Historic Area, which preserves this evidence of war on American soil and helps tell the story of the Native people who were interned by both the Japanese and Americans during the war (See "The Aleutians: The Quiet After War," below). U.S. Army Fort Schwatka, on Mount Ballyhoo, is about an hour's hike from the airport. The fort once had over 100 buildings. Many remain, including the best-preserved gun mounts and lookouts of all the nation's coastal defenses from the war. Besides, it's a spectacular site where you can see ships returning. Stop by the historic site visitor center at the airport first; besides learning the context of the park, your $4 admission fee is your permit for access to the ruins, which belong to the Native-owned Ounalashka Corp. (All use on their land requires a permit; see "Hiking," below).

That's about it for sightseeing in Unalaska, unless you take a walk in the port. The activity there is interesting for the size of the vessels and harvest and the incredible investment in buildings and equipment.

GETTING OUTSIDE

BIRD-WATCHING   Flip through the crisp, unused pages of your bird book to find out what you may see in the Aleutians. Several rare bird species nest in the area, and Asian birds occasionally drop in as accidentals. The whiskered auklet and red-legged kittiwake are among the birds commonly found around Unalaska that you probably haven't seen. You'll have the greatest success taking a boat to a seabird colony. The Grand Aleutian Hotel (below, under "Where to Stay") offers packages; it's also possible to combine halibut fishing and bird-watching on your own chartered boat (see "Fishing"). You're also likely to encounter sea lions and other marine mammals.

FISHING   You can fly out for salmon fishing from black-sand beaches, but Unalaska has become more famous for huge **halibut.** In 1995, a local sport fisherman caught a 395-pound halibut from an 18-foot skiff within a half mile of town; to kill the behemoth he had to beach it and beat it over the head with a rock. The next year, Fairbanks angler Jack Tragis landed the world's record halibut here, which weighed 459 pounds. If you're having trouble imagining a fish that big, drop by City Hall, where a replica hangs stuffed in the lobby. The convention and visitor bureau can refer you to a charter boat operator and has a few links to them on its website (see above).

HIKING   The island's green heather and rounded mountains of wildflowers are inviting for a walk. You can walk pretty much in any direction. Explore the abandoned World War II defenses; make a goal of a beach or one of the small peaks around the town; or, for the ambitious, head to the top of an active volcano, Mount Makushin. There are no bears and not many bugs, but there's great berry picking and beachcombing. The weather can be a threat, however, and fox holes can trip you up. As always in remote outdoor areas, you must be suitably dressed and leave word of where you're going and when you'll be back.

Hikers beyond the World War II historic area have to pay a higher fee to the **Ounalashka Corp.,** at 400 Salmon Way near the Grand Aleutian Hotel (© **907/581-1276;** www.ounalashka.com), the Native village corporation that owns much of the land around town. Hiking is $6 per person or $10 per family. They're open Monday through Friday from 8am to 5pm; or you can buy the permit from the historic area visitor center (see p. 420). For extended treks, also go to the Department of Public Safety (see "Fast Facts: Dutch Harbor/ Unalaska," above) for a travel-planning guide and to report your route on a travel plan that will assist with a search if you don't come back (not necessary if you're just going for a short ramble in the hills around town).

The Aleutians: The Quiet After War

Once thousands of men died for the rocky islands of the Aleutians. What began as a Japanese military diversion became a ferocious fight for honor, one of the worst of World War II's Pacific Theater. Yet when the fighting was done most of the islands were abandoned and left uninhabited, littered with military ruins, for half a century. Finally, with the construction of a new National Park Service visitor center in Unalaska, the battle for the Aleutians is just beginning to enter national consciousness.

The Japanese attacked the islands of **Kiska** and **Attu** at the start of the Pacific war to divert the main core of the American navy away from what became the Battle of Midway. But the Americans had intercepted and decoded Japanese transmissions and weren't fooled. Meanwhile, the Japanese had sent 24 ships, including two aircraft carriers, on a fool's errand to bomb the new American naval base at Dutch Harbor and occupy islands in the western Aleutians. Those ships could have tipped the balance at Midway, among the most important battles of the war. Instead, the Japanese met stiff antiaircraft fire in 2 days of bombing at Dutch Harbor; although 43 Americans were killed, the defensive function of the base was not greatly impaired.

The Japanese then took Kiska and Attu, meeting no resistance from 10 Americans staffing a weather station or from an Aleut village whose 43 inhabitants were all—even the children—sent to a prison camp in Japan to mine clay for the duration of the war. About half the prisoners survived to return to Alaska.

The Americans had their own plan to remove the Aleuts, but the idea of depopulating all the islands had been turned down. Now, with the Japanese attack, it was swiftly put into effect. All the Aleuts were rounded up and put on ships. Their villages were burned or trashed by weather and vandalism. With little thought given to their living conditions, the Aleuts were interned in abandoned summer camps and similarly inadequate facilities in Southeast Alaska. Shunned by the local communities and without the basic necessities of life, 10% died due to poor sanitation. The U.S. Fish and Wildlife Service took Aleut hunters to hunt furs as virtual slaves, much as the Russians had done 200 years before.

The Japanese and American military fared not much better on their new real estate. Although the Aleutians quickly became irrelevant to the rest of the war, significant resources were committed to a largely futile air and sea battle in the fog and endless storms. Flying at all was difficult. The Americans couldn't spare a land invasion force at first and had to rely on bombing Kiska and Attu to punish the Japanese and try to deter a further advance up the chain. To that end, they built a large base at Adak, among others, so shorter-range fighter escorts could accompany the bombers. Construction in the spongy tundra was difficult in any case, made more so by the length of supply lines.

The Japanese high command never had any intention of advancing up the chain, but also saw no reason to abandon their new Kiska air base when it was causing the Americans to exert such effort. The Japanese concentrated on fortifying Kiska, which became a honeycomb of underground bunkers and heavy antiaircraft guns and withstood constant bombing raids by the Americans.

Finally, on May 11, 1943, almost a year after the Japanese took the islands, Americans landed on Attu and a brutal 18-day battle for the rugged island began. The Japanese were massively outnumbered but heavily dug in. Finally, with only 800 soldiers left from an original force of 2,600, the Japanese mounted a banzai attack. Only 28 were taken prisoner—the rest were killed in battle or committed suicide. The Americans lost 549 killed, 1,148 wounded, and 2,132 injured by severe cold, disease, accident, mental breakdown, or other causes. In the end, it was the second most costly island battle in the Pacific, after Iwo Jima.

The battle for Kiska was less dramatic. The Japanese withdrew under cover of fog. After a massive bombardment of the empty island and the rallying of heavy reinforcements, the Americans landed to find that no one was there. Still, 105 American soldiers died in the landing in accidents and fire from their own forces.

After the Aleutian battle was over, American forces in Alaska declined drastically, but never went away altogether. Before the war, the absurd little Fort William Seward, in Haines, had been the totality of Alaska's defenses, with a couple of hundred men armed with Springfield rifles and no reliable means of transportation. Afterward there were large bases in several areas of the state. Military spending became the biggest economic boom the territory had ever seen, connecting it by a new road to the Lower 48 and bringing precious year-round jobs. A new wave of postwar settlers, many former GIs, brought a population boom. The advent of the Cold War, and Alaska's prime strategic location in defense against the Soviet Union, brought ever-greater increases in military spending in Alaska. To this day, the military is one of the largest sectors of the Alaska economy, and the state has been relatively unscathed in base closures except for remote outposts.

The end of the war was more bitter for the Aleuts. Returning to villages they had departed hastily 3 years before, they found homes and subsistence gear ruined and even historic Russian Orthodox churches and icons severely damaged. Many who had survived the terrible period of internment never returned. Some of the villages never revived; bureaucrats managing the evacuation wiped them off the map as a cost-saving measure.

Awareness of this injustice began to resurface in the 1980s, and in 1988 Congress and President Reagan formally apologized to the Aleuts and paid compensation of $12,000 to each survivor, then about half the 900 who were evacuated. That act also helped fund restoration of the five historic churches and construction of one replacement.

Today, the Aleuts own their islands. It's fitting that the National Park Service's Aleutian World War II National Historic Area is their guest, on their land, and the new visitor center belongs to a Native corporation. Stop in to learn about the lives sacrificed here, and wonder why.

To learn more, see Brian Garfield's readable *The Thousand-Mile War; World War II in Alaska and the Aleutians* (University of Alaska Press, $25).

WHERE TO STAY

Carl's Bayview Inn   The building, in town on Iliuliuk Bay, looks a bit like a Dutch Harbor warehouse from the outside, but the eight kitchenette units and six suites inside are comfortable and attractive, with many amenities, pastel colors, and sweeping views. The double rooms showed more signs of wear. Only four rooms are reserved for nonsmokers. They freeze fish for guests.

606 Bayview (P.O. Box 730), Unalaska, AK 99685. © **800/581-1230** or 907/581-1230. Fax 907/581-1880. bayview@arctic.net. 30 units. $110 double; $125 double with kitchenette; $150–$175 suite. Extra person $20. AE, DISC, MC, V. **Amenities:** Restaurant; bar; courtesy van; coin-op laundry. *In room:* TV.

Grand Aleutian Hotel ★★   It's almost unreal to arrive at this big, luxurious hotel in a hard-driving Alaska Bush community. The Grand Aleutian is the best hotel in the Alaska Bush, with rooms just as good as you find in Anchorage, but minutes away from some of the best halibut fishing and bird-watching anywhere. The accommodations are well designed and comfortable, many with good water views; the lobby is grand, with a huge stone fireplace; and there's a piano bar. As you walk outside into a driving gale, it's like teleporting from a big city hotel back to an exposed rock out in the North Pacific.

The **Chart Room** restaurant, on the second floor, allows bird-watchers to see waterfowl in the bay while dining on steak, seafood, or pasta. The menu, although brief, is Unalaska's most sophisticated. Dinner entrees range from $13 to $37. The **Margaret Bay Cafe,** downstairs, also has a good view, with grilled sandwiches and some lighter fare.

A 2-night birding package, which includes a boat visit to the Baby Islands bird colony to see the whiskered auklet, tufted and horned puffin, albatross, and other creatures, starts at about $750 per person, double occupancy, not including air fare.

498 Salmon Way (P.O. Box 921169), Dutch Harbor, AK 99692. © **866/581-3844** or 907/581-3844. Fax 907/581-7150. www.grandaleutian.com. 112 units. $179 double; $249 suite. Extra person $20. Packages available. AE, DC, DISC, MC, V. **Amenities:** 2 restaurants; 2 bars; activities desk; courtesy van; limited room service; laundry service. *In room:* TV, coffeemaker, hair dryer.

WHERE TO DINE

Two of the town's best restaurants are at the **Grand Aleutian Hotel,** described above. Here's the other contender.

Tino's Steak House AMERICAN/MEXICAN   Tino's packs in the commercial fishermen and other locals by serving huge portions of authentic Mexican food fast, as well as steaks, a few seafood items, breakfast, and lots of sandwiches and burgers. I'm told you save money but get virtually the same meal by ordering from the lunch menu—the dinner prices are on the Unalaska scale, with most over $20.

11 N. 2nd St. at Broadway. © **907/581-4288.** Lunch items $7–$14; dinner main courses $15–$40. AE, DISC, MC, V. Daily 10am–10pm.

5 The Pribilof Islands: Birder's Paradise

The Pribilof Islands of St. Paul and St. George sit out in the middle of the Bering Sea, due north of Unalaska, teeming with marine mammals and seabirds. Some 600,000 fur seals meet at the breeding rookeries in the summer, and two million birds of more than 200 species use the rocks. Bird-watchers visit St. Paul for one of the most exotic and productive birding and wildlife-viewing opportunities anywhere. It's best during the spring migration, from mid-May to mid-June, when great numbers of birds show up, including rare Asian accidental species;

the fall migration comes in late July and August. You can count on making rare sightings any time during the summer. Indeed, the National Audubon Society's *Field Guide to North American Birds* calls this "perhaps the most spectacular seabird colony in the world."

The islands are extremely remote, however, and the accommodations simple; if you're not interested in birding or in spending a lot of time watching wildlife, it's probably too much money and trouble. There is only one hotel, the **King Eider,** which has basic rooms and shared bathrooms. Guests are issued food vouchers for the mess hall at the Trident Seafoods fish-processing plant, near the hotel. Three meals a day come from a buffet there, and cost $10 for breakfast, $14 for lunch, and up to $17 for dinner; you settle up at the end of your stay depending on how many vouchers you've used. There is one restaurant on the island, **Duna's Kitchen,** open with soup and sandwiches for lunch or an early dinner (it closes at 7pm). There is also a grocery store, the AC Value Store, with an ATM, across from the hotel.

Visitors generally come on tours, which are sold as a package with airfare and guiding by Aleuts and expert birders. With the guides' help and radio communication, your chances of seeing exotic species are much enhanced. The tours are offered by **Tanadguix Corp.,** 4300 B St., Suite 402, Anchorage, AK 99503 (© **877/424-5637;** www.alaskabirding.com). Check the website for birding news and species details. Packages from Anchorage start at $1,361 for a 2-night visit and operate from mid-May through August. Travelers can choose to ride on a bus as a group or hike on their own. Permanent blinds are in place for watching birds and seals. The weather is always cool and damp.

6 Nome: Arctic Frontier Town

The accidents of history deposited the streets and buildings of this lusty little town on the shore of Norton Sound, just south of the Arctic Circle in Northwest Alaska, and gave it qualities that make Nome an exceptionally attractive place for a visitor. For once, the local boosters' motto—in this case, "There's no place like Nome"—is entirely accurate, and that's because Nome, although itself nothing special to look at, combines a sense of history, a hospitable and somewhat silly attitude, and an exceptional location on the water in front of a tundra wilderness that's crossed by 250 miles of road. Those roads are the truly unique thing, for Nome is the only place in Arctic Alaska where a visitor can drive or bike deep into the open country, coming across musk oxen, reindeer, rarely seen birds, Native villages, undeveloped hot springs, and even an abandoned 1881 elevated train from New York City. Elsewhere, you're obliged to fly from rural hubs to get so far into the Bush, a more expensive and ambitious undertaking for casual explorers.

The accidents of history have been rather frequent in Nome. History has been downright sloppy. Start with the name. It's essentially a clerical error, caused by a British naval officer who, in 1850, was presumably in a creative dry spell when he wrote "? Name" on a diagram rather than name the cape he was sailing past. A mapmaker interpreted that as "Cape Nome." Or so goes one widely accepted explanation. The original gold rush of 1898 was caused by prospectors in the usual way, but a much larger 1899 population explosion happened after one of the '98 stampeders, left behind in a camp on the beach because of an injury, panned the sand outside the tent—and found that it was full of gold dust. By 1900, a fourth of Alaska's white population was in Nome sifting the sand. Small-time operators and tourists are still at it. A huge floating gold dredge of the kind that makes for major historic sites in Fairbanks and Dawson City sits idle on the edge of town. In Nome, it stopped operation only in recent years. There are two other, smaller dredges in town, too. Historic structures are few, however, as fires and storms have destroyed the town several times since the gold rush.

Nome has a particular, broad sense of humor. It shows up in the *Nome Nugget* newspaper and in silly traditions like the Labor Day bathtub race, the pack-ice golf tournament, and the polar bear swim. The population is half white and half Native, and the town is run largely by the white group. Some see Nome as a tolerant mixing place of different peoples, while the town strikes others as a bit colonial. Booze is outlawed in Kotzebue, the Native-dominated city to the north; but in Nome there is still a sloppy, gold-rush–style saloon scene. That sort of thing is prettier as historic kitsch than when it shows up in the form of drunks staggering down Front Street.

But you can ignore that, instead taking advantage of the great bargains to be had on Iñupiaq arts and crafts. And, most important, you can use one of the pleasant little inns or bed-and-breakfasts as a base to get into the countryside that beckons you down one of the gravel roads. Nome is popular with bird-watchers, who find the roads especially useful.

ESSENTIALS
GETTING THERE   Flying is the only way to get to Nome. **Alaska Airlines** (© 800/252-7522; www.alaskaair.com) flies 90 minutes by jet direct from Anchorage or with a brief hop from Kotzebue. Prices are around $400 round trip. Many visitors come on escorted tour packages sold by **Alaska Airlines Vacations** (© 800/468-2248); as a day trip a tour package costs $385; an overnight in Kotzebue followed by a day in Nome costs $515 per person, double occupancy. Unlike some other Arctic communities, however, I think Nome is a better destination to be on your own, especially if you rent a car. "Which Arctic Destination to Choose," p. 433, summarizes the choices.

All taxis operate according to a standard price schedule you can get from the visitor center. A ride to town from the airport is $5. There are three companies, including **Checker Cab** (© 907/443-5211).

VISITOR INFORMATION   The **Nome Convention and Visitors Bureau,** Front and Division streets (P.O. Box 240), Nome, AK 99762 (© 907/443-6624; www.nomealaska.org/vc), provides maps and detailed information for diverse interests. The office is open from late May to mid-September daily from 9am to 9pm, the balance of the year Monday through Friday from 9am to 6pm.

The **Bering Land Bridge National Preserve Headquarters,** Front Street (P.O. Box 220), Nome, AK 99762 (© 907/443-2522; www.nps.gov/bela), is a good source of outdoors information from the rangers who staff a desk and are responsible for a rarely visited 2.5-million-acre national park unit, which covers much of the Seward Peninsula north of the Nome road system.

Also check the *Nome Nugget* website, at **www.nomenugget.com**, a real window into the community.

GETTING AROUND   The town is a street grid along the ocean. **Front Street** follows the sea wall, **First Avenue** is a block back, and so on. A harbor is at the north end of town, and the gold-bearing beach is to the south. You can mostly walk to see this area. Three roads branch out from Nome. I've described them below, under "Venturing Beyond Town, On the Road." To get out on the roads, you need to take a tour or rent a car, or bring a bike with you.

Several local car-rental agencies operate in town; the visitor center maintains a list, with rates. **Stampede Rent-A-Car,** 302 E. Front St. ((©) **800/354-4606** or 907/443-3838), charges $90 to $115 for SUVs and vans. The same people operate the Aurora Inn (see "Where to Stay," below).

FAST FACTS: Nome

Bank **Wells Fargo,** with an ATM, is at 250 Front St.

Hospital **Norton Sound Regional** is at 5th Avenue and Bering Street ((©) **907/443-3311**).

Internet Access **Nome Public Library** is at 200 Front St. ((©) **907/443-6626**).

Police At Bering Street and 4th Avenue ((©) **907/443-7766**).

Post Office At Front Street and Federal Way.

Taxes The sales tax is 4%; the tax on rooms totals 8%.

SPECIAL EVENTS   The **Tesoro Iron Dog Snowmachine Race** ((©) **907/ 563-4414;** www.irondog.org), in mid-February, is the world's longest cross-country snowmachine race, at over 2,000 miles, running from Wasilla to Nome and back each year.

The biggest event of the year is the **Iditarod Trail Sled Dog Race** ((©) **907/ 376-5155;** www.iditarod.com), a marathon of more than 1,000 miles that ends in Nome in mid-March. The sled dog racers and world media descend on the town for a few days of madness, with lots of community events planned. The activities last most of the month; contact the Nome visitor center, or download the calendar from www.nomealaska.org/vc. Among the most exciting vacations you could plan would be to volunteer to help put on the Iditarod; check their website (above) for information or an application, or call. They receive more volunteers than they can use, so apply early.

One of the March Iditarod events, showcasing Nome's well-developed sense of humor, is the **Bering Sea Ice Golf Classic** ((©) **907/443-6624**)—six holes are set up on the sea ice. The pressure ridges constitute a bad lie. Various similar silly events take place all year (see www.nomealaska.org/vc), including the **Polar Bear Swim** which happens around June 21 (ice permitting) as part of the **Midnight Sun Festival** ((©) **907/443-5535**). The festival celebrates the summer solstice, when Nome gets more than 22 hours of direct sunlight. A parade, handmade raft race, folk festival, bank holdup, and other events headline the festival. Winners of the raft race get possession for a year of the fur-lined honey bucket (known in some places as a chamber pot).

EXPLORING THE TOWN

Most of Nome's original buildings were wiped out by fires or by storms off Norton Sound that tore across the beach and washed away major portions of the business district. A sea wall, completed in 1951, now protects the town. Among the few historic sites that survive are the gold rush-era Board of Trade Saloon, a church, and a bust of Roald Amundsen, who landed near Nome, in Teller, after crossing the North Pole from Norway in a dirigible in 1926. Below the library, at Front Street and Lanes Way, the small **Carrie M. McLain Memorial Museum** ((©) **907/443-6630**) contains an exhibit on the town's gold rush. The museum is free and open summer daily from noon to 8pm, winter Tuesday through Saturday from noon to 6pm.

In good weather, a pleasant walk is to be had southeast of town, along the **beach.** Small-time miners may be camped there, but the gold-bearing sand extends for miles more of solitary walking. You can buy a gold pan in town and try your luck, but the sand has been sifted for nearly 100 years, so don't expect to gather any significant amount of gold. The **Swanberg Dredge** you can see from here operated until the 1950s; a large dredge north of town worked into the mid-1990s. The 38 gold dredges that once operated on the Seward Peninsula crept across the tundra, creating their own ponds to float in as they went. The **cemetery,** with white wooden crosses on top of a little hill just out of town, also is worth a look.

Several companies offer **organized tours. Nome Discovery Tours** (*C* 907/ 443-2814; discover@gci.net) has the asset of talented professional actor Richard Beneville as the van driver and tour guide. He'll pick you up and drive you anywhere in the area, sharing his quirky enthusiasm and extensive knowledge of the surroundings and culture. The highlight is the wildlife and scenery on the roads out of town, and he also visits an ivory carver and working gold mine. Half days are $45 per person, full days $85.

If you're in the market for walrus ivory carvings and other **Iñupiaq arts and crafts,** you'll find low prices and an extraordinary selection in Nome. Jim West has a legendary collection for sale, assembled in the bar room of the historic **Board of Trade Saloon** that is attached to a shop on Front Street. The **Arctic Trading Post** is more of a traditional gift shop and also has a good ivory collection. **Chukotka-Alaska,** at 514 Lomen St., is an importer of art and other goods from the Russian Far East, and is really worth a look. Alaska Native art you find in Nome is likely to be authentic, but still ask; see "Native Art: Finding the Real Thing" (p. 20). International visitors should see chapter 3 to find out about the special permit you need to carry ivory out of the United States.

VENTURING BEYOND TOWN BY ROAD

The modest attractions downtown would hardly justify a trip to Nome, but the city's surroundings do. The roads provide unique access to a large stretch of the Seward Peninsula. Unlike other Arctic Bush areas, where someone has to take you where you want to go, in Nome all you have to do is rent a car and go. There are few cars in Nome (they have to be flown in or shipped by barge), so you won't see many other vehicles on a huge expanse of spectacular territory, with wildlife-viewing opportunities as good as anywhere in the state. The **Alaska Department of Transportation** (*C* 907/443-3444) can provide current information on road conditions.

You have a good chance of seeing moose, reindeer, owls, foxes, bears, and musk ox anywhere you drive, but check in with the visitor center or the **Alaska Department of Fish and Game,** at Front and Steadman streets (*C* 907/443-2271), to find out the best locales to see animals. They can also give you guidance on fishing along the roads and a "Nome Roadside Fishing Guide," or download it from www.alaska.gov/adfg (click on "Sport Fishing," then the northern region, then "Northwest"). Check "Getting Around," above, to find a mode of transportation.

ROAD HIGHLIGHTS None of the three roads radiating from Nome has services of any kind—just small Native villages, a few dwellings, and some reindeer herders—so you must be prepared and bring what you need with you, including insect repellent and a good spare tire. The visitor center provides a road guide. Here are some highlights:

The **Nome-Council road** heads 72 miles to the east, about half of that on the shoreline. It turns inland at the ghost town of Solomon, an old mining town with an abandoned railroad train known locally as the Last Train to Nowhere. The engines were originally used on the New York City elevated lines in 1881, then were shipped to Alaska in 1903 to serve the miners along this line to Nome. This is a scenic spot for bird-watching, and fishing is good in the Solomon River, all along the road. Council, near the end of the road, has a couple of dozen families in the summer. A 3-foot-deep river separates the road from the village.

The **Nome-Taylor road,** also known as the Kougarok Road, runs north of town into the Kigluaik Mountains, 85 miles from Nome, eventually petering out and becoming impassable. About 40 miles out, you reach lovely Salmon Lake, with a lakeshore campground with picnic tables, grills, and outhouses. A few miles farther, a road to the left leads to the 125° Pilgrim Hot Springs, near a Catholic church. Access is limited to when the caretaker is on hand, so check with the visitor center before going.

The **Nome-Teller road** leads 73 miles to the village of Teller, which has 266 residents and a store. It's an opportunity to see an authentic Arctic Native village.

MOUNTAIN BIKING   The roads of Nome are one of the world's great, undiscovered mountain biking destinations—where else can you bike past musk oxen and reindeer? There is no bike rental in town, but there is a bike shop, Keith Conger's **Bering C Bikes** (© **907/443-4994**), and he also offers guided bike day trips and van-supported multiday camping expeditions. For bike enthusiasts, it may be worth renting a bike in Anchorage or bringing yours from home.

BIRD-WATCHING   Bird-watchers will make many discoveries out on the Nome roads, turning to previously unused pages of their bird books. A bird list is available at the visitor center, and they can tell you where to look—each of the three roads has a different habitat. The best times to visit for birding are right around Memorial Day, and from July to mid-August. There's a chance to see Siberian birds, and you can count on bluethroats, yellow wagtails, wheatears, Arctic warblers, and Aleutian and Arctic terns. Nome is the only place to see a bristle-thighed curlew without chartering a plane. You don't need a guide, although guided field trips do come to Nome (see "Bird-Watching" in chapter 2).

SEEING THE SIGHTS IN THE AIR

Nome is a hub for Bush plane operators. Flightseeing charters are available, or you can fly on one of the scheduled routes out to the villages and spend a couple of hours touring. The way to do it is to contact a flight service, explain what you have in mind, and follow their advice. Expect to pay around $160. Don't plan to stay overnight in a village without advance arrangements and don't go in bad weather—you'll see little and may get stuck in a tiny village. Among the operators is **Cape Smythe Air** (© **800/478-5125** in Alaska only, or 907/443-2414; www.capesmythe.com).

Bering Air (© **800/478-5422** in Alaska only, or 907/443-5464; www.bering air.com) also has a long and illustrious reputation and serves 32 villages from Nome and Kotzebue. They offer flightseeing trips by fixed-wing aircraft or helicopter on hourly charter rates (expensive if there are just one or two of you along). Or they will sell you a seat on a scheduled loop flight that visits various villages, charging the fare only to the closest village on the trip while you enjoy the entire round trip.

WHERE TO STAY

There are several good B&Bs and motel rooms besides those listed in full below, including the **Nanuaq Manor** (📞 **907/443-5296**), **Nugget Inn** (📞 **877/443-2323** or 907/443-2323), and **Ponderosa Inn** (📞 **907/443-5737**). Staying at a B&B makes sense, as your host can introduce you to the community in a less contrived way than a formal tour company. The visitor center and their website can provide information on them.

Aurora Inn Suites ⭐   Look here for the best traditional hotel rooms in town in a mock country inn on the town's main street. They're nicely furnished and even have some style. That's a remarkable contrast to the other hotels in Nome. Also unique in town, there are lots of nonsmoking rooms. Don't put too much faith in the rates listed here, which are expected to change; call and see what kind of deal you can work out. The same company owns the car rental operation in town, which is on site.

302 E. Front St. (P.O. Box 1008), Nome, AK 99762. 📞 **800/354-4606** or 907/443-3838. Fax 907/443-6380. www.aurorainnnome.com. 68 units. $130 double, $185–$225 suite. Extra person over age 15 $10. AE, MC, V. **Amenities:** Sauna; car rental; coin-op laundry. *In room:* TV, dataport, hair dryer.

Sweet Dreams B&B   It's the host—former Nome Mayor Leo Rasmussen— who makes this place special. A personable and funny man, he is a deep well of Nome history and local knowledge. The two-story house has a rustic, old-fashioned feel, with lots of Alaskan memorabilia and a sun room on top. A full breakfast is served when the hostess has time to prepare it.

406 W. 4th St. (P.O. Box 2), Nome, AK 99762. 📞 **907/443-2919**. leaknome@alaska.com. 3 units, shared bathroom. $90 double. Rate includes full breakfast. MC, V.

WHERE TO DINE

You wouldn't go out of your way to dine at any of the restaurants in Nome, but you can find an adequate family meal at various establishments along Front Street. Several are operated by immigrant families, who offer their national cuisine along with standard American-style fare. There sometimes is a language barrier with the servers.

Milano's Pizzeria (📞 **907/443-2924**), at 503 Front St., the Old Federal Building, serves Italian and Japanese meals; its pizza is recommended by the locals. **Twin Dragons,** on Front Street near Steadman Street (📞 **907/443-5552**), has made it for years with Chinese food alone, which is consistently good; it's probably the best you can reliably get in Nome. Both of these take Visa and MasterCard.

The other flavor of restaurant in Nome, and the most popular locally, is the classic American greasy spoon. The ethnic restaurants mentioned above all have a way to escape the smoke; these burger habitats tend to be smoky throughout. Both of the following take all major credit cards.

The **Polar Cub Restaurant,** at 225 Front St. (📞 **907/443-5191**), has an extensive dinner menu and prices that are reasonable for the Alaska Bush.

Fat Freddy's Restaurant, attached to the Nugget Inn (📞 **907/443-5899**) and right next to the Iditarod Trail finish line, is a local favorite. In addition to the usual sandwiches, the restaurant serves more expensive fare in the evening, such as steaks and fried fish.

7 Kotzebue: Big Village

Although its 3,082 residents make Kotzebue (*kotz*-eh-biew) a good-sized town, with a bank, a hospital, and a couple of grocery stores, I've heard it called a village instead. A "village," in Alaskan parlance, is a remote Native settlement in the Bush, generally with fewer than a few hundred residents, where people live relatively close to the traditional lifestyle of their indigenous ancestors. Kotzebue is a support hub for the villages of the Northwest Arctic, with jet service and a booming cash economy, but it's populated and run by the Iñupiat—fish-drying racks and old dog sleds are scattered along the streets, and Native culture is thriving. It does feel like a village.

For visitors, this characteristic makes Kotzebue unique because you can see real Eskimo culture without leaving the comforts of jet travel and standard hotel rooms behind. Or, if you don't mind giving up some of those comforts, you can get even closer to the Iñupiat way of life. For adventurous outdoors people, Kotzebue offers access to huge areas of remote public land through which you can float on a raft or canoe. **Kobuk Valley National Park,** with its bizarre sand dunes; **Noatak National Preserve;** and **Cape Krusenstern National Monument** are among the largest national park units in the country, and among the least visited.

It's important to realize from the outset, however, that outside of an organized bus tour, there's absolutely nothing to do in Kotzebue. As I was told, "You have to shoot something or burn a lot of gas to have any fun around here." Kotzebue is not set up for independent travelers except those of the most intrepid ilk, and they will most likely use the town as a way to get into the remote public lands. See "Which Arctic Destination to Choose," p. 433.

The dominant business in town is the **NANA Corporation,** a regional Native corporation representing the roughly 7,000 Iñupiat who live in this Northwest Arctic region the size of Indiana. NANA, which stands for Northwest Arctic Native Association, is a successful example of how the 1971 Alaska Native Claims Settlement Act gave the indigenous people control over their own destiny. With huge land and resource holdings and the cash to develop them, NANA is making money for its Iñupiat shareholders and providing them with jobs in institutional catering and oil drilling and jobs at the Red Dog zinc mine near Kotzebue, the world's most productive. More relevant for visitors, NANA also owns the main hotel and tourist businesses in Kotzebue.

ESSENTIALS

GETTING THERE The only way to Kotzebue is by air. **Alaska Airlines** (© 800/252-7522; www.alaskaair.com) has several daily jets from Anchorage in the summer. You'll pay around $400 round-trip from Anchorage. They also fly from Kotzebue to Nome. The cheapest and really the only sensible way for most tourists to go to Kotzebue is to take a package offered by **Tour Arctic** and **Alaska Airlines Vacations,** described under "Exploring the Town," below.

VISITOR INFORMATION There is no town visitor center. The National Park Service staffs the **Iñaigvik Education and Information Center** at 2nd Avenue and Lake Street (P.O. Box 1029), Kotzebue, AK 99752 (© **907/442 3760;** www.nps.gov/nwak), providing information and displays on the immense area of protected land in the region and offering classes on traditional Native crafts and medicinal plants. Employees will answer questions about the town as well. It's open in summer daily from 9am to 4pm, by appointment in winter. The **local headquarters of the National Park Service,** open during normal business hours all year, is in the Eskimo Building with the post office on Shore Avenue (② **907/442-3890**).

Even if you won't be going to Kotzebue, you can still get lost in the city's charming website, full of pictures and community communications, at www. cityofkotzebue.com.

GETTING AROUND Kotzebue is 26 miles north of the Arctic Circle on the Chukchi Sea. About a mile by 2 miles in size, it sits on a low spit of land extending into the shallow Kotzebue Sound. You can walk pretty much everywhere you need to go or take a cab if you have luggage. The main hotel is a 15-minute walk from the airport, and taxis are available from three companies, including **City Cab** (② **907/442-2229**). If you're on the Tour Arctic package, buses will pick you up at the plane and deliver you and your luggage to the hotel. The gravel streets are on a warped grid radiating from **Shore Avenue,** also known as **Front Street,** which runs along the water. Roads extend only a few miles out of town.

FAST FACTS: **Kotzebue**

Alcohol The sale of alcohol is illegal in Kotzebue, but possession for personal use is permitted.

Bank **Wells Fargo,** with an ATM, is at the corner of Lagoon Street and 2nd Avenue.

Hospital The **Maniilaq Medical Center,** with a 24-hour emergency room, is at 5th Avenue and Ted Stevens Way (② **907/442-3321**).

Police For nonemergency calls, contact the **Kotzebue Police Department** at ② **907/442-3351** or the **Alaska State Troopers** at ② **907/442-3222**.

Post Office You'll find it at Shore Avenue and Tundra Way.

Taxes Sales tax is 6%; the tax on rooms totals 12%.

EXPLORING THE TOWN

There is only one activity in town, and it's part of an organized tour. **Tour Arctic** (② **800/523-7405** or 907/442-3441; www.tour-arctic.com) hosts visitors in its cultural and natural-history program, the centerpiece of which is the seasonal **NANA Museum of the Arctic,** across from the airport. For most people, the packages, also sold through **Alaska Airlines Vacations** (② **800/468-2248;** www.alaskaair.com), are the only sensible way to go to Kotzebue. You'll learn about the Arctic and Native culture, but the tour is scripted and there are no spectacular sights on the way. Owned and operated by the Iñupiat, the company employs Eskimo guides who offer commentary for about 5 hours while keeping customers comfortable, mostly in buses and indoors. A show at the museum includes children dancing, a blanket toss, and a high-tech slide show about the struggle to save Iñupiat culture. The tour includes a talk and demonstration in a tent about the clothing and survival techniques of the Eskimos. There's also a brief opportunity to walk on the tundra.

Day-trip packages are $385 from Anchorage, less than a full-fare ticket. The same tour with an overnight stay at NANA's comfortable Nullagvik Hotel is $415 per person, double occupancy (why not stay?). The prices to add Nome to the tour are reasonable, too, compared to the cost of a plane ticket alone.

GETTING OUTSIDE

A FISH CAMP   Some rugged and curious travelers may want something a bit less pampered and scripted than the Tour Arctic program. **Arctic Circle Educational Adventures** (© 907/442-6013 in summer, 907/276-0976 in winter; http://fishcamp.org) offers a chance to stay at a camp similar to the fish camps where Native people spend the summer gathering food for the winter—and to participate in set-net fishing, fish cutting, food gathering, and other traditional subsistence activities as well as hiking, town tours, and bird-watching. You are a participant rather than an observer, and spend real, unmediated time with Native people. The camp on the beach 5 miles south of town is as simple and rough as Bush life; guests stay in plywood cabins without plumbing. Elderhostel groups sometimes come for a week. Rates are $145 per person per day for lodging and meals and an additional $100 per day for tour activities. The season is from late June to mid-August.

FLIGHTSEEING   Flying in a small plane can give you an idea of what this remote country and its Native villages look like. Of greatest interest is the **Kobuk Valley National Park,** including the Great Kobuk Sand Dunes, a desert-like area of shifting 100-foot dunes. If your group is small, you may be able to save by going on a scheduled flight rather than chartering the whole plane. **Cape Smythe Air** (© 907/442-3020) is one operator flying to the surrounding villages. They fly twice daily to Noatak and Kivalina, over the **Cape Krusenstern National Monument,** for $141.

FLOAT TRIPS   There are several remote rivers near Kotzebue with easy self-guided floating for experienced outdoors people. This is the best chance to get deep into the Arctic on your own. The great Noatak River originates in the Brooks Range and flows 450 miles through America's largest undisturbed wilderness in the impressive scenery of the Noatak National Preserve. The Selawik, Squirrel, and Kobuk rivers all have long sections of easy water. **Alaska Discovery,** and **Equinox Wilderness Expeditions,** listed in section 8, "Planning an Outdoor Vacation," in chapter 2, have float trips in the area, although not necessarily every year. Expect to pay $3,500 per person, including air travel.

Most river running in the region is self-guided. Get details from *The Alaska River Guide,* by Karen Jettmar, director of Equinox (Alaska Northwest Books). Obviously you should be experienced in the outdoors and in river floating before heading out for a multiday trip in the Arctic. And plan ahead, arranging details well in advance with the park service and your pilot. Most visitors bring all their gear from Anchorage. Buck Maxson of **Arctic Air Guides** (© 907/ 442-3030) flies many rafters, charging $330 an hour for anywhere you want to go. Minimize your costs by putting in or taking out at villages along the river and using scheduled air services (see "Flightseeing," above).

WHERE TO STAY & DINE

Dining options in Kotzebue are limited. Besides the hotel restaurant listed below, you'll find good breakfasts and burgers at the **Bayside Inn,** right next door (© 907/442-3600). I cannot recommend their rooms, however.

To save some money and meet friendly local people, stay at **Lagoon Bed and Breakfast,** 227 Lagoon St. (© 907/442-3723; mar81996@otz.net).

Nullagvik Hotel ⋆ The NANA-owned hotel is thoughtfully designed and comfortably furnished. The modern rooms have all the features of a chain hotel. Their windows angle out from the building so that all get at least some ocean view. It can be startling to see Eskimo women wearing summer parkas called *kuspuks* cleaning in the halls; they do a thorough job. By booking with an Alaska Airlines Vacations package, you save considerable money on stays here. The **restaurant** changes every year; at this writing, it is called "Shogun" and serves various oriental food. It sometimes closes in the winter, but that, too, is unpredictable.

Shore Ave. and Tundra Way (P.O. Box 336), Kotzebue, AK 99752. © **907/442-3331.** Fax 907/442-3340. www. nullagvik.com. 73 units. High season $153 double; low season $121 double. $10 each additional person. AE, DC, MC, V. **Amenities:** Restaurant. *In room:* TV.

8 Barrow: Way North

Half-liquid land comes to an arbitrary point at the northern tip of Alaska, Point Barrow, a long tendril reaching into the Arctic Ocean where bowhead whales pass close to shore during their annual migrations. The Iñupiat settled here more than a thousand years ago because it is such a good whale hunting spot, and that is still why they live here, dragging their skin boats miles out on the frozen ocean to wait for whales along the cracks in the ice pack. And, according to age-old tradition, here they still share the whales they catch among the entire community. Indeed, even visitors who show up on a Saturday in late June, during the *Nalukataq,* may be offered a piece of *maktak* (whale blubber and skin) and a chance to bounce high in the air in the blanket toss.

Barrow is the northernmost settlement on the North American continent, above the 71st parallel, but that's not all that makes it unique. The town of 4,417 is a cultural treasure. It's ancient, but it's also the seat of the North Slope Borough, a county government encompassing an area larger than the state of Nebraska, in which lies North America's largest oil field. The borough has everything money can buy for a local government, yet the people still must contend with crushing ice, snooping polar bears, and utter isolation. From these ingredients, they have concocted an extraordinary mixture of sophisticated modernity and wise tradition. Alaska's largest corporation is based here; its top executives are also subsistence hunters. At the Iñupiat Heritage Center you could see, on successive nights, traditional dance in the Iñupiaq language and avant-garde theater in the same language.

Geography and the natural environment also make the place interesting. This is the most heavily instrumented and intensively studied scientific site anywhere in the Arctic. At the labs north of town, cutting-edge work on climate change takes place that could affect the whole world. The tundra around Barrow is dotted with lakes divided by tendrils of swampy tundra no more substantial than the edges of fine lace. On this haven for migratory waterfowl, the flat, wet land and the ocean seem to merge. Indeed, for all but a few months, it's a flat, frozen plain of ocean and land. For 65 days in the winter, the sun never rises. In the summer, it doesn't set. Ice recedes from the shore only for a few brief months. Such extreme geography is a magnet for visitors.

ESSENTIALS

GETTING THERE　　**Alaska Airlines** (© 800/252-7522; www.alaskaair.com) flies a couple of times daily to Barrow from Anchorage, by way of Fairbanks. The round-trip fare from Anchorage is $450 and up. You can save by booking their 1-day and overnight tour packages, described in "Exploring the Town & Getting Outside," below. Book them through **Alaska Airlines Vacations** (© 800/ 468-2248).

VISITOR INFORMATION　　The City of Barrow's **visitor center**, at Momegana and Ahkovak streets, near the airport and Wiley Post & Will Rogers Monument, operates in the summer only from 9:30 to 11am, with a guide to talk to, maps (including a numbered walking tour map), and other publications. To obtain advance information, contact the City of Barrow, Office of the Mayor, P.O. Box 629, Barrow, AK 99723 (© **907/852-5211;** fax 907/852-5871; barrowmayor@cityofbarrow.org).

GETTING AROUND　　Facing the Chukchi Sea, Barrow has two sections, lying on each side of Isatkoak Lagoon. **Browerville,** to the east, has the Iñupiat Heritage Center and the Stuaqpak, or big store, which contains a small food court and many services. The old part of **Barrow,** with the hotels and airport, is to the west. The northern tip of Alaska, **Point Barrow,** is north of the town on a spit. The road leads 6 miles in that direction, but the absolute end is farther out, beyond the road. Other gravel roads lead about 10 miles out of town on the tundra.

Taxis are handy and come quickly, charging a flat $5 anywhere in town, $10 beyond town, plus $1 for each additional passenger. **Arcticab** (© **907/852-2227**) is one of the four cab companies.

SPECIAL EVENTS　　The return of the sun after 2 months below the horizon is met by traditional celebrations on **January 21.** The **Piuraagiaqta,** a spring festival, takes place in mid-April and includes many fun events, such as the **tea-making contest,** in which couples race to set up a camp stove and melt ice to make tea. If the traditional bowhead whaling season is a success, the **Nalukataq** takes place in late June, usually on a Saturday, but the actual date depends on the preference of the successful captain. It is his responsibility to feed the entire community. The Eskimo blanket toss is also a traditional element of the event. In the fall, generally from early to mid-October, the whale hunt launches from the beaches of town (rather than the ice, as in spring). If you're lucky, you can be on hand as a whale is pulled ashore and butchered by the community. This usually occurs at the NARL runway, north of town; ask around, as everyone will know if a whale has been landed.

FAST FACTS: **Barrow**

Alcohol Legality The sale of alcohol is illegal in Barrow and importation for personal use in your luggage is limited and controlled by a permit system. If it's an issue, call ahead to the **Barrow Alcohol Delivery Site** (© 907/852-2337) or the **Office of the Mayor** (© 907/852-5211). Bootlegging is a serious crime.

Bank **Wells Fargo** is at 1078 Kiogak St., with an ATM.

Hospital **Samuel Simmonds Memorial Hospital** is at 1296 Agvik St. (© 907/852-4611).

Internet Access Free at the **Tuzzy Library,** at the Iñupiat Heritage Center in Browerville.

Police Contact the borough **Department of Public Safety,** 1068 Kiogak St. (© 907/852-6111).

Taxes There is no sales or bed tax in Barrow.

EXPLORING THE TOWN & GETTING OUTSIDE

The **Iñupiat Heritage Center** (© 907/852-4594) is the town's main attraction. It is part museum, part gathering center, and part venue for living culture. Inside is a workshop for craftspeople and a performance space for storytellers and dancers. In the museum area, displays of Iñupiat artifacts change regularly, while a permanent exhibit covers Eskimo whaling and the influence of Yankee whaling on it (the quiet pride here carries a real emotional wallop). Iñupiaq dancing and drumming performances happen every afternoon in the summer from 3 to 5pm, included in the admission price; these are the same performances that are the highlight of the escorted tours. The center is open from May 15 to September 15 Monday through Friday from 8:30am to 5pm (to see the dancing on weekends, call ahead); if you show up in the winter, they'll happily show you anything you want to see, as well. Admission is $10 adults, $5 over age 55, $2 ages 6 to 17, free ages 5 or younger.

The main tourism business in town is **Tundra Tours** (© 800/882-8478 or 907/852-3900; www.tundratours.com). Arctic Slope Regional Corp., a corporation representing the Iñupiat, owns the company and the Top of the World Hotel. Their tour (the same one sold through Alaska Airlines Vacations) introduces the town to visitors who arrive with little idea of what to expect. The 6-hour summer tour, in a small bus, drives around the town to show off the modest sights, including an Eskimo skin boat, the cemetery, and a stop for a dip of toes in the Arctic Ocean. The highlight is a visit to the Heritage Center with a cultural presentation, including Eskimo dance and a chance to buy crafts made by Native artists. The day-trip tour is $399 from Fairbanks, or $450 per person, double occupancy, for the tour and a night in Barrow at the Top of the World Hotel, giving you time on your own without the tour group; both prices include airfare and save over buying a plane ticket alone. Book the tour through Alaska Airlines Vacations or with Tundra Tours at the numbers listed above. If you buy the tour separately when you are already in Barrow, it's $75. They also offer a winter tour for seeing the Aurora ($85 separately), which does not include the cultural elements.

Jim Vordestrasse (© 907/852-2010) offers a decidedly less conventional tour, by bicycle. You can even ride as a passenger on his tandem recumbent bicycle—you don't have to peddle if you don't want to. He has given Iñupiaq elders their first bike ride on this contraption. Jim's a fascinating guy, a former mayor (now his wife, Edith is mayor), well loved in Barrow, positive and full of knowledge. The tour is $50. He also rents bicycles for $20 a day. If you arrive when snow is on the ground, he will take you cross-country skiing for the same tour price, equipment and polar bear protection included.

Barrow is the only place in the U.S. with commercial polar bear viewing tours. The bears are always around when the ice is in; they're dangerous and people take extreme care to avoid them. Barrow and other North Slope communities have minimized the danger of bears in town by setting up sites outside of the villages to dispose of gut piles and other hunting waste. It's a way of bribing the bears to leave the town alone. In Barrow, heavy equipment hauls the leftovers from fall whale butchering—bones and a few non-edible organs—out to the very end of the point. Polar bears come for an easy meal whenever the pack ice is close to shore, which is October through June. Commercial tours take visitors out to the point in all-terrain vans or Humvees that can drive on the beach gravel. Arrangements change annually and these are casual home businesses, so if polar bear viewing is your goal be sure to make firm arrangements with someone before you go. **Arctic Tours** (© **907/852-4512** or 907/852-1462 cell) takes visitors out in a Humvee May through September on a 2-hour tour that costs $60 per person, with a 2-person minimum. I advise going only in May and June, when the sea ice is in and the polar bear sightings are much more likely than later in the summer or in the fall.

WHERE TO STAY

King Eider Inn ✪✪   The best rooms in town—indeed, some of the best in the bush—are found in this like-new building near the airport. They're crisp and airy, with faux rustic furniture, and kept up so well it's as if no one has stayed there before. It probably helps that shoes are not allowed in the hotel—you have to take them off at the front door. The halls and rooms are decorated with Native art and a teddy bear greets you in bed. A room with a kitchenette is $10 more, and the enormous and luxurious Presidential Suite (where Barrow's honeymooners and visiting celebrities stay) is $300 summer, $275 winter. Smoking is not permitted, creating a rare nonsmokers' oasis in Barrow. The lobby is comfortable, with a stone fireplace and free Internet terminal. Bathrooms have large shower stalls, not tubs.

1752 Ahkovak St. (P.O. Box 1283), Barrow, AK 99723. © **888/303-4337** reservations or 907/852-4700. Fax 907/852-2025. www.kingeider.net. 19 units. Summer $195 double; winter $175 double. Extra person $25. AE, MC, V. **Amenities:** Sauna; car rental. *In room:* TV.

Top of the World Hotel ✪   This is a good hotel with familiar standard rooms. Owned by the Native corporation that also operates Tundra Tours, this is where you will stay if you come on the package tour. Rooms were updated in 2004. They're clean and have light furniture and blue carpet, desks, and refrigerators. Those on the water side have good views of the Arctic Ocean. The lobby is large, with a stuffed polar bear and a free terminal for Internet access.

Agvik St. (P.O. Box 189), Barrow, AK 99723. © **907/852-3900.** www.topoftheworldhotel.com. 50 units. Summer $140–$210 double; winter $75–$125 double. AE, DC, DISC, MC, V. *In room:* TV, fridge.

WHERE TO DINE

There are several decent restaurants in Barrow. Generally, they stay open very late, always have a TV on, offer free delivery, and don't brew decaffeinated coffee—people around here run on lots of caffeine and sugar.

Adjoining the Top of the World Hotel, **Pepe's North of the Border,** 1204 Agvik St. (© **907/852-8200**), is the most famous place in town thanks to an appearance owner Fran Tate made with Johnny Carson on *The Tonight Show* some 20 years ago. They serve large portions of familiar American-style Mexican food, steak, and seafood. The bus tours come here for lunch and Tate hands out souvenirs.

Brower's Restaurant, just off Hopson Street at the west end of Browerville (© **907/852-5800**), occupies an important historic structure, the whaling station and later store owned by Charles Brower, a Yankee whaler who became father of one of the community's largest and most successful Iñupiaq families. His memoir, *50 Years Below Zero* (University of Alaska Press, $25), is utterly gripping and packed with amazing stories. The restaurant has booths with big windows right on the beach. Service is fast and respectful, and the diner food solid and tasty (although I would steer clear of some of the fancier selections).

Arctic Pizza, 125 Apayauq St. (© **907/852-4222**), has the best fine dining in town, as well as the pizza and burgers available everywhere. The current chef prepares masterful Indian cuisine. One menu is offered both in the elegant upstairs dining room, which has a great view over ancient village ruins to the ocean, and in the light downstairs dining room where the TV is on and children and teens are allowed.

Northern Lights Restaurant, in Browerville at 5122 Herman St. (© **907/ 852-3300**), has a very comfortable, clean dining room and is operated by a charming family. Their menu goes on and on, with the owner's own Chinese food, plus deli selections and burgers, and the best pizza in town.

9 Prudhoe Bay: Arctic Industry

The Prudhoe (*prew*-dough) Bay complex is more than a huge oil field, it's an amazing achievement. Massive, complex machinery must operate in winter's deep, dark cold and in summer must avoid harm to a critical habitat for migrating caribou and waterfowl, on wet, fragile tundra that permanently shows any mark made by vehicles. Workers are forbidden even to set foot on the tundra. As you look from the edge of one of the gravel pads the heathery ground looks as undisturbed as a calm sea.

But that doesn't make it a good place to go on your vacation. The grim town of **Deadhorse,** which serves the oil facility, is really more of an industrial yard, barely deserving to be called a town; it certainly isn't anything you'd travel to see. To get beyond it to see Prudhoe Bay, you have to sign up for a tour. The tour has never gone inside the buildings, and under post-September 11, 2001, security measures it doesn't even go close to the most interesting areas. Visitors do get to stop at the Arctic Ocean, the only way to get to the water for those who drive up on the Dalton Highway. That hardly justifies the trip, however, unless you are bent on driving the highway anyway (it is covered in chapter 9, section 4). Frankly, I can't recommend spending the time and expense required for a Prudhoe tour. If you're curious about the Arctic, a trip to Barrow, Kotzebue, or Nome makes more sense.

If you do go, you must reserve at least 24 hours ahead to clear security for the tour. Tours are operated by the **Arctic Caribou Inn,** P.O. Box 340111, Prudhoe Bay, AK 99734 (© **877/659-2368** or 907/659-2368; fax 907/659-2692; www. arcticcaribouinn.com). They will need your name and an identification number that British Petroleum can use to run a background check before allowing you on the oil field: a driver's license, passport, or Social Security number will work. The inn also offers the area's visitor services, including a hotel and cafeteria, open in the summer only. Rooms start at $125 double. The restaurant has a buffet for breakfast ($11) and dinner ($18), and menu service for lunch. The town is dry: sale of alcohol is illegal, although you can bring it with you. The hotel is near the airport in Deadhorse and serves as the starting point for the tours. The tour itself lasts 2 hours, including a 20-minute video. Visitors are carried by bus among oil field buildings (which look a lot like industrial buildings anywhere) and then stop for 15 minutes at the Arctic Ocean. It costs $37 per adult, $17 ages 12 and under. There is no other way to get from the end of the road to the water.

Alaska Airlines (© **800/252-7522;** www.alaskaair.com) has one flight daily to Prudhoe Bay from Anchorage. A round-trip ticket costs around $650 from Anchorage.

Several companies drive bus tours up the Dalton Highway all the way to Prudhoe, flying the other way. **Northern Alaska Tour Company** (© **800/474-1986** or 907/474-8600; www.northernalaska.com) offers these trips, with add-ons to make it more interesting: flightseeing stops, dayhikes, village visits, and other choices. The basic 3-day, 2-night tour is $749.

Appendix:
Alaska in Depth

An old photo album opens, emitting a scent of dust and dried glue. Inside, pale images speak wanly of shrunken mountains and glaciers, a huge blue sky, water, and trees, a moose standing way off in the background. No family photographer can resist the urge to capture Alaska's vastness in the little box of a camera, and none, it seems, has ever managed it. Then, turning the page, there it is—not in another picture of the landscape, but reflected in a small face at the bottom of the frame: my own face, as a child. For anyone who hasn't experienced that moment, the expression is merely enigmatic—slightly dazed, happy, but abstracted. But if you've been to Alaska, that photograph captures something familiar: It's an image of discovery. I've seen it on the fresh, pale faces in photographs stamped with the dates of my family's first explorations of Alaska nearly 40 years ago. And then, researching this book, I got to see it once again, on my own young son's face. And I knew that, like me, he had discovered something important.

So what, exactly, am I talking about? Like anything worth experiencing, it's not simple to explain.

Tour guides try to get it across with statistics. Not much hope of that, although some of the numbers do give you a general idea of scale. Once you've driven across the continental United States and know how big that is, seeing a map of Alaska placed on top of the area you crossed, just about spanning it, provides some notion of size. Alaska has 627,000 residents. If you placed them an equal distance apart, each would be almost a mile from any other. Of course, that couldn't happen. No one has ever been to some parts of Alaska.

But none of that expresses what really matters. It's not just a matter of how big Alaska is or how few people it contains. It's not an intellectual conception at all. None of that crosses your mind when you see a chunk of ice the size of a building fall from a glacier and send up a huge splash and wave surging outward, or when you feel a wave lift your sea kayak from the fall of a breaching humpback whale. Or when you hike for a couple of days to stand on top of a mountain, and from there see more mountaintops, layered off as far as the horizon, in unnamed, seemingly infinite multiplicity. A realization of what Alaska means can also come in a simple moment. It can come at the end of a long day driving an Interior Alaska highway, as your car climbs into yet another mountain range, the sun still hanging high in what should be night, storm systems arranged before you across the landscape, when you realize that you haven't seen another car in an hour. Or standing on an Arctic Ocean beach, it can happen when you look around at the sea of empty tundra behind you, the sea of green water before you, and your own place on what seems to be the edge of the world.

What's the soul alchemy of such a moment? I suppose it's different for each person, but for me it has something to do with realizing my actual size in the world, how I fit in, what it means to be just another medium-sized mammal, no longer armed with the illusions supplied by civilization. On returning to the city from the wilderness, there's a re-entry process, like walking from a vivid movie to the mundane, gray street outside—it's the movie that seems more real. For a while, it's hard to take human institutions seriously after you've been deep into Alaska.

Some people never do step back across that boundary. They live their lives out in the wilderness, away from people. Others compromise, living in Alaskan cities and walking out into the mountains when they can, the rest of the time just maintaining a prickly notion of their own independence. But anyone with the courage to come to Alaska—and the time to let the place sink in—can make the same discovery. You don't have to be an outdoors enthusiast or a young person. You only have to be open to wonder and able to slow down long enough to see it. Then, in a quiet moment when you least expect it, things may suddenly seem very clear and all that you left behind oddly irrelevant.

How you find your way back to where you started is your affair.

1 Natural History: Rough Drafts & Erasures

THE SURGING ICE

In 1986, Hubbard Glacier, north of Yakutat, suddenly decided to surge forward, cutting off Russell Fjord from the rest of the Pacific Ocean. A group of warm-hearted but ill-advised wildlife lovers set out to save the marine mammals that had been trapped behind the glacier. Catching a dolphin from an inflatable boat isn't that easy—they didn't accomplish much, but they provided a lot of entertainment for the locals. Then the water burst through the dam of ice and the lake became a fjord again, releasing the animals anyway. In 2002 it happened again (no rescue this time). Ships were warned away as the 70-square-mile lake, having risen 61 feet above sea level, quickly drained through a 300-foot-wide channel with a whoosh. Geologists say it could happen again in 2005.

Bering Glacier, the largest in North America (about 30×145 miles in area), can't decide which way to go. Surging and retreating on a 20-year cycle, it reversed course in 1995 after bulldozing a wetland migratory bird stopover, and speedily contracted back up toward the mountains. Yanert Glacier surged 100 yards a day in 2000 after moving 100 yards a year since 1942. The next year Tokositna Glacier started galloping after 50 years of quiet. In 1937, surging Black Rapids glacier almost ate the Richardson Highway. In Prince William Sound, Meares Glacier has plowed through old-growth forest. On a larger scale, all the land of Glacier Bay—mountains, forests, sea floor—is rising 1½ inches a year as it rebounds from the weight of melted glaciers that 100 years ago were a mile thick and 65 miles longer.

Yet these new and erased lands are just small corrections around the margins compared to all the earth has done in setting down, wiping out, and rewriting the natural history of Alaska. In the last Ice Age, 15,000 years ago, much of what is Alaska today was one huge glacier. Looking up at the tops of granite mountains in Southeast Alaska, especially in the Lynn Canal, you can see a sort of high-water mark—the highest point to which the glaciers came in the Ice Age.

Some 7-year-old children worry about the bogeyman or being caught in a house fire. When I was that age, living with my family in Juneau, I was worried about glacier ice. I had learned how Gastineau Channel was formed, I had seen Mendenhall Glacier, and I had heard how it was really a river of ice, advancing and retreating. I came to fear that while I slept another Ice Age would come and grind away the city of Juneau.

It's possible that a glacier *could* get Juneau—the city fronts on the huge Juneau Ice Field—but there would be at least a few centuries' warning before it hit. Glaciers are essentially just snow that doesn't get a chance to melt. The snow accumulates at higher elevations until it gets deep enough to compress into ice and starts oozing down the mountainside. When the ice reaches the ocean, or before, the melt and calving of icebergs at the leading edge attains a point of equilibrium with the snow that's still being added at the top. The glacier stops advancing, becoming a true river of ice, moving a snowflake from the top of the mountain to the bottom in a few hundred years. When conditions change— more snow or colder long-term weather, for example—the glacier gets bigger; that's called advancing, and the opposite is retreating. But most of the time, the advance or retreat is measured in inches or feet a year.

The earth is warming today in time with regular cycles of cold and warm, but the warming is also accelerating due to human release of carbon dioxide from the burning of fossil fuels, which far exceeds natural changes in atmospheric carbon dioxide. The warming has been felt more strongly in the Arctic than anywhere else on earth. Forests are moving north, wetlands are drying, sea ice is thinning and withdrawing, and permanently frozen ground is warming. Glaciers are shrinking. I've written a book on this subject, *The Whale and the Supercomputer; On the Northern Front of Climate Change,* published by Farrar, Straus and Giroux in April 2004, and you can read more about it on my website, at www.wohlforth.net.

THE TREMBLING EARTH

Despite my early glacier phobia, I never had a similar fear of earthquakes. Living in Anchorage, I'd been through enough of them that, as early as I can remember, I generally didn't bother to get out of bed when they hit. Alaska has an average of 13 earthquakes a day, or 11% of all the earthquakes in the world, including three of the six largest ever recorded. On November 3, 2002, Alaska felt the world's largest earthquake of the year and one of the largest ever in the United States. My car rocked as I drove in Anchorage. Waves slopped across the bayous of Louisiana and geysers at Yellowstone changed their size and period of eruptions. No one died and few people were injured because the quake occurred in such a sparsely populated area, the region between Anchorage and Fairbanks in the Alaska Range east of Mount McKinley. A 140-mile-long crack appeared right across that region, running over mountains and through glaciers. The land on each side moved laterally as much as 22 feet and vertically up to 6 feet.

It's all part of living in a place that isn't quite done yet. Any part of Alaska could have an earthquake, but the Pacific Rim from Southcentral Alaska to the Aleutians is the shakiest. The very rocks that make up the state are something of an ad hoc conglomeration, still in the process of being assembled. The floor of the Pacific Ocean is moving north, and as it moves, it carries islands and mountains with it. When they hit the Alaska plate, these pieces of land, called terranes, dock like ships arriving, but slowly—an island moving an inch a year takes a long time to travel thousands of miles. Geologists studying rocks near Mount McKinley have found a terrane that used to be tropical islands. In Kenai Fjords National Park, fossils have turned up that are otherwise found only in Afghanistan and China. The slowly moving crust of the earth brought them here on a terrane that makes up a large part of the south coast of Alaska.

The earth's crust is paper thin compared to the globe's forces, and, like paper, it folds where the two edges meet. Alaska's coast is bending down; and farther inshore, where McKinley stands, it is bowing up. At Kenai Fjords National Park you can see steep little rock islands flocked with birds: they are old mountaintops, shrinking down into the earth. The monolith of McKinley is a brand-new one growing higher.

Living in such an unsettled land is a matter of more than abstract interest. The Mount Spurr volcano, which erupted most recently in 1992, turned day to night in Anchorage, dropping a blanket of ash all over the region. A Boeing 747 full of passengers flew into the plume and lost power in all its engines, falling in darkness for several minutes before pilots were able to restart the clogged jets. More than 80 volcanoes have been active in Alaska in the last 200 years. Earthquakes between 7 and 8 on the Richter scale—larger than the 1994 Los Angeles quake—occur once a year on average, and huge quakes over 8 averaged every 13 years over the last century. The worst of the quakes, on March 27, 1964, was the strongest ever to hit North America. It ranked 9.2 on the Richter scale, lowering an entire region of the state some 10 feet and moving it even farther laterally. The earthquake destroyed much of Anchorage and several smaller towns, and killed about 131 people, mostly in sea waves created by underwater landslides. In Valdez, the waterfront was swept clean of people. In the Prince William Sound village of Chenega, built on a hill along the water, people started running for higher ground when the wave came. About half made it.

But even that huge earthquake wasn't an unusual occurrence, at least in the earth's terms. Geologists believe the same Alaska coast sank 6 feet in an earthquake in the year 1090.

THE FROZEN TUNDRA

The northern Interior and Arctic parts of the state are less susceptible to earthquakes and, since they receive little precipitation, they don't have glaciers, either. But there's still a sense of living on a land that's not permanent, since most of northern Alaska is solid only by virtue of being frozen. When it thaws, it turns to mush. The phenomenon is caused by permafrost, a layer of earth a little below the surface that never thaws—or at least, you'd better hope it doesn't. Buildings erected on permafrost without some mechanism for dispersing their own heat—pilings, a gravel pad, or even refrigerator coils—thaw the ground below and sink into a self-made quicksand. With the climate warming, sections of the trans-Alaska pipeline are leaning, and many miles of highway in Interior Alaska are being rebuilt each year because the ground they traverse has turned to mush with warming climate.

The Arctic and much of the Interior are a swampy desert. Annual precipitation measured in Barrow is the same as in Las Vegas. Most of the time, the tundra is frozen in white; snow blows around, but not much falls. It melts in the summer, but the water can't sink into the ground, which remains frozen. Liquid water on top of the permafrost layer creates huge, shallow ponds. Alaska is a land of 10 million lakes, with 3 million larger than 20 acres. Birds arrive to feed and paddle around those circles and polygons of deep green and sky blue.

The permafrost also preserves many things. Although few and far between, tractor tracks remain clearly delineated for decades after they're made, appearing as narrow, parallel ponds reaching from one horizon to the other. The meat of prehistoric mastodons, still intact, has been unearthed from the frozen ground. On the Arctic Coast, the sea eroded ground near Barrow that contained ancient ancestors of the Eskimos who still inhabit the same neighborhood. In 1982, a family was found that apparently had been crushed by sea ice up to 500 years ago. Two of the bodies were well preserved, sitting in the home they had occupied and wearing the clothes they had worn the day of the disaster, perhaps around the time Columbus was sailing to America.

Sea ice is the frozen ocean that extends from northern Alaska to the other side of the world. For a few months of summer it pulls away from the shore. Then, in October, icebergs floating toward land are cemented together by new ice forming along the beach. But even when the ice covers the whole ocean it still moves under the immense pressure of wind and current. The clash creates towering pressure ridges—piles of broken ice that look like small mountain ranges and are about as difficult to cross.

The National Weather Service keeps track of the ice pack and issues maps and predictions you can find on the Internet (www.arh.noaa.gov). Eskimo hunters traveling on the ice by snow machine need this information, as do crab fishermen who like to tempt the south-moving edge in the fall, and shippers looking for the right moment in the summer to venture north with barges of fuel and other supplies for the coast of the Arctic Ocean. There is barely time in the summer to get there and back before the ice closes in again in the fall.

THE RAINFOREST

By comparison, southern coastal Alaska is warm and biologically rich. Temperate rainforest ranges up the coast from Southeast Alaska into Prince William Sound, with bears, deer, moose, wolves, and even big cats living among the massive western hemlock, Sitka spruce, and cedar. This old-growth forest, too wet to burn in forest fires, is the last vestige of the virgin, primeval woods that seemed so limitless to the first white settlers who arrived on the east coast of the continent in the 17th century. The trees grow on and on, sometimes rising more than 200 feet high, with diameters of 10 feet, and falling only after hundreds or even 1,000 years. When they fall, the trees rot on the damp moss of the forest floor and return to soil to feed more trees, which grow in rows upon their nursery trunks.

Here at least, Alaska *does* seem permanent. That sense helps explain why logging the rainforest is so controversial. Just one of these trees contains thousands of dollars' worth of wood. Vast Southeast lands owned by Alaska Native corporations were stripped of their old trees for the money they brought to their owners. But the great majority of this rainforest land belongs to the federal government, and a combination of environmental campaigns and economics put a stop to large-scale logging on that land while most of it remained virgin. When the Southeast Alaska logging economy died in the 1990s, the towns there suffered heavy economic blows. Tourism is taking the place of logging (with its own environmental and cultural impacts), but deep antipathy remains against logging opponents.

TAIGA

Rainforest covers only a small fraction of Alaska. In fact, only a third of Alaska is forested at all, and most of this is the boreal forest that covers the central part of the state, behind the rain shadow of coastal mountains that intercept moist clouds off the oceans. Ranging from the Kenai Peninsula, south of Anchorage, to the Brooks Range, where the Arctic begins, this is a taiga—a moist, subarctic forest of smaller, slower-growing, hardier trees that leave plenty of open sky between their branches. In well-drained areas, on hillsides and southern land less susceptible to permafrost, the boreal forest is a lovely, broadly spaced combination of straight, proud white spruce and pale, spectral paper birch. Along the rivers, cottonwoods grow, with deep-grained bark and branches that spread in an oaklike matrix—if they could speak, it would be as wise old men.

This is the land of the moose. They're as big as large horses, with flanks that look like a worn-out shag carpet draped over a sawhorse, and huge eyes that seem to know, somehow, just how ugly they are. But moose are survivors. They thrive on land no one else wants. In the summer, they wade out into the swampy tundra ponds to eat green muck. In the winter, they like nothing better than an old burn, where summer lightning has peeled back the forest and allowed a tangle of willows to grow—a moose's favorite food. Eaten by wolves, hunted and run over by man, stranded in the snows of a hard winter, the moose always come back.

2 Politics & History: Living a Frontier Myth

The occupations of prospector, trapper, and homesteader—rugged individualists relying only on themselves in a limitless land—would dominate Alaska's economy if the state's image of itself were accurate. Alaskans talk a lot about the Alaskan spirit of independence, yearn for freedom from government, and declare that people from "Outside" just don't understand Alaskans when they insist on locking up Alaska's lands in parks and wilderness status. The bumper sticker says, simply, "We don't give a damn how they do it Outside."

But just because you wear a cowboy hat doesn't mean you know how to ride a horse. In Las Vegas you find a lot more hats than horsemen, and Alaska is full of self-reliant pioneers who spend rush hour in traffic jams and worry more about urban drug dealing and air pollution than where to catch their next meal or dig the mother lode. As for self-reliance and independence from government, Alaska has the highest per capita state spending of any state in the nation, with no state income or sales taxes and an annual payment of about $1,500 a year to every man, woman, and child just for living here. The state government provides retirement homes; it owns various businesses, including a dairy, a railroad, and a subsidized mortgage lender; it has built schools in the smallest communities; it operates a state ferry system and a radio and television network; and it owns nearly a third of the landmass of Alaska.

That conflict between perception and reality grows out of the story of a century of development of Alaska. The state is a great storehouse of minerals, oil, timber, and fish. A lot of wealth has been extracted, and many people have gotten rich. But it has always been because the federal government let them do it. Every acre of

Dateline

- **Approximately 15,000 years ago** First human explorers arrive in Alaska from Asia.

- **1741** Vitus Bering, on a mission originally chartered by Peter the Great, finds Alaska; ship's surgeon and naturalist Georg Steller goes ashore for a few hours on Kayak Island, the first white to set foot in Alaska.

- **1743** Russian fur traders enter the Aleutian Islands; Aleuts are enslaved to hunt sea otter and massacred when they try to revolt; Aleut cultural traditions are eliminated, and over the coming decades they are relocated as far south as California for their hunting skills.

- **1772** Unalaska, in the Aleutian Islands, becomes a permanent Russian settlement.

- **1776–79** British Capt. James Cook makes voyages of exploration to Alaska, seeking the Northwest Passage from the Pacific to the Atlantic, and draws charts of the coast.

- **1784** Russians build a settlement at Kodiak.

- **1799** Russians establish a fort near present-day Sitka, which will later become their capital; Tlingits attack and destroy the fort, but are later driven off in a counterattack; the Russian-America Company receives a 20-year exclusive franchise to govern and exploit Alaska.

- **1821** Russian naval officers are placed in control of the Russian-America Company, which begins to decline in profitability.

- **1824** Boundaries roughly matching Alaska's current borders are set by treaty between Russia, Britain, and the United States.

- **1839** The British Hudson's Bay Company, surpassing Russia in trade, begins leasing parts of Southeast Alaska and subsequently extends trading outposts into the Interior.

- **1843** First overtures are made by American officials interested in buying Alaska from the Russians, so U.S. instead of British power could expand there.

continues

Alaska belonged to the U.S. government from the day Secretary of State William Seward bought Alaska from Russia in 1867. Since then, the frontier has never been broader than Uncle Sam made it.

Yet the whole concept of ownership didn't fit Alaska well from the first. Did the Russians really own what they sold? Alaska Natives didn't think so. They'd been living on this land for more than 100 centuries, and at the time of the purchase, most had never seen a white face. How could Russia hold title to land that no Russian had so much as explored? As Americans flooded into Alaska to search for gold at the turn of the 20th century, this conflict became obvious. Alaska Natives, never conquered by war or treaty, soon began their legal and political fight to recover their land—a fight they would eventually win.

The concept of ownership has changed in other ways, too. For the first 100 years after the United States bought Alaska, it maintained the vast majority of the territory as "public domain," with federal land and its mineral resources free for the taking as in the Old West of frontier lore. Each piece of Alaska belonged to everyone until someone showed up to lay private claim. Today, amid deep conflict over whether to develop such areas as the Arctic National Wildlife Refuge (known as ANWR), federal control stands out far more clearly than it did during the gold rush, when the land's wealth was free to anyone with strength enough to take it. Alaskans who want to keep receiving the good things that a rich state government brings equate the frontier spirit of the past with their own financial well-being, whether that means working at a mining claim or at a desk in a glass office tower. But other Americans feel they own Alaska, too, and they don't necessarily believe in exploiting its

1867 In need of money and fearful that Russia couldn't hold onto Alaska anyway, Czar Alexander II sells Alaska to the United States; Secretary of State William Seward negotiates the deal for a price of $7.2 million, roughly 2¢ an acre; the American flag is raised in Sitka, and the U.S. military assumes government of Alaska.

1870 The Alaska Commercial Company receives a monopoly on harvesting seals in the Pribilof Islands and soon expands across the territory (the company remains a presence in the Alaska Bush today).

1879 Naturalist and writer John Muir explores Southeast Alaska by canoe, discovering Glacier Bay with Native guides.

1880 Joe Juneau and Richard Harris, guided by local Natives, find gold on Gastineau Channel and found city of Juneau; gold strikes begin to come every few years across the state.

1884 Military rule ends in Alaska, but residents still have no right to elect a legislature, governor, or congressional representative, or to make laws.

1885 Protestant missionaries meet to divide up the territory, parceling out each region to a different religion; they begin to fan out across Alaska to convert Native peoples, largely suppressing their traditional ways.

1898 After prospectors arrive in Seattle with a ton of gold, the Klondike gold rush begins; gold rushes in Nome and Fairbanks follow within a few years; Americans begin to populate Alaska.

1906 Alaska's first (nonvoting) delegate in Congress takes office; the capital moves from Sitka to Juneau.

1908 The Iditarod Trail, a sled dog mail route, is completed, linking trails continuously from Seward to Nome.

1913 The first territorial legislature convenes, although it has few powers; the first automobile drives the Richardson Highway route, from Valdez to Fairbanks.

1914 Federal construction of the Alaska Railroad begins; the first tents go up in the river bottom that will be Anchorage, along the rail line.

resource treasure. They may want the frontier to stay alive in another sense—unconquered and still wild.

White colonization of the territory came in boom-and-bust waves of migrants arriving with the goal of making a quick buck and then clearing out—without worrying about the people who already lived there. Although the gold rush pioneers are celebrated today, the Klondike rush of 1898 that opened up and populated the territory was motivated by greed and was a mass importer of crime, inhumanity, and, for the Native people, terrible epidemics of new diseases that killed off whole villages. Like the Russians 150 years before, who had made slaves of the Natives, the new white population behaved as if the indigenous people were less than human. Until Franklin Roosevelt became president, federal policy was to suppress Alaska Native cultures. Protestant missionaries had the authority of law to forbid Native people from telling their old stories or even speaking their own languages. Segregation ended only after World War II. Meanwhile, the salmon that fed the people of the territory were overfished by a powerful, outside-owned canning industry with friends in Washington, D.C. Their abuses destroyed salmon runs. Formerly rich Native villages faced famine when their primary food source was taken away.

It was only with World War II, and the Japanese invasion of the Aleutian Islands, that Alaska developed an industry that was not based on exploitation of natural resources: the military industry. The war brought the construction of the territory's first road to the outside world, the Alaska Highway. After the war, military activity dropped off, but only briefly. By the late 1940s, Alaska was on the front line of the Cold War. Huge Air Force

- 1917 Mount McKinley National Park is established.
- 1920 The first flights connect Alaska to the rest of the United States; aviation quickly becomes the most important means of transportation in the territory.
- 1923 Pres. Warren Harding drives the final spike on the Alaska Railroad at Nenana, then dies on the way home, purportedly from eating bad Alaska seafood.
- 1925 Leonhard Seppala and other dog mushers relay diphtheria serum on the Iditarod Trail to fight an epidemic in Nome; Seppala and his lead dog, Balto, become national heroes.
- 1934 Federal policy of forced assimilation of Native cultures is officially discarded and New Deal efforts to preserve Native cultures begin.
- 1935 New Deal "colonists," broke farmers from all over the United States, settle in the Matanuska Valley north of Anchorage.
- 1940 A military buildup begins in Alaska; bases built in Anchorage accelerate city's growth into a major population center.
- 1942 Japanese invade Aleutians, taking Attu and Kiska islands and bombing Unalaska/Dutch Harbor (a U.S. counterattack the next year drives out the Japanese); Alaska Highway links Alaska to the rest of the country overland for the first time, but is open to civilians only after the war.
- 1949 Massive Cold War military buildup feeds fast economic growth.
- 1957 Oil is found on Kenai Peninsula's Swanson River.
- 1959 Alaska becomes a state.
- 1964 The largest earthquake ever to strike North America shakes South-central Alaska, killing 131 people, primarily in tsunami waves.
- 1968 Oil is found at Prudhoe Bay, on Alaska's North Slope.
- 1970 Environmental lawsuits tie up work to build the Alaska pipeline, which is needed to link the North Slope oil field to markets.
- 1971 Congress acknowledges and pays the federal government's debt to Alaska's indigenous people with the

continues

and Army bases were built and remote radar stations were installed to detect and repel Soviet bombers and missiles. To this day, the federal government remains a key industry whose removal would deal the economy a grievous blow.

The fight for Alaska statehood also began after World War II. Alaskans argued that they needed local, independent control of natural resources, pointing to the example of overfishing in the federally managed salmon industry. Opponents said that Alaska would never be able to support itself, would always require large subsidies from the federal government, and therefore should not be a state. But the advocates pointed out that Alaska's lack of self-sufficiency came about because its citizens did not control the resources—Alaska was a colony, with decisions and profits taken away by the mother country. If Alaskans could control their own land, they could use the resources to fund government. The discovery of oil on the Swanson River on the Kenai Peninsula in 1957 helped win that argument. Here was real money that could fund a state government. In 1959, Alaska finally became the 49th state. Along with the rights of entering the Union, Alaska received a dowry, an endowment of

Alaska Native Claims Settlement Act, which transfers 44 million acres of land and almost $1 billion to new Native-owned corporations.

■ 1973 The first Iditarod Trail Sled Dog Race runs more than 1,000 miles from Anchorage to Nome.

■ 1974 Congress clears away legal barriers to construction of the trans-Alaska pipeline; Vice Pres. Spiro Agnew casts the deciding vote in the U.S. Senate.

■ 1977 The trans-Alaska pipeline is completed and begins providing up to 25% of the U.S. domestic supply of oil.

■ 1980 Congress sets aside almost a third of Alaska in new parks and other land-conservation units; awash in new oil wealth, the state legislature abolishes all taxes paid by individuals to state government.

■ 1982 Alaskans receive their first Alaska Permanent Fund dividends, interest paid on an oil-wealth savings account.

■ 1985 Declining oil prices send the Alaska economy into a tailspin; tens of thousands leave the state and most of the banks collapse.

■ 1989 The tanker *Exxon Valdez* hits Bligh Reef in Prince William Sound, spilling 11 million gallons of North Slope crude in the worst oil spill ever in North America.

■ 1994 A federal jury in Anchorage awards $5 billion to 10,000 fishermen, Natives, and others hurt by the Exxon oil spill; Exxon appeals continue today.

land to develop and pay for future government. The Statehood Act gave the new state the right to select 103 million acres from a total landmass of 365 million acres. Indeed, that land does pay for state government in Alaska, in the form of oil royalties and taxes—but, to this day, the federal government still spends a lot more in Alaska than it receives.

Oil revenues supported the new state as it began to extend services to the vast, undeveloped expanse of Alaska. Anchorage boomed in the 1960s in a period of buoyant optimism. Leaders believed that the age-old problems of the wide-open frontier—poverty, lack of basic services, impenetrable remoteness—would succumb to the new government and new money, while the land would remain wide open. The pace of change redoubled in 1968 with the discovery of the largest oil field in North America at Prudhoe Bay on land that had been a wise state selection in the federal land-grant entitlement. The state government received as much money in a single oil lease sale auction as it had spent in total for the previous 6 years. This was going to be the boom of all booms.

The oil bonanza on the North Slope would change Alaska more than any other event since the gold rush. Once, opening the frontier meant letting a few prospectors scratch the dirt in search of a poke of gold. But getting this immense pool of oil to market from one of the most remote spots on the globe would require allowing the world's largest companies to build across Alaska a pipeline that, when completed, could credibly claim to be the largest privately financed construction project in world history. With the stakes suddenly so much higher, it came time to figure out exactly who owned which parts of Alaska. The land couldn't just be public domain any longer.

That division wouldn't be easy. Much of the state had never even been mapped, much less surveyed, and there were some large outstanding claims that had to be settled. Alaska Natives, who had lost land, culture, and health in 2 centuries of white invasion, finally saw their luck start to turn. It wouldn't be possible to resolve the land issues surrounding the pipeline until their claims to land and compensation were answered. Native leaders cannily used that leverage to assure that they got what they wanted.

In the early 1970s, America had a new awareness of the way its first people had been treated in the settlement of the West. When white frontiers expanded, Native traditional homelands were stolen. In Alaska, with the powerful lure of all that oil providing the impetus, Native people were able to insist on a fairer resolution. In 1971, with the support of white Alaskans, the oil companies, and Pres. Richard Nixon, Congress passed the Alaska Native Claims Settlement Act, called ANCSA. The act transferred 44 million acres of land and $962.5 million to corporations whose shareholders were all the Native people of Alaska. The new Native corporations would be able to exploit their own land for their shareholders' profit. In later legislation, Natives also won guaranteed subsistence hunting and fishing rights on federal land. Some Natives complained that they'd received only an eighth of the land they had owned before white contact, but it was still by far the richest settlement any of the world's indigenous people had received at that time. Today, the Native corporations are Alaska's largest and most powerful homegrown businesses.

It was a political deal on a grand scale. It's unlikely that Natives would have gotten their land at all but for the desire of whites to get at the oil and their need for Native support. Nor could the pipeline have overcome environmental challenges without the Natives' dropping their objections. Even with Native support in place, legislation authorizing the pipeline passed the U.S. Senate by only one vote, cast by Vice Pres. Spiro Agnew.

But there were other side effects of the deal that white Alaskans didn't like so much. The state still hadn't received a large portion of its land entitlement, and now the Native corporations also had a right to select the land they wanted. There still remained the question of who would get what, and of the question of the wild lands that Congress, influenced by a strong new environmental movement, wanted to maintain as national parks and wilderness and not give away. That issue wasn't settled until 1980, when the Alaska National Interest Lands Conservation Act passed, setting aside an additional 106 million acres for conservation, an area larger than California. Alaska's frontier-minded population screamed bloody murder over "the lockup of Alaska," but the act was only the last, tangible step in a process started by the coming of big oil and the need its arrival created to draw lines on the map, tying up the frontier.

When construction of the $9 billion pipeline finally got underway in 1974, a huge influx of new people chasing the high-paying jobs put any previous gold rush to shame. The newcomers were from a different part of the country than previously, too. Alaska had been a predominantly Democratic state, but oil workers from Texas, Oklahoma, and other Bible Belt states helped shift the balance of Alaska's politics, and now it's solidly Republican. In its frontier days, Alaska had a strong Libertarian streak, but now it became more influenced by fundamentalist Christian conservatism. A hippie-infested legislature of the early 1970s legalized marijuana for home use. Conservatives at the time, who thought the government shouldn't butt into its citizens' private lives, went along with them. After the pipeline, times changed, and Alaska developed tough anti-drug laws.

Growth also brought urban problems. As the pipeline construction boom waned in 1977, the boomtown atmosphere of gambling and street prostitution disappeared with it, but other big-city problems remained. No longer could residents of Anchorage and Fairbanks go to bed without locking their doors. Both cities were declared "nonattainment" areas by the Environmental Protection Agency because of air pollution near the ground in cold winter weather, when people leave their cars running during the day to keep them from freezing.

But the pipeline seemed to provide limitless wealth to solve these problems. For fear that too much money would be wasted, the voters altered the state constitution to bank a large portion of the new riches. The new Permanent Fund would be off-limits to the politicians in Juneau, with half the annual earnings paid out to citizens as dividends. The fund now contains more than $20 billion in savings and has become one of the largest sectors of the economy simply by virtue of paying out $1 billion a year in dividends to everyone who lives at least a year in the state. All major state taxes on individuals were canceled, and people got used to receiving everything free from the government.

Then, in 1985, oil prices dropped, deflating the overextended economy. Housing prices crashed and thousands of people simply walked away from their mortgages. All but a few of the banks in the state went broke. Condominiums that had sold for $100,000 went for $20,000 or less a year later. It was the bust that always goes with the boom, but it still came as a shock to many. The spending associated with the clean-up of the *Exxon Valdez* oil spill in 1989 restarted the economy and it continued on an even keel for a decade after, but the wealth of the earlier oil years never returned.

Meanwhile, the oil from Prudhoe Bay started running out. Oil revenues, an irreplaceable 85% of the state budget, started an inexorable downward trend in the early 1990s. The oil companies downsized. Without another boom on the horizon, the question became how to avoid, or at least soften, the next bust. At this writing, that question remains unanswered, even as state savings run out. Meanwhile, government spending for visitor facilities such as state parks is cut each year. Ironically, polls show that Alaskans would support a personal income tax, but so far they haven't been given the choice. Politically, it's more expedient to look for the next big project that will get the good times rolling again, such as a natural gas pipeline from the North Slope to middle America or oil development in ANWR.

Culture moves slower than politics or economics, and Alaskans still see themselves as gold rush prospectors or wildcat oil drillers, adventuring in an open land and striking it rich by their own devices. Even as the economy blends ever more smoothly into the American corporate landscape, Alaskans' myth of themselves remains strong. Today, the state's future is as little in its own hands as it has ever been. Big petroleum projects will be decided in Congress and distant corporate boardrooms, not here. Ultimately, an economy based on exploiting natural resources is anything but independent.

3 The People: Three Ways to Win an Argument in Alaska

NUMBER ONE: WAIT FOR SPRING

A small town in Alaska in March. Each time it snows, you have to throw shovels of it higher over your head to dig out. The air in the house is stale and the view out the window is black, white, and gray. Everyone's going nuts with winter. It's time for a good political ruckus. No one can predict exactly what will set it off—it could just be an ill-considered letter to the editor in the local newspaper, or it could be something juicier, like a controversial development proposal. At some point, when the cabin fever gets bad enough, it almost doesn't matter what sparks the inferno. Alaskans can generate outrage about almost anything, with a ritual of charges and countercharges, conspiracy theories, and impassioned public testimony.

It's particularly amusing when some outsider is involved, thinking he's at the town council meeting in a normal political process to get some project approved, only to wind up on the receiving end of a public hearing from hell. I'll never forget a sorry businessman who was trying to lease some land from the town of Homer. He endured hours of angry public testimony one night. He was sweating, the only person in the packed city hall meeting room wearing a tie, surrounded by flannel shirts, blue jeans, and angry faces. Finally, he stood up at his chair and, in a plaintive tone of frustration near tears, declared, "You're not very professional as a community!" For once, no one could disagree.

He gave up. He didn't know that if he had only waited a couple of months, the opposition would dry up when the salmon started running. Then most of the city council meetings are canceled, and the rest are brief and sparsely attended. If anything really important comes up, the council is smart enough to postpone it till fall. In the summer, Alaskans have more important things to attend to than government.

The sun shines deep into the night so you can catch fish and tourists, not sit inside. It's the season when the money is made. The streets are full of new people, like a bird rookery refreshed by migrants. Everyone stays awake late pounding nails, playing softball, and fly-casting for reds. Office workers in Anchorage depart straight from work for a 3-hour drive down to the Kenai Peninsula, fish through the night, catch a quick nap in the car in the wee hours, and make it to work on time the next morning, with fish stories to share. Sleep is expendable—you don't seem to need it that much when the sky is light all night.

In the Native villages of the Bush, everyone has gone to fish camp. Families load everything in an aluminum riverboat and leave town, headed upriver. On the banks and beaches, they set up wall tents and spruce-log fish-drying racks, maybe a basketball hoop and campfire, too. Extended families work as a unit. Men gather in the salmon and the women gut them with a few lightning strokes of a knife and hang them to dry on the racks. Children run around in a countryside paradise, watched by whatever adults are handiest.

Suddenly, August comes. For the first time in months, you can see the stars. It comes as a shock the first time you have to use your car headlights. The mood gets even more frantic. There's never enough time in the summer to do everything that needs to get done. Construction crews can count the days now till snow and cold will shut them down. Anything that's not done now won't be done until next May. Labor Day approaches as fast as 5pm on a busy business day.

As September turns to October, the last tourists are gone, and T-shirt shops are closed for the season. The commercial fishing boats are tied up back in the harbor and the fishermen prepare for vacation. Cannery workers are already back at college. For the first time in months, people can slow down long enough to look at each other and remember where they left off in the spring. It's time to catch up on sleep, make big decisions. The hills of birch turn bright yellow, the tundra goes brick red, and the sky turns gray—there's the smell of wood smoke in the air—and then, one day, it starts to snow.

It's not the velvet darkness of midwinter that gets you. December is bearable, even if the sun rises after the kids get to school, barely cruises along the horizon, and sinks before they start for home. Nowhere is Christmas more real than in Alaska, where carolers sing with cheeks tingling from the cold. January isn't so hard. You're still excited about the skiing. The phone rings in the middle of the night—it's a friend telling you to put on your boots and go outside to see the northern lights. February is a bit harder to take, but most towns have a winter carnival to divert your attention from the cold.

March is when bizarre things start to happen. People are just holding on for the end of winter and you never know what will set them off. That's when you hunker down and lay low, watch what you say, bite your tongue when your spouse lets hang a comment you'd like to jump on like a coho hitting fresh bait. Hold on—just until the icicles start to melt, the mud shows around the snow-banks, and the cycle starts fresh.

The Iditarod

Few things fire up Alaska's residents like the Iditarod Trail Sled Dog Race, a 1,000-mile run from Anchorage to Nome that takes place in mid-March. Winners cover the distance in 9 or 10 days, which includes mandatory stopovers of up to 24 hours to rest the dogs. The race is big news—TV anchors speculate on the mushers' strategies at the top of the evening news and school children plot the progress of their favorite teams on maps. When the event hits Nome, the town overflows with visitors kept busy by the many local events and activities that coincide with the race. Even if the first team crosses the finish line at 3am in –30°F (–34°C) degree weather, a huge crowd turns out to congratulate the winner.

Some animal-rights activists outside Alaska, currently led by a Miami, Florida–based group called the Sled Dog Action Coalition, oppose the race on the grounds that it's cruel to the dogs, and have organized boy-cotts against some race sponsors. Several sponsors defected from the race a decade ago. Professional Iditarod mushers insist, however, that the dogs, worth thousands of dollars apiece, receive veterinary care superior to the doctoring that most people get; they say it doesn't make sense to harm animals that can run races for years if well cared for; and they point out that mushers who violate the race's stringent dog care rules are ejected.

If you want to plan your trip to coincide with the race in March, plan well in advance, because the event is extremely popular and hotels (par-ticularly in Nome) fill up quickly. For information, contact the Iditarod Trail Committee (© 907/376-5155; www.iditarod.com). To find out more about the controversy, here is the website of the Sled Dog Action Coali-tion (www.helpsleddogs.org), and of an Iditarod supporter responding to the coalition's charges (http://sunhusky.com/Facts).

NUMBER TWO: BE HERE FIRST

There's a simple and effective way to win an argument in Alaska—state how long you've lived here. If it's longer than your adversary, he'll find it difficult to put up a fight. This is why, when speaking in public, people will often begin their remarks by stating how many years they've been in Alaska. It's a badge of authenticity and status in a place with a young, transient population that's grown fast. No one cares where you came from, or who you were back there, and there's no such thing as class in Alaska—anyone who tries to act superior will quickly find that no one else notices. But if you haven't made it through a few winters, you probably don't know what you're talking about.

It's also traditional—although, sadly, a fading tradition—to treat strangers as friends until they prove otherwise. The smaller the town you visit, the more strongly you'll find that hospitality still alive. Visitors find it pleasantly disorienting to arrive in a small town and have everyone in the street greet them with a smile. These traditions of hospitality run deep in Alaska's Native people. (Alaskans use the word *Native* to mean all the indigenous peoples of Alaska.) But instead of beginning a conversation by stating how long they've lived here, Natives—who've always been here—try to find a relation with a new person by talking about where their families are from.

Theories differ about how North America was originally populated. However and whenever the first people arrived, they quickly spread through the Americas, creating cultures of incredible complexity and diversity. Most scientists believe migrants through Alaska were the ancestors of all the indigenous peoples of the hemisphere, from the Inca to the Algonquin. Those who stayed in Alaska became the Eskimos, who include the Iñupiat of the Arctic, the Yup'ik of the Southwest, and the Alutiiq of the Gulf of Alaska coastline. They also became Indians: the Athabascans of the Interior and the Tlingit, Haida, and Tsimshian of Southeast Alaska and British Columbia. And seafaring people in the Aleutian Chain became the Aleuts, neither Eskimo nor Indian.

The Native groups of Alaska have a lot in common culturally, but before the white invasion they had well-defined boundaries and didn't mix much. They didn't farm, and the only animal they domesticated was the dog—dog teams and boats were the primary means of transportation and commerce. But they generally were not nomadic, and no one in Alaska lived in ice igloos (farther east, in Canada, igloos were used as winter dwellings on the ice pack). On the treeless Arctic coast, houses were built of sod atop supports of whalebone and driftwood; where wood was plentiful, in the rainforests, large and intricately carved houses sheltered entire villages. Typically, a family-connected tribal group would have a winter village and a summer fish camp for gathering and laying up food. Elders guided the community in important decisions. A gifted shaman led the people in religious matters, relating to the spirits of ancestors, animals, trees, and even the ice that populated their world. Stories passed on through generations explained the universe.

Those oral traditions kept Native cultures alive. Twenty distinct Native languages were spoken. A few elders still speak only their Native language today, and only one language, Eyak, is essentially extinct. The languages break into four major families: Eskimo-Aleut, Athabascan-Eyak-Tlingit, Haida, and Tsimshian (the last two are primarily Canadian). The Eskimo-Aleut language group includes languages spoken by coastal people from the Arctic Ocean to the Gulf of Alaska, including Iñupiaq in the Arctic; Yup'ik, in the Yukon-Kuskokwim and Bristol Bay region, Aleut in the Aleutian Islands, and Alutiiq on the

Alaska Peninsula, Kodiak, and Prince William Sound. There are 12 Athabascan and Eyak languages in Alaska, and more Outside, including Apache and Navajo. In Southeast Alaska, Tlingit was spoken across most of the Panhandle. Haida was spoken on southern Prince of Wales Island and southward into what's now British Columbia, where Tsimshian also was spoken.

The first arrival of whites was often violent and destructive, spanning a 100-year period that started in the 1740s with the coming of the Russian fur traders, who enslaved the Aleuts, and continued to the 1840s, when New England whalers first met the Iñupiat of the Arctic. There were pitched battles, but disease and nonviolent destruction of oral traditions were more influential. Protestant missionaries, backed by government assimilation policy, drove the old stories and even Native languages underground. Lela Kiana Oman, who has published traditional Iñupiat stories to preserve them, told me of her memories of her father secretly telling the ancient tales at night to his children. She was forbidden to speak Iñupiaq in school and did not see her first traditional Native dance until age 18.

Oman's work is part of today's Native cultural renaissance. It's not a moment too soon. In some villages, children know more about Beverly Hills, which they see on television, than about their own culture. Some don't share a language with their own grandparents. But schools in many areas have begun requiring Native language classes, or even teach using language immersion techniques. For the Aleut, whose cultural traditions were almost completely wiped out, the process of renewal involves a certain amount of invention. On the other hand, some traditional villages remain, especially deep in the country of the Yukon-Kuskokwim Delta, where Yup'ik is still the dominant language and most of the food comes from traditional subsistence hunting and gathering, altered only by the use of modern materials and guns.

Alaska Natives also are fighting destruction fueled by alcohol and other substance-abuse problems. Rates of suicide, accidents, and domestic violence are high in the Bush. Statistically, nearly every Alaska Native in prison is there because of alcohol. A sobriety movement is attacking the problem one person at a time. One of its goals is to use traditional Native culture to fill a void of rural despair where alcohol flows in. Politically, a "local option" law provides communities the choice of partial or total alcohol prohibition; it has been successfully used in many towns, but remains controversial in others.

There are social and political tensions between Natives and whites on many levels and over many issues. The Alaskan city and Alaskan village have less in common than do most different nations. Although village Natives come to the city to shop, get health care, or attend meetings, urban Alaskans have no reason to go to the villages, and most never have made the trip.

The most contentious rural-urban issue concerns allocation of fish and game. Some urban outdoorsmen feel they should have the same rights to hunt and fish that the Natives do, and the state Supreme Court has interpreted Alaska's constitution to say they're correct. But rural Natives have federal law on their side, which overrules the state. A decade of political stalemate over the issue divided Alaskans until, in 2000, the feds finally stepped in and took over fish and game management in the majority of the state to protect Native subsistence. Many Natives were glad to see it happen, as humiliating as the move was for independent-minded Alaskans. Natives feel subsistence hunting and fishing are an integral part of their cultural heritage, far more important than sport, and should take priority. Darker conflicts exist, too, and it's impossible to discount the charges of racism that Native Alaskans raise in issues as diverse as school funding and public safety.

Alaska Natives have essentially become a minority in their own land. In 1880, Alaska contained 33,000 Natives and 430 whites. By 1900, with the gold rush, the numbers were roughly equal. Since then, whites have generally outnumbered Natives in ever greater numbers. Today there are about 98,000 Alaska Natives—27,000 of whom live in the cities of Anchorage and Fairbanks—out of a total state population of 627,000 people of all races. Consequently, Alaska Natives must learn to walk in two worlds. The North Slope's Iñupiat, who hunt the bowhead whale from open boats as their forefathers did, must also know how to negotiate for their take in international diplomatic meetings. And they have to use the levers of government to protect the whale's environment from potential damage by the oil industry. The Alaska Native Claims Settlement Act created a new class, the corporate Native, responsible for representing rural needs but also obliged to function as an executive for large, far-reaching business concerns.

Non-Natives traveling to the Bush also walk in two worlds, but they may not even know it. In a Native village, a newly met friend will ask you in for a cup of coffee; it can be rude not to accept. Too much eye contact in conversation also can be rude—that's how Native elders look at younger people who owe them respect. If a Native person looks down, speaks slowly, and seems to mumble, that's not disrespect, but the reverse. Fast-talking non-Natives have to make a conscious effort to slow down and leave pauses in conversation, because Natives usually don't jump in or interrupt—they listen, consider, and then respond. Of course, most Native people won't take offense at your bad manners. They're used to spanning cultures. When I was in a village a few years ago, I looked in confusion at a clock that didn't seem right. "That's Indian time," my Athabascan companion said. Then, pointing to a clock that was working, "White man time is over there."

Urban visitors who miss cultural nuances rarely overlook the apparent poverty of many villages. Out on a remote landscape of windswept tundra, swampy in summer and frozen in winter, they may secretly wonder why Natives endure the hardships of rural Alaskan life when even the most remote villager can see on television how easy it is in Southern California. Save your pity. As Yup'ik social observer Harold Napoleon has said, "We're poor, all right, but we've got more than most people. Our most important asset is our land and our culture, and we want to protect it come hell or high water."

NUMBER THREE: BE A REAL ALASKAN

Alaska's history books are full of the stories of economic booms, the people who came, what kind of wealth they were after, and how they populated and developed the land. In a largely empty place, you can make it into history just by showing up. But every wave is followed by a trough, the bust that comes after the boom when those who came just for the money go back where they came from. Those are the times when the real Alaskans—those who live here for the love of the place, not only the money—are divided from the rest. The real Alaskans stay; the others leave. It's the perfect way to settle an argument.

Other people have other definitions of what it takes to be a real Alaskan. One definition, which I once read on a placemat in a diner in Soldotna, holds that to be a real Alaskan, you have to know how to fix a Caterpillar tractor. Similar definitions require various feats in the outdoors—hunting, fishing, or shooting—and even acts in the barroom or the bedroom. They all assume that a real Alaskan is a big, tough, white, male, bulldozer-driving type of guy. But those can be the first to leave when the economy goes down the tubes.

The first group to leave were the Russians sent by the czar and the Russian-America Company. On October 18, 1867, their flag came down over Castle Hill in Sitka in a solemn ceremony, got stuck, and had to be untangled by a soldier sent up the pole. The territory was virtually empty of Russians before the check was even signed, as Congress didn't much like the idea of the purchase and took a while to pay. The gold rush stampeders were the next to leave. The population of Nome went from 12,500 to 852 after the stampede was over. The oil years have seen the same phenomenon.

But each time the boom went bust, enough stayed so that Alaska ended up with more people than before. Over the long term, the population has kept growing dramatically. And each set of migrants has been similar: young, transplanted mostly from the West, but from other parts of the United States, too. Most people who have come to Alaska have been white—minority populations are smaller than in the nation as a whole—but there are strong minority communities in Anchorage. In Kodiak, the canneries are run by a tight Filipino community started by just a few pioneer immigrants.

The non-Native part of Alaska, 100 years old with the anniversary of the gold rush in 1998, hasn't had time to develop an Alaskan accent. It's a melting pot of the melting pot, with a population made up of odds and ends from all over the United States. Everyone arrives with a clean slate and a chance to reinvent himself or herself. On occasion, that ability to start from scratch has created some embarrassing discoveries, when the past does become relevant. There have been a series of political scandals uncovered by reporters who checked the resumes of well-known politicians, only to find out they had concocted their previous lives out of thin air. One leading legislative candidate's husband found out about his wife's real background from such a news story.

Alaska's population is as mismatched and haphazard as a thrift store clothing rack, but we do have some cultural traditions, or at least accepted ways of thinking: tolerance and equality, hospitality, independence—and a propensity for violence. In the late 1980s in Homer, a gunfight over a horse left a man lying dead on a dirt road. In the newspaper the next week, the editorial called for people not to settle their differences with guns. A couple of letters to the editor shot back, on the theme, "Don't you tell *us* how to settle our differences." Guns are necessary tools in Alaska. They're also a religion. I have friends who actually exchanged handguns instead of rings when they got married.

The tradition of tolerance of newcomers has made Alaska a destination for oddballs, religious cults, hippies, and people who just can't make it in the mainstream. Perhaps the most interesting of the religious groups that formed its own community is the Old Believers, who in recent decades have built villages of brightly painted gingerbread-style houses around Kachemak Bay, near Homer. Their resistance to convention dates from Peter the Great's reforms to Russian Orthodoxy in the 18th century, which they reject. In Alaska they've found a place where they can live without interference—in fact, they've thrived as fishermen and boat builders. You see them around town, in their 18th-century Russian peasant dress. Until a few years ago, even the girls' high-school basketball team wore long dresses, with their numbers stitched to the bodice.

The fight against assimilation may be hopeless, as children will ultimately do as they please, but after several decades, it looks as if the Old Believers are here to stay. Whether they speak English or not, I'd say they're real Alaskans.

Index

Great Trips Like Great Days Begin with a Plan

FranklinCovey and Frommer's Bring You *Frommer's Favorite Places*® Planner

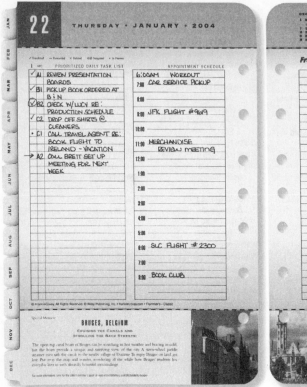

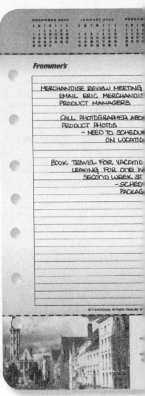

Classic Size Planning Pages $3

The planning experts at FranklinCovey have teamed up with the travel experts at Frommer's. The result is a full-year travel-themed planner filled with rich images and travel tips covering fifty-two of Frommer's Favorite Places.

- Each week will make you an expert about an intriguing corner of the world
- New facts and tips every day
- Beautiful, full-color photos of some of the most beautiful places on earth
- Proven planning tools from FranklinCovey for keeping track of tasks, appointments, notes, address/phone numbers, and more

Save 15%

when you purchase Frommer's Favo Places travel-themed planner and a binder.

Order today before yo next big trip.

www.franklincovey.com/frommer
Enter promo code 12252 at checkout for discount. Offer expires June 1, 200

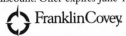

Frommer's is a trademark of Arthur Frommer.

FROMMER'S® NATIONAL PARK GUIDES

Algonquin Provincial Park
Banff & Jasper
Family Vacations in the National
  Parks

Grand Canyon
National Parks of the American
  West
Rocky Mountain

Yellowstone & Grand Teton
Yosemite & Sequoia/Kings
  Canyon
Zion & Bryce Canyon

FROMMER'S® MEMORABLE WALKS

Chicago
London

New York
Paris

San Francisco

FROMMER'S® WITH KIDS GUIDES

Chicago
Las Vegas
New York City

Ottawa
San Francisco
Toronto

Vancouver
Walt Disney World® & Orlando
Washington, D.C.

SUZY GERSHMAN'S BORN TO SHOP GUIDES

Born to Shop: France
Born to Shop: Hong Kong,
  Shanghai & Beijing

Born to Shop: Italy
Born to Shop: London

Born to Shop: New York
Born to Shop: Paris

FROMMER'S® IRREVERENT GUIDES

Amsterdam
Boston
Chicago
Las Vegas
London

Los Angeles
Manhattan
New Orleans
Paris
Rome

San Francisco
Seattle & Portland
Vancouver
Walt Disney World®
Washington, D.C.

FROMMER'S® BEST-LOVED DRIVING TOURS

Austria
Britain
California
France

Germany
Ireland
Italy
New England

Northern Italy
Scotland
Spain
Tuscany & Umbria

THE UNOFFICIAL GUIDES®

Beyond Disney
California with Kids
Central Italy
Chicago
Cruises
Disneyland®
England
Florida
Florida with Kids
Inside Disney

Hawaii
Las Vegas
London
Maui
Mexico's Best Beach Resorts
Mini Las Vegas
Mini Mickey
New Orleans
New York City
Paris

San Francisco
Skiing & Snowboarding in the
  West
South Florida including Miami &
  the Keys
Walt Disney World®
Walt Disney World® for
  Grown-ups
Walt Disney World® with Kids
Washington, D.C.

SPECIAL-INTEREST TITLES

Athens Past & Present
Cities Ranked & Rated
Frommer's Best Day Trips from London
Frommer's Best RV & Tent Campgrounds
  in the U.S.A.
Frommer's Caribbean Hideaways
Frommer's China: The 50 Most Memorable Trips
Frommer's Exploring America by RV
Frommer's Gay & Lesbian Europe
Frommer's NYC Free & Dirt Cheap

Frommer's Road Atlas Europe
Frommer's Road Atlas France
Frommer's Road Atlas Ireland
Frommer's Wonderful Weekends from
  New York City
The New York Times' Guide to Unforgettable
  Weekends
Retirement Places Rated
Rome Past & Present

Travel Tip: He who finds the best hotel deal has more to spend on facials involving knobbly vegetables.

Hello, the Roaming Gnome here. I've been nabbed from the garden and taken round the world. The people who took me are so terribly clever. They find the best offerings on Travelocity. For very little cha-ching. And that means I get to be pampered and exfoliated till I'm pink as a bunny's doodah.

Travel Tip: Make sure there's customer service
for any change of plans — involving
friendly natives, for example.

One can plan and plan, but if you don't book with the
right people you can't seize le moment and canoodle
with the poodle named Pansy. I, for one, am all for
fraternizing with the locals. Better yet, if I need to
extend my stay and my gnome nappers are willing, it
can all be arranged through the 800 number at, oh look,
how convenient, the lovely company coat of arms.

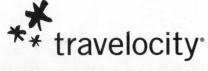